ERIC HILLEMANN

A Beacon
So Bright

THE LIFE OF
LAURENCE
McKINLEY
GOULD

"For Carleton College will be a cathedral,
not of bricks and mortar, but of ideas,
and with a spire so high, lighted by a beacon
so bright, that it will be a guide through
all the years of their lives to all who study here."

— Laurence McKinley Gould —
from his inaugural address as president of
Carleton College, October 16, 1945

ERIC HILLEMANN

A Beacon
So Bright

THE LIFE OF
LAURENCE
McKINLEY
GOULD

PUBLISHED BY CARLETON COLLEGE
NORTHFIELD, MINNESOTA

All inquiries and comments can be addressed to:

E-mail: bookstore@carleton.edu
Web site: www.carletonbookstore.org

Credits and Acknowledgments: Front cover photograph, Larry Gould with globe oriented to the South Pole, courtesy of Carleton College Archives.

Photographs herein are the property of the Carleton College Archives except those on pages 70, 77, 95, and 178, which are in the public domain, and those on pages 75 [Byrd7811_29], 87 [Byrd7821_29], 91 [Byrd7820_21], 113 [Album232_1_322], 115 [Album232_1_186], and 125 [Byrd7782_2], which are provided courtesy of The Ohio State University Archives, Papers of Admiral Richard E. Byrd [OSUA-BP].

Editing, Design, and Production: Nancy Ashmore, Ashmore Ink, Northfield, MN, www.ashmoreink.com.

International Standard Book No.:
978-0-9797423-2-3 (softcover)
978-0-9797423-9-2 (hardcover)

Printed in the United States of America

Keywords: Laurence M. Gould, Antarctica, Richard E. Byrd, Byrd Antarctic Expedition, Carleton College, college presidents, liberal arts colleges, geology, biography

This life of Gould, like so much of the original,
is dedicated to the alumni, faculty, and staff
of Carleton College—and most especially
to those who knew him.

ACKNOWLEDGMENTS

Work on this book started in one millennium and finished in another. There were times when it felt like that. Progress was not continuous, while attempting for many years to write a lengthy book in scattered spare hours, and though my Gould project was never abandoned, it was effectively set aside for several years in the middle for lack of sustained time to give to it. In a nutshell, nearly all of the research for this biography was completed from 1998 to 2002, and roughly a third of the text was written from 2003 to 2005, mostly in 2003. The last two-thirds was all written between April 2010 and August 2012. Thanks are due at both ends of this long arc.

Stephen R. Lewis, Jr., the president of Carleton College from 1987 to 2002, thought that a biography of Larry Gould ought to be written, and in 1998 he asked me, Carleton's college archivist, if I would like to write it. I am grateful that he asked. He rather hoped, at first, that the book might be finished while he was still president. That target was missed by a full ten years, but Steve stayed interested in the project throughout, and, as a critical reader of draft chapters sent his way long after he had left Carleton, returned valuable comments that improved the result.

It is my understanding that before commissioning me for the biography President Lewis received enthusiastic endorsement of the idea that I ought to be its author from Zoe Donnell (Carleton Class of 1955), the founder of the Carleton oral history program and a dear friend. While Zoe doubts that anything she said altered the request the president was going to make in any case, thank you, Zoe, nonetheless.

In 2000, President Lewis helped to secure a grant from the Harry A. and Margaret D. Towsley Foundation in support of our biography project. This grant allowed for the temporary addition to the Carleton archives staff of Susan Garwood, who for a period of two and a half years took over enough of my own regular work duties for me largely to finish researching Gould's life and to write the book's earliest chapters. Thanks to the Towsley Foundation and to Sue, both of whom were wonderful.

Appreciation is due to the capable archivists and librarians who assisted me during the researching of this book. These were, at the National Archives and Records Administration in College Park, Maryland, Marjorie Heins Ciarlante (Carleton Class of '65); at the University of Michigan's Bentley Historical Library, Kathy Marquis; at The Ohio State University's Byrd Polar Research Center, Laura Kissel and Bertha Ihnat; and at the University of Arizona Department of Geosciences' Antevs Library, Owen Davis.

ACKNOWLEDGMENTS

I wish to acknowledge the very kind hospitality extended to me, while I was conducting research in Ann Arbor, by Mary Ann Wilkes (Carleton Class of '55) and her husband James, the latter of whom encountered me quite by chance in the Bentley Library and knew, when he learned the subject of my research, that he simply must bring me home to dinner.

A very special debt of gratitude is owed to Clark and Ardith Arnold, of Tucson, Arizona (both Carleton Class of '62). The Arnolds sent to Carleton College most of the material now in the Gould Papers at the Carleton College Archives, documentation and memorabilia extremely valuable in the writing of this biography. They opened their home to me—and loaned me a vehicle—while I conducted my Tucson research and during a long taped interview patiently responded to all of my questions about Larry and Peg Gould's life in Arizona. At later points as the book was being written they answered numerous further queries by email. The last three chapters of this book in particular could scarcely have been written without them.

Other Tucsonans to whom I am grateful include George Davis, Peter Kresan, Paul Damon, and Ed McCullough, each of whom gave generously of his time for interviews during my 2002 visit. Pete Kresan has also sent a number of Gould-related items to the Carleton College Archives.

It was a stroke of luck for me as a biographer when Charles E. Hoppin (Carleton Class of '40) turned up in 2000 offering to donate to Carleton a collection of late 1960s to 1980s correspondence between Larry Gould and his late brother and sister-in-law, Dick Hoppin and Jean Rice Hoppin. These letters added much to the account I was later able to write of the Goulds' lives during these years.

I received encouragement, genealogical information, a number of family anecdotes, and copies of some family photographs through helpful early correspondence with two of Gould's grandnieces—second cousins to one another—Neita Trollinger and Dr. Elizabeth Wagar. I hope that they will be pleased with this account of their illustrious relative.

At the latter end of the timeline of this book's creation, I must thank Carleton's Dean of the College, Beverly Nagel (Carleton Class of '75), and Carleton's Associate Dean of the College from 2009 to 2012, Nathan Grawe, for deciding that my long-stalled project was worth completing and for coming up with a plan to free up enough of my time for more than two years to allow it to happen. Nathan also took steps to arrange the details of the book's publication by Carleton College, including the agreement with the book's editor, Nancy J. Ashmore (Carleton Class of '72).

Nancy Ashmore, who has both edited my writing and is responsible for the book's layout and design, has been a pleasure to work with. The end result owes a great deal to her competence, carefulness, and good sense.

Thanks as well to Sarah Entenmann (Carleton Class of '73), who undertook the art and craft of compiling the index.

Three of the reasons that I was finally able to be flexible enough with my work time to get the book completed during 2010 to 2012 were my new colleagues in the Carleton Archives: Nat Wilson, Carol Thunem, and Tom Lamb. Between them, this trio covered effectively for the time I spent writing rather than attending to other Archives' business. I am grateful as well to Carleton's former college librarian, Sam Demas, for all that he did in getting this crucial additional staff approved and hired.

I would also like to acknowledge those persons who read the book, or large portions of it, in draft form, and returned to me helpful comments and suggestions or simply praise and encouragement, which can also be helpful: Steve Lewis, Tom Lamb, Terry Kissner, and several Carleton alumni: Barbara "Putter" Beck ('49), Bill Beck ('50), John Street ('50), Bob Will ('50), Frank Wright ('50), Bill Huyck ('53), Jon Nicholson ('58), and John Hanson ('64).

My keenest regret in having taken the number of years I did to produce this book is in the thought of persons close to Gould who would have liked to have read it and who in some cases contributed to it, but who died before I could bring it forth. I think especially of Dorothy and Tony Obaid, Eiler Henrickson, and David Maitland.

Finally, there is Claire, who when I started to work on this book I was still nine years away from knowing, but who now resides at the very center of my life. Her love, support, and patience while I wrote have helped in ways that are innumerable and ineffable but important to acknowledge.

Eric Hillemann
Archivist
Carleton College
Northfield, Minnesota
October 2012

CONTENTS

A LEGACY THAT REVERBERATES

It is virtually impossible to study, teach, work at, or help steward Carleton College without repeatedly encountering the larger-than-life personality of Laurence McKinley Gould. Stories of this remarkable man and educational leader remain legion a half-century after he stepped down from Carleton's presidency. Gould mementos, both large and small, surround us and reinforce his lasting impact on this institution. Oscar, a stuffed penguin and "returning member" of the 1928-1930 Byrd expedition to Antarctica, graces the college library, which in turn bears Gould's name. College archives lovingly safeguard a collection of Gould's trademark red neckties—ties that were regularly mimicked by admiring students and alumni. Numerous Carls of the Gould era recount with pride how "their president" knew the name and pertinent details of every single student on campus.

The Gould legend, of course, is burnished by the fact that Carleton's fourth president had the singular good fortune to lead this institution during an era (1945 to 1962) that was truly a halcyon age not just for Carleton, but for liberal arts colleges and all of American higher education. It was a time when large cohorts of returning GIs brought energy and seriousness to their studies, when the prospects for college graduates were indisputably bright, and when the clarion call to respond to Sputnik led to a substantial influx of dollars and attention to the sciences, international relations, and other academic fields. Gould's timing was impeccable even when he relinquished the Carleton presidency. He departed several steps ahead of the raucous and much less comfortable era of student protests and social activism of the 1960s. Indeed, Gould's frosty relationship with his successor, John Nason, forms one of the interesting stories in this volume. But even accounting for Gould's exquisite timing, the passage of many years has only brought his remarkable qualities and achievements into higher relief.

Gould was a distinguished scientist—a geologist of great international repute who earned lasting fame as the chief scientific officer and second-in-command of Byrd's expedition. He was a teacher extraordinaire, with a gift for capturing and retaining the attention of his students. He was also a spellbinding public intellectual and speaker. All of these gifts led to his appointment as Carleton's president and helped make him singularly successful in that role.

Carleton under Gould continued its march to national prominence among liberal arts colleges. The college raised the quality of its faculty and students. Gould's charisma and vision led to significant fundraising success, creating a virtuous cycle that made it possible for the college to take even more steps toward distinction.

Surprisingly, despite his remarkable accomplishments, Gould has never before been the subject of a comprehensive biography. Therefore, it is most fortunate that Eric Hillemann has taken on the very considerable task of capturing Gould's family background, personal history, scientific achievements, and academic leadership in this detailed and thoughtful book. Through Hillemann's exhaustive search, we see aspects of Gould's character and life that have heretofore been obscured by his shining personality and celebrity. For instance, this volume establishes Gould as a prescient environmentalist, deeply worried about the fate of the planet. In his later years, he was engaged in educational and political activism to safeguard the Earth's natural resources. Gould also emerges as a committed internationalist, both through his personal involvement in the world scientific community and his foundation and higher education leadership roles promoting global understanding and student exchanges. Both of these issues are, of course, pressing concerns a half century later.

Readers will see a recurrent theme of Gould's commitment to recognizing and building academic quality. He was a masterful and charismatic recruiter of faculty talent to Carleton, and he continued to draw on those same skills when he joined the faculty at the University of Arizona. Those who know Gould best in his Carleton role often fail to appreciate how much of his career was actually spent in Arizona's Geology Department. Blessed with good health and longevity (he lived to 98), Gould helped to build an exceptionally strong geology program in Tucson—a program that to this day enjoys enduring links with Carleton.

One of the most striking features of Gould's life was his status as a first generation college student. The life-changing educational experience that the University of Michigan provided the young Larry Gould—and that Gould in turn made a hallmark of his career at Michigan, Carleton, and Arizona—is especially germane today, when colleges and universities rightly worry about ensuring educational access as a gateway to the American dream. Gould did not come from a family of educational accomplishment or distinction, yet he had a world-class mind. Through his own persistence and perspicacity, he made the most of his innate talent. The responsibility now weighs upon all of us to look for and nurture next generations of Laurence McKinley Goulds. Indeed, at a time when the science, technology, engineering, and mathematics disciplines are increasingly recognized as central to the intellectual and economic health of the United States and the world, developing such talent is an imperative. Eric Hillemann's timely and excellent biography reminds us of the transformative power of education, the reverberating effects of scientific discoveries, and the enduring impact of scholars, educators, and leaders.

Steven G. Poskanzer
President
Carleton College
Northfield, Minnesota
October 2012

Donald Cowling **Laird Bell** **Lindsey Blayney**

Laurence McKinley Gould, at the dedication of the Carleton Library in 1956

PROLOGUE

"WHAT WE WANT IS A PARAGON"

In the second half of the twentieth century Carleton College in Northfield, Minnesota, moved to the forefront of academic reputation and prestige among national liberal arts colleges. The achievement of institutional excellence may not be pinpointed to a moment, a year, or even necessarily to an era, as it is a moving target, complex, cumulative, and continual. Carleton's advancement to the front ranks of colleges of its type owes much to many persons, as does its subsequent success in maintaining that position and renewing excellence. Emerson's dictum that every great institution is but the lengthened shadow of a single man is an arresting oversimplification. Nevertheless, the institutional saga of Carleton's post-World War II leap to eminence does have a chief hero in Carleton's fourth president, Laurence M. Gould. It was during the seventeen-year Gould presidency (1945-62) that Carleton first achieved national renown as among the very best of America's small colleges. In a 1961 feature hailing Carleton as a "little Harvard in academic distinction," widely recognized as among the nation's top three coeducational colleges, the *Chicago Daily Tribune* noted that while the school had been "a college of distinction for many years … it rose to preëminence in the midwest only after Dr. Gould became president."

Of course he had help. To begin with, as president of Carleton Gould stood on the shoulders of another giant, Donald J. Cowling, who had presided from 1909 to 1945 over the shaping of that "college of distinction" out of the clay of a not-too-distinguished school of high religious ideals but rather modest academic accomplishment. Cowling established for Carleton the opportunity for greatness; Gould realized the opportunity. He did so in large measure by capitalizing fully on his own rich gifts of personality, leadership, and character.

It was Carleton's good fortune not only to enjoy outstanding administrative helmsmanship under Gould but also to benefit from the reflected luster of the fame and admiration flowing to her president independent of the college. Celebrated since the late 1920s as a polar explorer and scientist and subsequently prominent as an inspiring and much sought-after public speaker, as a distinguished holder of positions of leadership in scholarly and philanthropic organizations, and as a respected spokesman on issues of higher education or polar science, Gould was a headline maker whose position in the public eye kept Carleton there as well. Moreover he proved as president to be a shrewd judge of talent and potential, and his personal qualities attracted talent to Carleton. Time and again persons who had not thought of coming to a school like Carleton changed their minds upon meeting its president and discovering what pleasure it would be to associate themselves with such a man. Carleton morale soared when Gould became president and stayed high throughout his long term. All parts of the institution took pride in their leader, and communal outpourings of affection—students, for instance, organized annual Larry Gould Days to commemorate his selection as president—were genuinely felt. Gould's personal popularity within the college family, with students, alumni, faculty, and staff, was immediate and enduring, and stories relating to "Larry's" character and extraordinary charisma have become part and parcel of the college's sense of its own identity. In sum, there exists no figure in Carleton's remembrance of itself who stands higher in esteem and stature—no person more beloved and no presidency singled out as more successful or more crucial—than that of Larry Gould. It is indeed difficult to imagine by what paths a Carleton without benefit of Gould might have reached comparable heights.

***

In the first week of July 1944, however, all that lay in a future hidden from the men charged with responsibility for selecting a new president for Carleton College. The war news that week was headlined by bitter fighting in Normandy and, halfway around the world, on the Marianas island of Saipan. The Allies moved to occupy Siena, and a Russian army captured Minsk. German "robot bombs" were hitting southern England, and on the 6th Winston Churchill told the House of Commons that this weapon had since June 14 killed 2,752 persons and wounded about 8,000 in the London area. That same July 6, at a luncheon in St. Paul's Minnesota Club, a first joint meeting brought together the six-person Carleton trustees' committee asked to recommend President Cowling's successor to the full board and the five-professor advisory committee elected by the Carleton faculty, which had been invited by the trustees' committee to confer with them from time to time and participate in deliberations over possible candidates.

The faculty committee, headed by the college's senior professor Curvin H. Gingrich, a mathematician and astronomer, included a representative from each of the main divisions of learning within which Carleton's curriculum was then organized. One of its members, Ralph L. Henry of the English Department, was a Carleton alumnus, a graduate of 1917. The others were Professor of Hygiene and Public Health Neil S. Dungay, Professor of International Relations David Bryn-Jones, and Robert W. McEwen of the Department of Philosophy and Religion, who also served the small college (enrolling between eight and nine hundred students in a typical pre-war year) as librarian. Both Gingrich and Dungay had been on staff at Carleton for the entire span of the Cowling era, dating back to 1909. The youngest by many years, McEwen, was an especially able man with ambitions of his own for a college presidency.*

The six trustees included two graduates of the school, Louis S. Headley, Class of 1907, a St. Paul lawyer and banker who served as secretary to the full board, and Malcolm B. McDonald, Class of 1926, a Minneapolis banker who at age thirty-nine was the college's youngest trustee. Horace H. Irvine, another banker, was vice chairman of the board and chairman of its executive committee. Representing two of Carleton's historically important religious ties were the Rev. Thomas C. McQueen, pastor of the Pilgrim Congregational Church in Duluth, and the Rt. Rev. Stephen E. Keeler, bishop of the Episcopal diocese of Minnesota. Heading the committee, and inevitably the tone-setter and dominant decision-maker for the entire search, was the chairman of Carleton's board of trustees, Chicago attorney Laird Bell.

Each of these men knew that the choice of Carleton's next president would be a particularly important one for determining the future course of the school's fortunes, and they felt their responsibility keenly. In the case of Chairman Bell, family history added extra weight to the sense of responsibility. Bell's grandfather, William H. Laird, who had amassed great personal wealth through Minnesota lumbering as a cofounder of the Laird Norton Company, had been president of the Carleton Board of Trustees at the time that Cowling had been hired as president. William Laird's son-in-law, Frederic Somers Bell, had joined the board a few years after Laird's death and had himself served as board president from 1927 until his death in 1938. Both men had been important financial benefactors of the college. In 1938, the board vacancy occasioned by the elder Bell's death was filled by the election of his son, Laird, a graduate of Harvard College and the University of Chicago Law School. Within two months of becoming a trustee, Laird Bell was himself offered the board chairmanship, but he declined, citing the weight of other obligations. Rather than turning to another, the Carleton board got along without a permanent chairman for a number of years. In 1939, again in 1940, and once more in 1942, Bell repeatedly begged off appeals that he accept the chairmanship. "I simply cannot manage it," he wrote. Finally, in 1943 with Cowling's retirement now definitely on the horizon, Bell's sense of responsibility toward Carleton compelled him to reconsider the role he might play as the college approached a crucial decision. Cowling wrote Bell in September that the problem of finding a suitable presidential successor "will probably not be an easy one" but that the "continued progress of the College will depend very largely upon the success" of the coming search. Cowling was of the optimistic judgment that "no college of liberal arts in the United States has a better opportunity than Carleton" or stands "better adapted to meet the needs of the

---

* He would be named president of Blackburn College, in Carlinville, Illinois, in 1945, and a few years later began a long tenure as head of Hamilton College, Clinton, New York.

future," but he warned of unsolved financial problems, observing that "there is no college in the East … doing work comparable with ours which does not have an endowment of at least five million, as compared with our approximately three million." Asked once again to allow himself to be elected board chairman, Bell promised to give the matter serious consideration after the first of the new year.

Accordingly, on January 3, 1944, Bell produced, in a letter addressed to Horace Irvine but meant for the eyes of all his fellow Carleton trustees, a statement of principles he would follow should he become chairman. Predicting that he "might prove an unruly and eventually unwelcome incumbent," Bell cast this personal credo as a warning to the trustees "before they get too far" as to what they would be getting themselves into with Laird Bell at their head. "The trustees," he noted, "have the ultimate responsibility and the ultimate authority in all affairs of the college." In the financial realm this responsibility is relatively direct. While authority is rightly delegated to the college president and treasurer, still "by training and interest the trustees can make a genuine contribution … by prudent handling of these matters and by vigorous promotion of support to the college." With regard to educational policy, however, any trustee interference with the judgment of the president and faculty would be "disastrous to academic integrity." The ultimate responsibility, which the trustees cannot abjure in this area, becomes very real, however, when the question becomes that of the selection or retention of a president—a decision about to be faced at Carleton due to Dr. Cowling's intent to retire. Though that decision is one for the whole board, naturally the chairman "can have a great influence." "Before that power is given me," Bell cautioned, "I think the others should be warned that my views in that field are somewhat heterodox, if not even radical."

Bell, whose involvements with the University of Chicago had made him a great admirer of its energetic and independent-minded young president, Robert M. Hutchins—a man whose unorthodox proposals and willingness to experiment had made him by that time one of the most controversial figures in higher education—indicated that Carleton's next president should be "not merely a man of some vision and imagination—those are pretty general and vague qualities—but he should definitely have ideas that are forward-looking and that may seem revolutionary now." Bell feared stagnation and a "drift down to the level of the commonplace" if the school failed to go forward. "This means to me," he wrote,

> that we must not be content with some one whose ideas are conventional and correct by current academic standards. As Dr. Cowling undoubtedly realizes, I have been much impressed by Mr. Hutchins' views on higher education, which are anathema to a large part of the academic world. I do not contend that the new president should necessarily be a disciple of Hutchins; but I should be unhappy with one who did not give serious consideration to his ideas.

"I do not believe in a college as a school to grow a generation of young conservatives," Bell continued.

> I should want students to know the pros and cons of social and political questions, to be taught to reason honestly, and to reach their own conclusions. I should be willing to abide by the consequences. After all, it may be that conservatism is not the right equipment for the uncertain years ahead.

Undeterred by their prospective leader's declaration of heterodoxy, the trustees later that month formally elected Laird Bell chairman of the board. At the same meeting they authorized their new chairman to appoint a committee to recommend a suitable person to succeed Cowling as president. Such a committee having been duly appointed and the members of a faculty advisory committee determined in turn, the presidential search began in earnest with their first joint meeting in St. Paul.

Minutes were not kept of that July 6 meeting, which undoubtedly focused on procedure for the months ahead, but it is clear that there was at least preliminary discussion of possible candidates for the Carleton presidency. A few names had already been suggested to the committee for consideration. In particular, it is known from references in a later letter that one of the first names raised was that of an internal candidate, Laurence McKinley Gould. Gould had joined the Carleton faculty as head of the Department of Geology and Geography in 1932 and had quickly become the school's most popular professor. With star quality stemming from his fame as second-in-command on the much-celebrated Byrd Antarctic Expedition of 1928-30 and fueled further by his dashing good looks, charismatic personality, and powers as a public speaker, Gould had long been Carleton's best known, most admired, and highest paid teacher. He was then on wartime leave from the college, living with his wife in New York where he was administering the Arctic division of the Army Air Forces' Arctic, Desert, and Tropic Information Center (ADTIC), a post to which he had been appointed late in 1942.

By mid-1944, Gould was looking ahead to the end of his wartime service, expecting that he would be free to return to his work at Carleton sometime in the fall. However, he was also considering other options. Correspondence from April and May reveals that Gould was being considered at that time as a possible candidate to fill presidential vacancies by both the University of Oregon and the University of Minnesota. More immediately, he was being pressed by publisher John Cowles to accept a definite offer to become director of the editorial page for the *Minneapolis Star Journal*, something which would mean a "profound change" in Gould's life work but which was baited by a salary proposal Gould acknowledged as "far beyond anything a college professor could ever hope to achieve." During that first week in July, as the Carleton search committees were preparing to meet in St. Paul, the Goulds were in Minneapolis, at Cowles' urging, to "spend a few days looking the situation over." Gould promised Cowling that he would make no final decision about any plans "without first discussing them with you and having the advantage of your good advice."

On July 7, before returning to New York that evening, Gould spent the day in Northfield, some forty miles south of St. Paul, partly to confer with Cowling. It seems likely that the two spoke frankly about the Carleton presidency as another possibility for Gould's future, a thought that certainly had occurred to both men already and that Cowling may have been quietly endorsing to others for some time. That Gould himself was willing that week to confess his own preference for such an outcome is suggested by a letter sent a few days later, in which a member of Carleton's alumni board, C. Dexter Lufkin, passed along to his friend on the trustees' search committee, Malcolm McDonald, the "very hot scuttlebutt" which he "didn't know until today," that "Larry [Gould] would take the job here in preference to anywhere else and anything else." The basis for that statement is not made clear, but Lufkin's information appears to be good: He accurately reported Gould's presence in Minneapolis to consider the newspaper editorship and the consideration Gould was receiving for the two university presidencies, noting that Gould had recently been asked to go to Oregon as a serious candidate there. Lufkin also reported Gould's recruitment by Canadians wanting him to set up an Arctic transportation service. Lufkin himself endorsed the notion that Gould would be the best possible choice for the Carleton presidency and urged quick action to ensure that the situation be looked into.

McDonald passed Lufkin's letter along to the rest of the trustees' committee, prompting Bell to write to Headley, "I should think we ought to get in touch with Mr. Gould at once and at least not let him escape by default." McDonald agreed, writing Bell that "without attempting to rush into a premature decision, I think we should give very careful consideration to his selection." McDonald perceived that Gould possessed the "enthusiastic esteem of the faculty, students, and friends of the school" and noted that Gould's was the name most often raised when he sought suggestions from Minneapolis people.

Accordingly, on the 19th, the same day the national Democratic Party convened in Chicago to re-nominate President Roosevelt for a fourth term, Bell wrote to Gould regarding the committee's desire to talk with him whenever a meeting could be arranged. At the same time, in a letter to Headley, Bell raised a note of caution. Recalling that at the July 6 meeting Ralph Henry had indicated that while Gould's nomination would be generally agreeable to the faculty, yet "there would be misgivings on the part of a few," Bell sought amplification as to what those misgivings might be. He also queried as to whether Gould had ever expressed definite ideas about education or had written anything outside of his immediate field.

Henry then provided Headley with a long and thoughtful statement, "as wholly disinterested as I can make it," regarding what had been in his mind when speaking of some faculty "misgivings" about Gould. He wrote that he was aware of criticism—which he personally did not share and attributed to some extent to "professional jealousy"—that Gould's classroom work was entertaining but lacked rigor. He related that one full professor of long tenure had recently told him that he did not think Gould was "serious enough" for a very difficult position such as the presidency of Carleton College. Henry hastened to add that "only a very few members of the faculty have this attitude toward Dr. Gould," that "he would have most of the present faculty with him with their most cordial support from the start," and that the existence of some local opposition only reveals "what you must already suspect: that no faculty member can please quite all his neighbors." He thought that "those who feel that Dr. Gould is 'not serious enough' probably are implying that he lacks concentration on details and that he would not give Carleton the strong financial leadership that Dr. Cowling has." Finally, after mentioning two younger members of the faculty who wanted Gould "above all other candidates" and had come to him since July 6 "to make sure that Larry's name had gone in," Henry wrote:

> It is worth adding what one of them also said, for the question is bound to come up. "We don't think it will be as hard as some seem to think for Mrs. Gould to be successful as a college president's wife. We are sure she can readjust her social program to include all the faculty group instead of just a small group of intimate friends." That voluntary defense of Mrs. Gould indicates that they felt the need of bolstering up the situation somewhat. On the issue of Dr. Gould's splendid qualifications, they were 100% certain.

Henry concluded by saying that he should be "happy to serve under Dr. Gould if the trustees select him" but that "I should, of course, favor a long and searching effort to find other strong candidates. I do not think we should choose any one candidate just now even though he is available."

Bell's reaction was to acknowledge to Headley that "there is an extra handicap on any member of the faculty who has accumulated enmities and jealousies, however small" and that "that is a rather disturbing note about Mrs. Gould." Headley thought he sensed "the basis for some of the material in Mr. Henry's letter" and agreed that "the search should not stop at this point."

***

All the rest of that summer and on through the fall, machinery was in motion to canvass the field for other candidates. Lou Headley articulated the qualities sought in a letter soliciting suggestions from A. Calvert Smith, a friend then serving as secretary to the Harvard Corporation and Harvard's Board of Overseers:

> We need as president a man of large natural capacity and vision, and if these are present in good measure we will trust his judgment and

leadership in specific matters. He should be a scholar in his own right but he need not necessarily be a professional educator. He should have a genuine interest in education as such and perhaps for the years ahead his chief interest should be in education rather than in expansion. However, he should have business sense and the capacity to meet and deal with businessmen. He should be personable and capable of dealing with young people, faculty members and constituants [sic] in a way which will command their confidence and respect. He should be fortunate in his family relations.

You will gather from this brief statement that what we want is a paragon. If you know of one or more who might be available either at Harvard or elsewhere and will give us their names, we shall very much appreciate it; but knowing that paragons are rare and that less brilliant men often do a good job, we will welcome suggestions which may not match the pattern in all respects.

Similar letters traveled to educational leaders and friends of Carleton across the country, and the committee's file of names to be investigated grew large.

In mid-September, as units of the American First Army pushed into the German homeland through breaches opened in the Siegfried Line, Larry Gould received approval to resign from his ADTIC service and return to Northfield to resume teaching duties. En route, in Chicago on the 18th, Gould met for the first time with Laird Bell, who was just returned from a late summer vacation.

October brought a second joint meeting of the two search committees, trustee and faculty, held inauspiciously in St. Paul on the evening of Friday, the 13th. In preparation for this meeting the faculty representatives prepared a memorandum to convey the "general sense" of a conclave they had held. This memorandum stated "the following points of agreement" concerning Gould's candidacy:

(1) The faculty representatives have already stated their opinion that the advantages and disadvantages of appointing a member of the present faculty to the presidency probably "cancel out," but that statement should now be qualified as follows;

(2) They would regard relative unanimity among the faculty as a very important factor in weighing these advantages and disadvantages. They are convinced that such unanimity does not, at present, exist in relation to Dr. Gould. There is probably general agreement that he has obvious qualifications which the members of the Committee also recognize. That he is a possible choice would be admitted by most members of the faculty and is the definite opinion of this group.

(3) But there is a fairly strong feeling among certain influential members of the faculty that it might not be the best possible choice. At present it is a choice that would not be received with general enthusiasm nor perhaps with anything approaching unanimous approval.

(4) It is difficult to state the feelings which are responsible for

the reservations implied in this statement, for they do not concern Dr. Gould's personal relationships nor his reputation and ability in his field. They may be suggested rather than defined by saying that in a college of our type long range objectives and definite ideals are preeminently important—the shape of things to come for a college depends upon these objectives and ideals. In a college of our type the President's position is one of extraordinary importance and responsibility in furthering these objectives. It is here that doubts arise about Dr. Gould. Estimable, genial, and able, as he is, there is a sense that he has given no clear evidence of that vision of the place of liberal education in a philosophy of life which is the supreme justification for the existence of the liberal arts college. It is here that educational leadership, especially after the war, will be tested most severely and it is just here that doubts in relation to Dr. Gould are completely unresolved. What is attempted in this statement is perhaps impossible, viz. to make explicit in words the basic convictions which are responsible for such division as exists among the faculty, but enough has been said to indicate their nature.

(5) Whether this division goes deep enough to seriously jeopardize the chances of an administration begun while it exists, it is not possible to say at present. The Committee are strongly of opinion that it is deep enough to merit the most earnest consideration and to make caution a counsel of wisdom.

The reaction to this statement of the trustees' committee is unrecorded, but there is a hint of frustration over the progress of the search to that point in Bell's letter to his family describing the October meeting: "We started with 44 names, but plucked most of them by the time the professors and the ministers got through with them. New suggestions will be gratefully received."

Helpful evaluations of a number of names had been solicited and received from Carleton alumnus John W. Nason (Class of 1926), who had recently taken over as the young president of Swarthmore College. The suggestion was made by some, and echoed by Headley, that if Nason himself could possibly be enticed away from Swarthmore the Carleton trustees need look no further. Though it was doubted that he could be brought to accept, Bell was asked to discover Nason's attitude.* Bell met with Nason and others during a mid-November trip to Philadelphia, New York, and Washington. Also that autumn he met with other candidates in Chicago and, in late October, in Portland, Oregon.

Meanwhile, the search committee chairman now began to receive an almost regular succession of letters from Carleton alumni and faculty members urging

---

* Nason's final word on the matter was this: "If I were to leave Swarthmore there is no place I would rather go than Carleton.... Its spirit, progress, and well-being are in my blood. It would not be proper for me, however, to leave Swarthmore at this time." Nason did leave Swarthmore in 1953, becoming president of the Foreign Policy Association, and in 1962 succeeded Gould in the Carleton presidency.

the selection of Larry Gould as the college's next president. Dated October 24, from alumna Elizabeth Oliver Hosick '32. November 4, from history professor Nelson Vance Russell (asserting that "with the exception of a few and many of these will soon retire, a very large majority of the faculty support unreservedly the candidacy of Professor … Gould.") November 14, from former Associate Professor of Political Science Keith Clark. November 15, from alumna Peggy Muirhead '42. November 20, from Assistant Professor of Zoology Olin S. Pettingill, Jr. November 21, from former chemistry professor Azariah T. Lincoln. On the 24th, Bell forwarded these letters to the other trustee committee members, noting that "It looks a little as if some one were campaigning for Dr. Gould. However, some of the letters are quite impressive." Bell wrote Headley the next day that "particularly in view of the number of people that are writing about him, I should rather like to talk again with Laurence Gould."

Also choosing to write to Bell at about this time was crusty Professor of Physics Charles A. Culver, an alumnus from the Class of 1902. At age sixty-nine, Culver was one of Russell's soon-to-retire "exceptions" who did not look with favor upon a prospective Gould presidency. He made no bones about his opposition, asserting that "it would be unwise to select a new president from the Carleton Faculty," because "our group is small; inevitably too many personal equations would be involved" and because moreover "there is no one on our staff equipped to serve the College as chief executive, all factors considered."

A third joint meeting of the two committees was held November 28, after which Bell confided to Nason, "I am not sure what kind of paragon the faculty members of our committee have in mind, but we don't seem to have produced him yet among those that they really know about." Writing to the president of Bryn Mawr College, Bell confessed himself "painfully aware of the importance of making the right choice" and, as the third generation of his family to head the Carleton board, "particularly anxious" on that account "not to make a mistake." By the end of the November 28 meeting, the list of names under active consideration had been "reduced to approximately twenty," and plans were made for further refinement following "conferences which Mr. Bell and Mr. Headley had in prospect with certain persons in the east."

At this time Bell and the other members of the trustees committee were distressed to hear that the rumor was abroad in Minneapolis—and stated positively at a ladies' meeting—that the Carleton presidency was to go to Larry Gould. Members of the committee took steps to disconfirm this "news" and to stop its spread, but the incident was an annoyance.

Organized or not, the "campaigning" for Gould continued. Letters urging the selection of Gould came to Bell dated December 1, from alumnus Bill Stafford '38; December 2, from alumnus John Sirjamaki '34; December 7, from alumnus Carl Eklund '32, who worked under Gould in the Army Air Forces; December 14, from alumnus Victor Church '36; and December 19, from faculty colleague

Hans Weigert. On the 11th, Gould himself wrote to Bell, enclosing a letter received from another alumnus which was a declaration of support for Gould's "candidacy," on behalf of several Carleton friends in St. Paul and Minneapolis, and inquiring what they could best do to further his interests. Gould told Bell he had received others like it and that he had just learned that a number of other people had written directly to Bell "in similar vein." He declared that he was unaware of any organized effort in his behalf and that if such organized support did exist he considered it "unfortunate and to be regretted." "I have some idea of the heroic task which will confront Dr. Cowling's successor," he wrote, "and the job should seek the man—not the man the job." He indicated that "the conditions under which I could and would accept the presidency of Carleton College might well not be acceptable to the Board of Trustees."

The Board of Trustees, however, was not at all ready yet to offer the presidency of Carleton College to anyone. As December turned to January and Allied armies in Europe rolled back the last great German counteroffensive in the Battle of the Bulge, Laird Bell prepared to go "president hunting" on a trip to visit and screen several eastern prospects.

Before he left, his attention was called again to the merits of the local prospect, in the form of a particularly impressive letter from an Army Air Forces major familiar with Gould's wartime work as chief of the Arctic Section of ADTIC. Attributing Gould's success in this role to his "human qualities ... which made us respect him and want to work with him" and to his "knowledge of men—his ability to deal with them honestly, to evaluate their abilities, to put them to the best possible use," Major George Miksch Sutton praised Gould's unfailing ability quickly to find common ground with all men, consistently on a high plane, never as compromise: "Those who are with him step up a level or so. No one ever steps down." The major concluded with what may be as warm and pertinent an endorsement of a prospective college president as it may be possible to give:

> What I have said may not prove to you that Larry is the man for Carleton's presidency. Indeed, I'm not sure that I know exactly what a college president should be. But I know that if I had five sons and five daughters I'd want them all to live in Larry's shadow during their college days if possible.

The same day, however, that Major Sutton wrote to praise Gould, Professor Culver wrote hoping to bury him. In a letter addressed to Headley, Culver concluded: "The longer I turn the situation over in my mind, the more thoroughly am I convinced that it would be very unwise to select a man from the local faculty. Indeed we have no one here who measures up to the task."

Bell returned from his eastern "president hunting" trip without feeling that the picture was clearing. He was most impressed with President John S. Millis of the University of Vermont but doubted whether he could be drawn away from university work. As to Gould, he indicated an interest in arranging another visit with him—but at the same time, in response to President Cowling's having urged a committee decision soon, Bell confided that he was finding it "very difficult to get ahead. The simple solution which has of course occurred to you I do not believe can be accepted until we have pretty well exhausted other possibilities."

The faculty advisory committee, asked at this time to classify the remaining candidates in order of preference, grouped three names as "qualified" for the position, and thought that five others "might be found to be qualified" upon further investigation. Remaining names were "crossed out for the time being," with the exception of that of Gould, over whom the advisory committee recognized a divergence of faculty opinion and declared a willingness "to leave that situation with the trustees for appraisal and proper evaluation."

***

Louis Headley visited several prospective presidents on his own trip east during the first part of February. Thereafter the committee focused consideration on just a few individuals, giving serious scrutiny to each. Particular interest persisted in two men besides Gould: Millis—who it turned out could perhaps be interested in leaving Vermont for Carleton after all—and Eugene G. Bewkes, a Colgate University professor of philosophy then in Washington directing the Bureau of Manpower Utilization with the War Manpower Commission. Each met with members of both committees in March, and at the end of that month the five members of the faculty advisory committee were requested to compare the merits of these two men with each other and perhaps with others still under active consideration—meaning, effectively, Gould. Gingrich had not seen Millis but reported himself "very favorably impressed with Bewkes." Bryn-Jones was "very favorably impressed" by both men and without mentioning Gould by name offered the opinion that "either would be a decidedly better choice than any other available candidate whom we have considered." Henry limited his statement to Bewkes and Millis and concluded that "either would be an admirable choice." Dungay expressed a slight preference for Bewkes over Millis, while saying he would be pleased to have the trustees invite either to take the presidency. He placed Gould third out of the feeling that "a local man would suffer from faculty opposition," though he added that he did not consider this very serious and that he would personally find Gould a very acceptable choice and enjoy working under him. In any case, stressed Dungay, it would be unfortunate if a choice could not now be made as soon as possible. McEwen wrote that both Bewkes and Millis had made a favorable impression on him, but on the whole he would rate Millis slightly ahead. In relation to Gould, McEwen added:

> It is obvious, incidentally, that neither of these men has the knowledge of Carleton's present problems, the friendship of students and alumni, and the potential contacts in the immediate area of the College that Larry

Gould now has. Nor does either of them, in my opinion, make quite as forceful and dynamic an impression in meeting the public. It is equally clear that Larry has not had the experience in educational administration that both of these men have had. Nor has Larry, up to the present, shown the interest in general educational problems which Millis and Bewkes show. Any comparison of Larry with Millis and Bewkes seems therefore to depend primarily on the importance to be given to the public relations program during the next few years in the definition of the president's task, a definition which is not the province of the faculty advisory committee.

The power of decision, however, lay with the trustees' committee, and the weight of responsibility there lay most heavily upon its leaders, Bell and Headley—neither of whom, it now developed, felt easy about the selection of any of the remaining candidates. Vexed by doubts over perceived shortcomings in each of the men they had considered, as well as in Gould, they found themselves beset by indecision even while under increasing pressure to bring the search to a close in the next few weeks. Bell, aware that his opinion would likely be the decisive one, confessed his sense of "terrifying responsibility—the fate of a first-class institution for the next generation hangs on our decision." In a letter to his mother, Bell wrote at this time:

> I am not happy about *any* prospects. Gould is personally attractive, the students & alumni like him & urge his election, and yet I don't feel content. I don't think he has any very profound ideas about education. I think he would just make Carleton another college, a good one but no different from a dozen others and therefore without hope of being outstanding. On the other hand what are our alternatives? The one that was in St. Paul [Bewkes] has some ideas on the subject but they don't seem awfully profound either. You see, I'd like someone as outstanding, & as capable of making Carleton outstanding, as Dr. Cowling was when he went there.... And none of the people I've talked with really have seemed to me to have that touch of genius that I look for. Perhaps I ask too much.

Aware of their mutual unease, Headley regretted not having begun their search "a year or at least some months before we did." While he supposed that they could select from among the remaining candidates "one who would do a reasonably good job," he shared Bell's view that "there is lacking in all of them that overage which makes a man outstanding and which should be in a president of Carleton College." Declaring that "there must be such a person somewhere and it is our job to find him," Headley floated the idea that they make a temporary admission of defeat:

> How important do you think it is that we get someone before commencement time? If President Cowling can make the appointments

for next year and close out the present year without a deficit, might it not be possible for the College to get along a little time without a full time president? Perhaps as Chairman of the Board you would even be willing to assume the title of Acting President and to perform such broad administrative duties as might require attention. Such a program would give us time to look about still farther and as a result of more deliberative searching we might find exactly the right man. For my part, I am going over the file again to see if possibly we have missed some material.

A few days later, Bell responded, agreeing that he was not convinced that any of Bewkes, Millis, or Gould was "the man we must have." Gould, he thought, "has everything except the one thing I personally seek—a kind of flaming interest in education. I think he would do a good job but not an outstanding one."

The question that is troubling me is, therefore, whether to make an immediate decision or to face the grief of continuing the search for that ideal man. If we would give it out that we are not going to decide at once it amounts to serving notice on Gould that he will not do, and I judge from our talk with him that he will leave.

To his family, Bell wrote:

I'd like another year to hunt my ideal man, but I'm afraid the situation won't wait and that we'll have to take a man that's all right but not the knight in shining armour that I've been looking for. Maybe they don't wear armour any more.

That week, Bell's active options shrank further, as Bewkes wrote that he had decided to accept the presidency of St. Lawrence University, in upstate New York.*

The same day that Bewkes wrote to withdraw his name from consideration, Carleton's longtime dean of the college, Lindsey Blayney, addressed a letter to the chairman that Bell later told Blayney was "a genuine contribution to our thinking." Blayney, who as dean had been Carleton's second-ranking administrative officer since 1926 and was planning to retire at the end of the current year along with Cowling, began by observing that he had until now thought it best not to intrude himself into the selection process, but that with the year fast drawing to a close without the trustees' committee having yet reached a decision, he now felt it best respectfully to submit his opinion. In Blayney's judgment the principal qualifications needed for the position at Carleton were "intellectual integrity and dependability; courage of conviction; superior mentality; executive experience; breadth of interest and understanding; genuine respect

---

* Bewkes oversaw a period of great expansion at St. Lawrence in a presidency lasting from 1945 to 1963.

for religion; and personal achievement and recognition." To these he thought might be added for the immediate future "a knowledge of veterans' problems and of military affairs gained from personal experience." He then turned his letter to a ringing endorsement of Gould as rating "astonishingly high" under all of the above heads.

Blayney observed that Gould was a "profoundly spiritually-minded scientist" and that "the breadth of his interests and understanding outside the field of science is striking." He was, thought Blayney, more "widely-read in best literature" than any other scientist of his acquaintance and equal to few scholars in that way outside those actually in the field of literature. Gould's wide intellectual sympathies, Blayney thought, meant that he was already well acquainted with the subject matter of many of the "various departments of learning into which a college falls." Moreover, as a man who had personally come through the "searing but refining crucible of military experience," Gould would merit the respect and confidence of returning veterans. Observing that "the president of a growing college must be a platform speaker of ability," Blayney declared that "in this respect Dr. Gould has few rivals in the teaching profession." Carleton would be "seriously handicapped on losing Dr. Cowling, a persuasive speaker, if it does not have a magnetic interpreter such as Dr. Gould unquestionably is."

Blayney urged as well the advantage to the college of Gould's established prominence as a nationally known figure—"he enjoys far wider recognition at the present moment than do many college presidents after years of service"—and while he conceded that "only very exceptionally should the president of a college be chosen from its faculty," he judged that Gould's qualities merit "in every way that an exception be made." He concluded with words that could not have been better tailored to address Bell's continuing hope to discern, elsewhere in the field, a shining Galahad:

> May I suggest finally that Dr. Gould has been tested in remarkably many ways—by his classes, by student bodies, by audiences far and near, by army groups, by expeditions of "men's men", by national planning bodies, by thousands of readers, and yet unlike many, he has in each field won their loyalty, respect, and admiration. What more can we ask? If some hesitate to endorse Dr. Gould because he falls short of perfection in some small or fancied way, how much more ought we to hesitate to call someone less known, less tried, and possibly less talented? At least the fewness of local opponents to his appointment speaks volumes in his favor. May I, therefore, respectfully suggest to any who may be hoping for "two birds in a distant bush" that we should be thankful for the "one we now have in the hand."

Following this, the written record of Laird Bell's thinking regarding the "problem" of the Carleton presidency now falls silent for nearly three weeks.

***

On the 12th of April, with Germany nearing final defeat in Europe, President Roosevelt died in Warm Springs, Georgia. That day another senior member of the Carleton faculty, astronomer Edward A. Fath (like Culver also an alumnus of the Class of 1902), wrote to Malcolm McDonald of the trustee committee that he had changed his mind regarding a question that McDonald had put to him a week earlier, namely, if an outside candidate and Gould had equal qualifications, which one would he favor? Fath's first response had been that he would favor the outside candidate, but now he wrote that after further consideration, not only would he favor Gould if qualifications were equal, but he would even go further and state that he would now "favor Gould over an outside candidate even though his general qualifications fell somewhat below." His reasoning now was that Carleton in the near future would be faced with many problems which Gould was already in a position to know and upon which he could take prompt action, whereas an outside man "might require so long a time to acquaint himself with local conditions that the college would suffer seriously because of the delay." McDonald passed Fath's letter along to Bell the next day.

Meanwhile, Louis Headley continued to beat the bushes for a superior candidate who had previously been overlooked or who might yet be uncovered by another visit east, and he retained interest in the attitude of Millis. With regard to Gould, Headley wrote Bell that he found himself coming back to "the recurring proposition that Dr. Gould does not have the depth or breadth, referred to by someone as the 'stature,' nor the ardent interest in education which should be evident in the next President of Carleton College." He elaborated upon his feeling "that it would be unwise to select as president any member of the faculty group":

> I am not so much interested in the relative number of letters pro or con; they might not even reflect the balance of sentiment, as those who entertain doubts would naturally be less vocal than those who do not. It is the division itself which is significant and I cannot believe that it would be wise to launch a new administration with so pronounced a division in the faculty as seems to exist. It is conceivable that a member might have such outstanding qualities of leadership in education and enthusiasm for the task as to off-set in a measure the disadvantages of internal division, but I fail to find promise of these in Dr. Gould. If they exist, I am inclined to think that the division which seems to mark the faculty would not exist.

Headley concluded this letter with the hope that Bell was "planning another tour of the East and that you will find just the right man."

Two days later, trustees' committee member Tom McQueen wrote Headley that his feeling continued to be that "we have no candidate who can compare with Dr. Gould both in standpoint of preparation for the position and general ability." McQueen felt that the trustees should not take some local faculty opposition to

Gould too seriously and asked that the trustees "be very sure before we ask any other man ... that we are considering the best interests of the College regardless of what some members of the Faculty may have to say." Headley, however, continued to feel, in his response to this letter, that the division that existed "would be a serious handicap to a new administration."

Laird Bell, in the meantime, had indeed again gone east, to Washington, from where he arranged to have another lately suggested candidate, John Russell, an assistant to Harvard's President Conant prior to wartime service leave, meet with committee members in Minneapolis April 26. But Bell now had other news which left Headley feeling "sunk"—the Under Secretary of War had urgently requested Bell to go to Europe shortly as counsel to the Economic Division of the United States Group of the Allied Control Commission at Allied Headquarters. He would do his best to get "Carleton obligations cleaned up" before leaving but there was little time remaining. As Headley noted, "this means either that we must come to a conclusion at once or make some arrangements which will tide us over until you return."

On April 24, the eve of the opening in San Francisco of the founding conference of the United Nations, Bell was back in Chicago. That day he put on paper in a letter to Headley the trend of his latest thinking on the Carleton presidency:

> I don't believe we'll find Russell is the man. Of course he may change my thinking, but it seems a long shot. I talked with Millis by phone from Washington. He is still interested and wants to have "a long talk" with me but can't get away till May 5. That adds up in my mind to this: We have to take Gould, or one of these two men, or delay a year. Though we could do with Millis or Russell, I don't feel that they are enough better than Gould to warrant a last ditch fight for either of them. That leaves the question whether we should turn Gould down for some better unknown whom we can hope, but only hope, is going to be found. My conscience hurts with the realization that my own delay in getting to work on this is responsible for the difficulty. Be that as it may, that's where we are.
>
> Would Gould affirmatively hurt the institution? If so, of course we should suffer the damage now instead of over fifteen years. But I don't believe that—it is rather that he falls short of an ideal that you and I have.
>
> I think we are agreed on Gould's shortcomings, but they are not necessarily fatal. The fact of some faculty opposition doesn't bother me. Some men on any faculty would oppose any candidate if they knew him as well as they know Gould. (I suspect that if I found my own ideal he'd scare the faculty to death even at the start.) I should guess the faculty committee to be two for Gould, two against and one only mildly against; while certainly most of the other faculty people that have spoken out have been strongly for him.
>
> It might even be that Gould's lack of any deeply thought out ideas on education is an advantage. When he gets straightened around and

appoints the inevitable faculty planning committee perhaps educational ideas might be made to develop through that channel. Certainly educational thought is going to be forced upon us post-war. As Gould has no full-fledged program of his own we might well get a pretty good one in the end out of combined faculty thinking.

Gould has all the other and obvious things—personality, popularity with alumni, acquaintance in the Twin Cities, and the like, together with standing as a serious scientist.

I should feel a sense of personal failure at not getting more shining armor. But as I feel about it right now I think that, while we shouldn't be giving Carleton all the lift I had hoped, we shouldn't be doing her any harm.

In that reluctant manner was the man who would come to be seen as Carleton's greatest, most successful, and most *indispensable* president begrudgingly approved! The rest was anticlimax. Members of the committee met with Russell April 26 and again with Millis on May 5. Bell, in Washington again until his departure for Europe, remained in touch with Headley and the committee by telephone. On May 7—the day of Germany's final surrender and the end of the war in Europe—Headley wrote to Millis as a candidate who might still very well be chosen,* pending another telephone communication the evening of the 9th, but on Saturday May 12 representatives of the trustees' committee called on Gould at home in Northfield to offer him the presidency—which he accepted upon being assured that he had in the end been the committee's top choice.

* * *

Seventeen years later, at the final meeting of the Carleton Board of Trustees convened before Gould stepped down from what had indisputably been a stunningly successful Carleton presidency, a statement was read in connection with Gould's election that day to the title of president emeritus:

This Board cannot permit the president of the College to retire without some record, however inadequate, of its gratitude for what his administration has meant to us all. Building upon a college already distinguished, he has guided it to still greater stature. The new buildings are an expression of this growth; the endowment has increased many fold, thanks to his efforts; but his real contribution has been in his leadership in the academic field. His first concern has been the selection of a faculty whose primary devotion has been teaching, supported by genuine scholarship. He has maintained the College as a place of learning, without

---

* Millis went on to a long tenure as president and then chancellor at Case Western Reserve University, beginning in 1949.

compromise with the shallow or superficial. He has unfailingly supported the faculty in its freedom to teach. Above all, by his own example he has showed what it is to be at once a teacher, a scholar, a public servant, and a man of affairs. He has lived up to the Whitehead principle that he often quoted—"Moral education is impossible apart from the habitual vision of greatness."

Reading the statement honoring this paragon was a man who had become one of Gould's warmest friends and one of his most fervent admirers, Mr. Laird Bell. The board signified its unanimous approval with a standing ovation.

Ralph, Cecile, Neita, and Laurence Gould, c.1899

Gould's Updike grandparents

Parents Herb and Anna Updike Gould

CHAPTER 1

LAUNCHED: WHITHER BOUND?

Larry Gould's growing years were lived in the orchard country of southwestern Michigan, on a farm straddling the border between Allegan and Van Buren Counties near the village of Lacota. Forebears on both sides of his family had arrived in the area by the 1840s, and all branches were settled there by 1860. Each of Gould's parents and two grandparents were born within forty miles of Lacota. Seven great-grandparents and four great-great grandparents had lived within the same geographical circle. By standards of the American Midwest, these were deep roots.

One grandfather, William Gould, came to Allegan County from New Jersey, via Indiana. A number of William's siblings, and eventually his mother, did the same. William served in a Michigan infantry regiment for nearly four years of the Civil War. A few weeks after his 1865 discharge, at thirty-one years of age, he married Henrietta, the sixteen-year-old daughter of Herman Fisher, also a Michigan Civil War soldier, who had died of pneumonia contracted in the army in 1863 but whose widow Catherine would live on until 1916. William and Henrietta produced six children in the eleven years before William's death early in 1877, reportedly from disability incurred during service. Henrietta, whose family descended from colonials living in Maine prior to the American Revolution, would remarry twice. She was reportedly abandoned in old age by her third husband because she had become "unbearably bossy."

Larry Gould's maternal grandfather, Albert DeWitt Updike, was born in a cabin on the Kalamazoo River near Otsego, twenty-two miles east of Lacota. He was a descendant of Louris Jansen Opdycke, a seventeenth-century Dutch emigrant to New York. Four generations advanced from Louris, brothers Roliph, Abraham, Jacob, and Burgoon Updike were at the time of the Revolution living in New Jersey, where, descendants say, the battle of Princeton was fought partly on Updike land. Roliph's son Gilbert—Larry Gould's grandfather's grandfather—was but one year old at the time of the battle. As the British approached, the story is told, Gilbert's mother entrusted the child to a hired man, who was to take him on horseback to a neighboring farm. When the hired man was taken prisoner,

Gilbert was abandoned in a field; his mother eventually found him lying on the ground with nearly frozen cheeks. Passing English troops sympathetically called him a "poor little Rebel." The child survived to marry his cousin, Laney Updike, and to migrate with other family members by covered wagon and ox team to southwestern Michigan, where he died in 1845.

Gilbert Updike's son Garret married Eliza Loveless of Ithaca, New York, in that state in 1827, but by the 1840s their family and both sets of parents were all residing in Allegan County, Michigan, where Garret, a farmer and sometime carpenter with no formal education, is remembered as one of the first settlers of Ganges Township.

Albert DeWitt Updike was by several years the youngest of Garret and Eliza's five children, but circumstances made him, from a young age, his parents' principal support on the family farm. Two boys died as teenagers, one before Albert was born and the other when Albert was eight. The only girl, nearly fourteen years Albert's senior, was married before turning eighteen. The other boy, George, ten years older than Albert, was an epileptic. When Albert was four, Garret Updike placed a few pieces of furniture on a Kalamazoo River rowboat, transferred the load to wagon near Saugatuck, and brought his family to a new homestead on the Lake Michigan shore, some five miles north of South Haven. This farm would remain Albert's into old age and would be associated by Larry Gould with many happy memories of rustic childhood.

As Albert Updike grew he attended country school and helped on the farm. Eventually, he became a skilled carpenter and learned the trade of Lake Michigan shipbuilding as practiced in the yards of South Haven. By about 1867, the year Albert turned twenty-one, his mother's health had become poor and the family decided that she would need additional help with the strenuous duties of a farm household. Accordingly they hired the domestic assistance of an energetic girl of fourteen or fifteen, Sarah Ann Peck. Sarah's family had come to Michigan from Ontario several years previously. She was a small girl, talkative and friendly, and she soon caught the eye of Albert, who talked little but was equally, if quietly, friendly. They were married three days before her seventeenth birthday, and the first of their three daughters arrived some seven months later.

These Updike grandparents were important figures in Larry Gould's young life, and he spent much happy time on their farm, often in the company of two male cousins being raised there. Gould had a particular fondness for Sarah, or "Grandma Dike." She is characterized by descendants as a loving and industrious woman and quite bright though lacking in formal education. (She was taught to read and write only after her marriage, by a neighbor.) She lived to be ninety-four, long enough to see her grandson Laurence become a college president.

By all accounts Sarah and Albert Updike's second daughter, Anna Elizabeth, inherited her mother's industry, keenness of mind, and concern for others, as well as expert skills as a seamstress and cook. She was nineteen when she married a hardworking twenty-year-old farmer from an adjoining township, Herbert Gould.

Herb was cheerful and even-tempered, well liked by nearly all who knew him. The fourth of William and Henrietta Gould's six children, he was but five years old when his father died and from a young age had with his older brother Ellsworth become accustomed to difficult labor—both on the farm and, for a time during his hardscrabble youth, in a Michigan logging camp. Herb's schooling went no further than the third or fourth grade in a local country school; Anna had advanced through the eighth. One bond between them was music, for each was attracted to the fine singing voice of the other. Anna was able to play tunes by ear, on a foot-pedal organ.

They wed in mid-June, 1892. Their first child, Ralph, came at the end of October. Four more were born during the couple's first decade of marriage and then, after a nearly seven-year lull, two final girls, born when Anna was thirty-five and thirty-eight. In all, a family of seven children, two boys and five girls. The children were raised under humble circumstances, but in an atmosphere of love. Everyone enjoyed the evenings when Herb sang to them—songs of the lumbermen among whom he had worked when younger, or popular folk tunes such as the much-requested "My Grandfather's Clock." Anna quietly set for her children a tone of encouragement toward giving the world their best through self-improvement and service to others.

***

Herb and Anna Gould's remarkable third child was born August 22, 1896, joining three-year-old Ralph and one-year-old Cecile. The birth was registered in Allegan County, and the boy was christened Laurence McKinley—the middle name bestowed by the father in honor of the Republican man of the hour, nominated for the presidency at the convention in St. Louis earlier that summer.

Relatively little anecdote survives to paint details of Larry Gould's childhood in and about Lacota, but some picture does emerge.

Peaches and apples were grown in the family orchard, and Gould wrote later in life that he "always cherished the illusion that no apples were quite as good as those and no apple sauce quite as good as that my mother made when I was a lad." Like any farm boy, he was made to be useful early. At seven he learned to milk, whereupon this became his regular chore. "I disliked it heartily," he later recalled, "and decided not to do it permanently." Apparently the entire family soon agreed that Larry was not farmer material, that his aptitudes lay elsewhere. He was a youth prone to dreaminess—to "deep thinking" would be his preferred characterization. Relatives say that Herb Gould avoided sending Larry out with a team for fear he would kill the horses. His father "was afraid he would get distracted thinking about other things, and not stop to let them rest." Another relative reports understanding that "Uncle Laurence was quite the practical joker, and *very* devious!" Gould himself later began a speech with the information that he had been the kind of boy of whom his mother used to say that she wouldn't let him play with if he was the neighbor.

The village of Lacota was in those years essentially a railroad crossing surrounded by fragrant orchards. Located about eight miles east of the Lake Michigan shoreline at South Haven, it had previously been called Irvington in commemoration of the first white child born in Geneva Township, but this had been changed in 1884 upon the request of the Michigan Central Railroad to avoid confusion with the town of Irving, also on its lines. The name Lacota derived from the chief character, an Indian maiden, in a novel read by village resident Varnum Dilley. At the time of Gould's youth Lacota was a stop on the railroad that made three round trips daily between South Haven and Kalamazoo. Local boys enjoyed swimming in Spicebush Creek, and their elders were often to be found relaxing around the stove in Charlie Simpson's hardware store, swapping fish tales. In 1912 Lacota supported in addition to Simpson's a general store, two groceries, a livery, and a blacksmith and wagon shop for the manufacture of fruit wagons. It also contained a cider and vinegar factory, a lumberyard, post office, railroad depot, and two Protestant churches, the Christian and the Methodist Episcopal. The Goulds apparently associated themselves with the latter, located a little to the south of their home.

Larry attended the small one-room Crow School just north of Lacota in Casco Township. A profile by a boyhood acquaintance, printed some years later in the *South Haven Daily Tribune*, after Gould had begun to accumulate fame, gives one of the few glimpses into this period from a contemporary:

> Quite distinctly we remember the first time that we ever saw Laurence Gould—"Jake" he was in those days. It was on the banks of Spicebush creek, one of those little streams that have an unaccountable trick of becoming narrower and smaller as the years go by. It was a fishing trip of a pair of small boys. A big, rough awkward lad wandered into our path back in Lull's pasture near Lacota. As boys will, we became acquainted without benefit of introduction.
>
> Our memory of Gould at that time revives the picture of a boy with an amazing vocabulary of profanity and barbaric English. The barbaric language has gone now, but the vocabulary of weird epithets remains, to be used on select occasions. [...]
>
> Later Laurence Gould was—literally—the eighth grade at the Lacota school. With himself as the only individual in the class, he cometed through the school year. In the spring he easily won first honors in the Van Buren County eighth grade examinations.

On several occasions later in life Gould recalled how at about age thirteen he took his first paid job, picking strawberries for a penny a box. The money earned he spent on a book, a biography of his lifelong hero, Abraham Lincoln. Later he is known to have earned money picking sour cherries at the Ross Dilley cherry orchards.

This may have been close to the same time when Herb Gould, who was an enthusiastic hunter, gave Larry, who was not, the gift of a .22 rifle for shooting small animals. Larry later recounted a story whereby his father was trying to teach him to shoot, asking him to use as his target a sparrow sitting on top of the barn. Dutifully, Larry aimed and fired, but the bird did not move. A second try yielded the same result. "Well, let me show you how," offered the father, who in turn fired two or three times, the sparrow still unmoving. Finally the elder Gould gave up, concluding, "You know, it beats all how much space there is around one little bird."

From 1910 to 1914, Gould attended South Haven High School. When he entered, this was located on the second floor of the small, antiquated "Central School" built in 1858, but the elated student body marched downtown in celebration in the spring of 1913 when the South Haven electorate passed a bond issue to build a new high school. Gould rather wished to join the school's football team, but his mother forbade it, fearing serious injury. Instead, his focus was academic. In addition to the usual mix of English, history, and mathematics, the future scientist took coursework in botany, chemistry, and physics; he also studied both German and Latin. In his Latin teacher, Eva P. Carnes, Gould was fortunate to find an especially inspiring teacher he would always consider one of the greatest he ever knew.

During these years Gould's family experienced a number of important changes. Early in 1911 his youngest sister, Bonnie, was born. That fall, his older sister, Cecile, was the first of the family to marry, wedding Ed Dannison two days before her seventeenth birthday. Two months later, an uncle, Ellsworth Gould, was married at age forty-two. In December of the year following, Larry Gould became for the first time an uncle, when his niece Annabel was born to Cecile and Ed Dannison. Another family wedding followed in June of 1913, as older brother Ralph married Dott Sheldon.

Meanwhile, Larry was making a name for himself at South Haven High School, emerging as salutatorian of the Senior Class of 1914. (A friend later opined that "he might have carried away first honors ... but his sense of humor was not quite equal to the task of maintaining the necessary dead level of discipline.") On June 20, 1914, Laurence Gould addressed the forty-one other graduates of his South Haven class, assembled at the Congregational Church for commencement under the motto "Launched: Whither Bound?" His message, as reported by the local paper, was that the world demands educated men and women "filled with enthusiasm"; that "society is reinforced from the bottom, not from the top," and that "this is the day of the poor boy's opportunity." The "mainspring of life," he said, is ambition, but ambition "must be combined with industry, as we cannot dawdle through life." However, he urged, "the use of all labor is not merely to secure the physical necessities of life, but to fulfill the vision of the 'New Jerusalem, the Kingdom of Heaven on Earth.'"

Listeners agreed that young Gould showed potential as a public speaker.

Schoolmaster Larry Gould with students in Boca Raton, Florida

***

Gould's ambition now was to enter the University of Michigan in Ann Arbor. To do so, he would need money his family could not provide. He had already passed the teachers' examination in Allegan County and thought he would teach school for a year or two to save enough money to go on to the university. He had begun to investigate the local possibilities when he learned from a classmate, Ruth Chesebro, of high demand for school teachers in Florida and, specifically, of an opening in the village school at Boca Raton, which in 1914 had no more than a handful of residents and where Gould might succeed as teacher Ruth's sister Esther. Gould scored high on the Florida teachers' examination and secured the position, staying two years.

The Boca Raton school, established six years previously, was of the one-room variety, located in a small wooden frame building. Gould, who had just turned eighteen when the school year began, taught all grades one through eight. Photographs from the time suggest that this involved instruction for about twenty students. For at least most of the time he was there, he lodged with the Frank Chesebro family—though a story passed along by a grandniece suggests that he may initially have boarded with another. According to this story, told by "Uncle Laurence" to his relation decades later, the new country teacher was first placed with a family that was rather poor, entirely uneducated, and—the crux of the matter—served indifferent food, badly prepared. For a boy raised on the home cooking of Anna Gould and Grandma Dike, this was indeed a hardship! So, this story goes, Gould convinced the family that his upstairs room was haunted by a ghost and used this as a polite excuse to begin boarding with another family, presumably with a better household cook.

Several of Gould's students at this country school were Japanese from the Yamato Colony, a small settlement of Japanese immigrants two and a half miles north of the Boca Raton depot. These children needed to be transported twice daily over a rough road in a "bus"—first a horse-drawn wagon and later a Model T Ford—supplied by Frank Chesebro. Gould himself was the bus driver. On Sundays the school doubled as a community church, and Gould pitched in by organizing Sunday school classes.

Florida fauna

Many of Gould's pupils were the children of parents who themselves could neither read nor write; yet Gould's modest salary depended on his ability to maintain the attendance record. "So," he recalled years later, "I learned more about getting on with people in those two years than any other years of my life." His instruction included such topics as physiology and hygiene, and Gould enjoyed telling of an essay received from one youngster who reported, "The human body consists of three parts: the head, the chest, and the stomach. The head contains the brains, if there is any, the chest contains the liver and the lights, and the stomach contains the vowels—five vowels: A-E-I-O-U and sometimes Y." Another anecdote he related in later years concerned his prohibition of gum chewing in class. One day he spied chewing by one of the girls sitting in a rear row. Rather than call her down in front of the class, he asked her to stay behind when the rest were dismissed for a recess outside. When she did so he reminded her that gum was not allowed, to which she replied that she knew it well. "Then what are you chewing?" asked Gould. The answer came back: "My toenails." The young teacher was terribly glad that he had waited until recess to discuss the matter in private.

During his second year at the school, Gould and his students created a school paper, *The Boca Raton Semi-Occasional Newspaper*, with the teacher as editor. Officially registered with the Post Office as second-class matter on 6 November 1915, this is believed to be the first newspaper of any sort published in Boca Raton.

Gould would always remember this period, launching his career as an educator, with fondness and appreciation. The experience broadened his horizons, allowed for recreational treks into the nearby Everglades, revealed his aptitude for teaching, and introduced him to cultural surroundings quite different from his Michigan home but where he found he could mix with enjoyment and success. "These two years as a school teacher," he later wrote, "were amongst the most productive of my whole educational career. [...] There I made life-lasting friendships with people whom I loved and respected." More than four decades after returning north to begin college studies in 1916, President Gould's annual Christmas card mailing list still included Chesebros in Boca Raton.

***

In the autumn of 1916, even as a murderous toll of young lives continued to mount in Europe along the Somme and before Verdun, American colleges and universities welcomed to peaceful and picturesque campuses record numbers of students intent on the traditional business and pleasures of college life. European trench warfare, artillery bombardments, and gas attacks were seemingly a world away from the delights of football games, fraternity rushes, and glee clubs. The University of Michigan that year reported 3,254 undergraduate students present in Ann Arbor and enrolled in its College of Literature, Science, and the Arts. One of them was Laurence M. Gould, enrolled in the Literary Department for three credits of freshman rhetoric and four credits each of history, mathematics, and German. He entered college with the intent of emulating his great hero, Lincoln, by becoming a lawyer.

Two years of teaching in Florida had not relieved him of the necessity of working his way toward meeting university expenses. Thus it was that he occupied a room in the home of a Michigan professor, provided in exchange for working about the house at such things as lawn care and tending the furnace. The professor was the head of geology, William H. Hobbs; the hospitality shown by the Hobbs family toward their lodger was warm; and the eventual consequence of the acquaintance was to set Gould's academic and career aims running in a new direction.

Ann Arbor then was a most charming college town of pleasant homes, shady streets, and about eighteen thousand inhabitants—by far the largest community in which Laurence Gould had yet lived. The university lay atop and on the slopes of a gentle hill rising above the picturesque Huron River Valley. Life for Michigan freshmen involved conforming themselves to the accepted traditions of college life. Doubtless Gould wore one of the little gray beanies that were required headwear for all freshmen until the annual "cap-night" celebration when they were burned in a great bonfire in "Sleepy Hollow." Doubtless he proudly learned the words to school songs such as "The Yellow and the Blue." (*Sing to the colors that float in the light; / Hurrah for the Yellow and Blue! ...*)

Students that fall were caught up in the excitement of the national presidential campaign, with President Wilson's eventual reelection over Republican Charles Evans Hughes coming as something of a surprise. Though late returns from California tipped the balance to Wilson, the state of Michigan—not carried by a Democrat since 1852—remained safely Republican territory. At age twenty, Gould could not yet cast a ballot, but allegiance to the Republican Party was a family inheritance.

Gould did well in his fall classes—final marks of three Bs and an A—and appears to have fitted himself comfortably to life as a Michigan undergraduate. At some point during that first year at the university, Gould associated himself with a fraternal club known as Phylon. Organized in 1915 as the Philalethian Club, its stated goals were to encourage and promote among its members "higher standards of Christian living" and to encourage and support members in "deeds of service or acts of right." Membership in Phylon was based upon "Christian character, purposefulness of motive, and high ideals of service in life." The group included among its officers a chaplain, who was to direct the club's devotional enterprises.

Gould's coursework during his second semester at the university was a continuation of the year-long sequences begun in his first. Added to this was one earned credit in something new: military drill. The addition of this credit to the academic transcript stands as witness to the fact that during the first months of 1917 the University of Michigan was compelled to recognize that the United States was perhaps not going to avoid embroilment in the unpleasantness in Europe. Full wakefulness came slowly, as one observer recalled:

> The outbreak of war between the United States and the German Empire, in April 1917, found the student body of the University of Michigan almost totally unprepared for the immediate participation in the struggle. The attitude of the great majority of students had been one of apathy. This was also true of many of the faculty. Little interest had been taken in the "war news" which had filled the papers since August 1, 1914. Dances, parties, the opera and athletics had continued as usual. The first editorial published in the *Michigan Daily*, after the U.S. had broken off diplomatic relations with Germany on February 3, 1917, had to do with the baneful influence of co-education on intercollegiate athletics.
>
> It is true that Professors Hobbs and Van Tyne and a few others had been preaching "preparedness" and compulsory military training for months, but their voices had been those of men crying in the wilderness. They had succeeded in establishing an Ann Arbor branch of the National Security League, and a sort of voluntary system of military training had been instituted by the University. Two companies of Naval Reserves had been formed from the student body, and the officers had been chosen from the faculty. But on the whole, the war came as a shock to the university community.

It was on April 2 that President Wilson told a hastily convened Congress that "the world must be made safe for democracy" and four days later that a state of war with Germany was formally declared. At the University of Michigan there were immediately visible evidences of an eagerness to serve. Some three hundred students reportedly remained in Ann Arbor over spring vacation so as to spend four hours of every afternoon practicing military drill. By May, "315 men had been recommended for training camps, and 500 had left the University to enlist."

On May 8, a crowd estimated at thirty-five hundred or more attended a mass meeting in Hill Auditorium. Entertained by the university band playing patriotic songs of the U.S., France, and Belgium, the audience heard Madame Dupreiz give "a long and graphic account of her experiences with the Germans in Louvain in 1914" and witnessed the presentation of a large silk banner to a representative of the First University of Michigan Ambulance Unit, preparing to sail to France in association with the American Field Service.

A few days later, an article in the *Michigan Daily* informed students of plans to recruit a motorized Army Ambulance Service from various colleges and universities. Units would be formed of thirty-six men each, and it was anticipated that two such sections would be organized at Michigan. It was widely believed that volunteers for these units would be able to sail for France in only six to eight weeks—more quickly than with any other service branch. Within eight days of this article's appearance nearly a hundred undergraduates had put their names to the list, and in the end three sections were formed at Ann Arbor. Meanwhile, Congress had approved a Selective Service Act anticipating conscription and requiring registration of all men between twenty-one and thirty inclusive. Gould would not be twenty-one until August, but he took the lure of almost immediate service abroad and volunteered for the Ambulance Service.

In late May, those who had volunteered for this service began to meet almost daily for an hour or so of basic "foot drill"—not that anyone really knew whether such practice would be of any use to the members of an ambulance unit, but it could do no harm and "did enable the men to become better acquainted with each other." Then began a frustratingly long wait for the appearance of the promised recruiting officer who could accomplish their actual mustering in to the Medical Enlisted Reserve Corps. For days on end, the word was that the recruiting officer would "probably come tomorrow." Meanwhile,

> It was examination week at the University and many of the boys were at their wits end. The Naval Reserves had been excused from all work; but they were already in the government service, and the Ambulance men were not. Some of the students 'bolted' their final exams, but the great majority of them took their examinations as usual, though they were ill-prepared for them and trusted to luck—and the faculty—for their credits.

(Larry Gould's luck, or ability, was up to the mark. He fell to a C grade in mathematics, but held to a B and two As in his other courses.)

Finally, on Friday afternoon June 15, Captain W. B. Borden arrived in Ann Arbor direct from enlisting a unit formed at Oberlin College. Physical examinations began the following morning, and, in the Michigan Union at 11:30 on Sunday morning—though dated as of Saturday the 16th—Laurence McKinley Gould and 107 other men were mustered into three companies of the Army Ambulance Service, Medical Section, Enlisted Reserve Corps. Private Gould was assigned to Unit B. Captain Borden then proceeded to vaccinate each man before leaving for Battle Creek, "where he was being as anxiously looked for as he had been in the university town."

CHAPTER 2

DOUGHBOY

Almost the first thing Larry Gould did upon being inducted into the Army was to go home. He expected to have at least a week's visit with his family, but on his second day home a telegram arrived recalling him immediately to Ann Arbor, from whence the entire detachment was to proceed directly to the Army Ambulance Corps training camp in Allentown, Pennsylvania.

By noon on Friday, June 22, 1917, all who had scattered for visits home had reassembled in Ann Arbor for departure that evening. As the university was no longer in session and the night was a rainy one, the Ambulance Units' send-off was not so grand as it might have been, but a band was found to lead the men on a march from the Michigan Union between a double line of Boy Scouts and National Guardsmen to a train depot crowded with friends, relatives, and well-wishers from town. The train pulled away from the station shortly after 10 p.m.

Early morning found the entourage on the Canadian side of Niagara Falls, where the train stopped a few minutes to allow passengers a closer inspection. Gould's diary* records disappointment that the great cataract "was not nearly so great as I had always imagined." Later that afternoon he was more impressed with vistas of Pennsylvania's Lehigh Valley; the vicinity of Mauch Chunk was "wonderful scenery" such as he had never yet beheld. When Allentown was reached just after 6 p.m., the contingent marched straight to camp at the Allentown Fairgrounds and to a mess of boiled red kidney beans, bread, oleo, and blackstrap molasses. The men were each issued a cot and two blankets and passed their first night under only partial shelter—unfortunate, since the night was cold, with intermittent rain. The next day they moved into more comfortable quarters—nine-by-twelve-foot horse stalls sleeping five men each—and were further welcomed

---

* Gould was not a regular, long-time diarist but did from time to time keep a number of short-term diaries in connection with travel or unusual experiences, of which a record of his military service during 1917 and 1918 was the first. Later preserved diaries include those kept during his 1926 Greenland expedition, the 1928-30 Byrd Antarctic Expedition, his 1937 trip to Soviet Russia, and his 1969 Antarctic trip. There are also brief entries in a "pocket diary" kept during part of the year 1941.

to Army life by three days of digging latrines and making roads.

Then began many long weeks, indeed months, of encampment in Allentown. For Gould, there would always be pleasant memories of the place and appreciation for many fine people met there, but he was increasingly frustrated by the slow-turning

In training camp, 1917–18

wheels that failed to send his unit to France. Six months after enlisting in the Ambulance Service he noted in his diary that he had so far actually driven an ambulance but once. "Sometimes," he recorded, "it looks as though things are poorly managed."

All that summer and fall of 1917 the great events for Gould were also those of his training unit. The company was increased over the summer from a strength of thirty-six to forty-five, commanded by a lieutenant, with four non-coms. Days were filled with hiking, pitching tents, litter work, and classes in first aid and wig wag semaphore signaling. At the end of August one of the Ann Arbor companies sailed for France in the First Overseas Contingent; a week later the other two were combined into the 16th Battalion with three sections from Battle Creek, Michigan, and assigned to the Third Overseas Contingent commanded by Major Francis F. Metcalf—but with no prospect of imminent orders to sail. On September 1, Gould was among the eighteen members of his company promoted from private to private first class.

When it became evident that the Third Overseas Contingent would not be leaving by October 1, as per original expectations, construction began on real barracks for winter service. In what the men called "The Battle of Guths Station," beginning October 31, Major Metcalf's eighteen-hundred-man contingent encamped by a deserted iron mine six miles from town, waiting out the completion of barracks. Permission was granted to build dugouts, for those ingenious enough to do so using only the natural materials at hand. Gould and three others labored ten days, when free from drill, to build themselves comparatively comfortable shelter—with double-decked beds and a fireplace—dug into the steep riverbank. This was home for them and two others until the shift back to Allentown barracks on December 8. The shift involved dismantling camp in a blinding storm, followed by a march to Allentown through six inches of snow, pushing the section's trucks ahead.

Though many of the men went home for a Christmas holiday, Gould was among those remaining in camp. He wrote with appreciation of the citizens of Allentown who helped to see that the soldiers remaining "really spent a very merry Christmas." He was particularly grateful to the family of Section 590's special patron or "big brother," David Miller, editor of the *Allentown Morning Call*, whose home—"Millerheim"—was open to the men of 590 whenever they were in Allentown. The Millers "have quite taken the place of our home folks," reads Gould's diary as 1917 comes to a close.

Awaiting orders to embark for Europe with the US Army Ambulance Service

***

Late on New Year's Day, 1918, orders arrived for the 16th Battalion to prepare to leave for France within two days. January 2 was filled with the hustle and bustle of packing up—until about four o'clock in the afternoon when an ambulance drove up and took away a man from Section 600 who had measles. Another arrived later to collect a man diagnosed with scarlet fever. Instead of sailing for France, the battalion was dropped from the Third Overseas Contingent and confined to barracks under quarantine. Resigned to remaining in Allentown for some while longer, during the week that followed the men of Section 590 formed a section forum, or literary society, complete with forum officers, a program committee, and four honorary members including their Allentown patron, Miller, and Michigan's Professor Hobbs. The men also began a new daily schedule of a morning lecture on the "customs of the service," followed by an hour each of auto instruction and French, mess, and then two afternoon hours of drill or hiking. On Saturdays there were inspections. Evenings the men were often free to attend whatever was doing at the camp amusement hall, where Gould took pleasure in events as varied as wrestling and boxing matches, moving picture shows, and classical music performances but confessed himself unable to appreciate jazz.

Many weeks passed with little change in the routine, punctuated by occasional rumors that the battalion was about to be ordered overseas—hopes that repeatedly ended in new disappointment. Quarantine was lifted January 20, a Sunday on which Gould attended religious services twice—at the camp YMCA and then later at a Lutheran church in Allentown—and was unimpressed with both sermons. The next day he found more satisfaction in the hearty laughter produced by a Fatty Arbuckle movie at the Allentown Hippodrome. Local acquaintances made since arrival in Allentown the summer before resulted in occasional social calls or dinner invitations, often in company with other friends from the section. Measles, however, continued in the camp, and quarantine was reinstated early in February. It would last until the 4th of March.

On February 10 word descended that for Gould's ambulance unit there was no prospect for an overseas departure anytime soon but that qualified men might consider transfer to another branch of service where vacancies existed. Several men quickly had applications approved for transfer to aviation. Gould and some others were interested in the possibilities of a new tank company just being formed in New York City. Meanwhile, Gould also resolved to apply for a commission and to study hard to be ready for the examination should he be called.

The deflating news that there was no immediate chance of receiving orders for overseas service was followed within days by the floating of a new hope that, on the contrary, they would be going across quite soon; that their transport ships were empty and coaled up ready to go. The persistence of contradictory rumor left the entire camp feeling "uneasy and restless." Some from the section signed up for a course in the Army Medical College for men with electrical training to fill an opening in X-ray work. In mid-February, Gould told his diary:

I do not know just what to do. I should transfer to Aviation if I could be assured that I could get in line for flyer but I do not want to be in the aviation corps as a ground mechanic. I shall continue my studies toward taking an examination in this service until I can find something definite to stand upon.

Then came a "most joyous" statement by their battalion commander, Capt. McCurdy, that they would soon be going, not to France, but to Italy, as the first American troops being sent there. The next day rumor had it that this had "all blown up"; then that no, it was true, but not for the whole battalion, only for their section, separately. Then came a memorandum stating that these plans were after all only "tentative." Tentative though they were, the plans meant that for the moment section personnel were no longer likely to be approved for transfer, which scotched Gould's brief desire to respond to a talk he attended about opportunities awaiting in the heavy artillery. On the last day of February Gould turned in an application, supported by recommendations from Hobbs and others, to be examined for an Army Ambulance Service commission. At the same time, his diary records that he "would give up all hope of commissions in this service … [to] be even a buck private in a machine gun company." Made sanguinary by hearing a lecture on German atrocities in Belgium, he overflowed with indignation and martial spirit:

Oh God! How I want to get behind a gun and stop the Hun. I do want as never before to get into a real fighting branch of the service. I pray that some opening may be granted to me soon.

In mid-March, 175 men from the camp, including thirteen from Section 590, were sent to the Army Medical School for an eight-week course in bacteriology, after which there would be an examination for commissions in the Sanitary Corps. Gould had applied for this when the opportunity first arose early in the month but withdrew his application the next day after considering that it really would be no better "to sit over a microscope in a laboratory all thru the war than to drive an ambulance." Instead, he and three others did apply for transfer to a Coast Artillery battery, but battalion commander McCurdy refused approval. On March 21, Gould was promoted to sergeant, the section's original non-coms having by that time transferred to other service. By the end of the month, the company log reports, transfers had left so few men in the section that it appeared 590 might be broken up—but they were instead filled up again over the next few weeks by the addition of new personnel, "raw recruits mostly, but all very good men." Three men added that spring were Italian-Americans placed in the section to act as interpreters, for it did now seem to be the case that after long delays 590 was truly destined for service in Italy.

The month of May saw the 4th Overseas Contingent, of which Gould's section was now a part, working to get ready to ship out. On the 1st of April Italian had replaced French in the routine of morning language instruction. Sergeant Gould drilled his men in gas defense. He also served as best man at the wedding of one of the section's new men. Of new men there were many, as Section 590 was brought back up to a full complement of forty-five plus commanding officer. By June only eight men, Gould among them, remained from the thirty-six who first formed the unit in Michigan. In mid-May, Section 590 was placed under the command of a new officer, Lt. William H. Woolverton.

From Ann Arbor, Hobbs had responded to Gould's letters of anxiety about ever getting into action by taking up his case with Major General Leonard Wood, who, as Hobbs wrote later in the *Michigan Alumnus,* "was able to make arrangements for Gould to take examination for a commission in the fighting force." Near the end of May, Gould received a telegram authorizing his attendance at the 4th Officers Training Camp, but by this time the Italian contingent was really preparing to embark, and Gould guessed that now he was in the Ambulance Service to stay.

At long last, on June 12, cots were turned in and packs rolled, and the thirty sections bound for Italy left Camp Crane—the Allentown Fairgrounds where Gould had arrived nearly a full year before—to entrain for Jersey City, which they reached early the next morning. Waiting for them at Pier C was an Italian ship, the *Giuseppe Verdi,* which Gould noted "was painted in a strange manner with many colors, by way of camouflage." Gould was grateful for a berth "in the middle … way down near the water line so we do not get the rolling of the ship as much as we might in a different location." Late in the afternoon the soldiers were ordered below decks, portholes were closed, and the ship left harbor.

After a day in convoy the *Giuseppe Verdi* struck out on its own, beginning a largely uneventful crossing without escort. On June 23—exactly a year since Gould's arrival in Allentown—the transport met the American U-boat destroyer *Decatur,* which took them in between Moroccan hills and the Spanish peninsula to Gibraltar. There, while coaling to resume passage to Genoa, the contingent was greeted by American sailors "glad to see us," Gould wrote, for "we are absolutely the first American troops to pass thru this port. I suppose that is explained by the fact that we are actually the first expeditionary force to Italy." A day later they passed on into the Mediterranean, guarded against submarine attack by the company of a British torpedo boat ahead and the *Decatur* behind. On the 26th the *Giuseppe Verdi* was met by three Italian destroyers, and her passengers felt very secure to know that their single small ship now had five fierce escorts.

The next day they reached the port of Genoa, birthplace of Columbus, where the American contingent marched, four abreast, straight off the ship and into a parade through the city. Their reception was, to Gould, unforgettable:

> It seemed as though tons of flowers were thrown at us. Since I carried the Italian flag I got my share of flowers. Whenever I shook my hat or pack the flowers would fall to the ground. As the people on each side of the street saw us coming they began to press out into the already too narrow streets to cry out "Vive L'America" and touch the flags as we passed.

They were given speeches and a rendering of "The Star-Spangled Banner" before marching up to temporary barracks featuring the luxury of iron cots with mattresses, sheets, and pillows. After a day with leave to explore the city—which Gould did with fellow sergeants Reynolds and Muskatt—the Americans hiked to their "permanent" camp three or four miles out, where they set up squad tents.

For all of July and most of August Gould essentially lived an Italian idyll. The work needing to be done, preparing ambulances for duty, was not excessive, and Gould's diary is filled with accounts of swims in the Mediterranean, hikes for pleasure into the surrounding country, and advantage taken of cultural opportunities in Genoa. He indulged an interest in photography. His presence was required for several large parades, including a memorable Fourth of July turn-out, again carrying the Italian flag.

All this while the ambulance units expected to be sent up to the Italian front on the Asiago Plateau, but on August 19 telegrams arrived conveying the startling order that fifteen sections of thirty-two men each were to be placed for an indefinite period of time on detached service to the American Expeditionary Forces in France. Section 590, leaving thirteen of its men behind in Italy, would be the first to go. Three days later the section received definite word that they were departing for France by train on the morrow. The afternoon was spent packing—though Gould found time for a last swim in the Mediterranean—and then, as the day was also their popular sergeant's twenty-second birthday, some of the men threw a bit of a party at the Lido for Larry Gould. The company log recorded this event as "quite a success, what with a big moon shining on the sea and the champagne flowing … a fitting celebration both of Sergeant Gould's birthday and our last night in Genoa."

***

Three nights later the men of Section 590 were encamped—sleeping in their motorized ambulances—by the large hospital center at Rimaucourt, Haute-Marne *département*. The next day they received orders to report to divisional headquarters at Aignay-le-Duc, which they reached on the morning of August 27. They would remain in France through and beyond the seventy-seven days that remained to the war, working in earnest now at transporting patients, and moved by AEF orders from one site to another in an area stretching from the Langres Plateau in the Côte d'Or north through Champagne along the valley of the Marne and into Lorraine between the Meuse River and Argonne Forest.

By this point in the war the initiative along the Western Front had shifted permanently to the Allies, who had pushed back the last great German offensive into Champagne in mid-July and commenced an advance all along the line from Flanders to Lorraine. Sixteen days after Gould's ambulance section reported for duty at Aignay-le-Duc, General Pershing's First American Army undertook its first major action as an independent force with an offensive that successfully erased the German salient protruding since 1914 from their line at Saint-Mihiel. Section

590 had been brought north in support of this operation early in September, but when the offensive was launched September 12 Gould's unit remained behind the lines in reserve with duties confined to evacuating the sick. Stationed near Tronville on the Ornain River, on the 14th they did see their first Germans: some sixteen hundred prisoners being marched by under the guard of French cavalrymen. The next day Section 590 was ordered north to Souilly, in the vicinity of Verdun, as the American Army began to prepare the next big push along the Meuse-Argonne front.

From this more forward position, Gould and his ambulance service comrades now had daily reminders of their proximity to war, whether being overflown by a German plane about to bomb an ammunition train, seeing more "gaunt-looking" German prisoners marched past, or simply hearing the great guns, day and night. On the 19th, as they moved yet closer to the front, Private John McCarthy remembered:

> Larry Gould rode with me that night and we had a fine time. The night was black but the stars were bright and the air clean and crisp. Every few minutes a star shell lit up the sky frontwards. Under the spell of adventure and beauty we discussed many things—religion, our ambitions, our home and folks and friends. Later we changed to singing and went through all the old time songs. We sang "When you and I were young, Maggie" a dozen times and knowing myself, I imagine that song will forever remind me of that night.

Finally, on the night of the 25th, they were brought up quite near the front at Verdun to the town of Nixeville. At about 2 a.m. the French and Americans began the heaviest barrage yet seen on that front, and at dawn Americans between the Rivers Meuse and Aisne launched themselves over the top to commence a major offensive aimed at cutting the German rail supply line at Mézières.

Thus began what the men of Section 590 referred to as "our busy time." For most of seventeen days they kept their ambulance cars in almost constant use, evacuating wounded and pushing themselves to the point of exhaustion. From the distributing hospital at Fromerville to the front lines advanced beyond the old "No Man's Land" there was in their sector but a single road by which all traffic, artillery supplies and ammunition, as well as medical ambulances, had to move. Engineers worked on that road round the clock to keep it passable, but conditions and volume combined to tie it up so thoroughly that a round trip along the few kilometers between hospital and front lines could take twenty-four hours or more. On one such trip two days into the offensive, Sergeant Gould climbed onto the right mudguard in the front of his vehicle to better guide his partner from driving into shell holes with their cargo of wounded men.

Soon, Section 590 moved their kitchen and supplies up to Bethincourt, where a field hospital was established on what had been the German side of the line two days before. From there, they moved ambulances both ways, night and day, bringing wounded from battlefield and trenches to field hospital and, in the other direction, from field hospital to distributing hospital at Fromerville.

On the morning of October 2, a short period of "semi-rest" allowed Gould to take up his diary again, recording that:

> The place where we are now camped is under German shell fire and no night passes but what we hear the shells dropping around us and are wakened to put on our gas masks.
>
> I might write other pages about the wounded but I want to forget what I have lived thru during the last few days so I shall not write it to remind me.

During the same lull, Private McCarthy wrote with greater detail of two of his own ambulance runs to deliver stretcher cases from the front to the field hospital. On the first of these—twenty hours spent driving eight miles—the line of stalled traffic was strafed by machine gun fire from a German plane overhead, a bullet smashing the rear window of the staff car not three feet ahead. When he finally arrived with his patients, McCarthy noted, he helped the hospital orderly with the unloading. "We are not required to do this," he wrote, "and I'll never do it again, as three of my four cases were dead." Of a second run, to the village of Cuisy northwest of Bethincourt, McCarthy wrote:

> We oozed into town just at daybreak and the sight of that single street of the place I will always remember. On the left hand side of the street, about midway in the row of what had been buildings was the first aid station. That place had been picked for the shelter because it had at least half a roof and an empty basement. The flag was a welcome sight, but the row of bundles on stretchers which lay on the street for half a block each way from the aid station was ghastly in that first light of day. I don't know how many stretchers can be laid side by side in the distance of a city block, but my guess is that there were a hundred seriously wounded lying there. Many of them had lain there since the drive started, though we learned that many walking cases had walked or hopped trucks toward the rear.
>
> We drove up to the doorway of the aid station and were greeted with almost prayerful fervor by the three doctors and many orderlies. We were the first ambulance they had seen though they had asked repeatedly for them. All the medical corps men look tuckered out and hopeless. The wounded had poured in fast for about thirty hours, had filled the basement and the ground floor and then had to be put into the street.
>
> Tubbs and I went outside to the car to wait while the doctors picked out the lucky four men who were to be taken to a field hospital. The eyes of those men on their stretchers were pathetic with silent pleading to be among those taken. No one asked to be chosen, but we could almost read their hopes and fears in their faces.

Because his regular car partner, Yeckel, was, as McCarthy noted sourly, "always ailing when the time comes to go to the front" and the section's non-coms then had no regular cars of their own, Corporal Tubbs and Sergeant Gould were taking turns driving with "Mac" in Yeckel's place.

The nightly shell fire over their camp at Bethincourt was unnerving. Gas shells were included, and Gould wrote that "the night is unusual which does not contain two or three gas alarms." One night an uncomfortably close explosion showered earth on the fly under which men of the unit were sleeping, so everyone was "routed out" and carried blankets to sleep in shell holes farther off. The next morning it was found that shrapnel had passed through a car and knocked down a tent where various members of the section earlier had been sleeping. Gould was not present for that excitement, having taken a run delivering patients to Fromerville, but his own nerves were tested that night just the same:

> The road was mighty rough and I had one man in the car who was moaning continually. It was hard on one's nerves and it was nearly two o'clock when we arrived. To add to our discomfort it began raining on the way down and when we were driving thru [Chattancourt], where we thought we were far from the range of the German shells I was fairly scared out of my wits by a Boche shell bursting a short way in front of me, a second one burst closer to me but I didn't hear the third for I gave the car the "juice" and got out.

On the 9th of October Gould and three others took advantage of another lull to take a walk atop nearby "Dead Man's Hill," or "Mort Homme," which had figured prominently in 1916 as the German advance on Verdun reached its farthest extent. Here Gould "beheld such a scene of desolation" as he had never before encountered. "It is no exaggeration to state that not a square inch of the hill has not been torn to pieces by a shell," he wrote that evening, and there were "not a few human bones" lying about. After viewing the entrances of three of the famous German tunnels of 1916, their attention was brought back to the present by witnessing a live air battle above their heads.

The section stayed busy bringing in wounded until the 12th of October, when they were relieved and came back down the line to Fromerville. That same day they heard first rumors of an impending armistice. Gould and others began to hope that they would soon be returned to Italy. By the 14th they had moved farther back and were billeted comfortably in the village of Futeau, in the Argonne Forest. That same day, however, sad news came that two men from the section, "Rip" Taylor and "Judge" Williams, had both died of pneumonia shortly after being sent to hospital. Despite several "close calls," these were the section's first fatal losses. Regarding being relieved from duty at the front, Private McCarthy was doubtless expressing the view of all when he wrote that this was "jake" with him: "I don't care if this war quits tomorrow," he declared, "seventeen days of actual warfare is enough to brag about to posterity."

From then until the armistice actually came on November 11, Section 590 was employed only—with one banner exception—in transport of the sick and wounded well behind the lines. The exception came on November 7, when orders came to send seven ambulances to retrieve wounded from the advance dressing station in Beaumont, across the Meuse from the town of Dun, which had just been taken by American forces. Gould had already left on a supply-gathering expedition with Lieutenant Woolverton, but the cars were sent with seven drivers. Somehow, this group got onto the wrong road and ran straight through where they ought to have stopped—a fact of which they became aware only when "Jazz" Householder, in the lead, spied a German helmet and found he was being shot at by the German underneath it. Stopping the car abruptly, he jumped for the rather frightened German and knocked his gun away as the others came up. Then, as the section log relates, "spying more up the road, they took the German's weapons and sneaking up the road called on them to surrender which they promptly did on Householder's sending a ball over their heads." The group returned to Dun with five prisoners in tow, and by the next day the tale of this exploit "had spread among the hospitals like wildfire," as something "unprecedented in the ambulance service." In his diary, Gould expressed regret at not having been with them, for if he had not gone with the lieutenant it would undoubtedly have been him leading the seven ambulances—but then, he opined, they would doubtless never have gotten onto the wrong road in the first place, and so there would have been no excitement!

The guns fell silent on November 11, but Section 590's work evacuating sick and wounded or transporting medical department personnel went on some while longer. On November 20, section personnel learned to their general regret that they would not be returned to their "proper command" in the Italian contingent but were instead being attached to the Third Army for occupation service in Germany. After celebrating Thanksgiving in Luxembourg the section found itself by early December established in the German city of Trier, on the Mosel River. There Gould rather unhappily became "adjutant, stenographer, office boy and what not" for the Personnel Office of the Third Army Sanitary Train, essentially the prince of all paperwork and "doing nearly all the work." December 20 they moved up to Koblenz, where the Mosel joins the Rhine, and here they remained in service until their homeward journey began in March.

***

Long before Section 590 was relieved in Koblenz and started their way through the channels of returning home, its members were eager to depart. Ready they were to do their part in the war, but the section had not otherwise exactly embraced such attitudes as were proper to the military life. Already in December the Third Army Sanitary Train's Lieutenant Colonel Wilson had lost his temper and, in what the section log called "a bad attack of Silver Leaf-itis," told Lieutenant Woolverton that 590 was "the worst that ever came over, also the poorest disciplined, and so forth." The lieutenant then "had an attack himself" and "proceeded to pass the buck in good style," but, says the section log, "what the 'ell, we know damn well that this Section is the best one that was ever organized in spite of what the devil himself may say or think about it." The keepers of the log allowed as how "our hatred of military rot and poppy-cock might make us look inefficient to a damn fool medical officer" but stoutly declared that "we have never fallen down when there was real work to do." In March, as their impending transfer became official, prevailing feeling in the section was that their actual work was now finished, and that

> from now on until we are finally mustered out we expect nothing but military poppy-cock. We have resigned ourselves to it, however, for we know that however long we stay here, there is just so much red tape, etc. to be gone through with before we can expect to reach home and the sooner it is begun, the sooner it will be over.

On March 15, along with the other troops billeted in Koblenz, they were reviewed by General Pershing. The drill practice given them the day before by Captain Woolverton—the lieutenant had been promoted March 8—was "the first formation as such that we have had since we left Italy." Finally on the morning of the 17th they loaded their baggage and entrained for France. In Joinville, they were reunited with several of the old sections from Italy, now homeward bound themselves and about to leave for the harbor of Brest. Understanding that they would follow as soon as red tape allowed, Gould worked double-time on the paperwork. The section was given one last job, delivery of nineteen vehicles to a town near Tours, but was then permitted to proceed from there to Brest to await transportation home.

In the large camp at Brest, which was filled with others also waiting, they were pleased to discover about forty-five of the old Allentown sections, including another of the original units formed in Ann Arbor almost two years before, still with about twenty-six of their original men.

At last, on April 19, Section 590 boarded the *Koningin der Nederlander*, a converted Holland-Java trade boat, which docked on the 1st of May in Newport News, Virginia. There they were soaked by a steady rain as they marched out of town to Camp Morrison, where they dried off, were deloused, and "fixed out with new clothes." A few days later they proceeded by boat up the James River to Camp Lee near Petersburg, where after another day the section broke up, each man departing for his particular state cantonment for formal discharge and a return to family and civilian life.

CHAPTER 3

ENTERED UPON A SCIENTIFIC CAREER

As the University of Michigan returned to "normalcy" after the Great War, military demobilization caused student enrollment for the fall semester of 1919 to climb to some fifteen hundred more than in any previous September. Temporarily, classrooms were crowded and insufficient in number, and there was a shortage of rooms for rent in Ann Arbor. The campus, however, was growing too, with the addition in 1919 of two major buildings: a new university library and the grand and gothic Michigan Union, whose central tower became at once "the striking feature of Ann Arbor's skyline."

Larry Gould reentered the university at this time. A mature veteran of two years in the Army as well as two years teaching school, he was not now the typical college sophomore. Rather he was a tested twenty-three-year-old, confident as to his abilities, impatient to move forward, readied for hard work, and positively eager to focus on serious study. The university advanced him a semester's worth of credits for military service, and he determined that by adding summer sessions he could earn his degree in only two more years. First, though, must be decided the direction of his further studies—what was to be his major field and what his future career?

In this, Gould was influenced decisively by the friendship already established with Professor Hobbs, the eminent geoscientist. Among the classes in which he enrolled for the fall of 1919 was Hobbs' introductory course in geology. Hobbs' buoyant enthusiasm for his subject was infectious and intellectually stimulating, and it quickly turned Gould's ambition into a new channel. By November, Hobbs had arranged for Gould to receive a departmental assistantship, and Gould abandoned his original pre-law intentions, determined to become a geologist. "I probably owe more to Hobbs than to any other person I have known," Gould would write years later.

William Herbert Hobbs was a prominent and oftentimes controversial figure in the science of geology. His academic standing combined with full red beard caused students to dub him "the Lord in Sepia." Blessed with "a lively sense of humor," he had a wit that could be sharp and quick, but many of the jokes he most enjoyed were at his own expense—"he could take as well as give." To Gould he was inspiration and mentor.

During that first year back in classrooms, Gould studied Spanish, economics, physics, and chemistry—and took eighteen credits of geology or mineralogy.

Hard work and keen interest in his new subject resulted in stellar grades, nearly solid As from this point forward. After another year even more dominated by geological coursework, in September 1921 Gould would be awarded his bachelor of science degree with high distinction and earn honor society membership in both Phi Beta Kappa and the scientific research society of Sigma Xi.

Upon his return to Michigan, Gould also reestablished his connection with the Phylon Club—enough so that during his second year back in 1920-21 he had become the group's president. While still in this role the following year, Gould oversaw Phylon's amalgamation into the national fraternity of Pi Kappa Alpha, assuring alumni members that this entry into a larger fellowship involved no diminution of Phylon's ideals of

William Herbert Hobbs

Christian brotherhood. Throughout the years that Gould remained at Michigan, as graduate student and faculty member, he continued to be listed as "Faculty Brother" to Michigan's chapter of Pi Kappa Alpha.

As Hobbs' protégé, Gould was well ensconced in the Michigan Geology Department even before receiving his bachelor's degree, as both student and teacher. The Proceedings of the University of Michigan Board of Regents show him confirmed in June 1920 to continue as an assistant in the department at an annual salary of $400; in November, he was appointed teaching assistant, at $550; and the following June, his 1921-22 salary as instructor in geology was set at $1,800. He conducted his first major independent fieldwork in the summer of 1921, in Utah, traveling by train to Salt Lake City in company with Hobbs, who was on the first leg of a round-the-world trip. Entering the Graduate School in the fall of 1921, he continued advanced coursework in geology and mineralogy for two years, earning his MA in June 1923.

During this period as a newly minted instructor, Gould gained at least two valuable things. The first of these, chronologically, was experience as a lecturer. In later years, Gould would tell the story of how he delivered his first formal lecture to his first class of beginning geology students. Full of enthusiasm for his subject, he got off to a terrific start, holding his audience spellbound as his knowledge spilled forth. "I got all excited," he remembered, "and told them everything I knew about each phase of geology ... and then discovered that I had the last quarter of the class period and the rest of the semester to go."

Gould in 1920

The second valuable thing Gould gained as a young instructor was the admiration of one particular member of Michigan's freshman class of 1926, Miss Margaret Rice. "Peg," as everyone called her, was the tall, strikingly attractive daughter of an Ann Arbor investment banker. In 1922 she entered Michigan's College of Literature, Science, and the Arts from Ann Arbor High School, registering for rhetoric, French, Spanish, and—fatefully—elementary geology. The fatefulness of that choice was not immediately apparent for it was not until 1930 that Peg and Larry would be married, but the seeds of a romance were planted in 1922-23 when Gould taught and Peg, as she liked to say afterward, "lingered to marry the course."*

***

Gould was discovering, if he did not already know it, that he liked college teaching very much. To long continue at such work, he needed to secure his "union card"—that is, the doctorate degree—to be bestowed upon the successful completion of an acceptable thesis. His dissertation subject, suggested by Hobbs, was to be the geology of the La Sal Mountains of southeastern Utah, a district that had never yet been geologically surveyed. To complete the work, Gould would need to produce geological and topographical maps of the range.

It was Hobbs' hope, in assigning this survey, that his protégé might be able to provide evidence backing Hobbs' unorthodox theories about the formation of laccoliths—igneous intrusions into sedimentary rock that lift the overlying strata to form a characteristic dome. Hobbs thought that the standard explanation, advanced in the late-nineteenth century by Grove Karl Gilbert was doubtful and might be disproved in the laccolithic La Sal Range. Gilbert's assumption was that the doming of the strata over laccoliths was caused by the hydrostatic force of an ascending magma. Hobbs' hypothesis was that the arching was caused by folding stresses and that the presence of laccolithic magmas was due to the fusion of bodies of shale where pressures were relieved. Perhaps Gould, by investigating

---

* Margaret Rice's transcript shows grades for her freshman year of six As and three Bs. She earned an A in Geology 1, but that fell to a B second semester in Geology 2. Forty-three years later, in a note written for her husband's seventieth birthday ("Dear Prof. Gould" from "your oldest living student"), Peg teased Larry about his having taken so long to discover her intellectual competence, insisting that "I did deserve an A rather than that horrid B!" This delightful note concludes: "Since that time, so long ago, I have been studying, under the same tutelage, applied geology and a variety of other subjects too numerous to mention. I seem, indeed, never to graduate … Welllllllllll, anahoo, the teacher tried hard and the pupil wouldn't have had another by any stretch of her perfervid imagination."

   During 1922-23, Margaret Rice was elected vice president of the undergraduate class of 1926 and pledged the Alpha Phi sorority. She did not, however, return to school the following fall; her next courses at Michigan were not until the Summer Session of 1926 (earning another A in Geology 32, while Gould traveled with Hobbs to Greenland), and then she registered for five courses—three in the French department, her prospective major—in the fall of 1926, but withdrew due to "ill health" on October 13.

On the geology staff, University of Michigan

laccoliths other than those described by Gilbert, would be able to buttress his mentor's fusion of shales hypothesis.

In preparation for this dissertation Gould devoted two summers to arduous fieldwork, camping in the mountains and carrying out mapping and geological studies of his assigned district. In addition to his detailed survey of the La Sal Range, he conducted "reconnaissance studies" in the Abajo or Blue Mountains of Utah and in Colorado's Ute and La Plata Ranges. It was at the end of his second season in the western mountains that Gould had a closer scrape with death than he had ever had while under German shell fire in Europe. His work completed, Gould and a younger student companion had started the return trip by automobile. In a 1930 *Michigan Alumnus* profile of Gould, Hobbs describes what happened:

> While passing through Colorado they were running at a sixty-mile clip along an elevated highway above a deep canyon when suddenly without any warning they came to a sharp turn. The young man with Gould, who was on the side away from the canyon, jumped and was unhurt. Gould was behind the driving wheel and went over the cliff with the car, which after turning in the air struck bottom upward upon a ledge and left him unconscious lying on a portion of the torn car cover as the rest of the car descended to the bottom of the canyon seventy-five feet below. Gould was unconscious for hours after his removal from the ledge. He had sustained a broken jaw and severe contusions, but was in such excellent physical condition that within a fortnight he was again at his post teaching at the University.

Despite this frightening experience, Gould came away from his dissertation fieldwork with what was to be a lifelong love for the rugged mountains of the American West.

Gould's careful work in the La Sal Mountains did provide the wherewithal for a solid doctoral thesis. Unfortunately, much as he might have hoped for the contrary, his evidence regarding laccoliths tended to support Gilbert's ideas and not those of Hobbs. Not only could he provide no support for Hobbs' fusion of shale hypothesis, but he found such evidence in support of Gilbert as "a laccolith with clearly exposed base at the head of a cirque which showed with textbook clarity the feeder dykes through which the magma had risen" to form it. In some embarrassment, Gould wrote to his mentor, then in Europe, to convey the gist of his observations. Hobbs had to have been disappointed in the result, but he wrote back: "My boy, you have entered upon a scientific career, and you must report the facts as you see them no matter what the consequences may be."

Though Hobbs himself continued to hold to his contrary hypothesis, he made no attempt to influence Gould's conclusions differently. The dissertation was accepted with Hobbs' "championing" the work to other committee members, and the Doctor of Science degree was duly conferred upon Gould in June 1925. A few months later, the Michigan Board of Regents approved the promotion for 1926-27 of Laurence M. Gould, ScD, from instructor to assistant professor of geology, at a salary of $2,500.

The Geology Department was then housed in a four-floor section of Michigan's Natural Sciences Building, completed in 1916 as the largest building on campus. There Gould's daily routine reportedly included an hour set aside especially for reading outside his professional interests in geology, his tastes at the time running toward popular fiction and biography. This practice was an antidote, he claimed, to his becoming "a typical professor, as the average person understands him." Scientist though he was, Gould developed a fine literary appreciation. Enjoyment of books was one bond he shared with Peg Rice, with whom the acquaintance begun in 1922 as instructor and pupil had deepened into romance.*

By the late 1920s, Gould had established himself as a valued member of Michigan's geological staff, "accounted one of the two or three most popular faculty members." His personal qualities were attested to at the end of the decade by the journalist-friend who wrote that "no one of [my] acquaintance possesses a more active human contact, a readier wit, a finer and more active sense of humor than Gould." Liked and respected by those who knew him, from old friends and new, to students, to military comrades, to academic colleagues, Larry Gould before he reached thirty was well launched. "Whither Bound?" remained a

---

*   It is unclear precisely when Gould's romance with Peg Rice began, but it was evidently underway not long after Peg had taken Gould's introductory geology course in 1922-23. In a poem written for her brother-in-law's sixtieth birthday in 1956 (see Endnotes for text), Peg's younger sister Jean Rice Hoppin sets his appearance into the family circle as of the year she was ten and he was twenty-seven—that is, 1923-24. (Jean was born 28 May 1913.)

question full of possibilities. The Michigan boy had journeyed east, to European battlefields, and west, to the mountains of Utah and Colorado. In the years just ahead he would rechart his course through new journeys, first to the north and then far to the south.

Again, it was Hobbs who turned Gould's life. In 1926, Hobbs was making plans to direct a series of University of Michigan expeditions to Greenland. The object of the whole was twofold: first, to learn more about the circulation of the glacial anticyclone in Greenland's upper air, crucial for understanding the wind systems of the northern hemisphere; and second, to study how Greenland's continental glacier during its liquidation had modified the land around it, information that would be useful to geologists in interpreting ancient glacial deposits. The first expedition, to depart in June and return in September, was to lay the foundations for those that would follow. Its goal was to find a suitable base at which to establish an aerological station, to conduct preliminary meteorological observations both at ground level and in the upper atmosphere, and, simply, to gain practical experience in Arctic travel that would be useful for outfitting the later expeditions. Gould gladly accepted Hobbs' invitation that he act as second-in-command for this adventure.

It was necessary for Hobbs to raise funds for the University of Michigan Greenland Expeditions through individual solicitations, and expenditures could not be lavish. It was decided that the first expedition would consist of only six men: Hobbs, the director; Gould, assistant director, geologist, and photographer; S. P. Fergusson, aerologist, from the US Weather Bureau; J. E. Church, Jr., meteorologist, from the University of Nevada, but a Michigan alumnus; Ralph Belknap, surveyor, also from the University of Michigan Geology Department; and Paul C. Oscanyan, Jr., radio operator, from New Jersey. For transportation, Hobbs arranged for the expedition to be taken as passengers aboard Captain Bob Bartlett's double-masted motor-schooner *Morrissey*, which had been chartered that summer for a small American Museum of Natural History expedition to collect Arctic oceanic fauna, led by George Palmer Putnam, a prominent figure in New York publishing. The seventeen members of the two expeditions would all supplement the *Morrissey*'s own small crew by shipping as "able landlubbers," expected to assist with hauling on halyards but forbidden to go aloft. Hobbs' contract called for his men to be set down with their stores at the head of Greenland's Maligiakfjord early in July and then to be retrieved in September.

Eager though he was for the adventure promised by such plans, Gould regretted the many weeks of separation from Peg Rice, who was enrolling for classes in the university's summer session. He made a promise to Peg and to Peg's thirteen-year-old sister Jean, for whom Larry had become a favorite, that he would keep a summer diary. On June 23, in company with Ralph Belknap, Gould departed Ann Arbor bound for Nova Scotia, where they were to rendezvous with the rest of the expedition and board the vessel that was to carry them north.

CHAPTER 4

AN ARCTIC TENDERFOOT

On the northeast shore of Cape Breton Island, Nova Scotia, lies the small harbor of North Sydney. Visitors in 1926 found a maritime town stretched out along the waterfront, with small shops and strong-smelling fish markets lining a none-too-clean principal street, the scent of saltwater in the air, and a thriving population of noisy gulls. When Gould and Belknap detrained at its weather-beaten station early in the morning of June 26, they made their way directly to the office of Kelly, the ship chandler, where they learned that the *Morrissey* was in harbor, having arrived the day before. They also found the director of the American Museum of Natural History expedition that had chartered the *Morrissey*, George Palmer Putnam, who Gould characterized that day as impatient to head north, yet "as courteous and thoughtful as he is handsome—and that is saying much." Gould went aboard the crowded schooner and began the day's work of seeing to the loading of expedition supplies for which he was responsible. When he returned to shore he first met the living legend who was to be his host aboard the *Morrissey*, its owner and skipper, Captain Robert A. Bartlett.

"Cap'n Bob" was Arctic Adventure personified. A Newfoundland-born master mariner whose Harvard and Yale had been sealing voyages and the Labrador cod fisheries, he was famed as explorer Robert E. Peary's favorite ice pilot. In the winter of 1898-99, when Peary's feet froze and his toes had to be amputated, it was Bob Bartlett who administered the ether. From 1905 to 1909 it was Bartlett who commanded Peary's ship the *Roosevelt*, specially constructed for Arctic waters. In 1909, when Peary made his celebrated dash across the frozen sea to the North Pole, Bartlett's supporting party was the last to turn back, having accompanied Peary as far as the 88th parallel within 133 miles of the pole. When Larry Gould shipped with him in June of 1926—a month and a half after Richard E. Byrd and his pilot Floyd Bennett had electrified the world with their claim to have success-fully overflown the North Pole—Bob Bartlett could still enjoy the distinction of having stood farther north at ground level than any human save Peary, Matthew Henson, and four accompanying Eskimos.

Twelve years before this meeting, at a time when Larry Gould was preparing

Aboard ship, summer of 1926, ready for a summer of exploration and adventure

to graduate from high school, Bob Bartlett was in the midst of his grimmest Arctic experience, surviving the wreck of the *Karluk*, a ship outfitted for a Canadian expedition that had become trapped in ice it was not capable of withstanding. While a party of fifteen remained miserably stranded on remote uninhabited Wrangel Island north of Siberia, their only hope for rescue was Bartlett, who trekked with an Eskimo companion and seven dogs seven hundred miles across the ice to the Siberian coast and thence east to reach St. Michael, Alaska, a point from which it was possible to telegraph a report of the disaster and a plea for the rescue of those left behind. (Most of the castaways survived to be rescued almost five months after Bartlett's departure, a story sharing space in the press with coverage of the first battles of the 1914 war.)

The Bob Bartlett that Gould met in the harbor at North Sydney was now fifty years of age, with a "weather-beaten face, reddened and bronzed by much exposure." He had purchased the thirty-year-old *Effie M. Morrissey* (named for the daughter of her first skipper, a Gloucester fisherman) the year before and had just refitted her for new life as expedition transport in Arctic waters.* For all the impressiveness of Bartlett's Arctic résumé, what struck those who met him with greater impact was the force of the rugged mariner's colorful greathearted personality. "You never saw so much man in one body" is how he was eulogized years later by one member of the Explorers Club. Another recalled his "rolling, polar bear gait, his foghorn voice, his unexpected philosophical depths, his jovial good humor" and his "great warmth of heart." Bartlett was celebrated for—among those who were not scandalized by—the creative saltiness of his language, and within hours of making his acquaintance Gould was telling his diary:

> He is I think the most profane man in Christendom—the most amazing array of expletives flows from his lips with an unconscious ease that is very near to being art... . Hearing him talk I thought he was drunk but Putnam explained to me that he was just natural and was a most abstemious man—had never taken a drink in fact. He is just the sort of sea-captain one has to read about and just the sort to command such a ship as the *Morrissey*.

In later years Gould still spoke with admiration of Cap'n Bob's impressive ability to swear for ten minutes at a stretch, neither stopping nor once repeating himself.

The following morning the other four members of the Michigan Greenland Expedition—Hobbs, Church, Fergusson, and Oscanyan—arrived in North Sydney by train, and before noon the entire company had boarded ship and set sail. Gould quickly determined that the atmosphere tended to get "sort of close" below

---

*   This 1926 Greenland excursion would be the first of what would eventually amount to twenty major annual voyages Bartlett would take in northern waters aboard the *Morrissey*, a vessel that George Palmer Putnam later termed, in his biography of Bartlett, a "magic carpet of authentic adventure."

deck in the small cabin shared by a dozen or more men and that he preferred to spend as much time above as possible. On the other hand, the not-quite hundred-foot-long *Morrissey* was a small craft that soon began to roll—"to behave quite like a cork," wrote Gould, who managed to keep down his supper the first evening,

but at breakfast the next morning he got in only a few mouthfuls before turning green and having to hurry on deck and to the rail. Much recovered by evening, he was able to appreciate the special charm of viewing a glorious sunset through the rigging of an old sailing vessel, and the next day, after the cold fog that followed a heavy rain lifted, he declared, though bundled for warmth in chamois* and sheepskin, that he did not know when he had enjoyed a day so much. He now relished the "rolling sea, at times dashing spray over the vessel itself," and

With Cap'n Bob Bartlett (left)

that afternoon he thrilled to the sight of the first icebergs encountered. The day's only dampening moment occurred when taking exercise on deck after supper. Belknap challenged Gould to jump a rope, and on his fourth jump the loose rubber boot on Gould's right foot flew off and was lost to the icy waters of the Strait of Belle Isle. "It is funny," acknowledged his rueful diary entry, "but I shall have need of said boots in Greenland."

Part of the charm for Gould of the nine-day voyage to the Greenland coast was getting to know his shipmates. The small crew of Newfoundlanders was an interesting and picturesque group, starting with Bartlett, whose distinctive personality made a quick imprint on the young geologist. Cap'n Bob saw his life of sailing in northern seas as the destiny to which he had been called. Bartlett's mother had first hoped that he would become a minister, and at fifteen he was sent to the Methodist College in St. John's, where he stuck it out for two years before committing instead to the seafaring life. "I held the tack as long as I could," he once explained, "and then came about, eased off, and ran before the wind of what I was meant to do." If asked to trace the growth of Larry Gould's own call to polar expeditioning, one must begin with a pair of explorer's lectures he attended while still a student in Ann Arbor. These events sparked interest. Then Hobbs' readily accepted invitation to voyage to Greenland provided opportunity. But few things could more effectively have stimulated the spirit of ice-bound adventure than actually to be under sail for the Far North with Bob Bartlett, hearing him tell in his own high-pitched voice stories of blizzards and shipwreck, of Peary, Eskimos, and polar bear. Here, we can readily imagine, is where the spell of polar exploration fully began to work its magic on Larry Gould.

---

* Peg Rice's mother had given Gould the gift of a chamois skin coat, which Gould declared to his diary later in the summer to be "quite the most valuable piece of clothing I have."

Also aboard was Cap'n Bob's brother Will, the first mate. Will Bartlett asked Gould if he were married, to which the geologist replied that he was not and could not yet afford to be—the same state of affairs as held for Will as well. Gould inquired about Bob Bartlett's attitude toward matrimony and learned that when asked if he were married, Cap'n Bob had been known to reply, "Hell no! Why man I wouldn't marry the Virgin Mary!" As Bartlett was to reveal in his autobiography published two years later, he had once proposed marriage to a girl and been accepted, too, but almost immediately their "beautiful bark of happiness went to smash on the rocks" of an argument, and Bartlett, who was more relieved than not by the breakup, swore he'd never say another word about love to another woman in his life.

The American Museum of Natural History zoological collecting expedition that was the *Morrissey*'s principal cargo that summer was a party of eleven, headed by the dashing thirty-eight-year-old businessman and book publisher George Palmer Putnam. Putnam, a grandson of the original founder of G. P. Putnam's Sons, had joined the family publishing firm in 1918 and was responsible for the subsequent prominence in that firm's catalog of books on adventure and exploration. In his autobiography Putnam writes that "It seemed inappropriate to promote books about exploration without doing a bit of exploration myself. So I did."

For this 1926 venture into northern waters Putnam had gathered a colorful assortment of expeditioners that included a zoologist, a taxidermist, an expert bow and arrow hunter, a Pathé news cameraman, a Montana cowboy whose special role was to capture big game with the lariat, another hunter, a surgeon, a radio operator, and a chief engineer who happened to be Robert Peary's son and namesake. Also along was Putnam's thirteen-year-old son David Binney Putnam, already the successful author of a popular adventure book for boys, *David Goes Voyaging*, an account of a three-month sail in the Pacific. Gould found the whole contingent splendid company, and Putnam seems actually to have invited Gould to switch expeditions and stay with the Putnam group, which naturally was not a course Gould could seriously consider.

They sailed or motored through cold and fog, skirting ice floes along the upper coast of Labrador, and then across the icy Davis Strait, making for the southwest Greenland port of Holsteinsborg. For three days Gould endured a "continuous nightmare" of seasickness, during which he would gladly "have sold the ship and both expeditions for a nickel." Noting in his diary Mark Twain's description of the three stages of seasickness—you are afraid you are going to die; you want to die; you are afraid you won't die—Gould claimed to have discovered thirty-three stages beyond Twain's third. Describing how in open water the small boat rolled, pitched, and even turned like a corkscrew, Gould declared that he hoped the sea would freeze over by October so that he could skate home. His misery began to lift on July 4—a day the Montana cowboy saluted patriotically by firing off his six-shooter below the mess room table at 4 a.m.—and by the time they reached the west Greenland fjords on the morning of the 6th Gould was able to appreciate the ruggedly beautiful sight with delight. Encountering a group of Eskimos in kayaks at mid-day (a term of diminished significance in a latitude where there was now no darkness greater than a short twilight), the ship arranged for one of them to pilot the *Morrissey* in to Holsteinsborg. Daniel Streeter, a hunter on the Putnam expedition who later chronicled the summer in his book *An Arctic Rodéo*, described the arrival in port:

> Before us lay Greenland, theme of legend, song and story; yet so little known. Land of mystery and paradox. The spirit of adventure hovered over us; our thoughts wandered in vast virgin solitudes.
>
> For a moment the temptation to pose as the terrestrial representatives of Americus Vespucius, Pizzaro, Drake, Hawkins and the rest of the world's Great Rovers was almost irresistible. But only for a moment. A young man came off in a rowboat and requested George, in English impossible to misconstrue, not to land until the "Manager had examined our papers."
>
> That was the end of Americus Vespucius.

***

The expeditions' credentials were examined by the Danish authorities, and both groups were officially admitted to Greenland. They found themselves in a town of about three hundred persons, with a handful of bright blue- or green-painted frame houses and a brand-new red-hued church, ringed by sod huts, all arranged without streets on the slope of a steep rocky hill. The complete absence of trees made it difficult to judge the size of buildings from a distance, contributing to an impression for Gould of a doll-like toy village. The new arrivals were greeted by a mob of Eskimos eager to barter their merchandise—seal or dog skin moccasins, eider duck skin hats, bone carvings, and the like—in exchange for expedition supplies, especially shirts and pants. Gould wrote that the Eskimos, many of whom he judged very good looking, though "dirty beyond impression," were all laughing and colorfully dressed, "their beautiful head collars being especially bright." That evening the *Morrissey* hosted a banquet of sorts for the local manager and his wife, along with a group of their friends. This was followed by an informal dance in the ship's mess hall, described by one of the Putnam party as "six steps one way, a crash against a bulkhead, six steps back, and a violent collision with the tool chest," yet "all very enjoyable and no one was knocked unconscious." This Arctic cotillion was watched through the mess room skylight by a group of native Greenlanders who seemed to find the dancing highly entertaining, a number of them bringing their whole families and "all the necessaries for an indefinite stay."

After a time, however, the festivities were ended, the crew of the *Morrissey* hoisted anchor, and overnight—though there was no darkness—the ship proceeded another forty miles inland up the Ikertokfjord, toward the Maligiakfjord where the professors' party was to be unloaded to establish their summer base. An early morning stop was made at a small fishing village—seventy-some persons, sod huts, and one frame house—that was to be the Hobbs expedition's nearest approach to a local metropolis. Here was observed a pack of wolfish Eskimo dogs feeding on the carcasses of some beached sharks. The native dwellings were accessed by long earthen tunnels leading to dim single-room interiors, muddy, fishy, and with air described by one of the men who entered one that day as "'heavy,' all the oxygen having been extracted from it some days previously." The party introduced themselves to the inhabitants who were to be their neighbors, but did not stay long. At about noon, ten or eleven miles farther along, they reached the head of the fjord, where the *Morrissey* could proceed no further and where the Hobbs party disembarked. Their supplies were put ashore in three loads and hauled to their chosen camp within a rock-walled amphitheater by a stream. Farewells were said and the *Morrissey* departed until September. After she was gone the six men of the University of Michigan Greenland expedition discovered that their entire cooking outfit was still aboard—they were left with plenty of food, but "not a knife, fork, spoon, plate, cup, fry pan or anything." Cheerfully, Gould records, they were compelled to improvise "spoons from clam shells and various cooking vessels from empty tin cans."

The expedition's base camp, on what they called University Bay, lay about twenty-five miles north of the Arctic Circle. But the July weather, as they labored to unpack supplies and set up camp, was uncomfortably warm. "It seems like 85 degrees in the shade," wrote Gould on their second day in camp, "only there isn't any shade."

A greater trouble was the constant annoyance provided by tormenting swarms of mosquitoes and black flies. One witness to the unloading of the *Morrissey* on that spot disputed the notion that the mosquitoes were as large as quail, writing that they were not in fact "any larger than humming birds though much more ferocious." On the 8th, Gould told his diary that these pests could not be any thicker, for lack of space, and that he could scarcely see the page he was writing on, the mosquitoes were "flying about in such numbers." Their bites had caused his hands and face to swell "as though I had dropsy," and he was writing the entry clad in a head net and heavy leather gloves. During their first day in camp Gould and two others had attached an outboard motor to a canoe and gone about five miles up to the head of the fjord. There, he writes, "the motor began to sputter in a way which I knew wasn't a dirty gas line." The difficulty was soon diagnosed: "I found the stream in the gasoline clogged with mosquitos and black flies. So thick are they that just in the process of pouring gas into the tank enough had gotten caught to cause us all the trouble."

Over succeeding days the Michigan expedition was visited by groups of Eskimos—men, women, and children—arriving in kayaks and the larger craft for women known as umiaks. Gould, who acted as expedition cameraman in addition to other duties, filmed some of these arrivals, including the performance of one kayaker who demonstrated the trick of turning completely over and righting himself again—an operation which non-natives sometimes tried to copy, but at which they were generally only 50 percent successful.

Gould soon had good reason to be grateful for the presence of Eskimo visitors. On July 10, one Eskimo making a second visit to the camp from the neighboring village brought a number of the cooking and eating implements they previously lacked—cups, knives, forks, spoons, plates, and two other dishes. Another group of women and children and two young men also arrived in a large umiak. Meanwhile, Gould and Belknap again fastened the outboard motor to a canoe and after supper went out into the fjord to test the motor in preparation for an upcoming reconnaissance trip of a few days being planned by Gould and Hobbs. Church, Fergusson, and Oscanyan were occupied about the storehouse, while Hobbs and the Eskimo who had brought utensils were standing on shore. It took Gould several attempts to get the motor started, and so, as he wrote later,

> Before I half realized it we were out from our protected harbor into the main fiord where the wind got a full sweep at us. It was so rough I dared not try to turn the canoe around. The front end was so light that it bumped each wave triply. Suddenly it rose so high that the wind caught the front and blew us around into the trough. Instantly we capsized into the icy Arctic waters. I called to Belly to hang onto the canoe and not try to swim for we were fully 1/2 a mile from shore and I knew we should freeze. With the weight of the motor the overturned canoe would barely hold up.

Fortunately, their plight was immediately observed from shore, and the Eskimo who had been standing with Hobbs quickly launched his kayak and began to paddle swiftly toward the struggling men. Hobbs and Oscanyan followed in another canoe, and Fergusson and Church got a heavy dory into the water and struggled to make it move quickly with but a single pair of oars. The women's umiak, which had left camp shortly before, also observed the capsized craft and bent to the rescue.

Meanwhile, in the icy water the overturned canoe "seemed continually on the point of sinking." Its buoyancy was slight, and as whichever end they were clinging to would push down under waves they would frantically pull themselves along toward the other end. They fought to keep their heads above water, as the waves continually crested above them. The Eskimo kayaker, moving "with wonderful speed," arrived first, and helped to support the two men for several long moments until the umiak came up as well, and the crew of Eskimo women and two men pulled Gould and Belknap out of the frigid water into their craft. The canoe and dory now also approached but were immediately turned about, away from the rough water and back to shore, as the motor-canoe was also drawn up out of the water and laid across the stern of the umiak. When the shivering men were returned to *terra firma* a few minutes later, their companions who had hurried back first were ready with dry clothes, hot tea, and Arctic sleeping bags. "In a few hours they were quite themselves again," Hobbs wrote later, "but except for the opportune presence of the kayaker and the women in the whale-boat this accident might have had a tragic ending." Gould supposed they were actually in the icy cold water only a few minutes, but, he noted in his diary the next day, "it seemed hours. At any rate we no doubt owe our lives today to our good Eskimo friends. I liked them before but of course more than ever now."

***

For the next two weeks the expedition continued to prepare for the summer's real work. Gould and Hobbs took two multiple-day reconnaissance trips together, the second also with Fergusson, the aerologist, on which the three chief miseries for Gould seemed to be black flies, the drizzling cold rain of the first reconnaissance, and Hobbs' snoring.* A suitable spot was found on which to conduct Fergusson's work with weather balloons. Oscanyan set up what he believed to be the first short-wave length radio station in Greenland, made contact with the *Morrissey*, and also began to receive regular news reports from the United Press. Gould added to his other titles for the expedition that of chief cook, and claimed to have received good reviews for his ptarmigan pie.

Above all, preparations were made for four-sixths of the expedition to make a month's journey inland, onto the great ice cap. This group—Gould, Hobbs, Church, and Belknap, accompanied by four Greenlander Eskimos who were arranged for by a Danish contact—set out on the 26th of July. Their intent was to cross the miles of tundra separating them from the great ice sheet and then advance over the ice for a period of eight to ten days, experimenting with balloon ascents. Travel over the tundra was not easy in midsummer, when the lakes were no longer frozen and the torment of the insects was almost unrelenting. They made their first stage by umiak, bringing them to the head of a large lake where they cached the skin boat and continued on by carrying their gear on shoulders—"our strong man Gould portaging the seventy-five pound canoe," recorded Hobbs.

Gould got on particularly well with the Greenlanders, Abraham, Peter, Nathaniel, and Enoch. His diary is filled with indications of admiration for the Eskimos he encountered throughout the summer, and these four taught him some of their language while he shared with them some of his good tobacco. On the 27th he wrote:

> I have been learning a good deal of the Eskimo tongue today and find Nathaniel quite an apt student of English. Pardon my conceit but the Eskimos have come to like me even to the point of giving me a name. The name is Ivutiksek. I have no idea what it means but I have learned

---

* Gould described Hobbs' snore as "blood curdling gurgles and terrifying noises" louder than any he'd ever before heard. On the second trip he had Fergusson share the tent with Hobbs, while he took his sleeping bag off the distance of half a city block so as actually to be able to sleep. Fergusson, however, discovered that if the tent rattled, the chief would cease, so he proceeded to rattle the tent himself every time Hobbs started, and so got a modicum of peace.

to pronounce it. I have added about a dozen words to my vocabulary too.

The Eskimos brought their own food supply and eat apart from us. They were greatly delighted tonight when I showed them how to cook some oatmeal which they had brought along with them. They are the most happy hearted people I have seen—and courteous and gentle beyond compare almost. I have met few people in whom the qualities which we consider attributes of a gentleman are so deep rooted or so inherent as in these companions of ours.

On July 29, Gould and Belknap climbed a mountain near the party's path to attempt to determine what lakes lay ahead in which they could continue to use the canoe to advantage. From the mountain they were rewarded with their first glimpse of the Greenland ice shelf. Its edge, viewed through Gould's binoculars, looked rough and so heavily crevassed that Gould expressed some doubt as to whether they could actually climb onto it once they got there.

As the party proceeded inland they were continually lightening their load by caching food supplies to be retrieved on the journey back. On the 30th, Gould recorded that their diet now consisted only of hard tack, tea, oatmeal, bacon, pea soup, and pemmican and that on the ice they would have only tea and pemmican. Fortunately, he wrote, "our pemmican is a very good variety and I really like it."

What he did not like was the ongoing torment he suffered from the black flies and mosquitoes. Gould continued to carry the canoe on his shoulders during all portages* and found that the space his head occupied under the canoe was a favorite gathering place for mosquitoes. After one portage, which he described as "three of Professor Hobbs' miles, or five of anyone else's," he likened his face to a piece of beef.

The hardships colored Gould's reactions to the Greenland environment, though they did not prevent him from appreciating the positive. He was pleased that the nights were growing colder and the constant daylight beginning to give way to some midnight darkness. The end of each day now included "beautiful sunset effects and colors that suggest the desert." But he judged that he should not like to remain in Greenland through the long winter night. On the 31st, Gould's thoughts turned to contemplation of the explorer Stefansson's famous contention that "The Friendly Arctic" was really a most hospitable place for those who could sensibly adjust their ways to it:

> With my face raw from black fly bites and the knowledge that there is no life here—for we see no duck, geese, or anything of that sort here and the lakes … are devoid of fish—I am inclined to take issue with him. One would soon perish here if he attempted to live on the land… . On the other hand the natives are very friendly. The hillsides are often covered with the most gorgeous splotches of blue bells of the most massive

---

* Hobbs estimated that the canoe was portaged sixteen miles on the journey to and from the ice, saving the transport of nearly five hundred pounds a distance of about seventy-five miles.

size—and there are several other kinds of flowers. In some aspects it is friendly. But of course I have seen but a small part—other parts of Greenland and the Arctic may be more friendly. At best, however, the environment is severe and my respect and admiration for the ingenuity of the Eskimos grows daily.

The canoe was eventually left in camp at the last in the chain of small lakes they followed. From there the party still had three days of strenuous trekking over the spongy tundra with heavy packs to reach the ice. Food was becoming an issue, as Hobbs had reduced their un-cached stock to what Gould privately criticized as "starvation rations." He regretted the amount of very light dried food Hobbs had elected to cache earlier that might have been carried along without great effort. Moreover, the Eskimos had nearly used up their own meager food supply—meager, because they had trusted to get game, especially caribou, on the trail but had been disappointed in that. Some of the party, including Gould, had formed bad blisters on their feet, and one of the Eskimos had badly strained a knee. So all in all the party was not in the best of shape on the evening of August 4 when they finally arrived at a tongue of inland ice Hobbs named Otto Nordenskjöld Glacier, after the Swedish geographer and explorer.

The following morning the scientists began their balloon studies—the first ascents, Hobbs wrote, "ever to be made so close to the inland-ice either in the Arctic or the Antarctic. The courses followed by the balloons showed plainly the structure of the ice cap air circulation."

Meanwhile, the Eskimo Abraham made another discouraging hunt, again finding no trace of caribou. Gould records that in the afternoon he had "rather a plain talk with the Chief about our food situation with the result that he has agreed to shorten our time on the ice from 10 to 5 days." Hobbs' account reads:

> Our condition is not a pleasant one. We have now reached the ice-front only to find that we must feed eight men with the rations we had planned for four, even though for some days we have been keeping the rations too low for such heavy work as we are doing. Only one course is open to us. We must cut down the time for our ice-cap work to not more than four days at the most, after which it will be necessary to start back to our base on forced marches and with half rations until our nearest depot is reached.

Accordingly, the group's time on the ice was indeed cut short and the return journey commenced a few days later. Retracing their steps without notable incident, retrieving food stores and the canoe at camps along the way, the inland party arrived back at their base on the Maligiakfjord twenty-one days after first setting out, some ten days in advance of what had originally been planned.

At the base, Church and Oscanyan met them with news indicating the necessity of another change. On the 26th of July, the same day that the inland ice party had begun their journey, hundreds of miles to the north, off Northumberland Island in latitude 77° North, the *Morrissey* had struck an uncharted lava reef and gotten thoroughly stuck. This had occurred at high tide, which complicated the job of getting her off again—attempts could be made only when the tide was again at a full flood of similar height. Initial tries were unsuccessful. At last, after unloading all cargo, buoying the ship with empty petroleum cans, and putting on sail to encourage the Diesel engine, the crew of the *Morrissey* and men of the Putnam expedition were just able to scrape the schooner off her perch and slip her into deep water. The *Morrissey*, however, had lost her false keel and was found to be "leaking like a funnel." With passengers taking turns manning the bilge pump, the damaged ship limped south to Upernavik for emergency repairs. All this had been communicated to the men at the Maligiakfjord by radio and Hobbs now learned that the partially repaired *Morrissey*, though still leaking, was judged sound enough for the trip home but that the date of rendezvous for the Michigan expedition to reboard the ship in Holsteinsborg was being advanced to earlier in September.

While scientific endeavor marked much of the time left to the Michigan expedition in Greenland, the group did not overlook the August 22 arrival of their popular second-in-command's thirtieth birthday. One gift Gould received that summer was the pleasant sensation of having his name attached to a geographical feature on the map. The inland party had discovered along the southern margin of the Otto Nordenskjöld glacier a lovely half-mile-wide ice-dammed lake set like a jewel against vertical cliffs of ice. This Hobbs was pleased to name Lake Laurence M. Gould.

***

The expedition reunited with the *Morrissey* in Holsteinsborg and on September 7 set sail for home. The vessel was yet more crowded than it had been on the June trip out, as its passengers now also included the Danish trapper and explorer Knud Rasmussen, the blue fox "harvest" of two years at Rasmussen's Thule trading post, and all the results of the Putnam expedition's summer collecting, including a pair of live polar bear cubs destined for the Bronx Zoo. (Putnam and Cap'n Bob had nicknamed the cubs Tom and Jerry. Zoo personnel, taking a better look later, informed them that both cubs were female.)

A post-supper poker game was in progress in the after-cabin on the *Morrissey*'s first or second evening out from Holsteinsborg,* when Chief Engineer Peary became alarmed by the sound of the engine. He rushed off to the engine room, and for the next quarter hour the poker players could hear sounds of the motor stopping, starting, reversing, and speeding. Then silence. When Peary returned he announced that the propeller and shaft, damaged when the *Morrissey* had struck the reef, had separated and that the propeller had just gone to the bottom of the Davis Strait. Without a propeller the *Morrissey* was strictly a sailing vessel, and

---

* Hobbs reported it as the first evening. Dan Streeter, in *An Arctic Rodéo*, put it on the second evening. They agree on there having been a poker game.

the chief engineer declared himself henceforward simply a passenger. Putnam expedition chronicler Daniel Streeter summed it up:

> In the twinkling of an eye we had been converted from a lavish pleasure craft into a windjammer. Now all we had to do was beat our way across the twelve hundred miles of liquid mirth that separated us from Sydney. It might take ten days. It might take two months. Boreas would decide.

In the end, it was sixteen days after departing Greenland before the schooner put in again to North Sydney Harbor. Part of the trip was monotonous, as they made little headway while becalmed. Part of it was rather too exciting, as they were struck by gales. Streeter writes of great seas bearing down on them "like liquid mountains" and the wind howling in the riggings, filling one "with misgivings and a lively regret that he had not become a real estate salesman instead of a sailor." A nasty headwind kept them stuck for days in the narrow Belle Isle Straits, with "no recourse but to sail in the trough back and forth across the straits, jibing and nearly taking out the ship's masts with each turn." Hobbs writes: "This continued for days without relief. I shall not forget one morning when Bob, thoroughly worn out, came down to breakfast and after telling us he had almost lost his 'sticks' (masts) remarked, 'If any of you fellers are on intimate terms with the Almighty, you had better get busy.'"

Finally the wind changed, and "a roaring gale came out of the north and blew us through the Straits like a cork out of a bottle." Hobbs describes the sight of the captain "at the wheel, his sou'wester gone and strands of his long, thin hair flying free" while "great billows of following seas reared their black masses far above the taffrail." With canvas "shortened to a riding sail and a jumbo jib," the *Morrissey* "was making a good eight knots." "Riding like a Viking of the olden time," admired Hobbs, "Captain Bob was in his element."*

They reached North Sydney on the 23rd, where they learned to associate the weather they had encountered with the tail end of a major Miami hurricane that had blown north. Nova Scotia sailors were calling the resulting storm the worst off their coast in thirty years. For Gould, just turned thirty, the return to harbor at North Sydney marked the end of a summer's Arctic adventure which itself, however, marked only the beginning of a lifetime's fascination with the ends of the earth.

---

*   Some twenty years later the author of Bob Bartlett's obituary in *The Explorers Journal* wrote that "Captain Bob had a way of disregarding what others might call the violence of Nature. When the gale seemed ready to blow the sticks out of the *Morrissey*, he would lower his dripping bulk down the cabin ladder and write in the log book, 'Wind moderate, sea moderate.' The storm might increase; the quarterdeck might be awash, with water cascading into the cabin to send shoes floating about on the floor. Again, 'Wind moderate, sea moderate.'"

CHAPTER 5

BAFFIN TO BYRD

In the summer of 1927, sufficiently removed in time from the previous summer to dull over-acute recollection of the misery of seasickness or black flies—or perhaps already sufficiently pledged to the fraternity of true explorers that such discomforts simply did not signify—Larry Gould again went north. Again his transport to adventure was Bob Bartlett's *Morrissey*, and again he sailed in the company of George Palmer Putnam—this time at Putnam's express invitation and with the title of assistant director and geographer, Putnam Baffin Island Expedition. As the title suggests, their destination was Baffin Island in the Canadian Arctic. Their purpose was exploration—specifically, to penetrate into the Foxe Basin, north of Hudson Bay, visiting and mapping sections of the southern and western coast of Baffin Island that had hitherto remained geographically obscure. The expedition, organized and directed by Putnam, was sponsored primarily by the American Geographical Society.

The twenty-three person Baffin expedition sailed from Putnam's home of Rye, New York, on June 12. That was three weeks and a day after the biggest headlines of 1927 had hailed aviator Charles A. Lindbergh's safe arrival in Paris following his solo crossing of the Atlantic in *The Spirit of St. Louis.* In that interval, even while George Putnam the adventurer prepared to get his summer expedition launched, George Putnam the publisher stole a march on his book business rivals by succeeding, with the assistance of the Paris office of the *New York Times,*,

George Palmer Putnam, 1927

in getting a note promptly into the besieged new hero's hands that resulted in Lindbergh's agreeing before sailing home to an immediate book, to be published by G. P. Putnam's Sons. The resulting volume,

We, was rushed into print as quickly as possible and sold spectacularly.

By June 20, the Putnam expedition had arrived at Bob Bartlett's hometown of Brigus, Newfoundland, on the Avalon Peninsula. Here they stopped two days, during which they were made welcome by the entire village and in particular by

the senior Bartletts, the father and mother of Cap'n Bob and First Mate Will. From there the *Morrissey* sailed north along the coastal barrens of Labrador, taking some cod along the way and noting that ice was still present unusually far south for early summer. From Cape Harrison north, wrote Putnam in his article about the expedition, "vast drifting fields" of heavy pack were encountered that caused them to make their way "chiefly well in by the land, working along through loose pans and leads of open water, dodging behind islands, and 'cross cutting' through 'tickles.'"

The Morrissey, **beset by ice off the upper Labrador coast, 1927**

The schooner put in for brief visits at the Labrador villages of Makkovik, Hopedale, Turnavik, and Nain. Some twenty miles from Nain, a day was spent on Sculpin Island in a cursory examination of the ruins of a group of eleven stone houses supposed to be of Norse origin. The Moravian missionary at Nain informed them that the Inuit name for the ruins signified "the houses built by strange people" but that the natives had no real knowledge of who had built them. On Sculpin, Gould drew a map of the ruins, with careful measurements of individual structures, and the men attempted some excavation in one house without result. Unsurprisingly, Putnam concluded that "thorough-going archaeological study alone can determine with any definitude the comparative antiquity of the ruins and their possible historical significance."

On July 1 they passed the gorgeously fjorded Cape Mugford, at 57° 40' N latitude, but farther north, from Saglek Bay, they found themselves "well beset" by pack ice clinging close to land. The night of July 4 they were caught between heavy ice pans, with pressure sufficient to decommission the *Morrissey*'s propeller and shaft. For the next five days the injured ship battled the ice but was pushed slowly southward by pack ice cemented by a continuing northeast gale. Before, they had nearly reached Cape Chidley, the northernmost point of Labrador from which they could enter the Hudson Strait, but now the pack drove them back along the mountainous coast in a drift some fifty miles south. Bartlett had the *Morrissey*'s motor whaleboat and launch lashed astern to assist in shoving out of the pack whenever any chance of progress was perceived.

Finally getting clear of the ice jam, Bartlett made for the bight of a nearby bay where he beached his vessel for repairs. While engineer Peary oversaw the difficult job of installing the *Morrissey*'s spare propeller and shaft, a party including Gould and Putnam explored the neighborhood inland. Noting that their anchorage lay just at the base of the so-called "Four Peaks" supposed to be the culminating heights of the Torngat Mountains, Putnam reported that while repairs were in progress this party found "an unrecorded tidewater lake, some fifteen miles long, averaging over two miles in width, and possessed of a rugged Alpine beauty truly spectacular." To the west they found a second lake, connected with the first by a "freakish gorge over a mile long, narrowing to fifty yards in width, with precipitous walls."

With the Eskimo Avalisha

When the voyage recommenced, progress was better, and on July 17 the *Morrissey* passed between Cape Chidley and Resolution Island to the north to enter Hudson Strait. After stopping to take on water at Big Island on Baffin's southern shore, some three hundred miles beyond the mouth of the strait, on the 22nd they reached the Hudson's Bay Company trading post of Amadjuak, where they found a group of Eskimos encamped in summer homes of sealskin tents. Liking these people as much as he had liked their Greenland cousins the previous year, Gould took many pictures; his expedition photo album contains several pages of images of the Eskimo men, women, and several children encountered at Amadjuak and a few days later at Cape Dorset. One of the Amadjuak men, Avalisha, agreed readily to the expedition's suggestion that they arrange for his family to receive rations from the trading post while he accompanied them on into the Foxe Basin and along Baffin's western coast. According to Putnam, "In a matter of ten minutes Avalisha had bade his wife goodby, rolled his 'blanket' of caribou hide, hung about his neck the little skin bag containing his telescope and minor treasures, and was ready." Three days later, at the company post of Cape Dorset in Baffin's extreme southwest, they took aboard a second Eskimo, Kavaoo, in similar manner. Meanwhile, by prior arrangement, three members of the party concerned with the expedition's "collateral" purposes were established at Cape Dorset, there to conduct specialized studies among the Inuit until the *Morrissey*'s return.

From Cape Dorset Putnam intended to work his way north along the western shore of Foxe Land, but twin difficulties of fog and ice temporarily defeated Captain Bartlett's best efforts to oblige. The expedition was deflected to an anchorage on the desolate rocky mass of Mill Island, where its members became the island's first recorded white visitors. Continual bad weather kept them there six days, during which, Putnam complained, the total non-appearance of the sun made it impossible to make observations to determine their exact position. Assistant Director Gould, ever the geologist, approved the island as "remarkable" for the perfection of its fracture-fault system and for its "excellently preserved series of terraces." Finally, at mid-day on August 1, the heavy ice blocking further progress north loosened sufficiently for the *Morrissey* to resume her intended course, and on the 4th the ship completed its swing around Foxe Peninsula by reaching the "long finger of rocks and shoals" marking the northwest extremity of Cape Dorchester.

The bad weather that had driven the expedition to refuge on Mill Island was, unfortunately, typical of what they encountered all summer long—they learned from the testimony of natives and traders that 1927's summer conditions were unusually bad as compared with other years. Putnam observed afterward that

> Out of sixty days spent within the entrance of Hudson Strait, only eight were genuinely fair throughout. For thirty-two days fog was recorded as present all or most of the daylight hours, often with rain. On two occasions the sun was not visible for six days in succession; and fog, rain, and gales prevailed in about equal proportions.

Between Mill Island and Cape Dorchester poor visibility had prevented observations confirming their position or verifying their charts. At the cape, a hilly protrusion of barren granite and gneiss, they found a puzzling discrepancy between their charts and the shoreline before them. On the map, the western shore of Baffin proceeded on a northeasterly line after passing the landmark of Cape Dorchester. Instead, their apparent course in continuing to follow the coast now lay due east, and even slightly south of east. Assuming that the established charts were correct, it seemed that the discrepancy must be attributed to error in their magnetic compass, an instrument known to become eccentric as one approached near to the magnetic pole. Continual cloud cover disallowed immediate confirmations using the expedition's Bumstead compass, which operated on different principles and would be unaffected by magnetic whims.

The plan now called for the expedition to divide for a month into two separate parties. While Bartlett took the *Morrissey* farther on into the Foxe Basin, a smaller group set out to follow and survey the western Baffin shoreline so far as was practicable in a small-draft motor whaleboat. Transferring to the twenty-four-foot-long whaleboat, with thirty days' rations and 600-miles-worth of gasoline, was a party of seven: Gould, Putnam, Putnam's son David, Gould's surveying assistants George Weymouth, Monroe Barnard, and John Pope, plus the Eskimo Avalisha. Apart from a small tented area at the stern, the whaleboat was an entirely open craft, so that, as Putnam noted drily in his report, "the conditions were not notably luxurious, especially in bad weather—and the weather was almost continuously bad." Left behind at Cape Dorchester was a cache of food and fuel that would enable an emergency return to the Hudson's Bay Company station at Cape Dorset, if need be.

The shore followed by the whaleboat party over the next several days was truly a desolate one, as Putnam would later write, a "wilderness of ... dead monotony." Vast muddy flatland predominated, with the coastline no more than a thin "ribbon of granite rising just above the high-tide contour." Over a seventy-five-mile stretch the party could discern no appreciable elevations within a dozen miles of the waterline. The landscape's most distinguishing features were ice formations along the shore. As described by Putnam:

> The shore itself was festooned with an endless parade of grounded "growlers" and sizable pans, the bergs, high and dry on shelves of glacier-polished rocks, rearing aloft thirty feet and more at low water or again at flood tide showing but a fraction of their upper bulk. Every point was lined with them, as was also each protruding reef beyond the points. Picturesque they were, some of them huge, many of them fashioned by the tide-driven waters into grotesque shapes, a sort of gigantic mushroom *motif* predominating.

Shoals and ice made shoreline navigation often difficult and dangerous, even in their small-draft craft. Where the pack ice came in close to land, the party's only chance of progress was by what Putnam described as "cutting corners"—that is, "dodging along close inshore as tide and ice movement permitted, often in less than a fathom of water and pretty much at the mercy of six-knot currents." Where the pack prevented passing around a shoal, they had no choice but to try to cut straight through, "sometimes in veritable rapids where the tide raced madly over the shoals, often with only a few inches of water between us and bottom."

Through such hazards, they picked their way onward.

The cartographic mystery of the disjunction between what the charts said and where they in fact appeared to be was eventually resolved by the geographer Gould: It was the map and not the compass that was in error. A few days into the whaleboat excursion it was finally possible for Gould to make satisfactory observations, which placed the expedition "even more out of harmony with the map than the compasses hinted." Gould corroborated his results by a checkup of the chronometer, verified by using the portable radio to catch noon time signals broadcast from Washington and then by subsequent astral and further solar observations. The results showed that the whaleboat was in the rather novel position of being afloat on a seawater course that according to previously published maps ought to be some fifty miles inland. Gould's finding meant that the whaleboat party was engaged in exploring and charting a considerable stretch of coastline that was geographically new. It meant also that a considerable piece of "land," appearing as such on maps of Baffin Island for two centuries, did not exist—or rather, was now to be "cartographically … sunk beneath the surface of Foxe Basin."*

Over the next few weeks the seven whaleboat passengers were true explorers. The shape of the large bay they established in place of what had been charted as land was defined by the extent of their progress on an eastern course until reaching the head of the bay—they named it Bowman Bay, for Isaiah Bowman, the head of the American Geographical Society—and then continuing to follow the coast as it turned northward. An inland trek from the head of the bay resulted in the solving of another mystery, this time an ornithological one. Previously, no one had located the spot where blue geese went to nest. The Putnam party discovered this to be a flat soggy stretch of tundra southeast of Bowman Bay, which they mapped as "Blue Goose Prairie." It found rising from that a limestone highland that Putnam declared to be the "one distinctive landmark" they were to note in all that part of Foxe Land. This was startling in its contrast to the predominant drab mud flats, as if a Colorado desert mesa had somehow been transported to the Canadian Arctic. Gould was delighted to discover that the limestone of the Putnam Highlands, as they called it, was highly fossiliferous. He spent the two or three hours available to him there busily collecting as many of the Ordovician age fossils as he had time to secure and which could be carried forty miles in backpacks back to the boat.

Following its inland trek, the whaleboat party continued northward along

---

*   In the end, the Putnam expedition was responsible for the land area of Baffin Island being reduced more than five thousand square miles from what had previously been believed—a revision amounting approximately to the size of the state of Connecticut. In 1959, when Gould was at Dartmouth College to lecture on the occasion of explorer Vilhjalmur Stefansson's eightieth birthday, Professor Trevor Lloyd observed in his introduction of Gould that while Stefansson was renowned, among other things, for adding large areas to the map of Canada, Dr. Gould had just the opposite distinction, having been the only man to his knowledge to have *erased* a sizeable part of the Canadian map.

the coast for another hundred miles or so of renewed and unvarying flatness, then turned about and made its way back to the cache at Cape Dorchester, arriving there August 25 having covered in all about five hundred miles. At the Cape, Gould was now able to make additional solar and stellar observations that established without doubt its true position as being many miles south of where previous charts had placed it. The party was rejoined by the *Morrissey* on September 4, after which a return was made to Cape Dorset to retrieve the expedition members headquartered there and to disembark their Eskimo companions. After a five-day stop at Chorkbak Inlet they were truly homeward bound, passing out of Hudson Strait on the 17th and reaching Sydney, Nova Scotia, on October 1 to close the expedition. With two Arctic adventures now under his belt, Gould hurried home to Ann Arbor to resume his teaching responsibilities.

***

A great deal of news had been made in the world during the 111 days during which Larry Gould sailed on the *Morrissey* to Baffin Island and back. For forty-five of those days representatives of the United States, Great Britain, and Japan met in Geneva to discuss naval disarmament, ultimately failing to reach agreement. In Washington, President Coolidge confounded expectations by announcing that he did not choose to run for reelection in 1928. In Massachusetts, the anarchists Sacco and Vanzetti were sent to the electric chair. In New York, the afternoon before the Putnam expedition docked at Sydney Harbor (and one week before entertainment history was altered by the New York premiere of *The Jazz Singer*, a motion picture that *talked*), crowds in Yankee Stadium cheered wildly as Babe Ruth hit his record sixtieth home run of the season. Nobody, however, was being cheered more heartily across America just then than the handsome aviator hero Lindbergh, who, immediately upon completing his manuscript for Putnam, had embarked upon a three-month flying tour of all forty-eight states. Aviation—truly modern and truly dangerous—was a hero's business, and Lindbergh, that summer of 1927, was the public's darling, standing atop the highest pedestal of adulation.

He was not, however, the only hero raised to fame by exploits of aviation. If one American stood next to Lindbergh in public acclaim as a hero of the skies, that man was thirty-eight-year-old naval officer Richard Evelyn Byrd. Lieutenant Commander Byrd—he had been raised to that rank by act of Congress following his north polar flight of 1926—had had his eye early in 1927 on the same prize eventually seized by Lindbergh: the first nonstop flight across the Atlantic, New York to Paris. Sponsored by department store mogul Rodman Wanamaker, who financed a three-engine Fokker plane for a spring 1927 attempt, Byrd and his projected crew of pilot Floyd Bennett and radio operator George Noville had been widely considered to have a better chance of success than other contenders including the little-known Lindbergh. Byrd's attempt would have preceded Lindbergh's had not an April 20 test flight, with plane designer Tony Fokker himself at the pilot controls, ended in a nose-first smashup that broke Byrd's arm and put both

Bennett and Noville in hospital with more serious injuries. Byrd's attempt at an Atlantic crossing was thus delayed by many weeks, and in the meantime Lindbergh succeeded. (Byrd was gracious in his congratulations, as he had been in preflight assistance to Lindbergh, offering the solo flier his specially extended runway, his weather service, and navigational advice.)

Richard Evelyn Byrd

Though disappointed in his hopes to have made the first nonstop flight over the Atlantic, Byrd nonetheless continued to plan his own crossing in the craft he christened *America*, flying with a recovered George Noville and two pilots to replace the injured Bennett, Bert Acosta and a skilled young Norwegian who had been helpful at the time of the 1926 North Pole flight, Bernt Balchen. By the time this flight got off the ground on June 29, a second successful Atlantic crossing had already been made by Clarence Chamberlin and Charles Levine, so Byrd's attempt would be for number three. The transatlantic jump went according to plan until, upon reaching France the next day, they found that heavy clouds, rain, and fog made a Paris landing impossible. With the situation growing increasingly serious as fuel ran low, Byrd eventually directed that they come down in shallow water along the French coast, and Balchen successfully made a nerve-jangling emergency landing in the surf of Ver-sur-Mer.

Headlines were nothing like Lindbergh's of course, but even the third nonstop Atlantic crossing by air was news to celebrate, and when Byrd returned to New York he became the first person ever to be feted there with a second ticker-tape parade. Even before leaving France, however, Byrd announced to the press preliminary plans for a new and yet more ambitious undertaking: an expedition of science and aviation in Antarctica that would explore by air vast miles of unknown territory and include a flight to the remotest spot on earth, the South Pole. To this point, no plane had yet been flown in Antarctica, and the hazards involved would be daunting, both in the air and on the icy surface. .

Byrd's first idea was for an expedition of only a few months, departing late in October, but this quickly proved impractical and on August 4—while Gould and the *Morrissey* were reaching Baffin's Cape Dorchester—he announced that he would take another year to prepare, plan, and equip a more ambitious program, maximizing safety and solid scientific accomplishment while dramatizing the utility to exploration of modern technologies like aviation and radio. As one of Byrd's principal backers, the *New York Times* gave these plans great publicity; it was not long before scores of adventure seekers with and without specialized skills or relevant experience were besieging Byrd with pleas to secure a place on the great expedition.

Larry Gould was plagued by many insects during his two Arctic summers, but apparently none bit harder than the explorer's bug, with its bite of adventure. Whether it was he who first talked to Putnam about Antarctica or whether Putnam first raised the idea with Gould, within days of concluding the Baffin trip Putnam was enlisting American Geographical Society Director Isaiah Bowman as an ally in a campaign to get Gould onto the Byrd expedition. On October 11 Bowman wrote Putnam a note—duly passed along from Putnam to Byrd—expressing hearty concurrence in Putnam's suggestion that Professor Gould would make an excellent Byrd expedition geographer-geologist. "I do not think we could find a better man," wrote Bowman. "He is just the right age [and] has no dependents … to be concerned over risks he might run." Moreover, urged Bowman, "he is an excellent fellow, as you know better than the rest of us from your past summer's experience." Professionally, Bowman declared, one "can speak only in terms of the highest praise of his work, his ability, and his prospects." Gould wrote directly to Byrd on November 12 of his interest in accompanying the expedition, and Hobbs followed with a telegram on the 15th, expressing hope that the two of them could dine with Byrd prior to the commander's lecture in Ann Arbor on the 22nd.

The Tuesday evening of Byrd's lecture, Gould and Byrd were introduced at dinner by Professor Claude Halstead Van Tyne, whose guest Byrd was while staying in the city. The two were seated together and, as Gould recalled many years later, "hit it off extremely well." The following day a report in the *Detroit News* read that at his Hill Auditorium lecture later in the evening Byrd had announced "the probable selection" of Professor Laurence M. Gould to accompany him on his expedition as geologist.

Even so, Byrd hesitated for some months before confirming that Gould's selection was definite. On the 29th of February, for instance, Byrd wrote Gould that "I have really selected you but I must reserve the right to change my mind. That sounds hard but I must do things that way with this expedition." The scope of Gould's responsibilities was also left open some while—whether he was to serve Byrd only as the expedition's geologist or as geographer as well. Meanwhile, Gould was asked to "work up" the geographic end of things for Byrd, addressing the question of what geographic discoveries would be most interesting to attempt. For his part, Gould declared himself ready and eager to act either in the dual capacity or the single, and he began to prepare himself by "poring over the literature of Antarctic exploration" with an eye to learning exactly what had been done to date both geographically and geologically. Byrd wrote that, at least provisionally, he was depending on Gould to act also as geographer and authorized him to use his initiative regarding obtaining donations of necessary equipment.

In mid-March George Putnam came to Ann Arbor to lecture on the Baffin Island expedition and brought Gould an advance copy of Byrd's forthcoming autobiography, *Skyward*, which Putnam was publishing. At his lecture Putnam announced from the platform that Byrd had authorized him to state that he was taking Michigan's Assistant Professor Gould with him to Antarctica as geographer and geologist. Byrd, however, subsequently wrote Gould to contradict the commitment to both roles, saying that he had not yet finally decided whether or not to get a separate geographer but would let Gould know "in due course." Gould, no doubt starting to become a bit frustrated by the lingering uncertainties, wrote Byrd that it would be "splendid from my standpoint" if an additional man were taken for geography, as that would allow himself more time for geological study, but that he now wished to know as soon as possible one way or the other, as he intended to make plans, if he was to act as the expedition's geographer, to spend part of the summer preparing himself through study at the American Geographical Society. Finally, in April Byrd confirmed that he wanted Gould to take both responsibilities. He would head up the expedition's scientific unit and be the only member possessed of a doctorate.

Despite his now needing to absent himself from teaching for an indeterminate period, Gould's standing with the University of Michigan was excellent. He had just been named the recipient for 1928 of Michigan's Henry Russell Award, a medal and honorarium given annually to a young member of the faculty showing particular promise and brilliance in scholastic endeavor. *The Michigan Daily* hailed Gould's selection to go with Byrd as "one of the most signal honors which has come to the University through its teaching staffs in recent years." The Board of Regents readily approved a leave of absence, and Michigan's President Little wrote Byrd that "we are very glad to have him get the experience."

As Byrd grappled with the realities of what it would take to accomplish all of his announced goals, his plans expanded to assume a large party wintering over in the Antarctic, making preparations for a definite stay of a full year with the contingent ability to stay a second if necessary. For months on end leading up to the expedition's departure, Commander Byrd and aides such as business manager Richard G. Brophy wrestled with the considerable burdens of mounting so ambitious a private undertaking, facing thousands of questions of planning, equipment, personnel, publicity, and finance. The incorporated Byrd Antarctic Expedition's New York headquarters became a third-floor suite of offices donated by the Biltmore Hotel, and there Byrd and his staff waged what some of them came to call the "Battle of New York City." It was a war of fund-raising, expenditure, and an ocean of logistics. Byrd claimed that the multitude of problems large and small presented by the preparation phase of his expedition was far and away its hardest challenge.

Byrd's designated second-in-command during the early stages of mobilizing the expedition was his close friend and pilot on the north polar flight of 1926,

Floyd Bennett. Then in April of 1928, while flying with Bernt Balchen and a reporter en route to rescue the passengers of a German plane that had made an emergency landing in Newfoundland after completing the first east-west crossing of the Atlantic, Bennett took sick. His case turned to pneumonia, and—despite Lindbergh's flying to Canada to deliver serum—on April 25 he died, at age thirty-seven. Byrd and Bennett's wife, Cora, had hastened to his bedside when the seriousness of his illness was reported. Byrd sadly announced that the plane in which Bennett had taken his last flight, a Ford trimotor acquired for Byrd's use on his planned south polar flight, would be renamed the *Floyd Bennett*. Replacing Bennett as the expedition's second-in-command was Byrd's business manager, Dick Brophy.

Meanwhile Gould, who wrote Byrd that he was "fairly bowled over" by the news of Bennett's death, worked on recommendations for the expedition's scientific program and went forward with plans to spend, when he went east, some time in study at the American Geographical Society. He also, sometime prior to disappearing from Ann Arbor for nearly two years, established an understanding with his sweetheart, Peg Rice, that they were to consider themselves engaged to be married upon his return.

Gould came to New York in mid-July to assist with final preparations for the expedition. After two weeks, however, he began to shift regularly between New York and Ann Arbor, where he had agreed to finish teaching a summer school course for a Michigan colleague whose wife had become very ill. It was late August before he settled in New York to stay until the expedition's departure.

While Gould's duties in helping to get the expedition ready were centered on planning and procurement for the scientific program, he was also given the interesting assignment of gathering together the expedition's library—reading material for dozens of men of extremely varied background who would be entirely isolated for more than a year. Putnam helped him assemble a reference collection of works relating to polar travel, but the bulk of what became a 3,000-volume library, much of it acquired as gifts, was literature and other general reading, plus a set of the *Encyclopædia Britannica*. Byrd advised Gould that he personally liked to read "Dickens, detective stories, and philosophy."

In the end, when it was ready to leave the United States, the Byrd Antarctic Expedition consisted of eighty-two men and more than five hundred tons of supplies and material, including four airplanes,* ready to be shipped to New Zealand aboard four ships. Expedition personnel were given thorough medical examinations, as well as any needed dental work, as there would be no dentist among the party in Antarctica. (Gould later recalled going in for his examination, having the

---

* Three of these planes reached the Antarctic: the large Ford trimotor renamed the *Floyd Bennett*; a Fokker Universal monoplane, the *Virginia*; and a Fairchild folding wing monoplane, the *Stars and Stripes*. A small model built by General Aircraft was also transported as far as New Zealand but was not brought on from there to Antarctica.

dentist take one look inside his mouth and correctly surmise that his patient must be from the Middle West "because they don't do such good dental work as that here on the coast.") The *New York Times*, which was covering (and promoting) the expedition in detail and had assigned reporter Russell Owen to accompany it to

Studio publicity photo, 1928

the ice, made photographic studio portraits of each member. With less fanfare, the *Times* also prepared prewritten obituaries for each.

The newspapers and other institutions kept public awareness of Byrd's preparations high. Celebrities from Gene Tunney to Amelia Earhart offered financial contributions and public endorsements of Byrd's fundraising efforts. In the spirit of the late 1920s, a new dance appeared, dubbed the "Byrd Hop," with movements symbolizing the takeoff, flight, and landing of a polar airplane. New York's Gimbels store prominently filled two windows with a display of expedition gear. The month of August featured a number of farewell dinners or lunches for Byrd and other expedition personnel, as well as radio broadcasts of special programs about the imminent departure. Publicity was generated as well by a nationwide contest to select a worthy senior Boy Scout to accompany the

expedition to Antarctica. The scout who was selected, nineteen-year-old Paul A. Siple,* was notified of his selection just five days before he sailed on the first of the expedition's ships to depart.

That ship, the *City of New York*, was to the general public the romantic glamour vessel of the Byrd Antarctic Expedition. A stout, wooden, square-rigged windjammer with auxiliary steam engine built for sealing in 1882, she had been purchased by Byrd in Norway on the advice of polar veteran Roald Amundsen, who vouched for her thick-hulled sturdiness as an ice ship. Bought as the *Samson*, she was converted to a bark and renamed *City of New York* in early August. Though both photogenic and serviceable, the *City of New York* was also exceedingly slow, and was started on her way to New Zealand on the 25th of August, several weeks before any other ship in Byrd's flotilla was to depart. The *City of New York* carried thirty-three members of the expedition and two hundred tons of cargo. Most of the rest of the personnel traveled aboard a small iron cargo freighter Byrd had purchased on the cheap as a vessel confiscated for smuggling—the *Chelsea*, which Byrd renamed the *Eleanor Bolling* after his mother. In addition, a Norwegian

---

*   Siple, who would also accompany Byrd on several subsequent expeditions, would remain an
    active and prominent Antarctican throughout his life. Among his contributions would be the
    concept of calculating wind-chill factor when evaluating the effect of cold weather.

whaler, the *Sir James Clark Ross*, a much faster vessel than either of the first two, was employed to get ninety-four dogs, mostly Greenland huskies, and their human handlers, plus forty tons of dog biscuit, across the ocean to New Zealand as quickly as possible. Another Norwegian whaler, the *C.A. Larsen*, last to leave, carried airplanes and fuel, pilots, and mechanics, as well as Byrd, Dick Brophy, the *Times'* journalist, and a few others. The four contingents were to rendezvous in New Zealand, from where the whalers would set about whaling, and only the expedition's own ships, the *City of New York* and the *Eleanor Bolling*, would be available for transport on to Antarctica.

Boy Scout Paul Siple [OSUA-BP]

For the leg to New Zealand Larry Gould shipped aboard the *Bolling*, which carried three hundred tons and a crew of twenty-eight upon departure from Norfolk, Virginia. Sailing earlier from Brooklyn to Norfolk, the disreputable-looking freighter (described by one crewman as "a worn iron pot bent into the general shape of a ship"*) had been halted and looked over by the Coast Guard as a suspected rum-runner, but Gould did not board until after its arrival in Norfolk. Repairs and a restowing of cargo were necessary there due to the *Bolling*'s having been caught in a hurricane before limping into port, but all was accomplished and Larry Gould's adventure as an active sojourner with the Byrd Antarctic Expedition began in earnest the evening of September 25, when the *Eleanor Bolling* rolled out of the harbor of Hampton Roads, entered the Atlantic, and pointed south.

---

*   Gould's Byrd Expedition diary records a story concerning the father of the *Bolling*'s first mate, Harry King: When that man, an experienced sailor who had spent most of his life afloat, took a good look at the *Eleanor Bolling* prior to his son's departure upon it, he kissed Harry and said "good-bye son — god-dammit I'll never see you again."

CHAPTER 6

HIGH VENTURINGS

On his third day at sea, Larry Gould began a personal record or diary of his role in the great expedition. His first entry declares the *Bolling* the "rollingest" ship he ever saw, and confesses that "true to form" he "hit the rail four times" the first day out. (Those shipping aboard the *Eleanor Bolling* soon took to calling her the *Evermore Rolling*; some claimed she could roll in dry dock.) Even so, he recorded proudly, he never missed a meal, was now feeling great, and had become, he judged, "a much better sailor than of old." He had taken on the duties of ship's bosun—the world's worst, he predicted with perverse satisfaction.

Apart from praise for the work of the cook, nearly a month would go by before Gould put down in his journal any assessment of the qualities of any of his shipmates. Already in this first entry, however, he recorded early impressions of the man who had set them sailing but would not now rejoin them until reaching New Zealand. Critical of what he perceived as "waste in making preparations and numerous examples of bad management," he declared that Byrd was "not a business man and is scarcely less adept at sizing up men." He faulted Byrd already for "bad judgment" and found him "peculiarly naïf" and yet "altogether lovable." Though twelve years Byrd's junior, Gould likened Byrd in this early assessment to an attractive youngster one cannot help but like despite occasional bad behavior, and he concluded that

> even as one would run into the street at the risk of his life to save a foolish child who had strayed into the traffic so shall we all follow Commander Byrd's leadership wherever he designates and with utter loyalty—albeit he is still but a boy. He will always be one.

That "boy," to be fair, had exhausted himself, over the preceding months, to organize and launch the most ambitious expedition ever yet directed toward the Antarctic. Focused more narrowly on preparations for the expedition's scientific program, Gould was as yet hardly in a position to appreciate fully the magnitude of pressures, obstacles, and setbacks small and large that had sat heavily on Byrd's

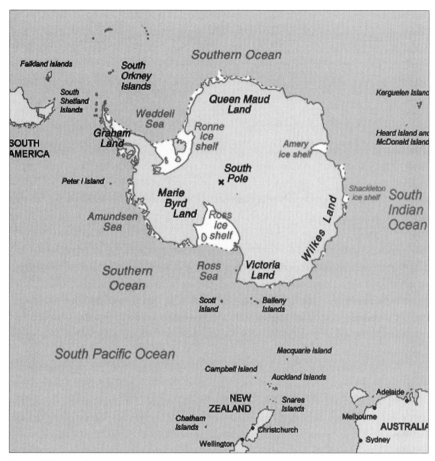

Map of Antarctica

Aerial photo of the *City of New York* in the Bay of Whales beside the Ross Ice Shelf

shoulders as the huge undertaking became real. Though the expedition was now afloat and moving south at varied speeds on four widely separated vessels, the pressures of ultimate responsibility would not really lift for Byrd prior to each man's safe return more than a year and a half later.

The month of October opened with the *Bolling* plowing through the Caribbean and ended with her refilling coalbunkers in port in Tahiti. The interval was largely given over to shipboard routine, without landfall from Panama to Papeete. Gould found the West Indies climate oppressive and wondered how he could return to New York after the expedition without recrossing the tropics. While their ship underwent minor engine repairs after traversing the Panama Canal, Gould and a group of others went to the arena in Panama City to witness a duel to the death between a declawed jaguar and a bull with blunted horns; a nauseated Gould closed his eyes to the bloody spectacle and left before it was over. Panama also gave the crew welcome opportunities to go ashore in a pair of "brazenly ... open" ports far from Prohibition America, prompting Gould to tell his journal that he hoped they could depart shortly, "before the whole outfit has to be poured aboard." The Pacific brought delightfully cooler weather, and Gould settled into a pleasant crossing, taking his turn with watches, never-ending ship painting, and rope splicing, but also with much time free for personal reading—selecting that month, in addition to a variety of novels and verse, Amundsen's *The South Pole* and Shackleton's *The Heart of the Antarctic*.

On the 18th, they slipped south of the equator and did not fail to observe the time-honored rites of sailors crossing the line. King Neptune, represented by third mate Harry Adams, oversaw the initiation ceremonies from which the ship's "landlubbers"—those like Gould who were crossing the equator for the first time—would emerge as "seamen and gentlemen." On this occasion the ceremonies began with a medical examination, proceeded to the purging of bodies by "medicine compounded of engine oil, salt water, rigging tallow and tar," and moved on to the ingestion of other "remedies" (Gould mentions pie made from bananas, mustard, salt, and pancake batter, as well as squid-filled doughnuts) before topping off with egg shampoos and the shaving of hair and beards with tin shears. "A welcome break in the monotony," recorded a good-humored Gould after the fact.

Tahiti was reached at month's end. Gould appreciated its beauty: "an inexplicably delicious breeze—the fronds of the cocoanut palm rustling mildly the while ... the moon through the trees ... sunsets through the clouds over the ragged peaks"—but concluded that he "should not want to remain long in such an environment" for fear that it might "get him" the way it had apparently gotten others:

> Perhaps the less said about the conduct of the expedition members in Papeete the better. They seem generally to lack any great sense of responsibility toward the expedition—at any rate they do not properly appreciate how their conduct reflects on the expedition. The second

night—a street fight with native police and one man locked up for two days—beaten up badly and a dislocated jaw.

Their sister ship arrived in Papeete a day and a half after the Bolling, and when their crews reunited onshore it quickly became evident to the earlier arrivals that the *City of New York* was a comparatively unhappy ship. Captain Frederick Melville of the *City* was an old-school sailing master who had divided expedition personnel into a privileged officer class and men designated as common sailors, despite Byrd's intention that on this expedition "special privileges will not obtain." Resentment followed, directed not only toward Melville but also at expedition "officers" who accepted the division, dined in the officers' mess aft, separate from the men in the forecastle, and in some instances seemed to enjoy "high-hatting" those forward. Gould's journal records his surprise at the "rampant discontent" prevailing aboard the *City* and his renewed appreciation for the contrasting spirit of good fellowship that was fostered by amiable Captain Brown* aboard the *Bolling*, "where Captain and coal passer alike eat at the same mess."

The early November voyage from Tahiti to New Zealand was marked by rough seas in which the "Evermore Rolling" well lived up to her nickname. Gould described as awe-inspiring the great hills of water that would seemingly engulf the little ship as she plunged with sickening speed into the valleys between and observed that whenever he raised a foot to take a step, he never knew just where it would land as he completed his stride. Unable some days to do much more than simply endure being uncomfortable, Gould retreated to his bunk where, for as many minutes at a time as he could manage, he reread *The Pickwick Papers*, enjoying it far more than when it had been required reading in high school. On November 11—Armistice Day—he remembered how he had once hailed the end of active military service in France as "the end of privation and hardship"—but ten years later here he was, "voluntarily embarked upon an enterprise which may well entail discomforts and hardships that will make those of the war seem petty." One stormy week later—a six-day week, after crossing the international date line—the much-buffeted *Bolling* docked near Dunedin on New Zealand's South Island, the hospitable point of rendezvous for the entire Byrd expedition to reunite and their final port of call before facing the unknown hardships of Antarctica.

The *Ross* and *Larsen* had reached New Zealand earlier, while the slow moving *City of New York* would still be another eight days. The crew of the *Bolling* by and large felt their arrival was well-timed, New Zealand prohibition having

---

* Gustav Brown, the 36-year-old master of the *Eleanor Bolling*, was a Scandinavian immigrant who had previously been second-in-command on the *City of New York*. Gould enjoyed the colorfulness of his Danish accent and habit of describing everything in terms of the feminine, such as "Commander Byrd—I tought she ..." In one journal entry Gould describes the "composite" manner of Captain Brown's singing, in which the words of several songs are rolled into one and matters are further simplified by singing all songs to a single tune.

been repealed four days before. The freighter was quickly unloaded so as to send it north to Wellington to pick up planes and other cargo left there by the *Larsen*. During the unloading Gould was distressed to discover damage to some of the scientific equipment stored in the afterhold, where a fresh water tank had sprung a leak during the voyage. While the *Bolling* made the round trip to Wellington and back, Gould and some others stayed behind to assess damages and see to possible repairs, as well as attend to other supply issues. In Dunedin, a lovely town of red-roofed houses set about green hills and overlooking the head of a narrow fjord-like inlet, Gould and aerial photographer Ashley McKinley became house guests of the expedition's local shipping agent, Harold Tapley, who Gould pronounced "the quintessence of hospitality and good humor." It was springtime in the southern hemisphere, and on the following Sunday Tapley's household and guests relaxed with a grand picnic into the back country, enjoying the golden patches of gorse and broom set against the brilliant green hillsides. Delightful hues and scenery at any time, these were relished all the more by men set to know only frozen whiteness for the next year and more.

The day after the picnic the *City of New York* finally lumbered into harbor, and Gould and all other hands now became hard-working stevedores. The season was getting on, and Byrd was anxious to make all possible speed getting his two-ship flotilla loaded and into Antarctic waters while the window of accessibility was still open. So the expedition's only professor stripped off his shirt and put his back into the sweaty task of heaving crates and coal sacks from dock to deck. As they labored almost around the clock, cargo was stuffed and piled high onto the *City of New York*, making sure that the greatest necessities—enough for a diminished "bare minimum" undertaking to go forward—went aboard her first, just in case the *Bolling*, unsuited to icebreaking, could never reach the continental ice with additional supplies. The plan, or hope, was to save coal and increase speed by having the *Bolling* tow the slower *City of New York* half the distance, to the northern edge of the Antarctic ice pack, then return to Dunedin to take on more coal and the supplies needed for a full-scale expedition, while the *City* reached Antarctica and began establishing a base. (With luck, their passage through the loosened pack and into the Ross Sea would be helped by a tow from the *C.A. Larsen*, though that rendezvous was uncertain and the Norwegian whaler would not wait for them if they were not at hand when she was ready to go through.) Then the *Bolling* would herself steam all the way to the Antarctic base, unload her cargo, and race back to Dunedin again in an attempt—recognized as something of a long shot upon which they must not depend—to take on more supplies, desirable items that were not absolutely necessary but would make the experience of the party that would stay in Antarctica less spartan, and deliver these to the Antarctic base before the advancing season shut down all access and escape. Both ships needed to be north of the Ross Sea before Antarctica's ice pack girdle froze them in; they would then winter in New Zealand and return the following summer when the loosened pack would again allow them to slip through and relieve the men who had wintered-over on the continent.

Thus, when the two ships set out from Dunedin early on Sunday morning, December 2, Gould was now aboard the *City of New York*, along with about sixty men, one plane, a mass of radio equipment, a mountain of additional cargo that caused the craft to ride alarmingly low in the water,* and the expedition dogs, whose incessant yelping and squalling, Byrd wrote later, was "a sound we were to know well, for it did not leave our ears for nearly a year and a half." Some fifteen hundred feet ahead was the *Eleanor Bolling*, pulling the *City* along by a quarter-inch steel towline anchored to the foremast. Before them lay ocean latitudes of legendary fierceness, long known to southern sailors as the "furious fifties" and the "screaming sixties."

Fine weather prevailed for a few days, but on the 7th of December they encountered a "frightful 'blow'" which severed their towline and which both ships rode out with some difficulty but no serious damage. The crew of the *City of New York* relashed cargo and strained backs to recover the entire thirty-fathom towline by hand winch hauling. The next day the wind lessened, and in calmer conditions the *Bolling* resumed towing. The 9th brought the excitement of sighting the first of the great tabular "barrier" icebergs that would thereafter be familiar companions; Byrd wrote that on the 10th (the first of two, as they crossed the date line again) they passed about fifty in the space of a few hours. That day, "in the teeth of a wind that was like a 'whetted knife,'" Larry Gould for the first time climbed into the *City of New York*'s crow's nest for a look out from a vantage point "so very high," he wrote, "that I seemed quite detached from the ship itself."

On the second December 10, hours after clearing up a minor Antarctic mystery by corroborating the location and existence of a small island reported years earlier by Robert Falcon Scott, the two Byrd expedition ships sighted both the boundary of the vast Antarctic ice pack and the great whaler *Larsen*, guaranteeing the *City* a tow through the pack when the Norwegian captain determined that the ice, still unusually heavy for the season, was sufficiently loosened to allow passage. Meanwhile, the *Larsen* and its satellite "chaser" boats were plying their trade where they were, and Captain Nilsen sent over some whale steaks, which Gould pronounced very good, though a bit coarse. That evening the *Bolling* came alongside and, for twelve cold, hard hours, transferred one hundred tons of coal to the *City of New York* prior to casting off and hurrying back toward Dunedin. A few days later, the *Larsen* ran out a towline for the Byrd ship and, after it was attached, started to nose a path south through the ice pack with the comparatively tiny *City* bobbing behind.

Movement through the pack was slow and nerve-wracking. Ahead, the ice

---

*   Byrd noted that the day before they sailed, an old sailing man who had marked the water showing above the *City of New York*'s Plimsoll line and the amount of cargo loaded above decks, warned that they were taking an awful chance with that load, predicting that "she'll ship green water every roll." Byrd, who had little choice if he were to realize his expedition plans, affected confidence, but, as he later wrote, "the incident suggested in an unpleasant manner the unhappy wedding guest impaled on the glance of the Ancient Mariner."

shattered or pushed aside by the *Larsen* had a tendency to surge back after the larger ship's passage, giving those following the constant feeling that the path might close again altogether between them. Behind, the narrow ribbon of black water spun out so thin that it was difficult to believe they had just passed through

Ashley McKinley and Gould

it. Always the watches aboard the *City of New York* needed to be alert, lest a stubborn floe halt the *Larsen*'s progress and the *City*'s momentum carry her right into the *Larsen*'s stern. Frequently the stout timbers of the *City of New York* were pounded by violent impact with walls or edges of the ice channel through which they were slowly being pulled. The *Larsen*'s help was a godsend, for the ice remained heavy enough that the *City of New York* would have been powerless to advance on her own and would doubtless have been delayed some weeks getting through the pack to open water. But the going was slow even for the huge Norwegian vessel, proceeding by fits and starts, using her power to force passage, often clearing no more than a few yards with each stroke. They were eight days pushing through the ice.

Larry Gould, meanwhile, noted with satisfaction unmistakable signs of the expedition's continuing progress southward—cold winds, sometimes bringing snow, but combined with summer's 24-hour sunshine; also snowy petrels, skua gulls, and, atop a floe inside the pack, a fine big Emperor penguin, that dress-suited emissary of the Antarctic, who saluted the passing ships most graciously. A number of its smaller Adélie cousins soon followed. A satisfaction yet greater had come to Gould just a few days before, when Byrd told him of his intent to name Gould his second-in-command in the field, saying that he needed a lieutenant of "calm sober judgment" to familiarize himself with all details of the expedition, take charge of a variety of matters as executive officer, and be prepared to assume overall command as necessary. Official confirmation and announcement of the decision came later in the month, bringing the popular professor much hearty congratulation from the men.*

---

* Of Gould's selection as second-in-command, Byrd wrote under the date of 26 December: "My mind as to the men is now made up. Gould I have made Second in Command. A splendid fellow, competent, a brilliant geologist, and popular with men. He has proper respect for the seriousness of the job. Naturally, he is greatly interested in the scientific results, and this is most important in the Second in Command. He will do well, I am sure, and I am fortunate to have him." Ashley McKinley became third-in-command, and Bernt Balchen was placed in charge of the aviation unit.

When the *C.A. Larsen* finally broke through to the southern edge of the ice pack, the two crews parted company. To the whalers, the great Southern Ocean they were now entering was itself their goal, the world's richest field for cetacean harvest. To the men of the Byrd expedition, the open waters ahead were the last to be crossed before reaching their own destination. Even as the *Larsen* launched a chaser after a whale already spotted, the wooden ship dedicated to quite another pursuit hove away and under her own power of sail and steam continued south. Soon, upon the cold waters of the Ross Sea, she was alone.

***

Many years later, as he faced an interviewer curious about his seventh trip to Antarctica at age 83, perhaps Dr. Laurence M. Gould was to remember that distant afternoon when, at an indentation of the Ross Ice Shelf known as Discovery Inlet, he first set foot upon "The Ice." At any rate, he told the inquirer that when he stood on the ice once again, more than fifty years after first doing so, he experienced a thrill almost physical; he had returned to his spiritual home.

Larry Gould's first steps ashore on Antarctic ice were taken the 26th of December, 1928. Christmas aboard the *City of New York* the day before had been given an added charge of excitement by the knowledge that the ship was at last drawing near her goal. A turkey and cranberry sauce feast was enlivened by songs, humorous toasts, and an appearance by physicist Frank "Taffy" Davies as Santa Claus, with pillow-padded stomach, red parka, and cotton beard. The revels were interrupted by a call from the crow's nest: "Barrier on the starboard bow!" As Byrd wrote later, "There was a clatter of dishes hastily dropped or pushed aside" and a "race of footsteps" to the forecastle head and into the rigging. "The thing we had come so far to see was before our eyes, a far-flung reach of lifted ice, stretching east and west as far as the eye could see." Byrd wrote of the crew's excitement, of enthusiastic cheers and back pounding. Pilot Bernt Balchen remembered a muter reception, as the entire crew stared in awe at the "majestic white precipice" rising "a sheer hundred feet above the sea, like a Great Wall of China carved in ice."

Hours later, having pulled to within a mile or so of the Great Ice Barrier's immense vertical face, the ship turned east, to run through the sunlit night alongside the great cliffs of ice. Crewman Jacob Bursey recalled "feeling like pigmies as we lined the rails of our little ship looking up at the mighty ramparts of Antarctica." Balchen was struck by the "white silence" of the scene, and Bursey wrote that "it was so still it seemed as if an overpowering presence was sleeping, and the men spoke only in whispers as if fearful of waking her."

The next day brought them into Discovery Inlet, an anchorage used by Scott in 1902 which Byrd wished to investigate for a potential base and landing field in case their anticipated location adjacent to the Bay of Whales proved unsuitable. At the head of the inlet, observed by a procession of curious penguins, men and dogs came ashore. While Byrd and four others set off on skis to reconnoiter, the rest of the expedition amused themselves for an afternoon and evening, tossing

snowballs, chasing after the penguins, practicing skiing, and with local exploration. Some members of the dog-sledge unit, wanting to provide their packs with
fresh meat, exploited the innocent lack of fear of the Weddell seal population
by killing thirty, of which only half were eventually hauled back aboard ship.
When Byrd's party returned, having found no location of suitable flatness for an
airstrip, the order was quickly given to reboard ship, and by midnight (one nearly
as bright as noon) the *City of New York* resumed its easterly course. Sailing all the
next day alongside the great Barrier front, Gould found the towering sheer ice
cliff forbidding, terrible, and ominous, but at the same time grandly and uniquely
beautiful. Sometimes dark and glowering, or slaty grey with an overcast sky, later
it would be a brilliant, dazzling white, with "patches and shadows of the most
delicate and indescribable blue."

It was early morning, December 28, when the *City of New York* reached the
entrance to the twenty-mile-wide indentation in the Barrier known as the Bay
of Whales. One member of Byrd's expedition, the Norwegian tailor/sailmaker
Martin Ronne, had been there before, with Amundsen in 1911, and though its
outline was much changed, due to the inexorable pushing out and calving off of
the ice walls, Ronne was able to recognize familiar features. The Bay of Whales had
received its name in 1908 when Ernest Shackleton passed by in his ship *Nimrod*
and found it teeming with killer whales, finners, and humpbacks. Fearing the
danger of basing a party on impermanent ice, Shackleton rejected any thoughts
of wintering there, even though it was as close as a ship might be brought to the
South Pole. Byrd believed it was this decision, resulting in Shackleton's basing
himself at a spot more solid but also more distant, that more than any other factor defeated Shackleton's ambition to be the first to reach the pole. A few years
later, Amundsen had judged the risks differently, concluding from his study of
all available reports that the persistence of the formation over a period of seventy
years—he identified the bay with a bight observed by Sir James Clark Ross in
1841—indicated a reassuring stability probably due to the presence of an under-ice
island to the south, solid land that would interrupt the glacial flow and provide
a grounding around which the Barrier ice spread sideways and crumpled so as to
form a lasting bay.* Amundsen, therefore, had located his base, Framheim, at a
suitable spot near the bay's southern head. Byrd hoped to do the same.

Unfortunately, the expedition discovered that in 1928 the bay ice extended
to a point well north of what had been open water for Amundsen in 1911. With

---

*   The eventual discovery of Roosevelt Island south of the head of the Bay of Whales matched this
     expectation. Nonetheless, the "lastingness" of the bay, while enough to serve Amundsen and
     Byrd, was in the end only semi-permanent. By the mid-1950s the indentation that had been
     the Bay of Whales was found to have disappeared, its sides having joined together. In 1987, a
     great section of the Ross Ice Shelf that included the long-buried bases of Amundsen and Byrd
     and the entire former Bay of Whales area broke off and floated out to sea. As Eugene Rodgers
     wrote to close his history of the First Byrd Antarctic Expedition, "All of Little America now
     lies somewhere at the bottom of the great Southern Ocean."

the *City of New York* halted as far south inside the bay as she could reach, at least eight miles of unbroken sea ice still separated her from the area where Amundsen had established his camp and where Byrd intended to site his own. Whereas Amundsen had moored his ship, the *Fram*, only 2.2 geographical miles from Framheim, if Byrd located in the same vicinity he was faced with the prospect of hauling supplies from ship to base over a considerably greater distance; it would mean trusting men, dogs, and heavy sledges to long stretches over floating sea ice that might yet break up under the summer sun. The first priority, though, was to locate a site for their permanent quarters, somewhere on the Barrier an appropriate distance from the sea and with surfaces suitable for a flying expedition. Byrd asked Gould to organize and provision a trail party of skiers and dog handlers that would go ashore with Byrd to look for Framheim and discover the best location for their own camp. Over the course of the next few days that group of six, remaining in contact with the ship by radio, failed to find any remaining sign of Framheim but eventually sent word that a good base site had been found and that preparations could begin for unloading cargo and bringing in supplies. Byrd decided that he would return to ship to supervise the unloading, while Gould would be sent in to take charge of the temporary camp on the Barrier. Gould would be responsible, as supplies came in sledge load by sledge load, to oversee construction of the base that soon received the name Little America.

As 1928 came to an end, but with his Antarctic adventure only now truly beginning, Larry Gould wished to be nowhere but where he was. There would be hard work ahead, but he was ready for toil. There would be physical discomfort in harsh surroundings; he relished the test. Real danger to life and limb might await in uncertain measure; that too was a risk accepted. At year's end he copied into his personal journal an inspirational poem that doubtless sounded an inner echo:

> Desire to Live
> by Jno. Edw Allen
>
> I would not have my life be one of bliss
> Untouched by heart-ache, agony, despair —
> A pale anemic thing: my nightly prayer:
> Is that with each new day I shall not miss
> High venturings, nor undeserve the hiss
> Of envious human moles who never dare
> To touch off rockets in their souls and flare
> Above their deepening grooves. O grant me this:
> That I shall scale life's peaks, explore its glooms
> Know mountained ecstasies, deep valleyed pains —
> That when my last red sands by time are sieved
> And Fate has struck my sinews from her looms
> I shall have earned three words o'er my remains
> Besides was born and died —"Between he lived!"

***

For the next month and more, the energies of all were bent to the collective task of unloading cargo onto the ice, moving it miles ahead to Little America, and building there a small village, ready for habitation and prepared for winter.

Gould went in to the camp on January 2, starting out on skis but being picked up by a dog team along the way. He was not an experienced skier; he had made his first somewhat awkward attempts at learning only three days before. But he had vowed to apply himself diligently to improving enough to get about. With Bernt Balchen he looked over the campsite and agreed that it was well chosen. The next day he rose early from his reindeer skin sleeping bag to return with the dog outfits to the ship. There he spent a pair of days going over plans with Byrd and helping to unload parts for Little America's first large pre-built house before returning to Little America on the 5th—this time skiing the entire distance. Taking charge of the men there with what Balchen termed "that quiet air of authority we have all come to respect," Gould oversaw several busy days excavating in the snow for the first house, leveling the foundation, putting in the floor timbers and raising the sides, interrupted from time to time by calls to assist the uphill arrival of heavily loaded dog teams. Since oversight for the building work was shared with expedition carpenter Charles F. "Chips" Gould (no relation), the pioneer Little Americans tacked up a sign reading "Gould & Gould Construction Company."

All work was halted January 9 and 10 by the expedition's first experience of a real Antarctic blizzard. Previously Gould had been impressed by the "overpowering quiet" of their surroundings, "a silence which fairly presses one down from all sides it is so deadly." In a blizzard that quiet was replaced by the tremendous noise of the wind, which filled the air with fine dry snow that found its way everywhere. As soon as it began, at about four in the morning, Gould ordered all dog teams in camp to hold there rather than attempt to make their regular return to the ship. As the storm grew worse, he concluded that there was "nothing to do but stay in the old reindeer sleeping bag and wait for it to blow itself out." Later, during an apparent lull, Gould got up to walk about the camp tents checking on the men and experienced the curious sensation of the loss of horizon with which to orient himself: Unable during a renewed gust of wind and dense flying snow to see even his feet, he felt as though suspended in a world of flying icy white dust where "but for the feel of the snow under one's feet he could scarcely have known that he was standing." When work resumed on the 11th, the first task was to shovel out the snow that had drifted into the unfinished house; over the two days following, they put on a roof.

Gould then went back to the ship to confer with the commander and to retrieve his remaining personal gear. This time when he returned to Little

Unloading the *City of New York* [OSUA-BP]

America it was neither by ski nor sledge but as an air passenger aboard the *Stars & Stripes*, piloted by Bernt Balchen.* With all of his belongings brought out from the ship, Gould noted that he was now the first expedition member to be permanently located on the ice.

The Fairchild plane, the *Stars and Stripes*

At this point, some twenty-five men were being housed and fed at Little America. Scientific work was getting underway in camp, as chief meteorologist William C. "Cyclone" Haines began pilot balloon observations. Crews were at work on a variety of construction projects: improving the large house (intended as the camp's mess hall, though it would also serve as bunkhouse for fourteen), erecting the smaller "Norwegian house" (at that point intended as a machine shop, though its eventual use was as living quarters for eight), digging a great storage hole for coal and other stores, and raising the three great sixty-five-foot radio towers that would be Little America's communication link with the outside world. When Byrd made a visit of inspection to Little America on January 25, he seemed well satisfied with the state of organization and progress. Meanwhile, everyone's spirits received a great lift when word arrived that the *Eleanor Bolling*, returning from Dunedin with another shipload of supplies, two more airplanes, and seventy-five hundred gallons of aviation gasoline, had cleared the ice pack and could soon be expected in the Bay of Whales. It would then be necessary for all possible hands to help with a rush unloading to get her promptly northbound again, in hopes that the season might yet allow an additional round trip to supply Byrd's Antarcticans with their full complement of desired provisions.

Even while the work of establishing living quarters on the ice proceeded, Byrd now felt ready to take a first stab at aerial exploration. Unknown territory lay to the east, and Byrd hoped to have a look in that direction as quickly as he could. Though this first longer flight would wait for an assurance of good weather from meteorologist Haines, all flying in this region was potentially hazardous, and

---

*   The Fairchild monoplane *Stars & Stripes* had been uncrated, assembled, and readied for flight by January 15 and made seven short test flights that day. These were not, however, the first flights over Antarctica: Byrd's Australian rival Hubert Wilkins had claimed that honor the month before, while the *City of New York* was still being towed through the ice pack. Wilkins' small-scale expedition departed the continent in January, as Byrd's men were digging in; he would return the following summer. In both seasons, Wilkins' presence and intentions were a worry to Byrd, who feared that the Australian might attempt to beat him with a flight to the pole.

when Byrd came out to Little America on the 25th he left Gould with written instructions for assuming full command should the commander and his plane be forced down or lost.

The meteorologist's go-ahead came on the 27th, and that afternoon the *Stars & Stripes* took off from Little America's newly graded runway with Byrd navigating, Balchen at the controls, and Harold June as relief pilot and radioman. The small plane turned east and disappeared from view. Two hours later, while Gould was outside taking readings with his theodolite, supply officer George Black came running toward him with the message that Gould was wanted immediately in the radio room, that the plane had gone down. For the next few minutes, as he hurried toward the house, Gould did some very heavy thinking indeed—followed with merciful quickness by great relief as radio signals were renewed; all was still well with the flight. In fact, the plane did penetrate some snow squalls that led Byrd to liken the situation to "flying in a bowl of milk," but Balchen steered them safely out again. Shortly after, while still in flight, radioman June received the welcome report that the *Bolling* had arrived in the Bay of Whales and would soon be tied up alongside the *City of New York*.

When the aerial explorers returned to base, their most exciting news—especially to geologist Gould—was their discovery of a hitherto unknown group of small mountains, unconnected to any continuous range and showing a surprising amount of exposed bare rock on their northern profiles. The plane had lacked fuel for any extended investigation of these peaks, encountered on its return leg, but Byrd's description set ablaze an eagerness in Gould to get there himself and explore their geological secrets. He hoped for an opportunity before the season advanced too far to allow it, and Byrd indicated that this might be possible after the unloading of the *Bolling*. The discovery of these mountains and other features were duly reported to the outside world, which through radio contact and Russell Owen's dispatches to the *New York Times* (subject to the filter of Byrd's approval) was kept up to date on expedition developments and achievements. Grateful for the financial backing of expedition patron John D. Rockefeller, Jr., Byrd named the newfound peaks the Rockefeller Mountains.*

The arrival of the *Eleanor Bolling* was most important to the expedition due to her heavy cargo, but it was also cheering because it brought happy reunions with shipmates and because she carried mail—the last that would arrive except as radio messages until the following year, if ice prevented the *Bolling*'s uncertain

---

* In his book *Little America*, Byrd likened the mountains to Rockefeller's inner life and austere character. He wrote that he could do no better than to name this range after a man who stands "steady as a rock, in the chaos of life" and whose great power was controlled "wisely and unselfishly for the betterment of the world." Gould's less-reverent comment in later years was that the mountains had been named "after the signature on the hundred-thousand-dollar check."

second trip. She would also take outgoing expedition mail back north with her when ready to depart. Speed being essential if another trip were to be possible, the task of getting her swiftly unloaded now became everyone's first priority.

Fortune appeared to assist when thinning sea ice permitted Captain Brown to bring the *Bolling* in closer, to within about five trail miles from Little America, and to use as a pier an ice foot only about fifty feet from the Barrier. A block and tackle rigged up to the *Bolling's* winch began hauling stores up to the Barrier at a rate of two or three sledge loads every half hour. Byrd established two twelve-hour work shifts so that the job could progress around the clock. The chief concern was that the ice foot to which they were anchored could break up before they were finished.

Gould stayed a day in Little America, where the top plate of one of the radio towers was being put on, but he went out to the ships the next morning—missing not only the first day of the *Bolling's* unloading but also, a few minutes before his arrival on the second day, the feared breakup of the improvised ice pier. Just as a crate containing a center section of the large Ford airplane, the *Floyd Bennett*, had been swung onto the sea ice, cracks appeared, and promptly split wide, causing the slope from the ice foot to the Barrier to collapse dramatically into the sea and separating the unloading area into three wobbling floes that slowly began to drift apart. Fortunately, no one had been hurt, and with some frantic scrabbling and sliding the men saved the plane section and other endangered cargo, losing nothing but some wooden crates and a sack of coal. The ships retreated from shore.

Gould spent that day working about the plane. Then, as four of the regular dog drivers were caught aboard ship in the bay, separated from their teams ashore, Gould and three others each chose a team and, learning by doing, drove loads back to camp. By the time Gould mushed back to the ships the next morning, the *Bolling* had resumed unloading, now anchored on one side by a face of the ice barrier and on the other by her sister ship, tied up alongside. Cargo was being discharged simultaneously by block and tackle onto the ice, starboard, and onto the *City of New York*, port. Gould continued to work a dog team, moving loads put onto the ice by the ship to a safer distance a hundred yards in from the Barrier's edge, from where they would eventually be hauled to camp. That day the great fuselage of the Ford plane was successfully brought ashore.

After supper, Gould was in the *City of New York* galley, talking with the cook, when there came a great noisy crash and a series of shocks jarring the ship, followed by shouts and exclamations: "Great God—something awful has happened!" With the *City* heeling sharply to port, Gould and others ran to the deck in time to see the *Bolling* heeling sharply the other way, apparently about to roll completely over. On her starboard decks lay a great mass of ice and snow dumped there when a piece of the Barrier cliff had broken off above. The *Bolling* stood up almost on her beam's end. Then, as witnesses' breaths caught in their throats, the lines connecting her to the *City* stopped her roll and righted her once again—though listing heavily from the tons of snow weighing to starboard. High on the cliff face, weatherman Henry Harrison was dangling from a line over the side; in the water below, clinging to a small piece of ice floe, was mechanic Benny Roth, a non-swimmer. As men on the Barrier hastened to pull Harrison to safety, others attempted to succor Roth. When four men clambered into a rescue boat lowered

from the *City* that was meant for only two, one of them who realized that they were dangerously overloaded immediately jumped into the water himself—"a more courageous thing I have scarcely seen in my life," Gould wrote later. Meanwhile, Byrd himself had dived into the icy water after Roth; hydrographer Ralph Shropshire went in after Byrd; and navigator Joe De Ganahl, who had tried paddling toward Roth astride a plank, pulled himself onto a drifting ice cake. In the end, the small boat reached Roth first; everyone else was shortly pulled from

The *Bolling* and the *City of New York* unload beside the ice barrier [OSUA-BP]

the water, given dry clothes, and massaged back to warmth. Miraculously, it was found that they had escaped the calamitous break without serious injury or loss of equipment. Still, the near-disaster had been sobering. Nodding thoughtfully afterward at the shattered edge of the glacial cliff, Taffy Davies remarked drily that this kind of thing could discourage immigration down here.

The major part of the unloading of the *Bolling* had already been completed, but Byrd resolved never again to tempt fate by trying to discharge directly onto the Barrier. The two ships were directed back to the *City*'s old berth on the bay ice, from where the *Bolling* as rapidly as possible transferred the last of her supplies onto her sister ship, while the *City* then unloaded more slowly onto the bay ice. On February 2, the *Bolling* departed again for New Zealand, hoping to return within the month with the last of the expedition's supplies.

In the weeks that followed, Gould and his companions continued the hard toil of unloading, transporting, digging, and building. Four dog teams worked together to haul the towering two-ton Ford plane fuselage from the edge of the Barrier to camp. A huge iron kitchen range was moved and installed, requiring that two standing sections of house be taken down to get it inside. Experiments began with a motorized snowmobile, a car outfitted with skis in place of front wheels, that Gould predicted would do the work of several dog teams.

Unavoidably, progress was slowed by a variety of difficulties, ranging from another work-stopping blizzard to missing house parts to the commander's decision to change the siting of the administration building after an initial excavation had already been made. As the days ticked by, every fresh delay added to Gould's anxiety over whether he would get a chance to do some geological fieldwork in the newfound mountains before the end of the flying season shut that door for months to come.

A further cause for anxiety was suggested in these days by the sight, described by Gould as both majestic and awful, of great masses of the barrier edge continuing to break off and either crash into the sea or float away. Having seen significant changes to the local geography over the course of just a few days, Gould admitted in his journal to nervousness over the stability of Little America's own section of ice over the coming year and more.

On the 18th of February, flights ventured in two of the expedition's aircraft, the Fokker monoplane *Virginia* and the smaller Fairchild *Stars & Stripes*, resulted in the discovery of another range of mountains to the east of the Rockefellers, in a previously unclaimed region now given the name Marie Byrd Land in honor of the commander's wife. Gould's own hopes to be flown out to do some work in the new mountains continued, for the moment, to be disappointed.

The next order of business, however, was to finalize the roster of men staying at Little America through the winter, and get the *City of New York* away to the north before she might be frozen in. The day after the flights of the 18th, Byrd noted in his journal that the thermometer was tumbling, the sun was curving lower on the horizon, and winter could not be far way. On the other side of the pack ice, the *Bolling* was again moving south, her crew still hoping to be able to deliver the expedition's remaining desired supplies, but within days Byrd would determine that all signs pointed to an early freeze and ordered that she should not make the attempt. This meant that the expedition would make do with only two of the five main buildings that they had hoped to assemble at Little America, though nothing essential to the wintering over was lacking.

Final selections as to who would form the winter party and who would have to return to New Zealand aboard the *City of New York* were deferred until the last possible moment, and it fell to Gould to inform many men who yearned to stay that they could not. One who was anxious over his status until the end but was ultimately given the good news that he was chosen was the Boy Scout, Paul Siple, who credited his late selection to Gould's request:

> Larry had promised the American Museum of Natural History that he would bring back a barrel each of seal and penguin skins, and now with his advance in status [to second in command], hard rock geologist Larry was quite anxious to turn over this messy job to anyone else who would take it. I was more than eager to do it for him. Even so, he apparently had to plead my case with Byrd before I was permitted to remain with

Little America, early 1929

the Little America contingent of the expedition as a taxidermist, dog driver and naturalist.

In the end, forty-two men were picked for the wintering team. Twenty others who had labored hard to bring the expedition to this point were now required to board ship and depart. Gould recorded that even on the day the ship was to sail there were still four people at camp whom he had to tell that they could not stay on the ice, though it had been the dearest wish of each "to somehow merit the reward of being a member of the winter party."

On February 22 those staying lined the ice to see off those sailing north. Cheers were raised by both contingents as the *City of New York* weighed anchor, and when her masts finally disappeared over the frigid sea horizon those left behind were profoundly and irretrievably alone. They would not be incommunicado, thanks to radio, but they would be entirely inaccessible, beyond the reach of any rescue or resupply, for months. On the globe's fifth-largest continent, in an area nearly double the size of the forty-eight United States, these forty-two men were the sole human inhabitants.

CHAPTER 7

FEARED LOST

In the United States the progress of the Byrd Antarctic Expedition was chronicled prominently in the nation's newspapers, which followed every stage of the enterprise from pre-departure preparations to the movement of ships to adventures on the ice. Regular reports and features filed by *New York Times* reporter and expedition member Russell Owen were positioned prominently by the *Times*, frequently as front page news, and were picked up and given similar prominence by scores of other papers around the country. From time to time Byrd himself, or other members of the expedition with Byrd's approval, received their own bylines for transmitting accounts specific to their experiences. Like a serialized novel, the story of the Byrd Expedition played out for the interested public at home chapter by chapter, incident by incident, in near-daily installments across an extended time span, and many of the characters involved, certainly including Byrd's dashing second-in-command, became names and faces well-known, at least temporarily, to the reading public.

Early in March 1929, stories sharing Page One space with the ongoing Antarctic adventure included the international ratification process for the recent Kellogg-Briand pact outlawing war, investigations into gangland violence intensified by the shocking St. Valentine's Day murders in Chicago, and the changeover in Washington from the administration of Calvin Coolidge to that of Herbert Hoover. Approaching the March 4 inauguration, the US stock market continued a brisk advance past already high levels established by what was being termed a "Hoover Boom." Byrd Expedition news concerned the hard, successful fight of the *City of New York* to get through to the north edge of the ice pack and beyond and the effects of an Inauguration Day blizzard that made Little America a swirling world of white, in the midst of which a dogsled driver and his team, out before the blizzard struck, became separated from companion teams and failed to return to base, resulting in uncomfortable hours of searching along the barrier by Gould and others before the man was found safe, dug into the snow half a mile from camp. A few days later Russell Owen reported from Little America that after a two-week wait for suitable weather geologist Gould and two companions, aviator

The *Virginia*, before its fateful trip to the Rockefeller Mountains

Bernt Balchen and radio operator/backup pilot Harold June, had flown in the Fokker plane to the newly discovered Rockefeller Range some 135 miles east of the base to conduct a survey and investigate rock outcroppings and that they had confirmed by radio their safe landing between two large peaks. Owen's article mentioned that the trio carried a tent and sufficient supplies to live comfortably for some while should renewed bad weather delay their return.

Meanwhile, stateside Americans were glorying in the fact that they could communicate with the distant Byrd Expedition by radio. The expedition had forwarded best wishes to President Coolidge and congratulations to President-elect Hoover just before the inauguration, and arrangements had been made for Byrd's men to receive messages through special Saturday night programs to be broadcast in alternate weeks by General Electric station WGY of Schenectady and Westinghouse station KDKA of Pittsburgh. On the first of these programs, March 9, New York Governor Franklin D. Roosevelt greeted Commander Byrd, wished him luck, and advanced the puckish suggestion that Byrd might help him greatly if he would invite New York's Republican state legislature to winter with him at the South Pole. A week later nearly one hundred messages were directed by the KDKA broadcast to members of the expedition at Little America, to crews of the supply ships at Dunedin, and to Gould's survey party in the Rockefeller Range.

Then suddenly the front-page news from Antarctica turned ominous.

On March 17, Russell Owen's dispatch to the *Times* reported that the base camp had received no radio communication from Gould's mountain party for the past three days. Byrd had grown sufficiently concerned over the silence that he was preparing to fly to the Rockefellers in the Fairchild plane the moment the weather showed signs of clearing for a few hours and was also readying dog teams for a possible overland rescue. While Owen's report stressed the likelihood that the silence was due to some failure of the radio apparatus rather than to a more serious mishap, it did acknowledge the "many hazards of landing away from the base at this time of year" and mentioned, even while holding it unlikely, the possibility of an aerial crackup after attempting a takeoff without notifying camp.

The follow-up news relayed by Owen the next day was frustrating:

> Commander Byrd was all ready to take off yesterday afternoon in the first
> few hours of clear weather we have had in many days, but the motor of
> the plane would not start. It is the first time it has balked in all the weeks
> we have been here and that it should have quit at such an important time
> was a great disappointment.
>
> When adjustments had been made and the motor was turning, the
> sky had clouded over, the wind was blowing, and flying was out of the
> question because of approaching darkness. There is a bare chance that
> the Commander may be able to go today, although conditions are not
> so good as they were yesterday.

Dog teams were expected to start for the mountains in a few hours, Owen
reported, despite weather conditions that would make such a journey "at best
extraordinarily difficult." Hope for the safety of the isolated men persisted, said
the *Times'* headline, but Owen's article confessed to puzzlement at the base as to
the possible causes of the now four-day silence and expressed fear that "a mishap
may be the explanation."

Other newspapers across the country also focused on the developing drama. In
Michigan, Gould's family and fiancée must have been chilled by the *Detroit Times'*
banner print: "BYRD TO HUNT LOST U.M. MAN: 3 AIDES MISSING IN
ANTARCTIC." Photos of Gould, Balchen, and June ran below, under the caption "Lost in Antarctic Wastes." "GOULD'S FATE IS NOT KNOWN," said the
Ann Arbor Times News. In South Haven, where Gould's parents were now living in
town, the *Daily Tribune's* headline was "LOCAL MAN LOST IN ANTARCTIC,"
and the paper featured an interview with the missing geologist's mother, headed
"Mother Tells Gould's Last Visit at Home":

> "Laurence didn't say good-bye this time," she said. "He threw me a kiss as
> he left the house and told me 'I'll see you again.' We expected him back,
> but he wrote me a letter a few days later and said that he might have stayed
> several more days at home but didn't because he hated to say good-bye.
>
> "Before he left, he changed his insurance so that Bonnie (Gould's
> 18-year-old sister, who attends South Haven high school) would be able
> to go through college if he didn't come back.' ...
>
> "Of course, I'm feeling pretty blue this morning. But Laurence
> has had so many hairbreadth escapes that we are not giving up hope."

At the University of Michigan, Professor Hobbs declared that the plight of the
missing trio "is not a case for despair" and expressed confidence that "Larry's resource-
fulness will bring him through." At Little America, men inside the radio shack kept
an uneasy vigil. A message to Gould's party that the Fairchild would fly in search of
them at the first break in the weather was transmitted hourly, but hour after hour those
straining for a response from across the frozen miles heard only a sickening silence.

***

It was with an eager heart that Byrd's chief scientist had flown to the Rockefeller Mountains eleven days before. Excited by the prospect of fresh discovery among hitherto unvisited rocks and anxious to make investigations there in the current season rather than adding to the already crowded program planned for the next, Gould had hoped since late January for an opportunity to visit the newfound range, but his chance had for weeks been delayed, first due to the priority of ship unloading and base construction and then to a persistent stretch of unsuitable weather. It had become rather late in the season for flying—the sun's movement now ranged from low on the horizon to beneath it, with lengthening hours of dark and twilight—but Gould pressed and Byrd yielded, allowing Gould to pick his men and prepare to go once the weather looked sufficiently clear. On the afternoon of March 7, with conditions better than they had been for some while, dog teams left camp to lay down some preliminary depots to the south in preparation for the following spring, and a short time later Gould and his chosen men, Balchen and June, took off in the *Virginia* from Little America's snow-covered field on what would be the first Antarctic flying trip to hazard a landing far from base to establish a temporary camp. Reaching the mountains just over two hours later, they selected a landing site at what appeared to be a flat expanse with good access to the hills for their work. Despite deteriorating visibility, Balchen brought the plane down safely, if a little roughly, on what turned out to be more rugged terrain than it had seemed from the air. While Balchen and Gould secured their craft with ice anchors and raised a tent, June rigged an external radio, using skis as an aerial mast, and sent Little America word of the trio's safe landing and approximate location. Judging it too late in the day to start surveying, the men ate a quick supper and turned in to rest until morning.

The next day they rose early and measured a baseline from which Gould, guarding his fingers against frostbite as he worked his theodolite in the face of a bitter cold wind, could fix the position of the main peaks visible from their camp. Finding after lunch that the breeze had lessened and the drifting they had experienced before noon had nearly ceased, the three decided to tramp over to the nearest mountain and climb far enough up its face to reach its exposed rock. Using ski boots and crampons to assist progress over the ice surface, they came to the mountain's foot and, after a short ascent, reached rock, which Gould was disappointed to find was nothing but granite, next to useless for establishing geological relationships with other known parts of the Antarctic. Sedimentary rock would have been a treasure; a fossil find better yet; and perhaps another sort of rock could yet be found higher up or beyond. But for now the overcast sky was darkening too much to risk any further climb that day. They returned to camp, planning to continue their survey on the morrow.

This would not happen.

Overnight while Gould, Balchen, and June slept soundly in their tent, the wind slowly mounted. Gould woke up at 6:30 to find that it was both snowing and blowing hard. The party had earlier agreed that with time precious and the March weather uncertain, they might work in good weather, night or day, and sleep during bad. Here was bad weather, and Gould, after advising his tent mates of the conditions outside, crawled back into his bag for another nap. By 11 he could sleep no more and got up, as did Balchen, to cook some oatmeal. June shared the breakfast, but without rising from his warm bedding. The wind had grown noticeably stronger. Suddenly there was, in Balchen's description, "a sharp retort like a .22 rifle," and half the tent collapsed. The men assumed that tent guys fastened to the *Virginia's* landing gear had snapped apart in the wind. Balchen peered outside, then yelled, "The plane has moved!" The tent guys had slackened, as the plane bucked and slid in the wind. Gould and Balchen scrambled outside, into a whipping wind difficult to stand against, and began shoveling snow onto the Fokker's landing skis to try to weight them down. June was delayed, throwing on clothes and dealing with an ill-timed leak of aviation gas from the primus stove, which had chosen that moment to catch fire in the bottom of the cooker. The wind grew stronger yet—Gould estimated it was now blowing 40 miles per hour—and as the plane slid again, Gould jumped on one of its skis himself while Balchen continued to shovel in alarm, shouting for June to come put his weight on the other ski. They then took turns cutting great blocks of snow to be piled atop the landing skis and before the fuselage. With four lengths of alpine rope, Balchen attached the landing gear to a deadman improvised out of one of their skis.

When the wind slackened in mid-afternoon, they caught their breath, refastened the tent guys, and felt assured that the worst was over. It was not. After no more than an hour the wind started up again with sudden strength more violent than before. Inside the plane Balchen found the air-speed indicator now registering a steady 60 miles per hour, with gusts up to 90. The Fokker slid backwards again, and then, as one powerful gust lifted the left wing, the plane quivered and appeared ready either to turn over or become airborne. Unable to stand upright against the gale, the men crawled over to the left wing on hands and knees. They found they could not brace themselves against the wind so as to loop a line through the wingtip eye, yet they knew they must somehow get this wing anchored. With June and Balchen grimly hanging on at the plane, Gould retrieved a ball of heavy mountaineering line from the grub chest and, keeping the free end, managed to throw the ball over the wing, grab both ends of the strand, and fling himself to the ground, holding to the line with both hands. Balchen and June soon put over another line, and while the heavier June acted as anchor Balchen worked "like a madman" at handling the shovel, despite the wind's blowing the implement's blade to and fro like a kite, and at again attempting to get a line through the eye of the left wing. Clinging to his cords, Gould felt his hands grow numb and feared he would lose his grip; he tied his end lines around a ski and then held on with both hands and legs. It grew colder and the wind worsened yet. Three times a gust lifted both Gould and June off the ground. "Another feather," Gould felt, "and it seemed the plane would have overturned." Balchen meanwhile got a securing line through the eye of the Fokker's right wing, if not yet the left.

For three "seemingly endless" hours they battled, Gould and June "lying flat on the ground and hanging to the lines ... numb with cold" while Balchen piled snow blocks about the plane and over its skis to hold it. Gould recalled the stinging of the wind-driven snow as "worse than needles" and the blizzard as "a veritable sand blast." In his initial hurry to exit the tent Gould had covered his hands with short mitts that left a gap between them and the sleeves of his parka. His wrists froze and became encircled by a bracelet of blisters. With his beard encrusted with ice, his face also lost feeling, and he was compelled to blink vigorously and frequently to keep his eyelids from freezing shut. When Balchen at last piled snow blocks high enough to reach and secure the end of the left wing, Gould and June were finally free to move again, though they could do so only with difficulty. They anchored the lines they had been holding to other deadmen, all buried beneath piled blocks of snow. With three guys on the left wing, it no longer seemed possible that any wind could now move the plane. Even so, they took the prudent step of removing certain supplies and the emergency radio apparatus from inside the craft.

The wind blew on without abatement, a force one could lean against with much the same solidity as a brick wall. A check of the barometer showed a precipitous drop of a full inch within four or five hours. Still the exhausted men worked to secure the *Virginia* as best they could, knowing not only how important the plane was to expedition plans for the following summer but also how serious their immediate situation might become should they have to walk back to Little America.

It was nearing midnight before a lull came and they felt able to leave the plane. Looking now to their tent, they found that it bore two great rips in the side where the guys had torn loose. The tent floor, sleeping bags, and everything else within was fairly saturated with soft, wet snow. With the temperature now risen to about 25 degrees above zero and the wind easing up considerably, they cleared away the slush as best they could, closed the rips with safety pins, crawled into their soggy "Turkish-bath" sleeping bags, and slept the sleep of the utterly exhausted.

Several uneasy days followed, filled with alternating periods of high wind and comparative calm. During gales, the three men mostly stayed within the tent, where the din made by the snapping canvas sounded to Gould like the broadside of muskets. Sometimes they would go out to shovel, keeping an eye on the Fokker. Buffeted by gusts, the plane "quivered and shook like a thing alive—ready to take flight" but held, secured by the guys and deadmen. On the 11th, they unloaded more from the plane, lest it be blown away, but otherwise recognized that there was nothing more they could do but wait. Though they had by no means completed the work they had hoped to do on the site, the danger to the plane had convinced them to fly back to Little America as soon now as the weather might allow. June communicated with the base that afternoon, learning that they had not there been hit by the same blizzard bedeviling the mountain party but had weather fit for landing. With local conditions also seemingly improving at last, the trio hoped to be able to take off that evening. They began to reload the plane in preparation, but snow continued, and it was 10:30 with a still overcast and now further darkening sky before the wind finally grew calm. With falling temperatures and a fairly high and steady barometer, Gould anticipated a probable flight back in the morning. "Little America will look good to us all," he wrote into his diary before turning in.

Less than four hours later, Gould was awakened by an ominous flapping of the tent. The barometer had begun to drop, and it looked bad enough that he dressed and went out to again unload food and other supplies from the plane. Somewhat later, flurries started, and another gloomy low-visibility day, impossible to fly in, had begun. It snowed through late afternoon, covering all with a five-to-seven-inch blanket. Nor could they fly on the 13th, a day of dead calm but with a completely overcast sky. Instead, they took advantage of the absence of wind to climb the mountains and do a good day's field work. They perfected their triangulation, establishing elevations for all of the surrounding peaks, collected more rocks, and even found in sheltered places rare Antarctic botanical life: bits of gray lichen and a greenish moss-like growth. These and other observations concerning ice melt made for a full day of successful science, enough that Gould felt he had now completed the work he had flown there to do. With the sky clearing at the end of the day and temperatures again falling—both good omens of improving weather for flight—optimism again ran high that they would be able to return to Little America the next morning. Conditions still looked favorable when they arose at 5, and the three started readying the plane for takeoff. While Balchen held a torch below the motor to warm it up and June began heating oil over the cooker, Gould shoveled away the snow wall they had so laboriously built atop the skis and under the fuselage. "But," as Gould wrote later,

> it was no use. We could not shut our eyes to the fact that it was slowly becoming overcast, and that soon the horizon would disappear in that curious chalky sort of day in which every direction looks the same and one can easily imagine himself suspended in a world of milk. On all sides an opaque white.
>
> First there came little puffs of wind from the north. That was warning enough. We began all over again building our snow wall and further securing the plane, and kept at it all the morning. Perhaps it was quite as well that we were not able to take off for Harold was able to establish radio communication by the middle of the forenoon and we learned that the weather at Little America was unfit for flying. As a matter of fact there had not been a single day since we arrived in the Rockefeller Mountains favorable to a take-off and flight back to Little America—only 135 miles away.... .
>
> About noon it let go again. Never was there another such blizzard. In one swoop the wind gathered up all the loose snow that had fallen

during the period of calm. Great clouds of the icy flying dust swirled and flowed about us. The air became liquid. So completely saturated was it with snow that one could not face the wind and breathe.

After a couple of hours of this, all the new loose snow that had been covering the ground had been blown away, leaving about them only a hard icy surface.

The men kept busy, doing what they could to restore snow walls about the plane and tent or otherwise re-secure the endangered plane, but their difficulties were enormous. As Gould described it:

> With infinite trouble we started cutting blocks of snow wherever we could find patches deep enough. Then we would try to put them on top of our snow wall. Often we would be caught broadside, tumbled head over heels and hurled 20 to 30 feet to leeward. Then we clawed our way back on hands and knees to try another block. Finally when we did get one in place on the wall we were trying to rebuild, we could lie back and watch it fade or melt away as it was eroded by the terrific force of the wind. We had never worked harder yet the wall always grew lower.
>
> One time Bernt and I were trying to anchor an additional line to an end of the wing, when a sudden gust blew me off my feet and held me streamlined horizontally in the air for some seconds.... . Once I was knocked off my feet by a blow on the side of my head. Though he could not possibly have heard me, I started to tell Bernt what a clumsy ass he was with the shovel. I looked up to find that he wasn't within 40 feet of me. I just had time to dodge a piece of hard snow half as big as my head or I should have gotten another crack. It seemed that the whole earth was being torn apart.

June tried intermittently that day to send messages to Little America, but none of these were in fact heard. These broadcasts were made from inside the Fokker, whose immovable transmitter was the better of the two with the mountain party, and during an attempt to meet an 8:30 broadcast schedule, with the plane "quivering ... and lifting in sickening way," it was noted that the Fokker's air speed indicator was registering nearly 90 miles per hour. Gusts ran the indicator up past 100. Two hours later, when it was time to meet the next schedule, the wind had further augmented, and Gould refused to allow June to enter the craft at all. Despite a cold motor, the plane's propeller began to revolve in the wind with increasing rapidity. Meanwhile, the protective snow walls were steadily eroding, as was the snow upon which both plane and tent were anchored. This was uncovering patches of blue ice, leading Gould to suppose that the flat area they had picked for a landing field and camp site was actually the edge of what in high summer was "a snow-bound lake formed from the accumulation of thaw water from the mountain slopes." With the areas of blue ice continually growing and merging, it "was evident," Gould wrote later, "that if the wind continued indefinitely, all the snow that was holding the plane and protecting our tent would be slowly eroded away and we should go with it."

By 10:30, when Gould deemed it unsafe for June to climb into the plane to use the radio, light was dimming and the wind had made it impossible for the men to get about except by crawling. A bone-tired Gould and his two companions now shouted agreement that there was nothing further they could do, and they crawled into damp, clammy sleeping bags inside a cold, wet tent, surrounded by the deafening noise of screaming wind and snapping canvas. Accounts differ as to the timing of what happened next. Here is Balchen's memoir:

> Along about midnight there comes a far-off moaning, building to a roar like an approaching express train, down the mountain and across the snow toward us. It hits with the boom of an artillery shell landing, and then everything is dead quiet. I sit up in my sleeping bag and look through a slit in the snow blocks we have piled around the tent. Where the outline of the Fokker's wing was above our tent, now there is only empty space.
> "It's gone!" I say to Gould and June and they both reply wearily, "Oh, the hell with it!" and we lie back in our reindeer bags and go to sleep."

In Gould's published account, it was the next morning before he awoke and stuck his head out of the tent somehow knowing that he would not see the plane. "I think we had all sensed that it had been torn loose and blown away a few minutes after we had crawled into the tent the night before," he recalled, "but none of us had dared to suggest it to the others. Certainly it was no surprise to any of us to find it gone now." His diary entry, written that morning, puts the anguish front and center—"There are no words to write what has happened"—and then describes the holding lines as having been parted by a sudden strong gust and the plane lifted up and carried backwards through the air half a mile before crashing onto the ice a total wreck—a status apparently not confirmed until Balchen fought his way across the ice and back on a mission to assess the damage. The three judged that the velocity of the gust that finally launched the plane must have been in the neighborhood of 120 to 150 miles per hour.

After what was undoubtedly a rather somber and thoughtful breakfast the men were faced by another unpleasant surprise: the transportable Burgess emergency radio set that had been brought into the tent was not working, the tubes all dead. The other transmitter was in the plane, now half a mile away, in uncertain condition. For hours they were unable to investigate the wreck further, as the wind blew hard continually, leaving the men to "sit still and contemplate the fairly dismal prospect ahead." Gould's diary entry that day shows the direction of his contemplation:

> Just sitting tight now and praying it will calm enough soon so that we can go over and see if June can make the radio work and get word back to camp of our loss and our present condition. I am sorry for the great

The Fokker plane, the *Virginia*, after the blizzard

worry that must be on the minds of Commander Byrd and our other friends at camp for we are safe—but not secure—our position is critical. I am hoping we can hear from camp and know whether the Commander will fly to us at the first break in the weather or send dog teams to our rescue. If we cannot establish communication we shall in any case wait for good weather—couldn't possibly travel now anyhow—with our eyes turned toward the western heavens hoping to see the Fairchild headed toward us. If the good weather comes and there is no plane to our rescue we shall start on the long trek back on foot—a cheerless task but not an impossible one—and whatever lies ahead I could search the wide world over for two better men with whom to face the future than these two companions of mine—Bernt Balchen and Harold June.

In his memoir written two years later, Gould was perhaps more realistic about how perilous an attempted overland return to Little America would have been:

We had brought a good month's supply of food with us and had an abundance of fuel in the gas tanks of the plane, provided they were still intact. But if we were forced to attempt to walk back to Little America at this late time of the year it might take us at least a month, for our experience had taught us that we could not depend on favorable weather for even half the time. I think Bernt could have done this trek with comparative ease. He is the ablest man out of doors that I have ever seen. But Harold and I were quite inexperienced on skis, and the long trek pulling a sledge load of supplies might have been too great for us. And of course before we had reached Little America the sun might have disappeared for its long winter sojourn, with the increasingly lowering temperatures that this would mean.

Finally, late in the day the wind lulled enough so that they went over to take a look at the wrecked plane and test its radio. They found a "disheartening" and "pitiful" sight: a crushed fuselage, smashed and splintered skis, and propeller blades twisted into corkscrews. Only the wings were little damaged, as the plane had apparently "preserved its equilibrium in the air and had literally flown itself, tail foremost," to its present position. June worked on restoring the radio, finding that he could hear camp but was unable himself to be heard. He learned that the extreme weather they had just experienced had not been duplicated at Little America, which did not suspect their plight, being unaware of the disastrous second blizzard that had caused it.

That night, freed of continuing worry about the plane, to which the worst had already happened, the men slept more soundly than they had in days. When Gould woke early the next morning he felt considerably "refreshed in body and mind." As if in apology for previous ill-treatment—or perhaps it was a gentle mockery, since it could now do them so little good—the morning of the 16th was both calm and sunny, good flying weather at last, had they only still possessed an unwrecked craft with which to use it. June returned to the radio, where hope of repairing the transmitter and informing camp of their situation lasted into the afternoon, then vanished permanently when the crankshaft belonging to the power set broke. Now while the mountain party could still hear Little America's periodic messages to them, there was no longer any possibility of being heard in return. By late in the day it was clear from what they heard that Byrd was becoming perplexed and alarmed over their continued silence, and the marooned trio hoped that he would soon send the Fairchild plane to investigate—if only the weather would cooperate in both locations!—but at the same time they also went on with preparations for a possible walk home.

Early on the 17th, Byrd radioed that Little America's weather was fine and that the mountain party should return at once, but that if they failed to appear he was preparing dog teams to start for their location, and if the weather held the Fairchild would also fly over to them. It was frustrating for Gould and his companions to hear that news of their "disappearance" was being communicated to the States, and therefore to loved ones whose worry they could not immediately allay with reassurances of well-being. Still, the morning hope was for an eventual rescue that day; Byrd would doubtless wait "a reasonable length of good weather time" for them to return on their own, but then send the *Stars & Stripes* to their aid. All they could do was "sit tight and hope the good weather lasts."

Again it did not. In mid-afternoon Gould noted glumly in his diary that their good day was short-lived:

> Now the sky is completely overcast and a bit of snow is falling. Visibility is poor. There is little chance or hope that the Fairchild can come to our rescue to-day. But dog teams are starting—barring accidents such as falling into crevasses and the like they might be here within a week. That is a more sure prospect and hope than is that of walking home. If there were only some way to tell the Commander that we are unharmed!

Knowing him I know this is his first, last and constant thought. For his sake and for those way back behind in the states we hope the Fairchild can come reasonably soon.

The next day the wait continued. A bright cloudless sky in the mountains seemed promising on Gould's end, but morning conditions at Little America were poor, forbidding flight. A takeoff authorized the day before had been scotched by failure to get the engine started. And to complete the vexing news from camp, the dog teams Gould had hoped were already heading toward them were reported—for a third day!—as still about to start. "It is so hard to sit and wait with nothing to do," reads Gould's mid-day diary entry. "We should be happier pulling on our hand sledges homeward bound." But really the only sensible course was to wait for relief where they were, where their position was known. "And so we shall sit tight and hope." Their foe, the weather, was at mid-day again starting to look troublesome—cloudier, with a falling barometer, though at least there was as yet no wind. ("'Tanks God,' as Bernt would say.")

For once, however, ill omens forebode no ill result; the weather stayed passable in the mountains and improved at camp. At about 4 p.m., June at the radio set picked up the welcome news that the Fairchild was airborne. The men laid out a "T" of orange flags to mark the best landing site, then kept watch over the western sky. It was now somewhat overcast and dimming, and so they heard the plane long before seeing it. Straining their eyes toward the sound of the motor, they finally spotted it high above and, when it appeared that they themselves had not yet been seen, hastened to signal their presence with smoke bombs and light. There was much relief when the plane circled back. It landed, and out came a three-man crew: pilot Dean Smith, radio operator Malcolm Hanson, and Byrd himself. The reunion was a happy one, the relief from anxiety being even greater for the rescuers, who had not known what to expect, than for the rescued. In Byrd's account, his first thought upon seeing the signal of smoke and light was "Thank God, at least one of them is alive." Before landing, Byrd could see the wreck of the Fokker, its "grotesque attitude show[ing] quite plainly that it had crashed." After Smith skillfully put the plane on the surface, Byrd emerged. At first he saw no one.

Then a figure came racing toward the plane—that gait could belong only to a Navy man, June: then I saw a man of bristling red whiskers advancing in our direction. No other face on the planet supported such a growth. Balchen's, of course. But where was Larry? In a moment I saw him as well. He, too, was on his way to the place, but his progress was casual, and he was the academician to the very end—making the dignified entrance of a professor who happened, let us say, to breakfast late and found his class already in noisy session. It was so very much in character that I had to smile.

No two accounts of this day of rescue are quite the same. Balchen's has the sound of the motor overhead being the castaways' first knowledge that the Fairchild was underway, and he has Gould as the first of the three to be spotted from the plane. Newspapers in the States printed Russell Owen's dramatic dispatch from the point of view of the men at base, following the flight by radio:

> All we knew was that they were flying into the unknown, facing dangers which all aviators avoid when possible, on an errand the outcome of which we dreaded.
>
> An hour and a half went by and then came word that they were at the first mountain. They passed another mountain, but there was no sign of the missing plane.
>
> Men were listening around the buzzing loud-speaker from which the sound of the motor of Commander Byrd's plane came like an echo of a distant wind.
>
> Signals ticked in, and looking over Howard Mason's shoulder as he copied the message one suddenly read:
>
> "See the plane now / Some one below waving."
>
> A shout went up, "They are safe!" But there was only one man apparently. The message said, "Someone."
>
> Where were the others? Were they dead or injured in the tent? We asked ourselves these questions looking at each other, sucking at forgotten and unlighted pipes.
>
> "Waving and working blinker," wrote Mason from the radio impulses.
>
> We could see that tiny light flashing up in the morning darkness. What dreadful message did it carry?
>
> "Landing," the pencil spelled out.
>
> We looked at each other in amazement and fear. The blinker must have told of something very serious if they were to chance a landing in that poor light after a storm that had bumped and torn the surface. Could they do it safely? We were a silent and worried group of men.
>
> There was a long period of silence. Mason looked up and said they had taken in the antenna and he could no longer hear the engine after it had been throttled down for the glide.
>
> We could imagine Dean, cool and resourceful, looking first to one and then to the other side, stalling in over a surface he could not see accurately, waiting for the first shock of touching. The moments dragged as Mason twiddled his dials, turning them back and forth without results. Suddenly he picked up his pencil.
>
> "Landed O. K., every one O. K.," he wrote.
>
> The shadow of gloom which had hung over us all day was lifted by those commonplace little words. Men jumped up and down and pounded each other on the back until Mason, the most imperturbable member of the expedition, looked up with a frown of annoyance.... .

The rescue plane could not, however, carry six men all at once on a return trip. Byrd's decision was to send Balchen and June immediately back with Smith, after unloading some food, a small sledge, and new working radio equipment; he, Hanson, and Gould would remain behind for now, to be retrieved the next morning—ominous words—"weather permitting." The hope was that the Fairchild could return twice more, to retrieve not only the men but also rocks and equipment.

Three days later, they were still waiting. While their own weather had mostly been clear and calm, continuously poor conditions at Little America had disallowed further flying. On the 19th, with possibilities for another flight uncertain, dog teams were started from camp at last, headed toward the Rockefellers as an alternate means of rescue—though it was doubtful whether sledges could reach the mountains and then return to base before the oncoming winter enfolded all in dark and cold. The men now in the mountains prepared to walk west themselves, if it appeared no plane could come, to meet the dog teams en route. Finally, early on the morning of the 22nd, word came that bad weather at base had relented, enough for the Fairchild to make another flight to their position, this time carrying but two men, Smith and June. All thoughts of two flights had been abandoned, and the small plane would be fully loaded just with five men and very minimal gear aboard, so a good deal had to be left behind, including a pair of rock hammers whose loss Gould felt deeply.* A short time after, Smith again brought the *Stars & Stripes* down on their icy field, Gould, Byrd, and Hanson squeezed aboard, and less than an hour and a half later they were back in camp. Flying westward, they passed over the sledge teams laboring on the trail toward them and signaled them to turn about. The drivers were happy to have their mission cancelled and made a sixty-three mile return trip in a nonstop thirteen hours. With all men returned safely to base and the stormiest month they would experience in Antarctica approaching its end, the Byrd Expedition now prepared to hunker down for the long dark winter.

***

Gould's trip to the Rockefeller Range was scientifically alluring, his keenness to get there entirely understandable. First investigation of a newly discovered mountain group was a rare chance, and the exposed rock reported there might yield answers to hitherto obscure geological questions concerning the relationship of this section of Antarctica to the rest of the continent. This was powerful enticement to a young scientist anxious to make a contribution. Apart from some glaciological studies in the near vicinity of Little America, Gould had as yet done

---

* Apparently, however, Gould simply could not bear to lose all of the rocks he had collected in the mountains. Decades later, Gould revealed that he had secretly substituted some of his rocks for food in baggage carried as emergency supplies. "I do not know what the record would have been if we had had a forced landing," Gould confessed at an Antarctican Society-sponsored talk half a century after the fact, "but Commander Byrd never discovered what had happened."

no real geology on the expedition, and he burned to accomplish something scientifically significant before the end of his first polar summer.

In risking the trip with winter so close, however, eagerness was allowed to trump caution. Gould's mature assessment was that attempting a flyover and fieldwork in March was "a silly, silly thing to do. Our total ignorance of Antarctic conditions might have been the end of all of us." "That was all my fault," he told an interviewer in 1981, adding, "Hell, today we wouldn't think of letting anyone fly over to the Rockefeller Mountains on the seventh of March." Doing so in 1929 proved to be an error and, with the wreck of the *Virginia*, a costly one. Losing the Fokker applied a serious check to established plans. As one historian of the expedition summed it up:

> Now that the aviation unit was down to two aircraft out of the original four, there were no extra planes. Since by Byrd's rules a plane could not fly without a standby for rescue, he would have to baby the aircraft he had left. As it was, the Fairchild could not make it over the polar plateau for a tandem flight or possible rescue, as the Fokker could have, so the wreck had made the polar attempt in the Ford that much more dangerous. Byrd would have to use the planes sparingly, when the expected payoff from a flight outweighed the risk. The sturdy, reliable dog teams would have to do much more of the depot laying and exploration than had been envisioned. With the high priority of the polar flight and other nonscientific aviation missions, the geological objectives would suffer the most.

Bad luck had wrecked the plane, but Gould blamed himself for pressing Byrd hard for permission to make the trip, though the commander had been doubtful about its advisability so late in the season and had perhaps relented out of concern to preserve Gould's morale. "He [Byrd] has been so kind and generous to me that it comes especially hard that my geological trip should cause him the loss," Gould wrote into his diary a day after the wreck of the plane: "There are no words to compass my regret."

And yet, paradoxically, that regret would in time be tempered by certain knowledge that it was the disaster of losing a plane in a blizzard in the Rockefeller Mountains in March that opened the way for the grandest experience of his life in November and December. In a way, Larry Gould would come to be glad for the circumstance that, because it forced adaptive changes in plans for the expedition's second summer program, deflected him deep into the Antarctic interior as a driver of dogs.

CHAPTER 8

FORTY-TWO MEN

"A man is not lost," Larry Gould always insisted, "if he knows where he is." Following the misadventure in the Rockefellers, reported to the world as a story of the rescue of men lost in the mountains, Gould's stout protestations that his party had never been lost but merely "marooned" were quite futile. Little America *would* continue to receive messages from home expressing relief over the safe recovery of those who had been lost in the mountains, until one expedition wag declared that Gould's monogram, L.M.G., surely stood for "Lost in Mountains Gould."

In any case, external fieldwork was now at an end for many months to come; to make ready for winter took over as the sole pressing task. Planes were buried, tunnels completed, improvements improvised on workspaces and living quarters for both men and dogs. By the end of March the sun was rising to no more than ten degrees above the horizon at noon and was visible at all for only a few hours each day. On Easter Sunday, March 31, Gould's diary recorded a daytime temperature of 40 degrees below zero. But it also noted the glorious, indescribable shimmering colors filling the air and imparted to the snow by the setting sun. Stratus clouds on the horizon were fringed with "rich reds and royal purples," and in the absence of clouds the sun "became a flame scarlet ball ... surrounded with the most complicated and fantastic halos and mock suns." Gould wrote of the sunsets of this time as phenomena seemingly only yards away in which one participated. "One had a very real illusion of being suspended in a world of soft pastel colors." By early April Little America was frequent witness during the lengthening darkness to the beautiful dancing-light displays of the *aurora australis*, spanning the heavens in shafts and arches of pale green.

On the 19th of April the sun failed to top the horizon at all and would be seen no more until late August. Save for a few minor tasks the expedition had completed its outdoor work until spring, and the men now settled into new routines that it was hoped would carry their forty-two-man community—the largest group ever to winter in Antarctica—safely through until then. For several months extreme cold and round the clock darkness dictated an altered, groundhog-like

(Top) winter approaches; (bottom) Gould with rime-encrusted theodolite, both 1929

existence for the Little Americans. For Commander Byrd and his executive officer Gould, winter would inevitably be a period of special concern, not only for the expedition's physical well-being in a harsh clime but also for the maintenance of morale and psychological health. Given their collective geographic isolation on the one hand but lack of individual privacy in cramped and confined quarters* on the other, given the depressing effect of the absence of sunlight, and the torpor bred of relative inactivity, the psychological dangers of winter were at least as worrisome as the physical.

Under the conditions of a polar winter, Bernt Balchen wrote in his later autobiographical memoir, "each man's true self will invariably emerge and stand revealed to his companions. There is no doubt that the type of man best fitted for a wintering party in polar regions is the man who is not only physically fit, but also even-tempered, with inner intellectual resources, and not overly sensitive." Larry Gould, who was just such a man, found the experience of wintering in Antarctica very much to his taste. He relished the time it gave him for reading and reflection. During the winter night, more than ever before, he emerged within the expedition as a natural leader, both popular and respected, whose cohesive effect on the small community of Little America was strongly positive and possibly crucial.

In his post-expedition memoir, Byrd acknowledged the psychological stresses that made winter a dangerous time for an Antarctic expedition and wrote of opposing them with the practical weapons of work and its ally, routine. Camp chores, mostly delegated by Gould, were assigned in such a way that each man had daily labor, with unpleasant duties such as dishwashing, snow shoveling, coal hauling, and latrine cleaning being rotated fairly. (Gould and physicist Taffy Davies themselves hauled coal and took care of other domestic duties for the Administration Building on Tuesdays.) Rousing the men in the various barracks from their bunks to begin each day was Gould's responsibility, performed, according to Byrd's later account, "with an unswerving fidelity to his office that was the despair of all." Popular though Gould was—Byrd wrote that "if any man was liked by all, it was he ... his friendly ways and his fairness endeared him to the Winter Party at Little America"—still from time to time he would

---

* Sleeping and living quarters in Little America would not have been so crowded as they were had the *Eleanor Bolling* been able to reach them again with hoped-for additional supplies including additional prefabricated buildings. As it was, the Administration Building (Edgar Barratt House) was remodeled to sleep seventeen, including Gould and the other scientists, as well as the pilots, doctor, engineer, *New York Times* journalist, Paramount cameramen, and a few others including Commander Byrd in a private room. Fourteen men bunked in the building (Roswell Barratt House) that also served as mess hall. Eight men, including most of the dog drivers, lived in an 11' x 14' room originally intended as a machine shop in the building referred to variously as the Norwegian House or the Biltmore. One man claimed private space in an improvised extension of canvas, boxes, and boards off of an outer wall of the mess hall, and the final two set up in a 9' x 12' hut fashioned from aircraft engine crates that was called "Blubberheim," as its heating came from a stove burning pungent seal blubber.

have to employ vigorous exhortations of one sort or another in order either to "help" someone rise out of bed or to get certain work done. This resulted one day in his being likened by dog driver Jack O'Brien to cruel Simon Legree, the slave master, and thenceforth he could not shake the nickname: "Simon" he affectionately remained.*

On a typical winter day in Little America, breakfast gave way to morning and afternoon work, separated by a small informal lunch spread with tea, coffee, or cocoa. After the afternoon shift came an early supper, the day's great social affair, generally comprised of soup, meat (most often dark mutton or roast beef, penguin, whale, or seal), dehydrated or canned vegetables, bread and butter with jam or marmalade, inevitably a dessert, and a hot drink, all seasoned with discussion of camp affairs, wherein some "special accomplishment of brilliance or dumbness always came in for approving or sarcastic review." A variety of amusements, individual or social, might fill the evening time after dinner, with "Taps" at 10 p.m. signaling "the one time of quiet during the waking hours of Little America." Then, after the main lights were put out and most were in bed, Gould and other kindred spirits with sources of individual light might enjoy the "luxury of an hour or two of reading in bed before it gets so cold that we have to stop." (Doors to the outside were opened at 11 to combat stale air.) Describing the last hour of a typical day, Gould wrote:

> As the cold air creeps upward and displaces the warm, the lights go out here and there and before midnight the room is quite dark, but it is not still. There are a few noisy sleepers, and to-night the wind has sprung up and as it sweeps across our tiny chimneys, which project up above the house, it sets up a sound much like the deep tones of an organ. It is rather restful.

Saturday nights were special, bringing the much-enjoyed weekly radio broadcasts from home, complete with personal messages for expedition individuals. Sundays might include the viewing of a motion picture. After supper on April 22, for instance, the men living in what was at that moment the world's southernmost human habitation entertained themselves with *Nanook of the North*. The remarks and catcalls of the audience reminded Gould of a lowbrow show at home or of a familiar Ann Arbor theater when it was jammed with students. While the movie nights were popular, Gould later observed that the camp came to be very greatly amused by the evident care which had been taken to provide for the isolated party of men only such pictures as by no flight of

---

* By midwinter, dog driver Eddie Goodale had already named one of his dogs "Simon," and Gould in his journal was anticipating the vicarious joy Goodale would get the following season swearing aloud at the animal, "Simon you — get up!" A second nickname Gould received that winter was "Doodle Bug," thanks to his having worn a pair of spectacled magnifying glasses that projected several inches beyond his nose. Sometimes the two were combined, and he became "Simon Doodle Bug."

3,000+ volumes of entertainment, information, and insulation [OSUA-BP]

fancy could lead minds to a recollection of their social and sexual deprivation.

Card games filled out many a winter evening for various groupings of the expedition. Gould now and then played bridge, and more frequently Hearts, with three or four other players and stakes of cigarettes or chocolate. But the single most important source of recreation, in Gould's view, was the camp library, arranged along two walls of the Administration Building, whose three thousand-some volumes he had assembled himself in New York prior to the expedition's departure. Detective stories and accounts of previous polar expeditions were Little America's most popular genres, though Gould reported that the most widely read single book was W. H. Hudson's Amazonian romance *Green Mansions*, perhaps because its lush setting was so opposite to their own. Gould followed his own reading of *Green Mansions* in May with two more Hudson works, *A Little Boy Lost* and *The Purple Land*. The catholicity of his reading that winter embraced authors ranging from Shakespeare to W. S. Gilbert, from Thomas Hardy to Earl Derr Biggers. "As for myself," Gould wrote after the expedition's return, "had the winter night given me opportunity for no other reading than Romain Rolland's *Jean Christophe* and Galsworthy's *Forsyte Saga* in its entirety I should still have considered it well spent."

Absent from the catalog of activities at Little America was any sort of formal religious observation. The possibility of services was discussed between Byrd and Gould but decided against given the denominational diversity represented in the men present. Gould did note that the Bible was much read in Little America on an individual basis, sometimes by the most unlikely people.

Another occupier of spare winter hours for many members of the expedition, and with which Gould was centrally involved, was the educational self-improvement program dubbed the "University of Antarctica." Early in May, Gould was planning to offer to five or six people (he supposed) a regular course in geology, using mimeographs of his University of Michigan lecture notes in lieu of textbooks. But about fifteen turned out for a preliminary meeting of the proposed class on May 6, and two days later at his first regular lecture more than half the camp was in attendance. Expecting at first that most would not stay long with the course, conducted as two lectures and two hour-long discussion groups per week, he was surprised by the number that persisted. Six weeks in, with some twenty Little Americans still maintaining interest, he noted how pleasant it was "teaching people who are entirely sincere in their attitude." Using other specialists in camp as teachers, the "University" also during this time provided instruction in radio operation and lectures on aeronautics and aerial surveying. Gould himself spent time studying navigation and attempting to master radio code, about which he confessed himself not really interested and therefore "quite wooden headed."

Navigation and radio were tools Gould wanted in anticipation of the altered plans now being made for the following summer. Adapting to the loss in the Rockefellers of one of the expedition airplanes, it was determined that Gould's desire to investigate the geology of the Queen Maud Range to the south might yet be met by means of an ambitious sledge trip of men and dog teams. Sledgers would go south along the line of Byrd's projected polar flight and lay a series of supply depots for possible emergency use in case anything happened to the plane on that flight. Then, having already pushed three or four hundred miles inland on this depot-laying mission, a party of six men and dog teams led by Gould would turn east and proceed along the base of the Queen Maud Mountains, mapping and making geological studies along their route before retracing their path in reverse. It would be a round trip of well over a thousand miles and would, Gould recognized, necessitate "infinite detail … in the way of making preparations." It would also necessitate his learning to ski, at least in a manner more passable than his very beginning efforts to date in the Antarctic. On a relatively warm May 3, one day after the first mention in his diary of plans for the summer sledge trip, Gould received a skiing tutorial from the proficient Bernt Balchen and resolved to practice every winter day, weather permitting. Subsequent diary entries show Gould acting on his resolution to take a ski run every possible day, usually with at least one companion. Intense cold did not often keep him inside—he noted on May 12 that he had been skiing one day at 58 degrees below zero. His daily runs were more frequently prevented simply by cloudy skies, which made the dim days altogether too dark.

Though the routine of the circumscribed winter months made them naturally short on dramatic incident and adventurous activity compared with the seasons of exploration that came before and would follow, Gould continued to journal those occurrences which seemed most worthy of note. One Monday less than two weeks after the disappearance of the sun was "just an average Antarctic day"

Radio broadcasts from home lighten the dark days of winter. [OSUA-BP]

in Gould's account but personally eventful in that he submitted like so many others had already done to Little America's winter fashion of a shaved head. He found the result, in combination with the Van Dyke beard he had grown, to be "grotesque ... worse than I thought it would be."

Some days simply offered no distinguishing variety. On one such, Gould noted that he was put in mind of Mark Twain's attempt to keep a diary: "He tried for three days and found that each day's entry consisted simply of the notation Got up, dressed, washed—went to bed again." More often, Gould found plenty to write about in his winter journal, whether his subject was his own activity, the doings of others in camp, vagaries of weather, or personal reflections on the strange beauty of their surroundings. A good example of the latter is his entry for May 13 after viewing "an aurora of auroras," particularly colorful and full of dancing life, in which he regretted that he lacked the power of poetic expression needed to describe its majestic beauty so that another could envision it, but recorded that for himself it would be unforgettable: "I close my eyes and see the reds the greens and the purples boiling over the dark rim of the night that is always with us and about us." It wasn't fair, he went on, that the enjoyment of its loveliness was limited to so small a privileged group, yet it belonged where it was:

> Without the bleakness of the all day night and the infinite solitude of the white desert everywhere it would lose some of its personality. Somehow I just can't imagine such a display over the green fields and the waving trees of my Michigan home. I guess the sky isn't big enough up there anyhow.

On the 9th of May, the third anniversary of Commander Byrd's north polar flight provided occasion for a celebration. Cooks prepared a grand roast turkey dinner with cranberry sauce and dressing, and the fourteen Little Americans who had also served Byrd in the north three years before were given first table. Liquid refreshment was wanted for a program of toasts, and Byrd approved, for the special evening, tapping into the supply of gin and other alcohol maintained by Doc Coman. The resultant cocktails were both potent and plentiful. There were few abstainers, and several expeditioners were soon feeling "pretty gay." Physicist Taffy Davies, at table next to Gould, declared that he could drink the second-in-command under the table. Instead, as Gould recorded in his diary when next he wrote, Davies' neighbors "surreptitiously filled his glass as fast as he emptied it" and "before he even had a bite of turkey he fell off his seat."

After the banquet about half of Little America kept the drinking party going in the shack known as Blubberheim There Gould, close-cropped though his scalp then was, let his hair down as executive officer. In his own account:

> It was a grand party—a bit boisterous—stories that by their very nature can scarcely be written and songs too. How pleasant and affable I did feel too. I am told that I made some such announcement as this: "I am second in command of this expedition and I order every one of you to get cockeyed drunk." It seems to have been a command that was pretty generously, I mean generally obeyed.

Another diarist, meteorologist Henry Harrison, described the result as "a spectacular and riotous drunken orgy." Thursday night's revel continued until about 4 in the morning, and most of the camp kept to their beds all the next day, with some hangovers persisting into Saturday. It was not until Sunday that Gould judged that everything had returned to normal.*

But everything hadn't, really. Instead, the alcoholic indulgence sanctioned for one night had awakened in some a thirst that persisted; it opened a door that then proved hard to close. Shortly after the north polar celebration, two men began siphoning off grain alcohol from a large drum kept in a camp storeroom for use in drying photographic film. Soon a handful was having regular drinking parties fueled by what they nicknamed "blowtorch," a mixture of the alcohol with jellied fruit juice provided to the expedition as an antiscorbutic. The accompanying drunkenness was sometimes violently rowdy. A week after the initial celebration

---

* In the interim, Little America nearly experienced a fatality. Taffy Davies, acting as Friday's night watchman, became groggy sitting in the camp's photographic darkroom after lights out. Assuming he was still hung over from the day before, he failed to realize that he was in fact beginning to succumb to carbon monoxide poisoning—a blizzard had filled the room's ventilator with snow. By a lucky chance, Davies and an unconscious puppy beside him were discovered by Jack Bursey, one of the camp's non-drinkers, who had been feeling restless and gone in search of the night watchman. Bursey fetched Doc Coman, and Davies and the pup both soon recovered.

one inebriated drinker, upset by some argument, punched one of the abstainers several times in the mouth and continued to rampage until another of the drinkers conked him on the head with a ski boot.

Gould had first viewed the wet celebration of May 9 (and his own part in it) with a highly tolerant eye:

> Sunday May 12th
>
> When I remember my rigid upbringing with regards [to] liquor and my almost total abstinence thruout most of my life and the confidence some of my best friends have in me that I don't indulge I wonder why I am not more disturbed by my occasional slips, as it were. But somehow there is nothing like a little wine to loosen the strings of one's tongue and promote a most delightful atmosphere of conviviality.

But the episodes of drunkenness that followed over the next two weeks changed his tune:

> Monday May [27]
>
> Liquor is a bad thing to have around! Our party of May 9th was somewhat of a mistake. There has been considerable drinking since then which came to a head as a decided brawl Saturday night which lasted thruout the day yesterday. And in the interim they have been at the alcohol barrel more often than we have guessed. And now it must stop and I find myself as second in command in a sense responsible. I wish the barrel could be emptied and temptation placed beyond the reach of those who do not know how to control their appetites... .

> Wednesday [May 29]
>
> The recent drunk was a bad thing it came nearer demoralizing camp than anything that has happened heretofore and can in no sense be tolerated again. It is so apparent that things which can be tolerated elsewhere take on very different aspects here. This is such a compact society—here are 42 men who rarely get more than 200 yards apart at most... .

The second-in-command was far from the only member of the expedition upset by May's ongoing boisterous drinking, but there were too many participants or unconcerned lookers-on for the behavior to be choked off by peer pressure. Byrd became concerned but, as a later expedition historian observed, "did not want to give anyone a tongue-lashing or punishment that would corner him into a position of defiance, a position that would seriously undermine the commander's authority over his civilian volunteer force and split the expedition." As Gould recalled it decades later, he and Byrd talked the business over and eventually decided that their best practical stance would be co-optive, to take the matter over themselves and allow for occasional binges to blow off steam: "So we had parties every two or three weeks. We put out a tub and we filled it with all kind of fruit juices and things, poured in a lot of alcohol, and then allowed people to drink."

Illicit drinking may have been for some a reaction to monotony. Late in May Gould himself could write of his needing to ward off a "dopey" feeling induced by a succession of lazy days. But more often he found the time speeding by all too quickly, his days too full of activity to be monotonous. Diary entries note variously: "There has been so much to do these last days ..." "Yesterday found me busy thruout the day ..." "There are so many details crying for attention in connection with our sledging plans for next summer that I find myself running around in circles ..." "Incredible how the time flies ..."

On June 12 a radiogram was received with an intriguing message for Gould from George Putnam. Putnam revealed a plan to organize a voyage by submarine from Spitsbergen to Alaska's Bering Strait the following June, traveling partly on the surface through leads and partly under ice. Would Gould care to join this adventure as sole scientist? The voyage would be dangerous but practical, Putnam thought, and of "obviously spectacular world interest." "If successful would establish you everlastingly." Gould told his diary that night that this was "quite the most fantastic thing" he'd ever heard of but that he should probably go. "It has most anything heretofore dreamed as a thriller pretty well backed off the map," he wrote. (In the end, nothing would come of the idea, Putnam informing Gould early in 1930, before the Byrd Expedition broke camp, that the proposed submarine trip was probably off.)

Midwinter arrived on the 21st of June. Gould was surprised to find that even then, when the direct rays of the sun were most distant, a pink glow remained visible at noon on Little America's northern horizon. Winter days were dark but not entirely so. They were also cold but not unrelievedly so. A blizzard early in June caused the temperature to rise 65 degrees over twenty hours, from 49 degrees below zero to 16 degrees above. The latter felt so "balmy" to Gould that he was "running around outside a good part of the day with but little clothing on—just a cloth parka" over his shirt.

Gould found that he was living in a world of fascinating contrasts. Here sometimes was calm stillness and "unparalleled quiet." "This is a land of silence," he wrote. "It is an expanding sort of silence," not at all oppressive as it might feel at home. "It is the natural state here and I like it—I have come to feel at home in the midst of it." But how different when the land of silence gave way to the howling din of a winter blizzard! Writing descriptively of "the whining and screeching of the wind as it sucks itself across the snow," Gould opined that "there are few things in nature more nearly approaching the weird or terrifying than a thorough going blizzard when it is so dark." In the brilliance of summertime the Antarctic landscape was sharp and clear cut; the light was dazzling. In winter, by moonlight, it became "a soft pastel world," with night shadows that were never sharp but full of "graceful curves." "The whole snowscape," Gould wrote, becomes bathed with the most delicate and far reaching opalescent lights." And then there were the auroral lights.

Gould loved it all, declaring that he "should be sorry for anyone who could watch an Antarctic night in all its varied splendor and beauty ... and not realize that he had had full compensation for any privation or hardship it had cost him to come."

**

Among the forty-two men living largely shut in together in close quarters throughout that winter personal frictions inevitably emerged. Later in life Gould noted, with reference to his Antarctic winter, that the way another man "butters his bread, or parts his hair, or eats his soup" can "drive you up the wall" when you're living "[as} the Irishman says 'contagious.'" To such frictions Little America was not immune. Experienced explorers had warned Byrd that no time would pose more difficulties for morale than the heart of winter, and the experience of the first Byrd Antarctic Expedition did not disconfirm the dangers. Personalities did clash; nerves were tested; some individuals struggled with depression. A falling out between veteran dog handler Arthur Walden and young driver Norman Vaughan apparently grew so serious that Vaughan began to fear a murderous attack. Pranks and practical jokes may have functioned in camp, as has been suggested, as safety valves for the hostilities engendered by winter living, but these, along with personally directed verbal wisecracking, sometimes had a sharp edge to them that may also have increased resentments in those who were the frequent butts of sometimes cruel humor.

A great deal might be, and has been, written about the complex personality and character of Richard Byrd. Somewhat reserved and formal, often ill at ease in his attempts to mix with his men though capable of great generosity toward them, prone to brood, frequently suspicious of others and obsessed with questions of potential disloyalty, a man apparently motivated throughout his life by tremendous insecurity and, despite his accomplishments, deep-seated feelings of inferiority, Byrd's psychic makeup was perhaps not ideally suited for managing the group psychological strains of a polar winter. He was, however, fortunate in having chosen a second-in-command who managed without difficulty the trick of maintaining both a high level of popularity and universal respect and whose mental equilibrium and wry sense of humor were assets to the entire ice-bound community. A number of Little Americans gave Gould significant credit for helping to hold the expedition together over the winter, and Eugene Rodgers, the author of the most comprehensive historical study of the expedition, agreed, writing that Gould "kept morale high and maintained a sense of group purpose under circumstances that had torn apart less well managed expeditions."

**

For the Fourth of July Little America cut loose with another very wet celebration. Festivities featured a comic show, "Midnight Follies of the Antarctic," which had been rehearsed in secret and for which the audience was given five-page programs interspersing information about the various numbers with joke "advertisements." The show mixed vaudeville-style skits with what Gould described as "a curious combination of musical comedy chorus and Negro minstrels." The chorus line was made as attractively feminine as possible, with wigs made of rope and gowns made of towels, but its members had not, Gould reported, "been selected for any particular vocal ability." The "minstrels" were Norm Vaughan as "Interlocutor" with Jack O'Brien and Mike Thorne as end men. Most of the show's humor was local, referencing expedition events or the personal foibles of expedition members, and by all accounts had the audience howling with laughter.

An all-out party then followed, with ensuing drunkenness that was not only sanctioned but also shared in and led by Byrd. When Gould and some others eventually had to pick Byrd up and help him to his room, the commander apparently became somewhat abashed over his fall from sobriety. "Don't tell Simon about this," he pled, seemingly unaware in his intoxication as to just who it was who was holding him up. As the group put him on his bed, Byrd further urged them above all not to let Igloo know—Igloo being the name of the commander's pet Boston Terrier that had accompanied them to Antarctica and was a sort of expedition mascot.*

This was a bitterly cold night, 60 degrees below zero, and Gould, fearing that an inebriate who got out of doors might freeze to death, stayed sober and patrolled between the houses until 3: 30 in the morning. Before reaching his bed at that hour he intervened to break up two fights.

Gould was observing that winter how different some men became from their usual selves when they got "tight." Aerial photographer Ashley McKinley, for instance, was normally as mild and loveable a person as Gould knew, but liquor made him meanly belligerent. More than fifty years after the Byrd Expedition, Gould recalled how at one of the winter parties both McKinley and supply officer George Black had had too much to drink. "Blackie," Gould remembered, walked up to McKinley and put his arms around him affectionately. "'Oh, Mac,' he said, 'You're wonderful—you're wonderful, everybody loves you.' Mac backed up and socked him in the jaw and said, 'I'm tired of being loved; I want to be a son of a bitch!'"

July now mirrored May, in that licensed celebration was again followed within a few days by a series of unsanctioned after-hours drinking parties. Byrd asked that these stop, and the result when they did not was that Byrd proclaimed a general curfew, whereby everyone after 10 p.m. was to be in either his bed or the library. Though this was the first time on the expedition that there had been any overt confrontation over discipline, there is no mention whatever of this matter in Gould's diary.

Despite the strains, overall morale seems to have been good that July, as

---

* The much publicized Igloo was lionized, if that may appropriately be said of a dog, by the media, featured prominently in the widely viewed Paramount film about the expedition released after their return, and was the darling of the public during Byrd's post-expedition lecture tours. In 1981, Gould described Igloo as "a pest of hell." He was so disliked by the community, Gould recalled, that some members used to feed him candy-like lozenges that they supposed would make him sick.

the expedition was over the "hump" of midwinter and the long night began to brighten perceptibly day by day. A spirited bit of entertainment was got up on Sunday the 14th, as members of the camp "arrested" Taffy Davies, arraigned him on a variety of humorous charges, and staged a mock trial. Donning a pair of protruding glasses and a long wig of white cotton, Gould was the judge. O'Brien and Black were prosecutors, and a three-man team provided defense counsel for the accused, pilot Dean Smith making a plea for his client that "would have caused the sphinx to smile."

Planning and preparation for the two major trips of the season ahead—Byrd's polar flight and Gould's overland geological trek—had gone into high gear, and those most involved had plenty to do. Over nearly a three-week period at the end of July and the beginning of August, Gould wrote in his diary but once, noting that he had been sleeping during the day and working at night assisting McKinley at photographic tasks, making a standard set of negatives for the *New York Times*, Byrd, and others. Late in July came some of the coldest temperatures that the expedition would experience, bottoming out on the 28th at 72 below. Gould wrote of shivering awake to find his pillow encrusted with ice where his breath had condensed on it. The coldest day was closely followed by several of the blowingest, including the highest wind velocity recorded at Little America during their stay, 75 miles per hour for a minute on the 30th.

"There is an increasingly genial attitude of the various men toward each other," Gould wrote on August 9. The sun was then within two weeks of topping their northern horizon, and each day brought significantly more light than the one before. "It is good," Gould declared. "It is worth spending a long winter night here just to watch the miracle of the returning sun." Camp was increasingly astir with activity. Gould was kept busy now overseeing dog operations, in advance of leading a sledge party, and with mapmaking necessary to the summer program. That day, he noted, he "finished the chart which Commander Byrd will use on the actual polar flight."

On August 19, Little America spotted what Byrd called Antarctica's equivalent to the first robin of spring—a Weddell seal poking its brown head through thin ice over a blow hole. A day later, fresh seal steak was served at dinner.

The theater of the sky was filled then with harbingers of the sun's imminent return. Gould wrote that "again the very atmosphere ... is suffused with those soft impalpable colors that were such a delight during the fall days when the sun was leaving us." "It is not difficult for us to understand," he added, "how man could worship the sun." On the 20th, Byrd and several other men climbed atop one of Little America's tall radio towers to catch a first glimpse of the topmost crest of the returning presence.

Official sunrise in Little America arrived on August 22—satisfactorily co-inciding, for purposes of celebration, with Larry Gould's thirty-third birthday. The long-awaited orb was greeted with a bugle call to arms played on the camp Victrola. American, Norwegian, and British flags were raised in a chilly windy-day ceremony before which all uncovered. Joyful celebration was the natural order of the day, and the conjunction with Gould's birthday doubled the occasion for merrymaking. Evening festivities commenced with a dinner at which Byrd, as master of ceremonies, presented his second-in-command with a certificate of appreciation and affection signed by every man of the winter party, illustrated colorfully with scenes of Antarctic life skillfully drawn by the omnicompetent Bernt Balchen. As with previous celebrations, the party was allowed to become, in Gould's words, "plenty wet." Diarist Henry Harrison recorded that Byrd gave an after-dinner performance "rigged up as a perfect dollar waterfront whore, and his takeoff nearly started a riot." In the course of the evening a football game was started inside the crowded mess hall, referenced later in the meteorological department's report that "A mild tornado struck the mess hall on the night of August 22nd-23rd and left a trail of wreckage in its wake." On this occasion, it must be admitted, Gould "was the first to pass out and be carried to his bunk."

In the by-now-probably-predictable aftermath to this celebration, the camp was again "stuck for the next two weeks with the problem of expedition members who would not stop partying after the party was over." Pete Demas, who earlier in the winter had volunteered to become regular night watchman, noted in his diary at the end of August that "those few who drink to excess have been taking advantage of the commander's good nature of overlooking a lot of things. ... The commander and all the rest are thoroughly disgusted with it." Early in September Gould summoned the small group of chronic offenders to the library and sternly lectured them on their responsibilities to the expedition. "Larry gave the boys quite a talk," Demas recorded, "which the commander seconded. [Gould] commanded them to stop drinking. If anyone drinks again without permission he will be sent back as a passenger." Demas appealed to them for cooperation as well, and these talks seem to have worked. Assurances of temperance reform were both given and, this time, kept.

The month of September proved to be a cold one, despite the return of the sun—it was in fact the only month of their entire stay in Antarctica in which the temperature never once reached so high as zero, and temperatures of 60 below and colder were frequent. Nevertheless, as the sun climbed higher and higher in the sky, there was a great deal to be done getting ready for summer undertakings, and Little America became more and more abuzz with busyness and activity. Indoor winter routines were sloughed off, new schedules implemented, and much of the working life of the community was moving back outdoors.

Most of Gould's attention now was focused on getting dogs, men, and material ready for his geological party's long southward sledge to the Queen Maud Mountains. Skiing practice was necessary, for it was "of paramount importance" that the six men be able to ski along with the dog teams, whose loads were to be heavy enough with food and equipment. The older dogs who had been idle all winter required training to be fit for the trail, and the new pups, born in camp since the previous summer, needed to be broken in before being used for the first time in teams. Maps and charts were required. Gould's written report to

Climbing the radio tower on August 22 to hail the return of the sun

Byrd detailing the plans of the Geological Party needed completing. Equipment needed testing. "There are accumulating so many details that must be gotten out of the way before we start our sledging journey," Gould wrote, "that I now find it necessary to write everything down and check off a number of items each day that must be taken care of."

With all in camp looking ahead with eagerness to their various summer missions, days flew past on "the wings of expectancy." Near the end of September, at the close of "another busy day getting ready for the long trek ahead," Gould observed that a pink glow now illuminated the southern rim of the darkened sky throughout the night. "Not long now," he anticipated, "until we shall have a midnight sun and then light—light, light—blinding, dazzling light for weeks and months on end."

CHAPTER 9

THE TRAIL SOUTH

On the 11th [of November, 1911] we made the interesting discovery that the Ross Barrier ended in an elevation on the south-east, formed between a chain of mountains running south-eastward from South Victoria Land and another chain on the opposite side, which runs south-westward in continuation of King Edward VII Land. ... We gave the name of "Queen Maud's Mountains" to the whole range of these newly discovered mountains, about 530 miles in length.—Roald Amundsen (first account, March 8, 1912)

Unseen, the mountains were there. For eons, they were silently there, across all of human history and prehistory and for long ages before. In human terms they had *always* been there, though in the immense span of geological time they did have a birth, millions of years before having a name. In recent millennia, while the busy race of man lived a tumultuous history in lands to the north, while successive civilizations and empires arose and disappeared in turn, the frozen world of these windswept, snow-clad peaks abided throughout, undisturbed in unknown solitude.

The first human eyes to look upon the icy majesty of these mountains belonged to men intent on approaching the southern pole of the Earth's rotation. The nearest to the South Pole that a ship could sail, and therefore a logical locale from which to begin a trek to its vicinity, lay in the Ross Sea region of the Antarctic coast. The Ross Sea was capped, between 77° and 78° S, by the great shelf of permanent sea ice then known as the Barrier, which blocked any further passage south by ship. Nobody knew at the beginning of the twentieth century how far south toward the pole the ice sheets stretched from the Barrier edge. And nobody knew that interposed between the head of the ice shelf and the polar plateau stretched a great and lofty chain of yet unseen mountains.

In 1908, the English explorer Ernest Shackleton and three companions headed south from McMurdo Sound on the northwest edge of the Ross Barrier. Traveling along the ice shelf on a course largely parallel to the north-south-running mountains of Victoria Land on their right, Shackleton's party eventually found

Crossing crevasses: no picnic even before the addition of hundreds of pounds of supplies and gear [OSUA-BP]

the chain swinging eastward and across their path to the south. Their way would have been entirely blocked save for the discovery of a huge glacier, the Beardmore, which proved a passable highway between peaks and a feasible means of reaching the polar plateau. Shackleton toiled up the glacier and pushed on to within ninety-seven miles of the South Pole before being forced either to turn back or to perish. He turned back. (Among the most familiar of Antarctic quotations is Shackleton's explanation to his wife, Emily: "I thought, dear, that you would rather have a live donkey than a dead lion.") From the Beardmore Glacier, centered at about 84° S, Shackleton and his men observed further elevations stretching off to the southeast.

Three years later, two expeditions, one British and one Norwegian, reached for the pole from bases at different points along the Ross Barrier. The ill-fated British party of Captain Robert F. Scott (successful in reaching the pole but destined to die in an ice shelf blizzard during the return journey) followed Shackleton's route from McMurdo Sound up the Beardmore Glacier. The Norwegians, led by Roald Amundsen, jumped off from the Bay of Whales, much farther east along the Barrier. When Amundsen, his four companions, and their dog teams reached the head of the Ross shelf ice on their eastern path, they found before them a towering range of peaks, evidently a continuation of the chain observed farther west by Shackleton, which they were pleased to name for Norway's Queen Maud. (The Queen Maud Range forms the land connection between Victoria Land, named for Maud's grandmother, on the western side of the Ross Sea and King Edward

VII Land, bordering the eastern Ross Sea, which is named for Maud's father.) Amundsen's party traversed the mountains to reach the polar plateau—and then, a month ahead of Scott, their South Pole goal—by ascending what they named the Axel Heiberg Glacier near the center of the range. After Amundsen's party returned safely to make their report, the Queen Maud Mountains, the world's southernmost major range, were unknown no more.

They remained, however, *little* known. Prior to 1929, only five men had seen their central portion, and a few others had glimpsed their western extremity. None of these men were geologists. While Scott's scientifically oriented *Terra Nova* expedition of 1910-12 had included three geologists (the Australians Frank Debenham and T. Griffith Taylor, as well as Raymond E. Priestley, who had also been with Shackleton on the 1907-09 *Nimrod* expedition), none of these men had been included in the southern party headed deep into the Antarctic interior. In 1928, in anticipation of the departure of the scientifically ambitious Byrd Expedition, the American Geographical Society issued a special publication on *Problems in Polar Research* with a section by Raymond Priestley and C. E. Tilley titled "Geological Problems of Antarctica." Therein, noting that, apart from a traverse to the south magnetic pole and a western probe from McMurdo Sound during Scott's 1903 expedition, direct observation of the interior had so far been limited to "the immediate vicinity of the converging lines of the Shackleton, Scott, and Amundsen routes to the pole," Priestley and Tilley declared that "at best, our present knowledge of the continent is not sufficient to provide more than the barest outline of its geological and paleontological history and the barest hint of its geological constitution." With regard to the Queen Maud Range, Priestley and Tilley regretted that Amundsen had neglected to make "at least a general survey of the geology of that most interesting portion of Antarctica it was his good fortune and privilege to discover and traverse" and that the only specimens collected were a few pieces of granite, mica schist, and other rock from the outcrop of Mt. Betty. "From the photographic evidence of Mt. Fridtjof Nansen," they wrote of the major peak adjoining the Axel Heiberg Glacier, "and our knowledge of the structure of the coterminous Beardmore Glacier mountains it is a reasonable conjecture that the summit of this mountain is partly composed of Beacon sandstone, but there is unfortunately no direct evidence of this."

When, then, in 1929 Larry Gould led a sledging party to the Queen Maud Range, he did so as the first geologist, from any country, to penetrate to those mountains and examine their structure or indeed to go so far south on the globe at all.* (85° 27' S was the Gould Geological Party's farthest south.) When Gould and his companions proceeded to chart the range to the east of where Amundsen

---

* Years later Gould liked to recommend to others this recipe for fame, though it had largely ceased to be possible: "Find out some place where no one else has ever been, go there, look at as many things as you can, come back and write a lot of things about it and get a reputation before anybody can check up on you!"

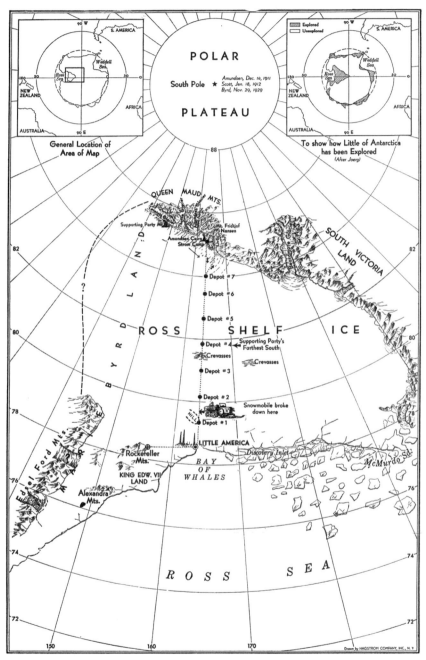

Reprinted from *Cold: The Record of an Antarctic Sledge Journey*

had traveled and where Byrd had meanwhile flown, they enjoyed the exceedingly rare sensation of knowing they were the first human beings ever to lay eyes on that part of the world. They were truly explorers.

***

The composition of the geological sledging party had been finalized over the winter. Gould was to be accompanied by five men and fifty-four dogs. The men—dog drivers all— would be George "Mike" Thorne, Jack O'Brien, and a trio of friends from Harvard who had early come to be known in newspaper coverage of the expedition as the Three Musketeers—Norman Vaughan, Eddie Goodale, and Freddy Crockett. Thorne, a Yale graduate from a well-to-do family—his grandfather owned the Montgomery Ward company—would also act as topographer. O'Brien, whose previous experiences included prospecting in Mexico and Canada, took on the role of surveyor. Vaughan was in overall charge of the dogs, and Crockett was made radio operator. Gould, in addition to geologist and overall group leader, would also be navigator and cook.

Their arduous journey had multiple aims. Part of their mission was in support of Byrd's flight to the pole. By advancing far to the south ahead of Byrd, Gould could radio weather reports to Little America that might be crucial to successful timing of the flight attempt. The sledging party would establish a base at the foot of the Queen Maud Mountains that Byrd could stock with gasoline and oil for refueling. Then, in the event of aerial misadventure, Gould's men and cached supplies could be turned to emergency relief. Their other objectives were scientific: to conduct geological and glaciological studies in the Queen Mauds and other highlands and to extend geographical knowledge of the area traversed. Specifically, Gould proposed doing three things after completion of the polar flight. First, to ascend Mt. Fridtjof Nansen in order to get a cross-section of the range. Next, to proceed eastward from the Axel Heiberg Glacier as far as the junction with Amundsen's reported Carmen Land. This Gould viewed as particularly intriguing, for Amundsen had plotted Carmen Land as highlands running at near right-angles to the main Queen Maud trend, a "curious and unnatural-seeming relationship" that would if confirmed be virtually unique. Third, to detour eastward between latitudes 81° and 82° on their return journey to investigate other unnamed highlands reported by Amundsen as existing in that vicinity.

Ninety days were deemed sufficient to carry out this program—allowing a 20 percent safety factor for bad weather delays—and so all calculations involving supplies and schedules were based upon a projected three-month journey. The logistical planning was extensive and detailed, with careful attention demanded by every aspect of the undertaking: man food, dog food, clothing, tents, sleeping bags, skis, sledges, safety precautions, and much else, all needing to be balanced against considerations of total weight. Much had been worked out over the winter, but as daylight lengthened in Little America and the anticipated season of adventure drew near, Gould faced a multitude of practical concerns in preparation for the trail.

Gould's six-man Geological Party was to be assisted in the first stage of its approach to the Queen Maud range by a four-man supporting party led by veteran dog-handler Arthur Walden. The Supporting Party, driving twenty-seven dogs, would begin the work by hauling a great load of supplies some two hundred miles south from Little America over what Amundsen had found to be a dangerously crevassed region, breaking trail and establishing carefully marked depots of food and fuel every fifty miles along the route later to be used both by the Geological Party and Byrd's polar flight. This would enable Gould's group to then speed relatively quickly over that difficult first leg of their longer journey, traveling more lightly than would otherwise have been necessary. October 7 was targeted as the Supporting Party's date of departure. As a dry run for themselves, Gould and most of the rest of the Geological Party planned to accompany Walden's Supporting Party with their own dog teams for about the first two days or at least as far as the twenty-mile depot that had been laid down the season before. They then expected to return to base before taking their final departure after another four or five days of making ready.

As trail time neared, Gould's personal preparations included his first clean shave since leaving New Zealand; he had found that the rime and frost that gathered in his beard and mustache during skiing practice was a great nuisance. He also contemplated trimming back his eyelashes a bit to prevent their freezing together in thick snow.

All Antarctic travel plans, however, are ultimately contingent upon the weather. As October 7 approached, it was clear that it simply remained too cold to take to the trail as scheduled. On the 4th, with a reading of 55 degrees below zero, Gould likened the behavior of snow at such temperatures to loose sand on a beach, noting that "there is no use attempting to travel when it is so cold. It is fearfully hard on the dogs and the sledges drag as though they were made of lead." Another problem emerged when dog food was being loaded into one of the large canvas sledge tanks to be used for supplies and the fabric tore. Finding that an orange dye had rotted the canvas, Gould was disquieted by the realization that all ten tanks would likely need repair and adjustments before the containers could be relied upon. Departure was retargeted for the morning of the 10th, and then, following more adverse weather and a few days of illness for Gould, who was "off his feed," for the 13th. A blizzard on the 12th was accompanied by an encouraging rise in temperature, but when the storm cleared the forbidding cold came right back. On the morning of the 13th it was bright and fair, but 34 below. Knowing how difficult it was for the dogs to pull heavily loaded sledges at temperatures lower than about -20 and himself still feeling "a bit queer amidships," Gould again postponed departure.

Repeated delay was vexing for all involved, but by this time Byrd's own frustration over the failure to get the southern parties started had apparently grown acute. Byrd called the sledge parties to a conference in the camp library, where he urged an immediate start of some kind despite the cold. Gould gave no account of this meeting in either book or diary, but there is evidence that it was strained. Byrd refused a suggestion that the idle planes be used to ease the dog teams' depot-laying burden. Meteorologist Henry Harrison, who was not present, wrote that night that it was "an unsatisfactory session," and a later historian of the expedition termed it "clearly acrimonious." The ultimate result was an afternoon sortie to haul and deposit some of the loads several miles south over the bay ice as a head start on the longer journeys. According to Harrison's diary, most of the drivers agreed with Gould that nothing would be gained by this effort, but several were persuaded to try, and there was a "hectic confused takeoff at one o'clock." Though Gould did not accompany this group, Byrd did. After four exhausting hours seven miles had been gained. The loads were then dropped, and a bone-weary party returned to camp on empty sledges with tired dogs and a certain amount of frostbite. At a second conference that night, Byrd vindicated Gould's original judgment by agreeing that the parties must wait for warmer weather, not lower than 20 below, to move again.

The next day did not reach that mark but moved decidedly in the right direction, rising from 47 below early in the morning to minus 21 later in the day. (This was close to the warmest Little America had yet recorded that October, though it was also within a degree of the *coldest* temperature experienced by Amundsen during the same month eighteen years before. When Amundsen left for the pole in mid-October 1911, the temperature at Framheim was a degree Fahrenheit above zero.) As conditions improved in the afternoon, O'Brien, who had not accompanied the group the previous day, decided to drive his front sledge load across to the head of the bay as well, so as not to hold up the others when the parties did finally leave. Gould accompanied O'Brien, as did Doc Coman. "Came home pretty cold," Gould scrawled into his diary that night. He then added: "It would be pretty miserable out on the trail in this severe weather but I guess we may start in the morning."

The combined parties, driving eight teams of dogs, finally left camp around noon the next day. The Geological Party drove four of the teams, as Crockett stayed behind for this venture, and Gould did not drive his own dogs but only skied along. They were accompanied also by Carl Peterson, to assist with radio operations, and cameraman Joe Rucker, who was shooting film. Gould's men left with light loads, as when they reached the head of the bay they would add on the supplies that had been left there earlier. Byrd and a number of other Little Americans came along that far as an escort to see them off. What followed, after the heavy loads deposited before had been picked up, was discouraging. As they struggled that day to advance their sledge loads a little farther—achieving only about eight miles before making a cold camp in temperatures that had fallen back to 30 degrees below zero—the heartbreaking truth was slowly borne in on them that, at least in these conditions, the dog power they possessed was insufficient to match the weight being carried. At every tiny rise in the snow, even of only a few inches, the men had to push on the sledges to help the dogs drag them across.

A second day of hard pulling brought the sledgers to their twenty-mile depot but piteously tired the huskies and further discouraged the men. It had, Gould admitted, become "evident beyond any question" that they should have to revise their plans. Gould was now bruised in body as well as spirit, for in the course of the day he had fallen in his skis on the hard-crusted snow beside Thorne's sledge just as the dogs were starting to pull. The dogs not only ran over Gould themselves but also dragged a heavily loaded front sledge across his arms and then the lighter rear sledge over his legs. Moreover, the party's cooker-stove had failed due to some undetected leak. Gould radioed Byrd that the Geological Party teams would return to camp the next day to work out significant changes of plan before proceeding farther. Byrd, who wanted the Geological Party to go on with the Supporting Party as far as a hundred miles south, urged Gould to reconsider and to make new plans where he was, with help by radio, but he recognized that Gould's was the judgment on the spot and declined to make his strong suggestion into an order. Gould returned. "Frightfully tired," he recorded that night. "Tomorrow we shall discuss other means of completing our mission."

What Gould wanted was air support. He hoped to persuade Byrd to allow the use of the Fairchild aircraft, the present mission of which was simply to stand by as emergency backup to the Ford, to fly supply loads south to the mountains or at least to a depot point along the trail. Recent experience had shown that the Geological Party program as planned could not be carried out without lightened loads for the sledges. Moreover, if their mission was to be accomplished with dogs and sledges alone, there was no way around the unhappy necessity of sacrificing dogs along the way,* but Gould held out the hope that more of the huskies might be spared killing if Byrd would only agree to drop a sufficient supply of dog food at a southern depot by plane.

Byrd, however, was not willing to do anything that might jeopardize the

---

* In his book *Cold*, Gould gave a clear explanation of this grim imperative. To have brought all the dogs back alive from so long a journey using dog power alone would have required hauling a weight of dog food and other supplies greatly in excess of what the dogs could pull at one time and could be done only by hauling a part ahead and then returning for the remainder— making three trips in all over the same ground and requiring much larger quantities of food, supplies, and time. The alternative, as Gould explained, was to make good one's journey "by sacrificing the weakest dogs as one proceeds." Noting that huskies would eat the carcasses of their own kind if fed to them, Gould explained that killing dogs en route both greatly reduced the amount of dog food that needed to be taken in the first place and greatly augmented the food supply on hand. Gould estimated that they would have needed to carry an additional three thousand pounds of dog food to have made their trip without canine sacrifice and that this would have required trail time at least half again as long as they had available. "There was not even a possibility of succeeding by this method," he wrote. "We had no alternative except to make our plans according to the second method."

flight to the pole, which from the standpoint of publicity was the whole crux of the expedition and the success of which was crucial to Byrd, financially and otherwise. The great risks of Antarctic aviation had already been borne in upon the commander with the loss of one plane, and at the conference convened the morning after Gould's return he insisted that the Geological Party revise their plans only in a way that did not depend upon aircraft. (Byrd later wrote in his own account of the expedition that he had secretly made up his mind to leave food by plane but that he did not want the Geological Party's plans to be based on it.)

Despite the refusal of a promise of air support, neither Gould nor Byrd wanted to reduce the scientific objectives of the Geological Party trek. Byrd did allow them to abandon their task of laying down a base at the foot of the mountains for use by the polar aviation unit, and he agreed to extend the time available to the Geological Party by promising to hold the *City of New York* in the Bay of Whales until February 10 and, if the party had not yet returned by then, to charter a Ross Sea whale chaser to stand by until as late as February 25 to take the party out before the bay froze over for another season. Furthermore, the expedition's primitive Ford snowmobile was to be promptly dug out and an experiment made to see whether it might not be useful in assisting with moving supplies on the early stages of the trail.

Two days later (October 20), five Geological Party teams started south again with the goal of picking up heavy loads left at the twenty-mile depot and advancing them to Depot No. 2, some one hundred miles from Little America, then returning for a brief rest and overhaul before making their final start for the mountains. Gould placed Norman Vaughan in charge of this trip and remained behind himself to attend to equipment improvements suggested by their recent experience.

Vaughan's depot-laying party returned on the 28th, having radioed reports over their eight-day absence that were sometimes encouraging and sometimes distressing. A satisfactory first day had seen them make camp at the twenty-mile depot, where they retrieved the loads left there before. But subsequent reports told of plummeting temperatures (down to 40 below on the 21st) accompanied by contrary winds and drifting that made it difficult to see the flags that the Supporting Party had planted as trail marks. Struggling against such conditions, the group's progress was discouragingly slow. On the 23rd, Vaughan had radioed Gould that a number of the dogs were weakening and needed rest if they were to serve the party later and that "important deficiencies" had been found in their gear, with "much overhauling necessary." He strongly advised returning, saying that he could not guarantee to bring all the dogs back if they pushed beyond seventy-five miles south. Gould replied that it was hard to see how they were going to be able to do their final journey as planned if the teams could not reach the hundred-mile depot now. He suggested proceeding with lightened loads and perhaps taking a day or two of rest for the sake of the dogs. Vaughan left seven hundred and fifty pounds of dog food cached beside the trail and carried on, finally reaching

Depot No. 2 the evening of the 25th. Their return to camp, with near empty sledges and in better weather, was swiftly accomplished in three days despite the weakened condition of some of the dogs. Sixty-five miles from camp they met the snowmobile and its three-man crew, still going strong on their experimental journey and hoping to help out by moving loads from Depot No. 2 to No. 3.

While the rest of his geological team was away on this final preliminary trip, Gould allowed his bruises to heal and busied himself with preparations in camp. He also had a chance to investigate some local geological wonders. The 25th, for instance, which happened to be Byrd's forty-first birthday, was a brilliant day of dazzling sunshine—shining now both day and night. Gould spent that morning lashing a new canvas tank to one of the trail sledges, then went out with Doc Coman to photograph some nearby "haycock" formations. (These were curious conical mounds of ice and snow found in places where the Little America basin met the higher shelf ice about it.) Coman added a dash of excitement to the excursion by putting his foot through the thin roof of a covered crevasse and partially falling in. In so doing, he unintentionally opened to view a sight that Gould termed one of the most beautiful he had yet seen in the Antarctic or anywhere else. As Gould and Coman peered down into the hole left by Coman's foot, they beheld a "celestial room" of pale blue light that deepened away from the top into darker hues of sapphire and ultramarine. The crevasse was layered over with just enough snow to let only blue light filter through, and the walls were covered with a breathtaking array of ice crystals so fragile that they would crumble and fall at the least touch. Gould later likened the revealed room to a fairy palace. A few days later, Gould, Coman, Tom Mulroy, and Clair Alexander went over to the eastern edge of the basin where they used an explosive charge to blow the top off of one of the largest haycocks, exposing within another grotto similarly "lined with the most glorious multitude of ice crystals of most fragile thinness." Gould happily recovered and photographed some of the largest examples. Some of the men crawled into the haycock's interior tunnel and followed it "for about thirty feet, at which point it narrowed down, although it continued as far as they could see."

It was October 29—a date remembered elsewhere as Black Tuesday. All week long radio carried even to the isolated outpost of Little America disquieting bulletins from New York of plummeting stock prices and panicked investors. It would take time for the full scope of financial collapse and its rippling effects to become evident, but in fact that week's news from Wall Street was a warning that when the expedition returned home a few months hence, its members would be discharged into an economic climate vastly different from the one they had sailed out of eighteen months before.

Meanwhile, radio also kept camp apprised of the continuing effort of Walden's sledging party to complete their depot-laying mission in support of the upcoming journey of Gould's Geological Party. A communiqué on the 30th told of their struggle to traverse a "frightfully crevassed area" that had begun with blind covered chasms encountered without warning a little south of the 81st parallel.

The Supporting Party's goal was to establish Depot No. 4 about 220 miles south of Little America, but due south of Depot No. 3, it was reported, the treachery of conditions were beyond imagination. "Great upheavals have taken place here since Amundsen's time," read a subsequent message. "Nothing he describes can compare with it. It was a restless sleep for all last night, for every few hours we were awakened by thunder announcing the birth of a new crevasse and shaking the hollow snow beneath us." The party, however, groped their way through this fearsome area at last, tapping their way step by step across narrow ridges between open chasms and thinly covered crevasses, and, after laying their fourth depot on the 1st of November, they turned back toward camp, retracing with greater speed their now marked trail.

In Little America the November 1 temperature soared all the way to 6 above zero, which seemed "positively sultry." News that the Supporting Party had reached their goal was equally warming, and Gould now anticipated getting his own party away at last after two or three more days of final gear improvements and still needed canine recuperation. "We shall all," he recorded that evening, "be awfully glad to get under way and headed toward the mountains."

***

Gould, Vaughan, Crockett, Thorne, O'Brien, and Goodale left camp to begin their great adventure in the early afternoon of November 4. They drove forty-six dogs—in five teams, one fewer than originally planned. Each team pulled two sledges, the trailing ones being somewhat lighter than the leads. In addition to scientific field equipment and a minimal number of personal items for each individual, the things they carried, kept carefully to the lowest feasible total weight, included: camp gear including tents, fur sleeping bags, a large vacuum jug, and a two-burner primus stove with fuel; ropes and material for making repairs; trail flags; a motion picture camera and two still cameras, with film for each; and a radio receiver and transmitter with hand generator. They hauled—or would be recovering at depots already laid down—pemmican dog food designed for the expedition by a New Zealand chemist. Three months' daily rations for the humans were provided by pemmican, biscuits, sugar, powdered milk, oatmeal, erbswurst, chocolate, tea,* and salt. To add variety as occasional delicacies, they also brought smaller supplies of butter, peanut butter, bacon, cocoa, and malted milk. For entertainment, they had playing cards and each man one book. (Gould's choice was a thin-paper, one-volume complete Shakespeare.)

---

* Nineteen years later, when asked his opinion about the relative merits of tea and coffee, Gould wrote the following: "Tea, not coffee, is the real man's drink. I have never known a polar explorer worth his salt who did not prefer tea to coffee. Admiral Peary marched to the North Pole drinking tea; Amundsen, Scott, Shackleton, Nansen have all found it a superior drink to coffee. Top notch men in the medical school at Harvard assured me before the Byrd Expedition that it was a better stimulant. I do not wish you, therefore, to have any illusions about my devotion to tea. Having said all of that, I am glad to record for your satisfaction and for the record of truth that I greatly prefer coffee."

When the Geological Party set off, two other groups of Little Americans were still somewhere to their south—the Supporting Party, on the trail back to camp but still several days' journey away, and the three snowmobilers, last seen by the Vaughan-led Geological Party during the earlier return from Depot No. 2—at that time still resolutely moving south but unheard from since. (The snowmobile party carried no radio.) The mystery of the snowmobilers' location was cleared up on the Geological Party's first day out, when Gould's group met the trio on the shelf ice some fifteen miles from Little America. The experimental snowmobile had broken down shortly after crossing paths with Vaughan's party the previous week and was abandoned approximately seventy-five miles out, leaving the threesome with a long walk back to camp, man-hauling tents, sleeping bags, and food on a small sledge. The news was radioed back to Little America that evening from the Geological Party's own camp at the twenty-mile depot.

For some days sledging would be relatively easy, as their heavy loads had already been advanced the first hundred miles by the previous effort. Temperatures stayed a comfortable few degrees above zero. The morning of November 6, some forty-four miles south of Little America, they reached the cache designated Depot No. 1 for that summer's sledging work. When they made camp that night they were sixty miles out. The next morning they met the northbound Supporting Party, which had broken trail for them as far as Depot No. 4, 220 miles out. Walden's crew warned Gould and his men once again about the great dangers and difficulties of the badly crevassed area lying south of Depot No. 3. A short time after this meeting they arrived at the abandoned snowmobile, where they salvaged some supplies, cached others, and had lunch. On the 8th, they reached Depot No. 2, where they took up their full loads for the journey to the mountains. Now the sledging would become tougher, with the dogs pulling much heavier loads and the men having to take entirely to their skis rather than adding their own weight any longer to the dog-pulled sledges. "For some of us amateurs that spells pretty hard work," Gould wrote into his trip log that evening, "but necessary if we are to see Mt. Nansen within the next month."

For the skiing amateur Gould, this was indeed hard work. "How many times I fell down and in what curious positions I arrived on the snow can hardly be described," he wrote on the 10th. The dogs were pulling well and maintaining their pep, but among the men, O'Brien and Thorne had begun to suffer somewhat from snow blindness and Gould, the unaccustomed skier, from a developing blister on one heel. Years later Norman Vaughan remembered Gould as trying to shrug off his pain and allowing Vaughan to take a look at its source only with reluctance:

> The blister, the size of a half-dollar, had broken open and was weeping. Although in intense pain, Gould kept insisting it would get better. The spot couldn't possibly get better as long as he permitted it to keep rubbing. After applying a liberal amount of antiseptic salve around the blister, I formed a doughnut-shaped pad from the left innersole of one of my boots.

After ensuring that the hole was big enough for air to get to the blister, I made the pad double thick, about one-quarter inch. Putting his foot into his boot the next day was difficult because of the thick spot around his heel, but Larry did get it on eventually. More than a week elapsed before he could walk and ski without great discomfort.

By refusing to complain or to hint that he might ride on a sledge until his blister healed, though that would have been acceptable to his companions, Gould set an example of toughness that Vaughan credited with inspiring the whole party.*

A heavy hoar frost on the night of the 12th made sledges and skis drag the next day, which also turned bitter cold, but despite frozen fingers and cheeks and generally slow going, late in the day the party reached Depot No. 3. Here, in preparation for crossing the badly crevassed area they had been warned about, they rearranged teams in order to rope themselves together in two lashed units. On the 15th they succeeded in bringing themselves over and around the crevasses without any greater mishap than one dog breaking his trace and lead line while falling in, but managing to pull himself out again. Though they worked their way through safely, they often held their breath passing over snow bridges between chasms on either side. Once a roof collapsed just as the last sledge had crossed, opening to view an eight-foot-wide chasm "so deep that the blueness of its depths seemed quite black."

By following the trail marked earlier by the Supporting Party, their experience in getting through was, all in all, milder than they had expected. Another two days of travel brought them to Depot No. 4 and the end of following where the Supporting Party had already gone. Here they were to take on another five hundred pounds of dog food, giving them for a time the heaviest loads to be hauled of the entire trip. (They carried now the wherewithal to lay down four more planned depots.) The six men had traveled half their distance to the mountains, but from this point forward, every mile traversed was new territory to navigate and new trail to be broken and marked.

The effect of added weight was quickly apparent the next day as men and dogs together strained to advance. "Disheartening and dreary" was how Gould remembered that day's struggle.

I tried to beguile myself with the thought that it was an exceptional day

---

* Though blistered in heel, Gould did receive a salve for his spirit at about this time, when news was relayed from camp to sledge party of the result of the Michigan-Harvard football game played November 9. Outnumbered three to one on the trail by Harvard men, who Gould later recalled as boasting repeatedly about their alma mater's gridiron prowess that year, Gould received word of the final score—Michigan 14, Harvard 12—with glee. He later recalled with satisfaction that he heard no more about the superiority of the Harvard team for the rest of the trip.

and that the soft snow surface could not continue much farther. Mike had relieved his team by carrying fifty pounds of dog food on his back; Norman had carried his heavy pack and the rest of us had tugged away at ropes attached to the sledges in vain attempts to help the dogs along, yet our combined efforts for the whole day brought us only 9 miles nearer the mountains than we had been in the morning.

Now that they were no longer following a pre-marked trail, they adopted an altered order of march. Thorne skied in front, with his own team following in his tracks. Gould skied beside Thorne's front sledge, from which he could keep an eye on the attached boat compass and make certain they stayed on course moving south. Goodale began planting new trail marker flags at half-mile intervals, for reference on their return trip.

About noon that day, they were overflown by Byrd in the *Floyd Bennett*, piloted by Dean Smith, en route to establish a fuel and supply depot at the foot of the mountains for the upcoming polar flight attempt. Shortly after passing over the "frightful mess" of the crevassed area and catching sight of the "crumbled dome" of Depot No. 4, the men in the plane glimpsed far below them the five teams of the Geological Party toiling up a long, rolling rise in the Barrier. Bringing the aircraft down toward the sledging party in a long, curving glide, the airmen could see men in harness, pulling with the dogs, and evidently having a hard time keeping the sledges moving. "The poor devils," Byrd wrote. "If ever a conclusive contrast was struck between the new and the old methods of polar travelling, it was then." The plane dropped a packet of letters for the toilers below, attached to a small parachute, and continued on its way—they were, as Gould would note later, "covering in about four hours a distance which it was to take us four weeks to cover."

One thought that heartened Gould and his companions as the *Floyd Bennett* passed overhead was that the plane likely would be landing dog food and other supplies for the Geological Party's use when they reached the mountains. Once it was confirmed that this was done, the excessive loads that they were currently struggling to move could safely be lightened where they were. Even better, a good supply of dog food left for them up ahead could mean a stay of execution for many of their faithful huskies, who under the harsh plan for self-sufficiency the party would otherwise be compelled to follow would soon have to start being sacrificed. When Gould next radioed camp, he asked Byrd, "Will you please tell me how much dog food you deposited for us?" Gould's message stated that several dogs would probably have to be killed within a few days and that present plans called for cutting all the way down to eighteen when they reached the mountains. "We like our dogs very much," Gould stressed, "and hope we won't have to kill so many."

Meanwhile, Byrd had not yet returned to Little America—the large plane had run low on fuel due to gas leaks and a malfunctioning carburetor and had been compelled to land eighty miles south of camp and wait for refueling by the smaller Fairchild plane. A few days passed before Byrd was able to send a reply to Gould's query about dog food dropped for the Geological Party. When the message did come, it was dismaying. Byrd had deposited no dog food on the recent flight, though the plane had left two hundred pounds of man food that the sledgers could use later if the polar flight went over without mishap. Byrd assured Gould that the aviation team would do all they possibly could for the Geological Party but that the whole thing was "so uncertain" that they "had better not depend on [air assistance] at all." This was very bad news—for the doomed huskies as well as for their unhappy executioners-to-be—and Gould was dryly understating its impact on the sledging party when he termed the communication one from which he and his companions "derived but little comfort."

On the morning of November 20, following another wearying day of struggle with the heavy loads through soft snow, Gould woke to prepare the group's usual oatmeal breakfast but found that the local weather had become "positively poison-ous." The wind had kicked up to 25 miles per hour and the temperature fallen to 20 below. Snow was blowing into fairly heavy drift. Considering that travel that day would be both exhausting and dangerous and that the hard-driven dogs in particular could benefit from a day of rest, Gould advised his men to return to their sleeping bags and spend the day in repose. The holiday seemed beneficial; Gould wrote later that from then on "things began to go better." Progress was satisfactory on the 21st, and on the 22nd they reached far enough to lay down Depot No. 5—the first to be established by themselves rather than by the Sup-porting Party. This was a meaningful milestone, for with this caching of supplies their loads would now be permanently lightened; the most physically grueling part of the long journey was behind them. At Depot No. 5 they left behind two heavy, rigid freight sledges, combining their cut loads onto the lighter flexible sledges that experience had taught them greatly to prefer.

It was at Depot No. 5 also that the party had to bow to necessity and shoot four dogs, no longer needed to pull, whose carcasses were then cached as food for those who would still be pulling on the return journey. Each member of the party had dreaded this moment. The carrying out of this terrible task was to have been shared among them all over the course of the trip, but in the end Vaughan, as head driver, volunteered to take the entire responsibility upon his own shoulders, and the others let him. Vaughan took four selected dogs behind a snow wall thrown up for the purpose. "The crack of the revolver as Norm shoots the dogs makes but a dull sound," Gould wrote, "yet I hate to hear it and try to keep myself as busy as possible at something else so as not to do so." Gould's satisfaction in knowing that they were drawing nearer the mountains was tempered by the knowledge that when they got there they must kill many more dogs, cutting down to no more than would be needed to bring them home.

From the crevassed area behind them to the mountains ahead, the surface they were now crossing was essentially flat and unbroken except by the rough snow ridges known as *sastrugi*. The normal trail day would begin with Gould rising about 6 a.m., to ready a hot oatmeal breakfast for everyone. If it were a day for meeting their radio schedule with Little America, they might not be underway until perhaps 9:30. After cutting down to four teams at Depot No. 5, O'Brien would drive the leading team with Gould skiing along beside, keeping an eye on the compass and occasionally shouting out directional corrections to Thorne, who skied out ahead. Around noon they would stop for a cold lunch, typically biscuits, pemmican, and chocolate, washed down with cold tea. Making camp hours later would begin with putting up tents and staking out and feeding the dogs, while Gould as cook would prepare the hot pemmican stew they called "hoosh" that was the usual foundation of supper.

In such a life, small amenities became large luxuries. Each member of the party carried one change of underwear. According to Vaughan, Gould forbade the men to change underclothes during their first three weeks on the trail, asserting that such was the way of explorers. But then, in Vaughan's account:

> At the end of the third week, Gould said to all of us one night, "Gentlemen, we've had a lovely dinner. We have a nice night. Tonight is the right time for all of us to change our underclothes."
>
> We made a grand party of the underwear-changing event, celebrating it as one of the high points of our first three weeks away from Little America. We put on our new set of underclothing and packed away our dirty underthings. What a grand feeling—as if I had just enjoyed a Saturday night bath. That change of clothes gave us such an uplift, we made five extra miles the next day.
>
> Everybody was happy, and we kept talking about how nice our bodies felt. We wore the second set exactly twice as long as the first. Then, at Gould's command, we put the first set back on, and they seemed clean by comparison. In that way, we had "clean" clothes for the whole trip.

Through twenty-one days of travel across the largely flat ice shelf surface the view ahead had been monotonously unchanging, but on the 25th of November the men were thrilled to be able to make out, far ahead on the horizon, their first sight of the mountain mass that was their goal. As a southerly haze that had partially obscured their view lifted, they could see clearly, though still at a great distance, a grand escarpment of snow-covered peaks. By 4 p.m. they could distinguish a large mountain almost dead ahead that they supposed must be Mt. Fridtjof Nansen. The next morning they completed the caching of food and supplies for Depot No. 6, and—though having to sacrifice another four dogs—pressed on toward the south with renewed eagerness to reach a destination still many miles distant but now in sight before them.

***

Meanwhile, back at Little America nerves were on edge and irascibility on the rise as the time neared to attempt the dramatic polar flight. Worried by the news that the Australian aviator Wilkins had just made a short flight from his own Antarctic base, Byrd determined that, with the Geological Party now close enough to the mountains to report on the weather there and to offer a possibility of rescue in the event of disaster, the attempt on the pole would be made just as soon as favorable conditions reported by Gould might coincide with an all-clear forecast in camp.

On Thanksgiving morning of November 28 perfect local weather and a steady barometer prompted Gould to radio Byrd that "this looks like the day." At the main camp it was neither so calm nor so clear as it was at Gould's position to the south, but expedition weatherman Haines nevertheless pronounced it good enough, and the sledgers were instructed to stand by in anticipation of the polar flight's departure later that afternoon. Enjoined from taking to the trail again until the flight was concluded, Gould decided that, although they were camped some fifteen miles shy of the planned location for caching Depot No. 7, they would use this waiting time to build that depot where they were, so that their stop would not be "a complete subtraction" from later traveling time.

At 3:29 p.m. the big Ford airplane, piloted by Bernt Balchen and also carrying Byrd as navigator, surveying photographer Ashley McKinley, and backup pilot Harold June manning the radio, took off on its historic flight. About four and a half hours later it overflew Gould and his men and dropped for them by parachute a bag containing some of McKinley's aerial photos from the previous flight to the Queen Maud Range, as well as messages including letters from Little America and radiograms for party members from friends in the United States. The plane then continued on toward a glacier pass from which to make its climb over the hump and onto the polar plateau; it soon disappeared from the Geological Party's view. The sledgers stayed in place until the dangerous flight was fully concluded—after it reached the pole vicinity and dropped flags there, refueled at the mountain base, and landed safely again at Little America on the morning of the 29th. Reported to the world by radio, the achievement commanded banner headlines everywhere.

While their expedition comrades were celebrating at Little America, Gould, his men, and their dogs ended their day of rest and returned to trail breaking, determined to reach within another two days the foot of the mountains which now looked so close. On the morning of the 30th the men, believing themselves from appearances now to be no more than about fifteen miles short of their goal, resolved that they would make the mountains that day "or bust." Bitter winds, "countless crevasses," and an actual distance to be covered of thirty-five miles, as it turned out, meant, as a weary and rueful Gould wrote into his journal that night, that "it came very near being the latter." After a certain point, having pushed into a region heavily crevassed, a "maze of chasms and cracks" with roof bridges that would sometimes hold them and sometimes collapse behind or about them as they hurried across, there was nowhere they could safely make camp, and going on became "an almost grim necessity." With great partially covered crevasses stretching diagonally across their course as far as they could see, they had no alternative but to continue to cross them. In places sagging snow and ice roofs had pulled away from chasm sides, exposing seemingly bottomless open spaces up to three or four feet wide. As Gould would later write:

> We were able to slide over these because of our long skis, but it was not so easy for the dogs. Individuals were always partially breaking through the thin roofs or falling in bodily to hang suspended in their harnesses until the forward surge of the team dragged them out.
>
> As we went on, the surface became more icy and slippery; it was increasingly difficult to manage ourselves on skis—and the crevasses were as large and close together as ever. Just as O'Brien and I cleared an especially big one the whole surface fell away behind us. Where we had crossed but a second earlier was now a yawning chasm, large enough to have swallowed our entire party.

Gould would term this region a "frozen inferno," but at last they came through it, leaving the shelf ice for land and finally stopping where they could safely make camp, only about a mile from the foothills of Liv Glacier. Dogs and men were both bone tired, the former falling in their tracks and into sleep "practically before they hit the snow," the latter deciding upon a hot supper before bed. "One of the boys," Gould would record, "with his spoon halfway to his mouth" was suddenly overcome by sleep, spattering the man beside him with hot hoosh as the bowl slipped from his fingers. "We were all just about as tired," Gould wrote, "but we had arrived. It was a moment for which we had been living. We were camped in the very shadow of our long sought mountains."

CHAPTER 10

"NO SYMPHONY I HAVE EVER HEARD ..."

Getting these six men to where they now were had been a tremendous and arduous logistical and physical undertaking. Now at last, however, could commence the scientific investigation that was the payoff to all of this effort, planning, and expense. They were a geological party; Gould was the geologist—at bottom all that had been done was done so that this one man, with his trained eye, could be brought to these mountains to look, and then report to the world's scientific community what it was that he saw.

Gould had begun to form some hypotheses about the structure and composition of the now visible Queen Maud Range even as the party was still some twenty miles distant and struggling through crevasses on their final approach. He noted that behind a series of ragged, angular peaks in the fore hills there towered a number of much larger flat-topped tabular mountains, including Mt. Fridtjof Nansen, that "immediately suggested horsts." These tabular masses exposed enough bare rock for Gould to observe they "were covered with great thicknesses of flat or nearly flat-lying rocks" that appeared to be sedimentary strata and which Gould was convinced would hold "the key to the geological story of it all." Their next challenge would be to find a means of ascending the range at some point where they could reach these flat-capped rocks.

Their first attempt, on the day following their arrival at the foot of Liv Glacier, was to climb directly up Liv in hopes of reaching an exposed mass near its head that was topped by the coveted flat-lying rocks. Eschewing their skis, Gould, Thorne, and O'Brien strapped crampons onto their boots, secured themselves to one another with ropes, and began an ascent. Gould found that the foothill rocks along the way were dark pre-Cambrian granites and gneisses, occasionally interrupted by light-colored veins of quartz, which were "examined in vain for minerals of any consequence." A mile or two up the glacier they found themselves amidst soft snow, which could dangerously mask the presence of buried crevasses. Indeed, an unsuspecting Gould had one too-thin roof collapse beneath him as he stepped and was fortunate to catch the far wall of the gap as he fell forward.

On the trail

"I turned," he wrote later, "and looked down the bare ice walls to the blue-black depths beyond which my vision failed." Though immensely deep, the crevasse was narrow enough to have been bridged safely by skis, and it became clear to the men that skis would be as important to their safe and efficient progress when climbing glaciers as they had been for weeks on the shelf ice and that it would be folly to attempt to continue their climb in soft snow without them. After a brief and futile attempt to make better progress on the glacier's other side, they gave it up and returned to camp.

All the while they had been climbing, the rocky mass that was their goal and which they had hoped to reach with ease in a few hours appeared to grow no closer. The next day by rough triangulation they found that their target was actually approximately twenty-one miles up the glacier. Mindful of numerous such instances of seriously underestimating distances gauged visually in Antarctica, Gould now endorsed Mike Thorne's dictum that the greatest reliability in estimation would be achieved by looking ahead, guessing the distance, multiplying by two, and adding ten.

Discouraged by a difficult and largely wasted day, Gould supposed that it might be better to ascend into the range to the level of the big flat-topped mountains via Axel Heiberg Glacier, which had been Amundsen's approach to the pole, rather than to continue battling with Liv. (The slopes of Mt. Fridtjof Nansen, which the Geological Party had made it a primary objective to reach, lie directly between the heads of these two glaciers.) As the polar flight had flown south up Liv to reach the polar plateau and then returned north down Axel Heiberg, Gould radioed Byrd for impressions as to the two glaciers' relative accessibility on the ground, receiving confirmation (which might have been communicated earlier, one thinks!) that Liv appeared "impossible because of crevasses," while Amundsen's route up Axel Heiberg would be better for reaching Mt. Nansen.

The team spent another day in their Liv Glacier camp, surveying and collecting foothill rocks, and then on the 3rd and 4th of December moved southeast along the line where mountains met shelf ice in search of an ideal place to establish their base field camp for an approach to Mt. Nansen and the rest of December's investigations. Large parts of these days were spent in fruitless search for the cache of supplies left for them by the polar plane. Its location had been marked on aerial photographs that had been subsequently dropped but with bearings that failed to yield success. Frustrated by more wasted time, they temporarily gave up the search and continued on their way east toward Heiberg. Late on the 4th they found themselves stopped on the lower end of a glacier between Liv and Axel Heiberg (which Amundsen on his chart had called the western spur of Heiberg itself) that seemed to offer many advantages—straight ahead and apparently smooth access to Mt. Nansen, good visibility and approachability from all directions, and a surface of loosely compacted snow that led them to believe the place was relatively free of strong winds. The party determined to make the site their new base of mountain operations. Lightening their load for a final time to create Depot No. 8, the party gave their location the name "Strom Camp" in honor of Sverre Strom, he who over the winter had made their highly valued light flexible sledges.

A "most depressing day" followed, first, because a morning attempt by Gould, O'Brien, and Thorne to explore farther east was cut short by heavy fog and then because harsh logic now called for the killing of more of their faithful, but now superfluous and resource-consuming dogs. "This has been our 'butcher shop,'" a sick-at-heart Gould wrote into his journal that night. Though arithmetic suggested that they should now cut down to only eighteen dogs (of the forty-six with which they began the trek), the men agreed to reprieve an extra three, maintaining two of these on a diet of human feces.

Alleviating the heartsickness to some degree was the prospect of soon achieving one of their principal aims in the field, reaching the exposed rock faces of Mt. Fridtjof Nansen. It will be recalled that geologists had already termed it a "reasonable conjecture" that Mt. Nansen's summit would be partly composed of Beacon sandstone—which would, for a start, link the Queen Maud Mountains as likely part of a single chain with a previously investigated range of far away Victoria Land—but that they were awaiting direct evidence on the point from Gould. Accordingly, on the 6th, skis and sledges loaded with an eighteen-day supply of rations began to ascend the glacier upon which Strom Camp had been established, which was a pathway leading directly to the slopes of Mt. Nansen. Though the ascent proved a "hard grind," all were resolute in making progress, and the party camped that night under a spur of Mt. Nansen, having traveled some fourteen miles and gained three thousand feet in elevation. The exposed rock that was their goal seemed close at hand, and—already forgetting Thorne's dictum, it seems—Gould anticipated an easy climb the next day.

But on the morrow, as Gould would write, "it was the same old story." The rocks were found to be still more distant than they had supposed, with the most direct approach to them effectively barred by numerous chasms and crevasses. There was no help for it, they conceded, they would have to break camp and move on up the glacier in search of a better path. "It seemed," Gould would remember, "that nature had outdone herself to keep her geological secrets to herself here in the Queen Maud Mountains."

Finally, three or four miles farther on, the party arrived at a point where no impassable crevasses appeared to separate them from the rocks. Accordingly, Gould, Thorne, Crockett, and Goodale herringboned up a slippery slope and over a steep ice falls to reach a saddle from which another eighth-of-a-mile climb along the edge of a great yawning chasm that Gould reported made his "spine sort of tingle" brought them at last to the desired outcrop. Here one cannot do better than to follow Gould's own description of his feelings:

> I had had the unhappy and almost dismal reaction of finding that the higher we climbed, the lower my spirits became, for the nearer we got to the long sought flat-lying rocks, the less they looked like the sedimentary layers I wanted so much to find, and the more they looked like a great series of volcanic flows. And even now, as I review the events of that day I realize that I did not overstate my enthusiasm of the moment when I sent Commander Byrd the following radiogram telling him about the day's work:
>
>> "No symphony I have ever heard, no work of art before which I have stood in awe ever gave me quite the thrill that I had when I reached out after that strenuous climb and picked up a piece of rock to find it sandstone. It was just the rock I had come all the way to the Antarctic to find."
>
> For I had climbed and clawed my way up over several thousand feet of glacier to the rocks and had actually to hold a piece in my hand before my very eyes, before I realized that it was after all not volcanic rock, but

sandstone. That little piece of rock which I first picked up and which was not half as large as the palm of my hand had repaid me for the whole trip. Had it been necessary for me to have turned around that moment and started back to Little America, I should still have felt that it had been a most profitable journey.

The significance of the sandstone justified Gould's elation. Here was geological news to communicate that was exciting in itself and upon which a young scientist ambitious to make important contributions could build a reputation. Confirming the lithological equivalence of the Queen Maud Mountains with the South Victoria Land ranges investigated earlier in the century by Scott's geologist Hartley T. Ferrar implied that the two systems were in fact one and continuous—it allowed Gould to identify the whole with confidence as "the most stupendous fault block mountain system in all the world."* The climbers were further interested to have discovered on rocks reached that day—spotted initially by Eddie Goodale—bits of living grey lichens, which they supposed to be the farthest south that indigenous life had yet been found.

Soon there was more. In Victoria Land, Ferrar's Beacon sandstone had been found in association with seams of coal, and Gould immediately anticipated that the same might be true here. This was confirmed the very next day, in a second ascent farther up the slopes and from a few miles farther up the glacier, when Mike Thorne, climbing the highest, reached dark bands in the rocks from which he extracted small bits for Gould's inspection. Holding a lighted match to the sample, Gould found that it would "with some reluctance" burn; the party had located, a little more than three hundred miles from the South Pole, a seam of low-grade coal. Here was a second discovery to match and augment the import of the sandstone. If coal was present both here and in the South Victoria sector of this single system, it implied that it might be present throughout many thousands of intervening square miles and make Antarctica's coal reserves possibly as extensive as any in the world. Coal upon Mt. Nansen also led to reflections of "vast interest" about past climates in this icy realm. The presence of coal was irrefutable evidence that the Antarctic had not always been cold—it tells us, as Gould was soon to write, "that for millions and millions of years it must have had a warm and even a sub-tropical climate."

Determining after another day's probing that they could do no more upon the north face of Mt. Nansen from where they were—at least without the hazards

---

* In time, the similarity of the Antarctic formations with systems present in India, South Africa, Australia, and South America would contribute evidence in support of the theory that these southern lands had once been joined together, furthering the eventual acceptance of the theory of plate tectonics.

involved exceeding any likely additional reward there—the party now made their way back down the glacier to return to Strom Camp. En route, they made for a hill or low mountain that they had previously been calling Mt. Betty in the hope and cautious expectation that this was indeed what it was—that is, that it would prove to be the location climbed by Amundsen and his party in early January 1912 and where Amundsen recorded that they had built up a great cairn of rocks inside of which was left a can of paraffin, several boxes of matches, and a short account, torn from Amundsen's journal, of their previously having reached the pole. They wished to definitely locate Amundsen's Mt. Betty both for the historical thrill of being the next persons on the spot to find Amundsen's cairn, if possible, and because doing so would finally allow them to orient themselves with certainty relative to Amundsen's own chart and the other features he had recorded therein nearly eighteen years before.

Alas, when they reached this peak* and climbed about on it, they were disappointed to spy no sign of prior human passage and were forced to conclude—particularly after finding the elevation to be twenty-six hundred feet above sea level, whereas Amundsen's Mt. Betty had been reported as a mere twelve hundred feet—that this could not be Mt. Betty after all. There were no other candidates in the immediate vicinity, but perhaps they would be able to locate it later before having to start their return trip north—it could perhaps be a little to the east, where they would soon be pointed.

Before making that departure, however, Gould decided to make one more effort, in the opposite direction, to find the elusive cache of supplies laid down for them at the time of the polar flight. Although this store of food and fuel was not expected to be needed for them to complete their mission and make their safe return, it would be comforting to have secured backup supplies in case of unexpected disaster, such as losing a fully packed sledge down a crevasse. Gould had radioed Byrd about the apparent inaccuracy of the marked aerial photograph as a guide to the cache, and Byrd had responded with new and detailed instructions that led Gould to believe that another effort would yield success.

On December 11, however, for the first time since leaving Little America, the expedition lost a day to bad weather, accompanied by visibility far too poor to risk the hazards of dangerous crevasses, much less going in search of a missing supply depot. Instead, the party kept in or near camp throughout a day in which the most remarkable event was the surprising appearance of a lone

---

* This was the first time in all their travels that they were able to drive dogs right up to exposed rock—and was therefore the first time that the youngest dogs, born on the ice in Little America, had ever seen such things. In *Cold*, Gould recorded the young huskies' initial caution and curiosity: "They ... approached very gingerly, sniffing eagerly for some familiar odor. Finally Bob screwed up his courage enough to lick the rock. Finding that he could neither bite it nor be bitten by it, he immediately lost interest."

skua gull come to pick at the bits of dog meat left from their recent slaughter. The men were at once amazed at finding a skua so improbably distant from its natural habitat near the open sea and tempted to turn the bird into fresh meat for themselves—a temptation declined, according to Gould, when the thought of this scavenger's "untidy ways" of feeding on whatever it could find became too much for them.*

The next day, with the return of good clear weather, Gould and Goodale sledged with Goodale's team approximately thirty miles back in the direction of Liv Glacier and, following Byrd's new directions, located the airplane cache "with but little difficulty." They found, Gould would later write, that its location as first given to them had been marked on the wrong photograph. Loading up the sledge with five gallons of gasoline and two hundred-some pounds of man food that gave them a "very safe margin" there, Gould and Goodale drove back to rejoin their comrades in Strom Camp, prepared to start eastward—in due course to reach land never yet seen by any human being—the next morning.†

***

Their first day of sledging east from Strom Camp was glorious, with brilliant sunshine overhead and mighty Mt. Fridtjof Nansen in all its grandeur silhouetted against a clear blue sky to their right. When they stopped to make camp it was on the lower slopes of Axel Heiberg Glacier, up which Amundsen's dog teams had driven eighteen years earlier during their successful race to the pole. Gould was charmed both by the historical resonance and by the magnificence of the surroundings, where a glacier, flooded with sunlight that was "pure gold," cut like an "ice stream" between two ice-clad peaks while the sky behind was colored a rare "apple green ... that one can see only over great areas of ice." He termed this camp's setting a "complete fairyland."

Enchantment ebbed, however, as fairyland had disappeared by the time the men awoke on the 14th and the party remained pinned in place, snowbound, for three monotonous days of zero visibility, constant snow, and, after someone produced a "godsend" deck of cards, many games of bridge and Hearts played

---

* The Geological Party at this point in its travels was itself hardly a model of fastidious tidiness. As one of Gould's early December radiograms to Byrd observed, they were "a disreputable looking outfit now for no one has washed or shaved since we left Little America." Gould likened Vaughan's appearance to that of an Italian bandit, Goodale to a backwoods Yankee farmer, Thorne to "a recent escapee from Sing Sing," and O'Brien to a generic thug, while Crockett was merely "a boy scout trying to grow [a] beard." Gould himself, he admitted, by this point resembled nothing so much as the dog rags.

† Inauspiciously, Wednesday's blizzard had delayed this departure to Friday the 13th, though nobody professed, as they got ready to drive their remaining dogs off the edge of all charts, to find the date in any way unsettling.

on a wet tent floor for chocolate ration stakes. Beautiful though the site became again when, on the 17th, the snow-covered mountains were again illuminated in brilliant sunshine, all concerned—including the now well-rested and reinvigorated huskies—were delighted to move on.

And so they beat on. Despite some of the familiar trouble with crevasses—it got so bad that they left land to go back out onto the ice shelf to the north for a time in order to keep moving east—the party traveled largely without notable incident or serious setback for the next several days, making frequent stops to take photographs or to make observations in furtherance of O'Brien and Thorne's ongoing surveying. Passing a stupendous glacier clearly larger than either Liv or Axel Heiberg, "quite the grandest unnamed feature we had yet seen," Gould had the pleasure of naming it for Amundsen. On the Amundsen Glacier's eastern boundary was a cluster of three towering peaks, which became Mounts Crockett, Vaughan, and Goodale. Subsequently, traversing an extensive ice field wrecked one of their fine sledges and damaged the runners on some others. That day, the 19th, when they finally reached patches of snow large enough to hold their tent pegs and so enable a stop, they found that they were camped directly north of another great glacier gap, the straightest and most clear cut they had yet seen. "There seemed," Gould would write, "nothing between us and the South Pole through this gateway." Gould determined that its name should commemorate the party's topographer, who charted its outlines, and so it became Thorne Glacier.*

The party's primary geographical mission, for this eastward jaunt, had been to follow the line of the Queen Mauds to the supposed "Carmen Land" highlands which Amundsen had reported sighting from afar in 1912. However, as Gould and his companions made their way closer and closer to where these promontories must be if they did exist, it became clearer and clearer that they did not. For a second time, Gould would be an agent for the erasure of a feature from accepted maps. Amundsen's reported sighting, Gould now supposed, was likely the result of an Antarctic mirage by which dark and distant clouds had been mistaken for mountains.

Although the definite determination that Carmen Land was a phantasm fulfilled their original geographical purpose in following the line of the mountains so far east, the party had no intention of turning back quite yet. First, every additional mile now refreshed the exceedingly rare and heady sensation of

---

* All of this naming of newly discovered features was tentative, pending the approval of Byrd—who, as the Geological Party learned that night during their regular alternate-day radio communication with Little America, had by special act of Congress and President Hoover's signature just been promoted from commander to rear admiral. For some features, even Admiral Byrd's endorsement did not bestow permanency of nomenclature. The Thorne Glacier, parallel to Amundsen to its immediate west, was eventually renamed Scott Glacier (for Robert Falcon Scott, Amundsen's heroic but unfortunate competitor in the 1911-12 race to the pole) by the US Advisory Committee on Antarctic Names.

knowing that theirs would be the first human eyes ever to see whatever would next come into view. Additionally, they most particularly wanted to be sure to cross the 150th meridian, and so be the first to enter the "American" sector of the continent, reinforcing the claim unofficially* made for the United States by Byrd when he had earlier flown past that meridian (the eastern boundary of British claims) along the coast five hundred miles to the north. Though Byrd had stated his claim and named the new sector Marie Byrd Land in honor of his wife, there was no precedent for claiming land that had merely been overflown, and so the party wanted to be sure to cross over into Marie Byrd Land on the ground before turning about.

Accordingly, on the 20th Gould and his companions spent a day slipping further eastward over an icy surface far enough to be certain of making camp well within the boundaries of Marie Byrd Land, and the next day they engaged in a small ceremony of claim-staking. Following their morning oatmeal the men gathered around the nearest rocks, where they planted a small American flag affixed to a bamboo ski pole, bared their heads, and stood silently at attention for a few moments, until Gould ended the makeshift affair of state with a gruff command of "Put your hats on!" Then, with Crockett remaining in camp to mind the dogs, the rest climbed the tallest nearby peak, which they decided to call Supporting Party Mountain in honor of Arthur Walden's team of sledgers who had broken the initial trail south from Little America and laid down the first supply depots. Atop this hill the men piled together a rock cairn in which Gould placed a tin can containing a note stating the composition of the Geological Party and that they now stood east of the 150th meridian upon land claimed as "a dependency or possession of the United States of America" and observing that they were "not only the first Americans but the first individuals of any sort to set foot on American soil in the Antarctic."

From the top of Supporting Party Mountain the Geographical Party could look out to the south over the foot of yet another stupendous glacier which they were the first to see, extending upwards into the mountains to the southeast. This massive ice flow Gould was pleased to name the Leverett Glacier in honor of Frank Leverett, the eminent geologist and specialist in glaciology who had been among Gould's most inspiring teachers at the University of Michigan.

---

* It was the official position of the United States, articulated in 1924 by Secretary of State Charles Evans Hughes, that "the discovery of lands unknown to civilization, even when coupled with the formal taking of possession, does not support a valid claim of sovereignty unless the discovery is followed by an actual settlement of the discovered country." Nonetheless, at the onset of his expedition Byrd had asked the State Department for advice as to whether or not he should claim sovereignty for the United States when entering previously unclaimed regions of the continent. In the absence of any clear answer from Washington, Byrd and other members of the Byrd Antarctic Expedition went ahead and stated claims that *could* be acted upon subsequently should the United States government later choose to take them up.

Attractive though it would have been to extend explorations still further into the unknown, both the calendar and the finitude of supplies dictated that it was now time to reverse direction. Deciding to travel by night as they sledged back to Strom Camp, so as to have the sun more nearly behind them, the men enjoyed an afternoon nap prior to departure. They had here reached both their furthest point east and their greatest distance from Little America. After supper therefore, when they broke camp and turned dogs and sledges toward the west, they were beginning the journey home.

***

Retracing a path over now-familiar terrain presented, for the next four days—or rather, nights—similar difficulties of ice and crevasse as were encountered in the opposite direction, but, lacking the excitement of discovery, may simply be passed over in this account as "largely uneventful."

On Christmas Day, still a night's journey away from Strom Camp, they camped again near the elevation that they thought best fit the description of Amundsen's Mt. Betty but where they had previously failed to find the cairn that Amundsen had reported leaving there. Arising at about 7 p.m., a time of day that had become their morning, the party decided "as a last hope"—so Gould would explain in his subsequent radio message to Byrd—"to look at a curious pile of rock far down on a low ridge from the main mountain." Because it was situated about a thousand feet below the mountain's point of highest elevation, the searchers had not previously paid it any attention, as it "did not seem conceivable that Amundsen would have referred to this little ridge as 'Mt. Betty.'" Peering at the ridge through Gould's field glasses, one could discern a small rocky projection that stood out but which "seemed to be just a single great piece of rock that had perhaps rolled down there from the mountain top or had been left stranded by glacial ice."

Gould and Thorne skied over to investigate. "The nearer we came to this curious projection of rock the more hopeful we became," Gould would later write, "yet we were almost upon it before we realized that it was really built up of a number of smaller pieces of rock. Such a pile could only have been put together by man and the only men who had ever been within hundreds of miles of here were Amundsen and his polar party." Gould waved his trail flags excitedly as a sign for the others to join them, and when they did, the entire party moved to the cairn and removed a few rocks from its side to gain access to what was within: a five-gallon can of paraffin, twenty small boxes of safety matches in a waterproof packet, and "a tin can with a tight lid on its top." Gould pried off the lid and found within what he already knew must be there: a note written by Amundsen and torn from his notebook. "We did not need to be able to read Norwegian," Gould wrote, "to make out the fact that he had on this paper told of his successful achievement of the South Pole. I do not think anyone could have appreciated more fully than did the six of us all that lay behind that bit of paper and its simple account."*

Gould decided that Amundsen's historic note should be taken back to the world and was his to safeguard. In its place he left his own note, on a page from his own notebook, commemorating the Geological Party's finding of the Amundsen cache. The others were each given permission to take a small bit of rock and some matchboxes. Otherwise, the rocks were all carefully replaced and the cairn left as it was. As they moved away from the cairn, Gould paused, turned back, and offered a silent salute. "His simple gesture," Vaughan would remember, well conveyed "the admiration for the Amundsen party that all of us felt."

That night the group completed the short jog from Mt. Betty back to Strom Camp, where they intended to stay put for a few days of preparations for the nearly five hundred-mile return to Little America, and so that the twenty-one remaining dogs could be thoroughly rested before setting off. Part of the preparations involved thinning now unneeded gear so as to lighten their homeward load to the extent possible. Accordingly on the 28th they returned to Mt. Betty to leave near the Amundsen cairn their own cache of excess gear. Building another cairn some two hundred feet from Amundsen's, the men filled it with a store of items such as heavy underwear, socks, mukluks, mitts, a gallon of gasoline, a bundle of trail flags, and several dog harnesses. Gould wrote another note detailing the work of the Geological Party and left that too, tucked inside a tin can. Outside the cairn they symbolically leaned one of their innovative flexible sledges, made useless by badly cracked runners, and Gould left one of his two geological rock hammers.† Finally, they marked the monument by planting atop it one of their trail flags. Caching complete, the Geological Party was nearly ready to say farewell to the Queen Mauds. Details of getting away occupied them for some while on

---

* After the party had returned to Little America, Bernt Balchen translated the note as follows:

6th -7th of January, 1912

Reached and determined the Pole on the 14th to the 16th of December, 1911. Discovered the connection of Victoria Land and King Edward VII Land at 86 degrees south latitude and their continuation as a great mountain range towards the southeast. Have observed this range extending as far as 88 degrees south. Under the conditions of visibility that we had, it appeared to continue on farther in the same direction across the Antarctic Continent.

Passed this place on the return with provisions for 60 days, 2 sledges, 11 dogs. Everybody well.

Roald Amundsen

† Decades later Gould's hammer would eventually be returned to him. The next group to visit Mt. Betty, doing so almost thirty-two years later, on January 13, 1962, was a party led by glaciologist Charles Swithinbank. Swithinbank found that the contents of the sledging party's cairn were intact, including the broken sledge still lying against the outside, and he took Gould's hammer, later mailing it back to him at the University of Arizona with the words: *"Here is the hammer that you left at Mount Betty some time ago. I hope that its absence has not caused any great inconvenience during the intervening years."*

The Geological Party at the cairn they built near the Amundsen cairn

the 29th, but finally at about 1 a.m., now on the 30th, they were off. "As though for a good omen," Gould noted in his journal, the clouds which had mostly obscured the mountains behind them for a few days now "lifted to give us one last grand view of Nansen before we headed northward."

Unanimous in wanting to avoid returning through the badly crevassed area below Liv Glacier that had made their last day before reaching the mountains so trying, the party struck out nearly due north from Strom Camp until they judged that they had passed beyond the latitude of that crevassed zone, after which they altered course farther toward westward so as to pick up their former trail, which they succeeded in doing late in the day on the 31st.

Nineteen more days saw them home to Little America, following the line of flags and snow beacons and the succession of seven supply depots that they had laid down weeks before. Weather and sledging conditions varied, and some days the going was rough, but in general they found the return trip far easier and swifter than what they had faced while breaking trail in the reverse direction. Their loads were lighter, and the men themselves had become veteran sledgers toughened into peak physical condition. Nonetheless, for the sake of the dogs they limited themselves to covering no more than twenty-three miles per day—a distance Gould called "scarcely a day's work any more," which on good surfaces they could attain in no more than six or seven hours.

One day the sun shone so brilliantly they all stripped off their outer clothing, and Vaughan spent the entire afternoon skiing naked, save for his boots. Other days they were much troubled by fog. Camping on the edge of the heavily crevassed area between Depots 4 and 3 that had given them so much trouble on the way south, they wisely decided to stay in place until visibility improved. When it did and they prepared to set forth once again, they found that they had unknowingly pitched tents and picketed dogs between two great parallel crevasses, each just a few feet away on either side.

It was in this area as well that a restless Gould, worried about the trail ahead and hoping to warm his feet through activity, crawled out of his sleeping bag and did "quite the most foolish thing [he had] ever done." Violating his own strict rule, he put on his skis and went on up the trail alone, assuming that the flag-marked trail could safely be followed. Instead, at some distance from camp, as he headed for the next flag straight ahead, the snow beneath him suddenly gave way and collapsed into a crevasse. He threw himself to one side as he tumbled, and his skis fortunately caught against the crevasse wall and saved him from a disastrously deep fall into oblivion. Pulling himself back to the surface, he "turned and looked down into the blue-black depths," then "very meekly" retraced steps to camp and quietly crawled back into his bag hoping never to have to say a word to the others about his folly. Alas for that hope, when they did set out again some hours later Gould's ski tracks were clearly visible. Though the culprit was clear enough to all, Gould's companions pretended wonderment over who could have been out skiing alone in this dangerous area in such clear contravention of their leader's rule. When the tracks then disappeared directly into a crevasse, O'Brien declared that, whoever the lone skier had been, he was clearly a stupid ass to have gone and jumped right into that crevasse. Teasing remarks were directed Gould's way for days; as Vaughan would later note, it was better to concentrate upon the humor of the situation than to contemplate how very nearly Gould's mistake might have been fatal.

Beset a day later by a gloomy white opaqueness that again reduced visibility to nil, the party was forced to halt in the midst of what Gould termed "a spider web of crevasses." Realizing that to halt here for long, short of the supplies needed from their next depot, would mean running out of their canine food within about a day and require the killing of more dogs, the men elected to see whether it might not be possible to escape the crevassed area more quickly by departing their marked trail and striking out more directly to the north. Thorne, Vaughan, and Gould roped together to investigate, and to their great satisfaction they found that the party could leave the crevasses behind this way within less than two miles—a route considerably quicker and less hazardous than following their old trail of flags would have been. After moving the party north in this way beyond the crevasses, they then changed course enough toward the west to again pick up their old trail only a few miles south of their next depot, where they were able to replenish their supply of dog food before continuing their northward march.

***

Meanwhile In Little America Admiral Byrd and the rest of the expedition were finding January an uneasy month. With no important work left to do for the majority, many men now were essentially just waiting to go home and becoming bored by inactivity. Drinking picked up again. Morale dipped, grousing increased, and camp discipline developed visible cracks. Making the situation considerably more stressful was growing uncertainty about the expedition's imminent departure. The pack ice lying between the Ross Sea and the rest of the world—impenetrable much of the year but generally passable during the latter part of the southern summer—was this season remaining unusually dense unusually late, and concern was developing about the ability of relief ships to pass through during the expected window of opportunity. The plan had been for two vessels, the Norwegian whaling factory *Kosmos* and a chaser sent by the *Nilsen Alonzo*, to visit the Bay of Whales early in the season, bringing food and some additional supplies that would be useful until evacuation. Then later, the expedition's own ships, the *City of New York* and the *Eleanor Bolling*, would arrive to reclaim the Little Americans and their equipment. But the whalers were reporting some of the worst ice conditions ever seen, and though the *City* left Dunedin on January 5, it seemed doubtful that she would be able to push through. (In these conditions, chances for the *Bolling* to clear the pack were rated as slim to none, and for the time being it simply remained in New Zealand.) The *Alonzo* finally did reach clear water south of the pack two weeks later than anticipated, but, needing to make up for the lost whaling time, delayed sending the promised chaser, and the *Kosmos*, finding the hunt better than usual north of the ice pack—the whales, too, were passing through to the south in smaller numbers—never did cross through that season.

All this led to increasing anxiety for Byrd and the others waiting in Little America. It was feared that the expedition could find themselves marooned and forced to spend a second winter where they were—an outcome for which they were in fact provisioned well enough, though some items enjoyed the first winter would be absent or in very short supply for a second, but this was a prospect that was pleasing to few if any and that would carry with it a disturbingly unpredictable psychological toll, given the cracks already evident in morale. Byrd would later write that no other situation encountered during the entire expedition brought him the worry that this one did. Out on the trail, Gould was kept informed—though Byrd noted that it was hard to give the Geological Party "bad news on top of such an arduous journey." In the middle of the month, recognizing that the *City* and the *Bolling* might not get through the ice at all that year, Byrd asked for help, requesting of the two whalers south of the pack, the *Alonzo* and the *Ross*, that they send chasers to the Bay of Whales to evacuate essential equipment and a number of men. After learning that, in light of the paucity of whales south of the pack that season, the *Ross* was already heading north again and the *Alonzo* preparing to do so soon, Byrd sent the captain of the *Alonzo* a message, almost amounting to an SOS, followed by a request for the big whaling factory itself to come evacuate the entire party. Gould was sent a radiogram advising that if the *Alonzo* agreed to come they could arrive in about two days and that Gould's party should therefore "hustle" all they could, as it would be difficult to hold the factory up. This was a distressing message for Gould and his men, still 104 miles away from Little America, to receive, and it occasioned "much discussion as to whether the dogs could cover such a distance within two days." However, the next morning brought the message that the whalers would not be coming, and so there was no need to hurry too much and risk running the dogs to death.

That day, the 17th, the party reached the abandoned snowmobile and then the final remaining depot. On the morning of the 18th, they made their last camp on the trail, knowing that the remaining distance could be covered in just one more trek. Gould wrote in his log that morning: "It has been a great trip—filled both with romance and achievement and I am somehow just a bit sick at heart to see it end."*

Setting out that night on the final push, the party was still twenty-five miles south of Little America when they came across fresh ski tracks. A short time later, they spied a lone skier headed toward them, which proved to be the expedition's Doc Coman, camped at the head of the Bay of Whales for some surveying with two others, and joined by the cameraman Willard Van der Veer, who, Gould would note, was thus in position to film the unkempt trekkers before they had any chance to clean themselves up back at camp. The rest of the Little Americans got their chance to give a boisterous greeting to the returning party a few hours later—about 9 a.m. on the morning of the 19th. Byrd would write:

> As they topped the last slope at the edge of the camp we recognized the figure of Larry Gould—but it was scarcely the same Larry who had gone away two and a half months before. His round, peaked cap stood up like a turban. His black beard, new to us, was bleached white around his mouth. Dark sun glasses hid his eyes. Around his waist was a twisted red and white sash.
>
> As he came toward me his teeth made a line of white in the mask of whiskers, glasses, and grime. No wonder the boys called him Abdul.

"A bath—and Paradise!" yelled Goodale, and soon the men were enjoying a good scrub down in the mess hall. As the layers of grime and soot produced by weeks around their camp stove slowly began to dissolve and flake away, it became clearer to the throng about them how very fit each of these lean, trail-hardened

---

* It seems he also wrote notes to his companions at this time, for we have a reply from Freddy Crockett headed "On the trail bound for Little America," in which Crockett says that nothing has pleased him more in a long time than Gould's note and that he wanted to tell him how much he had enjoyed serving him. "Never," Crockett wrote, "have I placed more confidence in any man, except my father, than I have in you. Never have I wanted to help more in accomplishing a task than this one." Now that their work together was completed, Crockett continued, "I feel sad that there is not more for it has been to me like a delightful dream."

The Geological Party returns to camp: (left to right) Thorne, Crockett, Goodale, Gould, O'Brien, and Vaughan

men now looked. Across ten weeks, five days, and approximately twenty hours of arduous journeying, Gould and his companions had traversed something in excess of fifteen hundred miles.

***

Once the Geological Party was safely back in camp, there remained no reason for the expedition's staying any longer on the continent, and the continuing uncertainty about when—or if, in 1930—they could get away became increasingly discomfiting. Though meteorologist Henry Harrison noted in his diary upon Gould's return that Little America was "a new place with Larry back," attributing to the force of his personality and ability "a better feeling of peace and security" in camp, it became clear to Gould that there was "great unrest" within the expedition now, with an unhappy group "impatient to be on their way out." As for himself, as he noted in his diary several days after his return, he was finding it hard after being so long active and away to get used to what he termed "the deadening lethargy that pervades the atmosphere here." "I am at once restless and yet dead," he continued. "There has been little to do here and the uncertainty about getting out this year has contributed to make [this] curious feeling." Thirteen silent days would then pass before he wrote again.

During those days the center of camp attention was the radio room, where updates were received on the condition of the ice pack and the likelihood that the *City* would be able to get through. At one point some American newspapers printed a report, entirely false, that the *City* had already reached the Bay of Whales and that the entire expedition was even then embarking. This "news" was duly posted on the mess hall bulletin board with the ironic commentary "interesting, if true." It was eventually determined that the *Bolling*, which on January 20 had finally set out from Dunedin towards the pack, should not attempt to force her way through, and at the end of the month the ship was ordered back. Meanwhile, the *City* was steaming back and forth along the pack's northern edge, waiting for improved opportunity to attempt to force her way through. The lack of positive development was frustrating to all, on both sides of the pack. In Little America, diarist Harrison wrote that January had been the "toughest" month of the whole expedition, "between uncertainty, lack of discipline and disciplined work, rumors and counter-rumors about ships and getting home ... all of which has resulted in a general loafing and probably a little too much 'free thinking.'"

During this period, Gould reportedly broached a proposal to Byrd that he, along with fourteen others, might be permitted to remain in Antarctica another year in order dramatically to extend the scientific program. The idea was supported by others interested in participating, including Coman and Siple, but was turned down flat by the admiral, who felt responsible for all the men and "feared that the ships would have just as much trouble another year." Putting aside the notion, Gould-the-scientist resigned himself to occupying the remaining time with such activities as taking pictures of snow formations and studying ice phenomena in the bay.

Finally, on February 7, the camp was electrified by the news that the *City of New York* had taken advantage of some breakup in the pack, pushed her way through, and reached open water in the Ross Sea on the southern side. Captain Melville estimated arrival at the Bay of Whales in five or six days if favorable conditions prevailed. He cautioned, though, that if temperatures dropped again behind him the pack could once again become impassable and therefore strongly urged that the Little Americans "be prepared to leave on arrival as any delay might prove serious."

As it happened, hoped-for conditions did not prevail, and the *City* had to battle through storms and foul weather on her passage through the Ross Sea. Her crew used axes and hammers to try to clear the ship as it became dangerously coated with tons of ice, and the *City* was blown significantly off course by ferocious winds. On the 15th Gould's diary records that the ship remained overdue, was still two or three days away, and was currently standing still in a hurricane headwind. "The uncertainty is disturbing," he wrote, "and there is a good deal of unrest among the folk here in camp."

It was early evening on the 18th when the *City of New York* at last reached the Bay of Whales. Supplies had already been sledged out from camp to the mouth of the bay in preparation for a quick loading. (The spot had unofficially been dubbed "Detention Camp" by expeditioners impatient to be off.) Gould sledged over with Crockett when the ship's arrival seemed imminent and was therefore on hand when the *City's* masts first came into view above the sea smoke round the Barrier cape. The reunion of Little Americans with the crew of the *City* was warmly felt but kept short so that loading could begin immediately. Temperatures in the bay had been falling steadily, and new ice cakes were forming. The bay was starting to freeze over, and Byrd estimated that in another week departure that year would have been impossible. At Little America, all but empty now, the flag was lowered for the last time.

Loading was directed through the night by Gould, McKinley, June, and Black. The last men leaving camp arrived in the early morning, and shortly thereafter the final pieces of equipment to be loaded (much else was left behind) were in place. Humans, dogs, and some penguins the expedition hoped to bring back alive for placement in American zoos were all taken aboard, and at about 9:30 a.m. anchor was hoisted and they were away. Gould's feelings were mixed. Planning as he was to marry Peg Rice shortly after his return, his emotions were "colored by romance." And yet, he wrote into his diary a few hours after setting sail, "I must confess that it was with a heavy heart that I saw my last of the Bay of Whales—these had been great days and I am loathe to end them."

Aboard ship and headed north, the morale of the Little Americans rebounded vigorously. This was aided by the sacks of mail brought by the *City*, the first received in paper form in more than a year by those who had wintered over. Within a day the swell of the ocean, though relatively calm compared with the ship's recent passage through Ross Sea storms, produced widespread *mal-de-mer* amongst the newcomers, with Gould reportedly suffering "more than most of them." Even so, spirits remained high now. On February 24 the *City* reached the pack ice and found it passable. Two days later they were through, and on the 28th the ship rendezvoused with both the *Kosmos* and the *Eleanor Bolling*, with Gould among those who transferred over to the latter for the return to Dunedin.

It was March 10 when the *City* and the *Bolling* together reached Dunedin Harbor, welcomed by a large waterfront crowd and bands playing "The Star-Spangled Banner" and "The Conquering Hero." For Gould, the most intense memories of the occasion, staying with him for decades to come, was how very green the landscape was and the taste of fresh fruit. A long voyage home still remained—Gould would not arrive in New York aboard the *Bolling* until the 19th of June—but with this setting of foot on the green land of New Zealand, the expedition *qua* expedition was at an end.

CHAPTER 11

ENDINGS AND BEGINNINGS

Departing New Zealand on different ships at different times, as they had when they left the United States to begin their adventure, most of the members of the Byrd Expedition were again crossing the Pacific by late March of 1930. Gould's return trip aboard the *Eleanor Bolling* saw him again serving as a shipboard mate and again suffering, predictably for some days following any significant time ashore, from seasickness. (His partner on the *Bolling*'s night watch, Hillton Willcox, wrote that during the first week or so out from Dunedin he and Gould were "a sorry pair together," often "sprawled over the rolling deck of the wheel-house, saying little except to commiserate ... and to agree that the 'Graveyard Watch' could not have been more aptly named." Following a week's layover ashore in Tahiti, the *Bolling* ran into a heavy squall, and the pair's nausea came right back.*)

The *Bolling* came into port in Balboa, Panama, on May 22, having given the more glamorous but slow *City of New York* a seventeen-day tow until the 17th. As before, Gould admitted to a loathing for the tropics, telling an Associated Press interviewer in Balboa, "I like the cold." The *Bolling*, after taking on new coal, returned to sea for a few days to meet her sister ship and tow her in. Then it was through the canal and, on June 3, departure from Colón, on the Atlantic side of the isthmus—the ships' last port of call before New York. With the *City* receiving a tow, first from a Navy tug and then from the *Bolling*, the ships' subsequent progress was so speedy that they had to be slowed down by Byrd's directive in order to time their arrival in New York Harbor to coincide with the municipal welcoming ceremonies that had been scheduled for June 19.

---

*   After the seasickness passed, Willcox's testimony is that he and Gould did much better than "saying little"—he wrote of the pleasure of listening, night after night during their watches, to the professor reciting "in his rich clear, baritone voice, some of his favorite poems" called up from his impressively "vast cultural memory." Willcox wrote that if his service with the Byrd Expedition, a diversion from his medical studies, did him no other permanent good, it would yet have been "entirely worthwhile for the inspiration and fellowship" of "that grand companion, Laurence McKinley Gould."

Both the *City of New York* and the *Eleanor Bolling* dropped anchor off Staten Island on the appointed day. Admiral Byrd, who crossed the Pacific on neither, had shipped on the *City* out of Panama so as to be filmed and photographed arriving in New York aboard his flagship, which to the public had always been *the* expedition vessel. The harbor teemed with activity as scores of craft filled both water and air to be part of the heroes' escort to shore. Three great airships circled overhead. Tugs and ferries hooted and tooted. New York Mayor Jimmy Walker, accompanied by radio announcers talking live to the nation, came out to greet them aboard the tugboat *Macon*, to which the crew and passengers of the *City* were transferred. Gould and others from the *Bolling* came in on the ferry *Riverside*. Both craft tied up at the Battery, on the southern tip of Manhattan, and, to the cheers of a tremendous crowd outside the ferry building, expedition members were ushered directly into a line of open automobiles which, under a sky filled with a dense snow of ticker-tape, and amidst the noisy huzzahs of thousands of onlookers, paraded them slowly up Broadway. In the lead car were Admiral and Mrs. Byrd and the crew of the polar flight: Balchen, McKinley, and June. Following in the second car were Gould and his fiancée Peg Rice, who had come to New York to greet her intended, along with the "three musketeers" from the sledge trip: Vaughan, Crockett, and Goodale.

The caravan unloaded at City Hall, where five radio microphones were ready to broadcast New York's official welcome, a ceremony before an estimated fifty thousand people, in which remarks by Mayor Walker and other dignitaries were followed by answers from Byrd and other expedition members. Then it was back to the cars and on to the Biltmore, where some rest was possible before the evening's grand dinner in the banqueting hall of the Hotel Astor—this an affair for two thousand guests given by the New York Merchants Association. Hilton Willcox recorded that after the wondrous meal "there were, of course, many speeches." His log had but one entry concerning them: "Larry Gould's was the best." It had been a long and memorably thrilling day, but it was not over yet. After dinner, a siren-sounding police escort conducted the expeditioners to Penn Station, where a special train chartered by the National Geographic Society carried them overnight to Washington.

On the 20th, shortly after noon the Antarcticans were ushered to the White House lawn, where commemorative photographs were taken with President Hoover. Then came a luncheon at the Willard Hotel hosted by the trustees of the National Geographic Society; then an introduction to Congress. After a further visit to the Navy Department, there was a drive past the capital's principal monuments and a pilgrimage to Arlington National Cemetery, where Byrd placed wreaths on the graves of polar heroes Robert Peary, Floyd Bennett, and Charles Wilkes. That evening's fete, attended by the president, the vice president, and "almost everybody who was anybody" in the capital, placed the Antarcticans on the stage of the Washington Auditorium. Hoover presented Byrd with a special National Geographic Society medal. After the ceremony the men were treated to an early screening of the just-completed Paramount film *With Byrd at the South Pole.**

A train carried most of the expedition from Washington back to New York, from where the group dispersed to their various homes and individual hometown welcomes. On the 24th several accompanied Byrd up the Hudson aboard a Navy destroyer en route to Albany, a welcome by Governor Roosevelt, and ceremonies at the state capitol. Gould instead returned briefly to Michigan, where on the morning of the 26th he applied at the Washtenaw County Clerk's Office in Ann Arbor for a wedding license. But then he was immediately off again to Boston for additional pomp mounted by state and municipality to honor Byrd and about a score of his associates, featuring another ticker-tape parade and a great dinner banquet at the Copley Plaza Hotel. "Never in the history of Boston," exulted one of the evening's speakers, "had there been such a large gathering of distinguished citizens."

In July, Gould seems to have divided his time between New York, where expedition headquarters remained open at the Biltmore Hotel, and Michigan, where the university had just promoted the returned hero from assistant to associate professor, with a $700 salary increase to $3,500 per year due to begin that fall. Late in the month he had a letter from Byrd, who wanted Gould's assistance with various factual and scientific matters as he commenced work with collaborator/ghost writer Charles Murphy on his book about the expedition, which the Putnam firm hoped to publish in time for Christmas sales. Gould, writing from Ann Arbor, advised Byrd that he hoped to have his plans there "consummated in a few days," after which he would hasten back east and to work on his post-expedition reports.

This nonchalant mention of "plans" soon to be consummated was in fact Gould's off-handed way of referencing his imminent wedding, then only four days away, and subsequent honeymoon idyll. Gould married Margaret Rice on August 2, 1930, a Saturday, in a garden ceremony performed at the bride's parents' house in Barton Hills, just outside Ann Arbor. The couple then repaired to an island camp on remote Lake Temagami in the north woods of Ontario.

---

* Though politeness and other considerations likely discouraged the expeditioners from outright hooting, the reaction of the members of the Byrd Expedition, who knew better, to the stunning disregard for accuracy of this exercise in myth-making, sentimentality, and melodrama presenting itself as a documentary despite faked scenes, rearranged chronology, and incidents severely distorted or entirely fictitious, must have ranged from raw disbelief to head-shaking cynicism. One who did record a reaction in his private log was Hilton Willcox, who complained that "The entire theme of the film was Byrd's flight to the Pole the previous November. All else was relegated to the background; even Larry Gould's geological survey in the Queen Maud Mountains, involving a sledging journey totaling 1,500 miles, was made out to be a depot-laying party for the polar flight (in case of accidents to that flight). Many of us were very bitter about it, and very sorry for Larry Gould; but Paramount had not been making a record of the scientific achievements of the Expedition; they had made a 'Spectacular' for the public [...]" The film did do well with the public and most critics, and it went on to win an Academy Award for cinematography.

Garden wedding, August 2, 1930: the beginning of a marriage of nearly 58 years

(There they received a note from Byrd offering congratulations to the groom and condolences to the bride.) They departed Temagami on the 18th, returned to Ann Arbor for several days that included Gould's thirty-fourth birthday, and— Gould having received a leave of absence from university teaching—moved on to New York to set about the serious business of enjoying life as newlyweds.

***

The Goulds would live in Manhattan for the next two years, settling within a short time into an apartment at 435 East 57th Street, a sixteen-story red brick building in the Sutton Place neighborhood near the Queensborough Bridge spanning the East River. Between their late-August New York arrival and the start of the summer following, Gould's non-marital energies were focused on three post-Antarctic expedition projects. First was to discharge his responsibilities, to Byrd and to science, to assemble, organize, and publish the scientific record of the expedition. In some ways complementing but in other ways competing with the timely completion of this goal were Gould's twin attempts to capitalize on the healthy public interest in the recent expedition by committing to a heavy schedule of participation on the lecture circuit and by readying for publication his own expedition memoir, focused on the planning and execution of the great sledge trip.

Assembling and presenting the mass of data collected and produced by the expedition's scientific team was no small task. It was envisioned that Gould, as chief scientist, would oversee and edit the production of several volumes of technical reports covering all of the varied scientific endeavors undertaken during the term of the expedition. On September 2 Gould informed Byrd that he was back in New York "reporting for duty as it were" and ready to devote himself "as far as possible to the task of bringing together and correlating the scientific results of the expedition." He stressed the importance of this work, saying that though mundane details about the expedition—"the kind of planes, the kind of food, how many dogs we use and all that sort of thing"—would soon be forgotten, "if there be any outgrowth of the expedition that will live for all time it will be these scientific records." Gould cautioned, however, that the necessary work would not be simple, that it would be time consuming, and that it would cost money—about $50,000 was his "conservative estimate," to include office space and work room, funds for making "necessary analyses, microscopic slides, maps etc.," as well as for "expert assistance" and "to defray most of the actual cost of publication." He stressed that his own financial prospects, on leave without pay from his university with "a wife and practically no income in sight," were "so uncertain that [he dared] not undertake this task without assurance that the wherewithal to complete it will be forthcoming" nor could he undertake the job "entirely as a labor of love."

Byrd responded reassuringly about the personal financial worries, stating that he would do what he could to see that Gould would have a healthy series of (paid) lecture bookings, which he predicted would "come up to … expectations," given the popularity of the expedition, and concluding "at any rate, you mustn't worry about finances because I am responsible for getting you into your present situation and I am going to see you through it." No arrangement or commitment was offered, however, concerning Gould's estimate of expenses for completing the scientific volumes.

Gould had already in July come to an agreement with promoter James B. Pond to hit the lecture trail with a talk and film presentation about his experiences with the Byrd Expedition. Byrd, whose own lecturing schedule was also being managed by Pond,* gave his approval for Gould to do this and to use expedition film footage in his appearances.†

Accordingly, in September Gould worked up an entertaining talk illustrated with colored slides and film footage, and Pond arranged for Gould to give his popular presentation to audiences all over the country. From the first week of October 1930 to the first week of May 1931, Gould delivered his "With Byrd to the Bottom of the World" lecture, running just under two hours in length, more than sixty times, traveling with it to at least seventeen states and the District of Columbia.

While trying to use September to get started with the scientific volumes as well as to prepare his lecture content and a University of Michigan opening convocation address, Gould received a number of requests from Byrd for assistance in connection with Byrd's book and with the film to accompany Byrd's own lecture presentation. Writing that he was in "a desperate situation in the matter of time," the admiral asked Gould, in addition to providing details of the Geological Party and supporting sledge trips, to write out for him "some humorous and human incidents" from the expedition, something Byrd confessed to having "no talent whatever for recalling and recounting," whereas he knew of nobody who could remember such things better or tell them so vividly as Gould.

---

*   Pond's list of lecturers that year also included Gould's old friend from voyaging to the Arctic, Captain Bob Bartlett, as well as such luminaries as deep sea explorer William Beebe, Mark Twain's daughter Clara Clemens, birth-control advocate Margaret Sanger, author and actress Cornelia Otis Skinner, and popular "Casey at the Bat" reciter DeWolfe Hopper.

†   Byrd was counting heavily on public interest in the story of his expedition to translate into healthy book sales, full lecture halls, endorsement contracts, and so forth, in order to assist him both in paying off expedition debts and keeping his own personal finances in the black. Having learned from past experience about the value of maintaining control over publicity and over the various means by which opportunities for "cashing in" derived from his exploits, Byrd had required each of the members of his Antarctic expedition to sign a contract stipulating that "all pictures and photos taken by any member … shall be the property of Commander Byrd, subject to his editing and returning what he does not require," agreeing to give no independent radio or newspaper interviews for the first six weeks after returning to the States, and setting an embargo of two full years' duration after the end of the expedition before being allowed, absent Byrd's permission, to "write or publish in any manner any story or book or deliver any lecture or address, relating in any way to the expedition."

Byrd also offered Gould the opportunity to write about the epic sledge trip as a special section within Byrd's own book. After first suggesting that Byrd might simply use the stories Gould wrote from Little America for the *New York Times,* which Byrd declined as not adequate for the kind of book he was trying to bring out, Gould eventually agreed to write and be given authorial credit for the chapter in Byrd's book dealing with the sledge journey. Late the following month, a draft was done—"a frightfully poor job" and "not ... as complete as I could wish," Gould noted apologetically, "but it is about all I could do on such short notice." The manuscript was left with Peg to type and send on, as Gould departed for Chicago and a series of Midwestern lectures.

Rushed though this writing may have been, it at least secured for Gould the privilege of publishing the first report in book form on the journey he had led. This had been in doubt because Jack O'Brien, the one member of the geological sledge trip team with whom Gould's relations had become a bit strained,* had managed to get, or believe that he had gotten, both Byrd's and Gould's rather grudging permission to write a quick "boy's book" about the sledge trip that would come out much sooner than the time otherwise stipulated for expedition members to wait to publish. Though Gould had not felt that he could forbid O'Brien from proceeding, especially as O'Brien had informed him that he had Byrd's approval, he told Byrd early in September that he had in any case "discouraged [O'Brien] in his desire to write a book about the sledge trip," doubting that O'Brien was "equipped to do a very good job of writing" and admitting furthermore, that he was "selfich [sic] enough to want to tell the story of the sledge trip myself, when it is told." Byrd was being petitioned by several expedition members for permission to publish material sooner than had been stipulated, and he was inclined to assent, so long as none were brought out before or within the first month after the appearance of his own account. "It does seem to me," he wrote Gould, "that the Leader of an expedition should be the first one to report in book form about the expedition."

Gould's lecture tours began in October. As Gould was a gifted speaker and as public interest in his topic was high, it is unsurprising that his lecturing was a decided success. At Denison University in Granville, Ohio, it was noted that his was "the largest lecture audience ever to assemble in Granville." At Wisconsin's Ripon College in November, he was pronounced "the most interesting lecturer that we have ever had in Ripon." A week later, people had to be turned away from his lecture to the American Institute of Electrical Engineers, in Lynn, Massachusetts, when the twelve thousand-person hall was filled to capacity. Two days after that, he spoke to some four thousand members of the National Geographic

---

*   Information is sketchy because nobody involved put into writing any of the relevant details, but O'Brien reportedly returned from the sledge journey with complaints about having received a "dirty deal," and Gould would eventually tell Byrd that O'Brien "was the one member of the geological party who failed to do his job."

Society at Constitution Hall in Washington. The society's president, Gilbert Grosvenor, called his appearance "one of the outstanding lectures given before the National Geographic Society in many years," citing Gould's "rare combination of dramatic narrative, human interest stories, humor and instruction." An

important lecture date later in the month was before the American Geographical Society in New York, where he became the tenth person presented with that society's prestigious Livingstone Medal.

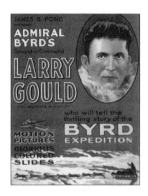

One of the earliest and, as it happened, fateful dates scheduled placed him on October 14 in Skinner Memorial Chapel at Carleton College in Northfield, Minnesota. This was, noted the Carleton campus newspaper, the *Carletonian*, the first public appearance in the Middle West of any member of the famed Byrd Expedition. Following his well-received Tuesday evening lecture Gould was a college guest overnight, and on Wednesday morning Carleton's academic dean, Lindsey Blayney, along with his wife, drove him the forty-five miles to St. Paul to put him on the train to Duluth. On the way, Gould recalled some years later, "Mrs. Blayney suggested that it would be a good idea for me to come to Carleton College and

"A rare combination of dramatic narrative, human interest stories, humor and instruction..."

teach geology. Dean Blayney agreed very warmly." Gould had little notion at the time that anything serious would ever arise from this casual conversation on the road to St. Paul, but in fact wheels were put in motion that morning that would in due course carry him back to Northfield, a community which for thirty years Larry and Peg would call home.

***

During the fall of 1930 Byrd, working with Charles Murphy, finished up work on his book about the expedition, to be titled *Little America*. In addition to having Gould contribute Chapter 15, "The Geological Sledge Trip," Byrd sought Gould's critical and editorial advice on the book as a whole. Enclosing page proofs, apparently of the first three chapters, with a letter of November 2, Byrd wrote that he considered it "vital" that Gould, as second-in-command, "look over these from the standpoint of accuracy, justice, etc.," and that he would appreciate frank suggestions as to any missing points that should be covered. Byrd asked Gould to read these "as promptly as possible and get the proofs back by special delivery," promising to follow with the other chapters as soon as he could. Unfortunately, subsequent deliveries seem to have misfired here, possibly in both directions, which led to some irritation when Byrd believed that his request had gone unheeded. Byrd wrote again on the 19th, complaining that he had "not had a word from you in answer to my urgent plea" and declaring himself to be within his rights as a leader in asking this of his former aide. Gould replied that he had indeed responded as asked relative to the first three chapters and that, after indicating to Murphy what he "thought might be done," he "dispatched them to you by Miss McKercher." Then, eager to help if he could, he waited for the rest of the galley proofs to reach him before writing Byrd directly about the whole, but none came. "I have been away from New York for a month and my itinerary has been very jumpy," he noted, "so it may well have been quite impracticable to get the proofs to me. But I am very sorry not to have had them." It was a misunderstanding quickly patched up and was unimportant in itself except that the episode foreshadowed further and more serious irritations and fallings-out between the two in the months ahead—divergences that would never be public and would never amount to an outright rupture but which created in their relations a mutual coolness that would never again entirely warm.

But that bumpiness remained ahead as December brought to a close what had been a very satisfying year for Larry Gould. Early that month he was asking his former sledging companion Eddie Goodale whether or not Goodale had already seen "the Boss's book," which began to sell briskly upon its arrival in stores and which Gould praised, though he did so with the slightly backhanded compliment that "Charley Murphy has done a great job for him." At year's end he and Peg celebrated their first Christmas together, after which they pleasantly passed a couple of weeks relaxing with friends at a lodge in Holderness, New Hampshire. (Writing to Goodale in prospect of this vacation, he indicated that he hoped to have a chance to drive over to see him, adding "but of course I expect to have my skiis [sic] there and can quite easily (?) put them on some day and slide over and see you if the distance is anything less than 1500 miles.")

In January the lecturing picked up again, starting with a presentation to the Boston Civic Club that was praised by the club secretary in a letter to Pond as "without question one of the finest talks we ever had in the history of the Club. … Our hall was packed with members only, who sat spellbound for nearly two hours. Everyone was thrilled, impressed and delighted." Out in Minnesota, Carleton College's Dean Blayney had followed through on making the attempt to woo Gould to join his faculty and had interested Carleton's president, Donald J. Cowling, in the idea. Their inquiries and enticements were gratifying, but Gould felt himself unable to consider the matter seriously for 1931, and, while certainly conveying encouraging interest in the proposal that he come to Carleton as a full professor and department head, he convinced the Northfield sirens to put off their blandishments for another year. Blayney wrote that "the postponement of your decision to enter into negotiations with us until next year suits us perfectly." Carleton intended to develop a full-fledged department of geology and hoped to have Gould at its head, if he and Cowling could come to an agreement about a position, but the college would be satisfied to begin with a half-time appointment to another man "who would get the subject started once more, ready for your complete reorganization." Blayney and Cowling were therefore willing to put the matter on temporary hold, but, Blayney concluded, "I certainly hope that we may eventually have you as one of the 'family.'"

To be applauded by admiring audiences and wooed and petted by college administrators felt very nice and fed the ego.* In contrast, to be scolded by his former expedition chief, perhaps especially where he considered the criticism unfair, but perhaps no less when he felt himself indeed somewhat at fault, caused Gould to bristle. No less did Dick Byrd bristle himself over any fancied slight or disrespect to his position or hint of disloyalty.† A scolding came, and much bristling followed, early in 1931. At issue, initially, were two matters, the slow-to-progress work on the series of volumes planned to present the scientific results of the Antarctic expedition and Gould's continued annoyance over Jack O'Brien's plan to bring out a boy's book about the sledge trip.

Toward the end of 1930, Gould had informed Byrd that he would be submitting for publication in the April *Geographical Review* "a brief semi-technical summary" of his own expedition work and had added the thought that it would be a good idea if other members of the expedition scientific staff, Davies, Haines, Hanson, and the rest, might do similarly "*in the light of the fact that our scientific series cannot possibly be published within a year.*" [Italics added.] Such a series, Gould suggested, "would demonstrate that we are at work and would by anticipating the full and complete reports whet the appetites of persons interested for the complete records eventually forthcoming." It is not clear whether or not Byrd was startled by the casually dropped "fact" that the scientific volumes could not be published within a year. But after also receiving a letter from aerial photographer Ashley McKinley in which McKinley referred to the scientific work as practically stopped, with expedition data in various scattered hands, Byrd asked Gould to "please outline for me what each scientist is doing" and to supply his current "plan of operation" for getting hold of and compiling the scientific data.

This letter immediately preceded Christmas and the Goulds' vacation in New Hampshire, and it had drawn no reply when Byrd followed it with another, dated

---

* Concerning ego, a history of Carleton's geology department printed in the 1970s contains the following anecdote: "Always sharp and quick on the comeback, [Gould] was confronted one evening in 1930 while on his lecture tour following the Byrd Expedition, when a reception was given in his honor in the home of one of the mining executives in Ishpeming on Michigan's northern peninsula. One dowdy woman, apparently a bit bothered by this dashing young man's somewhat cocky and confident manner, said to him: 'Dr. Gould, I want to tell you that was the most exciting lecture I have ever heard in my life; but I also want to tell you that I think you are the most egotistical man I have ever heard in my life.' Without batting an eye, as the mine manager relates the story, Larry replied with a question: 'Madam, do you know of anyone who has a better reason for being that way?'"

† Byrd biographer Lisle Rose, while also admiring Byrd's virtues of "genuine nobility and seriousness of purpose," identified Byrd's "chief vices" as "jealousy and pettiness." After his first Antarctic expedition was concluded, Rose judged, Byrd "became even more sensitive to slights, criticisms, and what he considered disloyalty."

January 10 in Spokane, where Byrd was then on his own lecture tour. In it, Byrd reiterated his desire to receive a report on Gould's plans for the scientific work and declared himself ready to do all in his power to help, though at the same time he complained of the "enormous burden" on his shoulders, the relentless demands on his time, and the heavy weight of his financial worries, claiming that the expedition debt then stood at $120,000. He somewhat transparently tried to inject a positive note by telling Gould that he had "started the ball rolling" to get Gould a number of medals he deserved, but the bite of the letter, and its impact as "scold," came next:

> In this connection and for your information, I think I should tell you that from a number of sources I have heard some criticism of you to the effect that you are not and have not been giving the time you should, since your return, to the scientific work of the Expedition.
>
> This must have started with several members of the Expedition who have though(t) that you should have done more to bring order out of the chaos of demobilization.
>
> Don't let this worry you because after all I am the one who should be the judge of these things, but I suggest that you stress the scientific end where possible and proceed vigorously in getting these articles written that you speak of.

Meanwhile, before this letter posted from the West Coast had traveled to him, Gould reintroduced the other thread in the weave of discord to come. On the 12th, Gould wrote to Byrd:

> I am genuinely disturbed over the fact that Jack O'Brien is rewriting his book and that it is to appear shortly. I have written to tell him that so far as I am concerned he can have no pictures and that I have asked you not to write a foreword for his book. I see no reason whatever why he should be granted permission to write as he is doing now. He did not distinguish himself on the sledge trip and I do not like the idea of his writing being accepted. I am going to turn my attention at once to the matter of writing a book on my own account for I want to have credit for the work done on that trip placed where it belongs.

Then on January 17, having received the admiral's letter of the 10th, Gould fired off to Los Angeles, where Byrd's lecture tour had taken him next, a bristling reply:

> First—About medals. I have received the medal which means most to me. Don't worry yourself about any more just now. It will be better if you give your attention to cooperating with me on the scientific work ...
>
> Secondly I naturally resent your statement that I have been criticized "from a number of sources" for having neglected the scientific work of

the expedition. I will not let that pass. I insist that you be specific both as to the nature and the sources of criticisms. I note that "this must have started with several members of the expedition etc." This seems doubtful to me since there is but one member of the expedition, namely Mike Thorne, who is conversant with what I have been doing. You owe me a prompt explanation Dick.

Thirdly You ask for "plans, etc. of the scientific work" and add "I will do everything in my power to aid all of you." May I in this connection remind you of a letter which I wrote to you on September 2nd outlining the needs for the scientific work? You acknowledged receipt of the letter but you have not yet given any answer to my proposals.

After reminding Byrd what his summation of necessities had been, Gould continued to vent:

You expect results but you have placed no tools in my hands to work with. ... I have been given to understand from a message you sent me by Norman Vaughan that you have four men busy on the scientific work. It seems a bit irregular to say the least that I was not consulted about this. ... To prepare any plan I must know what you have been doing. ... Things have been too vague and now I must have specific information.

Just what do you expect me to do? Have I the responsibility for the whole scientific program? That is what you have stated orally on numerous occasions. Does this still stand? If so maps are a prime essential. All of the data must be at my disposal. A scientific report cannot be written unless all the information is available. ...

I have naturally assumed that the general oral instructions were to be carried out in the spirit of the above paragraph and have made free use of aerial photographs but I am lead to believe that your own view of the use of this material does not correspond to my requirements. It is vital to clear up this and all other points with the least possible delay if the scientific work of the expedition is not to suffer.

I also want to reiterate my objections to O'Brien being granted permission to publish a book about the sledge trip before I have done so. ... Every member of the party is opposed to having O'Brien write such a book.

Gould repeated his objections to O'Brien's book in a January 19 telegram to Byrd sent after learning that Ashley McKinley was sending O'Brien photographs for his use. Byrd responded that he considered O'Brien's text "simply a narrative for boys," unharmful and unable to detract from anything Gould might produce; also, that he had gone into the matter thoroughly, making an effort to be just and fair, observing that O'Brien was now destitute, and asking Gould to trust his judgment. Gould would not let the matter rest, stating in another telegram on the 26th that he was

> not pleased with arrangement. If O'Brien is destitute let him undertake something he is qualified to do. … I think I have a sense of fairness too and it is decidedly unfair to every other member of party to let O'Brien write about it and they will all resent it. I shall not take it kindly if you carry out your plan to let O'Brien publish book.

"I cannot and will not stand for the tone of several of your communications to me lately," Byrd wrote from the lecture trail in Houston on February 3 in the first of three separate letters he directed to Gould that date. "There has been nothing," Byrd averred, "to warrant your using this attitude towards me. It is a pity for us to be fighting." Offering that he may have expressed himself badly, he said that "whatever injustice I have done you, I am ready to make every effort to correct." Observing that the burden on his shoulders was "almost more than a man can bear,"* he appealed to Gould to give him a fair break. The accompanying letters attempted to address some of the "points" Gould had brought up in his communications. On the O'Brien matter, Byrd repeated that O'Brien's short narrative was harmless, that in any case Byrd had insisted that it wait until at least a month after Gould's reporting on the trip, attached to Byrd's own book, had appeared, and that he felt he could not now retract permission already given. Byrd followed three days later with a fourth letter in which he proposed a number of conferences regarding the scientific work, as well as, "if you care to," a personal conference to get together and talk over the matters that Gould was holding against him. "Since we returned to the States," Byrd suggested, "our respective duties and work has kept us from seeing enough of each other." Byrd asked that Gould let him know his own particular needs for the geological work and the surveying work done by the Geological Party, but he told Gould it had never been his intention that Gould do the work on the maps resulting from expedition flights and aerial photography.

Gould's response to these various communications is contained in a letter of February 12. He agreed that it would be "a pity for us to be fighting" and claimed that there was no reason they should "if we but face the questions involved in the scientific program with full candor." However, he asserted, "none of your letters quite answers the specific things I asked about in my letter to you of January 17th." He introduced a new complaint, that without informing him

---

* Byrd's post-expedition burdens were very real, notably his struggles to retire the expedition debt, which he assumed as a personal obligation, in the deepening economic depression. His friend Charlie Bob, who had been one of the expedition's biggest benefactors, had been indicted in November for defrauding investors of $6 million and would in his resulting desperation sue for a refund of $150,000 that he claimed to have donated to Byrd. Historian Eugene Rodgers, writing decades later, judged that "Byrd's heavy financial burden must have played a large role in his tentative attitude toward the scientific project."

Byrd had "made certain commitments as to the disposition of scientific data before we had even left the ice," specifically "an agreement covering the division of material between the National Geographic and the American Geographical Societies." (His source for this information was Isaiah Bowman, of the latter.) He was puzzled by Byrd's unilateral decision to employ a friend, naval cartographer Harold Saunders, to undertake map work that he felt belonged properly to Ashley McKinley and furthermore was duplicating work already completed by others for the American Geographical Society. With regard to geology, he informed Byrd that he had done about all he could on that until summer when he would return to Ann Arbor, where his "analyses and microscopic sections should be ready by that time.* Gould agreed that a face-to-face conference had become necessary but thought that "just a personal one between the two of us will not settle all of the questions involved" and that "the only way out of this chaos" would require four or five who he named. On the O'Brien matter, he expressed himself as relieved that the book would be "the same manuscript [O'Brien] had submitted last summer," for Gould had been given the "very distinct impression" when he had last seen O'Brien in New York that he was planning to use his diary to have the whole thing "ghost written and rewritten." Finally, Gould concluded, "I hope you will understand that whatever I have written or may say is prompted solely by the desire to have the whole scientific record rightly assembled. If I express myself with the 'brutal frankness of a blood relative' it is purely for this reason."

The two did apparently meet around the end of February to discuss how best to progress on the scientific project. "Larry and I had a talk the other day," Byrd wrote to expedition meteorologist Bill Haines, "and it was agreed that I should jump in and help as much as I can with the compilation of the scientific data, since I have certain facilities such as a secretary. ... Because of the press of circumstances I have to some extent neglected my duty in this matter, but am now 'full speed ahead.'" When Byrd wrote Gould again at the end of March, reporting on a conference he had in Washington with several of the other scientists, which Gould could not attend, the tone of the communication seems to be restored at least on the surface to a cordial normality.

***

Larry Gould maintained a full schedule of lecturing that spring of 1931 while also working in earnest on his own book-length memoir of the expedition, drawn largely from his Antarctic diary and log of the Geological Party journey. He had agreed to publish the memoir with his good friend and former companion from Arctic travels, George Palmer Putnam. Putnam, who had sold out his interest in G. P. Putnam's

---

* The petrographical study of Gould's Antarctic rock specimens was being undertaken in Ann Arbor by one of Gould's former students, Duncan Stewart, who began the work that February and who would eventually turn the analysis into his 1933 doctoral dissertation. Gould would then bring Stewart to join him at Carleton, where Stewart would eventually succeed him as head of the department.

Sons the previous August, was now joining the smaller publishing firm of Brewer &
Warren, Inc., which in March would become Brewer, Warren & Putnam. Gould's
book would become one of the first projects of the newly titled house.*

Gould in this period was frequently on the road, but not always, and he and
Peg managed to have a wonderful time as a newly married couple living in New
York. For their first Valentine's Day together as husband and wife, Peg presented
Larry with a gift copy of Anatole France's novel *Penguin Island*. An anecdote of
their New York life which comes with no precise date is told by Gould's former
shipmate aboard the *Eleanor Bolling*, Hilton Willcox, who wrote of his pleasure
in coming to New York and again seeing some friends of Byrd Expedition days,
including his special hero, Larry Gould:

> This hero, now happily married to a beautiful and charming young lady,
> I now found in an apartment in East 57th Street, whither I had been
> invited, in company with Ashley McKinley … and his wife, for dinner. I
> arrived early (something I now regard as an unforgivable sin!): and it was
> a symptom of those strange days in America, that Larry after introducing
> me to his lovely Peg, should suddenly exclaim, "Good Lord!—I've
> forgotten hooch! Excuse me a moment while I call my bootlegger." I did
> not hear it, but within half-an-hour Larry heard the signal, and, giving
> the delivery-man sufficient time to remove himself from the scene of
> operations, opened the door to find that the beer and whatever else he
> had ordered was there. …
>
> It was a splendid evening with Larry Gould and his lady, and half
> a century has done little to erase its pleasure from my memory.

During the spring and into the summer of 1931, Gould seems to have flirted
more or less seriously with the idea of planning a return expedition to Antarctica,
not with Byrd, who was expected to organize his own second expedition there,
but in partnership with others. Aerial explorer Lincoln Ellsworth apparently
approached Gould with a proposal (or perhaps only with an idea for a proposal)
of going with him, but, as Gould informed Byrd in early June, nothing came
of that. Evidence exists that for a time Gould was considering an expedition
to be organized in partnership with Bernt Balchen. On April 24, Gould wrote
Paul Siple, who was interested in returning to the ice either with Byrd or with
Gould, that he was hoping, without trespassing "in any way on the Admiral," to
sometime "be able to announce the Gould-Balchen Antarctic Expedition." He
confided that he and Balchen were "on the search for contributions with which
to get started, but admitted that "these are frightfully hard days in which to raise
moneys" and that it was not at all clear "when or even whether our expedition is

---

*   Unfortunately, it was also not all that far from being one of the last, as well. As Gould noted
     ruefully during his March 1981 oral history interview with Peter Anderson, his publishers
     "went broke after they'd hardly gotten the book out." The Brewer, Warren & Putnam catalog
     would be acquired in November 1932 by Harcourt, Brace & Co.

going to materialize." He therefore gave Siple the advice, which the young man duly took, to "not in any way jeopardize your interests by waiting for us." Toward the end of May, Gould wrote Byrd that he would like to have a discussion about Byrd's plans for further exploration, saying that "some interesting possibilities have arisen for me" that he wanted to talk over with Byrd before making any decision. On June 5 he elaborated, claiming that "within the last ten days there has come a possible opportunity for me to return to the Antarctic … and of course I want to discuss it with you." He wrote that he would be meeting for lunch the following Wednesday with "the parties concerned" and advised that "if everything appears feasible then I should like to come to Boston at once to see you," stressing that much would depend upon Byrd's reaction and that "I should not want to start on an expedition without enlisting your good will both privately and publicly."

Gould informed Byrd on June 5 that the manuscript for his book was finished and that he thought the admiral would like it. "In the advertising," he stressed, "it is stated that it 'will be welcomed as a fitting complement to Byrd's own book.'" Five days later (the same Wednesday he was reportedly lunching with "the parties concerned" about planning a return expedition), Gould signed and dated the foreword to his book, subsequently brought out by Brewer, Warren & Putnam as *Cold: The Record of an Antarctic Sledge Journey.** Gould dedicated *Cold* to his wife and to Putnam. In his foreword, in addition to paying tribute to his sledging companions he highlighted the friendship of "three men to whom I shall always be indebted," his "teacher-friend" Professor Hobbs of Michigan, Putnam, and Dr. Bowman of the American Geographical Society. He headed each chapter with one or more apt quotations, usually a few lines of poetry—including, for one of them, verses of his kid sister-in-law, Jean Rice, who in Ann Arbor that June was just graduating from high school—and he closed the book with an eloquent expression of his desire to go back.

On the 17th, Gould and Byrd had a chance to discuss Gould's prospective plans to do just that when both were present for the commencement ceremonies at the Polytechnic Institute of Brooklyn, at which Gould was receiving an honorary degree. Though no record was made of their conversation that day and though the admiral had earlier written that he was "glad to hear" about the possibility that had arisen for Gould and that he hoped it would go through for him all right, it seems that Byrd may have expressed reservations, at least with any plans that would include reuse of the Little America site or that would poach too many members of the last expedition for future service with Gould rather than

---

*   An engaging and often exciting memoir, *Cold* was well received from the start and over time found a permanent place as one of the minor classics of polar literature. Though the publishers indeed went broke within a short while of bringing *Cold* out, this likely was rather less the fault of Gould's book than it was of the conditions of the Great Depression, which has a lot to answer for. In 1984 a new limited edition of *Cold*, with new fifty-years-later epilogue by the author, was published by Carleton College, which suffered no obvious ill effect or economic calamity as a consequence. The text of this edition was republished by Carleton in 2011.

Byrd. On July 2, Gould wrote that "when I discussed my prospective plans with you" on June 17th, plans he said were "still nebulous and indefinite," "I thought you would be glad to have us who shared with you in the task of building Little America use it again. Naturally if you do not wish it we shall make other plans." This followed an end of June telegram and letter from Byrd in which the admiral urged Gould to "not make any further move in connection with your expedition to Little America until you let me know what you propose to do" and suggesting that Gould neither approach "any more of my friends" (presumably potential financial backers) "until you and I have worked it out" nor "enlist for your expedition any more members of our last expedition until I can find out whether or not they want to go with me." With regard to plans "which take in any parts of Antarctica but Little America," Byrd allowed, "I naturally have no concern ... other than to wish you all success."

Active further contemplation in 1931 of a Gould return expedition to Antarctica does not seem to outlive the month of July.

***

During the summer of 1931 Peg Gould's fifty-five-year-old mother fell critically ill, which brought both Peg and Larry back to Ann Arbor for stretches. She then died, which Peg described as "a crushing blow." Admiral and Mrs. Byrd sent Peg a telegram of sympathy for her sorrow, but meanwhile Byrd had again begun to seethe with resentment over what he understood to be some of Gould's recent actions and statements to others. Byrd took exception to Gould's having implied in his letter of July 2 that Byrd had indicated that he did not want a Gould expedition to go to Little America, and he objected to Gould's having deflected his request for a statement of Gould's plans by calling them "nebulous," since he had heard from a number of sources that Gould had been actively trying to raise money for an expedition and that "raising money with nebulous plans is as a rule not possible."

More seriously, Byrd had heard that Gould had told someone that the recent resignation of Byrd's secretary Charles Lofgren had come about because Lofgren had gotten fed up with Byrd; also that Gould had been questioning the handling of the expedition debt and related financial matters. Byrd had a long history of seeing red where he saw or suspected personal disloyalty or being second-guessed or being talked about behind his back. On July 26 he wrote a complaining letter to McKinley, which historian Eugene Rodgers has characterized as sounding "as if he had reverted to the dark suspiciousness of the antarctic winter." He told McKinley that Gould's purported remark about Lofgren was "entirely disloyal" and that his questions about finances were off the mark. Going further, he protested to McKinley that Gould's statements were being made "in a malicious attempt to discredit me with the men of the expedition" and alleged that Mike Thorne had been saying "that he and Gould are going back to Little America to finish the work that I should have done there."

Byrd also brought George Palmer Putnam into his field of fire, claiming to McKinley that "there has been some pretty direct evidence that Putnam is after my scalp." Similarly, in a letter to Eddie Goodale, Byrd complained that "the finances of the expedition are not Gould's affair" and that a critical newspaper article to which he objected may have "been sicked on by Putnam, who used to be a friend of mine." Fulminating against newspapermen "who would crucify any one for a few pieces of silver," Byrd claimed that their information came from "this small gang of my enemies that play around together." "It has astonished me beyond measure," he continued to Goodale, "to find these two fellows apparently doing these things against me." (A handwritten insertion in this letter at this point admits "I may be doing Gould a grave injustice here.") Avowing that he could think of no unfairness done by himself to Gould, he said that he could not understand Gould's motive for "raking up these ... things that have nothing to do with him." "Where does Gould get his information about my financial matters?" he asked. "We have never discussed them. I don't see how he could know anything about them."

In September, some of the former members of the Byrd Expedition, evidently organized by Byrd loyalist Kenneth Bubier, threw a dinner for the admiral in Boston, at which they presented him with the gift of a Naval Academy ring (apparently replacing one that had been lost) for which a collection of small donations had been solicited from expedition members by mail. Perhaps due to several members' awareness of strained relations between Byrd and Gould, Gould was conspicuously uninvolved. A handwritten note sent at the time from Gould to Byrd reads as follows:

> Dear Dick,
>
> I am sorry not to be seeing you now—but I was not invited to the party and only learned of it accidentally. For some reason I have been completely ignored in the whole festivity except for my signature.
>
> I was not invited even to participate in the proposed gift and when I discovered that things were misrepresented to me to get my signature then I became much disturbed. I have the impression that the whole matter is designed to serve as personal aggrandizement for the person getting it up.
>
> When I discovered the "lay of the land" as it were, I protested to Bubier as he will no doubt tell you. I think the whole matter has been badly managed and there is little spontaneity about it.
>
> Mac [McKinley] has probably told you all this but I have written this hurried note so that you will not misunderstand my attitude. I should most certainly not like that to happen.

Byrd replied somewhat frostily that "I am sorry if the ring and testimonial have caused you any embarrassment on account of the way it was handled. When Mac phoned me I told him to do whatever was necessary to relieve you of any embarrassment and that I would agree to remove anything from the proceedings that was unfair to you ..."

For the most part, however, Byrd's sense of being persecuted or conspired against seems to have gone dormant by the fall, and his occasional correspondence with Gould resumed a more normal tone, with an ongoing chill between the two men rarely apparent on paper, unless between lines.

Early in October, Gould had the pleasure of arriving back in New York after a brief holiday in New Hampshire to find waiting for him a package containing a number of advance copies of *Cold*. Another signal pleasure came at the end of the month when he accepted a gold medal presented by the Chicago Geographical Society. From his lecture trail in Cleveland, a week later, he informed Byrd that the experience ranked among the most pleasant since the return from Antarctica and that he appreciated the role the admiral had played in it.

An additional pleasure worthy of note that fall was serving as the intermediary in introducing his friend, pilot Bernt Balchen, to his friend George Putnam's new wife—they had married in February—aviatrix Amelia Earhart. Putnam wished Balchen to instruct Earhart in navigation and in flying "blind" using instruments, in preparation for her planned attempt the following year to cross the Atlantic flying solo.*

Bernt Balchen and Amelia Earhart

An experience that fall and continuing on into 1932 was the distinctly unpleasant one of being sued for libel. The case was always ridiculous, and while an ultimate adverse judgment seemed an impossible outcome, it nonetheless occasioned considerable annoyance and expense before finally being dropped. The affair concerned a twenty-year-old, Raymond Mercola, who had made a small splash addressing audiences in Indiana as "the youngest member of the Byrd Expedition," claiming to have joined the crew of the *Eleanor Bolling* in Dunedin, and lecturing about the exciting adventures he had experienced traveling through the ice pack and on to Little America. Doubts arose as to whether the young man had in fact ever approached the Antarctic circle, and why the name "Mercola" did not appear on

---

*   Earhart had gained fame in 1928 for becoming, as part of a three-person team, the first woman to fly over the Atlantic, but for that flight, despite Putnam's insistence for publicity purposes that she had been in overall command, she had done no actual piloting and had felt herself to be "only baggage, like a sack of potatoes." Thereafter her ambition came to be to make the flight alone. Balchen, following Gould's introduction, became her trainer and technical adviser for the solo flight.

official lists of expedition members, to which Mercola improvised that he had gone to Little America under the name of M. W. Dobson. A friend of Gould's, Robert Pickard, who published a newspaper in Mooresville, Indiana, found Mercola's story improbable, wrote to Gould for reaction, and on October 22 printed Gould's reply under the heading "Investigation Proves 'Explorer' A Fraud." Gould wrote:

> I hasten to answer your good letter of the 16th apropos one Raymond Mercola.
> ... He was never a member of the expedition. He arrived in Dunedin, New Zealand, one day apparently penniless and out of the kindness of his heart Captain Brown took him aboard the *Eleanor Bolling* as mess boy. He was totally unsatisfactory even in this capacity and was discharged. He made no voyage to the Antarctic aboard the ship—was never near Little America and had no contact with the expedition beyond that mentioned above.
> In posing now as having been a member of the expedition under the name of Dobson, Mercola is laying himself liable, for Dobson was a member of the crew of the *Eleanor Bolling* and did excellent work. Doubtless Mercola thinks it safe to use his name now since he (Dobson) is very likely back in New Zealand. That Mercola was known to us on the expedition under any other name than his own is wholly untrue. ... Mercola is beyond any question one of the worst impostors I have ever had any contact with. You will surely understand that we do not want intelligent people to get the impression that a person of his calibre would ever have been selected for membership in the expedition.

The *Mooresville Times* added that it took "genuine pleasure in being able to present the true facts ... and hopes that it will in some measure help to curb Mercola's unscrupulous attempt to dupe an unsuspecting public."

Mercola's audacity was such, however, that at the end of October he visited Pickard with an attorney, informing him that they "would find it necessary to file libel charges." Pickard told Gould that "they volunteered the information that suit would be filed against you, so you may hear from them some of these days or may not. My guess would be that you won't." Pickard elaborated:

> During their call yesterday they attempted to convince me that Mercola has never told anyone that he had gone under the name of Dobson and that he had not represented himself as having gone to the ice as a member of the expedition. A trip to Danville last evening uncovered approximately five reputable people who heard him tell me that he went as Dobson. He was advertised on hand bills in Danville as the youngest member of the Byrd expedition and several persons who heard his lecture there can furnish plenty of testimony that he told many details of the expedition, such as conversation here and there and the details of Commander Byrd's take-off for the pole, as first hand information.

"I am wondering," Pickard added, "if you can possibly get a statement from Commander Byrd and forward it to us post haste."

Despite Pickard's prediction, suit was also filed against Gould, for $50,000 damages. Byrd promptly wrote the requested statement, affirming the truth of what Gould had said about Mercola's connection with the expedition. Though in a rational world the suit would then have been promptly withdrawn or quashed, the annoyance persisted all the way until May, causing Gould to retain a lawyer and go to the trouble of having the case transferred to federal court and resulting in Byrd's having to go through the inconvenience of giving a formal deposition in March. Mercola, Gould opined to Byrd in November, must either be "insane or making a cheap gesture for publicity," and he found it "all so damned stupid" that he could not "understand what manner of persons [Mercola's] lawyers are." "It seems to me," he told Byrd, "that if they only half realized the fallacies upon which they are working they would drop the case." They finally did so only after the taking of Byrd's deposition and his strong representations to Mercola's lawyers that they were being taken in by their client. Byrd thought "it helped that one of them had a son at the Naval Academy."

***

As 1931 disappeared and 1932 began, progress on the scientific reports continued by and large to be unsatisfactory to all concerned. Pressed in November for a statement to Byrd as to when he thought work on the geological report could be completed, Gould responded that he did "not see the end of it yet." Duncan Stewart was at work in Michigan on his part of the work, but there was more to be done. Gould asked for $500 to have a number of chemical analyses made; he also pointed out that his report on the glaciology could not be completed until the maps were finished, particularly the Bay of Whales mosaic, and asked whether anything was being done about that. "Finally," Gould concluded, "I don't know how long it may take me to coordinate the various reports of my colleagues and I must of course see them all. ... I do not know what progress the others are making and I should be kept informed about it." Byrd responded somewhat testily, "I think practically everybody but yourself have written that they will be able to finish by next summer." In January Gould would tell Byrd that though he thought it "vital to all of us that these reports be finished as soon as possible," there seemed to him to be, "with the present setup ... little hope of getting them done this summer or next summer or even the one beyond that."

Meanwhile, the deferred year had passed, and Carleton College was renewing its effort to bring Gould to Minnesota as a department head. The Goulds were visited in New York by Carleton's very persuasive President Cowling, who was able to make a definite offer: a full professorship as professor of geology or of geology and geography, as preferred, and a handsome salary of $5,000 per annum. After "much correspondence" with Professor Hobbs at Michigan, Gould and Hobbs together concluded that perhaps Gould's opportunities away from Ann Arbor "for the present at least" were superior to anything Michigan could then offer. In a Christmas Eve letter, Gould reported to Cowling that upon Hobbs' return from his holidays, about the 4th of January, he would "take up the matter of my resignation from the University of Michigan faculty with the proper dean and the president." "I am not so impressed with my own importance," Gould continued, "as to suppose that the announcement of my withdrawal will seriously affect the fortunes of my alma mater," and he looked forward to writing Cowling again early in January with his "unqualified acceptance of the position" offered at Carleton.

Cowling's offer, which would make the thirty-six-year-old Gould when he set foot on campus the college's highest-paid professor,* was being made possible by the personal commitment of the president of Carleton's board of trustees, Frederic S. Bell. Bell, whose fortune lay in his family's involvement in the lumber business, undertook to provide half of Gould's $5,000 a year salary out of his own pocket for the first three years "to make up the difference between what we can afford and what we ought to have."

In due course, after the New Year, the University of Michigan Board of Regents "regretfully accepted" the resignation of Associate Professor of Geology Laurence M. Gould "in order that he might accept a professorship at Carleton College." On January 9 Gould wrote to Cowling of his definite commitment to the position at Carleton, adding that "Mrs. Gould is delighted at the prospect of coming to Carleton next year" and that they were both "looking forward to happy days there under your leadership." They would start in September.

---

* Two other Carleton professors had the same salary as Gould in 1932-33, excluding housing allowances. Both were men decades older: Thomas Rankin, a very distinguished professor of English who had spent twenty-three years on the faculty at Michigan before coming to Carleton in 1928, and William F. Anderson in the History of Religion Department, who was a prominent Methodist bishop, held five honorary degrees, and had been a close friend of President Warren G. Harding. Anderson joined the Carleton faculty for two years at the same time as Gould. Only two administrative salaries were higher, those of President Cowling and of Dean Blayney. It was indeed a handsome offer.

In the classroom

CHAPTER 12

CARLETON PROFESSOR

W ord that Byrd lieutenant Larry Gould would join the Carleton faculty in the fall broke on the Carleton campus in mid-January, with President Cowling's announcement followed by excited reporting in the student newspaper. To a college with an enrollment of just over eight hundred, within a town of population four thousand-some, the pending addition to the community of a celebrity like Gould was big news indeed. (Though the faculty included a number of persons of distinguished reputation in educational circles and Cowling had become a widely respected and influential voice among college presidents, in 1932 the biggest newsmakers associated with Carleton were to be found on its board of trustees, which included both an associate justice of the United States Supreme Court—Carleton alumnus Pierce Butler—and board vice president Frank B. Kellogg, the former US secretary of state and recent recipient of the Nobel Peace Prize.)

The school which Gould had agreed to join was midway through its sixty-fifth year. It was in its twenty-third year of being lead by Cowling, who in addition to strengthening its academic standing had been its great physical builder; a majority of the campus halls and dormitories existing in 1932 had been constructed in the teens and twenties. (Ambitious plans for further development, though long ready, had been brought to a full halt by the 1929 crash and its aftermath.) Though its main campus, on the northeast edge of the city of Northfield, was only about ninety acres in size, Carleton's entire grounds comprised some eight hundred acres, including two major additions of the Cowling era: a college arboretum, primarily north of the main campus along the Cannon River, and to the north and east a three hundred-acre college farm. Between main campus and farm lay the picturesque, though artificially engineered, Lyman Memorial Lakes, created in the first decade of the Cowling administration where a meandering creek had run. In 1932 the college's endowment stood at a little under $3 million.

Gould would join a faculty that in the year before his arrival numbered sixty-five.* Except for some unclassified specials and a handful of graduates working toward master's degrees, the student body was entirely undergraduate and, the school having been coeducational from its founding, was about evenly divided between men and women. Carleton then drew its students mostly from Minnesota and adjoining states. For the college year 1931-32, of the total of 881 different students enrolled over two semesters 517 were Minnesotans; 275 came from Illinois, Wisconsin, Iowa, or the Dakotas; 41 more were from Michigan or Montana; and only smatterings (37) from elsewhere in the country. Eleven students came from outside the United States.

Carleton had been founded by Congregationalists and though under no denominational control had always maintained its essentially religious—and Christian—spirit.† Cowling was a Congregationalist minister, as both of his predecessors in the Carleton presidency had also been. Carleton's annual catalog made explicit the college's aims in this respect: "The College is especially concerned with the moral welfare of its students and strives to preserve a genuine Christian atmosphere." Under the heading of "discipline," the catalog added: "In all matters pertaining to personal conduct, students are expected to behave as responsible citizens and members of a Christian community. Any student who becomes antagonistic to the spirit and methods of the institution ... thereby automatically severs his connection with the College." In the early 1930s, on-campus chapel services, conducted by members of the faculty or with addresses by outside speakers, were held Tuesday and Friday forenoons, and on Sunday evenings students attended chapel vesper services, with music furnished by the Carleton Choir and speakers "of national reputation ... frequently secured." "A student may not be absent in one semester," the college rules warned, "more than four times from the vesper service or more than eight times from week-day chapel exercises."

Information about Northfield, printed in the Carleton catalog of 1932, stressed its easy connections to the Twin Cities of Minneapolis and St. Paul, some forty miles to the north, via the paved Jefferson Highway or by rail on a number of different lines. The catalog also noted that the city was "supplied with electricity, gas, water-works, and other modern conveniences," that it had well-equipped schools, and that it was represented by churches in denominations of Congregational, Baptist, Episcopal, Methodist, Moravian, Norwegian Lutheran, Danish Lutheran, Bethel Lutheran, and Roman Catholic. Northfield was very

---

* Among the associate professors, assistant professors, and instructors, nearly half were women, but in 1931-32 all twenty-six of those holding the rank of full professor were men.

† Also its essentially Protestant character. Church affiliations, though explicitly not relevant to the college's admissions decisions, remained overwhelmingly mainstream Protestant. The table of student affiliations printed in the annual catalog showed, among the 881 students enrolled during 1931-32, thirty-seven Catholics, seven Jews, three Unitarians, and a Mormon. Three reported "No Church." (In an apparent wavelet of rampant relative secularization coinciding with Gould's first year at Carleton, the number of those self-reporting as unaffiliated with any church would shoot all the way up to thirteen for 1932-33.)

unusual for a town its size in being home to not one but two fine liberal arts colleges, with Carleton being joined (and provided with a natural rival in athletic contests) across the Cannon River on the western edge of town by St. Olaf College, an institution distinctly Norwegian Lutheran in origin and ongoing character. The presence of the two schools and the resulting concentration in town of people who were faculty, or employees, or alumni of one or the other gave Northfield a highly educated citizenry and relatively cosmopolitan character that would have been otherwise unexpected given its small size and rural Midwestern setting. Close to the time of Gould's arrival, it has been noted, one out of every ninety-four Northfield residents (forty-four persons in town) had a listing in *Who's Who in America*, at a time when the *Who's Who* ratio nationwide was one in every 3,910.

About a week following the announcement that Gould would come to Carleton, college business brought Cowling to New York for several days, and the Goulds, characterizing themselves as "delighted about Carleton," invited him to dinner at their apartment in company with mutual friends President and Mrs. Kolbe of the Polytechnic Institute of Brooklyn. Conversation must have been very pleasant that evening, as Cowling doubtless supplied the Goulds with much information about what to anticipate that year as they prepared to recenter their lives on Minnesota. A few days later, Gould mailed Cowling a statement outlining his thoughts about the scope and work of Carleton's new Department of Geology and Geography together with brief descriptions of the courses he proposed initially to offer.*

***

Early in February, Gould alerted Admiral Byrd to the possibly alarming fact that a play had recently been written involving an American Antarctic expedition that faces mutiny when it appears that its rescue ship may have been wrecked, forcing preparations to dig in for another winter. The playwright, George F. Hummel, had collaborated on the script to some extent with Russell Owen, the Byrd Expedition's *New York Times* correspondent, whose involvement might naturally lead people to suppose that the play was based on that expedition's reality. The characters included aviators, dog drivers, a pompous publicity hound commander, a "capable" newspaper correspondent, and a geologist/college professor described in the script as "the conciliator of the crowd, a genial, kindly fellow who tries throughout to keep some sense of proportion." As Gould would inform Byrd, the play had actually been inspired by the ill-fated Greely Arctic Expedition of the

---

* The department had already begun work in a small way during the year before Gould's arrival as head, with George Gibson, a 1930 graduate of the University of Minnesota, present as a two-thirds-time instructor. Gibson, a former football All-American at Minnesota who was also appointed part-time instructor in physical education for men, gave one introductory course in geology each semester during 1931-32, enrolling forty-some students for each. This beginning would give Gould some students ready for more advanced coursework during his first year at Carleton.

1880s, but Hummel had moved it south to take advantage of popular interest in Antarctica since the Byrd Expedition and had brought in Owen to add "local color and to give the play a further boost with the public." Gould had learned about it after a news item had appeared stating in effect that Russell Owen was writing a play about the Byrd Expedition. This had troubled Hummel, who now regretted having involved Owen. Hummel spoke with Arthur Sulzberger of the *Times* about it, and Sulzberger advised Hummel to talk with Gould. After reading the script, Gould assured Byrd that it really "contained no parallel with the Byrd Expedition" and advised Byrd to read the play himself to see how silly the matter really was. In April, when Hummel let Gould know that he had found a producer, Gould repeated his advice that Byrd look over the script and offered the opinion that the admiral might "forever kill any tendency to tie it up with the Byrd Expedition" by publicly giving it his personal approval. In the end it is unclear that Byrd ever did anything at all about the matter, and the play, given the title *The World Waits*, eventually came and went, doing the Byrd Expedition no reputational damage.

Byrd, during this time, continued to press for progress on the wrapping up of the expedition's scientific reports but also continued to fail sufficiently to fund the necessary work; the result was a project that remained essentially stalled. With more and more of his own time focused on preparations and fundraising for a second Byrd Antarctic Expedition—announced first for expected departure in the fall of 1932 but eventually to materialize a year later than that—Byrd hoped to move things forward by asking the National Geographic Society, working through cartographer Harold Saunders, to take over coordinating the various scientific reports. In March, Saunders wrote Gould urging him to get a geological report submitted as soon as possible, but Gould replied that "as yet Admiral Byrd has not provided the moneys" for necessary laboratory work and that "we are waiting authorization from Byrd to go ahead with it at the expense of the expedition." A few days later, Byrd, who had suffered financial setbacks—by midsummer he was claiming to be "almost threatened with bankruptcy" and was announcing the indefinite postponement of his next Antarctic expedition—wrote to Ashley McKinley: "Won't you try to impress on Gould that I am not a multimillionaire. I have evidence from several sources that he thinks I am rolling in wealth."

In the end, the planned scientific volumes never would appear. Gould, of course, took up his duties at Carleton at the end of the summer of 1932. The following January Gould would optimistically project that he and Duncan Stewart might both be able to finish reports by spring, but in March Saunders told Gould that the overall project was "pretty much at a standstill." Byrd, the month after that, confessed to Dana Coman that he simply could not personally spend any more on the scientific work than he already had. Gould that month was still writing of his expectation to be able to complete a geological report "during the summer." By late September his revised expectation was that his and Stewart's

Aerial view of Carleton College, 1929

combined reports could "be ready for the printer by the holidays." But Byrd, in the fall of 1933, with his second expedition now departing, was finally forced to acknowledge that nothing further could be done towards comprehensively publishing the scientific and technical work of the first expedition until after his return from the second—a suspension of effort that would in fact never be resumed. (Never resumed, at least, in the systematic consolidated way that was first planned. It was the case that, as historian Eugene Rodgers notes, "most of the scientific findings were eventually published separately in scholarly journals.")

Rodgers, in his 1990 study of the expedition and its aftermath, hypothesizes that Byrd, when he took a post-expedition "hard look at the financial implications of the project," may have "privately decided not to go through with it," especially when considering that any "attempt at fund-raising to clean up the first expedition would have clashed with his campaign to finance the second expedition, difficult enough in the depression." Rodgers suggests that though the admiral could not say so outright lest he be criticized for shortchanging science, Byrd "may have wanted the scientists to find their own backing ... even as he lauded their goals and professed full support." Meanwhile Gould, Rodgers supposes, "no naïf, ... must have realized within a few weeks if not days of starting that the project was failing badly, for whatever reason," but chose to hang on, neither working hard at an unsupported enterprise nor choosing to abandon the project entirely and risk being blamed for its failure if he resigned. Guided only by the remaining correspondence, the matter is at this point, as Rodgers notes, all "guesswork."

***

A Day in the Life: May 19, 1932 … Throughout the spring of 1932 Amelia Earhart, working with Bernt Balchen, had trained and planned toward her attempt to beat out a number of potential competitors and become the first woman to pilot a plane solo across the Atlantic. Earhart and her husband, Gould's friend and publisher George Palmer Putnam, hoped to add to the drama of her attempt to claim the title "Lady Lindy" by timing her departure for May 20, the fifth anniversary of the start of Lindbergh's own solo crossing. For that to happen, the weather needed to cooperate. A favorable report was finally received on May 19, which was the last possible day to depart the New Jersey airfield where Balchen and Earhart had been training if Earhart were to jump off from Harbour Grace, Newfoundland—the nearest North American airfield to Europe—on the Lindbergh anniversary date. Putnam took the report from James Kimball, head of the US Weather Bureau, and passed the news on to his wife, who rushed home to Rye, New York, picked up her flying outfit (jodhpurs, silk shirt, scarves, and leather jacket), some maps and charts, her toothbrush, her comb, a thermos of soup, and a can of tomato juice, and then drove on to the Teterboro airfield to get away without attracting the inconvenient attention—yet—of any member of the press. Earhart was met at the field in Teterboro by her husband, together with Balchen, master mechanic Edward Gorski, and, at Putnam's invitation, Larry and Peg Gould. The farewells were short. Allowing Earhart as much rest as possible before going solo, Balchen piloted the specially prepared Lockheed Vega as it left Teterboro. Gorski also accompanied the plane to St. John, New Brunswick, and then on to Harbour Grace. As Balchen taxied the craft onto the runway, with Gorski and Earhart in the rear, the only witnesses seeing them off who understood what was happening were Putnam and the Goulds. As Earhart waved from a window, Gould noticed that nobody else present at the field seemed to take the least notice of her departure. Two days later, when Earhart and the Vega landed in Ireland (with, by that time, a malfunctioning altimeter, a cracked exhaust manifold, and a leaking fuel gauge), notice was no longer lacking: She was now the object of the world's adulation and, in the words of Earhart biographer Susan Butler, "had become the most famous, most celebrated woman in the world."*

***

In the summer of 1932, the Dow Jones Industrial Average bottomed out at its lowest point during the Great Depression, down 91 percent from its level three years earlier. The national unemployment rate stood at over 20 percent.

---

* In September Earhart joined Gould in the short list of authors published by Brewer, Warren and Putnam when her memoir *The Fun of It* was shipped to store shelves.

Ominously, in Germany that summer, Adolf Hitler's Nazi party doubled its strength in legislative elections, and in August Nazi Hermann Goering was elected president of the Reichstag. Yet for Larry and Peg Gould, looking ahead to a secure new job and exciting new responsibilities at Carleton College, the summer days rolled by pleasantly. In June, Byrd wrote Gould that he proposed, in connection with ongoing map-work to be published in the *National Geographic* magazine, to make a change in one name applied by Gould's geological party to a peak in the Queen Maud Mountains. Specifically, what the Geological Party had in the field called "Admiral Mountain," to the east of Thorne Glacier and near mountains named for Vaughan, Crockett, and Goodale, Byrd now gave instructions to be relabeled "Mount Gould." Some time in the latter half of June the Goulds returned to the nature camp at Holderness, New Hampshire, for a stay of a month or more. While they were there, a "Bonus Army" of World War I veterans camped in Washington, protesting defeat of a bill for immediate payment of compensation scheduled before the Depression for 1945. In Chicago, the Democrats nominated for the presidency Governor Franklin Roosevelt, who pledged himself to a "new deal" for the American people. After their long retreat to Holderness, the Goulds returned only briefly to New York, departing early in August to spend some weeks in Michigan prior to going on to Northfield.

When they did arrive at Carleton, early in September, they were a party of three. During 1931-32, Peg's sister Jean Rice had completed her first year of college in Ann Arbor, but, as the new head of the Department of Geology and Geography informed President Cowling, "economic conditions within the family" had now made it "expedient for her to come to Carleton" and to reside with the Goulds. Credits were transferred from Michigan, and Jean was duly admitted to Carleton's Class of 1935. In Northfield, arrangements had been made for the Goulds and Jean to live in the upper floor of a college-owned duplex house a block off campus.

For the academic year 1932-33, Professor Gould would be the sole member of Carleton's Department of Geology and Geography. His office and the department were located in Leighton Hall, a building erected in 1920 as a hall of chemistry and which now housed both these sciences as well as the offices of the dean of the college, dean of women, registrar, treasurer, and the director of admissions and secretary of the personnel service. Gould taught five courses his first year at Carleton. By far the largest enrollment—seventy students in the fall—was for the year-long general survey course in geology, divided into Geology 101 (Physical Geology) first semester and Geology 102 (Historical Geology) second semester. He offered one course each semester on the geography side of the department: Economic Geography for Semester 1 and the Geography of North America for Semester 2. These courses drew forty-three and forty-seven students respectively. Finally, building upon the offering of introductory coursework the year before by part-time instructor George Gibson, in his second semester Gould also taught a small seminar for advanced students—eight enrolled—in a subject dear to his heart, glaciation. Although he was his department's only instructor that first year, Gould was aided for 1932-33 by the presence of Helen Macgowan, a former Carleton student who had finished a geology major at the University of Minnesota, who assisted with the laboratory work for the survey courses in geology and who also helped with the "tedious and meticulous" task of arranging the department's fossil collections.

Gould and the other new members of the Carleton teaching staff were formally welcomed to the fellowship of the college in September at the first faculty meeting of the year, followed three days later by a reception at the president's house. Gould's real introduction to the student body, however, other than that portion of it enrolled in his first semester classes, came early in October, when he was the featured speaker at a special (and non-religious) morning chapel program that was attended—despite its being an extra and voluntary service—by nearly the whole college, students and faculty. Now a seasoned and practiced public speaker, it was no surprise that he "made an excellent impression" (as President Cowling reported to Trustee President Bell). Writing to Byrd later that day, Gould reported that Carleton was "as different from hectic New York as another world. Three chapel services per week which the faculty is expected to attend." Mentioning the chapel talk he had just given, Gould observed that he could not use quite the same language that he had been accustomed to employ in Little America and hoped that the discipline might benefit his vocabulary. "It is good to be in the country again," Gould told Byrd, "for I am essentially a farmer."

No longer supporting himself and Peg as a heavily scheduled touring lecturer, Gould nonetheless continued to make himself and his illustrated presentation on his Antarctic experiences available on a more limited basis—shifting his management, for this purpose, from the James Pond agency to the Emerson Bureau of Chicago. His public addresses remained frequent, by comparison with most college teachers, but now tended to be more geographically constricted or placed in locales he would be visiting in any case for reasons beyond lecturing, such as a mid-October address to the Michigan Educational Association in Ann Arbor. During his first year at Carleton, Gould is known to have spoken on Antarctica at public programs in Chicago, Milwaukee, Lansing, Saginaw, and Fargo, as well as to more than a dozen audiences in Minnesota, most frequently in the Twin Cities of Minneapolis and St. Paul. In his second year at the college, Gould reported making forty-six addresses concerning Arctic and Antarctic exploration in twenty different cities—all, however, within the states of Minnesota, Wisconsin, Illinois, Michigan, and Missouri.

During his first autumn in Northfield Gould very quickly, comfortably, and successfully fitted himself to the rhythm of Carleton life. Teaching the students proved to be a pleasure—some years later he recalled in a letter to a friend from Michigan days who had gone on to a deanship at Purdue that "one of the first impressions I had when I came to Carleton in 1932 was the superior quality of the student body compared with what I had known at Michigan. ... The longer I am here the more I wish somebody had urged me to take my undergraduate years at a college like this." The appreciation was mutual, as Gould enjoyed immediate and marked popularity with the student body. In October he accepted an invitation to become an honorary member of one of Carleton's women's societies, the Delians. A few weeks later, he and Peg acted as two of four faculty chaperones for a college dance held in the Sayles-Hill Gymnasium. In November, he gave an evening lecture to the International Relations Club on international aspects of Antarctica, and later in the semester his hour-long response to the question "Why Do Explorers Explore?" was broadcast on KFMX, the Carleton radio station. He represented the faculty at the special Homecoming chapel service for students, returning alumni, and other visitors. (The football game that followed was a defensive battle, resulting in a scoreless tie with Cornell College, good enough to clinch for Carleton a half-share in that year's Midwest Conference title.) Professor Gould's doings quickly began to be regular fare for reporting in the student newspaper, whether it was to feature his unearthing of a fifteen-foot Ordovician fossil mollusk in a bluff in nearby Cannon Falls or simply to take

"An engaging and often exciting memoir..."

him affectionately to task for his classroom habit of producing notoriously awful puns. The Carleton bookstore did good business selling copies of Gould's book.*

Gould, Cowling, and about three-fourths of the Carleton student body all saw eye to eye that fall with regard to the national political campaign. On what had traditionally been a solidly Republican campus, a straw poll conducted through the college post office found students overwhelmingly favoring the reelection of President Hoover over Governor Roosevelt's Democratic challenge. The country as a whole, as the economic depression worsened and worsened, voted otherwise.

Though Carleton had been a debt-free college at the beginning of 1929 and had suffered only lightly in a direct manner by the initial stock market crash later that year, by 1932 hard times had very much hit home. An optimistic campaign to raise four and a half million dollars for Carleton had been launched in 1930, but the Depression had soon made it "impossible to realize the hopes cherished in this connection." The spring before Gould's arrival the Carleton faculty, in recognition of the effect on the college of the general financial situation, had voted to forego 10 percent of their salaries for 1932-33 and additionally to donate to the institution 5 percent of their 1931-32 salaries to help with that year's budget. Nonetheless at the end of Gould's second month with the school, an agonized President Cowling was obliged to delay payment of faculty salaries due November 1. The situation, as Cowling reported to Carleton trustees on November 12, with

---

*   The student newspaper that fall told of the waggish bookstore worker accosted by someone looking for a copy of Gould's book on his Antarctic trip. "'Do you have Dr. Gould's *Cold*?' he was asked. 'No,' he replied, 'my voice is just a little husky.'"

salaries still unpaid, was due to a combination of delays in first-semester tuition payments from students—the college, recognizing the effect of Depression conditions on students' families, had granted numerous four-month deferrals in varying amounts and was then owed nearly $46,000 in unpaid tuition—and the imperative need to finance more than $28,000 in student loans that had been promised. The salaries were eventually paid, but then again in January "tuition delinquencies and limited borrowing capacity" compelled Carleton to omit payment in full of faculty salaries for that month until after second semester tuitions were received in February, and a deficit was projected for the end of the college year.

In the spring, less than a month after Mr. Hoover gave way to Mr. Roosevelt in Washington, President Cowling presented to the Carleton trustees his budget proposal for 1933-34. Taking into account—with prevailing conditions—an expectation of reduced student enrollment combined with a greatly expanded need for all forms of student financial assistance,* Cowling's budget—approved by the trustees in June—called for further salary reductions of 25 percent for the entire administrative, teaching, and operating personnel of the college. (Carleton's mean average salary for full professors would not again reach 1932's level until 1946. Mean average salary for all teaching ranks combined remained below the 1932 level until 1947.) When the fiscal year ended on June 30, 1933, Carleton was obliged for the first time during the twenty-four years since Cowling became president to close the year with salaries, wages, and certain outside bills still owing—a total of $91,289 in overdue obligations. Carleton suffered the embarrassment of having to issue on June 30, in lieu of immediate payment, notes at 6 percent interest for unpaid salaries. Though most overdue wages were paid over the summer, this was accomplished only by tapping current income for the following year, making necessary further borrowing in the months ahead to meet the already reduced payrolls of 1933-34. Though Gould had settled in very happily to faculty life at Carleton College, institutionally these were decidedly difficult days.

***

Larry Gould's popularity, so quick to bloom on the Carleton campus, also did not take long to root more generally in the city of Northfield. Gould would eventually make his religious fellowship Episcopalian, joining the congregation of Northfield's All Saints' Church. His skill as a public speaker was soon appreciated as widely by the town as it already was on campus, among the "gown." In February, Gould was the principal speaker before some twelve hundred Northfield

---

*   Awards for scholarships and grants in aid for 1932-33 amounted to $88,755, as compared
    with an average of about $31,000 a year for the previous ten years. In addition, according to
    President Cowling's statement of December 12, 1933, submitted to the Board of Trustees for
    their March 1, 1934, meeting, it "was necessary to assist an unusually large number of students
    with loans and opportunities for work. A considerable amount of student labor was employed
    in 'made work' which might have been postponed if students had been able to secure loans or
    work elsewhere."

With two geology majors of 1935, Charles R. Golden and Jean Todd

fathers and sons, gathered to celebrate the anniversary of the founding of the Boy Scout movement. A few days later he spoke and showed Antarctic movies at an evening program at the Methodist church, under the auspices of the Northfield Ladies' Aid Society. In March, he gave his regular "With Byrd to the Bottom of the World" touring lecture on successive evenings, the first at Carleton and the other across town at St. Olaf. (Even the veteran polar explorer, however, had to confess that he was not necessarily immune to the discomforts of a Minnesota winter. At one point during his first January in the state, Gould wrote Byrd that "last week I thought I was back in the Antarctic—it was 30 below zero on my porch as I started out in the morning to go half way across the state to give a lecture—and these people think I ought to go around coatless and hatless and not get cold!!!")

In April at the University of Minnesota, Gould spoke on glaciation as the luncheon speaker during the founding meeting of the Minnesota Academy of Science. Three other Carleton professors, zoologist Roy Waggener, botanist Harvey Stork, and astronomer E. A. Fath, also delivered papers at this inaugural gathering of the state's scientists, and Stork, who was becoming one of Gould's closest friends on the Carleton faculty, was elected the new organization's first president.

Also in April, Gould received a copy of Duncan Stewart's doctoral dissertation, completed at Michigan under Professor Hobbs and based on Stewart's petrographical analyses of Gould's Antarctic rock specimens. He then suggested to Stewart that it would be a good thing if Stewart were to join him in the Geology Department at Carleton, considering that he had approval to expand the staff for 1933-34 through the addition of a part-time instructor. Stewart, who was also pursuing a grant to support continuing research on Antarctic petrography, agreed that the opportunity at Carleton "sounds like a mighty good thing," assuring Gould that "the grant, if forthcoming, would have no effect upon my spending at least half my time instructing." Definite announcement of Stewart's subsequent appointment appeared in the *Carletonian* in mid-May. Two days after that, Hobbs, mentor to both Gould and Stewart, was at Carleton as Gould's guest, delivering a lecture on his explorations in Greenland and no doubt celebrating the fact that two of his protégées (both of whom had been with him on separate Greenland expeditions) were to be united on the Carleton faculty. Hobbs' visit was also timed so that he could see the 1933 Carleton May Fete pageant,* the theme of which that year was "Arctic Hay," a dance-burlesque upon Arctic life for which the original script had been written by Gould's sister-in-law, Carleton sophomore Jean Rice. It is to be supposed that Hobbs thoroughly enjoyed the performance, featuring "Koolita, a beautiful Esquimaux maiden," her lover, Inoukitsak, numerous giant auks, and, as its climax, the off-shore appearance of an impressive life-sized whale. The applause of six thousand spectators was a triumph for Jean Rice, still a week short of her twentieth birthday.

***

Gould spent most of the summer of 1933 teaching at the University of Michigan's summer session. Byrd was preparing to return to the ice with his second Antarctic expedition, and in July Gould sent him a note indicating, among other business, that he hoped to be able to see Byrd in the east before the admiral left, "to wish you bon voyage and to see that you do not carry back to the Antarctic with you any misapprehensions—back where there were none." Three years after the first Byrd Antarctic Expedition's homecoming, the chill that certainly had developed between the admiral and his former second-in-command had gotten beyond its iciest manifestations. Polite cordiality would characterize future relations between the two, and Gould—though private correspondence would occasionally show himself in definite sympathy with more estranged Byrd critics such as his friend Bernt Balchen—would always abstain from any public criticism

---

* Carleton's annual May Fete, a festival featuring the coronation of a May Queen and elaborately choreographed and costumed dances presented by the women of the college in a natural amphitheater on one of the islands in Lyman Lakes, had long been a premier event on the college calendar and a spectacle that regularly attracted more outside visitors to Carleton than any other event. Audiences viewed the festival's centerpiece, the dance pageant, from the hillside opposite the island.

of his former commander. Decades later Gould would observe that his eventual attitude toward Dick Byrd had settled into one that was far less critical than what he admitted it had been in the early 1930s, adding that "after any kind of expedition like that, when people have been penned up together for as long as we were, the reactions that emerge quickly are apt to be ephemeral, and highly critical—and I think shouldn't be taken too seriously."

As a fresh school year began for Gould and the first ships of Byrd's second Antarctic expedition were reported leaving the States, Gould wrote Byrd that the new expedition departure made him "downright homesick" but that he had his work cut out for him at Carleton. "When I met my classes yesterday morning," Gould told the admiral, "I found one quarter of the whole college enrolled in them."*

Interviewed by a *Carletonian* reporter as Byrd and his current party of scientists and explorers left for Little America, Gould acknowledged a keen desire to go back to Antarctica again some day but preferably to new territory not yet seen or studied. At any rate, he averred, he could not think of leaving Carleton at a time when the Geology Department was just getting under way. "I had to choose between exploring and teaching as my life work," he continued, and had made the decision that "teaching is my vocation; exploring is just an avocation." Larry Gould was thirty-seven years old. He would not finally leave classrooms until he was eighty-two. His chosen "life work" was just beginning.

---

* "One quarter of the whole college" is exaggerated, but only slightly. 162 students took one or another of Gould's three courses that fall, out of 752 present at the college: 21.5 percent. But, as noted in his departmental annual report for 1933-34, some twenty more students had to be turned away from his introductory course due to limitations of classroom and lab space. Twenty exactly would mean that 24.2 percent of the college sought to enroll in one or another of Gould's first semester courses; twenty-six more would have been a literal quarter of the college. For the spring semester he taught 166/738ths of the student body: 22.5 percent.

CHAPTER 13

ANY BRIGHT COLOR, SO LONG AS IT IS RED

Testimony abounds, from Carleton students of the 1930s and early 1940s, as to the exceptional quality and memorableness of Larry Gould's teaching and also as to the extraordinary quality of the man and the deep and lasting impact he so frequently had on those fortunate enough to have been his students. Remarkable encomiums have poured forth, across decades of subsequent remembrance, both from those who were influenced to become geology majors and those who simply took and never forgot the "must-have" experience of a course with Gould. They tell of his good humor and dry wit, of inspiring eloquence and characteristic expressions ("Holy Toledo!" was universally recognized at Carleton as an exclamation bearing the personal stamp of Professor Gould), and of an ability to make his subject mesmerizing. "The finest, most inspired teacher I ever had," wrote one student years later. "The most dominant and influential man I have ever been associated with," offered another. "Professor Gould is certainly 'the greatest' in all respects," concluded a third. Such expressions could be multiplied many times over. Gould "made geology so interesting that I felt I could not select any other profession," attested one who majored in the subject, while another called him the greatest "constructive influence" upon him of any man except his father. "Even more important for me in subsequent life than the geology I learned," wrote a former student who had gone on to a distinguished career in the State Department and an ambassadorship, "was having been closely exposed to a really great man like Larry Gould." A graduate of 1939 simply concluded, "it is impossible to put down in words what he meant to his students."

In the classroom Gould was both entertaining and effective. A magazine profile from 1934 authored by a Carleton senior attributed part of his popularity with students to his "delightful shafts of humor." "His lectures," it was reported, "are filled with witticisms and stories which he relates with the extremest of sober faces, and only the sparkling of his deep brown eyes tells his classes when he has departed from profound but prosaic facts." A student from one of Gould's first years at Carleton, hired the next to serve as a lab assistant and to operate the

Fieldwork at Mount St. Helens, 1938

classroom slide projector, reported that an extra part of his value to Gould was that he would laugh heartily at the professor's jokes, even those repeated from the year before—and as this particular student notoriously possessed the richest, most irrepressible, and infectious laugh on campus, he would inevitably help keep entire audiences appreciatively mirthful.* If Gould's classroom humor made an impression on his students, however, so did his success in sparking lasting interest and enthusiasm and in imparting substance. An alumnus of the Class of 1936 testified to the demanding nature of Gould's pedagogical method: "One hour each week is reserved for an oral quiz—and please believe me, it is nothing short of the third degree—which keeps the student posted on the weekly assignments. This method, obviously, meant a little more work in two hours but it was well worth it. When the end of the semester came, I had practically memorized my notes, doing so week by week, and to this day any question pertaining to Geography is right on the tip of my tongue."

Student demand for entry into Gould's annual introductory courses in physical and historical geology tended always to run up against lecture hall capacity, even after his second-floor Leighton Hall lecture room was refitted to squeeze in more. Carleton graduated its first geology major—Tom Jager—in 1934 and, as Gould successfully built up the program, would turn out forty-eight more over the next nine years. What was a departmental teaching staff of one in 1932 and two in 1933, with the addition of Duncan Stewart, grew to three in 1934—George Gibson returned as part-time geology instructor and coach of the football team—and eventually to four in 1941. As chairman, Gould pushed, in his early years at Carleton, for improvements in the department's laboratory facility, collections' storage and exhibit spaces, a departmental library, and capacity for providing students with meaningful fieldwork at locations distant from Northfield.

In the personal realm, Gould fitted himself comfortably into a small town college life that he found congenial, forming friendships among the professoriate and with others in Northfield that were sources of many pleasures and satisfactions. He praised as "near to the ideal" in a series of his annual reports the college philosophy of uniting in one faculty "a varied group of scholars and teachers and giving them opportunity to 'work out their own salvation'" in "an atmosphere of liberty and freedom" that he found "most conducive to intelligent and inspiring work." Repeatedly he told President Cowling how greatly he valued Carleton's "total lack of administrative intrusion into the fields of

---

* Alas, not even the most engaging of teachers can hope for universal attention all the time. A geology student from a few years later has put into print the memory of Gould interrupting his classroom lecture to ask a student in the back row to kindly wake up the unconscious man sitting next to him. "The response was, 'You put him to sleep, you wake him up.' So—Larry climbed the steps in Leighton 202 and did just that." In 1936 the student newspaper printed an account of a sleepy student arriving late to first-hour class and being told by Gould, "You should have been here at eight o'clock." Still bleary-eyed, the student asked "Why? What happened?"

teaching and research."

One sadness to which circumstances required him to adjust was that he and Peg would have no children. At some point early in their marriage—it has proved elusive to determine exactly when—Peg Gould did begin a pregnancy, but she miscarried, and, whether by the couple's own decision, by medical advice, or by subsequent physical inability is not clear, no other pregnancy ever followed. There would be, across the years to come, a number of younger people whose close relationship to one or both of the Goulds could and would justify being described as "like a son" or "like a daughter," but the actual experience of parenthood was not to be theirs.

***

Larry Gould had not been at Carleton long before the campus community began to notice and celebrate a number of appurtenances to the popular professor's personal style, such as the cane he then affected to carry and his large collection of pipes. Especially, however, the student press was instrumental in taking note of, and raising to the level of campus tradition, one particular aspect of Gould's visual presentation that would become forever associated with the man in Carleton legend and lore: his neckwear.

The *Carletonian*'s mythologization commenced early in the spring of 1933, when student columnist Marshall McDonough reported the "general and prolonged titter" that had arisen from Gould's geology students the previous Friday when the dashing explorer strode into class. "The trouble," McDonough observed, "proved to be a brilliant band of super dazzling hues wound 'round said professor's neck where ordinarily the average gentleman of today wears a cravat." The spectacle of Gould's tie that day was likened to "a Communist artist's modernistic interpretation of the aurora borealis sketched while astraddle a dog sled speeding over the Russian steppes." Gould, the paper's readers were told, "made only one comment with characteristic frigid brevity: 'Spring.'"

Gould continued his colorful ways, in marked contrast to the sartorially conservative professorial garb generally prevailing in Northfield in 1933,* and the following fall the paper publicized a November Friday as "Wild Tie Day" at Carleton, when all were invited to festoon themselves appropriately and attempt to outdo the day's patron hero, Larry Gould, in the brilliancy of their cravats. Solid red, the paper reported, was Gould's own favorite hue. Accompanying the

---

* Another exception to the dominant monochromaticism was art history professor Ian B. Stoughton Holbourn, a Scotsman who reportedly owned a haunted castle near Edinburgh and was Laird of the small Shetland island of Foula—the *Carletonian* declared him to be the only American college professor also a king—who, during the one semester per year during which he was regularly in residence at Carleton, was a conspicuous campus figure in his dramatic blue cape.

Sartorial flair

announcement of the special day was the following anonymous poetic effusion,
dedicated to Dr. Gould:

> Some may long for the soothing touch
> Of lavender, cream, and mauve,
> But the ties I wear must possess the glare
> Of a red-hot kitchen stove.
>
> The books I read, and life I lead,
> Are sensible, sane, and mild;
> I like calm hats and I don't wear spats,
> But I want my neckties WILD!
>
> Give me a wild tie, brother,
> One with a cosmic urge;
> A tie that will swear,
> And rip and tear
> When it sees my old blue serge!

O, some says a gent's cravat,
Should only be seen, not heard.
But I want a tie that will make men cry,
And render their vision blurred.

I yearn, I long, for a tie so strong
It will take two men to tie it.
If such there be, just show it to me—
Whatever the price, I'll buy it.

Give me a wild tie, brother,
One with a lot of sins.
A tie that will blaze
In a hectic haze
Down where the vest begins.

Wild Tie Day, always in Gould's honor, became at Carleton an annually recurring feature of the college calendar.

***

In the spring of 1934 Gould delivered a chapel talk to Carleton's senior class. This address, for which a transcript survives, ranges far afield from the familiar matters of geology and exploration upon which most of his previous public speaking had been centered. Concerning contemporary threats to liberty, it is an expression of political philosophy, broadly speaking, and is quite interesting as a reflection of some of Gould's thoughts at the time in relation to national and international developments and for the way in which one can see the early tracings of themes to which Gould would return in later years when called upon to speak far more frequently on larger political and societal concerns.

In his talk Gould recognized the challenge posed to democracy by dictators such as Mussolini, Stalin, and Hitler, saying that the question "Is Democracy dying?" is shaking the world and suggesting that within the next decade American youth may well be called upon to answer that question in more than the rhetorical sense. His own generation, he noted, was also faced with a great challenge to democracy and "we enlisted with all the fanaticism of religious fervor—we thought we were fighting the battle of Armageddon." "Our delusion," he warned, "was complete." He told the Class of 1934 that while he could never be ashamed of the impulse that had prompted him and those like him to enlist in that battle, he was now filled with shame at what he subsequently saw as "the cheapness and tawdriness of the propaganda" with which he was "beguiled into thinking [he] was on a high mission only to find [he] had been a pawn in a great racket." "Racket," he continued, was actually a polite kind of flattery to apply to the world war, the true name of which would be unspeakable. "Sherman's pallid old statement that 'War is Hell,'" he declared, "is like a kindergarten Sunday School lesson beside reality." "War," he said, "is not the way out. We tried it and it only accentuated all the problems that we had been told it would solve. There can never be a war to end wars."

Great as the dangers of European dictatorships and war appeared, Gould averred that threats to the ideals of liberty were "not entirely on the other side of the Atlantic Ocean." Made uneasy by the welfare state, he decried within current American life "the ease and even the eagerness with which increasingly large numbers of people are willing to surrender the adventure of striving and the fortitude of self-reliance for a sort of security in a state which will do all their planning, thinking and providing for them." "I do not believe," he declared, "in equality as an ideal or even as a political goal. No prospect could be more gray or barren than a social order in which there is not stimulation to one's aspirations beyond the achievement of mediocrity." At the same time, he recognized that "it would be sheer folly for anyone to pretend that the despotism of unchecked capitalism left entirely to its own interpretation of the doctrine of *laissez faire* would not result in financial fascism just as inimical to freedom as is political fascism." A Republican in Teddy Roosevelt's progressive mold, he acknowledged the danger where capital holds sway, noting that where the "owners of machines" control the courts and the press, citizens' rights such as free speech, free press, and the right of assemblage are prone to wither. Nonetheless, he doubted very much that freedom would tend to thrive more sturdily when politicians control the machine. "Shall we hand over for drastic regulation if not actual ownership," he asked, "the vast, complicated and delicate machinery of commerce and finance to the politician whose intelligence quotient is the greatest common divisor of a not too quick witted constituency?" That way, he warned, at least in times of crises, lies an appalling demagoguery, and he found that he would "rather trust the fortunes of liberty and freedom to an uneducated Henry Ford than to a Huey Long."

Gould told the assembled seniors that these remarks were not to be construed as unfriendly to the New Deal, much of which he believed necessary and corrective of some long-standing social injustices. But he did offer criticisms of some of its recent manifestations. To the extent that Gould offered a mechanism for defending his ideal of liberty from all that seemed to threaten it, he located it in schools such as Carleton:

> Long ago Edmund Burke sized up the matter which is still the root of our troubles and described the only really worthwhile tool that I know of that we can put into your kit. He said: 'Society cannot exist unless a controlling power upon will and appetite be placed somewhere, and the less of it there is within the more there must be without.' In other words if society is to direct its own fate, if we are to civilize ourselves then we must either submit to be made good or permit ourselves to be trained to be good. I know of nothing so very near the real heart of education as the quality implied in that statement by Burke. It is the old and the

obvious lesson mankind must learn and yet so few achieve—the task of self discipline. ...

In Tennyson's *Ulysses* is a line which is said to have pleased Queen Victoria so much that she granted him a pension of 400 pounds. That line is: 'I am a part of all that I have met.'...

Yes, you are a part of all that you have met and it is a part of you.[*] You will always be members of this college and will always be expected to have a deep appreciation of the necessity of schools and colleges such as this—for these are the very agencies which civilization has created to conserve and perpetuate the ideals of freedom which seem so precious.

***

The mid-1930s saw Gould continue to follow successful paths professionally and professorially. In both 1934 and 1935 he taught summer sessions at Utah State Agricultural College, after which he would engage in western geological work of one sort or another before returning to Carleton in the fall. Following the 1934 session he worked in southern Utah, where he discovered an ancient pictograph of some importance. The 1935 summer session was highlighted by Gould's heading up a twelve-day "scenic and scientific expedition" touring Yellowstone and Grand Teton National Parks in western Wyoming, followed by several days in the Bryce, Zion, and Grand Canyon region. After the responsibility of shepherding a party of forty-five for this adventure, Gould "took a holiday" by heading for the High Sierras with a friend from his Arctic exploration days for a three-day climb of Mt. Whitney, the highest peak in the continental United States. ("I surprised myself," Gould wrote President Cowling from Reno, "and find that 39 is not such an advanced age after all for I made the ascent much more easily than I had expected.") Then it was a few days in San Francisco, northward through Oregon to visit a friend in Eugene, and a return home via Glacier Park.

While in Utah that summer Gould received two communications of import, one giving him pleasure, the other not. Gould was touched and gratified to receive a telegram from his Byrd Expedition sledging companion Norman Vaughan, announcing the birth of a son and asking for permission to give him the middle name

---

[*]   Carleton alumni will here discern a pre-figuring of one of the most institutionally oft-quoted phrases of the Gould presidency, which has continued for decades to be repeated anew by Gould's presidential successors: "You are forever a part of Carleton, and Carleton is forever a part of you." There is no single phrasing of this sentiment which is canonical; President Gould voiced variants of the idea, in one formulation or another, probably every year from 1945 to 1961 in welcoming new freshman classes into the community of the college. Interestingly, in a November 8, 2003, letter Carleton alumnus T. Willard Hunter (Class of 1936) pointed out to the author the similarity of Gould's famous "you are a part of Carleton" phrase to his own remarks as student body president at a morning chapel service during the 1935 Homecoming weekend, presumably with Gould in attendance in the faculty section of the chapel. As reprinted in the 1936 Carleton yearbook, the *Algol*, Hunter spoke of feeling connected to the long historical heritage of Carleton as he gazed at various buildings and other parts of the campus. "And I felt," he said, "that all of that belonged to me, and that I belonged to all of that."

"Gould," in Larry's honor. (Permission was granted, though deemed unnecessary.) Less happily, Cowling wrote to inform him that Duncan Stewart had, for family reasons, decided to resign his position in the Carleton Geology Department in order to accept a permanent appointment at Michigan State College, closer to his Detroit home. Stewart's departure left Gould feeling downcast, but there was nothing to be done about it but accept the unwelcome change. Cowling and the Carleton board, still struggling with the Depression-era college budget, decided to leave the position vacant for a year, so Gould's department temporarily shrank back for 1935-36 to just himself and a halftime George Gibson.

Another alteration that year was in the composition of the Goulds' North-field household, for Peg's sister Jean Rice, who had lived with Larry and Peg on Nevada Street since 1932, graduated with the Class of '35 and subsequently returned to Michigan.

Gould continued in the mid-1930s to hone his skills as a platform speaker in a variety of contexts. During 1934-35, for instance, in addition to his usual collection of talks on polar exploration in Minnesota and nearby states, as well as special lectures on Antarctic geology at the Royal Canadian Institute in Toronto and at the Royal Society in Hamilton, Ontario, he delivered three Minnesota commencement addresses, gave several public lectures on behalf of charitable institutions in Minneapolis and St. Paul, and at Carleton was called upon to speak at a men's student societies dinner meeting, served as toastmaster at the annual athletic banquet and as referee for the Winter Carnival rink games, and was chosen by the senior class to give the address at the annual Cap and Gown Day service. Less public performance skills were apparently being honed as well, as the *Carletonian* characterized as "interesting" Dr. Gould's love of soloing his favorite church hymns afternoons when Leighton Hall was nearly empty and the vacant halls created a fascinating resonance.

By the fall of 1935 Admiral Byrd had returned from his second Antarctic expedition, and in October Gould sent him a cordial letter accompanied by copies of two recently published papers by Gould concerning the first expedition's geological work, and brought him up to date on the completion of Stewart's petrographical analyses. Gould informed Byrd that he expected to have one more paper at long last complete his own work from the 1928-30 expedition.

In 1936 the financial picture for Carleton College brightened as Cowling succeeded in a long fundraising effort to erase the college debt, meeting a stipulated condition of the General Education Board to qualify for a half-million dollar offer of assistance. The $500,000 would be paid over in mid-May, but already in early March Cowling was able to write to trustee Frank Kellogg that "the College is now in a more comfortable position than it has been since 1920 when we launched out on our enlarged program. Its work can now be carried on without the strain and tension of the past few years." Late in March the faculty celebrated Cowling's accomplishment with a gala dinner, which Larry Gould orchestrated as toastmaster.

With an easing of the severity in budgetary restraints, Gould received a green light to hire a replacement for the departmental position left vacant by the departure of Duncan Stewart. Citing increasing interest in international affairs, Gould decided to beef up the geography side of the department and—turning once again to Ann Arbor for personnel—brought in for the fall of 1936 a promising young Michigan-trained geographer, Leonard Wilson. Wilson would remain a fixture of the department until after Pearl Harbor, when he and his map information expertise would be called to Washington for war work.

In 1935-36 Gould served as vice president of the Minnesota Academy of Science. He was a member of the American Geophysical Union and the International Commission on Snow; a fellow of the Geological Society of America, the American Geographical Society, and the American Association for the Advancement of Science; and a life member of the National Geographic Society. In May he was honored to be appointed to represent the National Academy of Science and the National Research Council as delegate to the Sixth General Assembly of the International Union of Geodesy and Geophysics at their September congress in Edinburgh, Scotland. Committed to speak at the assembly September 7 on "The Origin and Dissipation of the Ross Shelf Ice," Gould made the appointment the occasion for enjoying with his wife a summer of extended travel throughout Great Britain. The couple sailed in the first week of July and returned to Northfield only in the first week of October (missing the first days of Carleton classes). Between, while European news was filled with reporting on the outbreak of civil war in Spain, on the Nazi-hosted Olympic games in Berlin, and on show trials followed by summary executions in the Soviet Union, Larry and Peg motored some five thousand miles through England, Wales, and Scotland, mixing tourism with visits to friends and connections of friends,* and indulging Larry with a ten-day stay in Cambridge, where he did work at the Scott Institute of Polar Research and was able to meet with many veterans of the British Antarctic expeditions of Scott and Shackleton. Their wanderings that summer ranged the length of the island from the geologically interesting chalk cliffs of Dover to the impressive Fingal's Cave on the Inner Hebrides isle of Staffa. They explored from Donald Cowling's native Cornwall north to Scotland's Loch Ness, failing however to glimpse the loch's fabled monster. Following their stay in Cambridge, which Gould told Cowling had been "a veritable festival of Antarctic explorers for me," they accepted an invitation for a weekend's stay at the country home of one of them. Altogether, Gould expressed himself as delighted with the "generous and warmhearted hospitality" of the people they met and "quite in love" with rural Britain.

Returned to Northfield following this congenial three-month holiday, Gould was soon faced, before the end of 1936, with the need to consider his future career path and the question of whether his course best lay away from Carleton.

---

* A particularly warm memory would be the time spent in Glasgow with concert pianist Ailie Cullen, the sister of Carleton faculty colleague and concert violinist Jenny Cullen.

Early in December the chancellor of Washington University in St. Louis wrote Cowling to suggest that Larry Gould might be an ideal candidate to become their next dean of the College of Liberal Arts and that he had invited Gould to come to St. Louis to discuss the possibility. In January Cowling informed Trustee Chairman Bell that it seemed likely that Gould would be offered this attractive position at a salary of $7,500 or $8,000 a year, as compared with the $5,000 that Carleton had been paying since 1932. "I am quite sure," Cowling wrote, that Gould "has no desire to leave Carleton"; nonetheless such a salary difference could not help but be seriously considered. Cowling sought Bell's endorsement of offering Gould an increase to $6,000 should that be helpful in trying to keep him. Bell responded that he thought such a step "would be good business" for the college. Gould, of course, was not privy to this resolve and, as it turned out, decided by May to remain at Carleton without any inducement of salary increase. He did secure from Cowling a special appropriation of $3,000 to purchase some additional equipment needed by the department and for a special one-year travel allowance. Gould noted with satisfaction in his year-end annual report that "the chief needs of the department will have been met during the coming year," with the details of several enumerated matters having "been worked out in detail by the Chairman ... in conference with the President."

During the winter of 1937 while he was considering his personal options, Gould gave a talk to the Carleton student body on the subject of taking stock of one's self. In these remarks, long-remembered by many in the audience that day, Gould challenged Carleton's students to ask themselves seven serious questions as a means of judging the efficacy of their Carleton education and the degree to which they had individually prepared themselves to put that privileged training to good use:

1. Have you achieved ease in communicating with others?

2. Have you learned enough about social organization to make use of your powers?

3. Have you learned that everything is useful, but nothing indispensable; everything wonderful, but nothing miraculous?

4. Have you developed a habit of will to do what is to be done?

5. Have you acquired college manners instead of mannerisms; college tone instead of taint?

6. Have your emotions and appreciations been more developed along with the development of your mind?

7. Have you acquired a sense of your obligations both to yourself and your generation?

The great majority of Gould's public speaking and writing continued to be concerned with science and/or investigations of the polar regions, but here, as in his 1934 chapel talk on threats to liberty, is more evidence of broad perspective and reflection about the purpose of a liberal arts college. Gould's own ability to give positive answers to his seven questions may be seen as firm foundation for fitting himself, within the next decade, for leadership of such a college.

***

The special one-year travel allowance that Gould negotiated with Cowling in the spring of 1937 enabled his extraordinary program during the summer that followed. This was participation as a delegate to the Seventeenth International Geological Congress in Moscow, to which was added both pre- and post-congress excursions to other Soviet regions, giving Gould altogether some eight weeks inside the USSR.

One of the first large-scale international scientific gatherings hosted by the Soviet Union, the Seventeenth International Geological Congress mixed 711 Soviet geologists with 238 delegates from forty-nine other countries. Abstracts were published before the opening for some 390 presented papers, and about 230 papers were read and discussed during the Congress itself, which divided into ten sections (including Gould's on the geology of the Arctic regions) and united for plenary sessions held in the Great Hall of the Moscow Conservatorium. Its *Proceedings* would eventually be published in six volumes issued in English and Russian.

Following an ocean crossing aboard the *Europa*, Gould arrived in Moscow on June 30 (two days, parenthetically, before the tragic disappearance over the Pacific of Amelia Earhart, wife to Gould's close friend G. P. Putnam), and then embarked on one of the pre-Congress organized excursions across the Caucasus Mountains into Georgia and Armenia, returning via the Black Sea coast and through the Ukraine, to reach Moscow again on July 19. Midway through this trip, the travel diary which he was keeping shows Gould exasperated by accumulated inconveniences compounded by an "internal upset, like dysentery," that he was willing to acknowledge was probably making his reactions less friendly than they might otherwise be. "For puerility, lack of common sense, [and] any sense of organization," he noted grimly, "these people cannot be beaten." "This whole trip has been arranged on impossible lines—from the first day in the field, schedules that could not be kept... . Far too many people are ill now, what with too much sun, terrible food and the indescribably rough, dusty roads." Traveling the next morning in a train compartment mercifully free of bed bugs, he slept well, and then found himself feeling so much better that he ate a hearty lunch. In a more charitable mood, he told his diary that he knew "full well that such inconvenience as we have suffered has not been occasioned by design" but was simply the result of inexperience with large groups of foreign visitors. Still, he wrote that evening, "a clean room with bath would look good now! I remember there are such places, but not in Russia, I fear."

While on this excursion Gould particularly enjoyed the camaraderie of the eminent Australian geologist Ernest Willington Skeats, whose company and generosity with his supply of cigarettes and cigars were both valued.

Seeing a newspaper on July 12, he learned that while their group had been in Tbilisi, an alleged Georgian plot against the Soviet government had been discovered and nine men arrested and shot. "So does the strong arm of Stalin keep this land in order," he journaled, adding a number of notes about "Russia, the jail of nations." He was also disgusted by the blatant "obvious and childish propaganda" that was fed continuously to the visiting scientists about the transformative wonders that had been worked since the 1917 revolution. "One would think (to hear them talk)," he wrote, "that even the geology has occurred as part of the U.S.S.R. plans."

The International Geological Congress formally opened on July 21. Its atmosphere was uneasy, at least within the ranks of its Soviet representatives. "A number of Soviet Congress participants," it has been observed, "were, sometimes at the last moment, refused permission to participate in the interesting excursions, and some of them, who in connection with their work, maintained contacts with foreign colleagues, were arrested during the Congress or immediately afterwards." Prominently absent from the international gathering were such eminent Russian geologists as Dmitrii Muschketov and Georgii Frederiks, each of whom had been arrested in June. (Muschketov, whose work, like Gould's, encompassed glaciology and Frederiks would both be executed the following February, victims of Stalin's "Great Purge." Gould took part in another brief excursion from Moscow while the Congress was in mid-course, in order to spend a couple of days taking a look at Leningrad, which he found much the more interesting city. Visiting the Hermitage on the 25th, he saw, as he recorded in his travel diary, more Titians, Rubens, and Van Dykes, etc., than he had previously known existed in all the world. Far duller, he found, was the arranged tour two days later, from Moscow, that he declared "quite the most childish example of Russian exhibitionism":

> The whole day was given over to a ride down the new canal connecting Moscow with the Volga River passing through 2 sets of locks. It appears to have been a relatively easy engineering feat yet we were told that it was one of the greatest ever. The locks were compared to those of the Panama Canal, to the disadvantage of the latter! And of course it was pointed out that it could not have been done under tsarist Russia. All progress here has happened since the October Revolution of 1917!!!! That is the tale which is dinned into our ears at every opportunity.

In Leningrad the party from the Geological Congress had been wined and dined at a Peterhof Grand Palace reception that Gould found splendid, but the splendor was surpassed, he admitted, by the affair put on for them at the Kremlin the evening before the close of the Congress. "We were seated at table at 7 o'clock," Gould reported, "and arose at 11:45. I stopped counting at the tenth course." Present were Molotov, Litvinov, and "all of the great Soviet leaders, except Stalin."*

On July 29 Gould cut out of the Congress's final morning session to go view Lenin's tomb. Writing to Cowling that day, he reported that he would depart the next evening on a trip to the Russian Arctic, the particular item of his summer travels to which he had most especially looked forward. Writing in his journal that night, he noted that the foreign geologists who were not participating in any of the post-Congress excursions had departed that day "seeming very glad to be on their way and ... feeling very sorry for us who are left behind."

The Arctic journey, in contrast to most of the rest of Gould's Russian summer, was an experience thoroughly enjoyed and which, he wrote to Cowling after its end, exceeded his highest expectations. The group went by train from Moscow to Archangel, where they boarded an icebreaker to take them north through the White Sea and into Arctic waters beyond the Kola Peninsula to reach the glacier-filled island of Novaya Zemlya. As the excursion moved north into the region of midnight sun Gould delighted in breathing in the invigorating "tang and real chill of the Arctic air" and called the day he wrote those words the best he had had in Russia. The waters around Novaya Zemlya they found to be free of sea ice, and so they were able to circle the large island completely, bringing Gould considerably farther north than he had been on either of his two previous Arctic expeditions. The ship stopped frequently during its circumnavigation so that Gould and his fellow glaciologists could make studies of the island ice from a variety of places. "Almost as good as having my own expedition," Gould wrote Cowling.

On the return leg of the voyage, which put in at Murmansk before sending the contingent on to Leningrad, Gould was tapped to give a pair of shipboard talks about the Antarctic, geographically about as far distant from where they then were as it is possible to get.

In 1929, in Antarctica, Larry Gould's August 22 birthday had happily coincided with the return of the sun following a winter of darkness. Now his 1937 birthday, on which he left Russia, was marked by a similar feeling of elation over a metaphorical movement from darkness into light. "Finland and Free," he wrote into his diary as his train crossed the border, "it is like getting out of prison to be out of Russia." A few days later, writing from Stockholm, Gould informed Cowling that "all in all" the summer Congress with its associated excursions had been

---

* Stalin may have been too busy planning domestic murder to greet foreign geologists. Within 48 hours of the close of the international congress in Moscow the Politburo enabled, and Stalin soon signed, the notorious NKVD operative order 00447, leading in short order to the arrest and either execution or transfer to labor camps of hundreds of thousands. During that same dismal week, in a competing dictatorship the Buchenwald concentration camp near Weimar became operational. A few days after that, Generalissimo Franco's artillery opened fire on Madrid, and the Japanese Army occupied Beijing and prepared to attack Shanghai. 1937: not the best of times.

"one of the most valuable professional experiences" he had ever had, particularly for "the privilege of being in the field with geologists from all over the world and watching them work," but that he had found Stalin's Russia itself "a dismal land" whose people "do not impress one as being happy." "In spite of their eagerness to do us justice," he wrote, "the Russians held us under constant suspicion as they do all foreigners now. All our geological discussions were listened to by members of the police." The world, he thought, had "but little to hope for from modern Russia," at least until there might be a change with regard to present policies and the people in control.

Gould finished his summer following a homeward path through Copenhagen, Hamburg, and Bremen to Cherbourg, from where he made a September return to the United States and a resumption of teaching duties at Carleton. He closed his travel journal with tongue-in-cheek disappointment over the woman at whose table he was seated for the voyage home: a "spinster instructor, professor, or something of the sort ... rather too high and thin of voice, skinny as a rail" and well past sixty. "So ends all hope of ... marine romance," his pen sighed, "and so all ends this journal."

***

Gould's speaking engagements continued at their usual high volume during the academic year 1937-38, with his subject matter (exclusive of four high school commencement addresses) being split fairly evenly between his accustomed talks on polar exploration and associated matters and reflections on Russia arising out of his experiences the previous summer.

In the classroom that year Gould introduced a new course that was somewhat experimental and innovative for its time in being team-taught and interdisciplinary. The Conservation of Our Natural Resources was given second semester under Gould's general supervision but with the teaching shared by a quinumvirate of area specialists: geologists Gould and George Gibson taught units, respectively, on water and mineral resources; geographer Leonard Wilson handled soil conservation; botanist Harvey Stork presented on the conservation of forests; and zoologist Olin Pettingill took charge when the focus moved to wildlife. Gould then concluded the course by considering how all aspects of conservation might be taken into account within the framework of regional planning. The twenty-seven students taking the initial offering of the course in 1938 had decidedly positive reactions—one senior called it the single best course he had taken in college—and with Gould, Stork, and Pettingill as the constant instructors when not on leave it would continue in the annual spring offerings for the remainder of Gould's teaching time at the school.

Gould had decorated his Leighton Hall faculty office with photographs and other memorabilia of his polar travels, and in the winter of 1937-38 he installed an eye-catching new item: a painted portrait of Al Smith, the lead dog of Gould's Antarctic team, contributed by an artistic admirer who executed the painting of

With the painting of his Antarctic lead dog Al Smith

Vacationing in Glacier Park, late 1930s, with Jenny Cullen, assistant professor of violin at Carleton, Dick Hoppin, Peg Rice Gould, and Jean Rice

the now-deceased husky from a supplied photograph. That same winter Gould lent to the zoology department, as the focal point for a display mounted in Laird Hall, a seventy-pound stuffed Emperor penguin* he had returned with from Little America. A third and far more animated reminder of his cold clime adventures of the previous decade also arrived at Carleton late that winter, in the form of a visit from his old friend Bob Bartlett, skipper of the *Morrissey*, the storied vessel which had carried Gould's first two Arctic expeditions. Bartlett stayed overnight in the Gould home and by Gould's arrangement returned the following week and delivered a well-received chapel talk to the student body on the subject of "Arctic Adventures." (Though Gould advised the campus that no one ought to place too much emphasis on any putative title, suggesting that a Bartlett lecture was apt to be like an omnibus act of Congress, "liable to cover anything and everything.") True to form, salty Captain Bob's personality made an indelible impression. The *Carletonian* reported that during his less than twenty-four-hour visit he expressed himself strongly on a great many subjects and that the famed navigator "astounds lecture audiences with his remarkable pictures, his friends with his remarkable store of information and learning and everybody else with his vocabulary."

That spring Gould was elected to a year's term as president of the Minnesota Academy of Science.† He was also featured in one of a *Carletonian* series of faculty interviews whereby the student body got brought up to date on biographical background and personal details. Through the interview with student reporter Alan Cason, the Carleton community learned that "the gentleman with the red tie" strongly preferred pipes to cigarettes though he had trouble keeping one lit when he'd get to talking and forget about it, that he thought roadside billboards ranked high in the evils of civilization, and that he identified photography and listening to good music, especially string ensembles, among his chief hobbies.

---

*   This penguin, which at some now unknown date and for some now unremembered reason had acquired within the Gould household the nickname "Oscar," remained a fixture of successive Gould homes throughout his life. The Northfield house built for the Goulds in 1939 contained a niche near the entrance designed specifically to display Oscar. After accompanying Gould to Arizona in the early 1960s, Oscar was finally given to Carleton College in 1995, where, wearing a bright red tie from Larry's collection, he was an onstage observer of the college's memorial chapel service remembering Gould that fall. Subsequently, he took up permanent residence in a special case near the entrance to Carleton's Laurence McKinley Gould Library and quickly became a popular mascot or symbol of the Gould Library.

†   During Gould's year as president, he and the Academy backed an initiative to preserve the state's last great stretch of primeval forest by supporting a bill to create a state park out of the Nerstrand Woods, not far from Northfield, which was the last extensive virgin remnant of the storied "Big Woods" that once covered vast territories of the old Northwest. Minnesota Governor Elmer Benson appointed Gould to a special committee created to draw plans for saving the unspoilt Nerstrand Woods, and as Academy president Gould subsequently published a public letter urging citizens to help the cause by urging their state senators and representatives to support the bill authorizing the Minnesota Department of Conservation to acquire the land to establish Nerstrand Woods State Park. The 1939 effort ran into difficulties, and it was not until 1945 that a bill authorizing the park finally passed.

The interview revealed his ongoing desire to lead his own Antarctic expedition, approaching the South Pole from the South American side this time, if he could find backing for it. It also mentioned that he was writing a book about glaciers and that he intended to work in Alaska that summer.* The feature concluded with a return to the subject of Gould's notorious neckwear, about which the professor was quoted as saying "I like any bright color so long as it is red." The piece averred that in contrast to his ties Gould's socks were a "sad let-down. Somehow he has never gotten around to taking the right kind of sartorial care of his ankles." However, it concluded, Gould made up for any deficiency in his stockings with pajamas that "are so loud that they keep the entire neighborhood awake."

Before leaving Northfield for his 1938 summer program in western states, Gould played a role in proposing and carrying out one of the pleasantest features of that year's Carleton commencement ceremony: the bestowing of an honorary degree on Carleton's retiring professor of chemistry, Franz Exner. A deeply moved Exner, who had begun teaching at Carleton when Gould was a seven-year-old, wrote Gould afterward that his last year of teaching had been brightened by many things but by nothing more than what Gould had done for him. "Your being one of the youngest of our Professors," Exner emoted, "would not be expected to take the initiative in an act of recognition of the oldest member of the faculty, and yet it was you who proposed the plan of the degree, made the most beautiful speech of presentation, and even furnished your own Doctor's hood for the occasion." Gould touched Exner further by leaving for him on his desk Commencement evening a volume of Gould's *Cold*, with an inscription that Exner found the finest statement that had ever been made concerning him. "Your book will be one of my most valuable possessions," Exner told him.

After half a dozen years teaching at Carleton, Gould had established himself as an unqualified faculty success, loved and esteemed by students and colleagues alike. President Cowling, clearly recognizing Gould's unique value to the college and grateful that his star professor had not yet been lured away by an unmatchable offer from another institution, now proposed that Carleton undertake to build a house for Larry and Peg's future occupancy, designed according to the couple's own taste and ideas. He suggested that they make some sketches of the sort of home they would like, and the project moved forward. During 1938-39, the design of the L. M. Gould residence was entrusted to architect John S. Van

---

*   Neither of these things was destined to come to pass. The glaciers book was never completed, and he did not work in Alaska. The same issue of the *Carletonian* that mentioned Gould's intent to go to Alaska that summer also reported, on another page, that he would be spending the summer lecturing in Minnesota and adjoining states. In fact, he would split the summer of 1938 between Portland, where he taught a University of Oregon summer session and found time for glacier climbing about Mount Hood and Mount St. Helens, and then Utah, largely in the region of Bryce Canyon and the Aquarius Plateau. Peg Gould spent most of the summer in Colorado and Nevada. Upon the couple's early September return to town, the *Northfield News* noted humorously that "Dr. Gould confesses that he 'left her in Reno' and that as a result Mrs. Gould has been subjected to considerable inquiry as to the object of her visit there."

Bergen of Highland Park, Illinois, whose daughter Nancy had just enrolled as a Carleton freshman and who had written to Cowling proposing the exchange of architectural services for partial payment of tuition. Van Bergen designed a handsome stone structure in the Prairie School style, and the residence would be constructed, close to the campus on the southwest corner of Third and Elm, during the summer and fall of 1939. Carleton retained ownership of the house, but it would be Larry and Peg's home for the next twenty-two years.

Still a year prior to that move, the second-floor flat on Nevada Street in which the Goulds had lived since 1932 was the setting for the wedding of Peg's sister, Jean Rice, to Richard Hoppin, an accomplished pianist and student of music from Carleton's Class of 1936. The ceremony, two days before Christmas 1938, was conducted by Professor of Biography Charles Mierow, a former president of Colorado College.

When the Goulds did move into their new home, one of the benefits for Larry was increased space to indulge a developing interest in gardening. Though uncooked tomato was one of the few foods to which he had a personal aversion, in Northfield tomatoes gifted from the Gould garden became locally famous. "You have no idea," he would write to Cowling in 1941 while on sabbatical leave, "what satisfaction and inspiration I get from digging in the earth and watching things grow. I could easily have become a botanist but I think it is better to have one side of the out-of-doors as my vocation and another as my avocation or hobby."

Gould's Department of Geology and Geography was now manifestly thriving. In June 1939 the department graduated eight majors, most of whom intended to continue their studies in the field with graduate work. Gould's annual report at that time counted an additional twenty-four non-seniors who intended to complete majors in the department and noted that it remained the case year after year that the introductory course in geology was obliged to limit enrollment below the level of demand in order to correspond with laboratory and lecture room capacity. In 1938 George Gibson had been promoted from instructor to assistant professor, but in 1939 he chose in mid-year to depart for another opportunity, which obliged Gould on short notice to take over two spring semester courses previously taught by Gibson. By the end of the academic year, however, arrangements had very happily been made for Gibson's place to be filled in the fall by the return to Carleton, after a four-year absence, of Duncan Stewart. During the following year Gould himself introduced a new field geology course that he had long planned, instructing students in the instruments and techniques involved in geological surveying and mapping.

Gould was also thriving professionally. In addition to his presidency of the Minnesota Academy of Science, he had become a member of the American Geophysical Union's Committee on Glaciers and continued his participation on the International Commission on Snow. A few days after Jean Rice's Northfield wedding, he traveled to New York to deliver a paper on the glacial geology of Boulder Mountain, Utah, at the annual meeting of the Geological Society of

America. In the summer of 1939 he served as chairman of a symposium on the Pacific Antarctic held in conjunction with the Sixth Pacific Science Congress meeting in San Francisco.

He continued through the academic year 1939-40 to maintain his now well-established pattern of frequent public addresses on geological and other topics. One special engagement, in Michigan, was a commencement address delivered at his old high school in South Haven.

In nearly every aspect of personal life* it seemed that Gould was thriving, and things were going well. In contrast, the grim state of the outside world at this time was quite another matter; things were going hellishly. Great nations were at war, and by the time of Carleton's 1940 graduation ceremony Hitler's blitzkrieg seemed unstoppable. Commencement that year was coupled with news of the fall of Norway and of Italy's declaration of war on Britain and France. Three days after Carleton's departing seniors marched into chapel in caps and gowns, gray-clad German soldiers marched into Paris. Though most Americans still hoped their own country's declared neutrality would keep them clear of the fighting, it seemed inevitable that at the very least a great deal of change and disruption was drawing near.

---

*   One sad, and sobering, personal note from the fall of 1939 was the sudden, unexpected death of Larry's older brother, Ralph Gould, of an October heart attack a few days before Ralph's forty-seventh birthday.

CHAPTER 14

WARTIME AND NEW TASKS

When much of Europe had gone to war in September 1939, Larry Gould's initial view of the conflict had been that of most Americans: that while Herr Hitler was appalling, the fight did not belong to the United States, which should stay uninvolved if it possibly could. His disillusion with the 1914-1918 war, which he had come to see as unimaginable carnage to no positive end, tainted by war profiteering, supported by manufactured hysteria and hate-producing propaganda, and ended by a treaty whose harsh terms upon the defeated had been unjustly punitive, had left him disgusted with militarism, repelled by war, and inclined towards pacifism. In November, while most of the European fighting had still been confined to Poland, and Britain and France remained uneasily suspended in a period of relative inaction labeled the "sitzkrieg," Gould had offered to a Carleton chapel audience a caution, in memory of the dead of the last war, to be very wary of wartime propaganda and a suggestion that the present conflict might at root be a battle of imperialism with an underlay of cold economic self-interest.

Within seven months, however, following the quick German conquest of the Low Countries, the military collapse of France, and the near-annihilation of the British army before Dunkirk, Gould's sense of the menace of the Nazi threat to democratic civilization had grown in clarity and dire immediacy. By the time the college reconvened in September 1940, the airborne "Battle of Britain" that had commenced over the summer had entered a new phase, the "Blitz," in which the *Luftwaffe* turned from primarily attacking airfields to targeting British towns and cities in an attempt to crush civilian morale; London was coming under nightly bombing attack. In this context, though isolationism had by no means left the field in America, the ground of public opinion had shifted sufficiently so that national military "preparedness" had widely come to be seen as prudent, and—the week before students returned to Carleton—Congress had passed and President Roosevelt signed into law an act authorizing the first US peacetime conscription, requiring all males aged twenty-one to thirty-five to register with local draft boards.

A national election campaign was underway that autumn, the Republicans having, immediately after the shock of the fall of France, confounded their isolationist wing by nominating an unconventional "dark horse" candidate—lawyer Wendell Willkie, who had switched parties only the year before and was supported most strongly by the more liberal and internationalist elements of his new party— to oppose Roosevelt's unprecedented bid for a third term. Shortly before the general election Willkie was found to have attracted the support of about three-quarters of the Carleton community, including Gould, who on the Saturday evening before Election Day acted as master of ceremonies for a large Willkie rally sponsored jointly by the Carleton, St. Olaf, and Northfield Willkie Clubs. (It has never, however, been seriously asserted that as Carleton goes, so goes the nation, and three days later FDR, undismayed by his poor showing in the *Carletonian* straw poll, was solidly reelected.)

Less than a week after the voting, on the eve of Armistice Day, Gould spoke to the Carleton student body at Sunday evening vespers about his evolving views concerning the war in Europe. He now portrayed the conflict as the barbaric assault of totalitarianism, of both the fascistic and communistic variety, on the ideals and values of Western democracy, and he identified embattled Britain's cause as being also America's. Material aid to Britain in her present struggle for survival, he now believed, had become imperative to our own national interest. Gould's "change of heart" vesper address occasioned much discussion and response, pro and con, in Carleton dorm rooms, at meals, and in the pages of the *Carletonian*. A columnist found it strange that he did nothing about "explaining away" the view that the war was at heart economic; a letter writer suggested that Gould's "about-face" was due to an unreasoning Anglophilia; a trio of students together objected to Gould's "lumping together the economic, social and political forces of fascism and socialism," which they held actually to differ greatly in philosophies and practices, and found it difficult to accept Gould's identification of Britain with the cause of "democracy" at the same time that the British were imprisoning the leaders of democratic forces in India. An anonymous parodist caricatured Larry McKinley Gould as Professor Varry Extremely Fooled, an Antarctican who "has now thrown away the pacifist toys with which he has been wont to play in times of peace" and who instructs an audience of eight hundred penguins that "the war is no longer a war for icepire and all true penguin lovers must rush to wings in defense of our antarctican principles," declaring that "the Battle of Cretin is our battle, for if we are to forestall the twin black images of forcism and ant-

From the Carletonian, *November 15, 1940*

Antarmistice Talk

To the Editor:

    ICEBELT, ANTARCTICA, Nov. 10, 1940.—In an Armistice day address here today, Professor Varry Extremely Fooled announced to an audience of 800 stratified and assorted penguins that he has now thrown away the pacifist toys with which he has been wont to play in times of peace and that it is the duty of every patriotic penguin to do likewise. "For," said Professor Extremely Fooled, "the war is no longer a war for icepire and all true penguin lovers must rush to wings in defense of our antarctocratic principles. The Battle of Cretin is our battle, for if we are to forestall the twin black menaces of forcism and antarchy, we must aid Cretin in every way. We must speed up production on icebergs and fight, if necessary, to the last penguin for the Antarcticos way. It is imperative that we disregard our selfish principles and idiotsyncrasies and follow in penguin waddle the Supreme Sphenisciforme down in Sloshington."

    —ANTARCTIC NEWS SERVICE.

Red Tape

To the Editor:

    For useless red-tape, the tea room exchange rules printed some weeks ago take first place among all the Carleton regulations. And they do not present the promised improvement over last year's.

    Isn't it still possible to work out a system for small groups of students to make use of these exchange privileges for informal gatherings?

If England stands in need these Friends of Britain assail with frenzied imperatives. For this cause, conscript, suspend thought, prostitute religion to chauvinism, proscribe the oh so sad truth that "our democracy" is a rather feeble gag, let loose the dogs of war, and GOD BLESS ENGLAND!

    —JACK BUNDAY.

Did Gould Forget?

To the Editor:

    Some of us who disagree with some of the statements made by Dr. Gould in his much-contested speech of last Sunday would like to present a few of our ideas wherein we differ.

    First, we think that the present battle is more than a barbarian attempt to destroy "Western civilization." Britain is fighting for a political democracy, for her own home, but also for an imperialistic empire which she has exploited for many years. This is a battle of economies as well as ideologies.

    Secondly, we fear the type of battle that Britain is waging. We have seen how the French people were betrayed by their own ruling industrial class. Pétain, Weygand, Laval and other leaders invited military defeat to establish their own fascistic state. Similar reactionary forces of the English conservative party rule England today with a few exceptions such as Bevin and Morrison. It is significant that while Britain fights for "democracy," Nehru, Ghandi's right-hand man in leading democratic forces in India, has been imprisoned for his liberal activities.

    We think that Dr. Gould errs in his lumping together the economic

archy we must aid Cretin in every way." In contrast, a writer responding to the
more intemperate of Gould's student critics pointed out that "he didn't ask you
to accept his ideas but only expressed himself, sincerely and inoffensively, as his
experience and knowledge shows the light to himself." She asserted that based
on the discussions she had been part of, the impression of most of her peers had
been that Gould's vesper talk had been "almost infallible."

Meanwhile, for another year at any rate, the wheels of American academic
life continued to turn in their accustomed grooves. During the second semester
of 1940-41, Gould enjoyed his first sabbatical leave since joining the Carleton
faculty. He spent it in the West, mostly in Arizona, based in the red rock country
of Sedona, and while he was away Duncan Stewart temporarily assumed the duties
of departmental chairman. In mid-January, before starting his leave, Gould took
a nine-day trip to the East, meeting with other members of a National Research
Council committee regarding work on a new glacial map of North America
and then lecturing in New York to the American Geographical Society and in
Rochester to the Rochester Academy of Science, before returning to Northfield
via Ann Arbor and Chicago. Early in February the Goulds again played host to
Captain Bob Bartlett, who gave a return lecture in the Carleton chapel the evening of February 3. This was also the first day of the new Carleton semester and
therefore the official start of Gould's sabbatical. He left town the next day, his trip
westward including lectures delivered en route in Iowa, Oklahoma, and Texas.

Larry and Peg arrived in Sedona on the 4th of March and made it their base
until early June, filling the days with fieldwork, ranch visits, trail hikes, canyon
climbs, and excursions to scenic wonders in all directions. Highlights included
Gould's exploration of ancient cliff dwelling ruins and his descent to the bottom of the Grand Canyon.* In May he spent a few days in San Francisco, Peg
remaining behind in Sedona, in order to confer further about the glacial map of
North America. Gould's particular assignment in relation to this map was the
assembling of data for all of the Cordilleran states south of the main ice sheets,
encompassing the Rockies and other ranges such as the Sierra Nevada.

Gould's pleasant sabbatical was, however, interrupted by one unhappy
surprise: an unexpected and somewhat sudden decision by Duncan Stewart to
leave Carleton a second time for a post with another institution. This time it was
Lehigh University which lured Stewart away from Carleton. Lehigh's former
specialist in petrography had resigned to go into commercial work, and the head
of the department there, who had known Stewart since 1928, urged Stewart to

---

*   "I had hoped," he reported in a letter to Cowling, "to be able to walk down, taking my own
time to examine the rocks, and ride up by mule. I found that the cost of the round trip by mule
was $18.00 and that strangely enough if I walked down and rode out—just one way—the trip
would cost me $21.00. This aroused my Scotch instincts and made me so annoyed that I hiked
down the canyon to Phantom Ranch—7 miles with a difference in altitude of 1 mile—spent
the night and climbed out the next morning by the longer Bright Angel Trail—12 miles. It
was an inspiring trek …"

consider a move. Alarmed by receiving Stewart's letter informing him of the possibility, Gould immediately wrote Cowling that he very much hoped it would be possible to make "whatever arrangements are necessary in terms of rank and salary to keep Dr. Stewart at Carleton." Cowling did offer to promote Stewart to associate professor but was informed the following day that Stewart had accepted the Lehigh offer, at no increase in pay.

When Gould heard the news he expressed himself to Cowling as both disheartened and puzzled that "conditions should have arisen which have caused him to leave … to accept another position at no increase in salary or rank." "Just what has happened?" he demanded of the president, probably writing in the first heat of his disappointment and surprise at losing Stewart a second time. "I think some explanation is due me. For the first time in nine years I have been at Carleton College I feel that I have been let down." Somewhat affronted by Gould's tone, though knowing it to spring from the distress he felt over the resignation, Cowling replied that there had been no lack of good faith in his attempt to convince Stewart to remain at Carleton but that Stewart had simply decided otherwise: "that they had five men in the department [at Lehigh], which permitted higher specialization than was possible here, and that an institution of Lehigh's type was more in line with [Stewart's] professional interests than an undergraduate college of liberal arts." With some asperity, Cowling responded to Gould's suggestion that he had been "let down" by reminding him that "the Department of Geology has been given more support since you came here than any other department in the College." "If Carleton had had resources to do for other members of the faculty and for other departments what has been arranged for you and the Department of Geology," Cowling wrote, "there would scarcely be any other college in the country to compare with ours."

A chastened Gould quickly wrote back confessing to a misunderstanding that would never have happened had he been present for a face-to-face discussion across the president's desk: "This has always been a satisfying way of arriving at conclusions." He both knew and appreciated, he now avowed, the generous support that Cowling had always given, both to him personally and to the department, and he pledged to continue to do his best to merit it. "It is because of the high regard I hold for you and Dr. Stewart too," he apologized, "that I was so upset by his resignation. It would be a real personal disaster for me to lose faith in you." Cowling concluded the exchange by telling Gould he appreciated "more than any sentence or two can convey" the kind expressions of Gould's last letter and declared that "this incident has at least had the happy result of giving us both the occasion for expressing our sentiment for each other, which in my case comes very near to affection."

From afar, Gould worked on finding Stewart's replacement, and in late May he finalized an agreement with one of his former students, William M. Fiedler, then concluding graduate work at the University of California, to return to Carleton in the fall as instructor in geology.

The Goulds left Sedona June 2 and meandered through Utah and Idaho en route to Portland, where Larry had agreed to teach another Oregon summer session. On the 14th, his pocket diary notes, they fell in with Carleton colleague Harvey Stork and his wife on the Columbia River. Two days later his summer session began, lasting until the last week of July, after which the Goulds returned to Northfield and Larry spent August investigating glacial drift in nearby Dakota County.

***

Yet new stages of violence were visited upon Europe that summer of 1941 as Hitler unleashed his invasion of the Soviet Union, but to the U.S. there still remained a last few months of non-combatant relative normality. Carleton College opened its seventy-fifth academic year in September, welcoming to campus 309 new freshmen excited to begin college life. A healthy 108 students enrolled in Gould's introductory survey course in geology for the fall semester. The annual homecoming festivities were calendared early that year, on the last weekend of September, and students organized the traditional elements: a band-led torchlight parade, pep fest, and bonfire Friday night upon the main campus green and a freshman snake-dance at Saturday's football game. Before the game, Gould presided at a morning convocation where students, faculty, and returning alumni were addressed by Minnesota's thirty-four-year-old "boy governor" Harold Stassen.

Early in October Gould wrote a friendly note to Dick Byrd, thanking him for having forwarded a copy of Byrd's late summer address at a Madison Square Garden meeting sponsored by the Council for Democracy. Gould told his former chief that the address, in which Byrd called for national unity behind the president in the defense of democracy, was a "grand job" that he hoped would help to counteract the irresponsible isolationist utterances of people like Lindbergh.

On the first Wednesday in December, Carleton observed its last pre-war "Wild Tie Day" in Gould's honor. Judging took place in the college Tea Room, with the winner chosen by popular applause.* That evening Gould attended a student play, the psychological melodrama *Ladies in Retirement*.

Normality continued another three days and a morning.

Sunday in Northfield was dismal—drizzly and gray. Shortly after noon, word started spreading rapidly from person to person about there having been some sort of an attack on an American naval base in Hawaii. By 2 p.m., all across town and on both college campuses people were huddled over radios, listening soberly to terse news reports. Unlike the supposed "Martian invasion" scare a few years earlier, this was no dramatization of fiction—the Empire of Japan had indeed launched a surprise military strike

---

*   Co-winners were chosen that year, sophomores Lucian Pye and John Solhaug, whose ties, respectively, were described as "unaccountable blue with a terrific diffusion of housemaid's knee pink here and there" and "a tropical-jungle-in-a-hurricane green on a background of what might be called yellow—and might not." Professor Gould confounded expectations by meeting his classes that day wearing a tie of conservative black.

against the United States. The words "Pearl Harbor," which that morning had meant nothing to most Americans, now meant: war. At Carleton, books were put aside, as undergraduates considered the immensity and uncertainties of what now lay ahead and how much their own lives were

sure to be rechanneled. As later remembered in that year's college yearbook, "the gyroscopes of self-control spun too fast and little whirlwinds of panic started up in people's minds. War had blasted off the back storm-door of naive security and the draft of reality was frigidly around us." That evening after vespers some five hundred students crowded into Great Hall to listen to an impromptu faculty roundtable discussion of the day's momentous implications, led by the advisor to Carleton's International Relations Club.

On December 8, the United States formally declared itself at war with Japan. At Carleton an evening meeting of the faculty concluded with President Cowling and Dean Blayney speaking tentatively about college problems

Building the Homecoming bonfire, fall 1941

anticipated due to the war. Within days Gould was asked to be part of a six-man Carleton Committee on Defense led by Blayney and charged with recommending a preliminary program of college responses. The Committee on Defense presented its first report at the morning faculty meeting convened December 17 in Leighton Hall. Noting that the country was now engaged in an all-out war which would determine the fate of democracy and that it had become a patriotic duty for individuals and institutions alike to aid in carrying that war to a victorious end, the committee recommended that the college undertake a defense training program, aiming to provide students—who were urged for now to remain in college, pursuing their studies with "renewed diligence"—with "rudimentary knowledge in special fields pertaining to military service, civilian defense, and technical employment in defense industries." A number of specific temporary courses were proposed, including one in military map interpretation and the elements of surveying, to be offered by Gould together with Fiedler.

In the end, for Carleton's 1942 spring semester Gould's Department of Geology and Geography provided due to the national emergency a non-credit course in elementary map construction and military map interpretation, and substituted a Gould-taught course in field geology, with special emphasis on map making and interpretation, for Gould's usual second-semester course in glaciation. The department's geographer, Leonard Wilson, was quickly called to Washington for war intelligence work, beginning an extended leave of absence from the college in January. Carleton was fortunate to secure as a replacement Trevor Lloyd, an English-born geographer lately working in Canada, who proved a gifted teacher and shared Gould's passionate interest in the Arctic.

Pearl Harbor's impact on college enrollment took some while to be felt, as college men were early advised that they could best prepare themselves for national service by continuing where they were and finishing their degrees if possible before volunteering or being called in the draft. At Carleton this goal would be furthered by instituting in 1942 (and repeating in 1943) the college's first-ever summer session, to help accelerate the completion of student degrees. Additionally, some students were able promptly to enlist in programs such as the Navy V-5 aviation cadet or V-7 naval reserve officer training (or for freshmen and sophomores, the preparatory V-1 program) that allowed them to stay in college for varying periods of time on inactive duty. But for college men for whom degree completion was still distant or boys still in high school whose expectations had been to enter college in the next year or two it was clear enough early in 1942—as the director of U.S. Selective Service announced a need for an army of 3.6 million by the end of the year with further increases planned for 1943—that the overwhelming majority would find themselves in uniform before long with college programs either interrupted or deferred, if not prematurely ended or entirely foregone.

Meanwhile, by late February 1942 the *Carletonian* was able to list a total of 91 former Carleton students then known to be serving in the armed forces—mostly, at that point, assigned to a variety of stateside training camps, though the list also included one alumnus serving with General MacArthur in the Philippines and two who were at sea in the Pacific aboard the *U.S.S. Lexington*, an aircraft carrier destined to be sunk three months later in the Battle of the Coral Sea.* The same edition of the paper also noted the first post-Pearl Harbor death of a former Carleton student in military service, Edward Crandall, an aviation cadet who had

---

* Both ex-Carls aboard the *Lexington*, Norman Sterrie '39 and Chandler Swanson '37, survived her sinking and eventually the war. Both received the Navy Cross for heroism for actions while aboard the carrier. Both men were former Gould students, Swanson having made geology his major. The alumnus serving with MacArthur in the Philippines early in 1942, Lt. Col. William Van Nostrand ex-'32, was reported missing in action on Mindanao on May 7, the day after the surrender of the American garrison at Corregidor and one day before the loss of the *Lexington*. In fact he had become a Japanese prisoner of war and remained so for thirty-two months before being killed in Taiwan on a POW transport ship bombed by American planes in January 1945.

spent three years at Carleton as a member of the Class of 1942, killed in a training crash in Illinois. By war's end, Carleton's "Gold Star" casualties would top fifty.

On March 31, following continued work by the Committee on Defense, Carleton rolled out its announcement of an ambitious war training program to begin in the fall. Known for about three weeks as the Carleton College Officers Corps, but thereafter as the Carleton Officer Training Corps (COTC), and informally nicknamed "The Flying Carls," this was to be a program of co-operation of the college administration with advising officers of each of the three major military branches, Army, Navy, and Marines, to combine college studies with special military training, particularly in aviation. According to the original plan, about three hundred Carleton men, half coming from the following year's freshman class, were to be admitted to the corps, whereby enlistees would receive training equipping them for a future military commission or for entry into the V-5, V-7, or similar deferment program while continuing work toward a BA degree. (Temporary deferments would depend on the

Preparing to go to war, spring 1942

continuance of satisfactory work and subject to future change in the urgency of the military's need for immediate manpower.) The college, it was revealed, would be acquiring nearby land suitable for the creation of a Carleton airport, for flight training and ground school studies. Under an arrangement with the Naval Reserve Aviation Base at Wold-Chamberlain Field in Minneapolis at least four training planes—by fall this would grow to twenty—were to be stationed in government-built hangars at the Carleton airfield, near the community of Stanton. Carleton announced that it would create seven new technical and military-related courses to be offered for college credit and that its faculty would also contribute a like number of non-credit lecture demonstrations useful for both flight and ground training. In mid-April came the follow-up news that Gould, as chairman of the college's division of science, would act as COTC commandant.

During the next month general oversight of the COTC and policy matters relating to the college's response to war was delegated to a new War Programs Committee reorganized out of the Committee of Defense and naturally including corps commandant Gould among its eight members. Also in May Gould agreed to be appointed official representative on campus for the Armed Forces' joint recruiting program. He wished to be doing all that he could in support of the national mobilization of talent and manpower to win the war. In mid-summer he wrote Cowling that "as the news from the Russian front grows more dismal I am more and more convinced that we must throw all of our resources into the war effort as though it were to last forever."

Feeling as he did that the struggle with Germany and Japan ought to lay first claim on all available talents, including his own, and despite his new responsibility as corps commandant for the nascent "Flying Carls," Gould was receptive that fall to a call upon him for emergency national service within the organizational command of the Army Air Forces. Late in October, even as aviation training under the auspices of the Hinck Flying Service geared up to commence operations at the new Carleton airfield, Gould traveled to Washington to confer about a role proposed for him to head up the Arctic division of a newly created Arctic, Desert, and Tropic Information Center (ADTIC). In Washington, where, as he wrote Cowling, he was "immediately on the merry-go-round"—sworn in, fingerprinted, and given an official identification badge allowing him to come and go—Gould's initial assignment had him for several days working at a desk and given secretarial help out of the office of Col. William S. Carlson, a fellow Arctic enthusiast and another former protégé of Hobbs at Michigan.* Although expressing early ambivalence about his proposed appointment—he wrote Cowling about "the sense of frustration that one meets here when he really wishes to do something" and about his surprise at "the lack of correlation among various branches of the service"—his assenting to take it on does not seem to have been seriously in doubt once it was agreed that even though overall ADTIC headquarters had been established at the Army Air Force Proving Ground Command at Eglin Field in the Florida panhandle, the Arctic section headquarters would be placed in Minneapolis. For the balance of the present semester, before the Minneapolis headquarters could be fully operational in any case, Gould would be able to divide his time between work there and teaching duties at Carleton.

Absence from Northfield continued the following week, but for quite different personal reasons, as on the first of November Gould's father died at age seventy-one; Larry and Peg traveled to Michigan for the funeral in South Haven

---

* Like Gould, Carlson had formerly participated in a University of Michigan Greenland Expedition. Commissioned in the Army Air Force while on wartime leave from the University of Minnesota, Carlson was also like Gould in that both men's postwar futures would lie in college or university administration—starting in 1946 Carlson was successively president of the University of Delaware, the University of Vermont, the State University of New York (SUNY) system, and the University of Toledo—where, like Gould at Carleton, he would eventually be honored as the namesake of the main university library.

and burial in Lacota.

Public announcement of Gould's appointment as chief of ADTIC's Arctic Section was made a few weeks later. The section was being set up to operate out of offices in Northrop Auditorium on the University of Minnesota campus, and Gould initially committed to being present Tuesdays, Thursdays, and Saturdays while completing his Carleton duties Mondays, Wednesdays, and Fridays for the balance of the semester. The mission of the Arctic, Desert and Tropic Information Center—quickly dubbed "Snow, Sand and Sarong"—was to collect and disseminate information on how warfare involving non-temperate environments might affect US military equipment and tactics and to prepare survival manuals for use in each. Gould sought to involve and draw on the expertise of many of the top men in pre-war Arctic study. Although even in his earliest public comment on his new position Gould emphasized the confidential nature of much of the work with which he would be involved, his later view was that as many as nine-tenths of the documents with which he worked in the assignment were absurdly overclassified. "A great many highly classified documents," he would tell a 1973 interviewer, "you could find in the encyclopedia or someplace else."

One of Gould's early acts with the Arctic Section was to draft into service as an ADTIC editorial staffer his sister-in-law, Jean Rice Hoppin, whose husband Dick had left a teaching position in Ohio to go into the Marines. With Dick in the service and eventually seeing combat in the South Pacific, Jean returned to Minnesota to work for Larry.

Gould's appointment with ADTIC and consequently his leave of absence from Carleton would extend until the early fall of 1944. For the first several months, while headquartered in Minneapolis, Gould followed a plan of returning home to Northfield, where Peg continued to live, on weekends. By mid-July 1943, however, he was forced by careful scrutiny of his paychecks to the "painful conclusion" that he could no longer afford to maintain the house in Northfield while living elsewhere, and he informed Cowling that, whether the Arctic Section was to remain in Minneapolis or not—a move was rumored—Peg would soon be joining him in a single household and accordingly he wished for Carleton to make temporary alternate disposition for the college-owned Gould house for the 1943-44 academic year. (He hoped that a reliable family without children could be found to rent it, and, as he had spent much personal time and money on the property's plantings and garden, he asked that provision be made in the rental agreement to prevent changes to his own plans in those matters.)

In the fall of 1943, despite the Arctic Section chief's best efforts to prevent it, an order came down that all sections of ADTIC were to be brought together in New York City, and by early December Gould was working out of new headquarters in Manhattan's financial district (25 Broad Street). Peg and Larry—and Jean, who liked her job and made the move to New York with her sister and brother-in-law—established themselves for most of the next year in a townhouse apartment in Midtown, in the Murray Hill neighborhood (115 East 37th Street).

As early as September 1943, though, as the section's move to New York appeared imminent but had not yet been finalized, Gould had informed Cowling that, as he foresaw that the Arctic Section's tactical contributions to the war effort would be largely complete by the following September, he was confident he would be able to be relieved from service at that time and would then be free to return to his work at the college.

***

The school Gould would return to in the fall of 1944 was significantly altered from the one he had left early in 1943. The three semesters of Gould's leave of absence saw surely the greatest departures from normal circumstances and normal operations in the college's history. The plans that had been so carefully crafted for the Carleton Officer Training Corps did not turn out to be of very long duration, following a national change of course announced in late December 1942 by the War Manpower Commission. New plans put most college men in uniform by the fall of 1943, calling up by mid-summer if not before most men enlisted in the various deferred reserve programs, but assigning a quarter million uniformed men to college campuses for specialized training, mostly technical in nature.

At Carleton, a group of twenty Army Enlisted Reserve Corps men began flight training in January 1943, and were housed in the football stadium. The first large detachment of soldiers—in uniform and under full military discipline accompanied by their own commanding officers—arrived in February in the form of some two hundred Army Air Forces privates following a pre-meteorology training program, for whom the Davis Hall dormitory was turned into a barracks. Reveille woke these men daily at 5:45 a.m. After mess they were marched to eight hours of classes, followed by military drill and physical training, evenings spent studying, and lights out by 10. The pre-meteorology program—formally at Carleton the 70th Army Air Forces Technical Training Detachment (AAFTTD) —conducted four twelve-week terms and concluded with a special graduation ceremony in Skinner Chapel in mid-February of 1944.

Meanwhile, a second large influx of soldier trainees took up residence at Carleton in the form of Service Unit 3716 of the Army Specialized Training Program (ASTP), the first wave of which arrived in June 1943. These men, divided into groups studying basic engineering and others following a course in either French or German language and area studies, had brought another four hundred-some uniformed men to campus. When combined with the pre-meteorology students and with a hundred or so Army Air Corps "War Service Flyers" (WSF) engaged in secondary flight training and ground school work, this amounted to over 740 soldiers present for part of the 1943-44 Carleton year. This compared with about six hundred civilian students, only a small fraction of whom were now men. (Only twenty-three men present in the original student body of 1942-43 remained at Carleton by fall 1943.)

All use of the campus for military training programs ended, however, with the February departures of the AAFTTD and the WSF. This was followed in the spring by the disbanding of the ASTP unit due to a government decision to terminate its student-soldier specialized training program. Therefore the campus to which Gould returned later that year was once again all civilian, but its student body was now overwhelmingly female, by a ratio of ten to one.

John Cowles

Another respect in which the college to which Gould returned in 1944 was now a different place involved the impending retirement of President Cowling, and the now ongoing institutional search for his replacement. The trustee committee charged with selecting Cowling's successor had been formed and held its first meetings in the summer of 1944. Gould was very much under consideration from the start. At the same time he was being scouted as a possible presidential candidate by representatives of the University of Minnesota and University of Oregon and was being pressed actively by publisher John Cowles to change arenas altogether and become director of the editorial page of the *Minneapolis Star Journal*. Committing to nothing but likely preferring the possibility of the Carleton presidency to any other alternative (and perhaps given quiet encouragement in that direction by Cowling), Gould took steps to secure release from his ADTIC post as of mid-September, in advance of another move of the Arctic Section headquarters, this time from New York to Orlando. Meeting with trustee Laird Bell in Chicago along the way, as sort of a preliminary "getting to know you" interview and discussion of the interest many were expressing over the idea that he might become Carleton's next president, Gould returned home to Northfield for what would be one final Carleton year in the classroom.*

Gould's department during that year was a shrunken one. Bill Fiedler, who had acted as chairman during Gould's leave, had departed, as had staff hired primarily to provide instruction in geography to ASTP students the year before. Taking up the geography mantle now (along with additional responsibilities in international relations) was a displaced German, Hans Weigert, who had fled Hitler's regime and come to America in 1938. For 1944-45 Weigert and Gould together formed the whole department. Gould offered his familiar year-long survey course in geology, as well as the fall Geography of North America course and, with Professors Stork and Pettingill, the team-taught Conservation of Natural Resources class in the spring.

Drawing on his recent ADTIC experience, Gould chose as his first on-campus

---

*   Here again, Larry and Peg were accompanied by Jean Rice Hoppin, who also ended her employment with the Arctic Section prior to its move to Orlando. Jean would continue to make her home with her sister and brother-in-law until after her husband was discharged from his Marine Corps service in September 1945.

public lecture after his return an illustrated talk on "Arctic Survival," with which he opened that year's natural history lecture program in October. The next month he was the featured speaker at two chapel assemblies, one in support of the annual campaign to raise money for the Carleton Service Fund and the other a part of the college homecoming celebration, which in 1944 on a campus almost empty of men was associated with no football game, most intercollegiate sports having been suspended for the duration in 1943. Instead it featured a basketball doubleheader: a student team vs. alumni players contest followed by a women's game between freshman and upperclass teams.

Also in November, Gould and Hans Weigert began working on putting together a special on-campus event, a conference on Arctic matters that would bring to Carleton several noted experts for a series of open lectures and discussions. Eventually scheduled for four days in March, after Gould-led planning that also brought in Professor of International Relations David Bryn-Jones, this Conference on Problems of the Far North began with an all-college assembly featuring a lecture on "The Northern Course of Empire" by the gathering's most luminous star, explorer Vilhjalmur Stefansson, who had recently, along with another of the conference guests, cartographer Richard Edes Harrison, co-edited a book with Weigert. The entire conference, which also included the screening of documentary films loaned for the occasion by the National Film Board of Canada, was a great success, with Carleton students attending in such numbers that meetings could be held only in the college's most commodious space, the chapel.

Leadership in the sponsoring of this conference went hand-in-hand with another of Gould's activities during the preceding year, which was active involvement in the founding and early direction of a new international organization, the Arctic Institute of North America (AINA). This institute grew out of a May 1944 meeting in New York of nine Americans and eleven Canadians concerned with assembling and disseminating Arctic region information of both scientific and strategic military value, followed by a formal founding in September at a meeting in Montreal. A key participant in both meetings, Gould—and his personal contacts with Canadian colleagues like Trevor Lloyd—had been instrumental in bringing them about. At the founding meeting in Montreal Gould was named to the new institute's initial board of governors and agreed to serve for a time as AINA acting director. (He would be relieved from carrying the duties of the latter responsibility in October 1945 by Lincoln Washburn, who had worked under Gould as an intelligence officer in ADTIC and who became AINA's first fulltime executive director upon receiving his military release.)

Just after the end of the Conference on Problems of the Far North, Cowling received a letter from his colleague, President Virgil Hancher of the University of Iowa, inquiring as to Cowling's view of the suitability of Gould's becoming Iowa's new dean of the College of Liberal Arts. (The vacancy had arisen because Iowa's present dean, Harry Newburn, had been called to the presidency of the University of Oregon, a position for which Gould also had been considered.) Cowling

At the Conference on Problems of the Far North, 1945: Hans Weigert, Vilhjalmur Stefansson, and Gould and an unidentified student

responded by saying that upon his own imminent retirement, "It would be entirely agreeable to me to see Dr. Gould selected as my successor. This statement is probably the best answer I could give to your inquiry." At this time and throughout the month following, Laird Bell, chair of the Carleton Board of Trustees, and the committee responsible for deciding upon Cowling's successor were wrestling mightily with the matter and becoming acutely aware that time was getting short. A working list of candidates that at one time had reached seventy-five names had undergone a sifting process that had reduced those still under active consideration to a few. Though nothing about this process had been public, both Cowling and Gould knew that throughout it Gould had been prominent among the possibilities, though standing in a decidedly different relation to the job search than other candidates due to a powerful presupposition against selecting a president from the ranks of a current faculty except under rare and extraordinary circumstances.

Almost certainly, had Gould not in the end been selected to take up the reins that Cowling was laying down, Gould's connection with Carleton would have been approaching its end, as he would sooner or later have accepted some offer elsewhere for some position, in or out of academia, that was too good to refuse. Omnicompetent as he was, he likely would have made a great success of whatever else it might have been. But, *mirabile dictu* for Carleton College, chosen he was. On the 12th of May—one day after Larry and Peg celebrated Peg's fortieth birthday; four days after Allied acceptance of German surrender—Gould was extended, and accepted, an offer to become Carleton's fourth president.

Two days later, shortly after 2 p.m. on Monday, May 14, at the Minneapolis Club, the Carleton Board of Trustees formally elected Laurence M. Gould president of Carleton. His salary was set at $10,000 per year and the use of the college house he was already occupying, plus an allowance for expenses incurred due to his office. That evening, at a dinner in the Carleton Tea Room given by the faculty in honor of President and Mrs. Cowling, Gould delivered laudatory

remarks on behalf of the faculty to which Cowling—who had also been informed of the trustees' choice on the afternoon of the 12th, to his decided satisfaction—responded warmly.

Public announcement of Gould's selection was made by board secretary Louis Headley the next day. In Northfield, word that their esteemed professor was to be the new president was received by the campus community with elation. As described by the *Carletonian*, "it took only a few minutes for the news to spread. The Willis [Hall] bell, long a herald of Carleton victories, rang out as an impromptu choir serenaded the homes of the president and the president-elect." The next day, in a united display of approbation, nearly the entire student body outfitted themselves in "Larry Gould red," the brightest they could muster.

The *Carletonian*, May 19, 1945

"Carleton is to be congratulated!" said the campus paper. Praising their hero's basic ideals, "truly religious beliefs," and "clear and broadminded thinking," as well as his organizational and leadership ability, the *Carletonian* editors declared with satisfaction that "there are few people anywhere today who so well portray the combination of both the arts and the sciences—upon which the success of a post-war America is dependent."

A few days later Gould wrote in separate letters to trustees Bell and Headley that he was feeling humbled by the trust being placed in him by the board, together with the "unbelievable enthusiasm" with which his selection had so far been met. Claiming to be fully cognizant of the difficulties of some of the problems that lay ahead and to have had some reluctance in agreeing to face the task, he reported that he was able to look forward to the job with confidence when he reflected upon the character of those who had elected him and would be standing behind him.

That year's Carleton yearbook concluded with the observation that at this moment with military victory approaching we "find ourselves standing at the beginning of a new era." In watershed 1945 this was unmistakably so—true for the world, true for the country, and true as well for Carleton College. At the level of personal biography this truth was equally apparent; the life of Larry Gould had arrived at a clear division—a new epoch was about to begin.

CHAPTER 15

BUILDING A CATHEDRAL

August 1 was set as the date for Donald Cowling to retire and for Gould to assume office, but already, from mid-May on, the two worked together on presidential matters of ongoing importance, and within days of his selection Gould had already begun to consider the pressing business of certain key hires he hoped to make before fall.

To begin with, he needed to replace himself. The problem of a new head for Carleton's Department of Geology and Geography had, however, a simple solution. Just four days after his formal election by the Board of Trustees, Gould wrote his old friend and colleague Duncan Stewart, then at Lehigh, urging him to return to Carleton—this time, he stressed, for good—as a full professor and department chair. Stewart quickly agreed.

Then there was the matter of a new dean. Lindsey Blayney, who had long acted both as Carleton's dean of the college and as dean of men, was retiring along with Cowling. One of Gould's most urgent early tasks as president-elect was to secure Blayney's replacement—or pair of replacements, as Gould thought it best going forward to divide Blayney's two functions into separate positions. By the end of May Gould was soliciting advice and decanal nominations from various contacts. In early July the young president of Swarthmore, Carleton alumnus John Nason '26, suggested that Gould consider Frank R. Kille, a zoologist on Nason's own faculty whose chance for advancement at Swarthmore was blocked by departmental politics but who Nason thought might make an admirable dean at Carleton. The forty-year-old Kille, Nason confided, had been one of his "chief supporters in attempting to persuade natural scientists that there is more to their function in a liberal arts college than to train professional scientists." Gould met with Kille in New York later that month, and an appointment as dean of men soon followed—though Gould was already that summer projecting accurately that Kille might subsequently be moved into the position of academic dean.

Meanwhile, Gould was also working on a third early appointment that he considered crucial: a dynamic individual to head and revitalize the English Department. English, Gould thought, by right ought to be a liberal arts college's most important and best department, and he hoped to make it such at Carleton. It was Louis Bredvold, chairman of the department at Michigan, who directed Gould's attention to Arthur Mizener, a thirty-seven-year-old Princeton-trained assistant professor at Wells College, previously an instructor at Yale, who was teaching part of that summer at the University of Minnesota. This was gracious of Bredvold, as Michigan itself was interested in Mizener. Gould followed up on a number of possibilities for the position in English but by early August had made Mizener a formal offer to come to Carleton as full professor and chairman of the department. Mizener's telegram of acceptance came to the new president as a very happy birthday present on the 22nd. Though President William Weld of Wells College protested that the hiring away of one of his teachers so close to the start of a new academic year amounted to an act of academic piracy, Gould wrote a note thanking Weld for his "understanding and generosity" in releasing Mizener to a larger professional opportunity. Mizener, Gould stressed, would begin at Carleton as the sole full professor in a department historically carrying three to five and which Gould intended to see become the college's strongest; he would have a "remarkable opportunity" to build around himself and his ideas an outstanding program.

How to build an outstanding college program around himself was, of course, now Gould's own primary concern. Writing to the new president-elect within days of his selection, Trustee Chairman Bell wrote that he hoped for "an aggressive, forward-looking program and policy" to move Carleton beyond what he sensed was "a sort of educational doldrums there now." "I do not mean just cooking up something to catch G.I.'s," Bell pressed. "I am thinking of something that will give new vigor and aim to those things, hard to define, which we all feel a liberal arts college stands for." Gould replied with an assurance that he would "not be content with the juggling of an old program" and that he hoped to find many friends on the Board of Trustees who would prove to share Bell's own "pioneering spirit in this direction." A month later we find Gould noting that the college's curriculum and graduation requirements had not been reexamined for nineteen years and that it was time to do so now. In a letter attempting to convey "a basic idea of what I wish to see develop here," Gould deplored Carleton's "sharp departmental lines" and the tendency of many department heads "to forget our primary function" as a liberal arts college and to concern themselves instead with "building up a little empire, as it were, around their own department." He wrote that he wanted to see Carleton reorganized more along divisional than departmental lines and further that the college could strengthen itself by sharpening its focus on its liberal arts core: "I think we have too many courses, too many departments, and too many majors."

Gould elaborated on his vision concerning Carleton's curriculum in a revealing letter to Bell later that summer, writing that not only would he

The Goulds at the door to their Northfield home, 1945

Frank R. Kille   **Arthur Mizener**

"not be content to go along in the same old rut" but that he thought "we face the need of a minor revolution." Some weeks earlier the president-elect had paid a visit to the University of Chicago to confer with Chancellor Robert M. Hutchins there and found that he and Hutchins saw eye to eye on many things. Gould now told Bell that he wished to study the work and aims of the college in Chicago more carefully before making specific and detailed recommendations for Carleton, but he was willing to provide an outline of the "minor revolution" he envisioned. "In brief," he wrote, "I want to see the College curriculum drastically reorganized. I want to see a closely integrated, carefully thought out, general education program which will be required of all students." He endorsed reducing the present two dozen separate departmental majors to "perhaps 6 or 7 field majors" and requiring each student at the end of four years "to pass comprehensive examinations both in the general education studies and in the field major." Institutional inertia would be a problem, with "too many of our professors [having] become contentedly established in their own sharply-departmentalized groups," but he was optimistic that most could be "re-educated to a vision of what Carleton College can really do and become." Gould was heartened by recent steps taken by both Harvard and Yale to constrict the elective system and saw in Carleton's small size a great advantage over a big university in attempting to dissolve well-established departmental empires and achieve "the integration which we seek." "Here in an institution this size," he urged, "we can really accomplish all that Harvard and Yale believe they can in the way of the establishment of the liberal tradition to meet the needs of the chaotic future."

In pushing forward, Gould told Bell, he hoped to capitalize on the evident good will and "pent up eagerness and enthusiasm to ... take a more active part in the new life of Carleton College" that he discerned both in board members and other college friends and in the alumni, who had been kept rather at arms length by Cowling. (Gould told the trustees when accepting the presidency that one of his major aims "would be to bring the alumni back to the college and make them feel that they belong to it and it belongs to them throughout their whole life.")

Another aim Gould expressed that summer prior to the start of his first academic year as president was to effect much-needed improvement in the matter of faculty salaries, which had languished throughout the Depression and war years. Crucial to this effort would be a larger college endowment, and the trustees authorized that summer the prompt undertaking of a five-year financial campaign to raise $5 million for Carleton. (A "huge figure," notes the relevant trustees minute, but "nevertheless, we believe that it is capable of attainment.")

While still president-elect, Gould managed in July to get away for a week-long holiday with Peg as guests of his publisher-friend John Cowles and his wife, Betty, at the Cowles' summer camp, Camp Glendalough, at Battle Lake, Minnesota. He used the excursion as an opportunity to broach the suggestion that Cowles accept appointment as a Carleton trustee, to be presented as Gould's own first candidate for election to the board. (Cowles initially demurred, suggesting that Gould consider asking him again after the expiration—in five years!—of his term as a Harvard overseer, but the persuasive Gould persisted and secured an acceptance the following month.)

When August arrived, on a Wednesday, the Gould presidency officially began—though the formal ceremony of inauguration was set for mid-October. There were other hiring decisions, for both the teaching and administrative staffs, with which Gould was concerned in his administration's earliest days. The first weekend after he assumed office found him off to Chicago where, among other appointments, he had a very satisfactory interview with a young Italian-born economist, Renzo Bianchi, whose addition to the ranks of Carleton faculty soon followed.

The Monday afternoon interview with Bianchi, in Gould's suite at the Palmer House, followed by a few hours President Harry Truman's electrifying announcement to the world that the United States had exploded an atomic bomb—the War Department was referring to it as a "cosmic bomb"—upon the Japanese city of Hiroshima. Little more than a week later, the war would end. For Gould, news of Japan's capitulation came just as he was returning from a short trout fishing trip of two or three days on Wisconsin's Brule River, which he had described in prospect to a friend as an excursion that would "positively be my last holiday, for how long I do not know." Now the glad news that the war was over stimulated all sorts of reflection. "These are times for rejoicing," Gould wrote in his correspondence that week, "but rejoicing with sobriety as we contemplate the tasks of peace ahead, which in many ways will be more difficult than those of the war itself." At home, Peg's sister Jean Hoppin, who had spent much of the war living with the Goulds, was filled with excitement and hope for the speedy return from the Pacific of her husband Dick, who had been wounded in action in June, taking a shell fragment in the hip during the Marine invasion of Okinawa. At Carleton, though it would still be another twelve months before the proportion of men enrolled in the student body could return to near normality, and the post-war environment would present innumerable thorny new challenges, the college relished the prospect of opening a fresh academic year, with its exciting new president at the helm, in peacetime.

Freshmen—still mostly female by a ratio of about six to one—arrived on campus September 16. Gould delivered a few remarks to the incoming class in the college chapel the next morning and an address, "The Educated Man," at a freshman dinner in the Carleton Tea Room the evening of the 18th. In between, on the evening of the 17th, came the first formal faculty meeting over which he presided. By his own account, Gould gave his teaching staff a "fairly brutally frank statement" regarding the "minor revolution" he hoped to bring about, and he professed himself as "amazed and delighted at the response, especially from the older, more conservative members," who claimed that this was just what they had been waiting for. "All of this encourages me to believe," Gould told Cowles, "that the re-education of our faculty will be much less difficult than I supposed; for, after all, if any plan is really to work and to achieve the unity and coherence which it must have, it must ... come from within rather than being super-imposed from above."

Since mid-summer a working group of Carleton faculty and trustees had been shaping plans and overseeing logistical details for a red-letter day, Gould's presidential inauguration, which was set for Tuesday, October 16. It was to be a gala celebration of the start of a new era at the college—a combination of emotions of solemn thanksgiving for having come through the difficulties of war, of shared satisfaction and communal pride in the person of the college's new chosen leader, and of exhilarating optimism over the possibilities ahead.

During the week preceding his inauguration, Gould made a brief excursion to Montreal for a meeting of the Board of Governors of the new Arctic Institute of North America, the acting directorship of which Gould was now turning over to new hands. This trip, however, was bracketed on both ends by a tragic occurrence in the life of the college community, which unhappily added anguish to the mix of Carleton's pre-inaugural emotions. In the forenoon of the 8th, the day Gould departed for Montreal, two cars violently collided at the intersection forming the campus entrance at First and College Streets. In one car, heading north into the college grounds, were Gould's geographer colleague Hans Weigert and his wife, Lili. In the other, speeding west along First Street, were two young men temporarily home on military leave. The westbound Ford crashed into the right rear of the northbound Studebaker, spinning Weigert's vehicle sideways until it hit the curb and throwing the 38-year-old Lili Weigert from the car onto the pavement with broken ribs, a broken pelvis, and kidney injuries. Over the next two days at the Northfield hospital, Mrs. Weigert received several transfusions of blood and plasma, some donated by members of the Carleton community, but upon Gould's return from the meetings in Montreal he was met with the news that she had died—leaving two young children and an emotionally shattered husband. Her funeral, at the All Saints Episcopal Church with which Gould himself was associated, was Saturday afternoon. Thus, three days in advance of the pomp, praise, and personal joys anticipated to accompany the celebration of his presidential inauguration a dampened Gould acted as one of Mrs. Weigert's six somber pallbearers.

***

In Carleton lore and legend, Larry Gould reputedly had the gift, highly useful to a college president, of being able to influence local weather sufficiently to guarantee good conditions for important college functions and ceremonies. In what was perhaps an early manifestation of these powers, Inauguration Day

College marshall Leal Headley leads the inaugural procession, October 16, 1945.

1945 was physically perfect. Indian summer warmth prevailed under a cloud-less blue sky; campus maples displayed their finest fall colors. At 10: 30 a.m. the scene became more striking still as the Carleton professoriate assembled in front of Laird Hall bedecked in the colorful variety of their academic regalia—bright-hued hoods proclaiming individual alma maters, set off by black robes topped by mortarboards or round Tudor bonnets. At the same time 106 similarly-garbed representatives of the nation's colleges, universities, learned societies, and other invited organizations gathered by Great Hall to form their own line of march to join the faculty, after which the entire assemblage made a stately double-rowed procession from Laird to the doors of Skinner Memorial Chapel. Leading this procession was the college marshal, Leal A. Headley. Following in order were a pair of student flag-bearers, carrying the American flag and the college banner; President Gould, paired with trustee vice chairman Louis S. Headley (Leal's brother, presiding over the inaugural ceremony because board chairman Laird Bell was in Germany on government assignment); Minnesota Governor Edward J. Thye, paired with guest speaker Alexander G. Ruthven, president of the University of Michigan; and then the whole panoply of institutional representatives, trustees, and teachers. Already seated inside the chapel was the Carleton student body and the rest of the non-marching audience, which had received programs from the hands of a dozen student ushers wearing red dresses in Gould's honor. Also waiting inside was a white-robed choir of a hundred. To the processional music of Guilmant's "Grand Chorus," played by college organist Henry Woodward, the marchers entered the chapel and passed down the aisle through packed pews to take their places in front. Somehow that morning an estimated fourteen hundred people were fitted inside a building which had a normal seating capacity of seven hundred.

After the choir led all in a singing of "The Star-Spangled Banner" (including the less familiar second verse), an invocation was delivered by the Episcopal Bishop of the Diocese of Minnesota, the Right Reverend Stephen E. Keeler. The choir, conducted by Professor Frank Kendrie, then sang an anthem, Bossi's "Cantate Domino," which was followed by Dr. Ruthven's guest address, "Thinking Toward the Future." Now Vice Chairman Headley called Gould forward to receive formal investiture into the office of the presidency of Carleton College. "This," said Headley, "is both a solemn and a thrilling occasion. It is solemn only in the sense that it is serious and important. ... The occasion is thrilling because of the possibilities which lie ahead." Declaring that the need for the sort of education that colleges like Carleton were fitted to provide had never before been so great, that "the education for which the world waits is not a further training in mechanics and the laws of matter but a statement of purpose," a rediscovery of "the high objectives of life," Headley addressed Gould directly:

> You, Sir, have shared in a great adventure. You have been at the South Pole and have seen the point about which the Earth turns so smoothly on its axis. It is a sublime thought to conceive of a world in balance. Great as that early adventure was, you must now face a far more important and difficult task. You must go in search of another pole. In a sense you, in company with all educators and prophets and practical statesmen, must create it. Your quest in the future must be for a way of life which will give meaning to individual existence and balance to society and send humanity running smoothly onward toward the realization of its highest hopes. ...
>
> You are now called to leadership in this undertaking. You must inspire others to follow. You must enlist here the aid of men and women of large vision and great heart. Teachers at Carleton must stir the imaginations and emotions as well as feed the minds of the young. Loyalties to ideals must be established, enthusiasm for service must be kindled, convictions must be rooted deep in the transcendent values of life and its measureless possibilities for growth. Carleton was built on this faith. It has labored in this philosophy for eighty years. Let it continue "as a light to the feet and a lamp to the path" as it moves out "with these festival rites from the age that is past to the age that is waiting before."

"And now," intoned Headley, "by virtue of the authority vested by law in the Board of Trustees and by it delegated to me, I declare you to be the Fourth President of Carleton College."

Stating that it was "with a deep sense of obligation and opportunity" that he did so, Gould accepted the office, avowing that it would be his "constant purpose" to foster Carleton's longstanding ideals, "that it may become, not only not less, but more beautiful and more noble than it has ever been before."

It was fifteen years (and two days) since Gould had first addressed an audience from the podium of Skinner Chapel, then as a visiting speaker relating his adventures on the Byrd Expedition. That talk had led to a job, and in that job he had further honed his skills as a commanding public speaker by addressing audiences again and again from this very spot. Now facing a larger assemblage than had ever before crowded into the building, he stood before them as their chosen leader. Most speeches Gould made during his Carleton presidency were delivered without prepared written text, often employing for effect a trick of shuffling, seemingly at random, through a stack of hand-held note cards that were not really needed. The speech he gave now, however, his formal inaugural address, had been carefully prepared.

He had titled it, provocatively, "Science and the Other Humanities."

Gould began by noting that from the perspective of a geologist it is clear that change is the one universal; the natural world, and life within it, has always been in constant flux—is always to be found in the process of becoming something else. The stream of life, he said, has been characterized by the interplay of two complementary but competitive qualities: "the struggle for individual survival or expression on the one hand and an equally constant groping for some kind of plan or order on the other." Both are necessary—without the one there would be stagnation; without the other, chaos. This eternal paradox is paralleled, he suggested, in the realm of man's activities, as the demand for freedom and the need for order. Because life always seems to tend to drift toward the side of order, with its dangers of stagnation and mediocrity, the development of individualism has depended upon a constant striving toward freedom, a quest which has become identified with the emancipation of the mind—which, he asserted, "is the end of all the studies we call the humanities." Gould counted the discipline of science as among the principal humanities for the distinctive contributions it, through rigorous application of the scientific method, has made toward the emancipation of mind.

He went on to criticize, however, the "ineffective and often indifferent teaching" of science, in which all too often students have been presented with "piled-up or accumulated facts which are but the results of scientific research, and too often by teachers so full of facts that they are 'all prickly with knowledge like a thistle and as barren of fruit.'" Too often, Gould warned, we have confused the mere accumulation of information with education, and too often science courses have been "aimed directly at the few who wish to specialize rather than toward the large majority who simply want to be liberally educated." "Science as a humanity," he urged, "must acquaint the student first of all with the methods by which science has accomplished so much" and develop understanding that "the means whereby knowledge has been achieved may be more important than the knowledge itself."

Gould stressed that science "is a part of the same whole as philosophy and the other fields of learning. They are not mutually exclusive disciplines, but they are interdependent and overlapping and must be so recognized in the curriculum of a liberal arts college." He likened the world of learning to a wheel with many spokes:

> The spokes represent the separate fields of knowledge which together merge in the rim or circumference. The rim is the field of general education. Here the integration and interrelations of the various specialized areas of knowledge are discovered to be parts of a larger whole.
>
> The student confronts the circumference of the wheel before he can study the rest; but to understand it, he must know how it is supported— what sustains it—what gives it strength. There is not time for any man to examine all of the spokes. Fortunately this is not necessary; for as the student follows one spoke from the circumference toward the axis, he discovers the pattern of the whole wheel. He finds that all the special fields converge at a common point which is the axis of the wheel. The methods of learning vary so that no two spokes ever run parallel, but they have a common purpose and a common dedication which bring them all together at the center, from where the universe of learning is at last seen to be one.

Gould then offered his proposal that, within the broad divisions into which the college had broken down the core for study there should be developed at Carleton "a few fundamental, carefully integrated courses which give coherence or unity to the whole." He identified the departmental system prevailing in higher education as the "chief stumbling block" to the achievement of the desired integration and coherence. "The arbitrary lines that have so long separated the fields of learning into small tight compartments," he asserted, "must be weakened and even disappear in certain areas." Moreover, while students should be required to develop competence in a particular field, overspecialization makes for a non-adaptable rigidity that is unwise in a world changing more rapidly than ever before. "The areas of specialization should therefore be broadened," he proposed, "and in place of the present thirty majors offered ... perhaps a third that number will suffice." Troubled that the curricula of most American colleges had become a "hodgepodge" of uncoordinated courses that have "grown up through overzealous departmental specialization and promotion," he favored a "considerable reduction in the number of courses and the elimination of the elective system over large areas of the curriculum."

Acknowledging that the sort of carefully integrated program he envisioned was unlikely to be brought about within the universities or the larger colleges, he observed that it is the small liberal arts college that is in a position actually to achieve the goal. Indeed, he declared, "this is its peculiar function; this is its mission; this is its birthright which it has nearly lost in its attempts to ape the university with its multiplicity of departments and plethora of courses."

The present moment, he urged, offers both great challenge and great opportunity, with the ferment of the war years causing academics to question much that had long been taken for granted. "We cannot sit still and we will not go back," he declared, turning to the poet James Russell Lowell for inspiration:

> New occasions teach new duties; Time
>   Makes ancient good uncouth;
> They must upward still, and onward,
>   Who would keep abreast of truth;
> Lo, before us gleam her campfires! We
>   Ourselves must pilgrims be,
> Launch our Mayflower, and steer boldly
>   Through the desperate winter sea,
> Nor attempt the future's portal with
>   The Past's blood-rusted key.

Elaborating upon just a few specifics within the subject matter of his ideal curriculum, he endorsed English as standing out "above all other subjects in the curriculum of general education," as all educated persons, regardless of academic specialty, needed to be able to use language to communicate ideas with clarity and intelligence. He then Identified knowledge of American civilization and American history as "a close second" common denominator for all students at a school such as Carleton—this due to a remembrance that "liberal education and liberal democracy are parts of the same idea," which commits American colleges to the importance of developing in their students "abiding and robust convictions about democracy." Thirdly, he noted that he should be betraying the high office to which he had just been inducted if he failed to point out that "the educated man, the whole man, is also a good man." He quoted with approval a recent report from Amherst College stating that "Our lives are spent against a background of tragedy which makes our selfish materialism and even our easy acceptance of social standards stand out as the sins they are. To combat them, we need a new commitment to the highest spiritual values and this we believe the right kind of religious teaching can supply." The hope of the world in the Atomic Age, he declared, "lies in the prospect of man's further spiritual evolution." How best to foster and stimulate this within the pattern of a school like Carleton is not easily seen, however. Formal instruction in religion was not enough. "We shall need men and women of character in the post-war world; or as the ancient Greeks expressed it—men of temperance, courage, moderation, prudence, magnanimity, justice." Evidence is lacking that these virtues can be instilled through curricular content. "If you can tell me," he appealed, "how the gift of humor, of laughter, and of a sense of spiritual uplift can be directly imparted to another, I shall be glad."

"... a beacon so bright that it will be a guide through all the years of their lives to all who study here..."

Turning then from the ideas "interwoven in our ideals" of liberal education to more mundane matters, he spoke of the college's pressing need for more buildings, most especially for a new library and then for a fine arts building. He noted that when Donald Cowling had delivered his own inaugural address thirty-six years before, he had called for construction of a women's gymnasium but that such a building—needed even more now than it was then—was still not in sight. Also wanted were a student union and an additional classroom building—"for the humanities other than science." "And these buildings will come," he foresaw, "—all of them ... and as we watch them grow, let us remember the story of the passerby who stopped to watch some men working on a building one day. He asked each of three workmen what he was doing. The first one replied, 'Carrying bricks'; the second one, 'Earning a dollar and a half an hour'; and the third one, 'Building a cathedral.'" He had reached his peroration:

> We do not need to wait for the ground to be broken for the new library to start building our cathedral; we are starting this day, for this will be a cathedral, not of bricks and mortar, but of ideas, and with a spire so high, lighted by a beacon so bright that it will be a guide through all the years of their lives to all who study here; and it will be a light that shall shine so clear that others too may see it from afar and know that here at Carleton College is a kind of twentieth century American monastery of sincere, scholarly men and women of all faiths and ideas, united by the common bond of the search for truth that it may be shared with others, realizing that at long last all definitions of colleges and education end in the simple concept that it is the truth and only the truth that will make men free.

When Gould finished speaking (and after the demonstrative audience had taken sufficient time to express its hearty approval), the ceremony concluded with an enthusiastic singing of the college's adopted hymn, "O God, Our Help in Ages

Past," with a benediction voiced by the superintendent of the Congregational Conference of Minnesota, and with the exit of the robed faculty and dignitaries, accompanied by an organ recessional. The ceremony was complete, having fully met the requirements of the occasion for academic pageantry and rhetorical flourish.

Gould and some two hundred of the invited select next proceeded to the Carleton Tea Room for an inaugural luncheon, featuring a menu of turkey breast and Minnesota wild rice, seasoned with additional speechmaking. Seated at the head table with President and Mrs. Gould were Louis and Mrs. Headley, Michigan's President Ruthven, and, with spouses where present, the eight luncheon speakers—trustee Merrill Hutchinson, presiding and providing opening remarks; Governor Thye, offering a congratulatory address; the new president of the University of Minnesota, James L. Morrill, conveying greetings from that institution; Clemens M. Granskou, president of St. Olaf College, doing the same from across the river; John Cowles, speaking briefly on the theme of "liberal education and the world today"; Professor of Biography Charles C. Mierow, on behalf of the Carleton faculty; Olive V. Seibert '17, president of the Alumni Association, on behalf of all alumni; and Thomas L. Hughes, of the junior class, with greetings of the undergraduates.*

After the luncheon a short meeting of the trustees was convened in Leighton Hall, during which Gould's nomination of John Cowles as a new member of the board was confirmed. Later, dinner with Ruthven concluded what had certainly been, for the freshly installed forty-nine-year-old president, an outstandingly memorable day.

Gould's celebrity status since the Byrd Expedition meant that his doings remained news, and *Time* magazine ran a short feature on the explorer-educator following the Northfield inauguration. The article, which highlighted the "husky, handsome" Larry Gould's "flaming collection of 150 red ties," was accompanied by an old photo from exploring days of a parka-clad Gould uncharacteristically sporting a full beard and whiskers every bit as wild as his wildest tie. Shortly thereafter his mail brought the gift of a razor sent by the father of one of his Carleton students.

***

It is entirely unsurprising that, as he settled into the role of college president, Larry Gould found that he had never been busier. Overseeing much, traveling frequently, always in demand, he found that the job required stamina—less

---

* Hughes, who in another year would be named a Rhodes Scholar and who would go on to a distinguished career in the State Department and eventually as president of the Carnegie Endowment for International Peace, told the luncheon guests that the hearts of the students were in this inauguration in part because "what we want is the spirit of the explorer—a curious combination of venturesomeness and everyday practicality ... purposeful stimulation, drive, freshness of approach, [and] clarity of goals—the type of vivid originality that is shot through the personality of Dr. Gould, the explorer."

dramatically perhaps than had his Antarctic sledge journey but just as real. The
month after his inauguration Gould wrote his old student and former colleague
in geology Bill Fiedler: "I had known, of course, that being President of a College
would be somewhat complicated but even so I am sometimes amazed at the curious problems that are dumped in my lap." Throughout that first post-war year,
for instance, one vexing problem was that of housing, which, with a sharp rise in
the numbers of both students and faculty, became very tight—and it is surprising
the degree to which the president of the college became personally involved with
questions of who would live where. Institutions like Carleton were under terrific
pressure to accommodate returning veterans, and would shortly be crowded like
never before. The situation "is hopeless," Gould wrote in April. "At the present
moment I can see the need for thirteen new faculty members for next year. So far
I have been able to find housing accommodations for only three. At the moment
we are somewhat at a loss as to just what we shall do."

A significant part of the mix keeping him relentlessly busy was his
schedule of speechmaking. It would be tedious to detail the occasions, but
it should be taken as never-changing background to any writing about the
Gould presidency that, month after month, year after year, his calendar was
filled with a steady succession of public speaking engagements, primarily
off-campus to audiences of all sorts. In the college history prepared in connection with Carleton's 1966 centennial it was calculated that while he was
president Gould delivered 764 important addresses, averaging about one a
week the year round. During Gould's first year in office the pattern was already
well established, with seventy-some speaking invitations accepted during its
course, including eight outside commencement addresses. Titles of his talks
that year were a diverse mix ranging from "Science and Society" to "Heroes
and Hero Worship" to "The Marks of an Educated Man" to "Exploring in
the New Age." Acknowledging that he had overcommitted that first year ("no
one can talk as frequently as that and still have much worthwhile saying,"
he wrote a friend), he resolved to be more selective in future*—though, as
he told Carleton treasurer Bruce Pollock, he did "assume ... that speaking
engagements outside are really part of my responsibility here." Where fees
were paid, Gould told Pollock, he would use them to defray expenses and
return to the college any surplus.

Whether combined with public speaking or not, large parts of Gould's
schedule would always be consumed by travel away from the college. Some of
this was due to commitments external to Carleton, though he often found that

---

*   A resolution fated to be only slightly successful. A few years later, in a letter to a trustee, Gould
      referenced another possible strategy for reducing his public speaking commitments: "I once
      suggested to a friend of mine in St. Paul that I was going to give the same speech all the time
      everywhere, and pretty soon people would stop bothering me. With real wisdom he said, 'Don't
      fool yourself. Nobody pays that much attention to what you say.'"

trips prompted by non-Carleton business could be made to include college matters such as faculty recruitment, meetings with alumni groups, or cultivation of prospective donors. Two weeks after his inauguration, for instance, he was off to New York for meetings of the board of the Institute of Current World Affairs, of which he had become a trustee, and of the Arctic Institute of North America, which was incorporating in New York. While in the city he also took the opportunity to interview Frank Verbrugge, a candidate he had in mind for taking over the chairmanship of the Physics Department following the upcoming retirement of Charles Culver. (Verbrugge already had briefly taught at Carleton in 1943 and 1944, in connection with the Army's program of specialized training, but as this had coincided with Gould's wartime leave from the college, the two men had not previously met.) The end result was Verbrugge's rejoining the Carleton faculty for the second semester of 1945-46 and succeeding Culver as department chair a few months later.

Gould was, however, able to rely upon help from many quarters in managing the demands made upon his time. Assisting him in the Laird Hall president's office—which he decorated across one entire wall with magnificent enlargements of photographs from his Antarctic explorations—was an extremely capable and experienced principal secretary, Sara Crandall, known as Sally. Crandall had been hired as an assistant in President Cowling's office in 1925 and had become secretary to the president in 1932, the year Gould joined the Carleton faculty. (She would stay in the role well into the administration of Gould's successor, retiring in 1967 after fully forty-two years employed in the service of three Carleton presidents.) The following spring Gould and Crandall were joined by a new secretarial hire, Dorothy May Peterson, a 1942 Carleton English major and former Gould student whose own service in the president's office would also span decades; she would eventually serve, until 1987, as secretary to the Board of Trustees. This grouping gave the Office of the President remarkable stability and a consistently buoyant *esprit de corps* throughout the Gould presidency.

As wife to the president Peg Gould found herself filling a role she had not sought that had attached to it certain expectations, particularly in the social realm, but which might to a large extent be shaped by the particular individual filling it so as to conform to a personality. Peg, whose natural inclinations tended more toward the private than to the public ceremonial, could better be said to have borne the necessary duties than ever to have embraced them, and to the extent that it was possible she preferred to keep her public role small. "Peg is not being swamped with her new duties as the wife of the President," Gould wrote in November to a former faculty colleague. "In fact, she insists on going her way as she should." To another correspondent he offered, "I don't believe Peg will let the social side of being the wife of the President get her down too much." In the spring of this first presidential year Peg would initiate a tradition for herself of long restorative vacations in sunnier climes—in this instance five and a half weeks in Arizona, joined for part of the time by her brother Jack. Describing this prospective spousal absence to a friend, Gould wrote that this would be less of a hardship on him than might be supposed, considering how much of the next six weeks he would himself be away. Furthermore, he wrote, "I am sure that Peg does need a rest after her first year as the president's wife."

Late that first fall Gould did manage to fit into his busy schedule one long weekend's worth of recreational getaway for himself in the form of a pheasant hunting expedition planned for a small group by two of Carleton's Minneapolis-based trustees, Malcolm McDonald and Atherton Bean. Participating in a repeat trip the next year as well, Gould found these manly trips to the Dakotas enjoyable, though his nonexistent experience as a hunter and consequent lack of any skill as a marksman occasioned a certain amount of ribbing from his companions. Bean, who both years loaned Gould a double-barreled shotgun for his use, subsequently took to calling Gould, with considerable irony, "dead-eye" or "Nimrod," the mighty hunter. Thanks to the generosity of his fellow sportsmen, Gould returned to Carleton from the first trip carrying with him twenty-six bagged pheasants. Unfortunately, as he wrote to Bean, this fact had generally failed to give people the desired impression of his prowess, as they *would* insist, regardless of how he tried to finesse the point, on knowing how many of the twenty-six he had shot himself. (Bean suggested in a recounting at a subsequent Board of Trustees meeting that Larry's personal total had been a single bird; Gould insisted that he could in fact claim six.) A lucky shot on the second year's expedition, according to a later retelling by Bean, resulted in Gould hitting a pheasant with both barrels at the same time, causing the bird simply to disappear in a cloud of feathers. Bean remembered Larry turning to him with the eager question, "Did I hit it?" To which Bean replied, "You not only hit it, you completely EXPLODED it!"

Hoping to move forward quickly on some of the curricular proposals outlined in his inaugural address, Gould asked Dean Kille to chair a new curriculum committee, comprised of representatives from each of the college's academic divisions, that was charged with reviewing the Carleton curriculum, studying developments at other institutions, discussing desirable changes, and reporting, with recommendations. On December 10 Gould announced to the faculty that henceforth no new courses could be offered without Curriculum Committee approval. In February, attempting to accelerate the committee's work, Gould proposed that it begin to meet every week rather than in alternate weeks. Fourteen tentative proposals would eventually be put forth, "primarily as an indication of the committee's thinking," when the committee issued its first progress report near the close of the academic year. In his published "President's Report" for 1945-46, Gould forecast that some of these proposals would "be brought to the faculty as early as the fall of 1946 for discussion and action" and that a comprehensive plan to place before the faculty could be looked for from the committee "in due time." Meanwhile, he had taken some steps toward his goal of combating the proliferation of departments by suggesting the consolidation of international relations with political science and moving to combine the separate Departments of Zoology and Hygiene and Public Health into a single Department of Zoological Sciences.

In December Carleton's recently inaugurated new president traveled to Iowa's Coe College for the installation there of Byron S. Hollinshead as a new presidential colleague. (Or, as Carleton's treasurer Bruce Pollock put it, to "inaugurate another unfortunate fellow human being into a college presidency.") On this occasion Gould, in addition to accepting an honorary degree from Coe, delivered a luncheon address on "The Independent College," in which he asserted that private schools like Carleton and Coe, supported by voluntary contributions rather than dependent upon taxes imposed by the state, were consequently freer than public institutions could ever be from governmental interference with the educational program. Among the advantages enjoyed by independent colleges, said Gould, was greater freedom to limit enrollment and maintain higher educational standards. Warning of a drift in American education towards "ever-increasing federal support, which means federal domination and eventually federal control," Gould argued for the importance of preserving independent institutions as bulwarks against centralized operation of American schools, which would provide "the perfect machinery for regimentation of thought." It was an early sounding of a theme to which he would return many times in years just ahead.

During the month following, Gould made an important hire, offering a position as associate dean of men and associate professor of history to a young Navy lieutenant anticipating imminent discharge to civilian life. This was Merrill E. Jarchow, universally known as "Casey," who had been an applicant earlier in 1945 for the dean of men position given to Frank Kille. (Jarchow had been urged to put himself forward for that position following a chance encounter with Carleton's once and future athletic director, Wally Hass, then also serving as a naval lieutenant.) Though hiring Kille that summer, Gould had continued to correspond with Jarchow and keep him in mind for another opening—or even the same one, should he follow through on his thought that Kille might shift from being dean of men to dean of the faculty. In mid-January Gould asked Jarchow to come out from Washington to interview at Carleton and at the conclusion of that visit offered him a job, which Jarchow accepted and began in mid-March. By June the decision had indeed been made to make Kille the academic dean— Gould had concluded that, with the financial campaign being planned, he would require such an officer to be present as more of his own time would necessarily be consumed by "what might be called 'public relations'"—and Jarchow moved up to begin a long tenure, lasting the rest of the Gould years and a few beyond, as Carleton's dean of men.

Also in January Gould asked the recently promoted college librarian, Marian Adams, to chair a committee to plan for a new library building consistent with Gould's view that the library, "more than any other building ... should be the heart of an institution like this." At this juncture Gould wanted to focus on the construction of a new library ahead of any other building, but within a few months he was reporting an altered timeline: "While the most critical building need of all is a library, the detailed plans for such a building and the solicitation of funds which will bring it into existence involve a relatively long-term project. The Building Committee, therefore, decided that the first new addition to our buildings should be a much-needed building for fine arts."

Late in the month, while on a ten-day eastern trip to attend various meetings in New York, Montreal, and Philadelphia, Gould took the opportunity to spend two days—from which he "profited much," he told Atherton Bean—in the company of Swarthmore College president and Carleton alumnus John Nason, who he had not previously met. Neither man could then know that sixteen years later—with Bean then chairing the Carleton board—Nason would succeed Gould in the Carleton presidency. Gould spoke to alumni groups on this trip in both New York and Philadelphia.* Better cultivation of the Carleton alumni body, which he repeatedly characterized (to alumni, at any rate) as the college's greatest resource, was an oft-voiced goal throughout his first year as president. "This is a resource that has scarcely been touched," he wrote one interested alumnus, "and I covet the hope that in the years ahead Carleton College will come to have the best Alumni Association of any college anywhere." Gould hoped to develop in alumni a "renewed interest in the life of the College," and he envisioned improvements in the existing alumni publication, *The Voice of the Carleton Alumni*, as a highly desirable means to that end. As a first important step there, he reached an agreement with the Alumni Association to allow the *Voice*, which he wanted to start appearing on a more frequent and regular basis, henceforth to be edited at Carleton itself, so that it would begin really "to carry news of intimate interest concerning the campus" and be "more definitely tied to the College." Gould proposed that he be given a regular column or page in the publication so that he "could keep the alumni continually informed of our hopes and aspirations and the progress we are making toward their achievement." The new *Voice*, edited by Associate Professor of English Ralph L. Henry '17, would make its debut in September 1946, also inaugurating the president's column, "President Gould Says."

Partially in the interest of better unifying the college with its alumni Gould also instituted a policy of granting honorary degrees more regularly than heretofore at college commencements—Carleton had presented only three over the preceding

---

*   At the Philadelphia meeting he was introduced by John Nason, who elaborated at length upon Gould's many honors, distinctions, and personal qualities. Gould then remarked that the effusive introduction reminded him of the story of the minister's daughter who was found by her father one evening kissing her young man goodnight on the front porch, leading to a parental scolding and an argument over the propriety of her behavior. Finally the daughter said, "Well, father, it didn't really do me any harm and did seem to do him a lot of good!"

ten years—and arranged for honorary degrees to go to two distinguished alumni at the first graduation ceremony over which he would preside, in June.

One week before Carleton's own commencement, Gould attended the graduation ceremonies of Macalester College in St. Paul, where he gave an address ("A Scientist's Faith") and picked up another honorary degree of his own. He passed along the $100 honorarium given by Macalester for his address to the Minnesota United Nations Committee, formerly chaired by Donald Cowling, an internationalist organization whose governing board he would join later that month.

***

Over the course of Gould's first semester as president the college's male student population had grown from its September count of sixty-nine to ninety-five, as Carleton had arranged to admit ex-servicemen in mid-term, making it possible for them, despite their late arrival, to complete full semester courses by doubling class hours per week the rest of the way. For the second semester the number of men climbed to 178, and the five-person admissions committee that was working that term to shape a freshman class for the fall admitted nearly twice as many men as women. (As Gould noted in early April, "by the very nature of the case this year we do have two standards of admission; the standards for the girls are very much higher than for the boys.") The enormous number of young men who had been compelled to interrupt or delay their educations during the war being so very great, all colleges were coming under great pressures to admit as many students as they could possibly accommodate for the fall of 1946 and for some time thereafter. A large proportion of new students would be veterans, a good number of them married veterans, for whom the college needed to make special housing arrangements. By June, an agreement would be in place for a loan from the Federal Housing Administration of prefabricated dwellings sufficient to house forty-six married couples.

Dramatic increase in the size of the student body required a corresponding increase in faculty to teach them, and in 1946 Gould had a great deal of additional hiring to do. This task took up much of his time during the winter and spring months and quite dominated his summer—though he did, in July and August, manage two in-state vacations: one simply a long weekend with Peg and the Cowles at Camp Glendalough in Otter Tail County (during which he caught a bass sworn by John Cowles to be the largest ever taken out of Annie Battle Lake) and the other a refreshing two weeks with Peg at the Northern Pines Lodge near Park Rapids, by the headwaters of the Mississippi, where the couple quietly celebrated Larry's fiftieth birthday and where, apart from working his way through the reading of a large stack of annual departmental and individual faculty reports, Gould was able for a short while simply to "fish and sit in the sun."

Between these two getaways, Gould visited his doctor for a checkup that included an electrocardiogram. "I was interested to know whether my heart was all right," he wrote Professor Mizener afterward, claiming that he wanted advice as to whether it was advisable for him to play tennis as strenuously as he had recently been doing. The doctor told him that he indeed could play tennis. "This was very gratifying," Gould told Mizener, "because so far as I know he is the first man who ever told me I could play tennis. It has set me up no end."

The number (as well as the quality) of hires he made that year was truly remarkable. Between February and mid-September he filled needs at the level of full professor in geography (bringing back Leonard S. Wilson after a four-year absence), American history (Carlton C. Qualey), sociology (Samuel M. Strong), and zoology (Thurlo Bates Thomas, brought in as department chairman). He hired new associate professors in chemistry (Ralph L. Seifert), psychology and education (Ralph W. Erickson), economics (Floyd Bond, who was brought to the president's attention by one of his old University of Michigan roommates, M. H. Waterman), zoology (Olin S. Pettingill, Jr., returning after a year's absence), and German (Siegfried Puknat). New assistant professors were secured in physical education for men (Joseph M. Platt), mathematics (Kenneth O. May), philosophy (Bernard Phillips), philosophy and religion (Philip H. Phenix), dramatic arts (Oliver M. Flanders), German (Paul J. Menge), music (S. Eugene Bailey, Mildred Sircom, and Leo J. Christy, the latter an appointment split also with chemistry), economics (Paul C. Mathis, Jr.), Romance languages (Donald S. Schier), English (James G. Benziger and Elisabeth L. Mignon), and health and physical education for women (Margherita C. Ciaramelli). Not new, but returning as an assistant professor from two years of military service was a Carleton alumnus of 1941 who had previously spent two years at the college as an instructor in Spanish, Antonio H. Obaid.* A dozen or so additional teachers at the level of instructor were also hired by the president in advance of the opening of the 1946-47 school year, some of them destined to stay long at Carleton and rise through the faculty ranks.† Additionally, over the summer he made an important administrative appointment, hiring Carleton alumna Leith Shackel '29 to direct the recently established fulltime Office of Placement Service to assist students in finding future employment.

---

* Gould's May 30 letter to Obaid telling him that Carleton would be very glad to have him back was typed by the president's new second secretary, Dorothy Peterson, still in her first month on the job. Two years later, Miss Peterson would become Mrs. Obaid.

† A notable name among the new instructors was a Carleton graduate of 1943 and former Gould geology student, Eiler L. Henrickson, who would retire from Carleton as an honored full professor in 1987 and who always credited Gould as the generative source of his interest in geology.

The housing shortage was responsible for all sorts of logistical headaches and complications in arranging and accommodating these appointments, and it was necessary for some married professors to arrive temporarily leaving their families behind. "The housing situation becomes ever more critical," Gould told one of his newly hired instructors at the end of May, though "at any rate, I assure you, you will not have to live in a tent when you come." In the letter of appointment as an instructor that was addressed to his former student Eiler Henrickson, who was about to be released from the Army, Gould foresaw that it might be necessary to set aside a few rooms in one of the men's dormitories for unmarried instructors like him and warned his protégé, "for heaven's sakes don't get married, else we couldn't find any place at all for you." In June he told another correspondent, "You have no idea of how this problem of housing ... is complicating matters for me. I am promising all of these new people whom I am hiring that we shall have a place for them to live. It may well be that come September 1, I myself will have to leave town."

Given that colleges and universities everywhere were engaging in similar frenzies of postwar hiring and the best available faculty were consequently in very high demand, Gould found that it could be a challenge to secure teacher/scholars of the caliber he sought. As he reported during his summer hiring, "there are plenty of mediocre people available, but the kind I want for Carleton College are rather scarce." He pressed the trustees for permission to make, or to plan soon to make, improvements in faculty compensation that would help him to recruit and retain the best. In January he had recommended to the board that the college strive to achieve a salary schedule involving a minimum of $5,000 per annum for full professors, with other ranks graded accordingly. (At the time, only one Carleton full professor was receiving more than $4,000.) In June the board did act to authorize salary increases of up to 15-20 percent at the discretion of the president. And at the end of July, Chairman Bell cheered Gould considerably by writing, in response to Gould's report on the market cost of new talent, "It may sound reckless, but I urge you to pay what you have to to get the men you want, even though it exceeds the formula agreed upon at the last Trustees' meeting. If the Executive Committee will not back you up let me know." By the beginning of September Gould was able to tell Bell, "Much of my summer has been concerned with the search for the kind of people we want here at Carleton College. Except for political science, I feel quite good about the results."

The results were beginning to be transformative. Extraordinarily, at the end of only thirteen months as president, Gould found that he had already personally hired fully 46 percent of his present faculty. Due to the increased enrollment and a high number of retirements, he had in that period already made forty-one academic appointments. As Gould's second year in office began, an impressed Arthur Mizener asked him,

I wonder if you can feel, having seen it accumulate bit by bit, what a really dramatic change there is in the faculty this year? Just being around the campus a day or so, meeting people here & there, I caught the thing right between the eyes. I'll bet you couldn't count the proved-good & promising-to-be-good instructors on less than 8 or 9 hands.

Gould himself told Laird Bell early in the fall of 1946 that the Carleton "complexion has changed greatly" and that "the intellectual level has risen considerably." The campus was crowded and the budget tight, but as the college opened its second year under Gould's leadership the spirit of the institution—like the spire of a cathedral of ideas—was soaring.

CHAPTER 16

THE WAY AHEAD

Prior to the end of World War II the highest fall term student enrollment that Carleton College had ever known was the 918 registered in 1930. For the five autumns preceding Pearl Harbor the student population had averaged 828. In 1946, as military veterans, assisted by the provisions of the federal Serviceman's Readjustment Act of 1944—the GI Bill of Rights—began to flood into American colleges and universities in an unprecedented tide, Carleton—a residential college that had constructed no new residence hall or classroom building since 1928—stretched itself to the utmost to accommodate 1,144. The 407 freshmen present that fall—262 men, 145 women—made the entering Class of 1950 the school's largest ever to that time. Among all classes, over 530 men were now enrolled (as compared with 69 the fall before), approximately 70 percent of them veterans. The demographic bulge that began at Carleton in 1946 was temporary. The college would intentionally reduce student enrollment back to under a thousand for the first eight years of the 1950s. But from the fall of 1946 through the spring of 1950 the on-campus count remained in four figures.

Crowding aside, in many respects the school was returning to "normalcy" by 1946. With the male population again robust, a full program of intercollegiate athletics was restored. Carleton had not fielded a football team since 1942, but it did so again that fall, returning to the Midwest Conference. In October, a football-centered Homecoming would be celebrated with relish and all the tra- ditional trappings of bonfire, pep fest, and freshman snake dance. (Homecoming had been on the calendar in 1945, but its only associated athletic contest that year was a touch football game with St. Olaf.) Although a few ex-soldiers now entering Carleton as older frosh balked at the idea of leaving the Army only to submit to freshman hazing traditions such as the wearing of green beanies and rules about staying off the grass, the great majority of student veterans embraced it all, determined as they were after the rigors of war to enjoy now the full college experience they had once feared to miss.

In September Gould welcomed the new students to campus with some vari- ant of the message he would voice to every newly entering class throughout his presidency—the observation that by matriculating at Carleton they had formed a permanent association that would never dissolve; that whether or not they stayed to graduate, from this day forward they would forever be a part of Carleton and Carleton would forever be a part of them.

Later that month Gould was honored by election as one of the twenty-seven governing senators of the United Chapters of Phi Beta Kappa, the national honorary scholastic society. At the same time, however, his mind was occupied by a number of other matters that were making him anxious. One was the persistence of difficulties regarding faculty housing. A group of prefabricated houses whose availability had been promised the college by mid-August was still unready in mid-September, leaving six faculty members as yet unsettled. Another concern involved Peg, who was in "somewhat low spirits," unusually tired or exhausted and complaining of back pain. "Thorough examinations and x-rays reveal nothing," he wrote the former director of the Carleton Health Service, "except a suggestion ... of low grade arthritis." Peg was advised to rest more and to take three heat treatments a week, and Gould noted that it might be best for her to spend most of the winter away from Northfield, where she could rest in warmth and "without any cares at all."

It is a rare and fortunate college president indeed for whom money, and the raising of it, is *not* a matter of ongoing anxiety, and Larry Gould's active engagement with fundraising to support his ambitions for Carleton grew noticeably during his second year in office and after. (He came to refer to college presidents collectively as "the fraternity of the itching palm.") This was an arena into which Gould advanced with almost no relevant prior experience. Before becoming president, the centennial history of Carleton would later note, "Dr. Gould had confined his efforts in soliciting money to asking Northfield neighbors to contribute to the community chest." Unsurprisingly, Gould in the earliest stages of his presidency relied heavily in this realm upon the advice and direction of members of his board of trustees.

A trustee committee formed in 1945 to plan and guide a financial campaign had decided against launching a high-pressure campaign with an announced goal and a definite timetable, favoring instead a deliberate, careful "long time low pressure effort" seeking "to build up a continuing flow of gifts to the College" from a broadened base of annual contributors. By the summer of 1946, however, Gould was ready to acknowledge to Chairman Bell, who had favored the low pressure approach, that the number of gifts received by the college during his first year as president had been "somewhat disappointing." During his July getaway to John Cowles' summer camp, Cowles had impressed Gould with quite a different, and daringly ambitious, vision. Cowles urged that Carleton openly aspire to a position as the country's outstanding liberal arts college and that it set its financial sights considerably higher than had previously been discussed. Cowles proposed a vigorous campaign aimed at providing Carleton with a $10 million endowment. (At the time Carleton's net assets totaled about $5.5 million.) Early in September Gould told Cowles that after much ongoing thought he had become convinced of the wisdom of Cowles' suggestion. "Except for such a campaign," he wrote now, "I do not know how we shall raise funds for the few necessary buildings and necessary additional endowment to back up the salary schedule which conditions make it necessary for us to install this coming year." Writing to Atherton Bean later that month, Gould declared that he now thought "we made a major mistake in not starting vigorously a financial campaign when it was first proposed at the Board meeting in July, 1945. ... Other colleges have been going ahead taking advantage of the good market conditions this last year, and I feel we may have lost several hundred thousand dollars that we might otherwise have had." Reminding Bean of the need to find funds to begin the new art building in the spring of 1947, with a new library to follow, he suggested that "the slow moving, cumulative kind of campaign, which Laird Bell seems to have had in mind" was insufficient. Bean responded with agreement that "we have missed the boat in not having a financial campaign going during the past year." He regretted that he and other trustees had not stepped right in to fill the gap earlier after it had become "quite apparent" that the trustee appointed to chair the committee on a financial campaign was "not going to devote much time or effort to the matter." "However that may be," Bean wrote, "we have to start from today."

At the end of October the trustees held a two-day meeting on the Carleton campus, a new tradition for the fall meeting of the board instituted by Gould and Bell so that trustees could get better acquainted with the life of the college. At this meeting, following Gould's outline of the efforts to date of the special committee on fundraising set up a year earlier (which seemed to amount to little more than halfheartedly starting a so-far-unsuccessful search for a public relations man for the college to hire as vice president), the board affirmed that "it is essential that vigorous action be taken in this area in the immediate future" and requested Bell to dissolve the original committee and appoint a new one.

Other notable business at this meeting included approving the preparation of detailed working drawings for the planned art building, discussion of options for the pension plan for college personnel to which the college had committed in principle, and approval of the president's recommendation that Carleton establish a mandatory retirement age for faculty of sixty-five.

When the full board next convened, in Minneapolis in January, Gould presented a rough summary of what he projected as the college's major financial needs over the next fifteen years—the years that would bring himself to sixty-five years of age and his own presumptive retirement. His forecast of need was for $5 million, a figure not including additions to endowment. Half of the total was to go to salaries, $500,000 to scholarships, and the remaining $2 million to building maintenance and the anticipated construction of a library ($750,000), a fine arts building ($250,000), a women's gymnasium ($300,000), and an auditorium and theater ($350,000).

That winter Gould was thrilled and heartened to secure what was to that point the most substantial individual gift made to the college during his tenure, $100,000 from Mrs. Edward C. Congdon of Duluth, to establish a professorship in government in memory of her late husband, who had had a friendship with President Cowling. Gould, in his visits to Dorothy Congdon, had found her impressed with his statements about the importance in his ideal educational curriculum of a program in American citizenship and of developing in students a sense of personal civic responsibility. (His letter of thanks to Mrs. Congdon, however, facetiously credited as crucial their discovery of a common bond of enjoyment of gumdrops.) Mrs. Congdon's check upon the Congdon Memorial Trust for the first $75,000 arrived in mid-March. In passing it along to Treasurer Bruce Pollock, Gould wrote that he wanted it in Pollock's hands immediately: "I am afraid to keep it here on my desk, because I can't concentrate on anything else." The Congdon gift would be announced publicly at Carleton's commencement convocation in June, along with announcement of an even larger gift ($200,000) from the Bell family to endow the Frances Laird Bell Fund, income from which would be used to further the religious and spiritual education and life of Carleton students.

Also in mid-March, Gould chose to express to Dean Kille, who had moved from the dean of men position to that of dean of the college and was continuing to chair the Curriculum Committee, a degree of dissatisfaction with the slow pace of progress on the sorts of curricular reform (the "minor revolution") Gould had called for in his inaugural address and his initial charge to Kille's committee. One development of significance had been committed to that year: the faculty had adopted the Curriculum Committee's recommendation that, effective with the Class of 1949, Carleton begin to require each prospective graduate to pass a final semester comprehensive examination set by his or her major department. This, Gould acknowledged, was good. But he was frustrated with the "inordinate amount of time that appears to have been spent" on matters subordinate to the committee's "primary opportunities," as Gould saw it, for "deep thinking" about the purposes of the college. What Gould hoped for, he reminded Kille, was the development of a more integrated liberal arts education, where specialized areas of training would be related to general education in an interdependent manner: "specialization like a pyramid, not like a flagpole." "Somehow," the president admonished his dean, "I do not see much evidence that the Curriculum Committee has really gotten its teeth into the basic problems concerned with the development of this ideal. … I do not want any misunderstanding about this memorandum. It is an indication of impatience."

It had become Gould's constant aim to push, pull, carry, cajole, guide, inspire, or otherwise direct Carleton toward continually becoming, by his lights, better. This involved presidential attention and leadership on numerous fronts. Sometimes it involved decisions, on personnel for instance, that were personally painful though right for the institution. ("I want to be a *good* president, even when it's unpleasant," Gould had vowed as recollected by Mizener.)

With regard to admissions, the large cohort of freshmen and other underclassmen admitted in 1946, coupled with the fact that the number of seniors—those who would be graduating in June—remained small, meant that Carleton could accommodate only a modest-sized freshman class for 1947. As entrance demand remained quite high, this meant that a greater level of selectivity was now possible (and necessary) than had previously been the case. This was good in that it implied an upswing in the academic caliber of admitted students but problematic in that markedly more rejected applications might engender bad feeling, particularly when it came to the children of alumni. In 1946, in order to provide a common denominator for evaluation, Gould caused Carleton to become the first Midwestern college to require all of its freshman applicants to take College Board aptitude and achievement examinations.

In the crucial area of faculty hiring, the foundation upon which institutional quality would ultimately have to be built, the pace would never again be so fast and furious as it had been during Gould's first year, but important appointments continued. Some now were essentially made by department heads rather than directly by the president—it was Arthur Mizener, really, who hired Scott Elledge and Reed Whittemore for the English Department in 1947; it was Lucile Deen in history who initially suggested that year the appointment of Catherine Boyd—but other times it was Gould alone who decided, as was the case that spring for instance with Charles Rayment, in classical languages, who Gould interviewed at the Michigan Union during an early April visit to Ann Arbor.

***

That same April, while speaking at a portrait unveiling in South Carolina, venerable US presidential advisor Bernard Baruch introduced to the public a new term, "Cold War," to describe the dangerously polarized state of relations of fear, mutual distrust, and conflict-by-proxy that had developed between the United States and its former wartime ally, the Soviet Union. A month earlier President Truman had, in a message to Congress calling for massive American aid to Greece and Turkey, outlined what came to be known as the Truman Doctrine, committing the United States to a policy of assisting the "free peoples" of other countries threatened by Communist infiltration and Soviet expansionism. He had also, nine days later in what amounted to a Cold War offensive on the home front (and defensive action to shield his administration, much weakened following the 1946 Congressional elections, against politically potent Republican charges that he and the Democrats were "soft" on domestic Communism), announced creation of a federal program establishing "loyalty screening" for millions of government employees in order to root out potentially subversive persons who might constitute security risks. The Federal Bureau of

Investigation was authorized to probe deeper into individual cases wherever initial inquiries yielded derogatory information or suspected Communist connections. A "Red Scare" that would poison American civil life for years to come now began to infect the body politic.

In 1946 Larry Gould had interviewed and hired a young mathematician from Berkeley, California, Kenneth O. May. May, who was just completing his dissertation at the University of California, had initially been brought to Gould's attention by Walter Rogers, the director of the Institute for Current World Affairs (ICWA) and a principal along with Gould in the establishment of the Arctic Institute of North America. May had previously been an ICWA Fellow. He had also, for about six years prior to joining the Army in 1942, been a member of the Communist Party. His membership had been somewhat nominal from joining during his senior year in college, for reasons common enough in idealistic youths of his generation, until 1939. Then as a graduate student he ramped up his political involvements and became a party spokesman at Berkeley. Publicity concerning his activities in 1940 led to a temporary but unfortunately very public disowning by his father, Samuel May, a University of California political scientist, and to his dismissal from a teaching assistantship at the university. In 1941 he had been the Communist Party's educational director for Alameda County and a (non-partisan) candidate for the Berkeley City Council. May, who declined to become reinvolved with the party after his return from military service, had made no secret of his past, and Gould in hiring him had satisfied himself that May now regretted his previous attraction to Communist ideology and had put such involvements entirely behind him.

Gould assured May in June of 1946 that as Carleton's president he was dedicated, "above all things else," to the maintenance of the tradition of academic freedom at its best. In the Red Scare atmosphere that grew more pervasive in 1947 and after, with the continued presence of an "admitted" ex-Communist on his faculty standing as an open invitation to criticism and attack, Gould's commitment to the tradition of academic freedom would indeed be tested.

Trouble was previewed in the spring of 1947 when one of three Carleton trustees elected by the alumni, Malcolm McDonald, handed Gould an unsigned and undated memorandum headed "Re: Kenneth Ownsworth May." The memorandum, coupled with a copy of a 1940 *San Francisco Chronicle* article concerning Samuel May's angry disinheritance of his son, appeared to be information and hearsay assembled, without any scrupulous regard for accuracy, by an anonymous FBI agent. It summarized Ken May's Communist involvements in a manner partly factual and partly fanciful, and implied the likelihood of continuing involvement while in the Army and after his discharge. Gould showed the memorandum to May, soliciting the latter's comments before attempting to reassure McDonald about the matter at the April 17 meeting in St. Paul of the trustees' Executive Committee. Early in the month of May Gould sent McDonald a long follow-up letter, with copies to Louis Headley and Atherton Bean, hoping to answer any lingering questions, returning the original memorandum, and enclosing a copy of May's own comments about the former document's careless blend of fact and error. Gould stated that he considered May one of the most desirable and promising hires he had yet made for Carleton. He also observed that he knew from his own correspondence with the chairman of the Math Department at Berkeley that May's dismissal as a teaching assistant there had been profoundly regretted and had been forced upon the university by the front page publicity generated by the senior May in intemperately blasting his son and publicly disowning him, accompanied by "such disgracefully insulting remarks that only a very genuinely tolerant person could ever forgive him." The father, Gould noted, has since "deeply regretted" his action, leading the two to a "reconciliation of sorts ... at any rate, the father was here visiting Ken this year and is tremendously proud of his son."

Kenneth O. May

Gould looked upon FBI information gathering of the sort represented by this memorandum with a very critical eye, observing that "prejudiced persons will give to [FBI] agents their prejudiced views" and that agents—who naturally are "more friendly disposed to adverse criticism than otherwise," given that "the continuation of the FBI depends upon the demonstration that there is a need for it in areas of this sort"—may do very little additional checking regarding the accuracy of statements made to them. Had this particular memorandum, he thought, "been put in the hands of some administrator who did not know May and who possessed a naive faith in the FBI, May's immediate dismissal would have been inevitable" and "a career destined to be of real service to his country might have been wrecked." Though he declared that he had never had any illusions about Communism, which he saw as "the greatest single hazard to the survival of the democratic tradition as we understand it" and he accordingly would not knowingly have an active Communist on his faculty, he feared the "sinister events which might develop" from memoranda such as this. "Innocent people," he foresaw, "could be crucified in this way."

The whole matter, Gould stated, filled him with apprehension. "The F.B.I. is taking on altogether too many of the aspects of a real secret police." This, he dictated, "is completely at variance with our democratic ideals.... . We should realize that we can lose our liberty through agencies of this sort just as well as through such agencies as Communism on the outside."

***

At the same April meeting of the Executive Committee at which he tried to reassure Malcolm McDonald about Ken May, Gould raised for the whole committee a possibility in the area of faculty hiring he now wished the college to consider. Six days, as it happened, after Jackie Robinson's historic first appearance as a Brooklyn Dodger began the integration of major league baseball, Gould asked trustees for opinions on the desirability of adding a "colored man" to the Carleton teaching staff. Reporting himself "greatly pleased and encouraged" by the response—"I find it difficult to justify any other position," he wrote Louis Headley—the following week at the Carleton faculty meeting he solicited information as to how a Negro professor would be received socially in Northfield. Writing shortly thereafter to Atherton Bean, Gould averred that "we cannot very much longer refuse to face frankly and honestly the whole question of race relationships both in the faculty and student body at Carleton." That summer he reported to Laird Bell that since April he had canvassed sentiment among faculty, alumni, students, and trustees and noted that "the reaction among the faculty and student body was unanimously, so far as I know, in approval of the whole idea. It seems to the students and faculty alike that if we are ever to have one world we must start in situations like Carleton College."

Desirous though he may genuinely have been of making such a hire, fully qualified black professorial candidates were not in abundant supply in 1947, and nothing then came of the matter with regard to faculty.* A few months later attention moved instead to the matter of admitting a "Negro student." Carleton had from its post-Civil War founding declared itself open to all applicants without regard to race, nationality, or denominational affiliation. In separate decades of the nineteenth century it had enrolled two African-American students in the sub-collegiate preparatory department or academy that had co-existed alongside the college proper until 1906. But no black student had yet been enrolled at Carleton at the collegiate level. (Whether or not any had ever even applied before 1947 is unclear but doubtful.) At the fall meeting of the trustees Gould informed his board that the college now had "one request for the admission of a negro student for the second semester of this academic year and that it is expected that he will be accepted." As Gould then reported to his director of admissions, Donald Klinefelter, the board had expressed "universal interest and approval. … No one questioned the desirability of welcoming qualified colored students." But, he advised Klinefelter,

> We are of the same mind that particular care should be taken with those who come first for the sake of the satisfactory working out of the whole idea. We certainly want objective colored students who will be adaptable. It would be a misfortune to have the first colored student be an aggressive type who had a sense of mission in immediately setting right the racial

---

* Although in other small ways the Carleton teaching staff's racial diversity was indeed slightly expanding in 1947. As Gould informed Bell, "We really have progressed, for we shall have this year a young woman doctor who is a Nisei and a young man in economics, Phi Beta Kappa, PhD from Harvard, who is Chinese in origin. This is the way Carleton College should go if it is to fulfill its highest purpose."

inequalities which are so rampant in our country. We all want these things corrected, but we recognize the necessity of the time element. I assume you will interview young Tinnin when you are in New York. Certainly his photograph suggests that he would be an intelligent and desirable citizen in the Carleton community.

The applicant, Alvis Lee Tinnin, had come warmly recommended by Carleton alumnus Buell Gallagher '25, formerly the president of Alabama's all-black Talladega College. Tinnin was, reassuringly, a little older than most students, a veteran with wartime service in the Philippines, who before his enlistment had completed more than half of his college degree requirements at Talladega. He would enter Carleton already a junior. He was also a talented singer and actor and had been appearing on Broadway since April 1946 in the musical revue *Call Me Mister*. Tinnin was duly admitted and attended his first class February 2. (In Washington that same Groundhog Day, Truman proposed to Congress passage of a federal anti-lynching law and desegregation of the armed forces—though the Gallup Poll found most Americans opposed to both measures.) During his first week at Carleton, Tinnin later recalled, Gould had a few words with him in his Laird Hall office. Telling him that he was very welcome at the school, the president said he hoped Tinnin would enjoy Carleton, but he was to realize that the same rules for everyone else also applied to him, "nothing different, nothing worse, nothing better," and that if he were to step out of line Gould would be obliged to treat him as he would any other offending student and show him the door. In fact, Tinnin made a fine record of success and in due course was followed by other black students—not, to be sure, by more than a handful prior to the start of sizable deliberate recruitment in the 1960s, but at Carleton a door had been opened and thereafter remained ajar.

***

Although in taking up the Carleton presidency Larry Gould to a large extent made his personal biography and the progress of the college for many years a single narrative, yet there are aspects of Gould's activities external to Carleton in the late 1940s that are worth recording. A given constant: He was making speeches continuously, sometimes on educational matters, often not. (Representative titles from 1947 and 1948 include "The Ends of the Earth: New Frontiers of Destiny," "Youth Today—Citizen Tomorrow," "The Crisis in Character," "Education for the Atomic Age," and "America's Real Resources.") He very much enjoyed active participation in the Minneapolis-based Skylight Club, whose members assembled monthly to hear speakers and conduct discussions on intellectual and cultural issues of the day. Early in 1947 he appreciated being put up for membership in Washington's prestigious Cosmos Club, an exclusive salon for men of any profession distinguished for their intellectual or creative attainments. Within the space of a few not atypical weeks he would find himself at Princeton for a meeting of the Phi Beta Kappa Senate, in New York serving as toastmaster for an Explorers Club dinner, and then in Montreal chairing the Board of Governors of the Arctic Institute of North America. He was named one of four civilian members of the Army and Navy Joint Research and Development Board's standing Committee on Geographic Exploration. In mid-1947, Minnesota Governor Luther Youngdahl pressed him to serve as chairman of the Twin Cities Airport Commission, an honor he ultimately declined. Accepted, that year or within the next few, were appointments to the board of Shattuck School, as chair of Minnesota's Rhodes Scholarship Committee, to the board of the Minneapolis Symphony Orchestra, and as a trustee of the Minnesota Community Research Council.

His hope that after settling in to the presidency he might sometimes find it possible to teach a Carleton geology course himself now and again proved unfeasible, given his schedule and commitments. Also in vain was his hope, for the summer of 1947, to spend a few weeks returning to his geological investigations on the Iowan Drift. Instead, he observed glumly to Dunc Stewart, he had to give his attention to the finding of "an economist, a chemist, a philosopher, and two resident heads, as well as many other things." Regardless of all, however, he insisted, for two weeks at least "I shall get away to go fishing." And so he did, spending the last half of August with Peg at the Square G Ranch on Jenny Lake in Wyoming's Teton Mountains. (The pleasures of summer stays at the Square G had been previously enjoyed by Carleton friends Alfred and Helen Hyslop and Jenny Cullen.) The Goulds loved it there in the Jackson Hole country and from 1947 on would return to this part of Wyoming for no less than four weeks minimum every summer for the rest of the Gould presidency, and after. For several years, prior to buying their own Wyoming property a little farther south, near the town of Wilson, this meant an annual return to the Square G Ranch, where year after year the gorgeous glacial lake proved an effective restorer of presidential spirits and energies. (The publisher Alfred Knopf, who stayed at Jenny Lake in the summer of 1948, wrote in his autobiography of falling in love with the matchless views of the mountains there, rising so abruptly out of lovely meadows, and how "the air seemed like the air nowhere else—one felt happy and lifted up just breathing it.")

***

One of the advantages Gould found in being a college president was that, if he should happen to encounter a voice or viewpoint he admired, and thought should be shared with the Carleton student body, he might well be in a position to make that happen. When in September 1947, for instance, he read with pleasure and approbation a recent address delivered at Colgate by the director of the CIO Committee to Abolish Discrimination he promptly arranged for the man to give a similar talk at Carleton later in the year. When that same month he read a timely paper on the importance of upholding civil liberties even for political subversives, lest they be lost to all, written by the dean of the University of California Law School, who was also a Carleton alumnus, he wrote in praise ("fear at this moment may be our more deadly enemy ... more dangerous than anything the native Communist is ever likely to achieve") and then arranged for the dean to be invited to give Carleton's next Commencement address and receive an honorary degree.

Freedom, besieged, was at the forefront of Larry Gould's mind in the fall of 1947. In October he spoke to the assembled college at a convocation in the chapel on the subject of academic freedom (he was "for it"), concluding by inviting faculty and students to write him with their own thoughts on the subject. "I want you to know how much it means to me as a Faculty member," replied Counselor in Religion Phil Phenix, "to know that I have full freedom to think and teach in accordance with my understanding of the truth." (Decrying the many evident indicators of "increasingly reactionary attitudes in this country," Phenix was "glad to see Carleton standing up for truly liberal principles." Phenix told Gould that with matters as they are he would "far rather have Carleton too far left than too far to the right," but affirmed that "even better is to have Carleton as it is—neither right nor left, but a place where the claims of all contenders may be fairly and fearlessly examined.") Replying to thoughts shared by an assistant professor of psychology and education, Gould declared that "how to defend free institutions while remaining free may turn out to be the supreme challenge."

For Gould the preservation of freedom of all sorts went hand in hand with the good health of privately supported educational institutions such as Carleton, and he lost few opportunities for spreading this gospel. A typical formulation of the creed appeared in the president's column in the Carleton alumni magazine for September 1947:

> We need to remind ourselves that the oldest secular institutions in western civilization are the independent colleges. They came into being in old Europe as an expression of man's quest for freedom; and down through the centuries they have drawn to themselves the intellectual life of the world, and it is doubtful if that life would be discernible in history without such institutions. It is in the independent college and university that academic freedom had its origin, and it is in these institutions that it is now being preserved. Should they disappear, then academic freedom and all of the other freedoms, such as freedom of the press and freedom of speech which stem from it, would disappear with it. I believe nothing is more important for the preservation of what is best in our democratic tradition than the preservation of the ideals inherent in such institutions as Carleton College.

In this instance Gould was stating the faith to alumni, but he said the same to all audiences. American businesses, he frequently and fervently pressed, should recognize the "very real ... interdependence between independent educational institutions and independent, free enterprises." With recognition of interdependence, he hoped to persuade, should come tangible financial support. Recommending to Laird Bell a recent like-minded article by the chairman of the board of directors of the Standard Oil Company on "The Stake of Business in American Education," Gould declared that if the point of view set forth were "largely adopted by great firms or great industries like the Standard Oil Company, it would mean the salvation of independent educational institutions."

Gould hoped as well to develop far greater ongoing support for Carleton from among its alumni than had hitherto been the case. In his travels about the country he met with and spoke to alumni groups with great frequency and found great continuing interest in and affection for the college, but there was much to be done to translate general good feeling into a tradition of regular alumni financial support. "It is a slow process," Gould had written in June to trustee John M. Musser, the Weyerhaeuser Sales Company executive who had joined the board earlier that year. "Dr. Cowling was able to finance the College in terms of the interest of relatively few wealthy people. We all appreciate the fact that security in the future lies in the broadening of our base of support." Addressing Musser again in November, Gould admitted that Carleton "has a long way to go to catch up with other colleges in the matter of its alumni relations and organizations. I do find everywhere a great reservoir of good will and potential interest in the welfare of the College, but since such an organization has never been encouraged we have to learn to walk before we run."

Fundraising in general was never far now from Gould's presidential mind. As he lamented early in December to his admissions director, "It beats the dickens how every worth-while thing one wishes to do around a place like this costs money!"

It was about a week later, while in the East for a Phi Beta Kappa Senate

Charles J. Miel

meeting, that Gould had his first personal interview with the man he would subsequently hire to help him pursue that money, filling at last the position first envisioned two years before of college vice president, with responsibilities primarily in the areas of public relations and, as Gould would put it in his letter of appointment, "for lengthening my arm, as it were, in our quest for funds." This was Charles J. Miel [pronounced MEE-el], a forty-nine-year-old University of Pennsylvania graduate with a variety of financial and alumni fundraising experiences, then working for the Treasury Department's US Savings Bonds Division as director for the state of Pennsylvania. During Miel's First World War service with a machine gun battalion in France, he had been cited for bravery in action during the Meuse-Argonne offensive. Miel was formally elected vice president of the college at the January trustees' meeting and arrived in Northfield to begin work at the end of April.

The building program for Carleton was at the center of Gould and Miel's quest for funds. Though a new library was clearly at the top of all needs and desires for the college, the library project would be so expensive that it had been deemed best to begin with a fine arts building. Architectural plans had been duly produced and approved—Gould himself, using his prerogative as a geologist-president, had insisted on the use of Mankato stone for the front facade—but that building, too, was proving challenging to finance. In January 1947 Gould had estimated its construction cost at $250,000. By December the estimate had risen to $275,000, and by the following April this had been further raised to $337,000. At the June meeting of the Carleton trustees Gould reported that approximately $240,000 was then available for the building—$140,000 from the George Boliou Fund* and $100,000 from other "free" funds. The project progressed that summer nonetheless, as in mid-July Laird Bell transmitted to Gould a proposal that he said he was authorized to make "on behalf of certain people who are interested in Carleton and who must remain absolutely anonymous" to complete the raising of funds for the art building by matching dollar for dollar up to $75,000 all funds raised for the purpose "within six months from the first of next October." "Whatever you think about the source of this is wrong," Bell added to his note of transmittal. Upon the strength of the offer from "Anonymous" and Gould's assurance that all fundraising efforts would be directed toward the art building project until $75,000 had safely been secured, the trustees' Building Committee agreed that construction should proceed. Shortly before leaving with Peg for their Wyoming vacation, Gould met with Building Committee chairman Merrill Hutchinson to open bids and select a contractor. Ground was broken in August on the selected site between Laird Hall and Goodsell Observatory overlooking Lyman Lakes to the north, and the new Boliou Hall eventually opened its doors

---

* The Boliou Fund was the result of a rather unusual bequest to the College. George H. Boliou, a farm-owner in Mower County, Minnesota, with a reputation as a bit of a tightwad, died in December 1933. The Austin *Herald* briefly noted his death and ran a formal obituary but otherwise took no notice—until the opening of his safe deposit box at the end of January put him on the *Herald*'s front page. "In that box," reported the paper, "was a roll of paper money as big as a man's head." Also present were notes, mortgages, certificates, securities, and farm deeds amounting to "the largest estate of personal property, money and credits probated in this county for over a quarter of a century." More surprises emerged with the reading of Boliou's will, dated two months before his death. An only child with no children of his own, Boliou established a trust fund with his estate providing his widow with $3,000 a year until her death, after which the rest of the fund was to go to Carleton College to erect an educational or recreational building bearing his name. This created a sensation, as Boliou had no known prior connection to Carleton and, said acquaintances, had evinced no particular interest during his life in education. "It doesn't sound like Boliou," said one neighbor, "he wouldn't give a nickel to a starving child for an ice cream cone." It was supposed that, disliking his in-laws and determined that they should not profit by his death he wanted to perpetuate his name in some charitable way and that his attention had been directed to Carleton College by the attorney who drew up his will, Lafayette French, a Carleton graduate. In any case, Carleton eventually received an estate valued at $150,000 at the time of transfer.

to use in the fall of 1949. It was the first major building erected on the Carleton campus since before the 1929 stock market crash.

Meanwhile, another building aspiration had begun to take shape, in the form of desire for a student union. In January 1947 the trustees had approved a War Memorial Campaign for funds with which to create a Memorial Student Union, to be dedicated to the Carleton gold star men of two world wars, and had requested the Carleton Alumni Association to allocate to the War Memorial Campaign all funds received from the alumni campaign for the next two years. Preliminary drawings for such a building were prepared by the college architects, with a sketch of a possible front exterior appearing in the alumni magazine of June 1947. A year later, more detailed architectural plans had been made, with the expectation that the building, of red brick with stone trim to match existing campus buildings, would probably be sited behind the Music Hall and Gridley Hall, a women's dormitory. It never happened. At the trustee meeting of June 1948 Gould provided a cost estimate for the building of half a million dollars but reported that funds accumulated through the Alumni Fund and other sources then totaled no more than $100,000, making it "obvious that it will be many years before a start can be made unless more determined effort is made to raise funds for this particular project." The following October the board approved spending $4,000 for increased promotion of the student union campaign among alumni, but little more than four months later, in February 1949, the college's administrative officers were being instructed to study the far cheaper alternative of adapting Willis Hall* to use as a memorial union, rather than putting up an entirely new building. In June, the decision was taken to do just that, looking to the Alumni Fund now to contribute no more than $150,000 for the rehabilitation job. By the time the trustees convened for their October 1949 meeting, with the art building finished and funds nearly in hand for the transformation of Willis Hall into Willis Memorial Union (though due to a variety of subsequent delays the renovations would not in fact be completed and the building rededicated until 1953), the board now agreed that it was time to turn "to the development of the library project as a goal for discussion with prospective donors." The Library Campaign would take years to complete, but it was time to begin.

***

On the curricular front, Gould was finding that it was quite a difficult thing to effect change or introduce innovations in a college like Carleton; the "minor revolution" he had hoped to bring about was not proceeding with speed. Early

---

* Willis Hall, the oldest building on the campus, had always been at the hub of Carleton life, but campus plans developed under Cowling had called for its eventual removal. This was reversed under Gould, even before there were thoughts of its being converted to use as a student union. In late summer, 1946, Gould had written to Professor Hyme Loss: "Probably one of the reasons no changes have been made in Willis Hall in many years is that the plans for campus changes involve the destruction of Willis Hall. This is a point of view to which I do not subscribe, and in our thinking in the years ahead Willis Hall will remain here as long as I do, at least."

Gould and Art Department chairman Alfred Hyslop (far right) with architects' model for the Fine Arts Building (Boliou Hall), 1948

in 1948 Gould pushed very hard to get faculty approval for institution of a year-long required course for freshmen that would be an interdepartmental course of introduction to the social sciences, to be team-taught by faculty from the Departments of Economics, Government and International Relations, History, and Sociology and Anthropology. The model was a course that had already been taught experimentally by Professor of History Lucile Deen, who had subsequently chaired a committee preparing a manual to use as a textbook for the new course. Gould called the development of Social Science 101-102 "one of the most exciting educational things that has happened since I have come to Carleton College." Personal enthusiasm for the new requirement is unmistakable in the pages of his presidential annual report as he anticipated its implementation in 1948-49:

> This course represents one of the most important steps in line with our desires to bring about a more unified and integrated curriculum. It is hoped that this course will provide the students with a common knowledge of the social and political sciences which will furnish a basis for intelligent communication and social activity. It is not just another course in the social sciences. It is a distinct experiment and contribution. The manual which has been prepared with so much care is a new kind of textbook which may well invite much comment and probably much copying.

Things did not work out as hoped with this class. Prompted by the receipt of an extraordinary number of adverse student comments during its debut year, both about its content and its teaching, in winter 1949 Gould asked Dean Kille to look into what was going on. He then wrote the chairman of the Political and Social Sciences Division, John Phelan, saying that, while he still believed in the validity of the idea and the ideal, "it is obvious to me that it is unwise to consider a continuation of the present course. ... It would be far better now to take a completely realistic view rather than blindly go ahead along a path which appears just now not to be leading where we had thought." Acknowledging his own "deep interest in the plan from the beginning," Gould nevertheless gave Phelan's division permission to pull the plug, if their consideration of the doubts which have been raised led to their own conclusion that it would be best not to repeat the course for 1949-50. "My own face might be a little red," he wrote, "but it is so often suffused with that color since I have been President of the College that that will not matter in the least." The experiment was duly ended, the requirement dropped, with Phelan acknowledging that "the success of a course of this type depends on securing a group of vitally interested teachers," and Gould concluding that "the idea has not failed, but people have failed it." He hoped that the integrated social science course might be revived later, avoiding the pitfall of having people teaching it who did not really want to be doing so and therefore were not giving it their full support. "I shall know how to proceed next time," he wrote. A disappointing educational experiment for the college, it had nonetheless contributed to Gould's own education as a president.

***

In the spring of 1948 there was more faculty hiring to be done, filling vacancies for the fall. The catch was a good one that year, bringing to the faculty as assistant professors a number of persons who would stay long and become highly celebrated Carleton teachers. Interviewed and hired within a few weeks of each other in May and June were future classroom giants Ada Harrison in economics, Ralph Fjelstad in government, and Milic Capek in philosophy. Another splendid development for the college at just that time was an announcement that Carleton had been selected as one of only six colleges nationally, chosen on a regional basis, to receive $50,000 from the George F. Baker Trust to establish academic scholarships for young men of outstanding merit but limited financial means. Selection as the host college for this program for the entire upper Mississippi Valley region was "one of the greatest compliments Carleton has ever had," enthused Gould after being informed of the honor.

Compliments were accruing to Gould as well. In June, he was asked by the chairman of Reed College's presidential search committee whether he would be willing to be considered for the presidency there. (He was not, replying that "if I am to remain a college executive, it should be here at Carleton so long as the fine confidence which I now have from the Board of Trustees continues.") Earlier in the year he had been informed that Captain Finn Ronne, leader of a research expedition in Antarctica that was mapping the Weddell Sea coastline—and the son of Martin Ronne, who had wintered over with Gould on the Byrd Expedition—had honored Gould by naming a newly discovered feature of the ice barrier coastline Larry Gould Bay.

Twenty years had now passed since Gould was preparing to depart for the

Antarctic on the adventure which did so much to launch his subsequent career. Although the thought he had once given to organizing a return expedition had given way to other endeavors, the far south would never be completely absent from his consciousness and concern. In June of 1948, sighing over the ongoing difficulties presented to him by the still-tight housing situation at Carleton, he confessed to one correspondent that "I ofttimes long for the opportunity to return to Antarctica, where peace of mind is an achievement easily within reach of any thoughtful person." The preceding January he had published an article on "Strategy and Politics in the Polar Areas," in which he had written of the realm of national claims in Antarctica as presenting a unique opportunity for resolving differences "in terms of one world." "No people are involved," he noted,

> and no questions of great economic or political importance have yet appeared. Perhaps if all interested states would renounce their real and fancied rights in favor of a world organization, techniques of co-operation and administration might be worked out which would help to solve some of the problems in the older populated areas of the world. Such a world control would help to achieve for all peoples their proper rights in whatever of good this continent holds for the future of mankind.

Dick Byrd wrote twice that June, the second letter being an invitation to Gould to join him in an effort to raise funds for Robert Peary's old Arctic companion Matthew Henson, who, with only a trivial government pension, was in some want. That letter had been preceded two days earlier by one in which Byrd described a "vivid dream" he thought to pass on:

> You and I and Marie, my better half, were in a plane and you were piloting. Suddenly something happened to the engine and we had a forced landing facing us. Marie got perturbed. I said to her, "Now, Marie, don't worry; good old Larry will get us down safely."
> You made a belly landing and smashed things up a bit; but I could see that Marie was all right. I yelled to you, "Larry, are you hurt?" When you said you were O.K. we all three walked away from the wreck. ...
> Perhaps it means that you were the pilot of our good plane friendship and when the engine got out of order for the moment due to my careless maintenance, you guided the plane of friendship down to a safe landing. And since Marie and I are one, she also would be in the plane.

Gould responded that he liked Byrd's dream "and especially your friendly interpretation of it very much," that he hoped to be able to have a leisurely visit with Admiral and Mrs. Byrd whenever he might next be in New England, and that he would be pleased to join Byrd in promoting tangible assistance to Henson. It was a friendly bit of icebreaking, but within the year Gould was again hearing complaints of bad Byrd behavior with which he sympathized. Finn Ronne reported Byrd upset to the point of "ranting and raving" that Ronne had not named a major Antarctic feature for him during his 1946-48 expedition. Not doing so, Ronne told Gould, seemed to Byrd to be a purposeful "blackening of his character," which Byrd would not stand for. "The reality of the situation is becoming extremely funny—with all his popular prestige, influence and power, he worries about an unknown struggling competitor—imagine." A few months later Ronne reported that Byrd had used his influence to "squelch" Ronne's hopes for another expedition operating under the Navy with wintering base at Gould Bay. "This, of course, was only to be expected." Gould replied that he was "distressed but not surprised" by Byrd's action, adding that "it is impossible to understand the selfishness of some people."

One other way by which Antarctica remained present to Gould that year involved his January 1949 trip to Scandinavia, in connection with which he had arranged to take the Amundsen note, the page from Roald Amundsen's log that in 1929 he had retrieved from its cache on Mt. Betty in the Queen Maud Mountains, back to Norway where it truly belonged. Gould had first thought to deliver the note to its rightful country in 1940 at the time of the International Polar Exposition in Bergen, but that plan had been canceled due to the war. Now this trip, which involved invitations to lecture in Copenhagen, Stockholm, and Oslo, was arranged by a member of the Norwegian Embassy delegation in Washington. Gould found it stimulating for several days to be returned to his "rightful role as a geologist and geographer." On January 26, the day of his evening lecture to the Norwegian Geographical Society, Gould was given an early afternoon audience at the royal palace with Norway's King Haakon. Gould found the king, who not only had known Amundsen and other great explorers but had read their books and could quote from them, astonishingly well-informed on Antarctic exploration. His Majesty's "detailed knowledge" about such history, he reported, exceeded that of any other person with whom he spoke. The scheduled fifteen-minute audience extended to a full half-hour of stimulating conversation and questions, at the end of which an unprepared Gould was surprised to discover Haakon making him a knight of the Royal Norwegian Order of St. Olaf. The royally bestowed medal became perhaps his most cherished decoration; he wore it proudly in his lapel that evening as he lectured to the Norwegian Geographical Society and presented to its president the precious Amundsen note. ("You can be sure," Gould wrote in March to Bernt Balchen, "that my standing among Norwegians here in Minnesota has risen very greatly since receiving the Cross of St. Olaf from the hand of the king.")

***

In the months following his Scandinavian trip Gould became preoccupied with a national fight over proposed federal aid to education. The immediate issue, in the spring of 1949, concerned Senate Bill 246, which would mandate federal grants to states to promote equalization of educational opportunity by reducing state-to-state disparities in educational expenditure. The bill aimed to make

Gould presents the Amundsen note to the president of the Norwegian Geographical Society, 1949.

federal tax dollars available to support teachers' salaries and other public school operating expenditures and would also provide federal funding to non-public schools for transportation and textbook purchases where such was not prohibited by state law. Strongly urged by the National Educational Association, the bill enjoyed robust bipartisan support, being endorsed both by the newly reelected Truman administration and by many key Republicans, notably including co-sponsor Senator Robert Taft of Ohio. Although previous versions of the same bill had foundered in either the Senate or the House three times in recent years, the Democratic gains in the 1948 elections led to widespread expectation among the proponents of federal aid that approval would come in 1949.

To Gould, who saw academic freedom as the mother of all freedoms and who feared that with federal support would inevitably come federal control, direct federal aid to education was anathema. He lambasted federal aid in a number of forums and accepted an invitation prominently to address the annual meeting of the United States Chamber of Commerce on the issue in Washington on May 3. In April, he first hoped that he would be able to state his objections to S.246 at public hearings on the bill that he expected would still be going when he arrived in Washington on May 2, but he was appalled to find that no public hearings were contemplated. On April 25 he fired off telegrams to Minnesota's two senators, Thye and Humphrey, protesting that the passage of this bill without providing public hearings "would be the most disgraceful kind of steam roller tactics" and a "flagrant betrayal of our democratic rights." Humphrey responded that the Senate committee had voted the bill out of committee without extended public hearings because it was seen as "relatively non-controversial and ... bi-partisan."

"The principle of federal aid to education is quite generally accepted," Humphrey asserted, telling Gould further that "the only large point of difference at this point that I am aware of is that undoubtedly the appropriations are not adequate for the needs of the states and of the schools."

Gould's address to the US Chamber of Commerce traveled widely; it was subsequently printed as a pamphlet titled "On Federal Aid to Education," and it received editorial comment in the *Saturday Evening Post*. In it he called the provision of direct federal subsidies for general school purposes "a radical departure from former practices." Stating that he agreed heartily with the proposition that schools ought to be more adequately financed at both state and local levels, he nonetheless argued that federal aid was an inadvisable and hazardous means to achieve that end. He observed that aid had not been requested from below, from local or state governments, and pointed out misleading statistics that had been used to imply that every state would somehow be receiving free assistance, omitting information about what each state would pay. (Minnesota, he noted, was shown as receiving a subsidy of about $3 million but would in fact pay about twice that amount in new taxes. "Do you subsidize someone," he asked, "when you give him one dollar and take two away from him?") Finally, he warned that despite protestations to the contrary, federal aid would ultimately imply federal control, centralization, and enforced uniformity that would be hazardous to democracy. "The strength of American education has been its variety. … Forcing all our educational institutions into a common mold would defeat the very purposes of democratic education." Granting that centralization in certain areas has been inevitable and desirable in the modern world, he argued however that it was important to know and stand firm on what should not be centralized in "our drift toward statism." Asserting that centralization of authority with regard to our schools would endanger academic freedom, he concluded that this was "a hazard we need not and indeed dare not take."

On May 5 the US Senate approved S.246 by the comfortable bipartisan margin of 58-15 (92 percent of Senate Democrats joining with 65 percent of Senate Republicans), and Gould and other opponents of the measure were left to pin their hopes for blockage on the House of Representatives. "I know there will be strong opposition in the House," Gould wrote in May. "We shall do everything we can to bring the issue into the full light of day which will help much, I do believe."

Gould continued to express his objections, alone and in concert with other college and university presidents, including his Carleton predecessor Donald Cowling. The 1949 legislation was in the end not fated to get through the House that year. Hearings were held by a special subcommittee on federal aid to education chaired by North Carolina Congressman Graham Barden, and this subcommittee eventually reported out instead a substitute bill proposed by Barden himself, which, as it explicitly prohibited the use of federal funds to aid private schools, was attacked as "anti-Catholic" and never emerged from the House committee to which it was reported. (The chairman of that committee, Representative John

Lesinski of Michigan, stated that he thought Barden had intentionally drawn his bill up that way because he was actually opposed to any federal aid to education and wanted to kill it entirely for that session.) Motions to report S.246 out from the House Committee on Education and Labor were subsequently lost twice—in August of 1949 and again, after President Truman had urged reconsideration, in March of 1950, the latter by a vote of 13-12.

Throughout this period Gould put considerable effort of pen and tongue into opposing federal entanglement in the educational realm, which he equated on occasion with "the coming of the welfare state." He worked with newspaperman Laurence Rossman and with editorial advice from Cowling to produce two other pamphlets on the subject which he proposed to mail "to members of Congress and two thousand other carefully selected people in the country." In March an address he had given the month before to the Minnesota State School Board Convention in Minneapolis was published as "Education and the Welfare State." Here he identified American greatness with "making the concept of freedom our guiding star" but warned that "today we are in danger of becoming ashamed of the things that have made us great." He feared that "the flame of freedom has grown dim" as security has instead become our social, economic, and political "Mecca." The movement toward a welfare state, he posited, had grown out of a growing enthusiasm for "economic rights" that has unfortunately been accompanied by an "element of indifference to political rights." "Freedom without bread," he acknowledged, was "difficult license," but he urged that "bread without freedom is the life of the beast." Calling himself "a middle-of-the-road man," he granted that there were a great many things that could and should be solved at the federal level, and that he didn't mind living in a "semi-welfare state," but he declared that he did not believe that all problems could best be solved from the top down and that he did fear too great a centralization of power in the state as a threat to the preservation of liberty. Injustices imposed by private enterprise, real though they were—he certainly was not calling for *laissez faire* capitalism—were, he thought, in history "small indeed, almost trivial, compared with those imposed by the state." "The history of the struggle for human freedom," he avowed, "is the struggle to limit the power of the state, and we may be very sure that as our federal state becomes more powerful it will become more corrupt." "Perhaps," he thought, "we could have socialized medicine and other things without losing the essential character of Americanism, but we should stop at a federally socialized system of education."

The culmination of Gould's year as a public crusader on the subject of federal aid to education came with an invitation to debate the subject with Senate Majority Leader Scott Lucas of Illinois, a federal aid supporter, on the widely broadcast radio program *America's Town Meeting of the Air*. The radio debate, airing the week after S.246 had been rejected by the House Education and Labor Committee, was to bring Gould considerable national attention and fan mail.

Lucas stated that federal aid had become necessary because in some sections of the country, notably in the South, state and local governments, despite "Herculean efforts," had "fallen hopelessly behind" in efforts to keep their standards of education up to the requirements of the times and needed "help from their richer state sisters" in raising their educational level. He argued that the bill passed by the Senate had been carefully crafted to maintain the American "tradition of keeping control of local schools in the hands of local people," blocking "every possible point of intervention by federal officials." "We simply would divide up the money among states, with those states where the need is greatest getting the most assistance." "Dr. Gould," Lucas concluded, "I believe this is federal aid without federal control."

Gould responded that no state was now making Herculean efforts, noting that all were spending a lower percentage of their income on education now than had been the case before the war and that no state should receive federal aid "when it establishes its case by refusing to tax its people properly or by neglecting its schools while it can afford to build great bridges and highways and things of that sort." "The current proposals to grant aid," Gould asserted, would do so "not on the basis of incapacity to support education, but on the failure to do so." Gould denied Lucas's contention that the bill in question was or even should be federal aid without federal control, observing that "Congress hasn't any business appropriating my tax monies and not exercising some supervision over them." "Saying that no control is authorized in this bill," Gould countered, "is like giving a man a sock in the jaw and saying at the same time, 'I wouldn't hurt you for the world.'"

A few additional addresses on the federal aid to education subject followed, but by the beginning of May Carleton's board chairman was urging Gould to heed the recommendations made by a management consulting firm the college had engaged to suggest improvements in operating efficiencies that the president disengage at Carleton from so much detail and also that he lessen the amount of his public speaking. "I think you ought to cut down even on your crusade against federal aid," Bell advised. "Isn't it pretty well staved off for the present?" It was, and he did.

***

In the spring of 1949 Gould again thought it important personally to deliver to the Carleton student body a convocation on the subject of academic freedom. The summer before, Gould had been appointed one of five members of a five-state civil service loyalty board to review cases where the loyalty of an applicant for a government civil service position had been questioned and where doubts still remained subsequent to FBI investigation. Referencing this work in his 1949 convocation address, Gould stressed that, contrary to the impression one might get from reactionary papers like the *Chicago Tribune* "and evil sheets of that sort … that about 98% of the people in our Federal Government are extremely pink or red," out of some 17,000 applications processed through the Civil Service in St. Paul, only twenty-eight persons had been questioned and only four or five disqualified from employment. Gould stated that active membership in the Communist Party today would automatically disqualify anyone from teaching at Carleton College, given that Communists "must toe the party line and surrender freedom of thought to enforced conformity under ideological control," which was irreconcilable with the fundamental aims of Carleton. However, he stressed, he saw very little reason for "all of this agitation and concern about Communism" in American public life and decried the damage that such agitation was doing to American institutions. Although the ideas underlying Communism were repugnant, he said, today "it's the irrational response to such ideas that constitutes the real threat to academic freedom." He observed that "in times like these there will be increasing pressure to teach Democracy or the American way," coming from "a variety of organizations that I need not name; you are familiar with them yourself." "One hundred percent Americanism," Gould declared, "isn't the way." "To teach one point of view," he urged, "is usually to tell only the partial truth. We want you to have free, critical minds which will discover for yourselves the value of democratic institutions."

Gould was not an advocate of the sort of anti-subversive loyalty oaths prescribed in that era by the Truman administration. In a commencement address from this time, titled "The Way Ahead," he offered instead the sort of oath of citizenship to which he would be most happy to subscribe. It would go, he suggested, something like this:

> I declare my loyalty to the great tradition of civilization, my belief in the freedom of the individual to develop his talents for the enrichment of the community, and my conviction that man's community is now the whole human race, within which each nation must play its characteristic part. I pledge myself to use every opportunity for action to uphold the great tradition of civilization, to protect all those who may suffer for its sake, and to pass it on to the coming generations. I recognize no loyalty greater than that to the task of preserving truth, toleration, and justice in the coming world order.

***

Larry Gould's fourth year as Carleton president ended with a "sunshine-favored" June commencement exceptionally featuring the presentation of four honorary degrees. One went to Congregationalist divine Dr. Albert Peel, of London, who preached the baccalaureate sermon the day before Commencement. Another went to eighty-three-year-old Elizabeth Wallace, a former professor of Romance languages at Chicago who had become a close personal friend of Gould's and a member since 1946 in the group of friends of the college organized as "Carleton College Associates." A third honorary degree was bestowed upon the Commencement ceremony's principal speaker, Carter Davidson, president of Union College, past president of Knox College, and before that, for five years

Commencement 1949: (left to right) Gould, Elizabeth Wallace, Donald Cowling, and Carter Davidson

in the 1930s, a Carleton professor of English and special assistant to President Cowling. The fourth degree, the result of a plot between Gould and Davidson, went to Cowling himself.

Writing to Davidson months in advance to arrange for the Commencement address, Gould observed that Dr. Cowling had been "the most perfect President Emeritus in the history of education," having told Gould upon leaving the college that from then on he would have no contact with Carleton except through Gould and as solicited by Gould. The problem was, Gould complained, he has been "too perfect!" "The marvelous support he has given me in a completely detached way," Gould told Davidson, "has been a source of great strength, but he over does it a little bit in that I have great difficulty in getting him to come down to the campus at all. He has declined to come to any Commencement since I have been President." Cowling had previously refused all suggestions that he be given an honorary Carleton degree himself, stipulating that he would attend a commencement and accept the attention concomitant with a degree only after his successor had completed five years in office. Gould would in 1949 be finishing only his fourth year, but the lure of a reunion with Davidson, his former assistant, had proved sufficient to get Cowling to "break his abstinence" and agree to be present for Davidson's address and degree hooding. Gould hoped that he might now also persuade Cowling to allow the college to move up by a year the presentation to its past president of his own honorary degree. Davidson directed Gould to inform Cowling how much more Davidson's degree would mean to him if he could receive it together with such a companion. Ultimately, Cowling was persuadable, and the most memorable moment of Commencement 1949 was the spontaneous standing ovation with which the audience erupted in appreciation for the man who had led Carleton for thirty-six formative years, building and strengthening the school all the while despite two world wars and the Great Depression. It was one of the great emotional demonstrations in Carleton history.

CHAPTER 17

THE THINGS THAT HAVE MADE US GREAT

The 1949-50 school year, Larry Gould's fifth as president, would be the fourth and final year of Carleton's post-war demographic bulge of enrollments exceeding eleven hundred students. The previous March Gould had advised the trustees' Executive Committee that pressure for entry had diminished relative to the last few years and raised the question whether it was now time to begin cutting the college population back down to a level more ideally commensurate with the physical plant. Commenting in a Carleton publication that summer, Gould identified that ideal as about 950 students. In a June letter to Bell, Gould had wondered at the policy of nearby Macalester College, which was boasting of the rate at which its enrollment had recently increased. "I am at a total loss to understand why a liberal arts college should want to go in this direction," wrote Gould. "They will lose their birthrights." Gould felt that Carleton's distinctive quality stood out all the more clearly for her insistence on remaining small.

Assisted by some extra year-end generosity from its board chairman, Carleton managed to finish the previous fiscal year in the black, and Gould had been told by Trustee Secretary Atherton Bean that he and Charlie Miel could look back with satisfaction at that year's money raising. ("A good enough job," Bean wrote, "so that you have laid a foundation on which to build for a wider base of giving in the future.") After paying attention in July to the filling of faculty vacancies in chemistry, economics, psychology, and German, he was able with good conscience to spend August enjoying with Peg their now customary summer holiday at the Square G dude ranch in the Tetons, inviting Treasurer Bruce Pollock to make free use of his home vegetable garden while he was away.

Carleton opened its new year in September with a sense of optimism over the direction in which the college was evidently moving. Hailing notable advances on numerous fronts, the alumni magazine declared that "progress" seemed destined to be the key word for the year ahead. Though the start of the fall semester coincided with unsettling developments in the outside world—President Truman's public announcement on Carleton's second day of classes that the Soviet Union had successfully tested its own atomic bomb was followed a week later by

"Red ties" — things of innocent amusement at Carleton at mid-century but accusations with dire consequences elsewhere in America during McCarthyism

news that in China triumphant Communists had formally proclaimed a People's Republic—campus attention continued its primary focus on local matters. The great festive event on the autumn college calendar was the dedication of the new art building, Boliou Hall, during Homecoming Weekend in mid-October.

A few days after that event, Gould delivered an address at the centennial banquet of the Minnesota Historical Society in which—stimulated, as he acknowledged, by his recent reading of Friedrich Hayek—he bemoaned the collectivist philosophy of security underlying the concept of the modern welfare state. "Security," he cautioned, "is a philosophy for a people which is finished, a people which believes no further improvements are possible. It is a philosophy of senility and defeat." Gould posited that "insecurity—the goading necessity of coping with changing conditions—has always been basic to human progress" and that "when you free man from all the risks of hunger, health and any others that might plague him, you free him of the things that have made him a man." He declared himself out of sympathy with the new liberalism which would eliminate all risks, for, he thought, it minimized the importance of the individual and "is not in keeping with the traditional concept of American freedom, which implies freedom to fail as well as freedom to succeed." "We are in danger of being ashamed of the things that have made us great," he warned. "For, trite as it may sound, it has been our capitalistic economic system of free enterprise, coupled with our political system, which has produced our opulent material civilization."

Gould reached a large audience through that address, particularly through excerpts printed in the *Minneapolis Star* newspaper. "As is so often the case,"

Gould wrote Laird Bell early in December, "the excerpts were not continuous, and certain impressions ... were not quite what I had in mind. One man in Minneapolis observed that 'For the president of a parasite institution, you are a dodo.' He then went on among other things to wish that I might be stricken down with polio and blindness." However, Gould noted, reactions in general "have not been quite so severe."

The high visibility, public speaking ability, and personal following enjoyed by Larry Gould continued to be materially helpful to Carleton, as was recognized in a major report on public relations put together that fall by Vice President Charles Miel. Miel's confidential "Comments on Public Relations," inspired in part by work that a new Carleton trustee, William Benton, had previously done for the University of Chicago, stressed that Carleton's great need in the area of public relations (the ultimate objective of which was acknowledged to be money raising) was to be better known among the public at large, rather than in academic circles where her prestige was already "tops." Miel said that what the college must do is to "keep everlastingly at it," generating publicity using various media that would break down the "major sales resistance" to Carleton, which was "widespread ignorance" about it in the general public relative to some of its competitors. Miel identified President Gould as a "distinct personality" whose public profile was a tremendous asset to the college—he quoted a Minneapolis feature writer as telling him, "Anything Gould says is news; send in something any time he speaks no matter where"—but warned of the danger of dissipating Gould's efforts. Miel urged (and Bell soon strongly seconded) that the president should become more selective about speaking engagements so as to more carefully emphasize "the kinds of meetings and addresses that help the College most, providing these are adequately reported." "One commencement address in the metropolitan areas of Chicago, New York, Philadelphia or Los Angeles, properly 'exploited' in the press, would do a lot more good for Carleton," Miel observed, "than a score of small town Minnesota high school talks by the President."

The goal was to be more intentional about "capitalizing on Carleton's greatest Public Relations asset rather than letting it become too 'localized.'" Strategic targeting of Gould's appearances, Miel argued, should "not lose sight of the basic objective of money raising. Talks to foreman's groups or employees of General Mills, Minneapolis Honeywell, Minneapolis Moline, [or] Minnesota Mining as a step toward gifts from these company executives would help." Miel also saw a need to involve the president in cultivating better alumni support. "As is well known," he wrote, "Carleton alumni have not been well 'educated' to give to Carleton. They have been allowed to feel that the College can too easily progress without their help. To overcome these years of 'neglect' is not easy, but last year's experience was encouraging ..."

In the years ahead, Gould's time and public speaking would increasingly (though never entirely) be "deployed" along the lines suggested by Miel in 1949.

***

With the art building completed and the decision taken to create a student union by remodeling historic Willis Hall, the next item on the college's "bricks and mortar" agenda was the big one: a new library. (Gould wanted, as he put it in his "Five-Year Report" as Carleton president, to put up a structure that would be "a worthy physical shrine of the intellectual heart of the College.") A faculty committee chaired by Librarian Marian Adams had begun assembling ideas for the building as early as 1946, and by January 1950 the process had moved forward as far as the drafting of preliminary plans by the same architectural firm that had just designed Boliou Hall, Magney, Tusler and Setter of Minneapolis. Tentative floor layouts and an architect's drawing of a proposed exterior, for a building estimated to cost $657,000 excluding stacks and furniture, were presented to the Carleton trustees at their winter meeting. Gould's enthusiasm for the architects' modernist proposals was, however, apparently not matched by that of his board—or, at the very least, by that of the one individual trustee whose endorsement was indispensable, Laird Bell. The day after the board first viewed the early plans, Bell wrote Gould: "As you probably guessed, some of the trustees were not too favorably impressed." Expressing doubt that Carleton required so large a building and suggesting that so assertively non-traditional an appearance might fail to appeal to a major potential donor, Bell thought the plans "will bear some consideration still." The same day Gould wrote Bell:

> I do hope that you will get over your allergy to contemporary architecture. The economy of building must be a guide in thinking of any kind of structure. It would seem to me immoral to add $50,000 or $100,000 or perhaps more to a building just so it would coincide with what we consider conventional design. The outward appearance of a building should reveal the purposes served within. That is part of the characteristic of contemporary architecture. I would guess that if we tried to build the library plans into a building with all of the gingerbread of Leighton Hall, it would make the cost seventy-five per cent greater.

So began a brief contest between the geologist and the lawyer over the merits of modernist architectural style and precept. Both claimed the mantle of trying to reduce costs: Bell by questioning the building's size and ambitious scope; Gould by objecting to conventional ornamentation and "gingerbread." Bell wrote:

> I don't think the plan and elevation which you showed us are good selling documents.... I do think that something that is likely to charm a donor is necessary. Perhaps it would be a good investment to get some other and more conventional exteriors sketched out, with the idea of building the kind of library you want behind it.

At the same time, Bell expressed himself as "from Missouri" in doubting Carleton's need for a library with the volume capacity being planned or for all of what he termed "the gadgets, lounging spaces, receptions space, etc." "I mistrust

the library experts," he wrote, doubting "whether they err on the side of economy."
Gould replied that he would see what could be done about having some other
exterior options suggested, but he said "it will be interesting to compare the costs"
and suggested that Bell was not remembering the plans accurately in speaking
about excessive "gadgets" and so forth. Bell responded with a reassertion of his fear
that Gould's plan might be "so ambitious that, quite independent of its startling
appearance, it will call for so much money that it will scare off possible donors."
"You are very stern with me about modern architecture," wrote Bell. "In return I
am tempted to charge you with infatuation for it." If Carleton's needed library was
to be realized by gift, Bell observed, "it has got to be something that appeals to the
donor rather than to the Art Department, if the matter must come to that issue."

By telephone, Gould promised a truce, but he still found it necessary in
next writing Bell to record his dissent from the opinion that he was "infatu-
ated" with modern architecture. "I think one reason why people like Peg and
I are so fond of you and find you so stimulating," Gould salvoed, "is that you
are such an interesting mixture of really enlightened liberalism and, shall I say,
gross reaction." Enclosing an article by Walter Gropius preaching architectural
modernism, Gould attributed his own liking for the modern style in part to the
economic factors involved: to the principle that "economy of building should be
a guide." He acknowledged that some of what "passes for modern architecture
... is incredibly bad," but he declared that "some of it is simple and beautiful
beyond description." He acknowledged that should he find a prospective donor
willing to give Carleton a library he would ultimately grant that donor full power
to stipulate "any style of architecture short of the Bahai Temple in Evanston,"
but, he said, he should feel it his duty "to encourage him to use the minimum
amount of money on the building as such and to give most of it ... to endow the
main purposes of the library." Bell closed the exchange, just before departing
on travel to Africa, still unconvinced but offering a draw, denying that he was
"reactionary" about modern architecture as a whole and maintaining that "it's
just that modern job I am objecting to."

In the months ahead Gould would engage in further discussion with the
architects about revisioned plans—for a library building, as Carleton's treasurer
put it in a July memorandum, "of such shape and appearance as to be pleasing to
the eye of the retrogressive older Trustees." He also acceded to a request from Marian Adams to be relieved of the chairmanship of the library building committee,
naming history professor Carlton Qualey to continue that work. Meanwhile, the
difficult job of financing the building got off to what Gould called an "auspicious
beginning" when the 1950 Commencement speaker, Willard Thorp, founder of
the American studies program at Princeton, returned half of his $200 honorarium
the day after Commencement as a contribution to the fund for the new library.
This was followed by a $200 gift from Adams. Though these were only two small
drops in what would need to be a very large bucket, the task of raising funds to
realize the dream of a new college library was underway.

***

On the 18th of January, 1950, two special agents of the Federal Bureau of Investigation called on Carleton mathematics professor Ken May at his office in Goodsell Observatory. The pair, Agents Stuart and Flaata, pressed May, whose previous membership in the Communist Party, ceasing in 1942, was no secret, to provide information about a physicist he had known at the University of California. May told the agents that if he knew of any illegal activities he would inform the FBI without being asked but that otherwise he would decline to answer personal questions about individuals other than himself, explaining that misuse or misinterpretation of such statements could be, and had been, harmful to innocent people. In response to the agents mentioning the possibility that he might be subpoenaed—for what or to what body was not specified—May observed that such a situation would be quite different and that he "would of course under such conditions answer all legitimate questions truthfully and refuse to answer only if proper legal grounds existed for doing so." Reporting the contact in a memorandum to Gould the same day, May concluded, "I do not anticipate that anything more will come of this." One week after the FBI's visit to May, a federal court in New York found former US State Department official Alger Hiss guilty of perjury in having denied personal Communist affiliation and involvement in Soviet espionage. Fifteen days after that, Wisconsin first-term Senator Joseph McCarthy, who had hitherto attracted little public notice,* seized national attention by claiming in a Lincoln Day speech to Republican women in Wheeling, West Virginia, to have in his possession a long list of names of active domestic Communists—"enemies from within," he called them—who he charged were known to the Secretary of State as being members of the Communist Party but who nonetheless were "still working and shaping policy in the State Department." McCarthy followed up with additional headline-grabbing allegations (and fluctuating numbers on his purported lists) in ensuing days, beginning a run of four years during which he kept himself and the sensational issue he made his own, that of Communist subversion allegedly permeating American life, continually in or near the limelight of public affairs.

Larry Gould was appalled and disgusted from the start by what he saw as McCarthy's recklessly unsubstantiated character assassinations. Decidedly anti-Communist though he was himself, he early concluded that the poisonous atmosphere of fear and distrust fomented by the less than scrupulous demagoguery of McCarthy and those who supported him did more damage to the fabric of American civic life than anything wrought by domestic Communists or "Communist sympathizers." Personal friendship with some of McCarthy's first targets—and personal awareness of the baselessness of the mix of accusation, insinuation, and innuendo with which these friends' reputations were smeared—undoubtedly contributed to the quickness with which Gould was alert to the loathsomeness

---

* He had, however, recently stood out in a negative way by topping a senate press corps poll as "the worst U.S. senator" then in office.

and dangers of "McCarthyism."

In response to McCarthy's original allegations about the State Department, the Senate Committee on Foreign Relations established a subcommittee, chaired by Maryland Senator Millard Tydings, a Democrat, to investigate. During the Tydings Committee hearings that opened in March, McCarthy finally made public charges impugning the loyalty of nine specific American individuals, only some of whom still, or had ever, worked at the State Department. Though little evidence was brought forward to support McCarthy's accusations and the Tydings Committee majority report eventually termed his charges "a fraud and a hoax" perpetrated on the Senate and the country, those who had been tarred by McCarthy all suffered, to varying degrees, from the experience. Two of the nine citizens individually attacked by McCarthy before the Tydings Committee were persons well known to Gould. One served with him as a national senator of Phi Beta Kappa; another was his former student at Carleton.

Judge Dorothy Kenyon, Gould's fellow Phi Beta Kappa senator, was a feminist and liberal activist, a US representative for the United Nations Commission on the Status of Women, and since 1930 a national board member of the American Civil Liberties Union. On the opening day of the Tydings Committee hearings, March 8, Senator McCarthy publicly labeled her a Communist and implied that she was of suspect loyalty for having been involved with numerous Communist-front organizations.

Not one to be cowed, Kenyon responded forcefully. "He's a lowdown worm," she pronounced, "and although it ought to be beneath my dignity to answer him, I'm mad enough to say that he's a liar and he can go to hell." Promptly arranging to appear herself before the subcommittee, Kenyon testified that while she certainly had lent her name to a multiplicity of liberal and anti-fascist organizations over the years, she had in no wise ever been a supporter, much less a member, of the Communist Party. McCarthy, she charged back, was "a coward to take shelter in the cloak of Congressional immunity."

As a relatively prominent figure whose reputation in academic, legal, and political circles was impeccable, Dorothy Kenyon was in an advantageous position relative to most subsequent McCarthy targets: She was promptly defended by Eleanor Roosevelt and received the editorial support of the *New York Times*. McCarthy then claimed to have little interest in pursuing her case. Although Kenyon's aggressive self-defense and unabashed condemnation of McCarthy and his tactics resulted in her formal vindication, the times were such that simply having had her loyalty questioned made her "controversial," and in fact she never received another political appointment.

Another of the nine Americans publicly besmirched before the Tydings Committee by Senator McCarthy was thirty-seven-year-old State Department official Haldore Hanson, who had made a name for himself in the late 1930s as an Associated Press journalist in China. Before that Hanson, a Norwegian-American Eagle Scout from northern Minnesota, had been an especially outstanding student at Carleton College, a Phi Beta Kappa graduate of the Class of 1934 whose scholarship and intelligence had brought him a number of college awards. In 1933, he had been an A student in Gould's "Geography of North America" class and had stayed in touch with Gould over subsequent years. Hanson's wife Berni, who had also been a very top student at Carleton (though taking no course with Gould), had also gone to China for a time, in her case to teach English in the "Carleton-in-China" school located in the north China city of Fenyang.

In 1950, Haldore Hanson was working in Washington as assistant director of the State Department's Asian development program. He and Berni were also trying to make a go of running a small cattle farm in rural Virginia. On the 13th of March, Hanson was abruptly pulled out of a meeting at work and was dumbfounded by being told that Senator McCarthy, in testimony that day before the Tydings Committee, had named him as one of the cases which would substantiate the senator's charge that there were Communists making policy in the State Department. McCarthy had characterized Hanson as having "pro-Communist proclivities" and as a man with "a mission to communize the world." His "evidence" in support of these statements was to quote, selectively and out of context, passages from Hanson's 1939 book on China's conflict with Japan, *Humane Endeavour*, purporting to show that Hanson was therein promoting the Chinese Communist cause. Hanson never returned to his meeting, spending the rest of that day, and practically all of the next, addressing a barrage of questions posed by reporters of the radio and press.

In his own subsequent statement before the Tydings Committee, on March 28, Hanson described the "groundswell of hate" he had experienced in the two weeks since his picture had "suddenly appeared in the newspapers under the caption 'Red in State Department.'" Following the initial shock, he said, he had acquired "a false feeling of optimism" from the letters and telegrams he received from friends reassuring him that the accusations were ridiculous and from the many editorialists, columnists, and commentators willing to state that Senator McCarthy had not proved his case. "I thought," he told the subcommittee, "that by the end of the week it would be forgotten, hoping that reasonable people who read the newspapers would know the charges were not true." Instead, new shocks were coming. Returning to his small Virginia farming community, a neighbor told him of having been visited the day before by several other neighbors exclaiming over the revelation that they had had a "Russian spy" living incognito amongst them all these years! Another neighbor, who Hanson had employed to feed his cattle through the winter, told him that in Leesburg, the county seat, he had been asked by a number of persons whether he intended to keep on working for "that Communist." Meanwhile, Berni got word of a petition being circulated in the community to drive them out, calling the family "undesirable." Some days later Hanson learned that at an agricultural committee meeting in Leesburg a state official from Richmond, who so far as he knew had never heard of him until McCarthy made his charges, had felt impelled to publicly denounce the "growing number of Communists in government" and had named Hanson as one of them. "I learned one thing from these experiences," Hanson would tell the subcommittee. "To many loyal Americans, who have read the assertions about Communists still in the Government, any American whose name appears in the newspapers charged with being a Communist is guilty until proved innocent."

Haldore Hanson

Gould was among those who wrote supportively to Hanson in advance of his appearance before the Tydings Committee, and he visited the Hansons during an East Coast trip immediately after, in early April. For his part, before testifying Hanson considered asking Gould to send the committee a character reference on his behalf but then decided as a matter of tactics to send no testimonials, noting that when another of those accused by McCarthy, Columbia Law professor Philip Jessup, had provided letters from Dwight Eisenhower and George C. Marshall, the prevailing response had been "So what? Alger Hiss has had better references than that."

The statement that Hanson did make to the committee at the end of March Gould praised as "masterly," adding that he hoped everyone who had given any serious thought to McCarthy's charges would read it. Hanson began his testimony by noting that the word "Communist" had become "the nastiest word in the American vocabulary," standing effectively for sneak, thief, liar, and traitor. "It makes no difference," he said, "whether you qualify the word and say a man is pro-Communist, or has an affinity for Communism," or, as McCarthy had said of Hanson, has "pro-Communist proclivities." In every case what is conveyed by such labeling is that he is the "dirtiest, lowest type of man." Hanson told the committee that he deeply resented the attack upon his loyalty, stating under oath that he was not a Communist, had never been a Communist, had "never belonged to an organization cited by the Attorney General as being a Communist-front organization," had "never knowingly associated with an espionage agent of a foreign power," had "never advocated the Communist form of government any way, at any time, for any people," and had "never committed any act which was disloyal to the United States." He challenged Senator McCarthy to "say directly what he has insinuated" and to do so without the shield of his Congressional immunity. He asserted that "the kind of public denunciation, labeling, and hate-mongering with which we are now dealing is alien to the traditions of the United States," bearing instead close resemblance to the Stalinist purges of another political system. After refuting specific allegations to the best of his ability, pointing out many ways in which McCarthy had misrepresented his writings or twisted facts about him, and after detailing the personal impact of McCarthy's accusations upon him in his community, Hanson concluded:

I am a loyal American and I believe that I am entitled to have the Committee say so. I deeply appreciate its attention. But the corrective action of this Committee cannot attain the same headlines, reach the same people, or fully counteract the suspicions and hatreds which Senator McCarthy's charges have unleashed. Congressional immunity may protect him from lawsuit, but it will not save him from moral accountability.

Despite subsequent closed-session testimony in April from ex-Communist-turned-paid-FBI-informer Louis Budenz that he knew "from official reports" that Haldore Hanson was a member of the Communist Party, testimony not corroborated by any other person, Hanson's name would eventually be cleared, not only by the Senate subcommittee but also by two loyalty review boards. His State Department service, however, would come to an end in 1953.

McCarthy pressed on with the issue he had found to be a political gusher, suggesting that the Democrats' failure to root out subversives in government amounted to treason. Gould was heartened in June when a number of his fellow Republicans were willing to object to McCarthy's "irresponsible sensationalism" and "vilification for selfish political gain." Maine Senator Margaret Chase Smith's "Declaration of Conscience," delivered on the Senate floor June 1, protested that, Republican though she was, she did "not want to see the Republican Party ride to political victory on the Four Horsemen of Calumny—fear, ignorance, bigotry, and smear." Gould was pleased that among the six Republican senators who joined in Smith's declaration was Minnesota Senator Ed Thye, the Northfielder and former state governor whose election to the Senate Gould had supported publicly with a radio talk in 1946.

***

Budget and personnel were the college matters claiming the lion's share of Gould's attention in the first months of 1950. With regard to the latter, in addition to the customary smattering of faculty hiring there was a ticklish changeover to be managed in the college chaplaincy—the termination of one appointment followed by securing the return of the man's predecessor, Phil Phenix, who Gould rather aggressively snatched from the jaws of a competing appointment at Vassar. Gould also began what would be a long and ultimately unsuccessful attempt to secure a favorable result on a visa application for a German national, Curt Friese, to stay in the country and continue to teach German at Carleton as a prospective permanent member of the department. For this Gould enlisted the aid of his friend in Washington, Senator Thye.

As to the college budget, financial pangs were such that in April Gould still needed to find $60,000 by the end of June to finish the year in the black. More consequentially, the decision to reduce enrollment closer to pre-war levels, with its negative impact on tuition income, had left the college facing greater than usual projected budgetary deficits. Although reductions in departmental allocations for the year ahead had been mandated and although Gould hoped for certain savings from implementing the recommendations of a spring consultant survey aimed at improving operating efficiencies and reducing operating costs, he was compelled to inform the faculty in May that there could be no general increases in salary for 1950-51. The following week Gould was heartened to receive a supportive communication from three senior professors recognizing the financial difficulties accompanying the decision intentionally to decrease enrollment. "It seems to us," the professors wrote, "that this is the most important decision for Carleton's future the College

Marking the fifth anniversary of Gould's selection as president of Carleton, Gould Day 1950

has had to face since we have been here, and we want you to know that we are whole-heartedly in favor of the proposed admissions policy." Declaring that to take in more income-producing students at a cost to admissions standards would be "defeat"—that to sacrifice standards to the budget is the way of the average college rather than the way of the distinguished one—the professors expressed willingness to share in financial sacrifice. "Almost everything Carleton has gained during your administration," the professors wrote,

> —its higher standards, its enormously improved Faculty, its intellectual liveliness and creativity, its greatly improved standing in the college world—depends on the quality of its student body. It seems certain to us that these painfully earned gains—how painfully earned only you, who have done most to earn them for the College, can fully know—will quickly be lost unless we commit ourselves now, when the shoe really pinches, to paying for the maintenance of our admissions standards.

Gould responded with thanks, saying that all that he was attempting to do at Carleton was predicated upon the assumption that if they built a high quality institution, the needed support would follow. "There is no alternative for me if I am to be president of the kind of institution of which I can be fiercely proud."

A gala dinner celebrating the fifth anniversary of Gould's selection as Carleton president took place in April in the Main Ballroom of the University of Minnesota's Coffman Memorial Union—and it was by this time abundantly evident that

Gould's Carleton was indeed a college in which he could take pride. In 1950 the dean of Yale College, William Clyde DeVane, in an article titled "Our Competition," listed Carleton with Amherst, Williams, Bowdoin, Dartmouth, Oberlin, Wesleyan, Swarthmore, and Haverford as the "distinguished small colleges" which constituted a "lively crop of rivals," in addition to the eleven leading universities with which Yale was annually competing for the best students.

In Chicago in May, Gould delivered an address at the annual convention of the Millers National Federation which was subsequently printed as a twelve-page pamphlet posing the title question "Are We Ashamed of the Things that Have Made Us Great?" Expanding upon some of the themes of his Minnesota Historical Society talk of the previous October, in this widely circulated address Gould said that the predicament of modern man was that he has become "a prisoner of the industrial collective society which his technology has produced. He is at the mercy of the social institutions he has created, and it seems as if these institutions are deliberately intent on crushing the individual." Gould said that while modern science and technology have provided unprecedented control of power, unprecedented material creativity, and unprecedented release from drudgery, these were "power without reverence," "creativity without an attendant sense of responsibility," and "freedom without restraint." The total result, as he articulated his diagnosis, "has conspired to make ours an age of violence, of force, of power—an age of unreason." Noting that trying to oppose change as such was wrongheaded, for change was both unstoppable and necessary to growth, Gould declared that "our greatest hope lies in directing or canalizing change in harmony with the values that underlie our western civilization. This we shall not do by being ashamed of those institutions which have preserved and nourished these values for us."

He then focused on four such institutions, which, though "they may appear prosaic," yet once were "surrounded by a glamour they deserved and which I would have us, in part at least, recapture." These were: this country's political system, which was "designed to make government our servant and not our master;" its economic system, "about which we do not need to be continually on the defensive;" its educational system, for which he emphasized the importance of "the existence of many competing voices," warning of the hazard of a "common mold" that would be the result should private independent institutions disappear; and finally, its heritage of faith, broadly conceived, of which he feared that we had become "if not most ashamed, most neglectful." Gould dreaded the result if, with a decline in religious faith, Americans as a society were to embrace the notion that there is no absolute distinction between right and wrong, no moral law:

> Nothing in the world makes a more profound difference to everything a man thinks or does than his attitude at this point. If he believes that there are no truths that are eternally right, then he believes he lives in a world with only such values as he himself gives to it. The

irresponsibility and lawlessness that can stem from this attitude are hardly to be exaggerated. On the other hand, if he does believe that certain things are eternally right and certain things are eternally wrong, then he believes that there is in the universe round about him a perfection to which he can aspire, a voice to which he can answer, and a love to which he can respond.

What is needed in order to prevail over the chaos of our time, Gould urged, is a return to "the sources from which our strength comes." The problem as he saw it was that "we have cut ourselves off from the sources from which our civilized traditions spring and upon which our institutions are founded." These sources he identified for Western civilization as essentially embodied in but two traditions, the classical heritage of Greece and the Hebrew-Christian heritage of Palestine. "We don't need a lot of new 'isms' of any sort," he concluded. "We need a return to those principles that have blessed us in the past. We need to renew our faith in the ideals of our youth from which our strength came when we were a young and growing nation."

***

The school year ended on the 11th of June, with the largest graduating class in Carleton's history to that time assembling under clear skies on the "Bald Spot" greenery* north of Skinner Chapel for Carleton's first-ever Commencement exercises held out of doors. One of the highlights of the ceremony was the surprise awarding of an honorary degree to retiring Carleton astronomer Edward Fath. Writing the following month to Fath's daughter, Gould related that he should "never forget the expression on your father's face" as it began to dawn upon him that the citation then being read was for him. It was a happy occasion.

Less happily, fourteen days into the college summer and half a world away masses of North Korean armored columns rolled across the border into South Korea—an aggression that would, among other more serious international repercussions, quickly require that most of Gould's short-term Carleton plans and budget projections be reassessed in light of new uncertainties. With the U.S. joining a United Nations coalition to support South Korea and President Truman calling on Congress in July to support a massive military effort, the question loomed: What would be the effect upon the male student enrollment or, if reserve officers were to be called into service, upon the ranks of the college faculty? Writing in July to former colleague Leonard Wilson, Gould acknowl-

---

* The June 1950 issue of *The Voice of the Carleton Alumni* informed its readers that this lawn space "previously (and lovingly) known as 'The Bald Spot' ... has now (and henceforth shall be) itself graduated to the more dignified title of 'The Commons.'" Language usage decrees, however, do not necessarily make things so. Six decades later, Carleton's central green remains (lovingly—and exclusively) known to all as "The Bald Spot."

edged that he and his trustees were at that moment somewhat bewildered and uncertain as to just what they should do; for the present they were "following the old Army game of doing nothing." "We go ahead," he wrote, with the "assumption that the Korean situation is a local one and will not spread into a world-wide conflagration." But he worried over the dark prospect that "it may be but one of many such events around the fringes of communism that will last over a period of years." Nonetheless, it was summer, and he was in need of his annual August rest and relaxation in Wyoming. Gould declared that he and Peg were preparing to depart July 27 with the expectation that they would "listen to no radio, no telephone, and read no newspapers for a month. There will be plenty of problems when the month is over."

In fact, trouble would not wait even so long as that. Carleton's ex-Communist mathematician Ken May had been overoptimistic in January when, after being questioned by FBI agents concerning a physicist he had known at Berkeley, he advised Gould that he did not expect anything further to come of the matter. Instead, he found himself called to Washington August 1, compelled by subpoena to give testimony before a federal grand jury considering whether or not to bring perjury charges against the man in question, Joseph W. Weinberg, now employed at the University of Minnesota, who was under suspicion of having passed classified atomic information from the University of California radiation laboratory to a Communist agent in 1943. The matter stemmed from 1948 testimony before the House Committee on Un-American Activities, which had initially kept secret the identity of the suspect physicist, giving him for public reference the anonymous designation "Scientist X." In 1949 the House committee had revealed that Weinberg was their "Scientist X" and recommended that he be prosecuted for perjury for having twice under oath denied Communist affiliation.

May's confidential grand jury testimony took two hours on Tuesday the 1st; Weinberg was then grilled for an hour and a quarter on Thursday. Although May himself was being accused of no illegalities, the simple fact of his being called to give testimony in a case connected with alleged Communist espionage resulted in newspaper headlines that he and Carleton College administrators would have preferred to avoid. "Teacher at Carleton Named as Former Red" ran one—front page, centered, with photograph—on Friday in the *Minneapolis Tribune*. It was a maddening lead, giving the impression that something which was not news and had never been concealed had just been sensationally uncovered. The same day the report in the *St. Paul Dispatch* headlined "Dr. May, Ex-Red Called in Sift, To Keep Carleton Teaching Job"—as if there had as yet been any contrary question.

With Gould vacationing in the Tetons with the hope of not reading newspapers, all statements called for from the college were left for the time being to Vice President Miel and Publicity Director Carolyn Pettet. May, before leaving for Washington (and then on to another month of personal visits and professional conferencing in the East), had left Miel with a short written statement, in case there were inquiries, to the effect that all of his connections with the Communist

Party had ceased in December 1942 with the beginning of his military service; that Carleton College and President Gould had been fully informed regarding his youthful past politics prior to hiring him; and that since August 1946 all of his time had been devoted to teaching and related research. "I have taken very little part in any political activities," the statement read, "and none at all in any which might be considered Communist even by the most careless." A week after testifying before the grand jury, May wrote Miel and Pettet that he "would rather be in continuous front line action for a year than go thru the last few days again" but that he was recovering with the aid of his wife and "nights under the stars" and that he had written Gould a long confidential report.

Gould's senior secretary Sally Crandall sent along to the president in Wyoming a copy of the *Minneapolis Tribune* article on May, about which Gould, thinking that it "gave quite a distorted picture," immediately complained to *Tribune* publisher John Cowles. A week after that, writing Charlie Miel that he hoped the Ken May problem was not plaguing him too much in the president's absence, Gould expressed sympathy for the "very difficult time" May had had in Washington, where he feared that the FBI and related agencies might be "looking for victories rather than the truth." "I will do what I can," he vowed, "to save this man from being crucified in a red witch hunt." (Gould wistfully concluded this letter to Miel from Wyoming by noting that his mother's funeral was that day—she had passed away four days before in a Michigan convalescent home—and that he should have been home with his sisters, but it had not been possible.)

Meanwhile, a certain amount of defensive thinking was going on at Carleton concerning the public relations aspect of the Ken May affair. In March, Miel had written a letter on May's behalf to the chief industrial engineer for the Ford Motor Company's St. Paul plant, who was a Carleton alumnus, making an introduction by letter to see whether May might not be able do some relevant temporary work at the Ford plant that summer in applied statistics. The day the "Teacher at Carleton Named as Former Red" article appeared, this alumnus sent Miel a curt note with clipping attached, demanding "an explanation of why you were interested in getting this chap in to the Ford Plant." A few days later another Carleton alumnus, a former trustee of the college, wrote Gould that he found it most unfortunate that "a man who was an active Communist on his own statement for a period of from six to ten years, and who … was discharged from former employment by the University of California and disowned by his own father" could have been "hired at Carleton with knowledge of these affiliations and activities." This critic was forthright in his opinion that "no man who has been an active Communist should be given a place on the faculty of any educational institution. … He should earn his living in some way where he does not instruct young people in the formative years of their lives." The writer asked for information as to whether there were any other faculty at Carleton who had in times past been Communists and for a decision as to what would "be done about this particular man." "The responsibility resting upon you and the trustees in a matter of such vital importance," he concluded, "cannot be overstated."

Responses to these letters were drafted carefully by Miel, following consultations in Minnesota with half a dozen of the Carleton trustees, Carolyn Pettet, Frank Kille, and Sally Crandall—with drafts then sent on to Gould in Wyoming, including one of a possible reply from Gould himself. Miel was concerned that the two letters received doubtless "represent an attitude which some other friends of the College are bound to have" and thought that "rather than try to dissuade them from their stand, we should go as far as we can to explain the situation." It was decided that the college would release no further statement on the matter at that time but that it would be in a stronger position to ward off future bad publicity if May would prepare for his file a signed statement further clarifying his present position, not only by declaring that he had severed his connection with the American Communist Party but by positively expressing strong opposition to Russian Communism. In words that were in turn communicated to May, Gould told Miel that he saw no reason why May should not be willing to make such a statement and that May needed to "understand the urgency" of the request. "He owes it to us to do this in a forthright manner," Gould indirectly directed. "Indeed he must do so else we have no basis for keeping and defending him."

May readily agreed to prepare such a clarifying statement for possible future use, taking pains to ensure that what he crafted be dignified and clear-cut—not open to misinterpretation—as well as honest and well-considered—"not a mere product of the present hysteria." Preferring to put his name to a positive affirmation of his present beliefs rather than to a mere disavowal, May hoped that such a statement would suffice to "settle the matter" and allow him to "get back to work." He stipulated in advance that he had no interest in entering into a debate on his current political beliefs and that he would "not become a professional anti-communist denouncer."

By late September, May had written his statement, highly autobiographical, in the form of a four-page letter to Gould. Ascribing his pre-war interest in communism, which he stressed arose from attitudes quite common among "the lively students" of his generation, to idealistic impulses coupled with "the urgency of the international situation" of the late 1930s, May asserted that his interest at that time was neither an abandonment of patriotism nor of the ethical principles with which he had been raised. He wrote that he had always remained "a loyal American," more willing than most to sacrifice personal interests to those of his country. "If I made mistakes," he insisted, "they were made in good faith." Even while professing himself a Communist, he said, he had "always believed in the best of our Christian and democratic heritage" and had "never knowing done anything disloyal" to family, friends, or country. Though focused more on explanation than renunciation, the statement was judged sufficiently useful to the college's public relations requirements concerning May that it was provided, in condensed form, to a number of newspapers when May next returned to public attention by being called in to appear at a late December hearing of the House Un-American Activities Committee, followed by a second appearance before a reopened grand jury investigation of the Weinberg case. In the interim, Gould's confidence in May's ongoing value as a member in good standing of the Carleton faculty had been demonstrated in November when Gould named him chairman of the newly combined Department of Mathematics and Astronomy beginning with 1951-52.

That fall, when pressed by a man who might be in a position to direct major foundation support toward Carleton for an accounting of this business of Communists on the Carleton faculty—the head of said foundation having expressed a disinclination to give to Carleton because of the presence and retention of Ken May on the faculty—Gould was able to state that not only were there no Communists on his staff and that none would be tolerated but that he knew Ken May's former adherence to Communism's avowed ends to have stemmed from misguided idealism. "Some few weeks ago," Gould related to his correspondent, Charles L. Horn, a trustee of the Olin Foundation, he had told May that

> if I ever discovered the slightest suggestion of any Communist indoctrination with his students or fellow faculty members, I would ask for his resignation. He laughed with complete frankness and assured me that he would expect that and would gladly give it. He is no more a Communist than you or I. On the contrary, because of his fine integrity, his friendly personality, and his genuine devotion to the basic ideas that underlie our institutions, he has probably done more to validate American ideals than the vociferous adherents of the good old times.

Carleton, Gould reminded Horn, had been founded by the Congregationalists and "still clings to the idea of being a Christian college." "The very basic thesis of Christianity," he maintained, "is that there can be no such thing in life as sinning without repentance and possibly salvation."

> Must we except youthful membership in the Communist Party as the one unforgivable sin? How shall we cure the world of Communism? Must we kill them all off? Must we isolate them and send them to the wilds of Siberia, as it were? I think one of the most stupid mistakes that could be made is the preventing of repentant people from getting out of the Communist Party. ...
>
> It is a tragic comment on our loss of faith in the dignity of the human being that the presence of this splendid young man on our staff should in any way jeopardize the welfare of this College. What would you do in my place, Charles Horn? How can I turn my back on a man with such an impeccable record as this young man has made with us? I should scarcely be able to abide my own soul if I did so.

***

As war gripped Korea and a major US military draft seemed increasingly probable, concern arose at Carleton and in similarly situated colleges over schools' ability to maintain the desired level of male enrollment. By the opening of the 1950-51 academic year, it was being suggested that Carleton might be well advised to depart from previous practice by securing a Reserve Officers' Training Corps (ROTC) unit associated with some branch of the armed services, so that Carls could get on-campus military training—or face losing young men to schools that could offer ROTC. Gould advised the Carleton professoriate of the likelihood that the college would apply for an ROTC program at a mid-September faculty meeting held a few days after the dramatic surprise landing of UN forces in Korea on the beaches at Inchon. In October the Board of Trustees officially directed Gould to explore this course of action and authorized him to install an approved ROTC unit "if he thinks it necessary and proper."

Whether he *would* see this step as necessary and proper seemed up in the air for a time. To a Quaker member of the faculty who questioned the wisdom of bringing ROTC to campus Gould wrote that

> Even now, young men who are applying to Carleton College for next year ask what facilities we shall have which will enable them to fulfill their military requirements here. Ripon College, Coe College, Knox College— all have R.O.T.C.'s. Young men are not going to enroll at Carleton College unless we are prepared to furnish such opportunities for them. We cannot run the College without filling the men's dormitories. We are confronted with a practical question and not a theoretical one at all.

But to his presidential counterpart at Lawrence College, Nathan Pusey, he wrote that he was "a little troubled" by the trustees' directive to aggressively pursue application for the ROTC unit because he was not sure that it would accomplish the desired end of keeping up male enrollment, and he queried whether they were also feeling confronted at Lawrence with the necessity of making such a decision. (Pusey replied that they were not, at least as yet, taking that course at Lawrence but were for the present maintaining their traditional reluctance to mix military training with liberal education. "It has been a long-standing prejudice of mine," Pusey added, "that in a small college the presence of an R.O.T.C. unit was an indication of an inferior institution, and I find it hard to give up this view.")

In any case, Gould did spend a considerable amount of time and effort over ensuing months in pursuing for Carleton an ROTC unit in one or another branch of the military. All efforts and applications, whether with the Army, the Navy, or the Air Force, were ultimately unsuccessful, occasioning much frustration at the time. Gould was particularly maddened—he termed it "a kick in the teeth"—when news came in April that Carleton had not been selected for one of sixty-two new Air Force ROTC units but that neighboring St. Olaf College *had* been. Writing immediately to Senator Hubert Humphrey in puzzlement and dismay, he noted: "Am not reflecting on St. Olaf but Carleton has facilities for housing and feeding more men and furthermore owns an airfield." Professing himself unable to understand any possible basis for such a decision and noting that the Air Force officer who had inspected the college following its application had given Carleton his highest rating, he even wondered, in a postscript present on his draft, but ultimately not sent to Humphrey, whether it was possible that the committee making the decision had settled on "Northfield" but had gotten its records mixed and accidentally selected the wrong college! Ultimately, an explanation arrived from the Secretary of the Air Force pointing to St. Olaf's larger male enrollment and greater desire to have a *permanent* ROTC program, whereas a poll (requested by the Air Force in connection with the application) of Carleton students and faculty had shown overwhelming support for ROTC only on a temporary basis during the time of national emergency. Efforts continued to some extent to establish an ROTC option for Carleton men until the summer of 1953, at which time Gould closed the file on the issue by stopping the application process for an Army unit, admitting that, with the trend of the times by then, there was no longer sufficient interest in the faculty, the students, or the trustees to continue to pursue the matter.

During the balance of the 1950-51 academic year, however, Carleton's president and trustees were placed in a state of great uncertainty by repercussions of the war situation, including the effects of spiraling inflation and concern over what might happen in the area of Selective Service. Estimates that in the fall the college might have 30 to 40 percent fewer men enrolled were considered conservative. In December, with the situation in Korea worsening after China's entry into the conflict, the Carleton trustees directed Gould to consider reducing the size of the faculty for 1951-52 by 5 to 10 percent, a course of action that seemed prudent, though painful to carry out. Soon Gould was speaking of the necessity of cutting faculty numbers even more, perhaps by as much as 30 percent, and he was compelled to alert faculty that those not tenured nor under contract for multiple years ought not to be surprised if it developed that they could not remain. "This is a dreadful task," he wrote one correspondent, "and one which I do not contemplate with anything but great regret. However we have no alternative."

In January, the trustees agreed to postponement of the planned renovation of Willis Hall into a Memorial Student Union, due to the Korean War by-products of "increased construction costs, scarcity of materials, and probable prohibition of this type of construction."

Budgeting that winter for a 1951-52 enrollment possibly dipping as low as only 750 students, Gould spoke with some discouragement early in 1951 about how so many of the dreams dreamt and progress actually made for the preceding half dozen years had now stopped in their tracks, likening the situation to the Red Queen's telling Alice about it taking all the running you could do just to keep in the same place. As it transpired, the pessimistic numerical projections of the winter of 1951 did not come to pass, and Carleton's fall enrollment the next year was in fact a healthy 890 students. But before that happy result was reached or in view Larry Gould had to endure many anxious months.

Also depressing to Gould's spirits at this time was the degree to which the demagoguery of Joe McCarthy and his unsavory allies then seemed to be riding high. In November elections, Republicans had gained thirty seats in the House of Representatives, and in every contest in which McCarthy had involved himself—including the defeat of Maryland's Senator Tydings and Illinois' Senator Lucas, prominent McCarthy critics—he had triumphed, increasing his personal power and influence within the Republican party. On the dangers he clearly saw in ascendant "McCarthyism," Gould spoke out forcefully. At a convocation address at Wisconsin's Ripon College, where in January he accepted his fourth honorary degree, Gould warned that

> never in our history has the climate of public opinion been so anti-intellectual and so authoritarian as it is now. ...
>
> Nothing in our current life more sordidly illustrates the anti-intellectual character of our time than the fact that a minor politician could launch a broadside attack upon persons in positions of responsibility and thereby be catapulted into a position of notoriety and influence which in no wise is lessened when not a single one of his charges is substantiated.
>
> Socrates and every other great teacher has known the power of the well told lie. History is full of examples of those who have known that it is the quickest way to power. In our day it has reached a kind of refinement which Richard Rovere has called the theory of the multiple lie. One tells a number of lies this week and while an investigation is going on which finds that none of the charges is true, a second set of lies is released to attract attention away from the fallacies of the preceding one. Thus a demagogue can climb to power.

He continued at Ripon by quoting Harvard professor Archibald MacLeish, who had recently written that if American fears had truly reached the point where cynically unsubstantiated charges and hearsay suspicions could produce the uproars and effects that had been witnessed that year in shame and disgust, then the country was in greater danger than at any time since the Civil War and that the danger was "something far more deadly than communist armies without or communist conspiracies within, deadly as these things are." What is in danger for the Republic, Gould quoted MacLeish, "is the loss of its own soul."

He sounded similar themes in a Carleton convocation address ten days later and then again in mid-February when speaking to the Minnesota Editorial Association. On the latter occasion Gould quoted "the observation of a great statesman," for whom he admitted that he never voted, who had proclaimed in 1933 that "the only thing we have to fear is fear itself." Now, he lamented, "our fear of Communism is causing a mounting hostility to all ideas," and in our fear we were unhappily embracing many of the attributes of our enemy, who suppresses and denies freedom of speech and substitutes smear and whispered words for due process of law. "We are in danger," Gould asserted, "of letting other things flock in under the name of anti-Communism that can be almost as counter-American as Communism itself."

Gould was delighted in 1951 to find the only United States senator who was also a member of the Carleton College Board of Trustees emerging as Joseph McCarthy's most vociferous opponent on the Senate floor. William Benton had been a Carleton student during World War I before transferring to finish his degree at Yale. After turning down a Rhodes Scholarship for a job as an advertising copyrighter—horrifying his mother, who wrote him "If you won't go into a respectable profession, can't you at least be a lawyer?"—he had gone on to co-found a successful New York advertising agency with Chester Bowles, which made him rich, but from which he had resigned in 1936 "to associate himself with things on a higher plane than soap and breakfast food." He had then become vice president of the University of Chicago, and eventually chairman of the board of *Encyclopedia Britannica*, which he had caused the University of Chicago to acquire. Subsequently he had been appointed an assistant secretary of state by Truman, in which post he had begun the "Voice of America" radio broadcast program and helped to establish the United Nations Educational, Scientific, and Cultural Organization (UNESCO), which "was very much his idea." Larry Gould had first met Benton in October of 1948 when in New York to attend the inauguration of Dwight D. Eisenhower as president of Columbia, and shortly thereafter, acting on Laird Bell's suggestion, had brought him onto the Carleton board. At the end of 1949 Benton, a Democrat, was appointed by his former advertising partner Chester Bowles, who had become governor of Connecticut, to fill an unexpired term in the US Senate left vacant by resignation. In 1950, Benton had narrowly won election in his own right to complete the two years remaining in the original six-year term.

At the beginning of February 1951, Benton stood up on the Senate floor to protest the appointment of Senator McCarthy to the Senate Appropriations subcommittee responsible for overseeing the budget of the Department of State. Benton, who observed that he was the only sitting senator who had previously served as a State Department operating executive, argued that the appointment was astonishingly inappropriate given that McCarthy had "proved himself an implacable and ... irresponsible enemy of the Department concerned." He warned that McCarthy, who had publicly expressed elation over his appointment, would gain the power to become "his own kangaroo court" when sharing in "the vast and almost unlimited inquisitorial power" of this subcommittee. Over a Republican's protest that Benton was in violation of Senate rules concerning what may be imputed to a colleague, Benton charged that McCarthy's performance in the past year, which had recently expanded to include public smearing of Secretary of State Dean Acheson as "the Red Dean of Fashion," could "perhaps be summed up in the slogan: If you can't make one libel stick, try another, and then try another." Gould wrote Benton the next day: "May I tell you that I was tremendously proud of you and your speech yesterday. If we do not somehow stop the demagogues, I do not know where they will lead us."

Later that year, in August, with McCarthy now elevated to the height of his influence and power, Benton would, without cosponsors, introduce a politically quixotic resolution calling for McCarthy's expulsion from the Senate for having been guilty of a "pattern of fraud and deceit" in his indiscriminate Red-hunting campaign. In testimony before the subcommittee to which the expulsion resolution had been routed, Benton supported his charge that McCarthy was guilty of corruption, dishonesty, and gross irresponsibility by identifying a catalog of abuses. Gould told Benton that fall that he was "so pleased and proud of what you are doing." "I hope," he added, that "your plan to expose McCarthy will eventually result in his being disposed of in some way or another. If you had done nothing except oppose him, you would deserve the thanks of all of us." McCarthy's initial response to Benton's resolution took the form of an imperious sneer, dismissing its source as "Connecticut's mental midget." Benton, said McCarthy, was becoming "the hero of every Communist and crook in and out of Government."

***

Filled as it was with worries about enrollment levels, concern over college finances, and the painful need for a significant reduction of faculty, Larry Gould found much about the winter of 1950-51 decidedly gloomy. For a time, troubles seemed only to mount: Carleton trustee Atherton Bean, a close friend and confidant on the board, upon whom Gould had come to rely heavily, was hospitalized in December and forced to conclude by the end of January that his recovery would mean withdrawal from "almost all general activities" until at least June. In February another trustee, Al Lindley, was killed in a private plane crash. The same month one of Gould's first and best faculty hires, Arthur Mizener, who had just published an important biography of F. Scott Fitzgerald to much acclaim, announced regretfully that he was tendering his resignation as head of Carleton's Department of English to accept a position at Cornell University. Days later—taking Mizener's new biography with him as reading material—Gould departed for Florida on what he termed a "fishing" trip among prospective Carleton donors at their winter homes. Unfortunately, the day he arrived in Miami he developed a terrific cold which plagued him the whole trip, making him "not as fit company for [his] fellow human beings" as he would have liked.

One thing that Gould actually enjoyed about that gloomy winter, however, is that it was an exceptionally snowy one in Minnesota. He was already commenting on it by mid-January, but the largest blizzards were yet to come. By March 19, a record-breaking eighty inches had fallen, half of it in the previous eighteen days, and Gould commented in correspondence that he hadn't seen so much snow since leaving Antarctica. Being Larry Gould, he naturally found that delightful and wrote that his only regret was not having "a dog team and proper sledging equipment to negotiate the snow." (Peg Gould, on the other hand, missed the worst of the storms as she left in February to spend six weeks in New Mexico where her brother was living and where her father had entered an Albuquerque nursing home. The timing of her absence was a good thing, Larry admitted, as she would have taken such excessive snowfall as a personal affront. Once, he recalled, when he had pressed Peg over breakfast at home to acknowledge how beautiful an earlier large snowfall was, she admitted it was so, "but in a revolting sort of way." It became a regular expectation for the couple that Peg would shorten each winter for herself by getting away somewhere warm on her own for a part of it.)

By the fifth of April the season snowfall total was eighty-five inches, and Gould was reporting it "still piled high out of my office window, where I am now looking at some boys playing snowball." The record-breaking winter was also the occasion for some fun between Gould and a couple of students he found himself seated next to at the opening of a college play early in March. A bet was made, with a treating to milk shakes the stakes, as to when the snow would be gone from the ground. Gould lost. He paid his debt handsomely on a sunny afternoon early in May, picking up the students—junior Anthony Downs and sophomore Nancy Neller—in his black limousine, taking them to a drug store for strawberry milk shakes, and then for a drive around town, visiting the St. Olaf College campus, up through the Carleton Arboretum, and so forth, before delivering them back to Nancy's dormitory. Downs, who was the Carleton Student Association president at the time, wrote in thanks, "as a lesser president speaking to a greater," that the experience had "far exceeded the obligation incurred."

Despite the many difficulties with which he was confronted at Carleton in the early part of 1951, Gould was reaffirming his commitment to the institution and to his place within it. Between them, he and Laird Bell had scotched the recent suggestions of others that Gould might become president of the University of Michigan or that he succeed Hutchins at Chicago. Although given at this time to statements like February 11th's "I suppose at no time since its origin has this college faced a more uncertain future," he could follow with "on the other hand, I have never been so sure as I am now that this kind of institution must be maintained." In April he wrote to a retired professor who had urged him to take good care of his health because Carleton needed him, "whether Carleton College needs me or not may be open to question, but whether this country or world needs Carleton College is not open to question. The continuation of this kind of institution is just about the most important thing I know of." Shortly before this he had dictated (in a letter ultimately not sent) that his belief in the importance of schools such as Carleton was so strong that he was resolved to "devote the rest of my life to this institution if the trustees so will." That summer Gould would tell his former student and present Carleton geologist Eiler Henrickson, who was eyeing more lucrative personal opportunities in business and industry, that he had once been offered a salary three times greater than what he was paid at Carleton. "You have to be slightly crazy to stick to a place like this," Gould advised, "but I think it is worth it."

Gould's popularity with students was certainly running as high as ever. In

May, the campus newspaper's announcement concerning the annual approach of Larry Gould Day, marking the anniversary of the announcement that Gould had been selected as Carleton president, was headed by the reproduction of a delightful student-created caricature of Gould's head combined with a red tie-wearing penguin's body. The celebrations that year included, not for the first time, the arrival of the (very red) local Northfield fire truck to escort Gould and a score of red-clad students from the President's Office to Willis Hall for the start of festivities. Nearly the entire student body, plus the campus dog, George, turned out bedecked in their brightest reds. Evening saw the traditional student serenading in front of the Gould home.*

As late as June 7, with the academic year 1950-51 coming to a close, Gould was still operating under the bleak assumption that enrollment for the year following would likely shrink to "probably 750 or less," and he reported in his June column in the alumni magazine that "we face the prospect of several relatively lean years" deriving from the war situation, the low birthrate of the early 1930s, and the combination of reduced income and rising expenses due to inflation. Within a few days, however, the outlook for the coming year improved considerably, with news that the college had done very well with its "yield" of admitted students choosing to enroll and that consequently, barring a summer change in draft regulations, expectations for the fall were now much brighter than heretofore. "So much brighter," a relieved Gould wrote to trustee John Musser, "that I think we shall be able to maintain our integrity, our standards, and all of the other things by which we live." By mid-July, college projections were for 863 students in the fall, and the eventual actuality was higher yet—allowing Gould in the end to make some merit increases in faculty salaries, something he had desperately wanted to do. "Our year starts splendidly" would be Gould's mid-September take on the brightened situation.

---

* The Gould home, by the way, gained an additional new occupant that spring, in the form of a black poodle puppy given the Goulds by Helen and Ellwood "Goley" Newhart; the Goulds named her "Jill." In a letter to the Newharts written on May 16, Larry Gould Day at Carleton, Gould reported that Jill "grows rapidly in intelligence and understanding, and captivates everyone who meets her." Though still very small, she had "already almost completely reorganized our household." Jill would be an important member of the Gould family for the rest of its time in Northfield, and beyond.

CHAPTER 18

I LIKE IKE

The Goulds spent nearly six weeks of the summer of 1951 at their accustomed vacation spot in the Tetons. Returning to Minnesota in early September, Gould reported to Laird Bell that he had done a great deal of fishing and, now that he was back at Carleton, was "going fishing again right away"—by which he meant angling for money, as he would be spending the upcoming weekend attempting to slip a hook into a businessman donor prospect. A few years earlier he had critiqued this aspect of his presidential performance to Bell by confessing that he had not yet learned the art of effective appeal or how to translate goodwill toward the college into dollars and cents—but by 1951 this was a realm in which experience had improved him. He was gratified that week to receive the first of what he hoped to be a series of gifts to Carleton from the richly endowed Olin Foundation. Cultivation of the Olin Foundation was and for some while would continue to be for Larry Gould a lengthy, delicate, and sometimes very trying process. Trying, because, as Gould had been told when the foundation had first been brought to his attention in 1949, the key person to be cultivated to secure an Olin gift, Charles L. Horn, was "a very opinionated, blunt man, who likes to express his own ideas and who likes to be flattered." Horn enjoyed making a college president sit up and beg and maybe run through a varied repertoire of tricks before tossing him any of the juicy scraps at his disposal. Horn, Gould was warned from the start, would resent any attempt to approach him below the level of the president himself. Keeping Charlie Horn happy, when Charlie Horn wished to make Gould dance for him—which meant repeatedly having to return small rudenesses with smiles and politeness—would be one of Gould's particular crosses to bear across the span of a decade.

Gould had laid out for Horn the college's principal needs in the spring of 1950: endowment to eliminate or reduce the annual deficit needing to be made up between income and operating costs; the raising of professorial salaries and retirement benefits; and the physical need for a new library building. In 1951, following Horn's recommendation as to what might be agreeable to the foundation, he requested a grant of $100,000 to be spread over three academic years, and this resulted in $35,000 being confirmed early in September, which Gould directed toward "some long overdue upward adjustments" in faculty salaries. (Soon after, however, Horn was indicating to a Carleton trustee that whatever he may have advised Gould to request, Carleton could not expect annual contributions from the Olin Foundation, which "would probably give to other schools next year." When Gould eventually wrote to request continuation with a like amount for the year following, Horn replied that Gould should not have inferred that a donation would be made each of three years, but rather that the $35,000 given the year before "would have to be used over a three-year period." Though it had been Horn who had given Gould the impression that Carleton might hope for $100,000 over three years, Gould was compelled to apologize for any impression that he was being presumptuous, express regrets for a possible misunderstanding, and good-humoredly restart the cultivation for substantial future gifts.)

A noteworthy undertaking at Carleton in the fall of 1951 was bringing an outside observer to campus in November to survey and evaluate the college's religious program, out of which Gould hoped there might come recommendations for breathing new vitality into and making "more effective" the school's loose but important historical relations with Minnesota's Congregationalist, Episcopalian, and Baptist denominations. The observer, Professor Seymour A. Smith, executive director of the National Council on Religion in Higher Education, was in the middle of his week in residence at Carleton when Gould was involved in a frightening "close call" on the highway that, at greater velocity, might have shortened the length of this biography by about a third.

Gould had spoken on "The Crisis in Education" at the Mt. Zion Temple Men's Club's annual Humanitarian Award dinner in St. Paul, and he and Peg were returning home in their Buick when they collided head on with a Jeep station wagon driving entirely on the wrong side of the road, fortunately at low enough speeds at point of collision that the worst injuries were to the cars rather than to people. Peg fractured a finger, and Larry came away with no worse than a pair of black eyes and several days' absence from work, though he would also be troubled for some months by recurring headaches. He claimed that since not infrequently in his job he felt as though he'd been run over by two or three automobiles, "the actual experience probably did less harm than might otherwise have been the case."

The aftereffects of Gould's accident slowed him down to some real extent that winter; late in February he was reporting that the results of the November accident "still cause me to tire more readily than I should." He used the slowdown, however, to do some carpentry—building a desk for a small room at home—and to get in some good reading. While he was incapacitated in the days immediately after the accident, the recommendations of both his wife and his board chairman got him started on the novels of Anthony Trollope, upon which by early January he had become so thoroughly hooked* that the "demoralizing result" (for which he asserted that Peg and Mr. Bell were responsible) was self-reproach for allegedly neglecting other things.

***

People frequently imagined alternative careers for Larry Gould. In that winter of 1951-52 Gould confided to a friend that he had been offered a job by one of the top men in the Central Intelligence Agency; he was advised that any time he wanted to come to Washington he "could walk into a number of good opportunities." From time to time he was urged to consider running for political office. In the latter half of 1951 it was suggested to him on at least two occasions that he become a candidate for governor of Minnesota. Though surely he was flattered, the possibility did not seriously interest him.

In February of 1952 Gould received an extraordinary letter from a former Carleton instructor in physics and astronomy, Andrew J. Galambos. Galambos, who was then a doctoral candidate in the Physics Department of New York University but who in later years would go on to be a stimulating if eccentric figure on the margins of intellectual libertarianism, thought that Larry Gould ought to succeed Harry Truman as the next president of the United States. In this letter (nine pages, typewritten) he explained why he thought this both desirable and realistic—having "a non-zero probability of success," as he wrote. Galambos thought that the perilous times called out not for merely a tolerable president but for "an outstanding one, a man who can rise to the occasion as Lincoln did when he saved the Union." (He found it appropriate that he was writing this letter on Lincoln's birthday.) "If liberty is to survive," postulated Galambos, "we shall need a man of the utmost intelligence, ability, and character. This brings me to you."

To Galambos it was clear that Gould's qualifications on these counts outshone by far those of any of the more conventional candidates for the presidency:

> You, sir, are an explorer among other things. You know how to go into uncharted seas and lands. You are not afraid of the unknown. You have a wonderful mind. You are honest to the core. You have administrative ability. You have a wonderful personality and know how to influence people and make them both like you and your ways of thinking. Besides the ordinary brand of honesty which most people have, you also have that rare commodity: integrity and a highly refined sense of morality and ethics. (This would be a welcome restoration to our government,

---

* The prolific abundance of Trollope novels—there are forty-seven of them—may have been welcome to Gould, given his remark in a letter to his sister-in-law three years earlier concerning another favorite author, Jane Austen, that he wished she had written eighty books: "I have read and reread her [six] novels so frequently that I can almost repeat them now, and when I get in a condition where I need a Jane Austen novel I am reluctant to pick one up. ... Somewhere I've got to find some equally satisfying source of relief." Jean had just gifted Gould with a volume of Austen juvenilia, which he called "sheer delight."

I might add.) You are a scientist and as such you know how to think logically. You have the affection of most of the people who know you. In short, you possess the qualifications that a man needs in order to make an outstanding president.

Galambos went on to paint a picture of Gould doing what he could to make himself better known nationally in the months leading up to the political nominating conventions and then becoming the Republican presidential nominee in a Wendell Willkie-like scenario, as a dark horse independent emerging out of a Taft-Eisenhower convention deadlock. Capturing the nomination was the difficulty, thought Gould's would-be kingmaker; Galambos had no doubt that, if nominated, Gould would then sweep the country in a general election, as his evident virtues would attract nearly all of the independent vote that held the balance of power.

Gould had happened, just a few weeks earlier, to read a friend's copy of Frank Scully's then-popular *Beyond the Flying Saucers*, about an alleged government cover-up of extraterrestrial "saucer" crashes in the American Southwest. He returned it with a pronouncement that it was "a fascinating book but seems to me to belong still in the realm of science fiction." He might have said much the same—arrestingly interesting but too far-fetched for belief—about Galambos's political fantasy. Politely, he replied to Galambos that he was "deeply touched" by the letter, the high compliment of which he wanted to be sure to bring to the attention of his wife (then away visiting her brother in New Mexico) but that he had by that point enthusiastically pledged himself to the candidacy of General Eisenhower. "I have a deep feeling that Eisenhower will be the man," he wrote, "and I think it best that we all concentrate our efforts in that direction."

Gould would get more actively involved in the national election of 1952 than in any other before or after. Although allegiance to the Republican Party was a family inheritance dating back at least as far as the bestowing of his middle name, within the party Gould was a relative liberal, identifying with the progressive, internationalist wing of the GOP and largely out of sympathy with the conservative brand of Republicanism epitomized by Senator Robert Taft. He had aligned himself with the World Federalist movement and the ideal of peace through world government. He was understood, in the late 1940s, to be a "Stassen Republican," and indeed in 1947 he had told a Carleton trustee that "if Stassen is not elected President, I shall be one of the most disappointed of all his admirers." Within Minnesota he had given radio talks in support of the 1946 Senatorial campaign of Governor Ed Thye and of the 1950 reelection effort of Governor Luther Youngdahl, both Republican "moderates." In September of 1950 he rejoiced to his friend John Cowles, who had that year become a trustee of the Ford Foundation, over the announcement that the new head of the foundation was to be Paul Hoffman, the former president of Studebaker and more recently administrator of the Marshall Plan, who Gould termed one of his "favorite Americans" and "my first choice for the next President of the United States."

Hoffman, despite Gould's admiration, was not widely identified as a possible 1952 candidate. Among those who were, Gould was affirming as late as September 1951 that "Harold [Stassen] is still my man." When the Twin Cities Carleton Club sponsored a meeting that month with the Republican frontrunner, Senator Taft, he attended (though disagreeing "violently" with the senator "in certain fundamental areas"). He admitted afterward that Taft's presentation and forthright responses to questions had raised his opinion of him but that he nonetheless did not think Taft could muster broad enough support among independents to defeat Truman if the president were again to be the Democratic nominee. And "we must beat Mr. Truman," he added. "To do that I think we must get someone with the stature of Paul Hoffman or General Eisenhower."

Eisenhower's stature, it was generally acknowledged, was then unique in American life, the military hero (who had left the presidency of Columbia University for duties in Europe as supreme commander of the North Atlantic Treaty Organization) enjoying popularity and respect across the political spectrum. As a potential political candidate, he was pure gold. The difficulty, for a time, was that nobody was quite sure what Eisenhower's politics were; he had been courted seriously by both major parties. (Illinois Senator Paul Douglas, a Democrat, proposed that Eisenhower carry the standard for both parties in the 1952 election, essentially entering the White House by acclamation.) Early in January 1952, however, Eisenhower disclosed Republican alignment. At the same time, while saying that he would not campaign for the Republican presidential nomination—that under no circumstances would he ask for relief from his military assignment in Europe to become an active candidate, nor would he "participate in the pre-convention activities of others" who might seek the nomination on his behalf—he did signal that he would accept that nomination if it were offered to him, as "a clear-cut call to political duty." An "Eisenhower boom" immediately followed among those Republicans not in ideological accord with the archconservative Taft. In Minnesota, which was scheduled to hold in March the nation's second presidential primary, seven days after New Hampshire's, Larry Gould was a part of that boom.

Gould liked Eisenhower's internationalist outlook and felt confident that as president he would have both the will and the power to cleanse the party of the stain of McCarthyism. (Taft, on the other hand, when asked about McCarthy, would only say that in his view Joe was "doing a great job.") Gould saw Eisenhower as a likely winner in November, if he could only be nominated by a party whose stalwarts were suspicious of the general's newfound and therefore possibly somewhat nominal party allegiance, whereas Gould saw Taft—known as Mr. Republican, but just the reverse of Eisenhower in being more popular with party regulars than with the broader public—as anchored too far to the right to have the appeal to independents necessary for electability.

Paul Hoffman, Gould's fantasy first choice for president, came out strongly for "Ike," and in February he asked Gould to become a member of the national advisory committee of Citizens for Eisenhower. Gould agreed to put his own name on an Eisenhower slate for the Minnesota primary, hoping to be elected as a delegate to the July Republican National Convention in Chicago. However, a couple of weeks in advance of the primary the entire Eisenhower slate was ruled off the ballot by a State Supreme Court finding that the petitions by which Eisenhower's supporters had hoped to enter him onto the primary ballot had not conformed to legal requirements. "I have lost my chance to be a delegate from Minnesota to the National Convention," Gould lamented in correspondence of March 10. "Harold Stassen had asked me earlier to be on his slate, and I declined because I told him Eisenhower was my man."

Taft had already declined to enter the Minnesota primary, and after Eisenhower was removed by court action the official Republican ballot would contain the names of just two candidates: de facto "favorite son" Stassen and Edward C. Slettedahl, a St. Paul school teacher running as a stand-in for General Douglas MacArthur. Stassen, it was assumed, would receive the vast majority of the votes of those who bothered to come to the polls with neither of the two principal contenders for the nomination listed. All of which would have made the 1952 Minnesota primary a matter of very little interest. But then, things changed.

In New Hampshire on March 11 Eisenhower's appeal was powerfully demonstrated when he—in Europe and not campaigning on his own behalf—received 50 percent of the vote (to Taft's 39 percent) as a write-in candidate. Elated Eisenhower supporters in Minnesota, headed by a political amateur, Bradshaw Mintener, the vice president and general counsel of Pillsbury Mills, then asked the state's attorney general (J. A. A. Burnquist, a Carleton College graduate of 1902) to rule on whether write-in votes would be included in the Minnesota primary tabulation. On March 14, a Friday, the answer came back that they would. Over the next few days before the Tuesday primary Mintener directed a whirlwind campaign to inform Eisenhower supporters in the state that there would be a write-in effort. This was a challenging task for the small Eisenhower organization, headquartered in a dingy Minneapolis storeroom where two of the three telephones had been disconnected to save on the bill. Volunteers each agreed to call five friends, urging each of them to call five more, about writing-in the general's name on election day. On the eve of the primary—the first held in Minnesota since 1916—Mintener estimated that only $600 had been spent on the write-in campaign and said that he would be "thrilled" if Ike received ten to fifteen thousand votes. The results were electric—what *Time* magazine termed "The Minnesota Explosion." On a slushy day of snow and drizzle that would normally make for light turnout nearly three hundred thousand Minnesota Republicans went to the polls, and 108,692 of them (37 percent) wrote in Eisenhower's name. (Election judges were lenient about spelling, taking many variations from Eisonhauer to Izenour to Ike as evidence of intent.) Though Stassen "won" the primary, with 44 percent, media coverage focused on the astonishing write-in totals for Eisenhower, the *New York Times* calling it a "political miracle" and "something unique in American political history." In Europe, Eisenhower reevaluated his position on resigning his NATO command, deciding that the popular groundswells in New Hampshire and Minnesota had amounted to a "clear call" for him to return home in advance of the convention and take more active steps toward securing the nomination.

Gould was thrilled by the surprising result and impact of the Minnesota primary, but he was not actually present in the state to witness it firsthand, having departed on March 14 for his biennial tour of Carleton alumni groups on the West Coast and in the Southwest. On the 18th, Primary Day, he was in Seattle, speaking to alumni gathered at the Olympic Hotel on "The College and You." He did not return to Northfield until three weeks later, finishing the trip with Peg, who had been visiting her brother in New Mexico* and was picked up when the alumni clubs tour reached Albuquerque.

At the end of March the nature of the broader presidential race in 1952 shifted abruptly with Truman's announcement that he would not be a candidate for reelection. In April, a month in which six more primaries were split evenly between Taft and Eisenhower (the former winning in the Midwest and the latter in the East), Gould made a friendly ten-dollar bet with Carleton trustee Howell Murray, a Taft supporter, as to which man would ultimately be nominated. In May, as Minnesota's state Republican convention approached, Gould told Murray that despite the way the "Stassen people" got the Eisenhower slate off the ballot in March it appeared there was still a chance he could find himself attending the national convention as a delegate or as an alternate. "I would certainly like to see one of these so-called smoke filled rooms," he said. A few days later, at the state convention, Gould was duly elected an alternate delegate to the Republican National Convention in July, which, as the contest between Eisenhower and Taft was looking more and more as though it still might not be resolved in advance, promised to be an intensely interesting experience.

**

Parallel to politics, other business in these months continued for Gould to run in its natural courses. He was appointed a member of the Committee on Scientific Personnel in Education for the emerging National Science Foundation (NSF). Observing that this group was "setting the pattern and policy for the granting of fellowships and many other benefits" that would come from the NSF program, he stated that of all the assignments that had ever previously taken him to Washington this one was of the "greatest potential importance."

At Carleton, Larry and Peg instituted during the spring semester of 1952 a practice of having dinner most Thursday evenings with small groups of senior students. Gould oversaw initiation of a five-year (three at Carleton followed by two elsewhere) joint program of engineering studies in cooperation with both the Massachusetts Institute

---

*   Peg's visit extended over several weeks, as was becoming her annual custom. "Somehow," Gould wrote a friend, "since this bachelor brother moved to New Mexico the Minnesota winters seem to get worse and worse for my good wife."

of Technology and the Columbia University School of Engineering. The president combined travels with faculty hiring. An early January interview in Washington resulted in appointment of a new college librarian, Jay Richards. A March interview in San Francisco, followed in April by several in New York, led to the hiring of Robert Adamson for psychology and education, Albert Elsen for art, Elvan Kintner for English, and Jean Calloway for mathematics. A quick trip to Chicago in May yielded William Butler for physics. Early in June he met on campus with a candidate to head the program in physical education for women, Eleanor Hansen, hiring her the same day. (As Hansen would later recall, Gould told her that her salary as an assistant professor would be $3,500. Hansen, who had not expected to be offered a position on the spot, bravely decided to try to negotiate: "$3,550!" she countered. Gould, as Hansen remembered it, looked at her silently for a moment, then laughed. "How about $3,600?" he said. "We don't deal in $50s.")

Fundraising marched on, successful in small ways but with the major commitments that would be needed to realize the library project proving elusive. After Gould wrote in some discouragement early in February, Laird Bell counseled patience:

> I don't think you should be depressed. Substantial amounts of money are not to be had for the asking. I am sure that it takes a long build-up in the creation of a genuine interest on the part of potential donors. A man must really have a fervent interest in the school and, I suspect, the same desire to perpetuate his memory as the Pharaohs of Egypt had before he is likely to let go of millions. You have been eminently successful, although at considerable agony, in getting current gifts and should not be discouraged about the possibility of larger ones. I am afraid that there is no way to get the larger ones except to ask for them bluntly, but I am quite sure that that can't be done successfully until some years of cultivation have created the proper atmosphere.

Patience was also required with regard to the ongoing cultivation of Charlie Horn of the Olin Foundation, who questioned the extent to which the college president seemed to be involving himself in partisan politics. Gould tried to reassure him in May: "I have never dabbled in politics until lately. Even now, not very deeply." But in September, following Gould's request for a continuation of the previous year's support granted Carleton, Horn erupted with a heated "blast over the telephone" to a Carleton trustee, who reported to Gould having been told that "Larry Gould's political activities make it impossible for him to contribute any money" from the Olin Foundation to Carleton. Gould told the trustee that this was nothing new from Horn, adding that he thought he had never been "treated more rudely by anyone" than he had by Charlie Horn. "If the College didn't need money so desperately, I would tell him to go to a more tropical climate." However, offered Gould, periodic blasts of this sort were "only symptomatic of his way of doing things. If he is serious about it, he will tell me."

In the meantime, Gould suggested, this might as a matter of fact be a good area in which Horn could safely "blow off steam."

An extra difficulty for Gould during the first part of 1952 was presented by the effective absence for much of the semester of his "right hand, so to speak," Dean of the College Frank Kille, who was hospitalized with internal hemorrhaging caused by a very bad ulcer. "This comes at a time when I have needed him most," Gould reported glumly, "and of course, it means that my own load will be nearly doubled for the rest of the year."

Kille recovered well, but Gould was shocked in March by the sudden death of Dr. Dana Coman, his former companion from the Byrd Expedition, who was within a year of his own age, and who Gould had just seen "in rare spirits and looking forward to [a] trip to the Arctic" at a January dinner at Norman Vaughan's house that had reunited them with the three "boys from Harvard" who had sledged with Gould in 1929. Additional reunions with a number of expedition mates Gould had not seen for a long time were occasioned by Coman's funeral.

Another of his closest friends from Antarctic days, Colonel Bernt Balchen, came to Northfield that spring to deliver an evening lecture at St. Olaf College, for which Gould provided the introduction. Balchen stayed two nights at the Gould home and was delighted when he was introduced to a prospective student of Norwegian descent who happened to be touring the Carleton campus that day and who was thrilled and dumbfounded to find himself unexpectedly meeting the famous Colonel Balchen, a family hero who he had been hearing about all his life. "Why," the young man exclaimed, "I was named for Bernt Balchen! My middle name is Bernt." Gould relayed the story to Balchen's wife Bess with great pleasure.

***

Certainly the standout personal experience of the summer of 1952 for Larry Gould was attending the Republican National Convention in Chicago as a Minnesota alternate delegate. While Gould hoped to see his man Eisenhower nominated, he feared in the days leading up to the July 7 convention opening that the prospects for this were none too bright. The primary season had concluded inconclusively, with Senator Taft overall winning six contests and General Eisenhower five. They had rarely entered the same state primaries to compete head to head. Taft had outpolled Eisenhower altogether in primary voting and, as a party insider who had entered the race much earlier, had had a large head start in lining up delegates outside the primary process. Taft supporters appeared to be largely in control of the national committee, which could provide a big edge in a close struggle. The committee had arranged for the convention keynote address to be delivered by General MacArthur, whose ideological alignment was with Taft. "The situation looks a little bit too much pro-Taft at the present time," Gould wrote a friend in mid-June, and a week later he confessed to Laird Bell that he felt "greatly depressed at the hold the Taft forces seem to have on the situation." He expressed some optimism that if Taft were not nominated on the first ballot, Eisenhower's chances would then be very good, as there would be movement towards Eisenhower as the surer winner in November. Gould had, for his part, become so ardently anti-Taft by this point that, despite feeling that the country was "desperately in need of a change" after five consecutive Democratic administrations, he had gone so far as to state publicly that if Taft were to be nominated by the Republicans and the Democrats chose Adlai Stevenson he should, for the first time in his life, become a Democrat. Writing Senator Benton the week before leaving for Chicago he told him "If you Democrats are smart enough to nominate Stevenson, you certainly ought to lick Taft." He also told Benton, whose almost solitary* fight against Joseph McCarthy continued in the Senate, that he was "desolated" to find that McCarthy had been invited to give a highlighted speech at the convention.

Gould left for Chicago on the 6th, staying during the convention at the University Club. Over the ensuing five days he was witness to an historic convention exceptional for tension and emotion as well as for bitterness of feeling. Eisenhower's managers mounted a challenge contesting the selection of certain pro-Taft delegates in Southern states, notably Texas and Georgia, claiming irregularities and illegalities that had amounted to delegate stealing. "Charge and countercharge flew back and forth." The Eisenhower camp demanded that "Fair Play" required that a number of the contested pro-Taft delegates be expelled and replaced with delegates that were pro-Eisenhower. At a hectic first session, the Eisenhower group won a critical victory when the convention approved a motion that disallowed those whose own seating was being challenged from voting on the credentials of others. Ultimately, the convention's 658-548 vote to adopt the "Fair Play" proposal was decisive in denying Taft the nomination, but the bitterness of the division within the convention hall was evident to all viewers when at one point Senator Everett Dirksen of Illinois, a Taft supporter, pointed with contempt from the podium to New York Governor Thomas Dewey, the GOP standard-bearer in 1944 and 1948 and a leader of the pro-Eisenhower group, and bellowed, amid a mix of boos and cheers, "We followed you before, and you took us down the path to defeat!"

The contested Taft delegates having been replaced, balloting for the nomination began the morning of the fifth day. It was slow, accommodating repeated requests for the polling of individual delegations. When the first ballot result was announced, Eisenhower had surpassed Taft's 500 votes with 595 of his own, nine short of the number needed to nominate. At this point, Gould's Minnesota delegation came to the fore. In accordance with its primary results, Minnesota had cast nine votes for Eisenhower and nineteen for Stassen. Stassen now asked

---

* Gould had recently written a friend that he thought it "positively disgraceful" that almost no one within the Senate had been willing to rise to Benton's support. The reason, he supposed, was that, as "such an unscrupulous demagogue," McCarthy "will shamelessly do anything to destroy those who oppose him."

to address the convention. He announced that all nineteen of the Minnesota delegates who had cast first ballot votes for him were now switching their votes to Eisenhower—making him the nominee. Minnesota's switch was followed by a tidal wave of other vote-changing, such that the official final tally summed to 845 delegates who "liked Ike."

With this result, Gould was elated. He was less happy when, at the suggestion of Governor Dewey, the convention chose freshman California Senator Richard Nixon, a fierce young anti-Communist with a reputation as a slashingly nasty campaigner, as Eisenhower's running mate. Gould was not an admirer of that half of the ticket, but it certainly would not cause him to back off from supporting Eisenhower in the general election. In correspondence from the days following, Gould dubbed the experience of having attended "illuminating … to say the least," but he expressed no interest in soon being present for another. "In spite of all the foolishness, steam-roller tactics, etc.," he wrote one friend, "I came away with the impression that the will of the delegates had made itself felt. The nomination of General Eisenhower actually was the result of a moral protest against the high-handed tactics that were attempted before and during the Convention by the Taft machine." He termed what had happened in Chicago no less than "a revolution in the Republican Party the like of which has never taken place before"—though Teddy Roosevelt had attempted it in 1912 and others had tried since. He looked forward to November, he said, "with no little enthusiasm," feeling that at long last his party had nominated a candidate who could rescue the party of Lincoln from political oblivion.

***

Progressing naturally from politics to money … By far the greatest focus for Gould's presidential energies during the next two years at Carleton was his ongoing campaign for funds for a new library. Though both the need and the desire was great and architectural planning had proceeded to an enticing degree of detail, it remained an open question when, if ever, the dream could be turned into reality. In the spring of 1951 Vice President Miel had worried in a confidential memo to Gould that the library project, which had seen a 75 percent increase in cost estimate in the space of a year, might be "pricing itself out of practical accomplishment." "I realize fully," Miel had written, "that a library as the 'heart' of the College is the most important building … but because of its cost it is likely to be one of the hardest to attain." Gould fretted similarly that week in a note to Library Building Committee Chairman Carlton Qualey:

> I like the plans enormously, but I am depressed at the prospective cost. We have no responsibility, of course, for the shriveling value of the dollar due to inflation, but perhaps the plans for the kind of library we need have priced it out of all probability for the near future. I shall, however, go ahead with the architects to secure the kind of presentation material I can use with prospective donors. One never knows but that lightning will strike and our dreams will come true.

Qualey agreed that the present plans fit Carleton's needs so well that they deserved a chance to be laid before the eyes of prospective donors, hoping that they might capture the imagination of "one or two of our wealthy friends," convincing them "to immortalize themselves on this campus."

In mid-1952 the drive to realize the library dream received a magnificent kick start from a familiar friend. Shortly before Gould's departure for the Republican National Convention the president received an eye-opening letter from his board chairman, Laird Bell. "I want," Bell began, "to share with Carleton some of my unearned increment, derived mostly from the foresight of my father and grandfather, whose interest in Carleton you know." Saying that he did not want to build monuments ("there's too much Laird and Bell on the campus now anyway") but that he wished to help with Carleton's greatest need, the library, Bell observed that funds for maintaining the building would be just as necessary as the building itself and proposed that his contribution lie there. Bell thought that although the cost of the building had grown to an amount beyond what a single donor could be expected to give, it seemed possible "that several substantial donors might be found to give enough to reach the necessary total if there were some way to get the project off the ground." He proposed to contribute "an amount for maintenance proportionate to what you can raise from any source for the building"—more specifically, "a teaser consisting of a contribution toward maintenance at the rate of 1,000 shares of Weyerhaeuser stock for each $100,000 contributed to the building" within a reasonable time limit and to a maximum of $1.5 million. (Given the 1952 value of Weyerhaeuser stock this amounted to an offer to match for the library maintenance endowment fund approximately 70 percent of all other contributions toward the library up to the $1.5 million cap.)

Gould shared early news about the gift and its officially anonymous source with a select few, including the college librarian, Jay Richards, and trustees Atherton Bean and Howell Murray. (Murray thought it "the greatest thing that has happened in your administration.") On July 16 he confidentially informed the trustees' Executive Committee, telling its members that he would "substantially limit his program of activities" for the next academic year so that the raising of the million and a half could take precedence over all else in the allocation of his time. Writing to Bell later the same day, he said "I don't think I exaggerate when I say that my spine is still tingling from the enthusiastic response on the part of the trustees there present to your wonderful proposal." He was departing in two days on his annual Wyoming vacation but would immediately consider how to proceed when he returned from the West. He reiterated for Bell what he had told the Executive Committee, that from here on he would avoid other undertakings to the extent possible so as to devote full energy and attention to the library building. When Bell formalized his proposal two months later, he made it "subject to the condition that the total amount raised … within two years from this date shall be at least $1,500,000." Accordingly, the imperative of securing a million and a half for the library by mid-September of 1954 became for Gould a goal that, for the next twenty-four months or until the threshold was reached, would overshadow all others.

***

1952 was the sixth straight summer that the Goulds spent some weeks in
the Tetons, always returning to a cabin at the Square G ranch, where Carleton
friends Alfred and Helen Hyslop were also again in residence. (Alfred Hyslop was
a Scotsman who had begun teaching art at Carleton in 1923 and now chaired the
department. Helen, a Carleton graduate of 1922, had, on and off, been employed
by the school as an instructor of French. They had begun coming to Square G
at least as early as 1940.) The place was in part a retreat from the world, where
Larry deliberately tried to avoid news. That summer he put away his portable radio
once the Democratic Convention nominating Adlai Stevenson was over. He went
there to relax, though his Wyoming relaxations* often had a strenuous quality. As
years passed, he climbed mountains somewhat less and fished somewhat more.
In 1952, he reported, he spent nearly all of his summer vacation time fishing for
trout, claiming that he was getting better at outsmarting them. (He also endorsed
what he claimed to be the "Moslem point of view about fishing," which he said
was that when a child was born, its span of life was completely determined and
could not be altered—except that time taken off for fishing did not count against
one's allotted span. "If this holds for me," he wrote a friend, "then the more time
I spend fishing, the longer I shall live. It is a convenient philosophy anyhow for
one who likes to fish as well as I do.")

Summer was followed as ever by the start of a new school year, and for Carleton there was a welcome repeat of the pattern whereby pessimistic estimates of
reduced enrollment, upon which spring budgeting had been based, turned by
September into robustly healthy actual registration. The failure of repeated attempts to bring a deferment-granting military unit (ROTC) to Carleton seemed
to have had no significant ill-effect on male enrollment after all.

The dormitories opened to returning students on September 16, and most
made a point of being back in time for that day's special late-morning event, the
appearance of General Eisenhower at a giant campaign rally at Carleton's Laird
Stadium. Eisenhower's speech, unique during that campaign season in being
addressed to a college audience, had originated with an invitation the previous
spring from then-junior Clifford Stiles, the student head of the Carleton Republican Club, who had suggested to the general that if he were nominated he
should give one speech specifically to youth. The result was an exhilarating rally
that filled Laird Stadium to capacity for the first time ever. In addition to those

---

* At home his chief relaxations were reading and gardening, with occasional matches of, he said,
  "very bad tennis." (He characterized himself as "one of the world's worst tennis players but one
  of its most enthusiastic ones. John Cowles when speaking at Carleton referred to Gould as "the
  second worst tennis player in Minnesota," adding a bit later that he himself was the very worst.)
  Gould did not play golf—he told one person who challenged him to a game at this time that,
  "strange to say," he had at age fifty-five never been on a golf links in his life. "Never having even
  taken a crack at a golf ball," he mused, "there is a possibility that I may be a brilliant golfer!
  This is a possibility which I wish to cherish."

Eisenhower's visit drew more than 10,000 to Laird Stadium, including scores of journalists.

from Carleton and St. Olaf, buses or caravans brought in students from at least thirteen other Minnesota colleges and the state university. A colorful throng that also included Republican-minded non-student citizens of Northfield and nearby communities crowded into the stadium in advance of Eisenhower's arrival, moving through an array of booths selling refreshments as well as Eisenhower buttons, ties, banners, and hats. Inside they were entertained by high school bands, the Northfield Men's chorus, three trumpeters from St. Olaf, and cheerleaders from Carleton and Macalester, who led the crowd in an "I Like Ike" cheer.

Gould, along with St. Olaf President Clemens Granskou, met Eisenhower's special eighteen-car train at the Northfield station, presented Eisenhower's wife, Mamie, with a flower bouquet, and escorted the general and his party to the stadium in a bright red convertible. The Eisenhowers and various dignitaries in attendance made their way to a seating dais set up on the football field, fronted by a microphone-lined podium from which Eisenhower's speech and the entire occasion was broadcast on live radio as well as kinescoped for later viewing on CBS-TV. Gould, acting as master of ceremonies, introduced Minnesota Senator Thye, who in turn introduced the candidate. In words that must have been sweet music to Gould's ears, Eisenhower in his address praised the role played by America's small colleges in preserving "the values that have made our country great and which in turn we must apply if we are going to lead the world toward peace, security and prosperity."

John Cowles, who had thought that Eisenhower's campaign was being potentially harmed by the belligerency with which Eisenhower foreign-policy advisor John Foster Dulles had been talking about an American obligation to "liberate" Soviet satellite countries, suggested to Gould in advance of Eisenhower's Northfield visit that, if he had a chance to talk privately with the candidate, he urge him to ask Dulles to "soft-pedal that line of talk." Gould in fact had "no opportunity ... to talk to Ike about things serious," but he did report that he had "lodged the idea about John Foster Dulles with one of his men," from which he expected it would reach Eisenhower's ear. He did apparently have enough of a talk with the general to feel certain that Eisenhower had also developed a deep loathing for Joe McCarthy and to expect that, in the White House, Ike would be sure to "pull the carpet out from under" McCarthy just as soon as he could do so without making a political martyr out of him.

Seven weeks lay between Eisenhower's Laird Stadium appearance and Election Day. At Carleton during those weeks work was begun on the physical remodeling of old Willis Hall into a new student union. The Board of Trustees met on campus for two days in mid-October, and during the afternoon session of the first day Gould read to the full board the text of a letter from the anonymous "friend of the College" (who was in fact not only in the room but chairing the meeting) formally stating the conditions for matching contributions toward library construction for the purpose of establishing an endowment fund to maintain the planned building. The board that Friday officially accepted the offer and its conditions, committing to "wholeheartedly cooperate" with Gould in the now imperative task of securing a million and a half for the library within less than two years.

One-sixth of that total came Gould's way before the weekend was out. On Saturday afternoon following adjournment of the board's late morning meeting Gould, accompanied by his wife and trustees Bell and Murray, drove to Minneapolis for tea with seventy-seven-year-old Trustee Emerita Carolyn McKnight Christian, who had retired from service on the Carleton board two years before but who remained a steady friend to the college. Gould had hoped for her attendance at the meeting in Northfield and was disappointed that she had not come. When the pleasant tea was over and the group was about to depart, Christian called Gould back into the room. In order to get the campaign for a library building "off the ground," she informed her friend, she had decided to make a gift of $250,000. Climaxing a long history of giving by this benefactress, this was, as Gould told readers of the next issue of the alumni magazine, one of the largest single gifts the college had ever received. Gould's drive home from Minneapolis that day must have felt wonderful; though the car was earthbound, his presidential spirits had been given cause to soar.

Gould's spirits were elevated as well by the results of the national balloting on November 4. At Carleton a poll of students and faculty had shown strong preference on campus, about 77 percent, for Eisenhower, and unlike 1948—indeed, for the first time with regard to presidential elections since 1928—this time there was agreement between Carleton and country. In neighboring Wisconsin the "unscrupulous demagogue" had won reelection, but Gould expressed himself as "heartened by the fact that McCarthy ran well behind his party" in that state. He wrote Laird Bell the day after the election that had Bell's candidate (Stevenson) been elected, subsequent attacks on McCarthy by Democrats would have continued to rally Republicans to McCarthy's support but that "if his own Republican Party pulls the carpet out from under him, we shall dispose of McCarthyism." "I predict," he told Bell, "that General Eisenhower will wring that man's political neck."

Election Day results did, however, disappoint Gould in one significant case, which was the defeat in Connecticut of McCarthy's Democratic antagonist, Carleton trustee and Gould friend William Benton. Gould wrote Benton:

> Though I am a Republican, as you know, I had deeply hoped that I might be able to send you, of all people, a telegram of congratulations. I hope you know that here in this college of which you are a trustee there is a group of people deeply devoted to what you represent. Whether you have been aware of it or not, there are many here who have been holding your hand, as it were, in your fight against McCarthyism.

Gould suggested to Benton, as he had to Bell, that, though it might sound contradictory, the election of Eisenhower over Stevenson would actually be for the best in furthering the destruction of McCarthy's political power.

Shortly after the election Gould flew to Montreal to attend a meeting of the Board of Governors of the Arctic Institute of North America, which body he had recently agreed to rejoin after a few years absence. December travels took him to New York, Princeton (for the Phi Beta Kappa annual meeting), and Washington, followed by Chicago where, in addition to speaking at a University of Chicago convocation, he and Peg were given the opportunity at a gathering at the Bells' home to meet Judge and Mrs. Learned Hand, as well as Bell's favored candidate in the recent election, Adlai Stevenson. "I can understand your enthusiasm for him," Gould wrote Bell at year's end.

During this time period ongoing interactions with Charlie Horn of the Olin Foundation continued to be typically difficult. Horn approved a check to Carleton for $10,000, which, while welcome enough in itself, was not a renewal of the $35,000 given the year before, which Gould had originally been led to hope for annually over a three-year period. After meeting with Horn in mid-November, Gould concluded that he needed to recast the nature of his Olin requests. To Miel he memorandized:

> I am convinced, as the result of my difficult conference with Mr. Horn day before yesterday, that the Olin Foundation, at least, is primarily impressed by pretentious presentations.
>
> I have no idea why Mr. Horn has hitherto given me the distinct impression that the Olin Foundation was much more concerned to help keep colleges going than it was to help them expand. In my contacts with him I have, therefore, emphasized our need for gifts to balance the budget. Now his position has completely reversed itself, and this is one area in which the Foundation seems to have little desire to help. Rather, they are concerned with buildings, and apparently every building is to bear the name Olin. By the time they get through, there will be Olin buildings on a number of campuses. There ought to be one here.
>
> Somehow I have the feeling that if we can get around Mr. Horn and discover how to handle him, here may be one of the chief sources of help in our expanding physical program.

Changing direction, in early December Gould wrote Horn that he had hitherto "dwelt unduly" on requests for current support because he "had the mistaken assumption that that was the area in which the Olin Foundation wished to help colleges like Carleton" but that he now hoped to give Horn better understanding of the wider range of the college's aspirations and marks of quality. Horn's immediate response was to inquire as to whether Ken May was still employed at Carleton, despite having admitted having Communist connections:

> The Olin Foundation is being investigated by the Cox Committee of the House of Representatives as to whether we are contributing funds to colleges which employ Communists. I would like to know if Professor May is to continue with your college. He has been named

as a participating individual in the Communist party and a soliciting individual. You cannot tell me, regardless of how young he was, that with his brilliant mind, he did not know what he was doing.

Gould had no intention of retreating from his position that so long as May's Communist affiliation or sympathies were confined to his pre-Carleton past forgiveness and second chances should be possible and that he should not be debarred from belonging to the Carleton community. Indeed, May had been promoted that year to full professor. Gould replied to Horn, much as he had already done two years before, that if May had continued to have Communist "leanings" he would not have a place on the Carleton faculty, but that "any implication or assertion that Dr. May has in any way whatsoever participated in or had any connection with the Communist Party since he left it in 1942 is completely misleading and entirely untrue." May's service to Carleton had been "superb," Gould stated, and he "could not possibly with clear conscience ask him to leave the College in the light of the record he has made with us." "You will tell me frankly," Gould wrote, "whether you think I have any other honorable course except the one I am following." To this no further response has been found.

***

On New Year's Day, 1953, William Herbert Hobbs, who had given Gould his start both in geology and in polar exploration, died in Ann Arbor at age eighty-eight. Gould's memorial tribute to his mentor was published a year later in the *Geological Society of America Proceedings for 1953*.

A few days into the new year Gould was off to Los Angeles to attend meetings of the Association of American Colleges and to dine with an individual being courted as one having the ability to complete the library campaign at a stroke, if only he would. (He wouldn't.) Later in the month, on the day that Eisenhower was inaugurated as president, Gould was in Chicago, giving an evening talk to an alumni group dining at the Normandy House. Less than two weeks after that he was in Illinois again, this time delivering a sermon* at the Winnetka Congregational Church on the subject "Does It Matter What We Believe?" (His

---

* It is unclear whether or not Peg accompanied him on this occasion, though in December Gould wrote Laird Bell, who was arranging the invitation to Gould to preach, that he hoped that he would be able to break down her resistance by assuring her that she need not actually go to church. Peg's stance toward organized religion was generally hostile, while Larry's was quite otherwise. When home in Northfield his attendance was regular at both the Carleton chapel and the Episcopalian church to which he belonged—though asserting that denominational ties hung "very lightly" on his shoulders. "I think religion is like democracy to the extent that it needs many voices," he had told a student early in his presidency. In January 1953 Gould stated one aspect of "what Christianity means to me" as follows: "It seems to me that while man belongs to the changing world of events, even more so does he belong to an eternal world of the spirit. I believe that man's destiny is essentially personal and that the fulfillment of personality, though it necessarily involves fellowship with other persons, can not be equated with social evolution."

answer: It does.) For the rest of February he stayed put in Minnesota—though Peg did not, departing on the 13th for another extended winter visit with her brother in warm New Mexico.

Two items of note pertaining to the first part of 1953 involved books. A study by two Wesleyan University professors, Robert Knapp and Joseph Greenbaum, published early in the year by the University of Chicago Press and previewed in the January issue of *Mademoiselle* magazine, identified Carleton—along with Antioch, Swarthmore, Reed, Oberlin, and the University of Chicago—as one of the six top coeducational colleges in the recent production of scholars going on to earn doctorates in all three academic areas of science, social science, and the humanities. The study, which focused its attention only on the years since World War II, coincident with Gould's presidency, proved useful to Carleton in highlighting the school's increasingly distinctive quality. Gould made certain to bring it to the attention of potential college donors; he wrote personally and promptly about it to Charles Horn. The other bookish development was that Gould learned early in February that his own book *Cold* was being dropped from Harcourt, Brace & Company's active catalog. He wrote to the publisher: "I have just learned that that immortal volume *Cold* is out of print and there will be no more copies available. You have no idea of the tragic implications of that situation for me. I shall now have to write another book in order to have some convenient item to give to people." The Harcourt, Brace president replied that, though the book had ceased to be profitable, he personally hated to see it go. "Even now," he wrote, "we would consider reprinting it if we had the plates, but unfortunately during wartime the government made us melt them." The irony, that melted plates should be the fate of a book titled "Cold," was not lost.

That winter also saw the intermittently problematic "issue" of Ken May's Communist past and Carleton future again become a concern demanding presidential attention. Notwithstanding Gould's stout declaration to Charles Horn in December that he was "positive" that May had put all connections with Communism behind him and that he knew of "no single reservation on the part of any student or member of the faculty" who had come to know May at Carleton, not two months later he felt compelled to write to the director of the FBI office in Minneapolis to say that "recent circumstances" had led him to some extent to doubt his faith in May. "I don't know quite how to phrase this inquiry," Gould wrote, "but I do need guidance which I believe can come only from your office."

The "recent circumstances" that had made Gould uneasy seem to have involved the circulation of disquieting rumors, apparently spread at least in part through talk by a colleague distrustful of or simply dissatisfied with May's ongoing political opinions. This colleague, whose history as a Czech citizen naturally made him personally sensitive on the issue of Communism, may have taken umbrage over unconsidered or not entirely serious remarks on Cold War matters that May might have offered in his typically "jocose manner"—Gould himself noted that May liked "to argue and take positions for the sake of argument." He also seems to have put a dark interpretation upon (or at least have been ready to raise questions about) the information that May had provided a recent Carleton graduate, then studying physics in Europe, with a letter of introduction to J. D. Bernal, a British scientist who was, in the political realm, an unrepentant Communist. It may also be that, given his desire to distance himself from his past, May acted with insufficient circumspection in choosing to sign his name to a letter to President Truman asking for commutation of the death sentences passed upon Ethel and Julius Rosenberg, the American Communists convicted of atomic espionage conspiracy.

In response to Gould's request the FBI promptly designated Special Agent Alden D. Sheffield, a Carleton economics major of the Class of 1932, to meet with Gould at his Carleton office to discuss the information or rumors that had led Gould to become uneasy. Gould spoke with Sheffield on a Friday afternoon and then had a lengthy talk with May the next morning. He emerged from these meetings once again "completely confident of [May's] loyalty and his integrity." With May he recited "some of the items that had caused people to worry" and did not doubt the mathematician's sincerity in being surprised over people's suspicious reactions. May remarked that "if he really were still a Communist, he would know how to be more subtle than these so-called suspicious circumstances suggest."

Both men knew that May's political past was likely to be splashed across the newspapers again very shortly. The perjury case against the physicist Weinberg, whom May had known at Berkeley, was now coming to trial in Washington, and May had been summoned to appear as a defense witness; he would testify six days after his Saturday meeting with Gould. Following his conversation with the president, May, as a "token of his sincerity," complied with Gould's suggestion that he offer Carleton a signed letter of resignation, which Gould hoped it would not prove necessary to accept. A few days later Gould wrote to three professors who had raised questions about May to say that he had "gone to some lengths" to inquire into the rumors that had lately been circulating and that he had concluded that they were "wholly unwarranted," that "a thoroughly honest man" had been "wrongfully accused and perhaps harmed," and that his policy going forward would be to "defend him without reservation." May's testimony in the Weinberg trial did indeed again bring his name and past Communist Party adherence into the newspapers, but with little repercussion to Carleton: Within two weeks of May's appearance at the trial Gould had received but one letter about the affair. Though language had been prepared (with the assistance of advice from trustees Atherton Bean and Malcolm McDonald) against the need to issue some sort of statement from Gould, it was finally decided that "the less publicity given to the matter, the better" and that no public statement then seemed necessary. Weinberg, in the end, won acquittal from his jury, and May, the following month, was awarded a prestigious faculty fellowship grant from the Fund for the Advancement of Education that occasioned his being on leave from Carleton during the next academic year. There would be no further storm clouds active on that front for the next eighteen months.

***

Aided especially by a $100,000 pledge from Atherton Bean, the Carleton library campaign total had climbed to half a million dollars by the end of March 1953, with a year and a half remaining to find twice that again and so secure the added endowment offered by Bell in the guise of "Anonymous." Gould maintained some hope that a portion of this might come from the Olin Foundation, now that he was being advised that Olin (contrary to what Charles Horn had first told him) was indeed interested in giving money for buildings. Three members comprised the Olin board, of which the "hard nut to crack," as Gould reported to one of his trustees, was of course "the cantankerous and capricious" Mr. Horn, who was sometimes "all friendliness and courtesy" and then capable of taking "one's hide off." On these occasions, wrote Gould, "I have never been treated as rudely by anyone in my life as I have by him." Gould described the situation to a new trustee, Olivia Coan, saying that this was a man "whom I have got to get around somehow" and hoping that Coan might help him to "cook up something to snare him." Meanwhile, his attention focused on William McKnight, chairman of the board of the Minnesota Mining and Manufacturing Company, with whom he had an invitation to go fishing on McKnight's yacht in Miami. The trip he made for that purpose at the end of March and beginning of April caught only a small fish—a pledge of $50,000 toward the library from a man who "could build us ten libraries" if he wished and who he had seriously hoped might contribute a full million, but Gould did think that this might prove to be but "the opening wedge" with McKnight.

With regard to the hiring of Carleton personnel, Gould's principal task that spring was to find the right person for the important post of college chaplain, as Phil Phenix had decided the previous November to leave for a position with the Hazen Foundation in Connecticut. An "extensive" search resulted in an offer being accepted in May by David Stowe, associate minister at the First Congregational Church in Berkeley. Gould was sorry to see Phenix leave, both because he had highly valued his services and because such departures inevitably added to his burdens in having to find a replacement. When a professor from another college appeared on campus that spring making an effort to lure away the chairman of the Carleton Physics Department, Gould claimed that he was "tempted to invite him to lunch and put arsenic in his soup." (When, however, Gould found that the coveted professor was not at all likely to be pried loose, he admitted that he thought the arsenic "will not be necessary.")

That April Gould was involved in another automobile accident, his second in eighteen months. On this occasion the president, in a new car, was smashed into on a Northfield street by a teenaged girl who had skipped school to take friends joyriding in her father's car. While Gould's vehicle was thoroughly crumpled, his body somehow escaped without a bruise, leading some of his friends to remark that it was increasingly obvious he was born to be hanged. After losing first his Buick and then a Chrysler to collisions which were not his fault, Gould claimed that his next car was going to be a tank, so that instead of getting run into he could start running into others.

Late in May, the Eisenhower White House made a short-lived attempt to interest Gould in making a political challenge for Hubert Humphrey's US Senate seat in 1954. Gould declined promptly and completely. To one correspondent with whom he confided about the suggestion he wrote: "I am sensible enough to know that I couldn't beat Humphrey. Besides, I cherish the thought that there is still some unfinished business for me to do here at Carleton College." But, when he informed Congressman Walter Judd that he had a responsibility to Carleton to raise $1.5 million for a library building in the next year and a half and Judd promptly assured him that Republican friends would make this a relatively easy matter if he committed to running, he did have some fun toying facetiously with "the temptation to be just a little devious and get the necessary funds" in that way.

June began with Gould flying to Memphis to deliver a commencement address at Southwestern College (now Rhodes) and accept his fifth honorary degree. The same day the news was released that Lawrence University President Nathan Pusey had just been selected as James B. Conant's presidential successor at Harvard—news which was greatly satisfying to Gould, as he had some months earlier made just that recommendation to Harvard through both Laird Bell and John Cowles, the latter of whom was then president of the Harvard Alumni Association. Cowles wrote Gould to say that "what you told me about Pusey and your all-out endorsement of him, which I transmitted in detail to the corporation, was apparently a substantial factor in the corporation's decision to take him instead of another possibility." Harvard's new president-elect himself wrote Gould later in the month: "In more lucid moments I have very grave misgivings about feeling grateful to anyone who played a part in getting me into the mess where I now find myself. But it is an honorable mess, and somewhere out on the other side of the present confusion, there is, I am sure, a very great opportunity."

Mess and opportunity: Such words from one college president to a fellow, Gould well understood.

CHAPTER 19

"CARISSIMA MIA"

The three-day Carleton Commencement Weekend of 1953 was troubled by bad weather. On Saturday morning (June 6) Northfield was visited by a mass of cool polar air that dropped temperatures to only about fifty degrees Fahrenheit. This had little effect on the day's planned activities for returning alumni, which concluded with a dinner that itself concluded with remarks by President Gould on one of his favorite themes—the important role of the small liberal arts college in keeping alive the best of our cultural inheritance, which the world could ill afford to lose. On Sunday, however, torrents of rain that arrived around the time of the morning Baccalaureate service turned into twelve steadily wet hours that washed out planned reunion picnics and class photographs and forced all other events indoors. And then on Monday morning high winds, continuing intermittent drizzle, and the threat of more caused that day's graduation exercises, scheduled to be held outdoors on the "Bald Spot" common, to be moved inside the chapel.

That Larry Gould had extraordinarily reliable powers of local weather control where important campus events were concerned—that he could somehow always guarantee sunshine when needed—had already become an entrenched article of expressed campus belief, and indeed this would be the only instance during his presidency when a planned outdoor commencement ceremony had to be relocated. Nothing observable in Gould's public performances throughout the weekend suggested to graduating seniors or campus guests that anything other than the weather was amiss with the president, but perhaps the weather itself—cold, wet evidence of a slippage in Gould's fabled meteorological mastery—should have been seen as an indicator that for some reason Carleton's red-tie-clad leader was a little off his usual game. He did in fact have cause to be.

Only a very few of the many observing Gould that weekend knew of the heavy added weight that was then on his mind. On Thursday night, June 4, Peg Gould had "collapsed," and upon the advice of Northfield doctor Bernie Street had been taken to Miller Hospital in St. Paul, suffering from what seems to have been severe clinical depression. With Peg's hospitalization, Dr. E. H. Hammes

Larry Gould, Bess Balchen, Peg Gould, and Bernt Balchen, at 1953 Carleton exhibit of Balchen's Arctic-themed artwork

became the authority overseeing the particulars of her observation and care, as well as judge as to when it would be permissible for her to receive visits or even communications from anyone, including her husband. Gould had early been told that Peg might need to remain in hospital for a matter of weeks for full recovery, but it was two days after Carleton's graduation exercises—six days from her collapse—before Gould received a preliminary report to the effect that although Peg remained depressed she was less so, and was "cooperating." "So we may hope the treatment may get started soon," Gould wrote Laird Bell. In addition to psychiatric evaluation, various metabolism tests were being ordered, and a specialist was called in with respect to Peg's developing troubles with arthritis.

The depression and illness that came to a head with Peg that June had been present and building for some time. "Mrs. Gould hasn't been too well for the last two or three years," the president wrote to one correspondent early in July, and the following winter he would reference problems existing "for the past four or five years." Sources are lacking to write with real assurance (or at length commensurate with genuine biographical importance, surely) regarding the history or nature of Peg Gould's depression.*

Gould cancelled the commencement address he had been expected to deliver at Winona State Teachers College the day after Peg's collapse, sending history professor Carlton Qualey as a last-moment stand-in. But otherwise during the ensuing weeks of worry he carried on with work—bringing Carleton's fiscal year to a close with the budget balanced—and with events as planned: a St. Paul commencement address at the Summit School, followed before the end of the month by addresses at Carleton, to an Episcopal conference meeting in the chapel, and in Minneapolis, to the Lions Club District Convention, and then to the Minnesota Retail Federation meeting at the Minikahda Club. He wrote to James O. Wynn, one of Charles Horn's codirectors with the Olin Foundation, about the foundation's interest in giving college buildings and seeking advice as to whether he ought to apply formally for the foundation to complete, and then name, the Carleton library. Despite Peg's absence, Gould carried on, with help from Jean Hoppin, Helen Hyslop, and Dorothy Obaid, with the hosting of a late June wedding reception for Peg's brother, Jack Rice, and his bride, Martha MacGalliard Leavenworth, a Carleton biology instructor who had been widowed with an infant son during World War II. (Following the ceremony at Northfield's Episcopal church the reception was held in the garden at the Gould house.)

During the fourth week of June, Dr. Hammes reported that Peg's feelings of "hopelessness" had subsided, that she was now "pleasant and cheerful" most of the time, and that Gould might now write to her—which he did immediately. "You will tell me, of course, when it is wise for me to see her," Gould replied. Gould also expressed hope that the doctor would approve Peg's release, if possible, to spend August at the Square G ranch in Jackson Hole, where their annual reservations were scheduled to begin July 26. "I do not know of any kind of atmosphere in which Mrs. Gould has been more relaxed and more completely herself than there," Gould wrote, himself convinced that "nothing could be better for her."

By the end of June, Gould had received his first hospital letters from Peg, who was eager and impatient to return home. He was finally allowed to see her early in July, and by mid-month he was permitted on occasion to take her out of the hospital to quiet dinners in St. Paul. An entire weekend away was granted

---

* Or, for that matter, to write with a desired level of penetration and understanding about most aspects of the Goulds' fifty-eight year marriage. Peg apparently did not take easily or naturally to mid-twentieth century expectations for the social role of college president's wife. It is known that she could not abide the length or severity of Minnesota winters. In Northfield, outside of a relatively small circle she tended to be seen as somewhat aloof. A woman of high intelligence who was, however, reportedly sensitive about the fact that she never finished her university degree and whose "career" as Mrs. Laurence M. Gould was defined by reference to her husband, subsuming to some extent her own identity—were these things the source of psychological difficulties and frustrations for Peg? In contrast to the richly documented "public" aspects of Larry Gould's life and work, so much as regards private life, marriage, and the clearly complicated character of his wife is difficult to write about with confidence. The biographer's dream of perfect narrative truth and balance arising out of perfect knowledge feels here impossibly distant.

them later in July, spent with their poodle Jill in the rustic surroundings of Dixie Lodge in Balsam, Wisconsin. Finally Peg's full release, with approval to fly out to Wyoming, was scheduled for August 2. Larry drove west first, a two-day trip starting the 31st, four days after the armistice signed at Panmunjom ended the Korean War. He met Peg at the airport in Casper when she flew in on the 2nd, and they drove together the remaining 260 miles to continue her recuperation for several weeks at the Square G.

Gould was concerned in 1953 that the long string of summers in which he and Peg vacationed at the Square G dude ranch on Jenny Lake might soon be coming to a forced end. Since the 1930s land in the Jackson Hole valley had steadily been bought up, parcel by parcel, by a conservationist group backed by John D. Rockefeller, Jr., so as to prevent overdevelopment and with an eye toward the land's eventual addition to an expanded Grand Teton National Park. Amid much controversy, Jackson Hole National Monument had been established in 1943, and most of its acreage then added to the national park in 1950. In 1951 the Rockefeller interests had purchased the Square G, and now the rumor was that the ranch was intended in the near future to be dismantled and its land returned to its natural condition. Conservationist though he was himself, Gould thought this plan was a shame as regards the Square G, whose modest cabins were quite the opposite of developed blight. He attempted, with the advice and support of his Wyoming friend, the noted naturalist Olaus Murie,* a resident of the Jackson Hole town of Moose who had been a major local supporter of the Rockefeller family's previous efforts in the valley, to make the case to Laurence Rockefeller for saving the Square G. Assuming (correctly), however, that such appeals were ultimately unlikely to win the Square G a reprieve from liquidation, the Goulds that summer bought a bit of land for themselves in the area, just outside of the national park, near the town of Wilson, "so as to be sure that the Rockefeller steam roller should not completely exclude us from the Jackson Hole country." Their purchase, made in tandem with several other Square G regulars including the Hyslops from Carleton, did result, after they all built cabins upon their collective forty acres in 1955, in Larry and Peg's maintaining a definite—and soon much loved—place to return to summer after summer for the next quarter-century.

***

That September Larry Gould reported to multiple correspondents that August in Wyoming had been very good for Peg's well-being; that though she was still tiring easily she had shown steady improvement in health and spirits and was now "better than she has been in a long time, and everything is going to be

---

* The Goulds' friendship with Olaus and Mardie Murie dated from the summer of 1950. In 1951 Gould arranged for Olaus to lecture at Carleton and a month later proudly accepted gift membership in The Wilderness Society, of which Olaus Murie was then the president and director.

all right." Gould thought it a part of her recovery that she put hard work that year into improving her Spanish with the help of Carleton professor Hyme Loss.

As the new academic year got underway, there was a temporary change of personnel in the Carleton President's Office. The usual working trio of Gould and secretaries Sally Crandall and Dorothy Obaid lacked the third musketeer all that year, as the Obaids were spending 1953-54 on sabbatical in Spain. Elaine Lyman was moved over from the Treasurer's Office to fill in.

Gould now had only twelve months remaining to complete the library campaign on time to earn Laird Bell's matching gift for the proposed building's maintenance endowment. This, until secured, clearly would be the president's top Carleton priority for the year ahead. In September, with half the time elapsed on the two-year period stipulated in Bell's offer, only a little over a third of the funds that were needed had been either pledged or paid. That month Gould was informed of an officially anonymous gift of stock valued at about $25,000 added to the Library Fund by trustee John M. Musser, which helped lower the remainder needed to $905,000 by the time of the fall trustee meetings. In October—a month highlighted at Carleton by formal dedication of the now renovated* Willis Memorial Union in ceremonies coinciding with Homecoming—Gould formally solicited the "serious consideration" of the Olin Foundation toward supplying the full cost of the new building, so as to give Carleton an Olin Library, but this appeal ultimately yielded nothing but an early January letter from Charles Horn stating that, though the Olin Foundation "never closes the door," it has "many projects ahead, which will exhaust the funds we have to spend this year and next." Concerned that autumn that the library fund was not "moving along as it should," Gould vacillated between optimism regarding certain prospects from whom he expected great things and worry that slow progress might be attributable to some diminished vitality in himself. (Disturbed by the latter thought, he decided to get a thorough medical examination from his old doctor Fred Schaaf, who, as Gould later related the story, ended up informing his patient that he found him to be in better shape than two years earlier, when he had last seen him. Nonetheless, being cautious, Dr. Schaaf solemnly advised the *ex officio*-ally burdened president to avoid "tension of any kind." "Upon having given that advice," Gould wrote Atherton Bean, "we both burst into uproarious laughter.")

Two signal honors external to Carleton came Gould's way during the fall of 1953. The first arrived in September, when President Eisenhower appointed him to the twenty-four-member National Science Board of the National Science Foundation, replacing James Conant, the former Harvard president who had resigned his NSB seat to become the US High Commissioner for Occupied Germany. Gould owed his position on the short list of candidates provided to the White House by NSB Director Alan Waterman to the effective job he had done as a member

---

* Though dedicated in the fall, work on the building would not be entirely finished until the middle of the following summer.

of the NSF Divisional Committee for Scientific Personnel and Education. Then, in November, Gould was elected a trustee of the Carnegie Foundation for the Advancement of Teaching.

That same month Gould's old friend Bernt Balchen came to visit, speaking at a Carleton convocation and opening a display in Boliou Hall of forty-one of his own watercolor paintings of Arctic scenes. Gould spent $200 buying one of Balchen's exhibited paintings for Carleton ("Bluie East 2, East Greenland," which he had framed and hung for a time in a "commanding position" in his own living room at home).

Balchen was at this time frustrated by the conviction that his promotion within the Air Force from colonel to brigadier general was being blocked, principally by the enmity of Richard Byrd working politically through his brother, Virginia Senator Harry F. Byrd. "There's no doubt in my mind any longer whom is behind all my trouble in the AF," Balchen had written Gould in October. "I talked to him last week and he sure gave himself away completely."

Gould sympathized entirely with Balchen's position regarding his blocked promotion, urging a number of Minnesota Scandinavians to write to senators and congressmen about the matter, though feeling unable himself "to be completely outspoken knowing the situation as I do." Gould did encourage his friend Senator Ed Thye to write to President Eisenhower recommending that special action be taken on Balchen's behalf lest the country lose Balchen's services to forced retirement due to the amount of time spent in his present rank. (These efforts were ultimately fruitless. As Gould later came to understand, "it seems that ... Senator Byrd went to the White House with his brother Dick and persuaded President Eisenhower on some pretext or other to kill the bill pending in Congress to make Balchen a General." Balchen ultimately was retired from the Air Force in 1956, still a colonel.) Gould, in correspondence with a Carleton trustee he took into his confidence about the matter, deplored "the mean extremes to which Dick Byrd is going." "I really believe the man must be ill," he confided. "If he saw things in their right proportions, he would be the first man to propose Balchen for promotion and would do his utmost to secure it, for Balchen got his start with Byrd and has always been grateful to him so far as I know." Gould concluded this frank letter by saying that he thought its recipient had better burn it after reading.* "I have been careful all these years," he wrote, "not to record any unkind attitude toward Dick Byrd, nor do I wish to do so now."

Peg showed continued improvement through that fall and winter. The weather cooperated, as a beautiful warm and sunny autumn that Gould termed "phenomenal" was succeeded by a winter that was, by mid-January, cold, but bright and sunny, with the result, Gould told his brother-in-law, that "Peg has not yet seemed to mind it or suggest that she ought to be on her way to a warmer

---

* The original may or may not have been burnt, but Gould's secretary-typed copy was duly filed, and ultimately archived, in his presidential correspondence files.

climate for an interlude." Gould credited an enjoyable Christmas visit from Jean and Dick Hoppin with having done Peg "a lot of good."

In January, while in Cincinnati between talks to Carleton alumni groups in Ohio and Michigan, Larry was moved to send Peg an affectionate handwritten note from the heart:

> Carissima mia, I wonder if you know how wonderful it has been to see your rapid recovery in these past weeks. Your progress has been phenomenal and it is again so comfortable to be with you. You are being the Peg I fell in love with. And others who love you are rejoiced too. ... Bright days and happier than any you can easily remember are ahead. Read Browning's Rabbi Ben Ezra again.* It is true. And you are such a help to me. I have noted with deep satisfaction how you are doing things so much more easily and how you wake up in the morning with a smile. Actually that frown which had almost changed your face is fast disappearing. I think you are wonderful and I wish I could see you right now.

Six weeks later, the day before a flight to Miami, he wrote another:

> Carissima mia, I am so depressed about going off to Florida without you—even though this will be really a business journey at college expense—that I may not be able to tell you so.
>
> For the past four or five years there have been times when I have been glad to go off on journeys and when I have looked forward to returning with reluctance. Now when I go away no sooner am I off than I begin to think how happy I will be to get back.
>
> From now on there must be a break at this time of year. The doctors give me a fine bill of health for a man of 58 but I know when I have pushed myself too far—doesn't do me any harm—but I get so inefficient. I fumble at my desk and in my speech. That is not good.
>
> You have no idea how eagerly I am looking forward to our journey down through the Mississippi Valley in early April.
>
> You might infer from this letter that I am in love with my wife and I guess that about sizes it up. What do you think of that? I like it.
>
> Some time take down a copy of Browning and read Rabbi Ben Ezra.

> All* my love, Larry

> *At your discretion you may share some with Jill.

The trip to Florida on which Gould was about to depart included an appearance at an alumni meeting but was largely undertaken to continue the cultivation

---

*   Presumably with reference to the famous opening lines: "Grow old along with me! The best is yet to be..."

of certain wealthy donor prospects regarding the ongoing library building fund campaign. The year 1954 had begun with close to $850,000 still needed toward the million and a half goal. "If the people I know who could finance it only had the insight I do the matter would be very simple," Gould noted semi-seriously in the first week of January. A few days later a check came in for $12,500 from a very wealthy man in whose potential philanthropy Gould had invested a great deal of attention and who was making provision for Carleton in his will but from whom Gould had hoped for much, much more in the near term for the library. When Gould passed the check along to Carleton Treasurer Bruce Pollock, who was well aware that Gould's hopes on that front had been aimed considerably higher, Pollock mused in return, "I suppose you are too young to remember the lines of a song which went something like this: 'I was only dreaming, blow the smoke away' ..." (With this man Gould continued with renewed pleas and suggestions and secured another $25,000 from the same source in July, though this remained a disappointing total as measured against the man's capacity to give on quite another scale.)

Nonetheless, the big breakthrough toward completion of the library program did eventually come that winter when half a million dollars—the campaign's major gift apart from Laird Bell's challenge for the building's endowment fund—was pledged by Reine H. Myers. Myers, whose husband Paul had been a Carleton trustee and whose son John was a Carleton graduate of 1933, signed the papers establishing the gift in February, asking initially that the donor identity be kept anonymous to the public. Eventually the special fund set up by the Myers family to make payments on the half-million-dollar pledge was designated the "M.P.M. Account," for Myers-Parish-Myers, the surnames of Reine Myers' three children. "We are all very happy about this gift," John Myers wrote Gould. "We feel privileged to be associated with the growth of Carleton in general—and with the administration of Larry Gould in particular." At a stroke, the Myers pledge left Gould and Carleton less than $300,000 away from reaching the million and a half target for which Mr. Bell's deadline was September.

***

Focused though Gould was at that time on fundraising, there were of course other matters that also received his presidential attention. In January and February he concluded a pair of what would be especially successful young faculty hirings in the sciences, securing Robert Reitz, from the University of Illinois, for the Physics Department and Richard Ramette, from the University of Minnesota, for the Chemistry Department. Each would anchor and grow their respective Carleton departments for decades.

Two other Gould appointments of particular note also enter the biographical narrative in the first part of 1954—these being, however, not appointments made but rather appointments received.

Early in March, during his eight-day excursion to Miami and Palm Beach panning for donor-prospect gold, Gould was called out of a dinner to the telephone. On the line was Detlev Bronk, president of the National Academy of Sciences, whom Gould had known since the days when they both were young graduate students at Michigan. Bronk wanted Gould to accept appointment as chairman of the committee being established to plan and implement US efforts in Antarctica in connection with the upcoming International Geophysical Year (IGY) of 1957-58. The IGY, under the overall coordination of the International Council of Scientific Unions, was being planned as a comprehensive program of global geophysical observations, data gathering, and related scientific activities, timed to run from July 1957 through December 1958 to coincide with a period of peak sun spot activity. The committee on Antarctica was being set up as a sub-committee of the US National Committee for the International Geophysical Year (USNC-IGY), itself chaired by UCLA physicist Joseph Kaplan. USNC-IGY members had been appointed the year before by the National Academy of Sciences. By becoming chairman of the Antarctic Committee, Gould would also be made a member of USNC-IGY.

Gould, concerned about his ability to commit to such an undertaking in light of his responsibilities toward Carleton, needed time to consider and to consult with Bell, as chairman of the Carleton Board.* Meanwhile, Bronk's request was reinforced by a follow-up call to Gould in Florida from another old friend, Lloyd Berkner, who, as a radio operator, had been one of Gould's comrades-in-ice on the first Byrd Antarctic Expedition. It had been Berkner who, needing better worldwide data for his work investigating the geophysics of the earth's atmosphere, had in 1950 as a member of the NAS made the original proposal for an International Geophysical Year, an idea modeled on the two previous International Polar Years of 1882-83 and 1932-33. By mid-March, Gould had tentatively committed to undertake this important assignment, though confessing that it was "not yet quite clear" how he would manage his time so as to be able to do it. Late in April, speaking at St. Olaf College to the Minnesota Academy of Science, he delivered the first of what would in the next several years be many addresses on the subject of the IGY.

On the evening of March 21, another unexpected phone call brought Gould his second weighty appointment of the month. This call, received at home, was from Henry Ford II, who was gauging Gould's interest in being named a trustee of the Ford Foundation. This was indeed a major honor, and recognition that was deeply flattering to receive. (Gould had undoubtedly been recommended for

---

* Years later Gould told an audience that he took the matter up with his board chairman and conveyed that he would like to do this job but that he didn't think the resulting diversion of his energies and necessary absences would be very good for Carleton. He said he had at first felt flattered by Bell's warm endorsement of his desire to accept the appointment—until, he told his laughing listeners, the less flattering implications of Bell's immediate assurance that, on the contrary, he thought the college might benefit from Gould's involving himself deeply in another concern, sank in.

consideration by his friend John Cowles, who had himself become a Ford Foundation trustee four years before.) The Ford Foundation, memorably characterized by Dwight Macdonald as "a large body of money completely surrounded by people who want some," was then by far the largest foundation in existence, by assets. Its board of trustees/directors was a select group of fourteen highly distinguished men (all male as they then were) that determined the allocation of enormous funds to philanthropic ends in five separate spheres: international relations, the strengthening of democratic institutions, the US economy, educational institutions, and human behavior research. Immediately confirming his interest, Gould was shortly thereafter duly elected. (This despite, he joked, the "bad impression" he made when foundation president H. Rowan Gaither informed him that the perquisites of Ford Foundation trusteeship included being able to buy any Ford product at factory prices. "Good Heavens!" Gould reported himself as having exclaimed, going on to confess that he had just bought a new Chrysler. "Don't ever say that word around here again!" Gaither whimsically advised.)

Public announcement of Gould's election to the Ford Foundation board, in tandem with another new director, Mark F. Ethridge, publisher of the *Louisville Times* and *Courier-Journal*, was made by Ford on April 4. A letter dated the next day from fellow foundation trustee Judge Charles E. Wyzanski, Jr. (to whom Carleton would give an honorary degree at Commencement in two months time) told Gould that "the unanimity with which we voted for you indicates how highly we esteemed your qualifications, and how much we look forward to being associated with you in what is a challenging, if frighteningly enormous, responsibility." Membership on the Ford Foundation board *was* an enormous responsibility, and Gould professed himself both proud and humble to have been selected, as well as bowled over by thinking of helping the foundation wisely *spend* millions of dollars a year, rather than trying to secure the few hundred thousand dollars which he was forever doing for Carleton.*

Early in May, Gould and Ethridge traveled to New York for a day or two of trustee orientation with Gaither and other officers of the foundation; their first participation in formal board meetings came later that month. Gould told Laird Bell, subsequent to these meetings, that he found the foundation board to be a stimulating group and that he was "glad to report" that he and Ethridge had both been able "to insinuate the idea that the Ford Foundation had not yet done enough for small liberal arts colleges." The resulting conversation was lively, Gould reported, adding that he had said that "when the time was ripe" he could tell them "exactly where to begin with such concerns." It was, he affirmed, a seed planted in ground he thought was fertile.

---

* The Carleton Archives contains an undated poetic composition by Carleton professor of French Donald S. Schier titled "Irreverent Reflection On the News of Mr. Gould's Being Made a Director Of the Ford Foundation." The poem begins: "Now shall the lion lie down with the lamb, / Now shall the sad song change to a dithyramb, / Now shall the leopard shrug off his spots, / For he who begged money now weighs and allots."

Gould joined the Ford Foundation board at an interestingly fraught juncture. Under the leadership of Paul Hoffman and Robert M. Hutchins (who had left the University of Chicago chancellorship to become Ford Foundation associate director), the foundation and its subsidiaries had become "one of the favorite targets of the militant anti-Communists," egged on by right-wing gadfly columnist Westbrook Pegler and others of his stripe who seemed to spy creeping socialism under every rock. A House select committee chaired by Georgia Representative Edward Eugene "Goober" Cox had in 1952 conducted an investigation into the programs of tax-exempt foundations and comparable organizations, the Ford Foundation principal among them, to "determine whether they were using their resources for the purposes for which they were established, and especially to determine which such foundations and organizations are using their resources for un-American activities and subversive activities or for purposes not in the interest or tradition of the United States." Although in January 1953 the Cox Committee report had concluded that "there is little basis for the belief expressed in some quarters that foundation funds are being diverted from their intended use," the Ford family and top officials of the Ford Motor Company had been stung by the controversies surrounding Ford Foundation programs, with ensuing periodic suggestions of conservative boycotts of Ford products, and Henry Ford determined to replace Hoffman and Hutchins and "clean house." Hoffman "resigned" early in February 1953 and was replaced as foundation president by Gaither, described by Waldemar A. Nielsen, a leading historian of philanthropic foundations, as "a mild and reflective man ... chosen as president partly because he was known to be a good problem-solver and partly because the trustees were confident, given his unforceful personality, that he would carry out instructions and not plunge the institution into new difficulties."

The foundation's critics on the right grew frothy again, however, when in the same month that Gaither replaced Hoffman the board announced a $15 million grant to the Fund for the Republic, a new organization with a focus on supporting American civil liberties as embodied in the Bill of Rights. (The creation of the Fund for the Republic had been approved in principle a year and a half earlier, but the grant prudently delayed until after the 1952 elections.) As Nielsen observed, "this fateful stroke, taken at the height of the McCarthy mania, infuriated the senator's supporters."* A few months later, Republican Congressman B. Carroll Reece of Tennessee, dissatisfied with the benign conclusions of the Cox Committee, called for and got a new congressional investigation of the foundations and

---

* Dwight Macdonald pointed out that "the Fund's first action was bold to the point of foolhardiness—granting $25,000 to the American Bar Association to make a study of the uses and abuses of Congressional investigating committees." Though established by the Ford Foundation with its founding grant, the Fund for the Republic was thereafter independent. In May 1954 its president became Robert Hutchins, who had been forced out as associate director of the Ford Foundation, and Hutchins later sourly described the Fund as "a wholly disowned subsidiary of the Ford Foundation."

particularly of Ford, which Reece characterized as taking "the last of the great American industrial fortunes, amassed in a competitive free market place," and using it in a "diabolical conspiracy ... to undermine and subvert our institutions." The aim of the conspiracy, he warned, was "the furtherance of Socialism in the United States." The Reece Committee hearings were set to begin in May 1954, just as Gould came aboard what was, therefore, a besieged ship.

The two trips that Gould made to New York that May, for Ford Foundation orientation and then his first board meetings, were both preceded by other business in Washington. Washington is a city in which history is continuously in the process of being made. This was at least as true as ever that month, which in the US Senate saw the middle portion of the Army-McCarthy hearings, which were televised gavel to gavel from late in April until the middle of June—exposure which was subsequently credited with decisively turning public opinion against Senator McCarthy and leading ultimately to his political downfall. In mid-month, over at the Supreme Court building, announcement was made of the historically momentous ruling of a unanimous court in the case of Brown v. Board of Education of Topeka that racial segregation in public schools was unconstitutional under the equal protection clause of the Fourteenth Amendment. Gould followed both developments with interest.

In Northfield, one day previous to the handing down of the Brown decision, the Carleton student body celebrated the annually popular Larry Gould Day. Following Sunday evening vesper services a large number of students garbed predominantly in red gathered behind Gridley Hall and then trooped over to the Gould home on Elm Street, where Holly Samuels, crowned the day before as Carleton May Queen for 1954, presented Peg Gould with a dozen red roses and Larry Gould with an old-fashioned red flannel nightshirt. Then, as reported in the local newspaper, a student band organized specially for the occasion serenaded the Goulds with renditions of the Carleton fight song, "When You Wore a Tulip," "When the Red Red Robin," and the Carleton Alma Mater.

When the Carleton Board of Trustees met early in June, Charles Miel's report on the Library Building Fund showed that as of that morning there remained $185,925.37 to be secured by the 19th of September so as to meet the goal set by the conditional gift. Looking past the library project at the next facilities needs on the horizon, Gould advised the trustees that "over-crowded conditions on both sides of the campus" dictated that the most pressing need would then be for two new dormitories, one each for men and for women, with the latter preferably to include a small gymnasium and swimming pool. Gould also observed that the college expected to enroll about 866 students for the fall semester, but that due to a coming upsurge in the student-age population there would in the next five years doubtless come pressures to matriculate larger numbers. In response the board resolved unanimously that Carleton's enrollment "for the predictable future shall not exceed 1,000 students." A report from Director of Admissions Donald Klinefelter concerning accepted students who ultimately chose to attend other schools indicated that Carleton's real competition had become by then "not so much in the middle west as it is among the better eastern colleges." The trustees approved for the year ahead an increase in the college's operating budget deficit, so as to allow for professorial salary increases upon which Gould was insisting.

Four days after presiding over the pomp and circumstance of Carleton's 1954 Commencement (and two days after the most dramatic confrontation of the Army-McCarthy hearings had culminated in Army Counsel Joseph Welch's incredulously asking McCarthy, "Have you no sense of decency, sir? At long last, have you left no sense of decency?"), Gould caught an afternoon flight to Ann Arbor, where he was the next day to deliver the University of Michigan commencement address and receive an honorary degree from his alma mater. Peg made the trip as well, to witness the honor. The degree was granted, but Gould's address was wiped out when a terrific storm broke upon the twenty thousand people gathered in the football stadium just as the exercises were getting underway. The winds blew and the heavens opened; mortar boards went flying over the field, the rain poured down, and amid the chaos that followed Michigan President Harlan Hatcher stood up, shouted that he hereby conferred on everyone whose name appeared on the program the degree to which they were entitled, and the ceremony came to a wild and abrupt end. Gould later learned in the pages of the *Michigan Alumnus* that it was the first time in a hundred and ten years that Michigan had finished the year without a commencement address. He wrote to Hatcher the week following the aborted ceremony, observing that he should have given a warning in advance that "if my Alma Mater ever attempted to give me an honorary degree there would be all hell to pay."

Gould claimed that the most unfortunate aspect of the episode of his un-delivered address was that Michigan then asked him to write it out, something he rarely did with his speeches, so that it might be published. Thus we have the full text for his address "Noblesse Oblige: What is Required of the Educated Man?" printed in the autumn number of the *Michigan Alumnus Quarterly Review*. The address is a reworking of ideas Gould first gave in a 1937 talk to the Carleton student body. In "Noblesse Oblige" Gould posed five questions to emphasize that being "educated" is an unending task: Have you learned to communicate with others, acquired manners instead of mannerisms, educated your heart as well as your head, learned that will is the basal fact of life and that authority is part of all living, and come to appreciate that the privilege of being educated imposes upon you a corresponding obligation to yourself and to society? When the university later sent along a check for $250 as honorarium for the address he didn't give, Gould turned to Treasurer Pollock for advice as to "what the ethics were." Pollock advised that he send the check back, along with the observation that he "ought to get paid a great deal more for not speaking than for giving the address."

***

Meanwhile, Gould was finding that the responsibilities he had agreed to take upon his shoulders in connection with the Antarctic operations of the International Geophysical Year were already accumulating and in need of his attention. In May he had asked Paul Siple, helpfully located in Washington, to assist him with regard to the USNC-IGY Antarctic Committee. (Siple had gone on from being picked as the Boy Scout to accompany the first Byrd Antarctic Expedition to a full career centered around the polar regions in continued association with Admiral Byrd and as an Army research scientist.) Gould early added Bernt Balchen to the committee, as well as Richard B. Black, a veteran of two previous Antarctic expeditions who was then with the Office of Naval Research. Gould also sought Siple's advice regarding Dick Byrd—what the admiral's stance towards the IGY's Antarctic program might be and whether he would wish to associate himself with it in some way. Initially, Gould thought of asking Byrd to serve as an "Expert Consultant" to the Antarctic Committee. Siple wrote that, while he thought that whether Byrd would want to take a very active part in the IGY was a "highly problematical" question, he found that with respect to any Antarctic undertakings it was always "wise to keep him completely informed and in a favorable frame of mind." (Eventually, later in the year, Gould would ask Byrd to be the committee's "honorary chairman," an offer Byrd accepted "with pleasure.")

National Science Foundation plans for the IGY depended heavily on securing adequate governmental support and appropriations, and not long after agreeing to his leadership role with the IGY Antarctic program Gould found that he was being called upon to act as a lobbyist for such support. Writing Lloyd Berkner following one of his May visits to Washington, Gould advised that the Bureau of the Budget was at that time "swamped with more supplemental bills" than ever before and that they "seemed a little dubious about the whole situation" of additional millions for the IGY. Among the USNC-IGY planners "there was a general feeling," he reported, "that it might be well for one of us to go directly to President Eisenhower, and Det Bronk, Hugh Odishaw, and Alan Waterman [NAS president, USNC-IGY Executive Director, and NSF Director, respectively], without me being present, agreed that I was the person to do it." He did not, ultimately, speak directly to Eisenhower about the needs of the IGY program, but he did in June and early July, once the commencement season was past at both Carleton and Michigan, make a pair of IGY-related trips to Washington, apparently conferring with Secretary of State John Foster Dulles and then appearing before the House Appropriations Committee in company with Bronk and Waterman. Gould's message was that the IGY was to be the "most important cooperative scientific venture ever undertaken" and that its potential political importance to the United States was also enormous. "I think," Gould ventured in a letter written the day after his Congressional appearance, "we persuaded them of the importance of this activity so effectively that I hope I shall not need to go to Washington again until fall." Later that summer both houses of Congress did agree on an initial $2 million appropriation.

As the calendar page turned to July, Larry and Peg looked ahead with keen anticipation to their late summer getaway to Jackson Hole, where the Square G ranch was to be maintained for one final season before being dismantled by the Rockefellers as its acreage was returned to natural park conditions. However, before he could, as he put it, "go fishing with a clear conscience and a light heart in the month of August," Gould hoped to secure most of the remaining balance needed to complete the library fund, the amount yet to be raised still standing at the midpoint of July at $140,000. Despite feeling again, as he wrote Laird Bell, that it was becoming therapeutically "imperative" to get Peg "quite a long way from here" and to the Grand Tetons, where he hoped that the "calm and peace of the mountains" would enter Peg's "tired and somewhat distraught person," Gould put off his expected departure for Wyoming by a week, "with the hope that we can find enough doorbells to push so that the magic one will be amongst them."

His conscience cleared and his heart was lightened by his morning mail on July 27, following a weekend spent with Peg at John Cowles' summer place in northern Minnesota. A letter came in from Mrs. Harry Towsley of Ann Arbor, whose daughter* had just graduated from Carleton with great satisfaction as to her choice of school. Gould had asked Dr. and Mrs. Towsley if they would like to "have an equity" in the Carleton library by contributing to the fund, hoping perhaps for a gift of about $5,000. What Gould now found in his mail was a pledge of Dow Chemical stock worth about $40,000. "I restrained myself from fainting," Gould wrote Bell. Three days later the Goulds left for Jackson Hole, now needing only the final $100,000, in the next seven weeks, to meet the challenge.

While in the West that August Gould managed one important piece of Carleton faculty hiring business, interviewing and bringing onboard for the English Department Wayne Carver, a young Utahan with a BA from Kenyon College in whom he discerned great promise.† Mostly, however, he recharged his personal batteries with the usual program of relaxation, hiking, and a great deal of trout fishing. Looking ahead to future summers without the Square G, he anticipated making arrangements to build a cabin on the bit of Wyoming land purchased the year before. In his intellectual idle time Gould had intended on this vacation to delve into Carleton history professor Lucile Deen Pinkham's new study of the

---

* The daughter was Margaret Ann "Ranny" Towsley, who as Margaret Ann Riecker, was herself destined to become a Carleton trustee in 1987 and chair of the Carleton board from 1999 to 2004.

† Carver would teach at Carleton into the 1990s. He joined the English Department at the same time as another young instructor, Owen Jenkins, who would be similarly central to that department's development for decades. Jenkins, however, had essentially been hired directly by department chair Scott Elledge rather than by Gould himself, who did not meet Jenkins prior to his arrival on campus in September.

Glorious Revolution of 1688, *William III and the Respectable Revolution*, but, as he reported to Pinkham in September, he had perused only a few pages when the book was appropriated by another of that summer's Square G guests, Professor Robert Dewey Horn of the English Department of the University of Oregon. A friend for decades who had been one of Gould's roommates in student days at Michigan, he was apparently so delighted with the book that Gould never got the opportunity that summer to continue with it himself.

Another familiar guest (plus wife and four children) arriving in the Tetons later in August was Carleton trustee John M. Musser. Before leaving for Wyoming, Musser had informed Charles Miel that the directors of the Musser family's foundation, the General Service Foundation, had just approved a contribution to the Carleton Library Building Fund of $10,000, plus the offer of up to another $5,000 as needed to complete the fund, if the college found that so small a final amount was still needed near the September 19 deadline in order for the goal to be reached. (Gould later apologized to Musser for not having commented on this generous gesture while Musser was with him in Wyoming, explaining that the news had not immediately been forwarded his way.)

On the night of August 29, Gould in Wyoming and Miel in Northfield each received a memorably momentous telephone call—Miel called his the most wonderful of his life—from Mr. James R. Thorpe of Minneapolis, together with his Carleton trustee friend, Bob Flanagan, who had for some time been assiduously interesting Thorpe in Carleton. Flanagan asked about the amount still left to go on the $1.5 million campaign and was told that, counting the $5,000 that John Musser's family foundation would give if it were still needed by September 19, the amount stood at about $45,000. Flanagan then put Thorpe on the line, and Thorpe conveyed the electric news that he would like to relieve Larry Gould of any further worry for the balance of his vacation and was prepared, in addition to an immediate gift of stock worth about $5,000, to guarantee to make up himself whatever balance might still be needed on September 19 to meet the goal. Success was assured! In order that further gifts prior to the 19th not be discouraged, the Carleton administrators kept this offer, and also the "if needed" pledge of an additional $5,000 from the Musser family foundation, confidential for the time being, reporting it to Bell and Pollock, but not to the rest of the trustees or other persons. Additional amounts would indeed still come in—notably a further $10,000 from Richard Drew Musser, adding to earlier gifts, and $5,000 from trustee and alumnus Wadsworth A. Williams—but with completion of the goal secured by the Thorpe pledge, Laird Bell went ahead and in advance of the deadline signed over the agreed-upon stock, which had risen in value to more than $1.3 million, for the library endowment. Responding to Bell on September 9 with the college's receipt for the gift, Gould wrote that this had been "the most important single financial transaction" in the school's history and that it was "now our task to keep the College worthy of this gift and your confidence."

Later that month, sending Carleton news to biology professor Thurlo Bates

Thomas, who was away on sabbatical, Gould noted that not only had the library campaign officially closed, but contracts had promptly been let and, not far from his Laird Hall office, "the bulldozer is just now pushing down the trees," creating a great gap which was the beginning of physical work on the long-sought library. At the trustees meeting in October, Gould reiterated that the library project, with its endowment, constituted "the largest single undertaking in the history of the College." He noted that the naming of the building "was to be left open for the time being." As it happens, it stayed open for forty-one years, though a number of names had been or would be suggested for the coming structure. Admirably idealistic but wholly unlikely was Professor Renzo Bianchi's suggestion later that autumn that the library be named to honor sixteenth-century Italian cosmologist Giordano Bruno. Gould himself hoped that it would one day be possible to over-ride Laird Bell's objections such that at some later time it could become the Laird Bell Library. History professor Carlton Qualey had gotten it right the previous March—telling the president he was certain "that there will be no more fitting name for the new building than The Laurence McKinley Gould Library." Indeed, that would eventually become its name, though only as a posthumous honor, following decades of campus service as simply the Carleton Library.*

Gould added to his report to Professor Thomas the comment that, with the long campaign at last concluded, he was left feeling "kind of let down and inefficient just now." "Now and again," he confessed, he was finding himself sitting at his desk "not doing much of anything." "I am almost persuaded," he wrote, that "I ought to take a holiday."

These were prophetic words. One month later, at the close of the first meeting of the Carleton board following the successful completion of the library campaign, the trustees requested that the president kindly absent himself from the room for a few minutes. As Gould later learned, Atherton Bean then informed the rest of the board that some of their number had been considering among themselves that "Larry" was then beginning his tenth year as president, that he had just completed a "most strenuous and successful two years" in raising the full cost of the new library, and that the board might seek some means of expressing to him their appreciation of these facts. As recorded by the board secretary, "Goley" Newhart, "the suggestion was made that Mr. Bell, as Chairman of the Board, order Larry and Peg to take a 60 to 90 day vacation away from Northfield at such time as best suits the college and their convenience." On the spot the collected trustees agreed to pool contributions out of their own pockets so as to make a sum of $3,500 available to the Goulds for such a purpose. Bell informed Larry of this action in private conversation after the trustees adjourned. "Isn't that sort of

---

*   At the small ceremony accompanying the unveiling of the new name chiseled over the entranceway to the Laurence McKinley Gould Library months after Gould's 1995 death, Emeritus Professor of Economics Ada M. Harrison was heard to say that Gould had during his lifetime consistently blocked suggestions that Carleton buildings be named for him. "But," she pointed out with some relish, "now we've GOT him! I'd like to see him object this time!"

wonderful?" Gould wrote to Thomas a few days later, sharing prospective plans already in formation for a long winter getaway to South America. (Before the Goulds' eventual February departure on this trip—in the end reduced from the 60 to 90 days originally suggested to a mere, but still substantial, seven weeks—a more tongue-in-cheek Gould would report to a fellow college president that "the trustees insisted that I needed a vacation. I replied that I didn't need a vacation, whereupon the chairman of the board said, 'Perhaps the faculty does.'")

The evening after this meeting of the Carleton board and of Gould's being informed of the vacation he was commanded to accept as a reward for hard work well done, a very special informal dinner for twelve was held in St. Paul "to celebrate the great new addition to Carleton College's assets." Celebrating along with the Goulds, Bell, and some Chicago trustees were the library campaign's major donors apart from Bell himself, Reine Myers and her children with their spouses. The Minnesota Club food that night was doubtless delicious, but it was probably also the case that at that moment Gould's sense of satisfaction over what had been accomplished was so elevated that, whatever was served, this was one meal he was sure to experience as exquisite.

CHAPTER 20

SOUTH AGAIN

Quite unexpectedly, the Carleton College football team (which had claimed only two victories the year before) won all eight of their games in 1954—the first undefeated season for Carleton football since 1916. Naturally, Larry Gould shared in the general campus satisfaction produced by this surprising result, though he offered the opinion to Laird Bell that by the law of averages this was bound to happen some time. Shortly after the final victory concluded the fairy tale season, Gould joined his fellow Minnesota college presidents in a group corporate solicitation of support for higher education among the Twin Cities business community. One of those called upon, who knew of the success of Carleton's recently completed library campaign, chided Gould for his sly deceptions: "Here," he said, "you have been persuading all of us that you were raising money to build a new library; whereas, obviously you were spending it to produce a championship football team!"

In fact, construction of the new library was now underway, following the plans that had been carefully developed by the college and its architects. Gould added one touch entirely his own: the suggestion that a wood-carved quotation be placed behind the charging desk in the completed building's main lobby. For this, Gould selected words from an address given at St. Andrew's University by his polar hero, Fridtjof Nansen: "The history of the human race is a continual struggle from darkness toward light. It is therefore to no purpose to discuss the use of knowledge. Man wants to know, and when he ceases to do so he is no longer man." Nansen's words struck Gould as "about as fine a statement of the real nature of a library as anything I have ever read."

Early in October Larry and Peg took Laird and Nathalie Bell up on a longstanding invitation to spend some relaxing time together at the Bells' cabin overlooking Lake Superior in the Huron Mountains of Michigan's Upper Peninsula. (Bell's instructions for the getaway were that clothes must be "old and tattered" and that Gould should warn his office to telephone him only "on great provocation," for the nearest phone was in Big Bay, ten miles away.) This respite was followed, however, by a series of working trips, each important, but cumulatively far from relaxing. In mid-month Gould flew to Washington for a National Science Board meeting as well as the first of what would eventually be eight formal meetings of Gould's USNC-IGY Antarctic Committee over a span of twenty-one months. Early in November Gould returned to Washington to attend the sixth meeting—his first—of the parent body, the US National Committee for the International Geophysical Year, at which it was decided to expand earlier plans and recommend that the United States ambitiously establish six major scientific stations in Antarctica as part of the IGY. He came to Washington again in December, combining an alumni club event (held on the same day that Joseph McCarthy was at last formally censured by his peers in the United States Senate) with meetings of both the United Chapters of Phi Beta Kappa and of the National Science Foundation board. And he returned yet again in January for the second meeting of his IGY Antarctic Committee. That was Washington. He also attended multiple-day Ford Foundation board meetings in New York on separate trips in both late October and mid-December. Gould's responsibilities external to Carleton—the actual meetings were only a part of it—were keeping him very busy indeed. In December he wrote Dick Byrd that Antarctic matters, in particular, "keep intruding in my mind more frequently than they should," stealing attention that belonged fundamentally focused on his college, and he told English professor Scott Elledge that it was a very good thing that his board-ordered holiday was soon approaching, as that seemed "the only way I can extricate myself from doing more than I should do but not more than I want to do."

Days later, his body possibly protesting over his recent pace, Gould came down with a nasty ailment that proved hard to shake. On Christmas Eve he told Bell that "that confounded virus" had not yet departed though it had already kept him low and partially out of commission for more than ten days—the longest such stretch of his life, he thought. All of which, he confessed, both annoyed him very much and probably was making him difficult to live with. (As antibiotics had failed to be of any help, so he informed Bell, he had turned instead to "the traditional libations, which though they do not cure, if taken in sufficient quantity do help one to forget the difficulty.")

Meanwhile, that December saw the issuance of a final report from Congress's Reece Committee, which had been investigating the role of American foundations—and the Ford Foundation in particular—in providing support for allegedly subversive activities undermining American traditions and furthering socialism. The Reece Committee had held hearings the previous May, June, and July, and after a delay of several months now issued a 416-page majority report, signed by its three Republicans, and a short dissenting minority report signed

by its two Democrats.* As a Ford Foundation trustee, Gould was promptly sent
a copy, together with a response prepared by Ford Foundation staff. The latter
statement Gould termed "superb." The majority report itself he found difficult to
slog through, it being, he said, "very hard on my religion," but in early January,
noting that he had yet to encounter anyone familiar with the report who had
not unqualifiedly condemned it, he offered the hope that it was "such a bad job"
that it would do the foundation no harm. Indeed, the report was being roundly
attacked in the nation's newspapers, predominantly Republican though they were,
and the Gallup polling organization eventually concluded that the overall effect
of the Reece hearings and report had been to increase the general popularity of
the Ford Foundation.

The sensibly judicious manner in which the Reece Committee's majority report was generally dismissed, paired with the censure of Senator McCarthy, were
welcome signs to Gould that the country might be beginning at last to dismiss
the paranoia upon which the anti-Communist demagogues fed and so reclaim
some measure of political sanity.

***

The Goulds' late winter holiday to South America was planned for a time when
the president's absence from Carleton seemed possible and when there was no great
difficulty with regard to IGY Antarctic planning. It did, however, require Larry
to miss one set of meetings of the Ford Foundation board. This seemed especially
unfortunate given that there were multiple proposals close to Gould's heart, in
the area of education, that the foundation was set to discuss at these meetings,
and he very much wanted his views to be considered. Accordingly, shortly before
beginning his holiday Gould sent Ford Foundation president Gaither a statement
endorsing foundation grants for a national scholarship program and for a program
of general support for private colleges. The latter initiative in particular received
much prominent press attention, virtually all of it favorable, when approved and
announced to the public early in March. A Ford Foundation staff officer wrote
Gould to say he believed that Gould's letter, which had been summarized for the
full board, had been "most helpful to the other Trustees in their consideration of
the various docket proposals in education."

Larry attempted some preparation for his upcoming vacation by studying a

---

* Dwight Macdonald characterized the Reece Committee hearings as "devoted largely to the
  animadversions of obscure crackpots and the scarcely more lucid testimony of the Reece
  Committee's staff," and he summarized the majority report as "a lengthy exercise in irrelevance,
  insinuation, and long-range deduction." He further described the report as "a patchwork of
  data botched together to support two major propositions—that the social and cultural changes
  that have taken place since the McKinley administration are the result of a conspiracy by the
  staff employees of foundations, and that these changes are subverting the American way of
  life." Though the Reece report could point to little evidence that any of the foundations had
  supported pro-Communist activities, it alleged that "subversion" properly understood had been
  supported nonetheless, by "undermining some of our vitally protective concepts and principles."

little Spanish "at odd moments," hoping to learn enough to get around without having to depend too entirely on his wife, who had been studying the language for a few years. The plan evolved: eight days in Peru, followed by close to three weeks in Chile, and then four days in Buenos Aires before a leisurely—nineteen-day, with port calls—return to New Orleans by ship.*

The first leg of the Goulds' seven-week holiday was an early morning flight from Minneapolis (6 degrees above zero and snowing) to Miami (75 degrees upon arrival, "bright sun, clear skies, spanking breeze"). The first glitch was that evening. Forty minutes into their night flight from Miami to Lima the plane turned back due to an oil leak, and after a delay of some hours the flight was postponed a full day. On the second attempt the next evening all went well and, as Peg recorded, "we were lulled to sleepiness by generous drinks on the house and good Chilean wine with dinner."

In Lima the day following, after checking into the Bolívar Hotel and rest-ing up for a time, Larry and Peg had seated themselves at a bar to sample their first pisco sours when they were happily astonished to have walk in a Carleton graduate of 1947, who was for his part thrilled to encounter the Goulds south of the equator. This was Dick Ajello, who the Goulds knew had married a Peru-vian girl, Marcella Pajares-Bedoya, of Carleton's Class of 1946. "Marcie," Larry remembered well, had been a student—one of the best—in the last class he had taught before becoming president. Unknown to the Goulds, the Ajellos had been living in Lima for the past year and a half. "What a reunion," chronicled Peg. "Dick kissed me, and almost Larry, and nothing would do but to drive out to their house and surprise Marcie. She almost jumped out of her skin and what squealing and kissing for her favorite professor and his wife."

---

* The trip's timing made Gould unavailable to participate in person in an important Carleton appointment made instead by Treasurer Bruce Pollock, but about which Gould and Pollock had had prior discussion and of which Gould had expressed himself "heartily in favor." This was the bringing back to Carleton of Frank I. Wright, Class of 1950, in the capacity of assistant treasurer, but with the explicit expectation that young Wright would so familiarize himself with all aspects of the business administration of the college that he would be prepared eventually to succeed Pollock as college treasurer. Wright was already well known to Gould as having been a top student and star athlete at Carleton. Prior to Wright's graduation the president had written him a glowing letter of recommendation, stating that "seldom have we had such an extraordinary student. In addition to his rare combination of intellectual and physical qualities he is a genuinely modest man. There are great days ahead for him." The great days ahead for Wright were, as it developed, to be spent at Carleton, to which Wright would devote more than three decades of outstanding financial leadership.

    A second momentous appointment that also began while the president was away was completed, with a campus interview followed by Gould's decision to make an offer, shortly after his return to Carleton. This was the hiring of Ian G. Barbour as assistant professor in the new Department of Religion, though also with an openness to Barbour's doing additional work in physics, the field in which he had first been trained. Barbour would go on to become an academic jewel of the Carleton faculty, holding appointments in both departments into the 1980s and establishing himself as a leading voice on issues at the common boundaries of science and religion. In 1999, Barbour would become the twenty-seventh recipient of the prestigious Templeton Prize for Progress in Religion.

Peg found the eight days in Lima "all too short." The Ajellos added greatly to their enjoyment, though arrangements had also been made to visit with a pair of Institute of Current World Affairs fellows, Bill MacLeish (the son of poet Archibald MacLeish) and Richard Patch, who flew over from Bolivia to see Gould. Larry and Peg explored Incan and pre-Incan ruins, spent a weekend visiting Huancayo up in the Andes, and had the experience in Lima of being shaken by a "first-class earthquake." On their penultimate evening in Lima they were the special guests at a dinner party arranged for them by the Ajellos, for which Marcie prepared a delicious Peruvian repast and invited fourteen guests, half *peruano* and half American residents of Lima. When the Goulds arrived, the rest of the guests were already at the house and were, in Larry's honor, all wearing red carnations. "I had all I could do to keep from bursting into tears," Peg wrote. After a lively dinner one of the guests broke out a guitar and entertained the company with a sampling of "enchanting" Peruvian songs.

When the couple flew on to Santiago, Chile, they found another "warm and royal welcome," this time from the family of Carleton professor Antonio Obaid, who was married to Larry's secretary Dorothy. The Chilean Obaids thoroughly charmed the Goulds with their immediate and abundant affection. To Luís Obaid and his family the Goulds became Don Lorenzo and Doña Margarita—or Doña Peggy. Santiago was followed by several days in the Chilean region of Los Lagos, which Larry termed "wonderful," and then on the Pacific at Viña del Mar, which was "lovely." (Connecting "wonderful" to "lovely," however, was an exhausting railroad leg which Peg declared "ghastly," "incredibly dirty," and altogether "the worst rail journey we have ever made.") In Buenos Aires, to which they flew on March 8, they were again greeted by a Carleton connection, here the brother of the wife of a Carleton professor of zoology. And here again they had an unexpected encounter, this time with an icebreaker. It turned out the Navy vessel USS *Atka,* which was returning from a reconnaissance mission to Antarctica to search out possible places to establish American bases as part of the International Geophysical Year program, was in port. Naturally Gould, as head of the Antarctic Committee for the IGY, wished to go on board and be brought up-to-date on what they had found out. The Goulds spent half a day aboard the *Atka,* which to Peg's delight turned out to be carrying eleven live penguins, a mix of Antarctic emperors and Adélies, which she said made her fonder than ever of Oscar, the stuffed penguin greeting visitors at the entranceway to their home in Northfield.

The cruise portion of their holiday, returning from Buenos Aires to New Orleans, was not either Gould's favorite segment. Tours at stops in São Paulo, Rio, and Willemstad were interesting, but, according to Peg's report, they had not really realized before boarding at Buenos Aires that they were booked on a bona fide cruise ship and, she wrote, "God deliver us ever from going on one of the damned things [again]." "It is hard to believe," Peg shuddered, "that adults can indulge in such adolescent goings-on." Her pre-conceptions were confirmed:

"Cruise passengers are just as I imagined them to be. Autobiographical & dull— one listens with only a small ear. Most people travel just to say they've been places." Moreover, the movies shown on board were "uniformly the worst Hollywood has to offer." Still, "at the risk of seeming queer and asocial it is perfectly easy to withdraw from the puerile nonsense and enjoy one's self—which is, for the most part, what we have done." Peg and Larry allowed the days afloat "to melt into each other and lose their proper identity, which is all very pleasant. We read, we sun ourselves on the afterdeck or swim in the salt water pool, sleep a siesta every afternoon and are lazy as all get out." When they docked in New Orleans, where neither had been before, they took a couple of days to see that city before return-ing home to Northfield on April 2.

***

Almost as soon as Larry was back, he was off again—to Washington in connection with IGY Antarctic matters. The thorny business of clarifying the command structure, as between the US Navy and IGY scientists, that was to pertain for the Antarctic program as a whole and for the individual bases to be established was clearly in need of attention. Whatever the answers regarding command were to be, it was important that responsibilities and assignments be clearly defined, so that the necessary collaboration with the Navy should work as smoothly as possible. The immediate result of these early April 1955 meetings was that the USNC Executive Committee empowered a group of six persons, including Gould, "to explore the need for solidifying the command structure of the proposed Antarctic expedition." "This," Gould wrote Paul Siple a few days later, "is a complicated matter." To William Benton, Gould wrote after these meetings that he was in need of limiting or reducing his Antarctica-related duties, which were threatening to grow quite heavy. "If I were fifteen or twenty years younger," he felt, "I might devote all of my time to it and look toward the direction of the Antarctic program." But he was not. "I shall continue as chairman of the com-mittee, " he told Benton, "but I may not participate as actively as I would like."

Later in the month, on the eve of yet another three-day return to Washington on Antarctic business, Gould elaborated further, to another correspondent, on the tensions between what he was being called upon to do, what he would like to do, and what he felt able to do, with regard to these responsibilities:

> We are now in the midst of discussing the command structure and selecting key people for the various positions. The president of the National Academy of Sciences and the director of the National Science Foundation were on the point of getting the president of these United States to request the Board of Trustees of Carleton College to release me for three years to take charge of the whole Antarctic program. I put a stop to it, for many reasons. I don't know at the moment just how deep my participation can be, but I do still hope I can eat my cake and have it.

Gould's late April visit to Washington involved talks both with Naval officer George Dufek and, twice, with Admiral Byrd. As Gould subsequently reported to Siple, he was "worried to see how much Dick Byrd had changed" since he had last seen him, citing alarm over "his great loss of weight and other indications of ill health." In May, Gould sent Byrd a diagram of a proposed command structure for the IGY's Antarctic work, and Byrd claimed that he was now "pulling up" again in both weight and endurance.

"Command structure" had, in a sense, arisen also that year as a matter claiming Gould's attention at Carleton. Laird Bell, seventy-two years of age in the spring of 1955, had some while earlier suggested that the time was approaching when he should step down as chairman of the Board of Trustees. Larry Gould had also been after Bell to assent to an honorary degree from the school for which he had done so much. Bell was amenable to taking the honor only if it were timed so as to either link with or follow his laying down of the chairmanship. Who then should succeed Bell? Both the president and the incumbent chairman felt that trustee leadership should ultimately pass to Atherton Bean, whose qualifications for the role were splendid. When sounded out about the matter Bean protested that Carleton should try to get another Laird Bell. Gould sensibly pointed out that unfortunately there weren't any more. Gould advised Bell in November 1954 that he now felt that "Atherton might be willing to succeed you directly if it could be done without offending Lou Headley." (Headley, a most devoted and senior trustee, had long been the board's vice chairman.) Ultimately Gould reached the conclusion that the chairmanship really must first be offered to Headley, who could be expected either to decline or to fill the post for only a few years, after which the board could turn to Bean. When it developed, by May, that Headley would indeed wish to become chairman for a time, Gould pressed Bean, with success, to allow himself to be nominated vice chairman. "I think this is a good arrangement," Gould wrote Bell, "for I believe it will mean Atherton will become Chairman before too long."

At the start of these discussions Gould assumed that, although Bell would be allowed to step aside as board chairman and had agreed to accept an honorary degree at Commencement, "under no circumstances" would Carleton allow him to leave the board altogether, at least prior to the 1958 completion of the term to which he had most recently been elected. Bell, however, thought that the time was now ripe for his daughter Margaret to be elected to trusteeship, giving the family a fourth generation of such service to Carleton. Father and daughter both felt that they ought not to overlap, that it would be a mistake for the family to take up more than one seat on the Carleton board. (Moreover, Bell pointed out, his resigning as a trustee altogether at this time would relieve him of some of the embarrassment he would otherwise feel at being voted a degree by a board over which he "might be thought to influence.") Accordingly, Bell urged Gould to reconcile himself to their clearing the way for "Maggie" to take a seat on the board by Laird's retiring to "emeritus" status, which would allow him to continue to

Laird Bell receiving his Carleton honorary degree, 1955

attend and speak at future meetings, though not to vote. He pledged to continue to attend with "decent regularity" but observed that the more he was "divorced from technical responsibility the easier it will be for Lou Headley." To this plan Gould did smother his protests, and so it happened.

The spring of 1955 marked the tenth anniversary of Gould's selection as president of Carleton, and the milestone was celebrated in that year's Larry Gould Day observations. As reported in the local paper:

> Immediately after vespers Sunday evening, May 15, the students marched from the chapel to the president's home, singing Gould's alma mater "Michigan Fight Song." Mrs. Gould was presented with a bouquet of roses, the couple was given an electric oven, and the Goulds were informally serenaded with several appropriate songs. On Monday there was a "red hangover" on campus and at luncheon at the Carleton Tea Room faculty table Dr. Gould was surprised with a huge tiered cake fantastically frosted in red and inscribed "A Decade of Progress with President Gould."

Three weeks later, Carleton's commencement ceremonies highlighted both Laird Bell, the only person upon whom an honorary degree was bestowed that year, and the completion of Larry Gould's tenth year in office. Gould himself had agreed to deliver the Commencement address. He said that he had been "drafted into doing this by the Board of Trustees" and that they had wanted him to speak about the accomplishments of the last ten years but that he was displaying his stubbornness by talking instead about the ten years ahead. Even so he did begin by touching on a few select achievements of his presidential decade, observing that the college's total assets had increased from $5.68 million to a little more than $11 million and endowment from $3.5 million to $6.27 million. He noted the new, remodeled, or then under construction buildings, the provision of an insurance annuity arrangement for all Carleton employees, and the adoption of a 40-hour work week for office workers and a 44-hour week for maintenance. (He claimed to have adopted an "84-hour week for administration.") One thing in which he took particular pride was the "great increase of the alumni interest and support." Alumni clubs, he noted, had increased in number from sixteen to forty-two, and alumni giving to the college had "increased several hundred per cent in amount and between 100 and 200 per cent in the number of givers."

Turning to the main thrust of his remarks, he foresaw that within the next ten years there would be new men's and women's dormitories and—at long last—a women's gymnasium. There would be a fine new academic building suited to the newest developments in physics and biology. There would be a modern gymnasium and field house for men. And possibly a combined theater and auditorium.* "Most important of all," he said, was that he expected "at least a 50% increase in the salary schedule of the faculty." One thing that would not change, he said, was Carleton's "dedication to the idea of quality."

Gould finished by reminding the graduating seniors of what he had said to them four years earlier when they were just entering the college. "I said then," he said now,

> that you were forming an association that nothing—nothing—not even death, could break because always you are a part of Carleton College. Whatever happens to you is of concern to us. I remind you of the ancient legend of Antaeus. And you, like Antaeus, will find your strength renewed and your faith revitalized when you return to this maternal ground.

Two days after Commencement, Laird Bell sent Gould a warm note expressing the pride that he himself felt with regard to "the accomplishments of your first ten years," which he observed that Gould had touched on only modestly in his address. "I hope you really have had satisfaction out of them," the retiring board chairman told Gould. "Everybody else has."

***

Gould's travel path for the rest of June took him variously to Albuquerque, where he delivered the commencement address for the University of New Mexico and visited with Peg's brother Jack and his family; to Chicago where he accepted an honorary degree from the Chicago Medical School and delivered yet another commencement address, this time on the subject of "What Doctors Should Know Besides Medicine"; on to Washington for a meeting of the USNC-IGY

---

* This would be the only item on his list of buildings not in fact to appear within ten years, though as a "Music and Drama Center" it was managed within sixteen.

Executive Committee; and then before the month was out to Colorado, where he had a speaking engagement in Estes Park and stayed two nights in Boulder at the home of an old friend, ecologist William Skinner Cooper, formerly of the University of Minnesota.*

Early in July Gould flew to Paris, as head of the US delegation at an international planning conference for the Antarctic phase of the International Geophysical Year, held under the auspices of the IGY Special Committee, known by its French acronym of CSAGI. To the charm of the famed City of Lights Gould "completely succumbed," even though, as he regretfully reported after, he was kept so busy by his duties in the days that he was there that he "neither had time to go to a show nor to take a single sightseeing trip." The purpose of the conference was to discuss and decide a number of fundamental matters regarding coordination of the IGY Antarctic programs of a dozen participating nations. Cold War politics and disputes among nations making territorial claims in Antarctica—claims not recognized by either the United States nor the Soviet Union but tenaciously held to by those countries asserting them—lay just under the surface, particularly with regard to the locations of the Antarctic stations to be established by each nation. They might easily have fatally disrupted the conclave. That they did not—that the 1955 CSAGI Antarctic Conference in Paris was in fact memorable for the spirit of cooperation that prevailed among the scientists—is why the meeting has been singled out as meriting "a significant place in Antarctic history" and credited with "providing the framework that was later developed into the Antarctic Treaty."

The potential for discord was evident at the conference's start. The United States had already announced, at a meeting in Rome the previous year, several locations where it thought it might establish stations in Antarctica. The USSR had not been in attendance in Rome, as at that time it had not yet indicated that it would participate in the IGY. But when the Paris conference began the Soviet scientist Vladimir Beloussov, speaking for the USSR before Gould did so for the United States, revealed that the Soviets proposed to locate stations at two locations, one at the South Pole itself and another on the Knox Coast, that were already among the sites for which the U.S. had previously mentioned plans. When it was Gould's turn to speak he pointed out that these sites had already been preempted by the American declaration at the IGY Rome meeting the year before. Georges R. Laclavère, the French cartographer who had been elected chairman of the conference, suggested that it might be preferable for the collect-

---

* While in Colorado Gould also met with a young design artist, Raymond Jacobson, who had been recommended by University of Colorado Professor Alden Megrew as a strong possibility for a one-year appointment as a sabbatical leave replacement in Carleton's Art Department. From that meeting came an invitation to Jacobson to visit Carleton in July and look the situation over. From that visit came a one-year job offer made directly by Gould. What came ultimately was Jacobson's spending more than thirty years on the Carleton faculty—Gould and the Art Department becoming so impressed with Jacobson's contributions during his one-year appointment that they created a new permanent position for him.

ing of scientific information if the Russians would establish a station not at the geographic South Pole, but perhaps at the Geomagnetic Pole, helping to fill a large gap in IGY coverage. With regard to the overlapping plans for the Knox Coast, Gould recalled, in a talk given years later to the Antarctican Society, that he asked Beloussov, "Why do you want a station on the Knox Coast? We've done a lot of work along there and we want to go back to it." Beloussov replied, "Because it's on the same meridian as Moscow." Gould said, pointedly, "Well, the scientific importance of that eludes me." To his credit, Beloussov admitted, "It eludes me too." Fortunately for the spirit of cooperation the Soviets did not insist on either site, agreeing to shift to alternate proposals.

Laclavère set the tone for the conference at the opening meeting, insisting that its deliberations must be about science and not politics. The delegates unanimously adopted a resolution endorsing this statement. As Gould would later write: "This was a significant decision of historic importance. Matters of strategic and political concern were set aside as the Antarctic IGY program was dedicated to the sole purpose of scientific exploration." An "enthusiasm for collaboration swept through the meeting." Among the important decisions reached in this atmosphere was agreement that there should be exchanges of personnel at the various national stations and that, in particular, the "weather central" station to be set up at Little America should be internationalized. (The agreement that a Russian meteorologist would be included there was coupled with Soviet assent to the stationing of an American at the main Soviet base.) Gould would thereafter laud the Paris conference for the participants' remarkable degree of "willingness to adjust national programs for common goals" and point to the moment as marking "a flexibility and a simplicity and freedom from political considerations perhaps without precedent in international scientific cooperation."

Meanwhile, an ocean and the greater part of a continent away from Paris, the small cabin the Goulds had caused to be built on their "G2V"* parcel of land near the town of Wilson, Wyoming, in the Jackson Hole valley was ready for its first use. The Goulds left for the West on July 15, just a few days after Larry's return from France. Moving into their new summer retreat was exciting, but unfortunately on their very first day in the new cabin Peg slipped, injuring her knee. She chafed through an immobilized week and then, putting aside her doctor's recommendation, returned to her feet—too soon, as became clear when, after the couple's mid-August return to Minnesota, the knee flared up again and her Northfield doctor sent her to the hospital for some days. By the first of September she was again home but for a time "moving about with a cane and crutches."

Early in September Gould attended the 24th triennial council of the United

---

* The group buying property on Fish Creek, north of Wilson, incorporated in the state of Wyoming as "Gros Ventre Ventures, Inc." commonly abbreviated G2V. The G2V subdivision thus created was divided into six parcels, upon which were built six summer residences, including that of the Goulds.

Chapters of Phi Beta Kappa, conveniently meeting that year in nearby Minneapolis. The council elected Gould the organization's vice president for the next triennium.

The following week public announcement was made of the establishment of the National Merit Scholarship Corporation, aimed at helping to identify America's brightest high school students and to promote and assist their college educations, with a founding grant of $20 million from the Ford Foundation. Through his position as a Ford Foundation trustee concerned particularly with grants to education, Gould had, in his own words, "been concerned with the development of the idea," and he was instrumental in bringing about Laird Bell's appointment as chairman of the board of the new corporation.

As Carleton readied to begin a new school year, construction was moving forward on the new library. A ceremony celebrating the laying of the building's date stone, with suitably grand remarks to be delivered by Gould, was scheduled for early October, following Carleton's Homecoming football game. Looking ahead to the completed building's formal dedication in 1956, which he wished to make "one of the outstanding academic festivals in the history of the College," Gould wrote to former Librarian of Congress Archibald MacLeish, a warm friend of Carleton trustee John Cowles, inviting him to come and give the dedicatory address for the new building.

At the end of September Gould headed for New York for several days of Ford Foundation meetings. To foundation staff members he gave a talk on the "International Geophysical Year and Antarctic Experience." Ten days later it was back to Washington for IGY and NSF meetings. His Antarctic Committee held a pre-departure briefing session with the officers and staff of Task Force 43, the first ships undertaking the expeditionary phase (Operation Deep Freeze I) of IGY Antarctic operations. It was a few days after the conclusion of these meetings that a piece by journalist Carl Rowan of the *Minneapolis Tribune* confirmed that Gould would himself return to Antarctica late in 1956 and probably remain until March to direct at first hand "a major portion of 'the most comprehensive study of man's physical environment ever undertaken.'" The day after this news appeared in print, Gould gave a dinner address on the IGY to the Twin Cities Carleton Club, titling his talk "South Again."

In November, as the first two Operation Deep Freeze I mission ships (the USS *Arneb* and USS *Wyandot*) prepared to leave for the Antarctic from the naval station in Norfolk, Virginia, Gould was on hand to see them off. In remarks delivered at the departure ceremony, he reviewed their mission—the delivery of construction materials for the Little America and McMurdo stations to be established in the Ross Sea area and the unloading and caching of equipment for the inland stations to be constructed the following year at the South Pole and on Marie Byrd Land—and placed it in the context of overall plans for what Gould termed "the most ambitious program in international scientific cooperation ever undertaken."

Early in December (the same week the arrest in Alabama of Rosa Parks sparked the historically momentous Montgomery bus boycott), Gould was again in Washington for a meeting of the National Science Board. This was followed in New York by another meeting of the Ford Foundation trustees, memorable for finalization of a stunning decision, announced days later, to award grants totaling more than half a billion dollars to colleges and universities, medical schools, and hospitals. This was, to that date, the largest sum ever granted in the history of philanthropy. Of the $260 million total to be given collectively to 616 privately supported liberal arts colleges and universities, $210 million was to go into endowments to produce income that for ten years was to be used exclusively for much-needed improvements in teacher salaries. (The other $50 million for colleges, to be divided among only 126 selected schools, of which Carleton was one, could be used for any pressing academic need. Gould estimated that Carleton's share of the combined gift would be at least $550,000.)

The opportunity for what a St. Paul newspaper referentially capitalized as "The Great Grant" arose out of huge increases in the profitability of the Ford Motor Company, whose stock shares at that time still provided the foundation with most of its income. Tax codes required that the bulk of the income of philanthropic foundations be distributed in accordance with their charitable purposes rather than "unreasonably accumulated," and as the value of its Ford Motor Company shares shot upward the Ford Foundation was finding it difficult—such a problem to have!—to spend enough of its money to stay within the tax guidelines. The result was the Great Grant, a huge "one shot" package—dispensing at a single stroke $150 million more than it had given away in total over the previous eighteen years of its existence—that allowed the foundation both to dispose of its problematic excess of income and perhaps also, as a foundation historian has suggested, to "appease some of its political attackers by making a large distribution of string-free general support grants to established, uncontroversial institutions throughout the country." Naturally, Gould found the opportunity to participate in the deliberations leading up to the great giveaway "an exciting, thrilling privilege." He was careful, however, in his writing about the matter in the pages of the Carleton alumni magazine, to stress that the gesture, important though it was for the college, would not by itself be enough to raise salaries to the level at which he felt they ought to be. "The trustees of the Ford Foundation," he wrote, "hope the main result will be to focus attention on how great the continuing need is."

***

The honorary doctorate of letters given Gould in 1955 from the Chicago Medical School had been his seventh honorary degree. In the six years from 1958 through 1963 he would collect fourteen more. In 1956, he accepted no honorary degree, but it was not for want of invitation: In January—in the course of a single week, in fact—he turned down offers to be hooded by Yale, Dartmouth, and Hamilton College, due to conflicts, respectively, with Carleton's own commencement exercises, with the baccalaureate service preceding Commencement, and with the traditional senior breakfast hosted by the president and his wife on the Sunday preceding Baccalaureate Sunday.

Gould's service to Carleton, during the first months of 1956, included attention paid to financing the ongoing building program (he wrote Charles Horn of the Olin Foundation of how he would like to hear him giving the dedication speech at the opening of an Olin Hall of Physics and Biology at Carleton or perhaps in connection with a new men's dormitory), to alumni relations (he and Peg made another two-week swing through the alumni clubs of the Pacific Coast and Southwest in March and April*), and to appointments (he himself handled the hiring of new men to fill two important college positions: college chaplain, where David Maitland was brought in to replace David Stowe, and athletic director and football coach, where, after interviewing "more people than for any other position I have filled since I have been president," he hired Warren Beson to take over from Wally Hass).

More than a week of March was spent in Washington and New York on what had by then become the usual mix: hearings before the House Appropriations Committee in connection with a request for more IGY support, Ford Foundation meetings, a National Science Board meeting, and a USNC-IGY Antarctic Committee meeting. Late in April Gould was in Washington again, this time participating in a National Academy of Sciences symposium on Antarctica sponsored by the American Geophysical Union; he had served as chairman of the symposium committee. Alongside other presenters such as Admiral Byrd (on US Antarctic Programs) and Admiral Dufek (reporting on the recently completed Operation Deep Freeze I), Gould offered a presentation on "Highlights of Antarctic Exploration."

As always, the scope of his concern during this time was a blend of the great and the small. A personal note in April to English professor Charles Shain reflected on how "yielding to demands on his time" the president of a small college often has to be, reporting by way of example the surprising number of parents who expect him to have full acquaintance with individual students. "I get a goodly number of letters from parents every year," he told Shain, "who ask me to talk to their sons or daughters and see if I can't help straighten them out. I usually try to do this." (The greatest satisfaction he had in his position, he also told Shain in the same note, was derived "from watching others do what I have enjoyed more than anything else I have ever done; namely, teach.") Another personal note, from the next day, informed Assistant Professor of Geology Eiler Henrickson, his former student, whose research for his doctorate had not yet quite been completed, that he had "secured $200.00 from an anonymous donor" to help Henrickson

---

* Near the end of this trip a Denver newspaper's interview reflects Gould's ahead of his time thinking about renewable energy, quoting Gould as warning that "man will not be a permanent resident of this planet until he learns to live on current income—direct solar energy—instead of on his bank account of fossilized fuels like oil, coal and gas."

acquire some material needed for him to progress. The same day, Gould's memo to Treasurer Pollock read:

> Herewith is my check for $200.00 as a gift to Carleton College. It is to be made available to Eiler Henrickson for the purchase of some necessary thin sections to complete his research. I am most anxious that this young man get his doctorate this spring. The source of this gift must be kept confidential from Mr. Henrickson.

He also, that month, corresponded with Professor of International Relations Reginald Lang about Lang's anxieties in caring for his ailing mother. Lang described his reading while under this strain as "escapist": rereading Carlyle's 1837 history of the French Revolution and some Dickens. Gould thought such fare "about as good a prescription as I could give" but also heartily recommended that Lang revisit the novels of Jane Austen, if he had not read them lately.

All of this time the new Carleton Library building had been approaching nearer and nearer to completion. The ceremony of dedication, with principal address from Archibald MacLeish, was scheduled for May 19. However, on the first of May Gould received the following telegram from MacLeish:

> Am undergoing wholly unexpected surgery at Massachusetts General Hospital tomorrow. Profoundly regret inconvenience to you and to college. Will mail manuscript of address I had hoped to give. Its interest, if any, will be wholly academic now, but you may wish to see it. Regards.

Within a day Gould and the library dedication committee had taken the decision to postpone the event until September, with the hope that MacLeish could still make his speech when fully recovered. (As he indeed would be. A few days later Gould, who had received further news through John and Betty Cowles, wrote to Mrs. MacLeish, "What a wonderful word 'benign' is, isn't it?" Early in June MacLeish confirmed that "21 September will suit my severed colon simply fine and me also.")

Meanwhile, although the spring dedication was postponed, Carleton went ahead with the physical moving of the book collection out of the old Scoville Memorial Library, along about a thousand feet of sidewalk and into the new building. In what was dubbed "Project 'L' Day," all classes were cancelled for Tuesday, May 22, as roughly a thousand volunteer members of the campus community—students, faculty, and staff—worked together throughout the morning to transfer, without losing call number order, library collections of books and periodicals from shelves in the old library directly onto waiting shelves in the new. As described afterward in the school paper:

> Women manned their stations while men manned Med-O-Milk boxes filled with books, and thus began a weaving line to rival any academic procession.

Moving books into the new Carleton Library during Project "L" Day, 1956

> For four hours men traversed the distance from old to new library
> with successive loads while women shelved books into their new homes
> in the stacks. …
> At the close of the morning workers had walked an estimated
> 2,000 miles and the only bottleneck that developed was in the line of
> eager beavers waiting to get their boxes of books and head for the trail.

At the conclusion of this impressive feat of planning and community cooperation, an outdoor lunch was served to all on the terrace of Burton Hall. Fitting
remarks were made by three speakers: Minnesota Attorney General and former
Governor J. A. A. Burnquist, who as a Carleton student in 1896 had helped move
books *into* the library from which they had just spent the morning moving them
out; Vice President and Treasurer Bruce Pollock; and a beaming President Gould,
"in fine form," according to the student reporter. The new Carleton Library was
fully open for business at 8 a.m. the next morning.

***

During the summer of 1956, the Goulds' traditional holiday in Jackson Hole
ran from the latter part of July into early September. Before that Larry and Peg
spent a few days at John Cowles' retreat of Glendalough, following which Gould
sent Cowles "in line with our talks" his suggestions regarding "great areas of potential service" ripe for philanthropic attention. (Gould's top five areas, in order,
were world overpopulation; the maintenance of peace, especially in Southeast
Asia and the Near East; securing in the U.S. closer ties and better understanding
with Latin America; guaranteeing adequate salaries to the faculty of outstanding
small liberal arts colleges; and a "world-wide primary education program designed
to teach all mankind to read, write, and do arithmetic, and to make elementary
improvements in personal standards of health sanitation.") Gould also, before
departing for the West, chaired in Washington the eighth and final meeting of

his USNC-IGY Antarctic Committee, which was completing its prescribed preparatory work. In Wyoming, Gould unfortunately broke a rib, which kept him from fishing but which he nonetheless termed "sort of a mixed blessing," for it forced him to give attention instead to a piece of long overdue writing, an article on Antarctica for the *Geographical Review*.

While in Wyoming, the Goulds celebrated Larry's sixtieth birthday. Though reaching a round number demanding notice, Gould claimed to feel no different after the milestone than he did before—perhaps, he claimed, because "I continue to define a middle-aged person as anyone ten years older than I am." Back in Minnesota, the *Minneapolis Tribune* took note of the occasion by running a profile, written by Victor Cohn, under the title "A Man of Books and Blizzards." Making the story more about Gould and Carleton than about Gould and the Antarctic, Cohn wrote that this was intentional because Carleton was, in Gould's own estimation, "by far the more important part of his life." Cohn wrote that Gould's immediate answer to the question, "What is Carleton's special reason for existing?" was "Quality!" Cohn quoted Gould as identifying his goal for Carleton as "the highest possible quality in a student body never to be more than 1,000"—"large enough to sample the great society all around us, yet small enough to have a sense of community," where "the student is a participant, not a spectator."

In September, with the start of Gould's twelfth year as president, came the delayed ceremony of dedication for the new Carleton Library. Archibald MacLeish, now in fine health, arrived to give his long-awaited dedicatory address, accompanied for the trip by former Secretary of State Dean Acheson.

MacLeish painted a compelling picture of libraries, in an America not yet clear of the evils of McCarthyism, as "strong points of defense" for the party of freedom of the mind as against the party of "ignorance and bigotry and fear" in the "spiritual civil war" that had quietly but bitterly been dividing the country since the end of the Second World War. He pictured librarians, when they are worthy of the name, as active and noble champions of the cause of freedom of the human spirit and deplored any notion that in this struggle "which can never perhaps be won for good and all" they could ever in good conscience remain neutral. "No librarian," he declared, "who believes in the freedom guaranteed by the Constitution, and who detests authoritarianism, can avoid taking positions on controversial issues; indeed on the most controversial of all issues—for the issue of the freedom of the mind in America today is precisely that." And so he celebrated in the dedication of a new library at Carleton College an affirmation that "one more bulwark has been raised against ignorance and bigotry and fear: a tower which will not yield."

MacLeish's speech had been worth waiting for. Gould declared afterward to College Librarian James Richards, Jr. that he thought the address had been the greatest he had heard in his twenty-four years at the school.

Gould's subsequent activities that fall continued to be the usual mix of Carleton business and matters connected with his external involvements. The

Ford Foundation trustees, at the end of September, named New York University President Henry T. Heald as the foundation's new head, replacing Rowan Gaither, who had become too ill to continue. In mid-October, after attending National Science Board meetings in Washington, Gould spent a couple of days at the naval air station in Davisville, Rhode Island, helping to indoctrinate scientific personnel selected for IGY Antarctic service. He finished his advice to the Antarcticans in training by telling them: "Remember, if you fall into a crevasse, you'll be in a hell of a lot better shape in 500 years than any of the rest of us!"

His Antarctic Committee had held its final meeting, but Gould's IGY work was far from over. Not only was his own extended tour of inspection of the scientific stations being established in Antarctica coming up soon, but he was asked that autumn to accept a new title, with ongoing responsibilities, that of director, United States International Geophysical Year (US-IGY) Antarctic Program.*

At Carleton, one memorable early November event was the convocation performance of folksinger Pete Seeger, whose career had suffered from the effects of McCarthy-era blacklisting, but whom some Carleton students now hoped to bring to campus. One of those students, Tom Blackburn (Class of 1958), later remembered that he and his roommate were thinking of trying to raise money towards Seeger's appearance through bake sales but that Gould had proved not only sympathetic toward extending what could be a controversial invitation but went further and paid the costs of bringing Seeger to Carleton out of his own discretionary fund.

On the evening of November 14, at the Waldorf Astoria Hotel in New York, Gould delivered to the Grocery Manufacturers of America an address later published under the title "Use It or Lose It." In it he called for greater encouragement for the emergence of excellence in individuals and in particular for giving "every stimulus ... for the gifted to advance as far and as fast as they can."

The next day, in Northfield, Charles Miel, Carleton's vice president in charge of public relations and development, who for years had occupied a Laird Hall office next to Gould's own, was found slumped at the wheel of his car near Carleton's Goodsell Observatory, dead of a heart attack at age fifty-eight. It was a shock and a sadness and it deprived Gould of the presence of someone upon whom he had come to depend more than he realized until he was gone. In a tribute published in a subsequent issue of *The Voice of the Carleton Alumni*, Gould wrote that in thinking of Miel he was reminded of these lines of Lao Tzu:

> He does not make a show of himself,
> Hence he shines;
> Does not justify himself,

---

* This appointment came through Det Bronk of the National Academy of Sciences, who wrote Gould that as the IGY's Antarctic program moved past planning phase and into its operational phase he and others recognized that it had more and more required Gould's "actual direction" and not merely his "wise advice as chairman of the Antarctic Committee."

Hence he is glorified;
Does not boast of his ability,
Hence he gets his credit;
Does not brandish his success,
Hence he endures;
Does not compete with anyone,
Hence no one can compete with him.

Consideration of the matter of Miel's replacement began almost immediately, with Gould telling John Cowles that he would be anxious to find "a young man who not only has organizing ability but who can also help me in the outside contacts. I can't possibly get around to cultivate all of the prospects that need such attention." Already in the first part of December Gould had himself identified a strong candidate in Carleton alumnus Robert L. Gale (Class of 1948), but for such an important appointment the trustees wanted to have a search committee investigate many possibilities, and it would not be until well into the spring that Gale would ultimately be offered the post, which he promptly accepted.

A faculty appointment of note that was finalized during November and December of 1956 was the bringing back to Carleton of an outstanding graduate of 1950, Bob Will, as assistant professor of economics. (Decision in this case was made jointly by Gould and economics professor Renzo Bianchi.) In conveying the offer to Will, with whom he had had some continued correspondence through the young economist's inter-Carleton years, Gould wrote of his pleasure in hearing about Will's imminent marriage, shared personal perspective on Christian denominational affiliation ("I was a Methodist for many years but have found in the Episcopal Church more than in any other gathering the avenues to the resources which I think religion should bring one"), and urged upon his newest faculty colleague a measure of his own enthusiasm for what was being built at Carleton: "Carleton College is an exciting place, and I want people to come here who are willing to stick their necks out and take a chance that it can become an even greater place."

Gould was scheduled to leave Northfield on the first leg of his IGY journey to Antarctica on the morning of December 21. Before that, he gained much satisfaction out of successfully concluding one further piece of Carleton business that he described as very close to his heart: the raising of $250,000 to be added to the endowment to create the Donald J. Cowling Foundation in Philosophy. To his relief, that campaign was completed on the 17th. He immediately wrote the good news to President-emeritus Cowling, saying that as a result his Christmas would be merrier and that he could now leave for Antarctica "with a much lighter heart."

***

The word that Larry Gould himself used to sum up the personal importance to him of his return to Antarctica at age sixty was "healing." Before leaving he had allowed himself, for quite an extended period of time, to be overworked, driving hard on so many fronts of activity and care. His travel schedule, shuttling so often to New York and Washington and frequently elsewhere could be wearying. There had been difficulties with Peg, whose struggle with depression continued. The sudden death of Charlie Miel hit hard—tangibly, by adding to his burdens, but also perhaps in another way, as he considered the sudden heart attack of the man two years his junior. He was not sleeping well. At the end of November he had been "struck low physically," having to cancel planned attendance at an important meeting in Chicago of the presidents of the colleges of the Midwest Conference. (Dean Frank Kille was sent in his stead.) However, the enforced caesura of his Antarctic trip at this juncture proved a restorative godsend. Decades later, writing to another Carleton president with advice to "have the good judgment to take a long long holiday" when needed, he recalled his own experience: "I did not realize how almost desperately I needed a holiday in 1957 until I went to Antarctica to set up our scientific bases. I had quite lost proper perspectives. I regained them in the ice clad continent and came back refreshed to finish the race."

As in 1928, Gould would approach Antarctica from New Zealand. He had first expected to fly that far before joining a Navy ship bound for the Ross Sea, but he changed his plans so as to cross the Pacific instead aboard the USS *Curtiss* leaving from San Diego. Admiral Byrd was expected to do the same, and Gould wrote him that he looked forward to the opportunity for leisurely visits with his former chief. "You have no idea, Dick," he wrote Byrd, "how exciting it is to me to think of going back once again to the places where I served with you back in 1928-30." That now long-ago adventure, he said, "opened vistas for me that have made my life infinitely more rewarding than it could otherwise have been. I would like to recapture some of that excitement and I think I may." Unfortunately, only a day or two before embarkation Byrd sent Gould a telegram communicating his distress at finding that he could not make the trip after all—"that will be a tremendous loss to me," he wired.

Peg left Northfield a few days before Larry did, spending Christmas and New Year's with Jean and Dick Hoppin in Austin, Texas, before continuing on to Mexico to live there for two months practicing her Spanish. Larry sailed from San Diego on the *Curtiss*, in company with numerous IGY scientists and Naval support personnel, on December 27. It is clear from his own testimony that as he started this voyage Gould's spirits were at a low ebb. Eleven days in he wrote Sally Crandall, at Carleton: "I was very, very tired when I came aboard this ship." To Peg, two days later, he confided: "When I got aboard the ship I felt as though I might be on a one way journey—and I was so depressed after talking to you—let's not do that again."

Apparently, however, shipboard life began almost immediately to improve his state. With Byrd having decided not to go down from San Diego, Gould was berthed in the admiral's quarters, a creature comfort to which he was not insensible. Most afternoons featured meetings of the scientific and support personnel with questions and discussion so that everyone could get acquainted with the people and programs represented. Gould called the ship "wonderful" and the voyage "perfect." Already on New Year's Day he wrote Peg that this was his "healing voyage." A week later he repeated the phrase, adding that though he was "springing back slower" than he could wish and was still not sleeping well, "that will come." "These days," he wrote his wife, "have forced me to look at myself as I have refused to do for years." He assured her that "I shall be all right and I shall put behind all the mistakes and misgivings of the past that have risen to remind me how I have insulted my body. I promise you that it shall not happen again." He told her that the young ship's doctor had taken his blood pressure and found it to be considerably lower than what had been measured in Northfield three weeks before. "Obviously the voyage is doing its work," he wrote. "The fact that most of my trouble is above the collar complicates things but that will be all right too." On the voyage's tenth day Larry wrote Peg that one of the signs of how much he loved and missed her was that he was continually picking up and looking at a favorite color picture of her—she looking up into the camera while patting a dog—that he found particularly lovely.

The *Curtiss* arrived at Port Lyttelton, New Zealand, near Christchurch, on January 12. She was met by Harry Wexler, chief scientist for the US-IGY Antarctic Program, who brought Gould a letter from Peg. (Two more were received after another two days.) Gould and others from the *Curtiss* were escorted into Christchurch by the American consul, and Gould established himself for a couple of nights in a quiet hotel. He reboarded the *Curtiss* on the 14th, and the following morning before renewing the journey south he sent Peg another note to be picked up in the last mail to leave the ship. Once they were again underway, Gould wrote her, "the Antarctic will begin to become very real. I have been shedding cares and past mistakes all the way down. I'm going to dump all the rest overboard as we depart here."

The *Curtiss*'s destination was McMurdo Sound, on the western side of the Ross Sea, where Admiral Dufek's naval task force had built an operational base the year before as part of Operation Deep Freeze I. (That operation also established another base, Little America V, at an eastern indentation of the Ross Ice Shelf at Kainan Bay.) At the edge of the ice pack the *Curtiss* was met by the icebreaker *Glacier*, which escorted it through. Before reaching the Sound, a helicopter was employed to transfer cargo from the *Curtiss* to the *Glacier*. It needed to make quite a few trips, all of them involving careful piloting given the ships' susceptibility to rolls and pitches where they were. Gould thought to have himself flown over to the *Glacier* to confer with personnel there concerning the location of the IGY's Wilkes Station on the Knox Coast but was dissuaded by the pilots' disinclination to carry passengers given the tricky nature of the takeoffs and landings. Not long after, Gould was at luncheon when the ship's flash alarm sounded, calling all hands on deck immediately. The helicopter had just cracked up taking off

Harry Wexler and Gould, en route to McMurdo Sound, January 1957

from the deck of the *Curtiss*. A boat put over the side rescued the two pilots within minutes, unhurt, though the helicopter and a load of paint intended for the *Glacier* were lost.

Later, as the *Curtiss* sailed into McMurdo Sound, dominated ahead by towering Mt. Erebus, an active volcano with steam visibly rising from its top, Gould was able to look through a telescope at the still-standing remains of the camp from which Shackleton had made his historic 1909 journey to within ninety-seven miles of the South Pole. At the McMurdo station Gould conferred with Admiral Dufek, who, when asked about the disposition of the *Curtiss* now that she had arrived in Antarctica, replied that for the duration of his stay the *Curtiss* was Gould's ship and would take him wherever he wished.

During the 1956-57 Antarctic summer, Dufek was overseeing Operation

Deep Freeze II, a major part of which involved the construction of a permanent scientific base at the South Pole, to be named (following a suggestion advanced by Byrd) the Amundsen-Scott Station. The delivery, by air, of all of the cargo needed for this task was assisted by the establishment of an intermediate weather station and refueling camp that, although named Beardmore Camp, was actually located at the foot of Liv Glacier, some 120 miles east of the Beardmore. Although in late January the supply, building, and manning of the South Pole station was still incomplete, the facility was formally dedicated on January 23—not at the pole itself, but in a grand ceremony at McMurdo. Gould served as dedication master of ceremonies and gave a short concluding speech of his own, ending with a declaration that, by the authority vested in him by the National Academy of Sciences, he hereby dedicated the Amundsen-Scott IGY South Pole Station "to the high purposes which have brought us all to this place, confident that the men at this historical station will write one more brilliant page in the long record of man's endless struggle from darkness toward light."

Following the dedication Gould made a short trip by Jeep over to Scott Base, a couple of miles away, where just three days before New Zealand's Sir Edmund Hillary had officially opened a facility in support of the Commonwealth Trans-Antarctic Expedition (which would the following year complete the first overland crossing of Antarctica via the South Pole). Visiting with Hillary, who had gained worldwide fame four years earlier with his successful ascent to the summit of Mount Everest, Gould looked across McMurdo Sound toward Antarctica's Royal Society Range and, as he later recounted, while acknowledging that he had never yet seen the Himalayas himself, wondered whether Sir Edmund thought that these mountains before them could compare at all favorably. Hillary, whether in earnest or simply displaying the tact of a diplomat, replied, "Yes, they do."

The next two days Gould took flights in a plane placed at his disposal by Dufek. The first of these airborne days, northward along Victoria Land towards Cape Adare alongside what Gould termed "one of the most stupendous mountain landscapes in the world," was "fascinating," but it was the second day that was for Gould the more thrilling. In his own account:

> We were in the air for nearly eleven hours and flew from McMurdo all the way along the Antarctic horst clear over to Leverett Glacier, which was the end of my sledge journey 28 years ago.* The pilot is a superb master of the R4D in which we flew. He is Commander Shinn who landed the first plane at the South Pole. All I needed to do was suggest that I would like to get a closer view of something and away we went. We flew up Beardmore Glacier, the unbelievable stream of ice which Shackleton and Scott had climbed on their journeys toward the Pole. Then we landed at what is called Beardmore Camp. ... I got out of the

---

* It had actually been only twenty-seven years, but Gould in this letter wrote twenty-eight—three times.

plane and looked up at Liv Glacier and realized that I was standing where my five companions and I had sledged 28 years ago. … When we took off again, I asked the pilot if he would fly along the front of the Queen Maud Mountains so I could see how they looked from the air as compared with my memories of 28 years ago. The scenery is even more spectacular from the air than it is from the ground—mountains thirteen, fourteen, some probably fifteen thousand feet high, for the most part swamped with glaciers, among which are the longest known anywhere in the world.

When the plane returned to McMurdo Gould had covered roughly the same ground, in under eleven hours, that he and his companions had once taken more than three months to traverse by dog sledge. Across two days of flying he had viewed almost the whole length of the world's greatest fault block mountain system, clearly seeing, to his delight, its "geology duplicated time after time with the great flat-lying Beacon sandstone series with its seams of coal and sills of dolerite." Nowhere else on earth, he marveled, could he find anything like it.

Gould stayed aboard the *Curtiss* for transportation to the fifth incarnation of Little America, on the other side of the Ross ice shelf from McMurdo, some thirty miles east of the old Bay of Whales location. Here, with the bay ice completely gone, the ship had to be moored to the ice shelf, which was much too high to unload onto, so Gould, along with the rest of the cargo, had to be transferred from ship to base by helicopter. Gould found Little America, just at this time, to be quite crowded, with men who had already wintered over and were awaiting departure overlapping with new personnel just arriving. For the moment, nearly three hundred men were sleeping, in shifts, in quarters designed for eighty-three. Gould himself temporarily bunked down in the dentist's operating room. On January 31 he rode along in a twin-engine plane carrying a load of fuel out to an inland depot. That the inherent dangers of Antarctic flying had not disappeared since Byrd Expedition days was borne in upon him when shortly after takeoff the craft flew into an enveloping whiteout, where all that could be seen was a uniform milky whiteness in every direction. Then one of the plane's two motors began to hiccup. Gould, sitting alone in the rear of the plane, put on headphones so that he could listen in on the pilot's communications with Little America—and heard the pilot give "a great oath" and say to prepare for an emergency landing. After some tense moments the pilot used radar to successfully return them to within a few miles of Little America where they landed "safely enough," though skiing on the ground into a large snow drift which might have knocked off a wing. It was, the pilot told Gould, the first time all summer that there had been such a difficulty. Close call or not, Gould was back in the air the next day in a smaller plane, overlooking the great tractor train route now connecting Little America to Byrd Station—and reflecting on the difference in payload between a single tractor train, carrying 180 to 200 tons, and his own sledging experience of 1929 in which the total load of dogs and men might have amounted to "about a ton and a half." "I am inclined to think," he wrote, however, "that our way was … more fun."

During one of the days spent at Little America V, Gould followed through on arrangements made prior to his departure from Northfield, making radio contact

George Dufek

with Carleton sophomore Edward Douglass, a ham operator, who at 1: 30 a.m. local time tape recorded an interview with Gould that was later broadcast to the campus on the college radio station, KARL. Gould told Douglass that he had that day flown over the site of the original Little America, the construction of which he had superintended in 1928. (Little was then left that was visible, except for the tops of the radio towers, still projecting above the level of the accumulated snow cover.)

The *Curtiss* redelivered Gould to McMurdo Sound on February 8, and on the 9th he had another lengthy talk with Dufek concerning the progress of various operations. (A few days later, while returning to New Zealand aboard the *Curtiss*, Gould wrote Peg of his satisfaction in working with Dufek, confiding that "I have found in George Dufek the qualities I wish I might have found in Dick Byrd 28 years ago.") That day Gould and Chief Scientist Harry Wexler were flown over by helicopter to visit the well-preserved site of Robert Scott's 1910-12 base camp, from which Scott had departed on the trek to the pole from which he and his party did not come back. The next day Gould was flown over the South Pole itself in one of the giant four-motored Globemaster planes that had been supplying the Amundsen-Scott South Pole base by air drop but which had been unable to operate for some weeks due to insufficiently frozen bay ice at McMurdo, the only surface on which the great planes were then able to land on the continent. Gould was able to see the camp plainly, watch the parachute drop of ten tons of supplies, and have a good air to ground conversation by radio with Paul Siple, now the South Pole station scientific leader. Reaching 90° S latitude by air was a grand climax to Gould's Antarctic return, just prior to reembarking for his return north.

Before flying out of Auckland, New Zealand, on March 1, Gould spent some days in Wellington. There he had a "heart-warming" reunion with the former Jocelyn Tapley, who had been "a lass of 7 or 8" when Gould had enjoyed an extended stay in her parents' Dunedin home in 1928 at the start of the Byrd Expedition. In 1957, Jocelyn was now Mrs. King, and a mother of five.

Gould returned via Honolulu, southern California, and—with Peg still in Mexico for a few more days—Tucson, before flying on to Washington to confer with both the National Science Board and the National Science Foundation and for a debriefing with a White House staffer. From Tucson, he wrote Peg that in Washington his "busy work begins," but, he insisted, "I promise you and me that

I will never again let it get as busy as it has been at times in the past." Three days later, he in Washington and she now revisiting the Hoppins in Austin before her own return to Minnesota, he wrote her a love note, saying that he had always found it difficult to tell her how much he depended on her and upon her "approbation and applause." The letter continued:

> You are so handsome and you do make such a grand impression and I am so proud of you. Please when I tell you these things don't shrug them off for it is so and it won't do your ego any harm if you will practice believing them—just a little bit at least! And that's that.

On Monday, March 11, Gould was still in Washington, reporting that day to the National Science Foundation. He was due in New York later that week, with a commitment on the 15th, but in between he had a little time, and that afternoon he indicated to USNC-IGY executive director Hugh Odishaw that he would call Dick Byrd in Boston the next day to see whether it would be alright for him to fly up and pay the admiral a visit. That night Byrd died in his sleep of a heart ailment. He was sixty-eight. Late the following afternoon Gould flew instead to New York.

***

Gould's "commitment" in New York on March 15 was to attend the gala annual dinner of the Explorers Club at the Waldorf-Astoria and there accept the prestigious Explorers Club Medal. The award, first bestowed in 1914 upon Robert Peary, had previously been given to only twenty-one illustrious persons, all extraordinary contributors in the field of twentieth century exploration. Some of Gould's predecessors in the honor were his revered idols, such as Nansen and Amundsen. Several were his personal friends: notably Stefansson, Bartlett, Bowman, and Balchen. The predecessor who was most on the mind of that evening's banquet attendees, however—both because the news of his sudden passing was so fresh and because his association with that night's honoree was so strong—was of course Byrd, who had been the medal's fourteenth recipient, twenty years before. Gould felt "very humble to be included in such a list."

CHAPTER 21

THE PURSUIT OF EXCELLENCE

Half a day after accepting the Explorer's Medal in New York, Larry Gould was on a Saturday morning flight back to Minnesota. When he stepped off the plane at the Minneapolis-St. Paul airport shortly after noon he was bowled over to find himself greeted not only by his wife but by more than four hundred enthusiastically applauding members of the Carleton College student body, faculty, and staff, led by cheerleaders and the Carleton band, all eager to welcome their popular president home after his nearly three-month absence. Larry was embraced first by Peg, looking radiant and carrying roses presented to her by the Carleton Student Association. Following additional welcomes and acceptance of a student gift of dish settings for the Goulds' summer cabin, Gould submitted to an on-the-spot press conference with print and television reporters. Afterward a motorcade of faculty autos and eight chartered buses received police escort back to Northfield. Gould called his reception that day "one of the most heart-warming experiences" he had ever known.

At Carleton, the most dramatic change greeting the president on his return was the twin excavations, at opposite ends of campus, for two new dormitories, one for men and one for women. As arranged prior to Gould's departure for Antarctica, these projects were being financed with the help of an $800,000 loan from the federal Housing Finance Agency, plus the loan of an additional $400,000 from Carleton's own endowment funds. Construction contracts had been executed in January, and the new dorms were expected to be ready for occupancy by fall term of 1958.

After the dormitories, the next item on Gould's list of future buildings to aspire to at Carleton was a new home, with greatly improved laboratory facilities, for physics and biology. These departments were then housed in parts of Laird Hall (built more than fifty years earlier for a much smaller college) with spillover into a barracks-style temporary annex of World War II vintage. A large and shiny new building, Gould decided, really ought to be provided by the Olin Foundation, the hope of which rested on the continued cultivation of Charles Horn, who continued to blow sometimes hot and sometimes cold in terms of be-

Returning to a reception by Peg and more than 400 cheering students, faculty, staff

ing encouraging or dismissive toward Carleton's approaches. Gould wrote Horn about the need in April and followed up in May with a more explicit request and presentation of the case to the Olin Foundation. The immediate answer to the latter was Horn's typically curt "blow cold" response: "I must warn you against too much optimism as we have many other requests."

Having reached age sixty the previous summer, Gould now expected to re-tire from the Carleton presidency within something like four or five more years, and he wanted to deploy that time to the best possible effect. Moreover, with the death of Charles Miel and the hiring of a new and very young replacement to take over as vice president for public relations and development, Gould saw Carleton as arriving at a crossroads where it might now be especially desirable to employ outside professional services to help in analyzing the college's present position and developing a concrete plan of action for meeting the college's goals for the years immediately ahead. He drew up a statement of what he saw as Carleton's most important five-year needs and ambitions. Then, with the approval of the trustees' Executive Committee, he came to an arrangement with the John Price Jones Company of fundraising consultants, which came highly recommended for its previous work on behalf of other colleges and universities, for the prepara-tion of a "survey, analysis and plan" pertaining to Carleton's public relations and gift solicitation program, so as to best position the college to attain its objectives.

At the June 1957 meeting of the Board of Trustees Gould stated that in order to see certain highly desirable things accomplished before his retirement at age sixty-five it would be necessary for Carleton to raise $8 million in additional capital. This sum would be apportioned as $3 million to support ten newly endowed professorships, a million and a half each for scholarship endowment and for the biology and physics building, another million and a half in total for a men's field house, a women's gymnasium, and an administration building, and a final half million for maintenance. No action was taken that day in response to the president's statement, but the faint outlines of the ambitious capital campaign that would be the major focus of Gould's final years in office were beginning to take shape.

Earlier the same day, at the graduation exercises for Carleton's Class of 1957, attendees had heard the featured speaker, Joseph Kaplan, chairman of the United States National Committee for the International Geophysical Year, express hope that the spirit of cooperation characterizing the IGY program might help move the globe away from the peril of World War III and in the direction of "World Peace I." The IGY, a "year" to be eighteen months in duration, was officially to begin July 1, and near the end of June Gould traveled to Washington for a meeting and ceremonies in connection with its opening. Then early in July he drove Peg and Jill the poodle out to the cabin in Wyoming. After seeing them established in residence, he flew back to Minnesota to continue working through the balance of the month before rejoining them the first of August. From then until the second week of September, his attention was primarily given over to Snake River trout.

***

In September, Gould received the results of the John Price Jones Company's consultant study of Carleton College, together with its recommendations. The JPJ report, which would be discussed extensively in October, first by the trustees' Executive Committee and then at a meeting of the full board, was titled "Development and Public Relations Potentials at Carleton College." It noted that Carleton's educational quality was frequently given high ratings in various tabulations, including a recent survey by the *Chicago Tribune*, which had ranked Carleton as third among the "ten-best co-educational colleges" in America, the first two being Oberlin and Swarthmore. But the JPJ report also warned that Carleton's achievement of excellence was made precarious by the small size of its endowment relative to most of its peers. In that area, critical for many reasons, but above all because Carleton's maintenance of quality depended upon its ability, through its salary scale, "to hold its faculty intact and attract, in replacements, the calibre of teaching it requires," Carleton was outranked by many with respect to absolute size, dollars per student, and relative rate of endowment increase. "The survival of all that Carleton does and stands for," the report concluded, "relates crucially to this matter of very, very substantially enhancing the capital endowment. To our eyes this is a condition not of casual, but of urgent need."

The JPJ report was critical of the college's development program as it then existed, calling it "still rather shapeless and rudderless":

> In fact, it never really got under way. The Library campaign was successful, the Cowling professorship was raised, and the alumni-parent annual giving program has been well established—but these facts alone do not add up to a well-organized, long-range, capital-gift, development program. ... That all-important work still remains to be done.
>
> Now is the time to put all this preparatory work into action, to carry out the necessary operations that will get this ship launched.

The report recommended preparation of a printed "case statement" for fund-raising, a pamphlet or other publication that would set forth the "big picture" of Carleton's "achievements and potentials" as an institution of academic eminence. Carleton's case, it advised, "may become very largely *the case for the superior student*—the well-trained student who is equipped to serve meaningfully in the world of today." Rather than a "lowest-common-denominator" philosophy of attempting to provide educational services to the greatest number of individuals, Carleton in building its case for support must stress "education for quality, high selectivity, rigid standards, and intellectual pioneering."

Carleton also enjoyed, the report emphasized, a uniquely valuable asset in the person of its president, who was "internationally acclaimed" and "universally admired and respected for his personal qualities." Gould's off-campus obligations, said the consultants, though they did compete for his valuable time, were nonetheless helpful to Carleton for lending "prestige to the College, both educationally and public-relations-wise." It would be important, the report stressed, in light of Gould's intent to retire at age sixty-five, that the "fund-raising opportunities that revolve around his presence" be leveraged heavily while they still could be, "during the next four or five years." The consultants doubted that Carleton had the capacity to raise, prior to Gould's retirement, the full $8 million that Gould had indicated as his objective, but thought that the college might aim to raise $8.5 million in new capital assets within the next ten years, culminating in Carleton's centennial year, with about half that amount to be expected by the end of the first five years, the phase of the campaign that could and should center on Larry Gould.

Trustee review of the JPJ report elicited much discussion of specific details and overarching goals. The Executive Committee, noting that its members had "certain reservations about the priorities of certain goals, the time schedule, and the context itself," therefore determined to ask the full board not to approve and adopt the JPJ plan *in toto*, but rather to endorse "a concept of the importance of establishing a long term capital fund campaign and use the survey as a guide to the Board's future action."

In discussion by the full board, trustees John Musser and William Benton both suggested that the fundraising goals set forth in the JPJ plan were too low—Musser emphasizing that inflationary forces would likely mean that the stated dollar amounts would not, over a ten-year time frame, actually produce the improvements anticipated and Benton favoring a much bolder and more ambitious program, which he coupled with his own view that Carleton should expand beyond the self-imposed limit of one thousand students that the board had previously declared to be its policy. The board approved the creation of a new trustees' Committee on Development charged with "redefining the goals and continuing top policy setting responsibility for the entire development program." The board also approved a motion that Gould additionally appoint a separate faculty task force to work with the trustees' Committee on Development as to questions of objectives and needs.

Finally, Atherton Bean observed that the fact that the trustees had determined that parts of the John Price Jones framework of strategy and goals for a capital campaign needed to be rethought "should not cause any delay in the technical work necessary in setting up the staff and organizing the volunteer workers." Bean subsequently agreed to take upon himself leadership of the new trustees' Committee on Development. The outlines of the capital campaign to come were becoming that much less faint.

***

The world changed a bit that October, with particular repercussions for education and for fundraising possibilities for education, by the shock to American confidence that accompanied the Soviet launch of Sputnik I, the first artificial satellite placed into Earth orbit. Sputnik was sent into space on October 4. Before the month was out Gould was speaking a great deal about what he thought it ought to mean for American education. October 19 was Parents Day at Carleton, a memorable one that included the dedication of four murals by Carleton artist Dean Warnholtz for placement in the Carleton Tea Room—paintings commemorating various aspects of Gould's scientific contributions in Antarctica through the Byrd Expedition (one panel) and the IGY (three panels). Gould spoke to some nine hundred parents at a morning convocation on the implications of Sputnik. Later in the week, in what was described as remarks in "extension" of what he had said at the Carleton convocation, Gould was widely quoted in newspapers as calling for significantly more money to be spent on science education. "We must recognize and encourage our talented youngsters," he said, and "stimulate our children to an interest in the sciences." The Soviet Union, he observed, "has stepped into scientific leadership primarily because the Soviet does 'an extraordinary job of identification and segregation' of young people with talent and a scientific bent." Gould called for making sure that "real physics, chemistry and mathematics are taught in our high schools," rather than merely general science courses, and for making sure that "every qualified student" is able and encouraged to go on to

Gould and artist Dean Warnholtz with mural marking Antarctic milestones

college or university. He said that after Sputnik it was clear that "we have to do everything we can" in helping colleges and universities pay their faculties well and expand facilities. Asked whether the United States government ought to subsidize good students through college if necessary, Gould replied: "I've always been one to oppose federal aid to education. But the situation now is so critical that every talented child and high school graduate should be subsidized if necessary wherever the money may be found. If it is necessary to do it by government, so let it be."

During the same week, in correspondence with Minnesota Senator Hubert Humphrey, Gould tried to steer Humphrey away from favoring proposals being made, in response to Sputnik, for the establishment of a federal "Department of Science," noting that Congress could stimulate interest in science simply by better funding the agency it had already established to do this, the National Science Foundation. (Humphrey himself had long been a warm supporter of the NSF and its programs, and Gould had written a number of times before to commend him for his fine efforts on behalf of NSF budget requests.*)

---

*   The tone of correspondence between the Republican Gould and Democrat Humphrey had been growing increasingly warm and personal over the preceding two years and more. In addition to Humphrey's strong support for the NSF, Gould appreciated his stances on civil rights. In 1956, for instance, Gould had written that it was a "source of immense pride" to him that Humphrey was among "the liberal senators leading a campaign to limit the historic filibustering activities in the Senate. More power to you!" In the same October 21, 1957, letter referenced above, after his comments about the NSF Gould added: "I am very glad you are where you are, Hubert, even though Governor Faubus may not like you." (Humphrey had sent Gould excerpts from a speech in which he had lambasted Governor Orval Faubus's use of the Arkansas National Guard in Little Rock to prevent compliance with the Supreme Court's school desegregation decision as a national shame that gave the Soviets a significant victory in the court of world opinion.)

The Carleton College world also changed a bit that October, with Dean of the College Frank Kille's decision, after more than a decade guiding the College's curricular affairs, to submit his resignation in order to take up a new post, beginning February 1, as associate commissioner for higher and professional education with the State of New York. The press release announcing Kille's appointment as associate commissioner was issued October 29, a day that Gould was in Chicago for a gathering of Midwest college presidents, prior to going on to Washington for a meeting of the USNC-IGY Executive Committee. Just before leaving for Chicago, Gould completed and sent off a promised article on Antarctica for the 1958 *Encyclopedia Britannica Book of the Year*. That day also, Peg Gould departed for New Mexico to spend time with her brother and sister-in-law and to go with them on a car trip to Mexico. She was doing this to coincide with her husband's second, considerably shorter in duration, return to Antarctica within the space of a year.

Gould had been asked a couple of months before whether he would be willing to accompany half a dozen members of the House Committee on Interstate and Foreign Commerce, which had jurisdiction over both aviation and science and from which the National Science Foundation had been born, and a senior advisor to that committee on a November tour to McMurdo and some of the other IGY bases in Antarctica. Other commitments made it impossible for Gould to attach himself to the congressional party for its entire journey, but he agreed to join the group in New Zealand, from where they would fly down together to the white continent. He had written ahead to George Dufek at McMurdo: "I know that having a bunch of Congressmen around is something of a nuisance, but as you know this committee is a very influential one. ... It seems to me that it may be a very good thing to impress these people with the potential importance of aviation in Antarctica."

As he prepared to leave Northfield, Gould dictated a note to Sally Crandall and Dorothy Obaid in the president's office to say that they should have a good time while he was away and "have tea frequently." (Gould was in the habit of taking afternoon tea breaks in his office with Sally and Dorothy most afternoons when he was present, fixing the tea for the three of them himself.) "I know very well," he told them, "that when I return things will be in much better order than when I depart." "No one," he said, "could have more complete confidence in those who work with him than I have in the two of you and I am grateful to you beyond any means I know of expressing it."

Gould left campus on November 10, going first to New York where, on the 11th, he was featured on a nationwide NBC television broadcast, "The Ends of the Earth," on the subject of US-IGY Antarctic activities. From there he flew to San Francisco and then, via Honolulu, on to Christchurch to meet the congressmen. On November 21, the party flew from New Zealand to McMurdo Sound in a DC4. A week later, Gould and Representative Oren Harris, the chair of the committee, took part in the Thanksgiving Day service held at McMurdo's Chapel in the Snow. Gould enjoyed finding in Antarctica Carleton alumnus Tom Morgan (Class of 1949), there on assignment as a staff writer for *Look* magazine. At some point during these days the entire delegation was flown over the South Pole to observe an airdrop of supplies for the Amundsen-Scott station. Despite some misgivings in advance of the trip as to what escorting a group of politicians might be like, Gould found the journey both enjoyable and worthwhile. As he wrote Laird Bell following his return to Minnesota:

> The Congressmen were interesting, personable, and I became very fond of them. It was no idle jaunt on their part either. They were sincere, hard working people. The kind of journey we took is not one that would entice anyone who was afraid of toughness. Just the flight from New Zealand to Antarctica, which is a fourteen hour, tiresome, non-stop flight would in itself discourage the 'tourist.' We did have one Antarctic blizzard, which reminded the Congressmen of what conditions could be like. They came back convinced of the importance of continuing our scientific program there, and that of course was precisely what I wanted to happen.

To Dufek he reported that after leaving McMurdo he had continued to have further discussions with the congressmen about Antarctica and that they had "parted in Honolulu the best of friends." "I am sure," he wrote, "we have six friends dedicated to the importance of continuing the scientific program in Antarctica." (Indeed, in January Representative Harris would forward to President Eisenhower a list of Antarctic recommendations that included strong endorsement of the importance of continuing US scientific efforts at several sites in Antarctica beyond the conclusion of the IGY. By the end of that month American intent to do just that was announced.)

Two sad things awaited Gould's December return to Carleton. While he was away, economics professor Renzo Bianchi, a decade younger than Gould, succumbed to cancer at his Northfield home after a long illness. A day after getting back, Gould conducted a December 15 memorial service for Bianchi in the college chapel. The other was the tragic and highly sensitive case of a full professor who had developed a mental illness, manifesting itself through disturbing behaviors that included a compulsive petty kleptomania, about which some members of the community were moving from suspicion to full awareness. The professor was initially in denial about his sickness, and the whole matter came as a very great shock to the professor's wife. Gould endured difficult, private, post-Christmas conferences with them both. Of his talk with the wife, who had been unaware of the severity of her husband's difficulties and the disturbing things he was doing as a result of them, Gould said that he had had "few sadder experiences." But as the year turned, the professor agreed to psychiatric treatment and to the necessity of a terminal sick leave.

The year 1958 would eventually see public announcement of Carleton's new development program and capital campaign. In preparation for that, the first part of the year was notably marked by a high level of serious consideration, and potentially reconsideration, of what the college was and where it should be going in the years ahead. The trustees turned their attentions to that at their January meeting, following a certain amount of routine business and a number of significant announcements from Gould. These included the news that the college would be receiving a substantial gift from the Andersen and Hulings families to establish the Fred C. Andersen Foundation for American Studies, that he was appointing Professor of Music Henry Woodward as acting dean of the college until a successor to Frank Kille might be found, that he had invited the other presidents of the Midwest Conference to meet together to discuss matters of common concern regarding tuition fees and scholarship aid, and that he had recently been appointed US representative to a newly established international organization to be known as the Special Committee on Antarctic Research (SCAR).

The group then focused on the major business of the day, consideration of "certain hypotheses" reached in the early work of the trustee and faculty committees on development formed the previous autumn. Atherton Bean read in full the preamble to the faculty committee's first preliminary report:

> Carleton should continue to be a small, coeducational, liberal arts college. She should continue to attract the most promising students possible, from as wide a range of social and economic backgrounds as possible, without regard to race or religion. She should continue to aim at excellence of intellectual training, conducted in that atmosphere of Christian ethics and Christian liberalism which is her fortunate heritage. She should continue to send out graduates distinguished by their ability to make critical and independent judgments, by their desire to enhance their civilization with the works of their reason and their imagination, and by their will to challenge any threat to the freedom and dignity of man.

While it was well to put the college aims into words so as to be able to communicate them effectively to the outside world, on this subject there already existed a clear consensus among nearly all persons connected with the school. Less clearly shared were opinions concerning the next matter to which Bean turned, that of the potential size and composition of the student body.

It had long been Carleton policy, and had frequently been affirmed by Gould, that the college would resist pressures to expand the size of its student population beyond one thousand. ("Carleton will never go above 1,000 students as long as I'm its president," Gould had flatly declared in a 1953 interview.) By the end of 1957, however, Gould's mind was being changed; in letters of December he was acknowledging that growth well beyond that limit might be desirable, so long as it would be done "in steps" which could be adequately financed, involving no "sacrifice in faculty salaries," and which did not lower the school's scholastic stature.

At the January board meeting, Bean reported that trustee Paul Christopherson, charged with thinking particularly about physical plant issues for the trustees' Committee on Development, had reached the conclusion that "it might be possible to accommodate up to thirteen hundred students without incurring much more expenditure than outlined in the John Price Jones Survey, which was, of course, based upon an enrollment of one thousand." This result could be reached, Christopherson had determined, by adding to the construction of the already hoped-for new science building another new dormitory along with dining room facilities to seat three hundred, and by expanding seating capacity in the chapel by extending existing transepts eighteen feet.

Bean also spoke in favor of gradually altering the student gender ratio so as to increase the percentage of men from the existing 54 percent up to a maximum of 65 percent. He expected that this would give the student body somewhat greater stability, given that the rate of attrition was lower for men than for women, increase the proportion of students taking courses in the natural sciences, and might improve the campus social environment.*

Following discussion, there was ultimately no objection expressed to "the concept that the student body gradually be increased as other conditions permit to a total enrollment of thirteen hundred students" and additionally that "in so doing more emphasis be placed upon increasing the percentage of men to women" not to exceed a ratio of 65 percent to 35 percent.

That same week, Hazel Lewis, whose tenure as Carleton's dean of women went back to the Cowling administration, advised Gould of her intent to retire at the end of the academic year. Knowing that this transition was approaching, though its exact timing had been uncertain, Gould had already reached agreement with Carleton alumna Leith Shackel, who since 1946 had done an outstanding job as director of the Placement Service, to succeed Lewis.

At the end of January, Gould was in New York to deliver the Isaiah Bowman Memorial Lecture at a dinner meeting of the American Geographical Society. In his remarks, published as "The Polar Regions in Their Relation to Human Affairs," Gould asserted that it was true now and probably would remain true for a long while that Antarctica's major export was scientific data. "These data may," he prophesied, "turn out to be of vastly more value to all mankind than all of the mineral riches of the continent and the life of the seas that surround it."

From New York, Gould flew to the Hague to attend a three-day conference as US representative to the newly formed Special Committee on Antarctic Research. The first charter or constitution for SCAR—the acronym would later be changed to stand for "Scientific Committee on Antarctic Research"—was

---

* How a significantly widened gender imbalance was seen, in 1958, as likely to improve the campus social environment was spelled out in the draft "case statement" for the financial campaign circulated that autumn: "With such a ratio, the women enjoy a variety of opportunities for dates and social gatherings, since there are more than enough men to go around. This is good for morale, male as well as female."

written and approved at this meeting, and Gould himself wrote the first statement regarding what SCAR's geological program should be. Plans were prepared
for continuing the scientific exploration of Antarctica beyond completion of the
IGY. General Georges R. Laclavère of France was elected the organization's first
president. (Gould would eventually, in 1963, become its second.) Gould was back
in Northfield on February 6.

***

Carleton's president continued, in the first part of 1958, to speak frequently
about the critical importance of education in meeting the "crisis" posed by Sputnik.
In January he testified in closed-door session to a House Appropriations subcommittee that America needed to do a better job of recognizing and encouraging the
relatively small percentage of young students with the capacity to become great
physicists and mathematicians. In February, a speech delivered at a luncheon
in St. Paul, "Education for Citizenship," was featured prominently in the *Minneapolis Tribune*. In it Gould was quoted as warning that the Russians "believe
they can win with education—and maybe they can." Terming the situation one
of "critical danger," he warned that "all we need do is continue as we are and our
children, or our children's children, will grow up speaking Russian." While the
Soviet Union focused on developing young scientists, America, Gould felt, was
focused on mediocrity and group values. "Like penguins wrapped in blubber,"
he said, "we have wrapped ourselves in such a layer of luxury we are virtually
impervious to what goes on in the world around us." Part of his prescription for
change involved money: "We spend four and one half times as much on alcohol
and cigarettes as we do on education—and then say we cannot afford to build
new schools," and "we praise teachers as our most important citizens ... but we
don't increase their prestige or their incomes." Another part involved values: "We
need more individual responsibility, more individual sense of obligation to work
for a better world," and what we must stress to meet the challenge of the satellite
age is "discipline, hard work, and quality."

Discipline and hard work had never been lacking in Larry Gould's own
makeup, but that month he acted on his resolutions of the year before about
relaxing his pace in future by taking advantage of "a gap" he had found in his
speaking engagements and booking a short vacation with Peg at the Desert
Willow guest ranch east of Tucson. (The ranch was owned by "Brownie" Cote,
Carleton Class of 1921, whose son Bob had graduated from Carleton in 1956.)
Gould's purpose in going there, he wrote a friend, was to do little more than "sit
as quietly as possible in the sun for ten days."

Shortly after carrying out that purpose in Arizona, however, several weeks
of busy working travel ensued, filled with meetings to attend and speeches to
make. Gould's out-of-state stops included Schenectady, where he spoke on the
IGY at a founder's day convocation for Union College and picked up his eighth

honorary degree, and New York and Boston in March, where in the former city he was part of the Cooper Union centennial program, went on to the latter to address the Harvard Travellers Club and speak to a Carleton alumni club, and then returned to the former to finish as the dinner speaker for the annual banquet of the Explorers Club. Five days at home were followed by New York again, for a Ford Foundation meeting, and afterward Washington, giving the keynote address at the general assembly of the American Congress on Surveying and Mapping and the American Society of Photogrammetry. At the end of March it was time for another of his circuit tours of Carleton's western alumni clubs, bringing him over eleven days through Seattle, Portland, San Francisco, Los Angeles, and Denver. After three days at home he returned again to Washington for a meeting of the USNC-IGY Executive Committee. Clearly, the more relaxed pace he had promised himself and Peg was only intermittently followed.

Gould's close friend Bernt Balchen, now retired from the Air Force, was at this time preparing to publish an autobiography, *Come North With Me*. Early in April Balchen sought Gould's advice concerning portions of his proposed book that were highly critical of the late Admiral Byrd and which conveyed Balchen's belief that Byrd and Floyd Bennett had not actually reached the North Pole on the 1926 flight upon which Byrd claimed to have done so. Balchen told Gould that he had long ago made up his mind to, as he saw it, write honestly about Byrd as soon as he was out of uniform. Gould, for his part, found himself "very apprehensive" about the wisdom of Balchen's taking such a step himself, especially so soon after the admiral's death. He sent his friend an eight-page letter on the matter, expressing relief to have learned the day before that Balchen and his publisher had "mutually agreed to remove the portions exposing Admiral Byrd," which is exactly what Gould had meant to advise "in the strongest possible way." Expanding upon the matter, Gould wrote that while he knew "that ground well enough to realize the justice of what you have to say," he felt that public reaction would be highly unfavorable and that a controversy over Byrd would sadly obscure the rest of Balchen's autobiography, which was "a document of great achievements." Gould counseled that the timing was all wrong; if Balchen were to expose Byrd's shortcomings now, "people would inevitably say that you had waited until he was dead to do so." Moreover, Gould thought, both the powerful National Geographic Society (which had verified Byrd's original North Pole claim) and probably also the Navy, "much as they hated him," would rise to the admiral's defense and denounce Balchen as a detractor. A couple of months before, Balchen had written Gould that the truth about Byrd's flight was "common knowledge in English polar circles." Gould's response now was that, in that case, "possibly what goes on abroad about the North Pole flight will emerge in publication" but that it ought not to be Balchen introducing an attack. "If such an article appears by someone else and you are invited to comment about it, you can only say the truth of course."

On the matter of Byrd's complicated psychological flaws, Gould wrote that he tended to agree with Balchen's theory that Byrd was strongly motivated by "a deep-seated inferiority" which required him "over and over to prove himself to himself... I think I have never known a more unhappy man or a man less secure, a man more suspicious of the motives of those round about him." He thought, however, that that it would be unwise for Balchen to put much of this into his book. Byrd the hero, Gould concluded, "is an established myth and I think we shall have to leave it to history to take care of that. I honestly believe that none of us who was intimately associated with him should be concerned directly with it." Whatever he might to commit to private communications, this advice to Balchen would essentially be Gould's own lifelong policy with respect to public comment on Byrd.

***

That spring, radio station KUOM's University of Minnesota School of the Air selected Larry Gould as one of the twenty outstanding Minnesotans of the Twentieth Century and featured his contributions to state history in a late April broadcast.

In May, Gould, who had earlier in the year been appointed chairman of the National Academy of Science's new Committee on Polar Research, was pleased by President Eisenhower's call for the international demilitarization of Antarctica. By early June, eleven countries including the Soviet Union had accepted Eisenhower's invitation to a conference regarding an international treaty dedicating Antarctica to peaceful purposes and scientific inquiry.

Gould was pleased also by Senator Humphrey's co-sponsorship of legislation to strengthen American education at all levels, including federal assistance to college students through scholarships, low-interest loans, and work-study provisions, plus a new loan program for college and university building construction. Gould's favorable reaction to the federal aid proposals eventually embodied in the National Defense Education Act represented quite a post-Sputnik reversal of the staunch opposition he had expressed to any sort of federal aid to education a few years before. By 1958, in order that American education might "rise to the challenge which confronts it," he was willing to support certain forms of federal aid that would "encourage us and at the same time not jeopardize our freedom of action." He praised the bill being brought forward by Humphrey for having "safeguarded these things."

Yet another event pleasing to Gould from that same spring of 1958 was the decision by Phil Phenix, who had resigned as college chaplain five years before, to accept Gould's invitation to leave his current position at Columbia University and return to Carleton to guide curricular matters as the new dean of the college. Phenix would take over for acting dean Henry Woodward in September.

Not so pleasing was the illness with which Gould was hit in the latter part of May, sending him home early from a trip to Washington* and straight to bed with a high temperature. Although he tried to follow his doctor's advice to take it easy and mostly confined himself to bed for his first week of feeling unwell, his malady persisted. On June 8 he was diagnosed with a case of viral pneumonia and directed to follow a program of complete rest for several weeks. The next day being Carleton's Commencement, however, coupled with an important meeting of the Board of Trustees—the board chairmanship passed from Lou Headley to John Musser, and Atherton Bean presented the written report of the trustees' Development Committee, which was accepted and its recommendations for the upcoming financial campaign adopted in principle—Gould struggled through one more strenuous day before he could really think of complete rest. Three days after commencement, however, another doctor decided that Gould now had two kinds of pneumonia and packed him off to a Minneapolis hospital for several days of more serious treatments and enforced rest. Finally on the 23rd he was allowed to return to his office, though only for a few hours a day until leaving July 3 for the Gould cabin in western Wyoming, where he would spend most of the balance of the summer recuperating. Biology professor Thurlo Thomas saved Gould the effort of driving by himself transporting Larry and Peg to the Tetons.

During the summer months of 1958 the trustees' Committee on Development and the John Price Jones Company collaborated on producing a "case statement" for the development campaign, with the goal now defined as the raising of $10 million by the target year 1962. At the same time, a faculty committee on curricular revision completed a report, transmitted to Gould in Wyoming, that recommended that the college plan to shift from a semester calendar to a "3-3" plan of fall, winter, and spring terms.

Saving the resting president the trouble of writing his usual summer annual report to alumni and friends, the college instead published and distributed one of Gould's recent addresses, "Education and Survival." His theme here, a frequent one for him at the time, was that the contest with the Soviet Union was more about education than it was about hardware and that it then appeared that the Soviets were doing a superior job in identifying intellectual talent early, cultivating it, rewarding it, and "making teaching the dignified and reputable profession it ought to be." What was required of America, Gould posited, was no modest change, but rather "a veritable intellectual revolution which will bring about proper recognition of the teacher and the scholar and their elevation to the position of prestige in our society which they deserve." But more than that, what was also needed was "a reorientation of our sense of values." He acknowledged that the United States must continue to be militarily strong, that survival in these frightening times "demands greatly increased

---

* Before leaving Washington Gould met with John K. Bare, a psychologist at William and Mary, whom he subsequently hired to come to Carleton as cochairman of the Department of Psychology.

expenditures for defense." And yet, he said, in what was subsequently the most widely quoted statement of his address:

> ... somehow I do not believe the greatest threat to our future is from bombs or guided missiles. I don't think our civilization will die that way. I think it will die when we no longer care—when the spiritual forces that make us wish to be right and noble die in the hearts of men. Arnold Toynbee has pointed out that nineteen of twenty-one notable civilizations have died from within and not by conquest from without. There were no bands playing and no flags waving when these civilizations decayed; it happened slowly, in the quiet and the dark when no one was aware.

"I believe," Gould went on, "that a free society will survive only on ideals that are always beyond human attainment." Also, "it is the function of liberal education to introduce the student to himself and to this kind of world, for liberal education is concerned with man's chief purpose, which is the creation and preservation of values." This means, he concluded, that "education must be both moral and intellectual" and that the pressing task now must be "to rediscover and reassert our faith in the spiritual, nonutilitarian values on which American life has really rested from its beginning."

One more occurrence of that summer is well worth the telling. The Goulds' Wyoming cabin had no telephone. One July day less than three weeks into Larry and Peg's 1958 stay there, at a time the Goulds were being visited by Bob and Barbara Gale, a rather excited messenger arrived at the Gould cabin with the news that a phone call had come in for Dr. Gould at the general store in the nearby town of Wilson and that it was from the White House. A White House operator had learned from Gould's Carleton secretary where he was and that the best way to reach him was to phone the store and have them send a runner up to the cabin to bring him to town. When the renewed connection was made a bit later, to the great interest of the unusually large number of Wilson town folk who had found some reason to be in the store as Gould took the call, Gould found himself talking with Carleton alumnus Robert K. Gray, Class of 1943, who had recently been appointed secretary to the Cabinet in the Eisenhower administration. (Gray had literally "dropped in" at Carleton for a brief visit with Gould only a few weeks earlier, landing by Navy helicopter on the campus baseball diamond while on his way to represent Eisenhower at a ceremony in connection with Minnesota's centennial of statehood.) Gray's purpose in now telephoning Gould in Wyoming was to ask him, as Gray put it in a later account, "if he would accept from the President of the United States nomination to one of the biggest posts in Washington." More specifically, the proposal was that Gould head up a new and soon-to-be-prominent government agency that Congress and the administration would shortly be establishing. Gould's answer apparently was not immediate, for his correspondence includes the following to Gray, dictated in Wilson on August 18, though typed and sent from Carleton:

> It was very nice to talk with you some days ago and, of course, I was immensely flattered by the implications of your queries concerning me. Naturally I have thought much about our conversation and have come to the conclusion after sober reflection that I must give a negative answer even if the imposing proposal which you suggested were made to me.
>
> Our Board of Trustees is in process of reorganization. We have a new chairman of the Board and we have a new Dean of the College coming to assume his responsibilities September 1. On top of that we will be starting the biggest fund raising campaign in Carleton's history. Your devotion to your alma mater will convince you of the wisdom of my decision, I am sure.

In this way, putting foremost the interests of Carleton College and its upcoming campaign to raise the ambitious total of ten million dollars by 1962, Gould declined the chance to become the first administrator of an agency whose annual operating budget over the same time period would grow from three hundred million to over a billion dollars. That brand new agency would shortly be named NASA, the National Aeronautics and Space Administration.

Gould returned to Minnesota at the end of August, but almost immediately departed again for New York, where at the triennial council meeting of the United Chapters of Phi Beta Kappa he was elected president of that body for the next triennium. Labor Day weekend was spent with John Cowles at his place north of Alexandria. This was followed, prior to the start of the new academic year at Carleton, by meetings in Washington of Gould's National Academy of Sciences' Polar Research Committee. On the morning of September 14, he addressed the incoming Class of 1962 in Skinner Chapel. "Every time I greet a new class," he put into a letter later that day, "I feel sorry for myself that I cannot remove forty years and begin my education under the exciting days in which we now live."

The next day he answered a letter that had arrived over the summer from the daughter of the American ambassador to New Zealand. In it she asked him to respond to this question: "If you had to choose one man as the greatest, excluding Jesus, who would it be?" Gould's choice, "without hesitation," he wrote, was his lifelong hero, Abraham Lincoln, who he said had long been, to him, "the most absorbing individual." "Here in my office," he told his young correspondent,

> ... is a magnificent lithograph of Lincoln. It is a kind of talisman. When I find myself getting irritated at the things that sometimes happen in conferences, lest I lose my temper I glance upward at this lithograph, which no one can see but me. It is a talisman that helps me to keep myself in line. I think history does not exhibit a more splendid example of what the human spirit can be.

***

Friday, October 24, was that fall's red-letter date, for Gould and Carleton both. That morning, the Board of Trustees convened in the library at 9:30 a.m. for what Gould said would be one of the most important meetings of the board in

the history of the college. There Atherton Bean, as chairman of the Development Committee, presented the report and recommendations upon which that committee had labored through the summer and early fall. The trustees had all been sent in advance a thirty-two page draft statement, titled *In Pursuit of Excellence*, that in more concise final form was to be widely distributed as the Carleton Development Program's case statement. The financial goals specified were to increase annual giving by at least $100,000 per year and to raise $10 million by 1962, "the year when retirement falls due for President Gould," with the aim of increasing faculty salaries, strengthening the endowment for scholarship and loan funds, and enabling the construction of six new buildings (a science hall, two

**Atherton Bean,
October 24, 1958**

dormitories, a men's gymnasium, a women's gymnasium, and a music and drama center) as well as the remodeling or enlargement of others. Following Bean's highlighting of certain aspects of the report, the trustees by unanimous vote formally adopted the $10 million development program and financial campaign outlined therein. The board then adjourned for Bean's presentation of the program to the Carleton faculty and student body at a special 11 a.m. chapel convocation.

Bean told the convocation that to do the job laid out in the development program within four years will strain "heart and nerve and sinew," but that he was confident it could be done and that it would mean that Carleton could "look forward to constantly rising stature in the educational world and to constantly increasing value in our free society." The convocation then continued with ceremonies of dedication of the two new dormitories that had opened on the campus that fall, one for men and one for women, now named, respectively, Richard Drew Musser Hall and Reine Myers Hall. (Both names honored major Carleton donors. R. D. Musser was a recently deceased former trustee of the college; Reine Myers was the widow of a former Carleton trustee, Paul N. Myers, and mother of a then current one, John H. Myers, Class of 1933.) Tributes to the namesakes' generosity were voiced by the longtime dean of men, Merrill Jarchow, and the recently appointed dean of women, Leith Shackel, and thanks offered by two students, officers of the Men's League and Women's League. Finally, senior Robert Stout, president of the Carleton Student Association, came to the chapel platform to present Gould with a gift from the student body—a gold-plated shovel, tied with a Gould-red ribbon, "to be used in turning over the first shovelful of earth for each of the proposed new buildings on the Carleton campus." Convocation was

Gould accepts Golden Shovel from student body president Robert Stout and senior Martha Calhoun.

then brought to a "ringing close" by thunderous applause and spirited singing of the Carleton Alma Mater.

Carleton's announcement of the launching of its $10 million program received wide and in some cases detailed coverage in newspapers of the upper Midwest, and was carried as well by the *New York Herald Tribune* and the Sunday *New York Times*. Twin Cities television stations gave the news prominent play, and both the Associated Press and United Press International news services sent the story, with photographs, out nationally.

Gould, addressing himself to alumni, called the development program to which the institution was now committed the "most ambitious effort ever undertaken by Carleton College" and "an act of faith" in the continuation of the college's role in education "of recognizing talent and encouraging its fullest development," which he summarized as "in other words ... the pursuit of excellence." Success in this undertaking, he indicated, would demand greater understanding and support from all the friends of the college than had ever been asked of them before. "So let it be."

CHAPTER 22

A NEW RENAISSANCE

Following the excitement of public presentation of Carleton College's ambitious development program and financial campaign on the morning of October 24, 1958, the trustees reconvened for further business. Two honorary degrees to be given at the 1959 commencement were approved, as was the appointment of William Kolb to a full professorship in sociology. A resolution was passed authorizing Carleton's membership in a new organization, the Associated Colleges of the Midwest, which was being formed by the member colleges of the Midwest Athletic Conference to "promote the educational effectiveness and the operating efficiency of the constituent colleges." (ACM schools, the resolution stipulated, would cooperate with one another in making studies, exchanging information, and potentially undertaking "cooperative programs in the fields of teaching, educational evaluation, research, finance and administration," but without any diminution of autonomy in the management of internal affairs.)

When the board subsequently turned to discussion of implementation of the development program, Atherton Bean stressed the importance of getting the campaign off to a good start by being able to demonstrate to prospective donors that the college trustees themselves were backing the program "not only by word but also by deed," and he reported that a small sub-group of the board had already indicated that they would start out the program with gifts totaling $1.75 million. It was further hoped that publicity might soon be able to be given to a prospective gift of a million and a half covering the campaign's first priority, the new science building. (In correspondence earlier that month with Charles Horn of the Olin Foundation, the possible source for such a grant, Gould—knowing that Horn would insist upon maximum publicity for any large Olin donation—had taken pains to assure Horn that Carleton would be sure to attach to the announcement of any major forward step "all possible fanfare, so as to attract the greatest possible amount of public attention and enthusiasm.")

In light of it now being the declared intent of the college to add six buildings to its campus in the near future, the chairman of the trustees' Buildings and Grounds Committee, John H. Myers, had been urging Gould to engage

Gould and architect Minoru Yamasaki, November 1958

the services of "the very best possible architect" to guide the college not only in the design of individual buildings but also as to overall campus planning, in the interest of maximizing harmony and beauty "from a placement on the campus viewpoint." The first celebrated architect approached, Eero Saarinen, declined Carleton's invitation due to other commitments but helpfully offered suggestions of alternate names. The end result, by the close of the first week of November, was the tentative selection of Michigan-based architect Minoru Yamasaki as "master planner" for the buildings associated with the Carleton Development Program, and an arrangement that Yamasaki would visit the campus to confer with Gould and a number of the trustees on November 20.

Gould told Yamasaki when first conferring with him that there would be a need for speed regarding plans for the science building. A tentative design prepared earlier by the firm of Magney, Tusler & Setter had been rejected as too pretentious and too expensive for Carleton's needs, but meanwhile Gould was being pressed by Horn for new preliminary plans for a more modest building to be delivered as quickly as possible due to the Olin Foundation's need to make its allocation before the end of 1958. Horn called Gould on November 15 (a Saturday morning) to remind him of the importance of moving along briskly and to lecture the Carleton president again regarding Horn's concern for getting "the maximum amount of building for cost" and lack of interest in "fancy" design. Before Yamasaki's November 20 visit Gould was worried by an article in *Time* magazine featuring a recent Yamasaki building that had cost 40 to 45 percent more than the estimates. "I grow increasingly concerned," he wrote Myers, "that we do not have some down-to-earth architect who can proceed at once with plans of a science building. We cannot afford to lose $1,500,000." On the morning of the 20th, while waiting for Yamasaki and Myers to arrive that afternoon, Gould wrote board chairman Musser:

> We are in a terrific "bind" concerning the science building, as I have tried to point out to the members of the committee from time to time. Few, if any, seem to realize the pressure under which we have to operate and the urgency of quick action. All of this I hope we can clear up satisfactorily to secure the promised gift; but we must move fast; for this building we have no time for the leisurely deliberations which we should have and which were part of the preparation for the library and Boliou.

Fortunately, Yamasaki that afternoon did much to allay Gould's worries, impressing him as being "thoroughly competent" and with a comforting "combination of imagination and practicality." He assured Gould that he appreciated the need for haste and that by the 8th of December he would be able to provide a preliminary design for the science building and other information required by the Olin Foundation as prospective donors.

And so it happened. Early in December Gould provided Horn with a summary presentation of the Carleton need and request, which Horn then had in hand for a trip to New York to confer with his codirectors. On December 16, the gift was officially confirmed. Gould wrote Horn: "I have just concluded a telephone conversation with you which is perhaps the most thrilling one I have ever had. I promise you, my good friend, that you will never regret the action you have taken. I shall call our architect in a few minutes and tell him to proceed with his plans ..." Public announcement of the gift would be delayed until early February.

Thus the development program was off to a good start. Late in November a gift arrived which directly advanced the distance to the $10 million goal by only .001 percent, but which had value to the campaign well beyond that. Gould's fellow Ford Foundation trustee, Judge Charles Wyzanski, who had received a 1954 honorary degree from Carleton, sent along what he called a "symbolic contribution" of $100. Accompanying the check was a letter, in which Wyzanski put forth the "compelling cause" for his wanting to contribute:

> I should like to pay tribute to that special excellence, characteristic of Carleton—an excellence rarely found anywhere, but when found, more likely to be in a small group or a small institution, than in the macrocosm. Just as we think of Western civilization's debt to the tiny city state of Athens, to the hardly larger Medieval and Renaissance community of Florence, to the Cavendish Laboratory and other small units at Cambridge and Oxford Universities, so we Americans have a right, nay a duty, to reflect on our obligation to Carleton College. It is one of the significant centers for the growth of our sense of higher value. Other institutions may, and indeed do, perform a role of wider dimension. But none is deeper in its concern for ultimate value; none is finer in its immediate products.

Gould was happy to publicize and otherwise put to good fundraising use such a statement as that, which had, he wrote Wyzanski, warmed the cockles of his heart beyond his capacity to convey appreciation. He took the letter with him when meeting shortly thereafter in St. Paul with major prospect William McKnight, and in December he passed it along to Bob Gale with the directive that it be made widely available in targeted campaign publications.

In mid-December, in the waning days of the International Geophysical Year, which would officially close on December 31, Gould traveled to Dartmouth College to attend a two-day conference on the objectives and organization of future US polar research, particularly with regard to participation by academic institutions. This conference resulted in a recommendation to the National Academy of Science's Committee on Polar Research (L. M. Gould, chairman) "to draw together representatives of academic institutions having an interest in basic polar research programs to consider how this interest might best be employed." Gould would subsequently convene the first meeting of the University Committee on

Polar Research on May 5, 1959, a meeting which resulted in a new organization of university representatives initially chaired by Michigan's James H. Zumberge.

For Christmas 1958, Larry had thought to surprise Peg with the gift of sending her, sometime in 1959, on a two-month holiday to Italy, in part to visit Bette Bianchi, the widow of Carleton's late economics professor Renzo Bianchi, in Florence. This thought was taken up with enthusiasm by Jean and Dick Hoppin, who transformed it into plans for Peg, who had never yet been to Europe outside the British Isles, to accompany her sister and brother-in-law on a ship crossing, starting February 11 in New York, with subsequent stops in London, Paris, and Brussels before going on to Florence. Two days after Christmas Larry wrote Bette Bianchi that he had "never seen Peg as pleased by any prospect as the one that now faces her. She was, indeed, quite speechless but she recovered rapidly." Gould's own best gift of that holiday season, perhaps, arrived the same day he wrote to Bianchi, in the form of news that Bernt Balchen's wife Bess had just given birth to a son and that the boy had been named "Larry," partly in Gould's honor. (The name was "Lauritz," the same as that of Balchen's father. But Gould was asked to be his godfather.)

As 1958 drew to a close the year's final issue of *Time* magazine ran a feature on Gould and Carleton, titled "Penguins & Scholars," that reported on the financial campaign to raise more than twice the school's current endowment. *Time* told the nation that Gould's method for finding money was "to bedevil the rich with reports of the U.S.'s conspicuous complacency." Gould was quite pleased with *Time*'s assessment that Carleton was one of the country's best colleges but that it numbered among the "respectable poor" and needed "a whale of a lot more money." And Peg was amused by the description of Larry as "running the college with casual, kindly autocracy, waving to undergraduates as he stomped about the campus"—though she thought her husband did not actually "stomp" when he walked. Meanwhile, Gould had, by request, sent in to the *Minneapolis Star and Tribune* a pair of New Year's resolutions for 1959:

> I resolve not to be bewildered by the rockets and man-made moons we are shooting into space, knowing that none of these celestial travelers can ever be as far-reaching as the minds that created them.
>
> I resolve also to remember that the last Spirit to emerge from Pandora's box (whose opening lid released so many ills on the world) was Hope, with the iridescent wings.

With the start of a new calendar, the International Geophysical Year was now concluded. The heavy responsibilities Gould had undertaken in connection with that effort had claimed a great deal of his time over several years of planning and execution, but he was happy to have had his active involvement in polar science so firmly reestablished. His IGY participation, he told one former Carleton science faculty colleague, had given him "a new intellectual lease on life."

In January the Twin Cities' educational television station, KTCA, finished work on a series of twelve movies about Antarctica that were then distributed nationally to thirty-one other educational TV stations. Gould served as the overall series host, and the dozen programs were described by project manager Betty Girling as embodying a concept she attributed to Gould: "to explore the continuing victory of man's spirit over his environment."

At Carleton that month, Gould reported to the trustees that the college had been approved to receive money to make student loans under the National Defense Education Act, but that he was troubled by the act's provision that student applicants must sign an affidavit and loyalty oath disclaiming belief in the overthrow of the U.S. government. As he wrote to John Musser, Gould found this requirement an obnoxious "holdover of the evils of McCarthyism," singling out educators and students for an indignity "not imposed on any other segment of our citizenry." His worry that this might constitute an infringement of academic freedom appears not to have been shared by most of the Carleton board, though it was stipulated in the minutes that "if at any time in the future this form of Federal aid to education involved any serious attempt of control of the educational process by the Federal Government, the College could decline to accept benefits." It would never come to that. A year later Gould reported that Carleton had in fact elected to withdraw from participation in the federal loan program at that time but that the reason had been "simply because the sums of money involved were too modest to make it worthwhile."

***

Two Days in the Life: February 6-7, 1959 ... At 11 a.m. on a Friday morning shortly after the start of a new semester of classes, an overflow crowd of students, faculty, and staff filled Carleton's Skinner Memorial Chapel for an all-college convocation that had been preceded by campus rumors of an important surprise announcement. That something unusual was afoot was confirmed by the presence of reporters and cameramen setting up in front of the podium. On the platform were President Gould, Dean Phenix, Treasurer Pollock, Professors Reitz and Thomas of the Physics and Biology Departments, and two other men in three-piece suits—one a strapping man with a waxed moustache and sporting a carnation in his lapel; the other slighter, white-haired, and balding. (These were Olin Foundation president Charles Horn and vice president James Wynn.) Gould rose to speak, causing "a buzzing semi-silence" to fall over the crowd. He quickly introduced Dr. Horn, who, he informed those gathered, "will say whatever he pleases."

Horn came to the podium, said a few words about the financial problems of colleges and universities, and then began talking about the Olin Foundation and what it could do to assist worthy institutions. Then, suddenly, the secret was revealed: "The Olin Foundation proposes to give $1,500,000 to Carleton College to build and equip an Olin Hall of Science. Now if anybody will accept it, I will be glad to give it to you."

Gould with Olin Foundation vice president James Wynn (left) and president Charles Horn (right) in February 1959

As the size of the gift sank in there was, for a moment, in the audience a stunned silence, punctuated by sharp intakes of breath, audible gasps, and a few low whistles—followed by a storm of thunderous applause which gathered, as Gould rose to make formal acceptance, into cheers and a standing ovation. Gould said that he was deeply moved and overwhelmed. Wynn added some words of his own, followed briefly in turn by Phenix, Reitz, Thomas, and then Pollock, who noted that Dr. Gould had shown multiple times that his dreams had a way of becoming reality and that he trusted the president would continue to dream. Finally Gould rose again, informing the assembly that this grant of a million and a half was the largest single gift in the history of Carleton College and one of the most munificent to any Minnesota institution.

The next day former Carleton dean Frank Kille, who had heard the news in New York and who knew of the many trials and tribulations which had beset Gould over years of dealing tactfully with the often irascible Horn, wrote Gould a note of hearty congratulations, saying that Carleton was deeply indebted to its president for his "persistence and patience in pursuing this particular source." That Saturday evening the Goulds—Peg was a few days away from embarking on her two-month trip to Europe—hosted the Mussers for dinner at home and afterward attended a concert given by classical guitarist Andres Segovia in the same chapel space that had so recently contained so large a measure of institutional exultation.

***

Early in 1959 Gould was caught up to some extent in controversy over the scope of ongoing post-IGY US programs in Antarctica and over whether or not to continue work at the Little America base. After Representative Oren Harris, who had toured IGY bases in Antarctica with Gould as his guide at the end of 1957, wrote President Eisenhower on February 7, with a copy to Gould, of his concern over plans to abandon the Little America base, Gould replied to Harris that he shared his concern and that, indeed, "I was so disturbed when I learned about the closing of Little America that I decided to resign as Chairman of the Committee on Polar Research and [as] our representative on the Special Committee on Antarctic Research." (He had changed his mind about protesting through resignation, however, "because I still want to see what can be done.") Gould termed the decision to shut down Little America "a scientific disgrace" and told Harris that it had been made without consultation with him or his committee, though he "should have been kept informed all the way along."

A few days later, Gould sent a telegram to the chairman of the House Appropriations Committee. Regretting that an indisposition would keep him from attending hearings on the matter the next day, he stated that "the closing of Little America is a major disservice to science. It is unfortunate for our prestige as well as for science that we have relinquished our scientific leadership in Antarctica to another nation." The other nation was of course the Soviet Union, which was expanding its operations to nine bases at the same time the U.S. was contracting from five to two. To Lloyd Berkner, Gould confessed that he would be somewhat embarrassed when representing the U.S. at the third meeting of SCAR, convening shortly in Canberra, Australia,* to have to make a report for his nation that would contrast so poorly with what the Soviets were doing.

Meanwhile, Gould's overall summary evaluation of the International Geophysical Year and its accomplishments was glowingly positive. Typical of his many public talks on the subject at that time were comments he made February 19 at Chicago's Palmer House hotel, where the Geographic Society of Chicago was having its 60th anniversary celebration dinner. Gould said on that occasion that advances during the IGY had exceeded scientists' loftiest hopes. "Not since Copernicus," he declared, "have the horizons of knowledge been so suddenly and dramatically enlarged. It well may be that we are at the beginning of a new Renaissance, with science and technology proving a brilliant new approach to unity and world peace."

Soon Gould was giving address after address incorporating the theme of a new Renaissance. "The IGY—A New Renaissance" was, for example the title of

---

*   Gould left for Australia on February 25 to attend the SCAR meeting March 2-6. He returned
     via Honolulu, where he remained an extra day because he "bumped into some pretty good
     prospects" there and then flew directly to Washington for National Science Board meetings, a
     Carleton alumni gathering, and a breakfast meeting with the secretary of the United Chapters
     of Phi Beta Kappa. He returned to Minnesota on March 14.

his April 17 Founders Day address at New York University (where he also picked up honorary degree number nine). The evening before that, at a black tie dinner at New York's Harvard Club on behalf of the Carleton development program, Gould said, in remarks later published as "Education's Greatest Task," that he believed "the thirst for knowledge—the desire to know for the sake of knowing"—had been the "unifying force in the IGY" and that this had "brought us a giant stride nearer to the kind of international co-operation which alone can bring peace to our troubled world." We are, he said at the Harvard Club, "staggered and frightened by the brilliance of science and its technology," but, he thought, if we hold fast to some "transcendent aim"—the development of which was education's greatest task—there was "good reason for hope." Quoting Bertrand Russell, he said that "we are equal to all that we can understand." His conclusion was that "to the extent that we can understand this new power, this new knowledge that science has given us, and apply it humanely, we have the radiant hope that a new renaissance can be ours." "A New Renaissance?" was subsequently the title of two Gould speeches delivered in the next eight days, a Phi Beta Kappa oration at the University of Michigan and an honors convocation address given at Carleton.

In May, Peg returned home from Italy, and in mid-month Gould returned to New York to address a symposium on basic research sponsored jointly by the National Academy of Sciences, the American Academy for the Advancement of Science, and the Alfred P. Sloan Foundation. There Gould spoke on basic research in the context of the liberal arts college, which, he stressed, was different from the university in ways other than size. "A liberal arts college," he said, "is primarily a society of teachers," and in such a college it is the quality of teaching that should always be primary—though participation in productive scholarship and research activity will always be vital to the makeup of good teachers. It was another occasion for Gould to preach the gospel of the liberal arts:

> I cannot too strongly reemphasize the fact that the academic climate which is hospitable to science must be no less friendly to intellectual values in other fields. No greater disservice could be done to science than to raise the level of science education without raising the level of all education. It is a chief task of the liberal arts college to emphasize the fundamental unity of knowledge—to hold before its students the idea that the pursuit of wisdom is still basically a single enterprise.

Gould remained to attend dinner and a reception that evening at the Waldorf-Astoria, where symposium scientists and invited guests heard President Eisenhower deliver a speech that Gould termed "a superb statement of the faith which I hope motivates all of us."

A pair of contrasting commencements highlighted June. Ideal weather graced Carleton's own exercises, featuring an address by alumnus Buell Gallagher (Class of 1925), president of the City College of New York. Board chairman John Musser made the gorgeous Monday morning even more pleasant by announcing a new

The Carleton Board of Trustees, 1959

unrestricted gift to the college from a group of unnamed trustees amounting in aggregate to $435,000 and bringing the running total of the campaign for $10 million to just over $3 million pledged since the announcement of the goal the previous October.* Six days later, at Dartmouth College, where Gould and his friend and fellow polar explorer seventy-nine-year-old Vilhjalmur Stefansson were receiving honorary degrees, the weather for the outdoor exercises was notably and uncomfortably chilly—so much so that when the shivering ceremony was over, the chairman of the Dartmouth board approached and told Gould he was glad the school had honored Gould and Stefansson together, but he hoped to hell that the next time Dartmouth might give degrees to explorers they would be tropical explorers!

As usual, summertime included several weeks of relaxation at the cabin in Jackson Hole, but in 1959 there were complications. Larry and Peg left for Wyoming on July 6, but Larry absented himself from the 14th to the 26th to attend a Sloan Foundation conference in Hot Springs, Virginia, followed by a week's work at Carleton. After returning to Wyoming for what he hoped would be a relaxingly undisturbed month of August, it was discovered that Peg had a case of pneumonia which she had probably been carrying around for some time

---

*   Gould had been able to make the second major gift announcement of the campaign in April, welcoming the receipt of a $750,000 pledge from a trustee wishing to remain anonymous, designated for the endowment of faculty salaries.

and which necessitated a period of hospitalization. Even after treatment and release, she remained troubled by a severe, lingering cough that tired her out and handicapped her activities. Late in the month the National Science Board met at Jackson Lake Lodge. Larry had promised to take the director and the president of MIT fishing for a day or two afterward, but following that the Goulds cut a week or so off of their intended stay and returned to Minnesota in hopes that the lower altitude would be helpful to Peg's cough. Back home, both were somewhat amused by the admonition of a Minneapolis doctor that for the sake of her throat Peg ought not to talk for two months. Successful or not at following this instruction, Peg did get better.

***

As Gould's fifteenth presidential year got underway at Carleton, the campaign for the Carleton Development Program, now designated "A Commitment to Excellence," entered its second year. The president appointed faculty, and two deans, to a pair of ad hoc committees to work out plans for two future buildings, a proposed center for music and drama and at long last—the pressing need having been highlighted not only in Gould's inaugural address of 1945 but also in Cowling's of 1909—a women's gymnasium.

A number of administrative changes were effected or presaged at the college that fall. In October, Gould received a consultant report prepared for Carleton by the president of the College Entrance Examination Board with recommendations that led, within a year, to a change in the directorship of Carleton's Admissions Office. (Longtime director Donald Klinefelter agreed to a lateral move to become college registrar and associate director Charles Gavin became head of admissions.) At about the same time, Vice President and Treasurer Bruce Pollock resigned the latter office to focus on a new role as coordinator of campus development, and his assistant, Frank Wright, moved up to become treasurer. Then in November Dean of the College Phil Phenix, after only fourteen months as dean, confidentially advised Gould that he had decided to return to the Teachers College at Columbia at the conclusion of the academic year, cutting short his third separate stint in a Carleton position,* and creating for Gould the problem of identifying the right new individual to fill this most important office.

Away from Carleton, honors and responsibilities each continued to accumulate. Chief among the former that autumn was the presentation to Gould in Washington of the US Navy's Distinguished Public Service Award—the highest honor the Navy could give a civilian—for his leadership during the IGY. He was honored October 12, together with USNC-IGY executive director Hugh Odishaw and US-IGY chief scientist Harry Wexler, all three having been sponsored by Rear Admiral George Dufek, who made the presentations. (Gould had written Dufek

---

*   Phenix's Carleton posts were assistant professor and counselor in religion, 1946-1948; associate professor and college chaplain, 1950-1953; and dean of the college, 1958-1960.

in September that he had rather receive the award from Dufek's own hand "than from the Secretary or the President or anyone else.")

Of added responsibilities pertaining to this period, perhaps the most significant was Gould's election to the Executive Committee of the Ford Foundation's Board of Trustees. Gould had long been a very active participant in Ford Foundation board deliberations, having faithfully attended all but one of the meetings held since he joined the board. (The only exception to that date was one coinciding with his South American vacation of 1955.) In the fall of 1959, however, Gould had expressed a measure of distress over his perception that the foundation had for some time been overlooking the best of the independent liberal arts colleges in favor of educational support directed almost exclusively toward large universities. He worried that "perhaps the Ford Foundation is succumbing to the idea that size and quality are synonymous" and characterized his internal protests on this score as "boring from within." Finally, at the December meeting, foundation president Henry Heald announced plans to develop a program of continued support for a limited number of independent colleges, with the expectation that Gould would help in formulating the program. It was at this meeting that Gould was added to the Executive Committee.

Another new responsibility, or at least a potential one, had been placed on Gould's shoulders in October when he was named to head a committee of six scientists who had been requested to advise the United States delegation to the international conference meeting in Washington to draft a treaty that would prohibit any military use of Antarctica and keep it open to scientific inquiry. Although the forging of the Antarctic Treaty was a matter near and dear to Gould's heart—he saw it as a direct outgrowth of the success of the IGY—this assignment in fact never amounted to much tangible labor for the busy president. The diplomats finished their work on the final draft of the Antarctic Treaty on December 1, 1959 (though ratification by all signatories was not accomplished until June of 1961), and Gould's committee was apparently not called upon for much service.*

Also in October, Minnesota Representative Walter H. Judd gave Gould an honor of sorts, or at least paid him a notable compliment, by making the public suggestion that Gould would be the ideal Republican candidate to challenge for Hubert Humphrey's seat in the US Senate in the 1960 election. Judd said that he could think of no present senator, of either party, with Gould's stature and general knowledge. Gould immediately indicated absolute disinterest in putting

---

* In his 1979 talk to the Antarctican Society, "My 50 Years of Antarctic Exploration and Research," Gould said this: "I was the Chairman of the National Academy of Science's Committee, an advisory committee to assist in the preparation of the treaty. Don't hold your breath, because they never asked for my advice. I didn't have a thing to do with it really. Nevertheless, on the walls of my study at home I have a photograph of which I am very proud. It's a picture of Ambassador Daniels standing, and Herman Phleger in front of him signing the treaty. At the bottom of it is inscribed, 'To Laurence Gould, without whom there would not be an Antarctic Treaty.' That isn't true at all, but do you remember what Mark Twain once said? 'A man would much rather be complimented for one thing he doesn't deserve than for fourteen that he does.'"

himself forward as a candidate, saying that his first obligation was to Carleton College and that he had too much to do there in the next few years to even think of running for political office. Nonetheless, in November the First Congressional District Republican convention, meeting in Rochester, passed a resolution officially inviting him to become an active Republican candidate "at his early convenience." To this Gould made no direct response—which perhaps accounts for the fact that in January he was compelled to restate his unavailability more forcibly. Former state Senator Elmer L. Anderson, who was running for governor, said early that month that it would be "wonderful" if either Representative Judd or Gould would top the Republican ticket that fall as the GOP nominee for US Senator. Though both men had already said "no" to running, Anderson offered that he thought it more likely that Gould might in fact make the race than that Judd would. The state GOP chairman then indicated that Gould would be "sought out" that week by party leaders hoping to discuss his availability. Three days after Anderson's remark, however, Gould said flatly that he was "not available under any circumstances" including a draft—that he had committed himself to remaining at Carleton for the duration of the four-year, $10-million building and expansion program that had been launched in October 1958 and that he thought he could serve his country best from his present post.

Even so, in March 1960 Gould would be formally endorsed for senator by the Goodhue County Republican convention. This was followed by an editorial in the *Northfield Independent* acknowledging that Gould had said he would not enter the race of his own volition but suggesting that "there is always that faint ray of hope that his job at Carleton might be well enough along by state convention time to answer the call of public service if a draft should materialize." The editorialist thought that the Goodhue County endorsement served notice that many Republicans would be "on the Gould bandwagon should a groundswell arise in his favor" and that it could "touch off a spark that would spread like a prairie fire should Larry Gould make himself available." Gould, the paper asserted, "has all of the qualifications of a great statesman" and was "one of the very few men on the scene at the present time who would stand a chance" of beating Humphrey. Gould remained uninterested. In fact (getting well ahead of biographical chronology at this point), by the time of the November 1960 election, which ultimately saw Minneapolis mayor P. Kenneth Peterson standing as the Republican senatorial candidate, Gould had decided that he would cast his own ballot for the Democrat Humphrey.

On November 2, 1959, Gould delivered an address, reported upon by major press services and carried as well over many radio and television channels, that attracted as much attention and favorable comment as any he had made before. The occasion was the one hundredth anniversary convocation of Cooper Union in New York. Four centennial addresses were given at Cooper Union that day: "Education and Society" by Gould, "Art and Society" by Sir Kenneth Clark, "Science and Society" by Nobel laureates Sir John Cockcroft and Harold C.

Urey, and "Government and Society" by the Honorable Lester B. Pearson, also a Nobel laureate. What Gould said that day was no more than a weaving together of what had become, in previous speeches, all familiar themes, but he prepared his remarks especially carefully for Cooper Union, and, as he wrote Peg afterward: "Carissima mia, ... the 'blood, sweat and tears' which went into my talk paid off. Even the conductor of the orchestra listened and stood up to applaud when I had finished. ... It was one of the great days of my life which I shall always cherish."

Gould told his audience that day that our salvation as a civilization depended upon "a reorientation in our sense of values." "We pay lip service," he said, "to spiritual values, but we give top priority to mink coats and expensive automobiles. ... We must change our motto from 'more and more' to 'better and better.' The most important resources, the only ones which will enable us to survive in this competitive world, are our intellectual resources."

There was "no major problem facing our society which does not point directly toward education" as the best hope for its solution, said Gould. But it must be a humane, integrated education: "Neither science nor all the humanities combined can save the world; but with a united front we can move forward in a broad humanism which visions the pursuit of wisdom as a single enterprise." The business of education, he said, was "to reassert our faith in the spiritual, non-utilitarian values upon which our society has really always rested"—defining "spiritual" not as an antonym of "secular," but as Webster did: "Of or pertaining to the intellectual or higher qualities of the mind."

Gould argued further that Western societies, where all major intellectual currents flow from Greco-Roman and Hebrew-Christian traditions—need to hold in common certain basic beliefs and that chief among these is the "great idea or assumption that human beings are to be treated as ends and never as means, and that respect for personality is the value that includes all other values." Education, he said, "must rescue the individual from the mass. ... The role of education is to create a community of persons, not a mere aggregation of people." Gould saw in the present moment great dangers, to be sure, but also, he affirmed, greater possibilities than any man has previously known. Scholars across all fields could today, he believed, lay the groundwork for a glorious new Renaissance, if they could only come together in the same spirit of cooperation as had recently motivated physical scientists during the IGY. This example, he declared, gives us "reason for radiant hope."

The next day Gould ran up to New Hampshire to deliver at Dartmouth a different address ("The Polar Lands in Human Affairs") on the occasion of Vilhjalmur Stefansson's eightieth birthday. He then returned to New York for several more days that included, in addition to a meeting of the Ford Foundation Executive Committee (to which he had been invited, though he had not yet been made a member), a series of personal conferences with men associated with foundational money: James Wynn of the Olin Foundation, James Perkins of the Carnegie Corporation, Dean Rusk of the Rockefeller Foundation, W. Homer

Turner of the US Steel Foundation, and Alfred P. Sloan, Jr., of the Alfred P. Sloan Foundation. Though Gould had, over the years, developed a great deal of experience in asking for gifts, this was a role, necessary though it was, that he would never really relish. A few days later, when the *Minneapolis Sunday Tribune* ran a three-page feature on "Gould the man," Carleton's fundraiser-in-chief was quoted as looking forward to the end of the four-year development campaign and then being ready, in 1962, to "turn the place over" to his successor, who, he hoped, would not "have to push doorbells to raise money. I want him able to spend more time at Carleton than I could."

In mid-November, a group of Twin Cities businessmen sponsored a black tie reception and dinner at the Minneapolis Club in honor of Gould's fifteenth year as Carleton president. University of Minnesota president James L. Morrill was chairman of the event, and Gould's Carleton predecessor Donald Cowling was honorary chairman.

James Killian, chairman of the corporation of MIT and until recently science adviser to President Eisenhower, delivered the evening's principal speech. Killian called for more "statesmen-scientists" with educations and interests "sufficiently broad to permit them to take a greater part in shaping public policy and in evolving our social strategy." Naturally, he identified Gould as a "shining example" of a man who, "at a time when we are troubled by barriers between the specialist and the generalist, between the scientist and the humanist, between the scholar and the man of action, is giving clear demonstration that it is possible to break down these barriers."

Required to offer some sort of a response to the evening's accolades, Gould said that applause was "a wonderful thing if you don't inhale too much of it" but that he had been sadly unable to hold his breath through an entire evening of praise and that he found himself now "in a kind of euphoria," which he intended to keep intact until falling asleep. However, he promised, borrowing a thought from his dear friend Dr. Elizabeth Wallace, "when I get up in the morning and look in my mirror I shall say, 'Larry Gould, you are an old fraud' and then I'll go on with the day's work."

***

As 1959 came to an end and 1960 began "the day's work" continued as a rule to be lengthy and demanding. Though it was still known only to a few that Phil Phenix would soon be leaving the Carleton deanship, one of the most important of Gould's tasks at this time was to line up his successor. Knowing that "doorbell pushing" for the development program would necessarily be claiming an increasing share of his time during his final years in office, he recognized that he needed "a dean to whom I can assign the full responsibility for the academic program and not have to worry about it."

Gould found his man in Richard C. Gilman, then executive director of the National Council on Religion in Higher Education, who had first been suggested for the post the *last* time Gould needed to fill it, when Phenix had ultimately been brought back to the college. Phenix himself, in his November letter of pending resignation, had recommended that Gould consider Gilman's qualifications to be the next dean. Gould met with Gilman in New York in December and subsequently invited him to visit Carleton to look the place over and himself receive further inspection. Gould pondered the problem into February, interviewing a number of external possibilities and thinking as well about people already at Carleton in other positions. In a confidential letter to former dean Frank Kille, inviting Kille's own recommendations for someone who might "fit the situation," he underscored the importance of this appointment, noting that, in light of the fact that he would turn sixty-four in August and his own retirement as president was on the near

Richard Gilman and Phil Phenix

horizon, "the Chairman of the Board and other trustees believe that if we could find a top notch candidate for Dean, we should not eliminate the possibility that he might be so satisfactory that he would be the next President." Before the end of February his mind was made up; on the 25th he telephoned Gilman and secured his acceptance of the position of dean of Carleton College effective with the academic year 1960-61. In order not to reduce Phenix's effectiveness over the intervening weeks, announcements to the faculty of his resignation and Gilman's appointment were delayed until mid-April.

Meanwhile, in January, the "Commitment to Excellence" campaign passed the $4 million mark on the strength of a gift of $500,000 to establish a foundation in economics given by the widow of longtime Carleton trustee Wadsworth A. Williams (Class of 1900), who had died in 1959.

Gould picked up another honorary degree in the first part of February, participating in mid-year commencement exercises at Detroit's Wayne State University. While there, Wayne State's dean of the College of Liberal Arts, Victor Rapport, told Gould that when he was ready to retire from Carleton he would be welcome to take an $18,000 a year professorship at Wayne State, teach as little or as much as he wanted, and be on the campus or off as he wished. "Some time," Gould mused afterward in a letter to Frank Kille, "I may go someplace like that and teach a course in the Geography of the Polar Regions, to which I have given so much attention over the years."

Although Rapport's interesting offer did not result in Gould's attaching himself post-Carleton to the Wayne State faculty, it may yet have indirectly germinated what did come to pass. Larry and Peg had long ago identified Arizona as a place to which they might possibly wish to retire upon leaving Minnesota. (As early as 1949 Gould was telling a correspondent that the Southwest appealed to him above all places and that he "should not be surprised if Mrs. Gould and I would some day retire somewhere in that part of the country." A few months later, to another friend, he wrote: "I am so exceedingly fond of Arizona. Mrs. Gould and I expect to live in that part of the country some time when we retire.") Now, in 1960, the Goulds spent the first two weeks of March in Arizona—attaching a late winter desert clime getaway to a two-day meeting of the National Science Board in Tucson that was paired with the dedication ceremonies for a new national astronomical observatory. While in Tucson Gould visited with Professor Reuben G. Gustavson, the former chancellor of the University of Nebraska, who, following retirement from administrative work for the Ford Foundation, had recently joined the University of Arizona's Department of Chemistry. Later that month, Gould wrote Gustavson:

> I shall be 64 years old in August and there lurks in the back of my mind that I may try to do something of the sort you are doing now. Some weeks ago I was on the campus of Wayne University in Detroit and was astounded to have the Dean of the Liberal Arts College tell me that any time I wanted to come to Wayne University and teach as little or as much as I wanted that a professorship with a generous salary awaited me there. However, I don't think I want to spend any winters in Detroit. I do hope, however, that when I have finished my tasks here I shall be able to do a little teaching and perhaps return to a bit of geological research. If I have ever done anything well in my life, it is teaching. ...
>
> I have been in Tucson from time to time and I was impressed anew with the tremendous progress the university is making under the presidency of Richard Harvill. Obviously his appointment was a fortunate one.

Gustavson replied:

> I can readily understand why any number of places would be delighted to have you on their faculty. In fact, I took the liberty of talking to President Harvill about your letter, and he said, "I wonder if he would be interested in coming out here." You may hear from him. ...
>
> What I am trying to say, Larry, is that I would love to welcome you as a buddy!

Thus was the ground prepared for what would in fact turn out to be Gould's path of choice two years later.

Throughout his presidency, quite in contrast to the involved group processes that would become the institutional norm in later years, it remained possible for Gould to make on occasion very quick, non-consultative, but in the end, more often than not, very sound, hiring decisions. An example from this time is the March 1960 hiring of a new Carleton basketball coach. The need arose out of the death due to a heart attack of Carleton's thirty-five-year-old football coach and athletic director, Warren Beson, in the fall of 1959. Mel Taube, already the coach of the basketball and baseball teams, had succeeded Beson as both head football coach and athletic director. He was agreeable, given his new responsibilities, to step aside as regarded basketball. Gould quickly thought of Jack Thurnblad, a star player from Carleton's Class of 1949 who he remembered as "a first rate human being" in addition to his having become a highly successful high school basketball coach. (Thurnblad's Wayzata High School team had won the Minnesota state high school basketball championship in 1959.) Years later, Thurnblad described the entirety of his interview for the position:

> I received a phone call one day from Sarah Crandall, who was then the secretary to President Gould. And Sarah said, "Jack," this call was on a Monday morning, she said, "President Gould would like you to come in and visit with him for a while on Wednesday afternoon, could you possibly make it?" Well, I almost jumped out of my chair because, for one thing, this reverence, you know, that we had for Larry Gould was still quite prominent in my thinking ... and I had never been in the president's office for another thing, and I always wanted to see what his office looked like. ... On the appointed day ... I walked in the office and Sarah Crandall said, "Good afternoon, Mr. Thurnblad, President Gould is waiting for you, go right in." And I walked in and President Gould got up from his chair and he put his hand out, and he said, "Jack, how are you?" and I said, "I'm fine, thank you, President Gould," and he said, "How would you like to be Carleton College's head basketball coach?" I said, "I'd love it," and he said, "Well, that's taken care of," and he picked up the phone and he called up Mel Taube, who was then the athletic director, and said, "Mel, you're going to be the football coach next year and Jack Thurnblad's going to be our new basketball coach."

Within days of hiring Thurnblad, Gould finalized another important and highly successful faculty appointment, that of Bardwell L. Smith* in the Department of Religion, in this case a more truly collaborative decision that involved both the president and the head of the department. Although Gould in the later years of his presidency involved himself directly in a significantly smaller share of college appointments than had once been the case, such decisions remained among his most important tasks and over time had been as institutionally transformative as anything he had done. A feature article on Gould that appeared that spring in *Look* magazine mentioned that 90 percent of Carleton's "yeasty young

---

* Smith, one of Carleton's most popular teachers for the next thirty-five years, would also serve two presidents as dean of the college, 1967-72.

faculty of 110" had now been hired during Gould's fifteen-year tenure in office.

***

As a governing body with authority over curricular matters, Carleton's "yeasty" faculty discussed, deliberated over, and decided, early in 1960, the fate of

a Curriculum Committee recommendation that Carleton switch from the two-semester calendar which it had followed since 1904 to a so-called "3-3" plan such as was in use at Dartmouth College for example, that divided the academic year into three terms of shorter duration than semesters, with students taking three courses per term. The Curriculum Committee had originally proposed this change in 1958, but in November of that year the faculty as a whole declined to approve the recommendation of its own committee. (The proposal had at that time narrowly carried a majority, 45-43, but the faculty had earlier passed a motion requiring a two-thirds majority for

Gould at a 1958-59 meeting of the faculty, many of whom he hired

passage of a curricular change.) In January of 1960, however, Gould had asked Phenix and the Curriculum Committee to reintroduce the issue. He suggested that it might be helpful if two or three Carleton professors arranged to visit an institution where the 3-3 plan was in successful operation. As was usually the case at Carleton, Gould's suggestions were followed: Charles Shain of the English Department and the Department of Chemistry's William Child were duly dispatched to Dartmouth to gather information and make their report. Ultimately on April 11 the proposal to adopt a 3-3 plan was carried. When Richard Gilman took over as dean of the college some months later, it was clear that a great deal of the substance of his initial year at Carleton would involve planning for and overseeing the changeover, which eventually would go into effect in September of 1961.

With regard to another decision concerning Carleton made early in 1960, Gould's preferences were not followed; he chose to yield. This involved the exact siting of the soon-to-be-built Olin Hall of Science. By January Yamasaki had developed a campus master plan, with tentative sites and designs for the new buildings included in the development program. Charles Horn of the Olin Foundation, however, kicked up an objection to the planned placement of Olin Hall and in February came to Carleton himself to look over the locations and argue the matter out. Horn insisted on a siting for the building farther east than either Yamasaki or Gould had desired. Although Gould then had to write Carleton Superintendent of Grounds D. Blake Stewart (universally known as "Stewsie") an apologetic note of explanation for thus having to destroy more campus trees than

The Golden Shovel put to use breaking ground for the Olin Hall of Science, 1960

expected, he saw no option but to agree. "One has to be very careful about looking a gift horse in the mouth," he told Stewsie, "when the mouth holds $1,500,000."

A ground-breaking ceremony for Olin Hall on May 10 employed the gold-painted shovel presented by students to Gould at the announcement of the development program in 1958. The first shovelful of earth was turned over by Horn, with seven others and finally Gould following in turn. During the accompanying speeches, Horn was informed by Carleton Student Association president Robert Fliegel (Class of 1961) that he was now a permanent honorary member of the Carleton student body; to mark this high status he was presented with his own student activity card. The building was slated for completion sometime in 1961.

The school year ended for Gould with four memorable ceremonies.

On May 21, Carleton's honors convocation featured an address ("My C- in Biology") by Associate Professor of English Reed Whittemore. But Gould ultimately stole the show. At the convocation's end he came to the podium and told the assembly: "Now I have the privilege of making one of the most important announcements ever made from this platform and one which closes this convocation." Gould then announced a gift of $1 million to the college, from a trustee who wished to remain anonymous, to supplement faculty salaries in the humanities. With this thunderbolt of news—the third largest single gift in Carleton's history to that moment—Carleton's "Commitment to Excellence" development campaign had passed the halfway mark on its way toward the $10 million goal.

On June 1, Gould accepted his twelfth honorary degree, this one from Columbia University. The same day, through the introduction of Carleton alumnus and trustee Henry S. Wingate (Class of 1927), the president of International Nickel, Gould met for an hour with top officials of U.S. Steel and the U.S. Steel Foundation, presenting "the most vigorous case I could for the same kind of 'leadership institution aid plan' for good independent liberal arts colleges" that U. S. Steel was then embarking on with universities. In his report on this conversation to Dartmouth's President John Dickey, Gould promised that he soon would be "on his neck, as it were," with Don David of the Ford Foundation and with Henry Ford of the Ford Motor Company, with regard to what the heads of Carleton and Dartmouth saw as the shortchanging of liberal arts colleges in favor of large universities in their current programs of support for higher education.

On June 3—a Friday, a change of recent pattern from Mondays—it was Carleton's own commencement ceremony, the fifteenth over which Gould had presided. Graduation speaker Julius A. Stratton, the president of MIT, took as his subject a theme with a Gouldian echo: "The Need for Excellence and Leadership in Our National Life." At the trustees meeting which followed, Atherton Bean, chairman of the Development Committee, cautioned that the development campaign's second half would be harder than the first, given that "now we must sell our story to people outside the Carleton family."

On June 5, it was a case of another day, another commencement, another honorary degree—this time from the University of Notre Dame. Lest we worry that this third graduation exercise within five days was pomp and circumstance too familiar and repetitive to be memorable—it assuredly was not: Gould received the honors and privileges of Notre Dame in company that day with ten others, a group that included both the president of the United States (who delivered the main address) and Cardinal Giovanni Battista Montini, the future Pope Paul VI. The boy from Lacota had certainly traveled far.

***

The summer of 1960 began with an urgent call for Gould to go to Washington to testify before J. William Fulbright's Senate Committee on Foreign Relations on behalf of the Antarctic Treaty. The treaty, which Gould thought just about the greatest, most hopeful diplomatic development in the history of the world, was facing powerful opposition through the lobbying of groups such as the Daughters of the American Revolution (which Gould characterized as "against various things including the twentieth century"), as well as a number of influential senators who, as Gould later expressed it, "just didn't think they should ever, ever have a treaty with Soviet Russia, no matter what it was about." Gould's statement to the Senate committee was ad-libbed, as his appearance had been called for on short notice and he had had little time to prepare remarks. Testifying on Tuesday afternoon, June 14, Gould said that he believed the Antarctic Treaty to be "a break-through of historic importance ... a document unique in history which may take its place alongside the Magna Carta, and other great symbols of man's quest for enlightenment and order." "A peaceful world," he said, "depends on the chance of international cooperation." The cooperative spirit that characterized the IGY, and especially the Antarctic Program, had now found itself carried forward and expressed in this treaty, he said, which gave him hope for the future. Moreover, he stressed, the Antarctic Treaty was "indispensable to the world of science, which knows no national or other political boundaries."

The following week, Gould went to New York for Ford Foundation meetings and other business, flying there and back with John and Betty Cowles in Cowles' private *Minneapolis Star and Tribune* plane. Peg had at first thought to come, but in the end her knee was bothering her too much and she stayed home. Gould had been invited by Sidney Weinberg (head of Goldman Sachs and a giant in the investment banking world) to be one of a party of twenty that would dine the evening of June 20 at the 21 Club and then attend a much anticipated prizefight at the Polo Grounds, the heavyweight rematch between Ingemar Johansson and Floyd Patterson. (Johansson had beaten Patterson the year before, knocking him down seven times in three rounds, and Patterson was attempting to become the first heavyweight ever to regain a championship after once losing it.) Gould was no boxing fan, but he could not pass up the experience, particularly as Weinberg's fight party would include numerous philanthropists Gould hoped potentially to influence. (Weinberg's group included, for instance, Henry Ford and publisher Walter Annenberg. It also included J. Edgar Hoover and Clyde Tolson from the FBI. Gould was the group's sole academic.) Gould was provided with a $100 ringside seat in the front row and reported afterward that when Patterson scored a fifth round knockout, "Mr. Johansson almost landed in my lap. I was so startled at the suddenness of the termination of the fight and the effectiveness of the knockout that I thought the man was dead." Indeed, Johansson did not rise from the canvas for a full five minutes.

In addition to Ford Foundation meetings at which Gould reported vigorously recommending "a great increase in our program in Latin America," these days in New York also included separate luncheons with Alfred P. Sloan, from whom Gould had high hopes for major support, and then Arnold Zurcher, executive director of the Sloan Foundation, a man Gould now knew well and with whom he could speak quite frankly. At their lunch Gould asked Zurcher whether, in his opinion, "it was time to shake the tree, as it were," with regard to the Sloan Foundation—that is, if the fruit was sufficiently ripe that it was ready to fall. Zurcher answered that he thought a little more cultivation of Mr. Sloan was still desirable. Gould subsequently suggested, through Zurcher, another New York meeting with Sloan in September, where he would be accompanied by select trustees and development program staff, as well as the presentation materials needed to give Sloan "a comprehensive picture."

Sadly, the night of Gould's return to Minnesota Carleton history professor Lucile Deen Pinkham, who chaired the department, and whose teaching ability and scholarship Gould admired enormously—he had once called her "one of the most nearly indispensable members of our faculty," and one of the "two or three best teachers"—died at her Northfield home of a sudden heart attack. By telegram the next day Gould asked Carlton Qualey to take over as History Department chairman, assuring Qualey that he and the dean would work quickly to provide the department with her replacement, impossible though actually replacing her would be. Services would be held at All Saints Episcopal Church, where Gould was a communicant, and he would be among Mrs. Pinkham's pallbearers.

Early in July Gould returned again to Washington on behalf of the Antarctic Treaty, the fate of which in the US Senate had him concerned. Minnesota's Senator Humphrey, a staunch supporter, was speaking very effectively on its behalf, but nonetheless Gould fretted that "it is going to take something of a campaign perhaps to secure the final passage." He had learned that Senators Russell (Georgia), Thurmond (South Carolina), Engle (California), and Gruening (Alaska) were standing in vigorous opposition, and he was worried that because Senator Russell's stature in the Senate was so great he might effectively be able to block ratification. "This," he warned, "would be a great disservice to science and a great setback to international good will." Failure to ratify would damage US prestige among Latin American friends and "give the Soviet Union a basis for claiming that our professed willingness to reduce armaments and ban nuclear explosions was mere hypocrisy." As chairman of the National Academy of Science's Committee on Polar Research, Gould alerted all of his committee members to the importance of writing the senators they knew, and he pledged to "make sure that the National Science Foundation makes its voice heard." To Humphrey he wrote that he was "deeply concerned that no stone be left unturned to secure the ratification of this very important document."

On the morning of July 10 the Goulds left for their cabin in Wyoming. Larry was not there long before flying off again, this time to Chicago at the invitation of Senator Thruston Morton of Kentucky, the chairman of the Republican Campaign Committee, to make a televised statement on education to the Republican Platform Committee on July 19, in advance of the GOP national convention beginning July 25.

Gould had remained uninvolved in the Republican nomination process in 1960. Although he found Vice President Nixon unappealing and would have preferred a ticket headed by Nelson Rockefeller, Nixon was essentially the inevitable nominee that year, and, unenthusiastically, Gould made his peace with that fact. He hoped at least that he might influence whatever plank his party adopted on education. He was invited to take twenty minutes to express his view on federal responsibilities in education as well as the importance of education in the definition of national goals.

In his statement to the platform committee Gould called on Republicans to spark an "intellectual renaissance." He wanted more and earlier encouragement and attention for the gifted and unusual student, not only in the sciences but across all fields. He approved a federal role in supporting education, but only supplementally, through loan programs and assistance in building construction but not through direct federal subsidies for teacher salaries, where he continued to see a danger that this would lead toward "a single federal system of education, and eventually to the consequent overarching, single philosophy of education" which would be a disaster he hoped never to see. Gould spoke in favor of a forthright Republican pledge to eliminate racial segregation in all public places, with all possible speed, saying that "the fact that thirty percent of our people whose skin happens to be darker than mine do not have [equal] opportunities should weigh heavily on our national conscience." Education, he thought, was the best means of raising "this now handicapped thirty percent of our population to the level of the rest economically, politically and culturally." He wished that Americans would cease as a people to continue to heap "ridicule on learning and the learned" and called upon Republicans to help destroy the prevalent "heresy abroad that the major part of the brains of our people is in the Democrat Party and [that] said Party is the Party of the Intellectuals." He concluded with advice to the platform committee: "Don't be afraid to be a bit idealistic as well as practical. Your fellow citizens are hungry now for a new and higher vision of our national purpose."

"I shall be interested to see," Gould wrote a fellow college president a few days later, "whether they paid any attention to what I said or not."*

Following his service to the Republican Platform Committee, Gould returned for a month to his summer cabin, his wife, and his mountain trout. He was committed to leave Wyoming on his birthday, August 22, for a joint meeting in Minnesota of the trustees' Executive Committee and the Buildings and Grounds Committee, prior to a week of meetings in Cambridge, England, of the international committee on Antarctic research (SCAR) . While still in Wyoming he was much relieved, and greatly elated, to receive the news that on August 10 the United States Senate approved the Antarctic Treaty, which was then formally ratified by the president on August 18. (It entered into force internationally on June 23, 1961.) Before leaving for the SCAR meetings in Cambridge, Gould wrote his bipartisan ally Humphrey to express his "deep appreciation" for the senator's vigorous support for the treaty and confessing that he should have gone to his meetings in Cambridge "with a heavy heart indeed had the Senate not ratified the Treaty, which is so important to our scientific enterprise." Instead, he attended the international conclave of Antarctic scientists unembarrassed, proud, and full of hope for a peaceful future.

---

*   With regard to federal aid to education, they seemed to. The Republican platform called for federal assistance to be selective, supporting aid for school construction, but not for teacher salaries, whereas the Democratic platform called for both. In a sentence squarely in line with what Gould had said, the Republican platform stated, "We believe … that any large plan of federal aid to education, such as direct grants for teachers' salaries, can only lead ultimately to federal domination and control of our schools." The difference between the Democratic and Republican platform planks in this respect "became one of the major domestic issues of the presidential campaign."

CHAPTER 23

SHAKING THE FOUNDATIONS

On September 21, 1960, an unprecedented number of world leaders were present in New York for the opening of the 15th General Assembly of the United Nations. That noon, about nine-tenths of a mile away from the UN headquarters complex, Larry Gould and other key representatives of Carleton College were gathered at the University Club to make a high-stakes luncheon presentation to Alfred P. Sloan, Jr. and other officials of the Alfred P. Sloan Foundation. The Carleton contingent's collective hope was to secure significant Sloan support for the Carleton Development Program: "Commitment to Excellence." Gould's team for this meeting included Carleton's vice president in charge of development Bob Gale; three trustees (Atherton Bean, president of the International Milling Company, Henry Wingate, president of the International Nickel Company, and Stewart McDonald, vice president of Stanley-Warner); and two of Carleton's distinguished alumni (John Nason, formerly the president of Swarthmore College, now president of the Foreign Policy Association, and Dr. Frank Stinchfield, president of the American Academy of Orthopedic Surgeons). In the other corner, so to speak, was the eighty-five-year-old Sloan, a colossus of the business world and of philanthropy, now retired as chairman of General Motors but still very much the president of his namesake grant-making foundation. Sloan was accompanied by two of his foundation officials, Albert Bradley and Frank Howard.

Sloan and Gould had been on friendly personal terms for some while. One Sloan Foundation trustee, James R. Killian, Jr., the former president of MIT, recently had been the featured speaker at a black tie Twin Cities dinner in Gould's honor. Another Sloan trustee, Frank W. Abrams, the former chairman of the board of Standard Oil of New Jersey, was also Gould's co-trustee on the Ford Foundation and had become a member of Carleton's advisory Development Board. In light of these relationships, Carleton's development campaign consultant with the John Price Jones Company had, earlier in 1960, concluded that "the potentialities and special considerations of the Sloan situation make it the number one prospect situation at this time. ... A case where as much as $1 million might be asked for." Following a lunch with Gould in June, Sloan's parting words had been "Remember, if you have any educational problems in which we can help you, be sure to let us know." Sloan and Gould had expected to talk again late in July at an event at the Homestead resort in Hot Springs, Virginia, but Gould had had to cancel attending due to Peg's having trouble in Wyoming with her knee and her inability for a time to walk well on her own. The September meeting in New York, then, was where Gould hoped to "shake the tree" with regard to a Sloan contribution to Carleton.

Sloan himself, as it developed, had a surprising additional agenda item in mind. Precise details are unavailable as to when it was that day that Gould received news that hit him like a physical blow: Overnight, in Northfield, Bruce Pollock had, quite unexpectedly, died in his sleep. The longtime college treasurer and vice president who recently had become coordinator of campus development, someone upon whom Gould had relied quite heavily since his own first day in office, was just sixty-seven. Whether Gould and his group learned of Pollock's passing before the Sloan luncheon or only after, the Carleton presentation went forward as planned: Gould wrote a week later to Sloan Foundation executive director Arnold Zurcher that "we had a thoroughly good time with Mr. Sloan and I believe he was interested in the program." Afterward Gould, missing Ford Foundation meetings for which he had intended to stay in New York, hurried home to Minnesota along with Gale and Bean in Bean's private plane.

It appears that at some point during or immediately after the luncheon Sloan had an opportunity for private conversation with Gould, for according to Gale's recollection years later, it was while they were on the way home in Bean's plane that Gould told the others that Sloan, in his mid-eighties and perhaps starting to feel mortal, had asked Gould to consider succeeding him as Sloan Foundation president starting the following summer. Surprised, flattered, and intrigued, Gould apparently did not reject the appealing offer out of hand but probably indicated—along with real interest—the existence of certain difficulties that stood in the way of his leaving Carleton as soon as that. (The development campaign was in mid-course, and at least one potential major gift would likely be endangered if Gould were known to be retiring as early as next June. Carleton's new dean of the college had just started and would take time to be brought up to speed. And Bruce Pollock's death that morning—if he had already heard about it when first reacting to Sloan's startling offer—left Carleton bereft of Pollock's experience. Young Frank Wright, being groomed to step into Pollock's shoes in most administrative respects, was still untried apart from Pollock's tutelage.)

Further discussion of these interrelated matters—Gould's interest in securing Sloan's support for Carleton and Sloan's interest in securing Gould to head his foundation—probably waited until Gould's next trip to New York in November. In town then for meetings of the Carnegie Foundation for the Advancement of Teaching and of the Executive Committee of the Ford Foundation, as well as for a Saturday night dinner of the Institute for Current World Affairs, Larry and

Peg both attended a Sunday evening gathering at Sloan's fourteen-room Fifth Avenue apartment, and Larry then lunched alone with Sloan at noon on Monday. Gould reported to the development program steering committee afterward that with Sloan "things were pleasant but the subject of a gift was not discussed."

Duncan Stewart

He reported as well, however, that at the Sunday night dinner he had also spoken with Sloan Foundation officers Albert Bradley, Warren Weaver, and Devereux Josephs, and indicated that "all three of them felt that we should let Mr. Sloan make up his own mind, and that things looked pretty good for us." Gould asked the steering committee to think of particular projects that might best fit Sloan Foundation support.

That would be November. Before that, in September and October, Gould carried forward with other concerns.

Pollock's loss was hard—he had been "my right arm," Gould wrote trustee G. Slade Schuster early in October, "and wherever I turn I find need of him" But, Gould affirmed in the same letter, "It is a great good fortune that Frank Wright was on his way to succeed Bruce. I know he will grow into full competence to carry on all of the things that Bruce did." Shortly before his death, Pollock had attended with Gould a special weekend conference on science and the news, cosponsored by Carleton, the University of Minnesota, the Mayo Foundation, and the *Minneapolis Star* and *Tribune*, which brought together at a Minnesota camp resort ten leading scientists and an equal number of top newspaper editors to discuss the public understanding of science and how to improve it. As chairman of the relevant planning committee, Gould had played a major role in organizing the conference, originally suggested by the National Science Foundation.

At Carleton during these weeks Gould found he had to put time and energy into taking on the role of a personal relations counselor, trying to ameliorate what had become a venomous rupture of good working relations between his alumni services director and Vice President Gale. Rather more positively, new Dean of the College Dick Gilman was settling in very well. Already by mid-October, Gould would tell Laird Bell with satisfaction that Gilman was "the best man we have yet had in that position." Gilman would be introduced to the Carleton board at the trustees' fall meeting, a meeting that also saw discussion of the establishment at Carleton of the Laurence M. Gould Science Fund and a progress report by the Buildings and Grounds Committee on the construction of Olin Hall, on the planned addition of a fourth floor to the Reine Myers women's dormitory, and on preliminary plans for a new men's dormitory to be occupied by the fall of 1962.

Circumstances that fall resulted, in what for the president was reportedly a mixture of trepidation and joy, in Gould's returning for a few weeks to the role of classroom geology teacher. Professor Duncan Stewart had long ago established himself—thanks originally to his doctoral work with rocks brought back by Gould from the Byrd Expedition—as one of the world's foremost authorities on Antarctic petrography. But this had all been done as laboratory analysis; Stewart had never yet himself set foot in Antarctica. Then on September 21, the same day Gould was hurrying home from New York in Atherton Bean's plane, Stewart received an invitation from the US Antarctic Research Program, in

The "sub" who volunteered to cover Stewart's class when he traveled to Antarctica in October 1960

recognition of his thirty years' work on the rocks of Antarctica, to visit the continent himself. As Stewart related it: "I pondered for two days wondering how to approach President Gould relative to the trip. On the second day he phoned me and said he was happy to hear that I was going to the Antarctic." Gould followed up with this note:

> When you know the more precise details, Dunc, about your proposed trip to Antarctica I hope you and Eiler [Henrickson, Stewart's departmental colleague] will come and talk with me. If I can fit it into my schedule, I should be very glad to give all or most of the lectures in Elementary Geology while you are gone. This would relieve Eiler of the heavy burden of looking after everything and would give me a great deal of joy. Though I have forgotten much of my geology, I think it would not be too much trouble to refresh my mind about the elementary aspects of it.

Stewart left campus October 9, to be gone a month, and Gould gave his first classroom lecture in sixteen years at 8 a.m. on Monday the 17th. Nine days later he was reporting that class preparations—three mornings a week for 120 students—were being a bit more work than he had expected, thanks to how long it had been since he had last taught but that it was all "so rewarding that Dunc may find himself out of a job when he comes back. In other words, I may try to trade places with him."

In the third week of October, Charles Horn of the Olin Foundation, accompanied by his wife, came down to the college for a visit and to take a look at the rising framework of the Olin Hall of Science. That evening the Goulds entertained the Horns at home with a dinner in the congenial company of college chaplain David Maitland and his wife Betsy, and "with plentiful supplies of fresh mango ice cream," a rarity (in 1960) for which Horn had previously expressed great affection. The week before, in a phone call arranging his visit, Horn had, quite intentionally, piqued Gould's interest by saying to him, "Hurry up and get that building finished so we can take on another one. I want to live long enough to see a second Olin Building at Carleton College." That tantalizing prospect was a subject which would reappear later.

***

That Bruce Pollock's death prevented Gould's attendance at September's Ford Foundation meetings had been particularly unfortunate because Gould was at the time continuing to be somewhat disgruntled over the thrust of the foundation's educational initiatives, and there were conversations about this fact that he had hoped to have on that occasion. When John Cowles filled him in on what he had missed at the meetings, Gould replied that he was "doubly sorry not to be present" because he had "wanted to record once again" his "disappointment that a program for independent liberal arts colleges is again sidetracked for a proposed program to help urban universities." "This," he submitted, "is not putting first things first. If the Ford Foundation is to support excellence, it can't neglect too long the Amhersts and the Dartmouths and the Wesleyans and the Carletons." In this Gould was voicing not only his own concerns, but those of a number of fellow college presidents who were corresponding with him on the matter, including John Dickey of Dartmouth, who wrote Gould of his increasing concern that the view seemed to be spreading "that the independent college is some sort of 'lesser thing' as compared with a university." Dickey urged that "the time has come for some of us to take the offensive" in voicing what was special and indispensable about their sort of college.* Gould agreed, pledging to "continue to be the fly in the ointment" at the Ford Foundation, even as Dickey himself was doing the same at the Rockefeller Foundation.

---

* "The independent college," Dickey wrote, "is today almost the last vestigial remnant of the *institutional* sense of purpose that historically has been so important in the work of American higher education." Observing that the great universities, "for good and understandable reasons" had "lost even the possibility of this institutional impact as contrasted with the disciplinary and departmental sense of purpose," Dickey asserted that "any possibility of retaining this kind of impact must be won and retained in our kind of institution or it will disappear everywhere."

Gould had been discouraged by Ford Foundation president Henry Heald's confidential memorandum attached to the trustees' docket for the September meetings. "Here again," Gould complained in October to Ford Foundation board vice chairman Donald K. David, "is a proposal to launch another program for selected universities, none of which compare in quality with Amherst, Dartmouth, etc." He termed as "only a passing nod" Heald's casual statement in the last paragraph of the memorandum that "a good argument can be made for extending this program or establishing a similar one for a limited number of independent liberal arts colleges." To Ford Foundation vice president Clarence H. Faust, Gould wrote of the sense of discouragement presently felt by many of the heads of top-notch liberal arts colleges over the perception that their institutions were being bypassed by the giving programs of both corporations and foundations. Though confessing to Faust that his being the only small college president among the Ford Foundation trustees gave him "some temerity about being too aggressive lest people will think I am concerned with one college," he hoped that the fact that he would soon be retiring might "disinfect me from the onus of pleading for a particular institution."

Gould's vigorous boring from within at the Ford Foundation would soon yield (or at least precede) something like the desired result. Following board meetings of early December, a better satisfied Gould wrote Faust that "the new program to strengthen liberal education in selected private colleges" that had there been extensively discussed was, to quote Henry Heald's own words, "an experiment in excellence" and an important parallel to the program the foundation had already established with regard to a selected group of universities. Differences he had expressed at the December meetings with just a few items in Heald's memorandum about the parallel program were, he told Faust, "largely a matter of semantics."

In another respect, Gould had cause at that time to be very happy indeed with his Ford Foundation connection, for he was that fall planning details of an exciting globe-circling excursion to be undertaken that winter at the foundation's behest to inspect certain supported programs abroad. Expenses for Mrs. Gould were included in the foundation's largesse. (Gould told one correspondent that he had hoped at one point to take himself again to Antarctica that season, but that after Peg heard about the Ford Foundation offer, with two months of travel "luxuriously arranged" for the both of them, the couple had "compromised"—and were going around the world.) The Carleton board, through its executive committee, had at the end of August granted the president leave to make this trip in January and February.

In November of 1960 the biggest news nationally, of course, was Senator John F. Kennedy's victory over Vice President Nixon in a very close presidential election. Gould had, without much ardor for the nominee, held to his party and cast his vote for Nixon, but JFK had impressed him. Later in the month he wrote one of the congressmen he had escorted to Antarctica three years before, Massachusetts Representative Torbert H. Macdonald, who had been Jack Kennedy's college roommate at Harvard: "Had I known that Torby Macdonald was such a close friend of President-elect Kennedy and would be one of his close advisors, I would have been tempted to vote twice for him!" "The next few years," Gould predicted, "are going to be exciting, indeed. However, for me life means adventure and I am not disturbed by the outcome." Early in January Gould would tell former US senator William Benton that he was "immensely impressed by the quality" of the president-elect's announced appointments. "My opinion of him rises," he wrote Benton, adding, "If I don't watch myself, Bill, I will end up by being a Democrat!"

Late in November Gould spoke in Chicago at a dinner honoring Laird Bell at the Sheraton-Blackstone Hotel. "You sounded like an ancient prophet—in modern dress," Bell offered in a letter of thanks the following day. (Gould replied: "I am immensely pleased and proud of my favorite human being, named Laird Bell.") In December, at a meeting in New York, Gould was elected chairman of the board of the Carnegie Foundation for the Advancement of Teaching. Later in the month, he participated in a conference on "Science in International Educational and Cultural Affairs" at MIT that was jointly sponsored by the National Science Foundation and the US State Department. In his invitation to Gould Secretary of State Christian Herter had characterized the conference as "informal conversation by thoughtful men from many walks of life." Gould's talk at this event, "Science, Engineering, and the Humanities in the University," would substantially reappear in 1961 as a Carleton College *Bulletin* publication under the title "One Culture Only" His thesis was that science, letters, art, and religion all ranked as among "the great human endeavors" and that "neither science nor technology nor all the humanities combined can save the world; but with a united front we can move forward in a broad humanism which visions the pursuit of wisdom as a single enterprise."

***

On New Year's Day, 1961, Gould jotted a short note to his wife, accompanying a small symbolic gift. "I always make New Year's Resolutions," he wrote Peg. "This year I am making but one and that is to do my best to make my wife the happiest woman in the world."

Larry and Peg were leaving to begin their around-the-world trip on Sunday morning, January 8. On the morning and afternoon of Saturday the 7th the Carleton Board of Trustees met on campus. It was the fifty-second meeting of the full board held since the election of Gould to the presidency in 1945. The trustees that day accepted a report on the new 3-3 curriculum which had now been formally adopted by the Carleton faculty. They approved an approximately 8 percent overall increase in the faculty salary schedule for 1961-62. Very importantly, they heard a report from Atherton Bean, chairman of the Development Committee, which included a review of cost increases that had occurred since 1958 in the buildings and equipment targeted in the decision, two and a half years before, to set the Development Fund goal at $10 million dollars, and then adopted a recommendation that the goal total now be revised upward, to $12 million. And, the meeting minutes read: "Since he was in his sixty-fifth year, President Gould stated he wished to retire in the predictable future and recommended the trustees appoint a committee now to begin the search for a successor." A motion was passed authorizing Chairman John Musser to appoint such a committee, to work with the assistance of a faculty committee to be selected in the spring. Although no precise timetable was yet set for what retirement "in the predictable future" might exactly mean, when Larry and Peg departed the next morning on the first leg of their world trip, they left with a clear sense that great life changes were drawing palpably nearer on their joint horizon.

Gould's travel mission was to inspect Ford Foundation-supported programs abroad, principally educational initiatives in Indonesia, Burma, and India, followed by four short stops in Europe. The itinerary took them completely around the world in sixty days, beating Phileas Fogg by 20 percent. They would leave January 8 and return March 9.

Peg's travel diary recorded that they left Northfield at 8:30 a.m., being driven to the airport for their flight to Los Angeles by Associate Professor of Zoology Bruce Guyselman, and checked in later that day at the Wilshire Boulevard Statler-Hilton. The next morning before breakfast they received a phone call from Frank Wright, informing them that their Northfield home had been broken into overnight. Apparently, publicity concerning the Goulds' trip had made it too evident to burglars that the house would be empty, and a person or persons, entering through a basement window, had ransacked every room, emptying drawers on the floor. The break-in had been discovered by a local woman who had arranged to call daily at the house during the Goulds' absence. As subsequently reported by the *Northfield News*, "the extent of property missing from the house is not known since some valuables had been taken to the bank before the Goulds' departure and it is not known for certain what jewelry and clothing the couple had taken with them." With nothing to be done from afar, the Goulds were left simply to sigh, worry about what might be missing, and catch their evening flight to Honolulu.

Two days were spent relaxing in Hawaii before an eleven-hour flight on the 11th-12th (losing a day by crossing over the international dateline) brought them to Manila. There they were met at the airport by Albert Ravenholt, a noted foreign correspondent and founding member of the American Universities Field Staff. The Ravenholts (Al and Marjorie) gave them dinner that evening at their Manila apartment, though Peg recorded that she and Larry, still jetlagged following their long flight from Honolulu, "were moderately dull because of biologic depletion." Three days in the Philippines were spent under the Ravenholts' wing, where, Peg acknowledged, "we learned more and met more significant people than would have been possible in three months under our own steam."

On the 16th they flew on to Java, their plane touching down briefly en route in Saigon and Singapore. In Djakarta their hosts were Mike and Marjorie Harris, who threw them a dinner party their first evening. The next day local staff of the Ford Foundation arranged a reception to which some four hundred persons came, representing, in Gould's description, "a most interesting cross section of people from government, education, and business." Altogether, the Goulds would spend twenty-six busy days in Indonesia, most of them tropically hot and humid. (It was the rainy season and a notably heavy one at that. The Ford Foundation offices in Djakarta were flooded three times during this period.) On the 20th—a memorable, quotable, inauguration day in the U.S.—the Goulds were flown to Bali, which Peg found particularly beautiful. There the Goulds enjoyed two unforgettable evenings of dance entertainments. One, by young boys and girls to gamelan accompaniment, Peg described as spellbinding and "so very beautiful in the strange light." The second, a sword dance and then monkey dance performed by a hundred men, she recorded as "absolutely thrilling and at times almost frightening." Unfortunately, the return flight to Djakarta in an unpressurized plane seems to have produced ear trouble in Peg: a deafness that vexed her for days afterward, as the Goulds commenced a motor tour eastward into central Java—to Solo (Surakarta), Salatiga, and Djokja (Yogyakarta), and then looping back toward Djakarta through Bandung. (From Bandung, where Larry stayed longer, Peg returned early to Djakarta with the Harrises to see a doctor about her "wonky ear." The doctor prescribed sulfa pills, which failed to clear up the trouble. Eventually, on February 8, two days before leaving Indonesia, Peg underwent a small operation in Djakarta to relieve fluid behind her eardrum. "Pain minimal and relief enormous," she would write in her diary that day. "I can hear once again.")

Gould was worked hard in Indonesia, meeting with government ministers, university presidents, deans, and many others. Altogether, during his twenty-six days in the country interviews or visits were arranged for him with eighty people. Perhaps the most memorable was the half hour he and Peg were given February 5 with President Sukarno. Although Peg's diary notes that Sukarno had been "pleasant and easy to talk to," with his "charm fully turned on," Larry did not hesitate upon his return to criticize the Sukarno dictatorship as being economically disastrous for Indonesians and ultimately politically unstable: "Whereas I did not hear anyone accuse Sukarno of being a Communist, his 'guided democracy' is leading his country toward a monolithic state which would be the easiest kind to be taken over." Gould's report to the Ford Foundation indicated it was "clear that the Indonesian bitterness toward Dutch colonialism causes them to oversimplify and equate colonialism with capitalism," that they were driving out capitalistic enterprises and non-Indonesians both, and that "the result is unbelievable bureaucracy, incompetence, and corruption."

On February 10, the Goulds flew on to Rangoon and five days in Burma. On the second day they attended the opening of an art exhibit ("very poor & dull & representational," thought Peg) at which a speech was given by Prime Minister U Nu. Afterward the Goulds were able to meet a bit with the PM, who presented

The Goulds with Indonesia's President Sukarno

them with a small gift—a "terrible water color in traditional style," recorded Peg.*
Larry judged that among the Ford Foundation's most successful grants in Burma
to date was one to the International Institute of Advanced Buddhistic Studies,
from which support much goodwill had flowed—Gould thought that particular
gift had helped make the Burmese realize that here in the Ford Foundation were
"people not concerned to make Americans of them but to help them understand
and take pride in their own institutions." Despite Gould's approving view of that
good work, little headway was made with him by the Burmese proselytizer who
at one luncheon, according to Peg's amused diary entry, attempted to convert
Larry to Buddhism.

Burma was followed by six days in India. This was a country which, Gould
frankly admitted afterward, he had never previously wanted to visit, a "crowded
land" he had not expected to like. Although some of what he viewed there was

---

* Peg's negative judgments were further extended that day to the foreign service VIPs present
at dinner: the British ambassador was a "diplomatic Col. Blimp" and the Dutch minister
"something of a playboy sportsman who thinks well of himself." As for the American
ambassador: "arrogant, rudely boorish, considers himself intellectual and is far from same.
A sorry representative." Earlier, an American host for one of their Indonesian evenings had
entered Peg's diary attached to "two dull daughters" and a wife who was "incredibly stupid."
Peg's bar of approval was perhaps a high one, but there were those on this trip who easily cleared
it. In Indonesia, for instance, her discernment had been impressed by both Mike and Marjorie
Harris and by Cornell graduate student Dan Lev; in Rangoon her assessment of Burmese UN
Ambassador U Thant, near whom she had been seated at luncheon, read "intelligent, interesting,
English good." (The luncheon food, however, was that day "absolutely ghastly.")

indeed appalling and India's precarious balance between population and food supply was frightening, Gould would ultimately identify India as the one place visited on this trip from which he got "the greatest lift"—this from the "courage and clarity" with which its "competent ... civil servants and educated ministers" were attacking its basic problems. He likened India's position with regard to industrial development to where the United States had been after the Civil War, "with the same great vistas" of development ahead, and predicted that the future direction of India "will be the key to Asia and indeed perhaps to all the world." "Of all the places I visited," he would write, "the one to which I would like most to return to help if I could would be India." To the Ford Foundation he recommended "no retreat from nor curtailment of our program" there. Stressing the dangers of what would happen "if India does not keep its face turned toward the West," Gould posited that "the contributions which have been made and are in the making by the Ford Foundation may tip the balance toward the West."

From New Delhi they were supposed to fly to Berlin, but a Pan Am strike forced an alteration of plans, and instead they were carried by BOAC to Zurich, via a stop in Teheran. Deciding to bypass Berlin altogether, they spent several enjoyable days in Zurich, including a day trip to Lucerne and back on February 24. In Zurich, Larry bought Peg a watch similar to one he had given her as a wedding present, though "somewhat smaller and in red gold." Then came a handful of days—too few for them both—in Greece. Athens they toured in the company of their friends-in-residence, the Shepards. Of seeing the Acropolis, Peg wrote, "thrilling beyond belief." Larry wrote afterward that standing "in the Parthenon, and again down in the market place where Socrates had held forth, and again at the site of Plato's Academy" had given him "one of the supreme thrills" of his life. In Delphi, also, they were "utterly enchanted" by the setting and the antiquity.

It was not, however, for the sake of the antiquity that the Ford Foundation had sent Gould to Greece. Rather, he went there essentially to meet architect and urban planner Constantinos Apostolos Doxiadis, the founder of the Doxiadis Associates firm of consulting engineers, who had been and would continue to be the recipient of a great deal of Ford Foundation support for his town planning work, most recently the design of the master plan for the planned Pakistani capital of the future, Islamabad. Gould was very impressed with the visionary Doxiadis, then forty-six-years-old, calling him in his trip report "one of the most exciting men I have ever known."

When the Goulds returned to Athens from Delphi on March 2, they received a letter with follow-up news on the January burglary of their Northfield house, confirming the loss of many items of value, both monetary and sentimental. Peg's subsequent diary entry was anguished:

> Nothing left & I fall apart once again, for this knowledge has been
> hanging like an albatross around my neck the whole journey. I'm not

particularly possessive but it tears me apart to know the things my beloved Tia left me are gone—as well as other old things I've loved for years.

"Two double tots of Scotch" helped Peg recoup and feel up to bathing and dressing for that evening's dinner in Athens with their friends the Shepards and Lew and Freda Morrill.*

Between Greece and home lay a few days each in Geneva and Paris, delights somewhat spoiled for Larry by the onset of a frightful cold. Peg's diary indicates that on the 6th the March weather was so lovely that "despite Larry's malaise we walked for blocks on the Champs Elysées," stopping for refreshment at a sidewalk cafe. On the 7th, though Larry was "still feeling miserable," they toured Notre Dame, after which, while strolling in a garden, they enjoyed a chance encounter with a Carleton graduate of 1957, Dan Brower. The next day they "picked up Ste. Chapelle & had hours and lunch in [the] Louvre." By evening (local time) of the day after that, following a quick plane change in New York, the Goulds were returned home to where they had started their great circle two months before, having proved to Larry's scientific satisfaction that the world was indeed round.

***

Early in January 1961, at just about the same time that Gould was departing on his world trip, the Ford Foundation invited Carleton College to put in a proposal for a share of the large grants expected to be made later that year to a select group of liberal arts colleges, a plan paralleling the matching grants program for universities already in operation. Aware before he left that information was about to be requested of Carleton in connection with the proposed grants, Gould told Dean of the College Dick Gilman, who would essentially be acting president in Gould's absence, to expect a call from Ford Foundation executive Jim Armsey, who had recently become director of the foundation's higher education programs. Before leaving, Gould sent Gilman a memorandum noting that the particular criteria of selection for the Ford Foundation's proposed program for leading liberal arts colleges would be, firstly, "excellence of leadership" (in president, staff, and trustees); secondly, evidence of a "strong constituency of support"; and thirdly, "a well-conceived long range plan or program." "I think on the basis of these Carleton College will stack up pretty well," Gould advised.

Gould left on his trip, and Gilman flew to Denver for the annual meeting of the Association of American Colleges. While there Gilman did get a call from Armsey, asking whether Gilman could come to a meeting in his hotel suite. In the suite, Gilman was introduced to Armsey and, as he later recalled, "about half a dozen other people ... and they wanted to know

___

* James Lewis "Lew" Morrill, after retiring in 1960 as president of the University of Minnesota, had now begun serving as a consultant for the Ford Foundation.

about Carleton; they had about forty questions." Finally, the group asked Gilman whether he could promptly get together certain material about the school in order to be considered for this major grant program, making clear that the amounts being discussed were seven-figures large. As Gilman related the story many years later, he was so impressed with the importance of this "major stakes game" that he decided to cut short his planned stay in Denver in order to hurry back to Northfield that same day and get to work on preparation of the college's proposal. ("I went back to my hotel room," Gilman remembered, "and I called Frank Wright, and I said, 'I'm taking a plane in an hour.'") In Northfield, Gilman, Wright, Bob Gale, and a bottle of Jack Daniel's Tennessee whiskey all gathered around Gilman's kitchen table late that night and got to work. Into the wee hours of the morning the three went through, "point by point by point, what the Ford Foundation was after." The next day Gilman told his secretary, Ruthmary Penick, that he, Gale, and Wright "would not be taking any appointments in the morning for the next week or ten days, and we wouldn't take any appointments morning *or* afternoon for a time" in order for the three to put together the requested material. The foundation wanted data from the past ten years and projections for the next ten. Gilman remembers: "I wrote most of the narrative, and Frank provided the figures, and Bob provided the projections." The resulting document, "Profile of Carleton College 1951 to 1971," was reviewed and approved, with minor modifications, by the trustees' Executive Committee early in February and submitted to the Ford Foundation on February 13 while Gould was in Rangoon.

Well before Gould returned to Carleton from his travels, the business of the Ford Foundation grant proposal was well and satisfactorily taken care of. But meanwhile, matters with two other foundations had not been running quite so smoothly.

What had once been high hopes bordering on expectation for a substantial gift to Carleton from the Sloan Foundation had come to nothing—as had, in parallel fashion, Alfred Sloan, Jr.'s interest in securing Gould himself for the foundation. Apparently Sloan, whose personal decisions remained for his foundation dispositive, did not take well to being turned down by Gould—or to Gould's intimations that the only way by which he *could* become available to the foundation on Sloan's timetable would be if Carleton's campaign were wrapped up quickly via a very major Sloan contribution. In any case, Sloan's final judgment regarding the appeal from Carleton was a negative one. In a mid-January letter to Gould forwarded to the president in Burma, Sloan Foundation vice president Warren Weaver expressed his "severe disappointment at the way things are turning out." Although Weaver characterized the outcome as "pure tragedy," he wrote that it was clear to him from recent discussions with Mr. Sloan that there was nothing he could do about it. In February, John Nason, who had been part of the Carleton team that met with Sloan in New York in September, lunched with Sloan Foundation Executive Director Arnold Zurcher, after which he reported to Gould that "our appeal to the Sloan Foundation is bogged down at dead center." Nason had the impression that Zurcher himself would like to help Carleton but that "he works for a very difficult boss who holds very strong opinions and who makes decisions at times in a rather arbitrary fashion." With Gould away, Bob Gale—pretending for the written record to less information than he actually had about the matter—responded to Nason:

> Apparently something strange is going on here since Larry has sort of dropped the matter since his last meeting with Sloan. Apparently Mr. Sloan approached Larry very confidentially about something and from all that I can gather Larry did not agree to whatever they wanted him to do. This seems to have colored our chances of having a proposal go through. Larry is apparently not able to divulge the problem that has arisen.

When Gould returned from his travels he directed Gale and others to drop entirely for the present all negotiations with regard to the Sloan situation. He wrote Sloan of his deep regret that circumstances did not work out differently. "Up to the very last minute," Gould told Sloan, he had "coveted the hope" that he might manage to secure some gifts to Carleton substantial enough to have enabled him to be released from presidential responsibilities "with no residue of ingratitude or ill will here." "As you know," his letter sighed, "the gifts I had hoped for were not forthcoming at the time and I had no alternative." A letter of the same day to Warren Weaver, marked "personal and confidential," was most frank:

> It pleases me to know that you too are depressed at the outcome of my various conversations with Mr. Sloan. I can't tell you how sorry I am. I was terribly stimulated by the prospect of working with you and for the Foundation.
>
> Somehow I think Mr. Sloan is blinded by his singleness of vision. He never quite understood the problems and responsibilities that confronted me here. In our last conversations I pointed out the necessity of a substantial gift by way of releasing me here. It would have been easy for this good man to have given Carleton College a gift from his own great personal fortune. The two things could have been unrelated in such way that I would have been free to insist on my release from the College.

The job of foundation president was an undeniably appealing one to Gould. In an address the following June he praised the American foundation—the "new dimension in philanthropy"—as being able to do things that government could not do or would not dare to: "It can be discriminating. It can select problems and single out individuals and institutions. It can pioneer ahead of public opinion." Attracted as he was by the constructive power belonging to foundations, Gould's remembrance of the opportunity foregone with Sloan would always be tinged with a touch of regret for the sadness of "it might have been."*

The other foundation with which a bump in the road had arisen while Gould was abroad was the Olin Foundation, through the ever-bristly person of its president, Charles Horn. Horn's ire was ignited, while Gould was in India, by an item appearing in the *Minneapolis Morning Tribune* of February 17, reporting a grant to Carleton from the Rockefeller Foundation in the amount of $175,000. Reading that most of this grant would be used to equip Olin Hall, Horn hit the roof. "I do not know what they are talking about," he promptly fired off to the Carleton president. "You know we have a definite plan that at the time of the dedication no equipment can be in the building except that supplied by the Olin Foundation, Inc." The same day Horn called A. W. Pickford, acting during the construction of Olin Hall as the foundation's on-site representative in Northfield, asking for an explanation. Pickford replied to Horn on February 22:

> I have discussed this matter with Mr. Frank Wright, Secretary-Treasurer and Mr. Richard C. Gilman, Dean of the College and they have advised me as follows. In the first place, this news release did not originate from the College but was given out by the Rockefeller Foundation. In the second place, the release was not entirely correct as written. This Grant is to be used in its entirety for movable equipment in Olin Hall for use in their Research work with the exception of that to be used to pay part time teachers replacing Faculty members whose teaching loads interfere with important research.
>
> According to the above statements, I can see no violation of the Contract between Olin Foundation Inc. and Carleton College. In view of the above, I believe that the College is at liberty to get the equipment ordered so that it will be ready to move into the building when the building is completed and turned over to the Owner. In as much as the tentative date for the Dedication is not until October …, which is after

---

* The rest of the story is this: In June of 1961 the Sloan Foundation announced that the president of Colgate University, Everett Case, would take over as the new president and chief executive officer of the foundation effective July 1, 1962. (The same date, as it transpired, that Gould would himself retire as Carleton president and so would have, after all, been … available.) Upon reading the news, Gould wrote Sloan a note to congratulate him on "this wise selection," adding: "Even so, of course, I shall always be sorry that circumstances did not work out for me to serve you and the Foundation." Sloan replied, with appreciation for Gould's gracious words: "I agree with you it is too bad that the chips fell where they did, so to speak, but I am sure you appreciate that nothing could be done about it." After Sloan sent another "very friendly letter" in October, Gould responded with "sort of an elaborate reply" which spelled out again, "as we go our ways," the reasons Gould had felt he had had to react as he had to Sloan's offer of the year before. Saying that the reason he may have "prolonged our dialogues longer than necessary" was that he had "kept hoping the way would open,—but it did not." Gould concluded: "Now may I tell you once again that never in my life have I wanted to do anything so much as I wanted to accept the proposition you made to me. Life has been good to me; honors of all kinds have come to me; and yet, Mr. Sloan, you paid me the greatest compliment I have ever received."

the start of the school year, it would be the writer's suggestion that the College be allowed to place this equipment in place prior to the start of the school year.

Gilman also wrote Horn the same day. Two days later, an unmollified Horn replied to Gilman:

> This will acknowledge your letter of February 22, 1961. I telephoned Mr. Pickford this morning and asked him to discuss the matter with you and tell you we could not approve the program.
>
> We expect things of this kind in some places and we try to avoid them. If we give a college $1,500,000 to $1,600,000 we supply the equipment. Then somebody comes along with 25, 50 or 75 thousand dollars to be used for equipment and they expect to receive six pages of publicity. We are giving the building to Carleton and not the Rockefeller Foundation. After Carleton College accepts the building and the key is delivered to you, it is a different story. In the meantime, please remember that until the building is accepted by Carleton, it is the property of Olin Foundation, Inc., although it is on your grounds. You do not seem to understand that Olin Foundation, Inc. is the complete owner until the key is turned over to you. Up until that time, we can say what goes into the building.
>
> In the first place, the article in the paper was not entirely correct. This indicates that a group, which gives a small amount of money to be used for movable equipment, seems to think it owns the building.
>
> I trust you will understand that until the building is dedicated in October, and the key turned over to Carleton, we cannot approve the plan. It has been necessary for us to take this position in order to keep out "free riders" who seem to think that by giving a small sum of money they can obtain a great deal of publicity.

Following his return, Gould wrote Horn both to try to restore good feeling and to request reconsideration of Horn's insistence that Carleton move no equipment other than what the Olin Foundation was supplying into the building prior to its dedication. Acknowledging that the Rockefeller grant announcement as released by that foundation had been "unfortunate," he regretted the concern it had caused Horn and assured him "that there will be no repetition of anything of the sort." He pointed out, however, that "over and above the magnificent gift from the Olin Foundation, which includes fixed equipment and the splendid electron microscope, the College is responsible for movable equipment which totals $329,750." Gould said he thought "it would be most unfortunate if we had to dedicate Olin Hall without all of the new equipment installed and the building in full operation." He observed that, although formal dedication would not be until October, the building was expected to be completed July 20 and that "we had hoped to begin moving in as soon after that as possible." "Moving out of our present quarters in Laird Hall into the new Olin Hall of Science involves a major operation," he pled, and members of our staffs in biology and physics are prepared to spend the summer doing it." He concluded:

> We have not consciously violated any part of our contractual agreement with the Olin Foundation, and I am sure, my good friend, that you know I do not wish to do so. If I am guilty of any shortcoming, it has been one of misinterpretation, which I hope you in your generous way will understand and excuse. I do covet the hope that you will give me the go-ahead sign so we can have a completely equipped, functioning Olin Hall of Science for you to dedicate [in October].

It required further lobbying of Horn in April and May, partly working through Pickford and then through Olin vice president James Wynn, but Horn ultimately unbent, allowing for the move of equipment into Olin in late summer.

***

In contrast to "situations" that vexed, one of the nicest things waiting on Gould's desk when he returned from globetrotting was a copy of a highly complimentary feature article in the *Chicago Tribune* calling Carleton a "little Harvard" now widely recognized as ranking, with Oberlin and Swarthmore, as among the nation's top three coeducational colleges. The article noted that for the most recent graduating class 71 percent of men and 41 percent of women had gone on to graduate school and that 48 members of the Class of 1960, almost a fourth of the class, had been awarded fellowships, scholarships, or assistantships, including "six Fulbright fellowships, six National Science Foundation fellowships, eight Woodrow Wilson fellowships, a Danforth fellowship, and a French government assistantship with a Fulbright travel grant, all won in national competition." Carleton, said the *Tribune*, "is not a snob college. ... But it is a highly exclusive college, dedicated to an aristocracy of intelligence and character." (A few months before, Gould had described his job, in a letter to one of his trustees, as "trying to help make this college as good as people think it is.") The article placed much of the credit for Carleton's rise to preeminence squarely on the shoulders of its president, observing that in fifteen years Gould had "increased the average salary of all ranks of the faculty by 248 per cent and has assembled a teaching staff of extraordinary distinction."

Helpful though positive publicity surely was, fine words could never by themselves substitute for the solid growth in endowment and other capital giving truly necessary to sustain Carleton's "commitment to excellence." About $5 million in new gifts was still needed to complete the $12 million development program as planned, and, as chairman of the trustees' Development Committee, Atherton Bean was becoming worried that progress toward the goal seemed to be slowing. On March 13, 1961, Bean wrote Gould a confidential expression of his concern:

I think we have reached a rather critical point in the campaign. We have not had a major gift which we have generated ourselves for a long time. We are running out of major announcements that we can make, and there is real evidence in the organization of let-down and some discouragement. We furthermore have to consider that we only have a year and a half to go in the campaign and that is not a very long time within which to raise roughly $5,000,000. In order to put life back into our organization, I think that we should aim to get at least two major gifts (and by that I mean in general $250,000 or more) between now and the first of June—items of such importance and interest that they would be worthy of special announcement at commencement time, for instance.

We might have half-hopefully, half-jokingly said before you left that we were going to try to prove that we could do just as well raising money when you were away as when you were here, but it is quite obvious not only that we have not done so, but I think that we cannot do so. We need the force of your personality and the persuasiveness of your diction to put over the really big projects that we must sell. I would like therefore to put as strongly as I can the necessity of your planning on devotion of a very major portion of your time from now on to fund-raising activities. I suggest that other public activities—important though they may be—be subordinated in substantial measure to the requirements of the campaign until it is quite clear that we are going to have our $5,000,000 in hand. I don't know how long this will take, but whatever time and whatever effort is necessary we need to apply to it and I am quite confident that everybody else in the organization will be delighted to follow your lead. … You are the key to our success. None of us, however well intentioned we may be, can add the spark of leadership that you and only you can provide.

Bean went on to outline particular major gift prospects, both individual and foundational, for which Gould himself was "the key to the situation" and that Bean therefore felt must fall to the president to pursue. Five of these happened to be persons then located, permanently or seasonally, in Florida, and Bean urged that Gould give the Florida prospects "special priority" at just this time. Bean aimed high: "As I sit here in my den this Sunday evening and dream about raising about $5,000,000, I can really see it all coming out of those five prospects in Florida."

During the first week of April, sandwiched between Ford Foundation business in New York and a meeting of the Executive Committee of Phi Beta Kappa in Washington, Gould occupied himself with prospect visits in Florida. Unfortunately, Bean's vision of $5 million possibly to be realized in a stroke—or five quick strokes—under the Florida sun was not to be realized. A successful end to the campaign would not be so easy as that. As Bob Gale subsequently reported to Robert L. Conway of the John Price Jones Company, "Larry's Florida trip was not very successful." Two prospects of whom high hopes had been entertained—the Ordways and William L. McKnight—were now reported as "pretty definitely a no for a large gift." Gould was received very cordially by the wealthy I. A. O'Shaughnessy, who Bean had thought "should be given an opportunity to contribute to the Men's Dormitory and possibly the Men's Gymnasium"—the two spent an afternoon and evening sailing together on Biscayne Bay—but Gould was told that despite O'Shaughnessy's personal affection for Gould, his commitments as a trustee at two other educational institutions precluded a really substantial gift to Carleton. Gould revised Bean's hopes downward to a subsequent approach to O'Shaughnessy to contribute to the Gould Science Fund. Similarly, businessman and foundation head Archie Bush, who Bean had said "ought to give us the Music and Drama Center entirely," told Gould that his ability to give handsomely to Carleton was preempted by commitments to two other colleges, Rollins and Hamline. (The president of Hamline, in fact, was arriving later that day, Gould was informed.) Archie Bush did provide Gould with an introduction to another of Bean's targets, Rose Skillman, who was looked to as a "principal prospect on the Women's Gymnasium," but here too, following some initial optimism, no significant deal was ultimately closed.

In May, as national attention focused on savage attacks on "Freedom Riders" challenging segregationist practices in the Deep South and prompting Attorney General Robert Kennedy to send federal marshals to Alabama, Gould was in Washington testifying once again to a Congressional committee concerning the US Antarctic Program and then "involved in further conferences about the Antarctic Treaty," which would receive its final ratification by all signatories the following month.

Perfect weather graced Carleton's graduation exercises on Friday morning, June 2, the sixteenth commencement over which Gould presided. He had the pleasure that day of awarding honorary degrees to two close friends, William Benton and John Cowles, each of whom were retiring from long service on Carleton's Board of Trustees. At the conclusion of the trustees meeting conducted later that afternoon, further change was effected on the board as the chairman of the Nominations Committee announced that John Musser preferred not to continue as board chairman, though he would remain a member. Atherton Bean was then duly elected to take over as the new chairman.

Earlier in that June 2 meeting, as chairman of the Development Committee, Bean had reported that "although seven and a half million dollars of the twelve million dollar program has been pledged," the program had for several months "been in a trough" and that it would be needful for every trustee to help and participate in gift solicitation over the next six months. Despite the fundraising "trough" for the Development Program as a whole, the college was nonetheless ready to go forward with the next building to follow Olin (and the fourth floor addition to Reine Myers Hall), a Yamasaki-designed men's dormitory to be placed north of Lyman Lakes. Construction bids for that project had been opened the day before, and the board now authorized the execution of construction contracts.

The next evening, Gould addressed the alumni gathered for Carleton's post-commencement reunion weekend and then on Sunday morning participated with Peg in the twenty-five-year-reunion breakfast of the Class of 1936—a class claiming a special bond with Gould, as he and they had all first arrived at Carleton together in 1932. The Goulds—well-fed that day—were then special guests at lunchtime with the Class of 1926, with whom Gould had no such close association as with '36, but—a college president must dote upon all his children.

All activities associated with the academic year 1960-61 were brought to a pleasant end for Gould eight days later in Los Angeles, where Occidental College awarded him his fourteenth honorary degree.

***

In mid-June, Gould visited and had dinner in Ann Arbor with his trustee Margaret Bell Cameron and her husband George. He also on this trip called on the Towsleys, Carleton benefactors since the library campaign, who now were looked to as possible principal donors for the women's gymnasium project. "I think something may come of it," Gould wrote hopefully to the Camerons afterward, "though unfortunately, Mrs. Towsley thinks modern education has gone overboard in deference to the 'A' students," having become convinced that the average student is more apt to be successful than the top one. "Of course, statistically this is nonsense," Gould told the Camerons, "but I didn't dare say so."

Gould could and did on occasion mask some level of difference of opinion with potential donors, but, much as he coveted securing significant gifts for Carleton, he did have limits in this respect. Earlier that month he complained in a letter to Carleton alumnus Bob Matteson how "depressing" he found it "that so many possible sources of support for this college are surrounded with such ultra-conservatism that they are unapproachable on terms that would be acceptable to me personally without a loss of self-respect and confidence in Carleton College and its primary mission."

One case in which Gould did apparently reach a limit he flatly refused to cross was, ultimately, that of Charles Lilley Horn. Gould had for years, in pursuit of grants from the Olin Foundation, danced to Horn's oft-changing tunes and flattered Horn's outsized ego. (Richard Gilman, in an oral history interview many years later, described Horn's ego as both "a mile wide [and] a mile long.") Late in 1960, the Olin Foundation had added the gift of a powerful electron microscope, costing $34,750, to its grant for construction of the Olin Hall of Science. As Bob Gale remembered decades later, when he and Gould went to Horn's Minneapolis office to get the check for the microscope, Horn intentionally knocked the check off the table onto the floor. When Gale moved to pick it up, Horn told Gale to sit back down; he wanted Gould to pick it up off the floor himself. Which he did.

Starting the year before, Horn had begun to allude to the possibility of the Olin

Foundation giving Carleton a second building. As Gilman related long after—and Gale independently said much the same thing—it was "common knowledge" at the time among college and university administrators that the Olin Foundation was giving two buildings; if all went well with the first, a second was possible—but only if there was an honorary degree for Horn in between. "This was," recalled Gilman, "as close to being literally true and widely understood as anything I could say on this matter." So the question arose within the Carleton board: Should we not give Charles Horn an honorary degree and put ourselves in line for a second building? In mid-May of 1961 Gould reported to John Musser that two trustees, Bishop Hamilton Kellogg and Paul Christopherson, had spoken to him in favor of recognizing Horn. "Quite frankly, it is embarrassing," Gould protested to Musser. "The Olin Foundation is unique in that it even permits members of its staff to accept any kind of recognition." Gilman, in his Carleton oral history interview, recounted that when the matter was raised at a board meeting—nothing of this made it into the written minutes, but that is not surprising—"Larry stood firm, and he said, 'I will not be party to an honorary degree for Charlie Horn. I have crawled on my hands and knees across his office often enough, and I will not submit myself to making him an honorary alumnus of this college.'" In Gilman's account, Gould's "firmness and force" on the matter carried the board with him, and Horn received no honorary degree.* (It is also true, in the end, that Carleton received no second Olin building.)

The latter part of the summer of 1961 included for the Goulds, as usual, several weeks of retreat to their Wyoming cabin. There in August Larry celebrated his sixty-fifth birthday. The following week he traveled to Salt Lake City to attend the Triennial Council meeting of the United Chapters of Phi Beta Kappa, where he chaired the council sessions. Though this meeting completed his three-year term as United Chapters president, he was elected to another six-year term as senator-at-large.

Gould returned to Minnesota on September 13. A week later, he flew to New York for two days of Ford Foundation meetings. These September 1961 meetings were, in the history of the Ford Foundation, momentous ones. Although foundation president Henry Heald had perhaps given Ford Foundation trustees exactly what they wanted when he took up the position in 1956—extricating the foundation from numerous controversial involvements that had gotten it into deep water with conservative critics in the first part of the 1950s—times had now changed, and Heald's board was now desirous of changes within the foundation as well. Heald, though strong on support for educational institutions—so far, so good, from Gould's perspective—had other characteristics that were now coming to be seen by most of his trustees as drawbacks. In the view of observer

---

*   Instead, at the October ceremony of dedication for the opening of Olin Hall, Gould would present Horn with a framed "citation of honor" conferred upon him by the faculty and trustees of Carleton College "in testimony of their appreciation and respect." It was also arranged for Horn to speak to Carleton students on his private scholarly interests in religion and Biblical literature.

Waldemar Nielsen, a Ford Foundation staffer until 1961, Heald had little interest in international programs, which he deemphasized, had "no natural sympathy for 'impractical men of ideas,' including social scientists in general," and "actively disliked 'reformers,' including such black spokesmen as Roy Wilkens and Martin Luther King, Jr., whom he considered 'propagandistic politicians.'" By 1961, in Nielsen's view,

> most of the trustees ... had become dissatisfied with him and his style. In large part the difficulty stemmed from Heald's unbending insistence on his executive prerogatives and his aloof, uncommunicative manner in dealing with the board. His practice was to inform the trustees about major program and policy decisions only in the final phase and, in the opinion of board members, after many of the preliminary decisions had already been made. In addition there was a widespread feeling that although the foundation's program had not stagnated under Heald, it was hamstrung by his negative attitude toward new ideas. In September 1961 the trustees, over Heald's strenuous objection, set up a committee to conduct "a general review of the programs and procedures of the foundation." Ostensibly it was to help define policies and programs for the coming decade but, to a number of its proponents, the study had at least two additional purposes: first, to redress the imbalance of authority which, in their opinion, had developed between the trustees and the president and to make the board more influential, particularly in relation to program development; second, to force Heald to open the foundation's program to a number of new areas of activity. At least a few members of the board also entertained the hope that the study might precipitate Heald's ouster.

The "revolt" of the Ford Foundation trustees—perhaps better characterized as the board's "diktat" to the president, to which Heald had no choice but to accede—was effected on Thursday and Friday, September 21-22. On the 23rd, Gould wrote foundation vice president F. F. "Frosty" Hill that he thought the meetings had been "very productive" and that he had high hopes for the "enlarged vision" to which they had made up their minds. In particular, he had been happy to hear Heald acknowledge that "it would be possible to double our overseas operations." To Heald, the same day, Gould wrote that he thought it had been "good for the trustees to talk freely and at length as they did" and that the "many cross currents" which had been aired were "important to a vital Board of Trustees." On a personal note, Gould praised Heald for how he had handled himself in the face of the board's reassertion of directive control: "You must have been in great discomfort on Thursday and Friday and yet no one was aware of it. You were a good sport and I am sure you know all of us appreciated that fact very much."

Gould was not made a member of the committee authorized at those September meetings to review the foundation's programs and procedures, but John

Cowles was, and later that fall Gould would write Cowles of his interest in that committee's work in "lifting the sights of the Ford Foundation." He quoted to Cowles part of what Waldemar Nielsen had written to him following Nielsen's recent decision to leave the foundation, done "with a rather heavy heart because the institution continues to function at a level far, far below its potential." "This," Gould told Cowles, "is but another way of stating the concern that you and I and many others have found about it. It ought to be vastly more exciting and fruitful." Following the next meetings of the foundation in December, Gould would write Henry Ford II that he approved the "ferment which is going on." "Somehow," he would then write, "I believe a veritable revolution is necessary to get that great foundation where it ought to be."

Meanwhile, within days of the significant Ford Foundation meetings of September, the foundation publicly announced its Special Support Program for "Liberal Arts Colleges, a program planned eventually to total at least $100 million. Carleton was one of eight colleges in the initial selection, rewarding the hard work months before by Gilman, Wright, and Gale in putting together the Carleton presentation document around Gilman's kitchen table. The Ford Foundation grant to Carleton offered the college up to $2 million for general support over a three-year period, on a matching basis of three to one; that is, the school would get the full amount if it raised $6 million on its own, from sources other than the federal government, by June 20, 1964. Gould praised the program as "recognition of the fact that the top-flight liberal arts colleges are among the purple threads of quality in the fabric of higher education" and observed with satisfaction that "assuming that we shall carry out our matching responsibilities, which I know we will, this then turns out to be the largest single gift in the history of the College."

In Northfield, two days after public announcement of the Ford Foundation's program for liberal arts colleges and of Carleton's inclusion in the first round of it, classes began for what would be Larry Gould's seventeenth—and last—year as president.

CHAPTER 24

"YOU CAN DO ANYTHING YOU WANT"

"I must tell you," Larry Gould once wrote to a Carleton professor being considered as a candidate for the presidency of Grinnell College, "in the light of my experience, there is probably no more complex or difficult task than that of being president of a small liberal arts college." The crux of the difficulty, as Gould expressed it, was that a college president "is expected to be all things to all people." The person filling that role, he explained, must "to the faculty … be a scholar and to the Board of Trustees a business man, and never the twain shall meet. He must be a counselor and an expert, a diplomat and a worker and a Christian and at the same time a man of the world." He developed his theme further in metaphor:

> A college president should have the diligence of a beaver, the adaptability of a chameleon, the complacency of a camel, the cheerfulness of a cricket, the wisdom of an owl, the innocence of a lamb, the vision of an eagle, the patience of an ox, the endurance of an elephant, the tenacity of the bulldog, the strength of a lion, the nerves of a cow, the stomach of a boa constrictor, the epidermis of a rhinoceros, the brass of a monkey, the presence of a peacock and the charm of the domesticated deer.

"If these things do not scare you," Gould concluded to the younger aspirant, "then I shall not have recommended you in vain."

Impossible though it may be to combine all desirable characteristics of the ideal college president within a single human being, by the end of Gould's Carleton presidency there were many who agreed with the editorial opinion of the *Minneapolis Tribune* that "Larry Gould has come as close as anyone" to doing so. A few years before, University of California physicist Joseph Kaplan, then chairman of the US National Committee for the International Geophysical Year, had remarked at a social gathering, when college presidents had come to be discussed, that his work had brought him into contact with the presidents of many schools and that he regarded Gould of Carleton as being "in a class absolutely by himself"—that "no other president was quite in the same league."

Gould indeed found he could do the job well, and he relished the role, but even so there were aspects he found frustrating. On the one hand, he could complain that much as he might wish to delegate authority small matters that should be resolved elsewhere were endlessly coming to his desk. Yet, he could also sigh regretfully over having, as a result of the imperatives of fundraising, to dissociate his personal attention from educational matters into which he would have preferred to delve—"I would like much more," he told trustee John Musser in 1956, "to be doing the work of the Dean of the College. However, as you know, most of my time has to be spent in pursuit of the elusive dollar."

Though the job demanded much, Gould was well suited to fill it with success—he had developed within himself the talents and capacities of mind that were wanted. When given the role, he was ready. A tale told about another academic president, Robert M. Hutchins, could never have applied to Gould. This story goes that in the 1920s the Rockefeller Foundation's General Education Board had given its secretary, educator Abraham Flexner, discretionary control over a special fund to assist talented young men to realize their potential. Flexner reportedly offered Hutchins, then the "boy-wonder" assistant dean of the Yale Law School, $10,000—two years' handsome salary at the time—to allow him to take a couple of years off from administrative work in order "to read, reflect, and generally deepen his wisdom." Hutchins, however, was a young man in a hurry; he turned down the offer, was promoted to dean, and a few years later became president of the University of Chicago. At some point thereafter, Hutchins was said to have encountered Flexner at a function and said to him, with some satisfaction, "If I'd taken your ten thousand, I wouldn't be President of the University." "Maybe not," Flexner answered, "but you would have been prepared to be."

Even within the busy schedule of a college president, Gould felt it was important to set aside regular hours simply to read—oases of time conducive to serious reflection and providing for the ongoing "deepening of wisdom." Although, as Gould once wrote, "finding time for leisurely reading is one of the more difficult aspects of the life of a college president," he took care that the time be found. His "normal" daily schedule, to the extent that such a thing was ever possible, included this self-report: "I usually lunch in the Tea Room at a table with various faculty members and reserve the time until two o'clock to read." Personal correspondence also mentions "my customary hour's reading before I go to sleep." Consuming though his administrative responsibilities usually were, Gould still made sure in every year of his presidency to keep his balance by finding time to feed the soul—not only through his reading, but also through music,* religious observance, gardening, and fishing for trout.

---

* Brahms was for Gould a longtime particular favorite, though he found enjoyment in many other composers as well. For his sixtieth birthday, Bernt and Bess Balchen gave Gould a three-record set of Jascha Heifetz playing Bach's unaccompanied works for violin that Gould termed "beautiful beyond belief," adding that he never seemed to tire of Bach. Two years later he was thanking Jack Lucas for pressing Bartok upon him, saying that "I've become sufficiently fond of him to put him almost up with the long-established three B's." On other occasions, however, he declared himself "indifferent" to jazz and said that he had "not received sufficient musical education" to enjoy all of Mahler.

***

As classes started at Carleton College in September of 1961, Gould thought it most likely that he would retire in June, and the trustees had quietly begun the process of selecting his successor. The timing of retirement was not yet certain, however, and no public announcement had yet been made that it was imminent. With the "Commitment to Excellence" campaign still in full swing, Chairman Atherton Bean was chary of diminishing Gould's fundraising potential by prematurely having it widely known that he would soon be stepping down.

Early in October Gould traveled to Boston to accept an honorary degree bestowed by Brandeis University. At Carleton six days later, he presided over the ceremonies, including convocation and luncheon, connected with the formal dedication of the Olin Hall of Science, into which the Departments of Biology and Physics had moved in late summer. Charles Horn addressed the convocation, accepted the framed "Citation of Honor" devised for his benefit, and turned over the keys of the building to Gould. The ceremony

With biology professor Thurlo Thomas and Charles Horn at the dedication of Olin Hall

was kept relatively simple at Horn's request. (Gould had told Bean in August that the college, which had originally thought of a grander celebration, had best go along with what Horn wanted, adding that "quite frankly, the kind of speech Charlie may give is unpredictable, and it might not be too good an idea to have a lot of people there.") Distinguished guests for the occasion included former president Cowling; Professor Emeritus Charles Culver, chairman of the Physics Department for much of the Cowling presidency; and the building's architect, Minoru Yamasaki, whose daughter Carol Ann was then a Carleton freshman.

The next day Gould flew to Tucson, where he enjoyed a week at the University of Arizona. This was a visit ripe with consideration on all sides as to what Gould's post-Carleton plans would turn out to be. He was met at the airport by his friend Reuben Gustavson—the man who the year before had spoken to President Richard A. Harvill about Gould's possible interest in joining the Arizona faculty after retiring from Carleton. At the university, Gould gave a public address ("Antarctica Old and New") and had what he termed a "splendid" visit with Harvill, at the end of which, Gould later recalled, Harvill said something like: "When you retire from Carleton College, come down here and you can have a job as long as I have, and you can do anything you want." Nothing was decided at that time, but Gould promptly wrote to Gustavson that his impression of Harvill had been extremely positive: "Here is a man of complete integrity and with a vision of what the University of Arizona can be. Perhaps I may be of some use to him some day."

At the same time, Gould was giving some consideration to a suggestion made in September by Frank Sparks, president of the New York-based Council for Financial Aid to Higher Education, that Gould consider succeeding to that presidency as Sparks reached the mandatory retirement age of seventy. His friend Frank Abrams was also urging this course upon Gould. The Council possibility remained an open one until the latter part of November, when Gould finally asked that his name be withdrawn from further consideration for the post—partly, he explained, because he did not in his "retirement" really wish to take on so exacting a new commitment as this would be, with obligations extending "beyond the normal academic year of nine months," and also because "quite frankly, the idea of moving back to New York and living there" no longer appealed either to himself or to Peg. Their eyes were increasingly focused on the Arizona desert. In a follow-up letter to Abrams, Gould wrote: "It may well be that we shall end up at one of the universities in the Southwest. I have had some tempting offers, and I think it might be fun to return to the classroom on a limited basis. Of all the things I've ever done, I think I enjoyed teaching most."

The Carleton Board of Trustees held their fall meeting on the campus October 27-28, with business that included the election of Elwood "Goley" Newhart as the board's new vice chairman, authorizing the Executive Committee to increase the student "comprehensive fee" for tuition and other items by up to $200 for the year following, and discussion of the current status of building projects and the Development Program. In addition to the completion of Olin Hall, the fourth floor addition to Myers Hall was done, the Gridley Hall dining facility had been expanded, and Williams Hall, an 1880 building which had outlived its usefulness, had been demolished. The new men's dormitory and dining hall was progressing on schedule, and a final decision on where to site a new men's gymnasium was imminent. The only hitch was with the women's gymnasium, a stated college need for more than half a century, where the Buildings and Grounds Committee was recommending that construction "be deferred indefinitely unless a specific gift is received for this purpose." Bean reported that gifts and pledges toward the $12 million goal now totaled $8,080,000. This included a not-yet-publicly-announced bequest forthcoming from the Charles L. Denison estate—eventually designated to establish, in the president's honor, the Gould Science Fund, supporting professorships, scholarships, and loan funds across the sciences. Bean's total did not include the $2 million Ford Foundation grant, which would be earned only on a matching basis.

Coinciding with this meeting of the trustees, the college mailed out a letter to alumni from Bean "confidentially" revealing the "distressing" news that President Gould had decided to retire. "Considerable work has already been done," the letter reported, "but no public announcement of Larry's decision, nor of our search has been made." Appointment of a successor was "at least several months in the future," and no specific date for Gould's retirement had yet been determined. The letter stated that the college did not plan to announce Gould's intent to retire to the general public until a successor had been chosen—though it is difficult to see how it was somehow expected that the news would remain unreported following a mailing to thousands of persons. Indeed, within days Gould was writing to Bean that he feared the letter had been "a tactical error"—that his telephone had been ringing constantly since it had gone out* and that two newspapers had already asked about it, to which he had tried to reply as vaguely as possible. On November 2, the news was reported prominently in the *Minneapolis Morning Tribune* and then on radio.

Meanwhile, the information from that week that actually *was* "distressing"— that Carleton's plans to build a women's recreation center might be postponed indefinitely absent substantial gifts toward that project—happily produced an almost immediate result. Trustee Margaret Bell Cameron, with her father Laird Bell, together offered to give Carleton $100,000 to get the building off the ground.

---

* No one at the college had realized ahead of time that Charlie Horn of the Olin Foundation would directly receive a copy of Bean's letter, having been placed on the relevant mailing list by being made an honorary member of the Class of 1960. Horn called Gould on October 31, saying that the news had "greatly disconcerted him." Horn indicated, Gould told Bean, "that they had been caught in between administrations in another college" with less than satisfactory result; Gould tried to calm him down by assuring him that there would be "no change in the hopes, the aspirations, or the quality of the administration" at Carleton.

(Following his usual pattern, Laird Bell's commitment to pay half of the joint pledge was to be kept anonymous; the eventual publicity for the gift would be all Margaret's.) Although the pledge would officially be dated December 1, Gould was already on October 31 able confidentially to advise Ele Hansen of the Women's Physical Education Department of the impending gift. Mrs. Cameron's largesse would be conditional upon the college's raising the remaining $350,000 for the building within three years. In the January press release making this announcement, Alumni Capital Gifts Campaign Chairman A. D. "Bill" Hulings stated that this challenge would be a "great incentive to our Alumni Program," as many of Carleton's female graduates had been highly interested in the status of plans for this particular building.*

In November and December, Gould made multiple trips to Washington and New York, attending several of his long-customary meetings: the Carnegie Foundation for the Advancement of Teaching, which he was now serving as chairman of the board; the United Chapters of Phi Beta Kappa, of which he had first become a senator in 1946; and the Ford Foundation, where he was now an experienced and influential trustee. Within the Ford Foundation Gould was at this time advocating greater strategic expenditures of the foundation's vast resources. "At current prices," he wrote a correspondent in mid-December,

> the Ford Foundation is worth about $4,230,000,000. We think we ought to lift our sights and spend more money which would involve not only income but sizeable pieces of the corpus, as well. It would do no harm if the Foundation were whittled down to $2,500,000,000. It would still be bigger than the next twenty foundations put together. Surely it is difficult to imagine a time when the needs of the world are going to be more critical than now.

The late-1961 travel that was to have the most profound personal consequences for Gould, however, was not a trip of his own, but rather his wife's holiday visit to her sister and brother-in-law in Columbus, where Dick Hoppin was now a professor of musicology at Ohio State. Peg left on December 18 for what was expected to be a long stay past Christmas. Larry, with Jill the poodle as company, was anticipating a quiet time in Northfield, hoping to make some progress on throwing away a lot of "useless" things accumulated at home and office since the early 1930s. ("I am the principal offender in this, I guess," Gould wrote Mrs. Cameron, "for Peg says I am a magpie.")

Larry later confessed that he had known Peg to be in a fragile mental and

---

*   The release noted that the need had been pointed to since 1909 and that Carleton was "probably further behind the times in the area of women's physical education facilities than in any other part of its physical plant." In July 1962, Gould's successor just taking office would write Mrs. Cameron: "I understand that Dr. Cowling as well as Larry both mentioned in their inaugural addresses the need for this new building. I am grateful to you for absolving me from the necessity of reiterating the refrain."

emotional state prior to this trip and said that he ought to have given Jean and Dick a warning regarding "how frazzled her nerves were." In any case, on Christmas Eve, in the Hoppins' home, Peg blew up. Or melted down. Exactly what happened is uncertain, except that it started, as such things can, as an argument over something quite trivial, possibly involving a copy of *Time* magazine in the Hoppins' living room, where Peg and Dick were reading, while Jean was in the kitchen. In Jean's memory eight years later:

> Suddenly, Peg threw the magazine in Dick's face and charged out of the living room into the kitchen … to keep the dynamite that had all at once built in her exploding until it was spent. She kept falling apart thereafter until she reached the point of saying: "Dick, get me a room at the Deshler, and call a cab. I'm going home." Me, I collapsed on the kitchen stool, and when Dick asked what he should do, I said: "Do as she asks … but go with her down to the Deshler." Dick did go with her.

As Peg remained bound and determined to return home, Jean called Larry to tell him so and—as Larry later described—"intimated that she was quite mad." Apparently before leaving, Peg pronounced the Hoppins henceforth dead to the Goulds, after which Dick may have said (Peg's version) that all of Peg's friendships "turn to ashes" or (Dick's version) that "we've just joined a distinguished company of people you've declared have ceased to exist for you." In any case, Larry remembered Peg literally falling into his arms when she returned, "weeping bitterly." (He also remembered—nearly nine years later—that "she even thought she might return to her psychiatrist in St. Paul but this idea didn't last long.")

Peg stayed adamant. When, a few months later in March 1962, Jean sent to Larry's office a post card informing him of the death of Dick's father Claude (Carleton Class of 1907), Larry took the card home to Peg. In Jean's subsequent retelling (to Gould, years later), after this there came in the Hoppins' mail a small envelope from Peg:

> I opened it with joy, thinking she had recovered and would be asking—as often she had done in the past when she had been particularly harsh to me—if we were kaput. Always, I had the answer to that one: No! Instead I read that, it didn't matter who had died—Claude or anybody else—we were never again to communicate with you two. Her rider was that, as far as you and she were concerned, Dick and I had ceased to exist.

Jean and Dick and Peg and Larry had shared many happy times together for decades—for three of them their history as a trio extended back to Jean's childhood in the 1920s, when Larry had begun courting her big sister. Peg had enjoyed many previous visits and a trip to Europe in the Hoppins' company. Yet now Peg cleanly cut them out of her life—and insisted that Larry do the same. (Larry later, during the term of the banishment, remained in some contact by mail, sent to and from his office and not home. The Hoppins understood and accepted that it was necessary for him to some extent to abide by Peg's decree. Jean would later write to him: "Of course, Larry, we never charged *you* with our sudden extinction.") The separation between sisters would last more than twenty-three years—until a few months before Jean's death in 1985. Across all this time the rupture between Peg and the Hoppins, resistant to his several unsuccessful attempts to heal it, would be Larry Gould's great personal sorrow.

***

As 1961 came to an end, Gould's post-retirement plans were still not definitely fixed. In November he reported himself to be sure of one thing only, that he and Peg would remove themselves from Northfield so that his continued proximity would in no way handicap his successor: "I shall say to [Carleton's next president] what Dr. Cowling said to me, 'From now on I will have no contact with the College except through you and only then if you ask it.'" To Cowling himself he wrote in December, "I am almost swamped with offers of things to do when I retire. At the moment I am undecided but may do a limited amount of teaching in one of the great universities."

At 9:30 a.m. on January 13, 1962, the Carleton trustees convened in executive session in Minneapolis and received the report and recommendation of their presidential search committee, following which they unanimously elected John W. Nason as Gould's successor, the college's fifth president, to take office July 1.

Nason, though eight and a half years younger than Gould—he was a Carleton graduate of 1926—had been the first of the two to head a college, becoming president of Swarthmore in 1940. He led Swarthmore until 1953; since then he had been serving in New York as president of the Foreign Policy Association. Although Gould was neither expected nor invited to play any significant role in the selection of his successor and it would have been inappropriate for him to try to exert any unsolicited influence on the choice, there is evidence that his own preferred candidate at the time was his dean, Dick Gilman. Gilman was indeed among those receiving very serious consideration until late in the process. Gould likely was to some degree disappointed that Gilman was not chosen. His "on the record" responses to Nason's selection were, however, of course all properly enthusiastic. The day after Nason's formal election by the board, Gould wrote one of the consultants for the development campaign that Nason was "a superb choice" and that he could "think of nothing better for Carleton College." The next day he assured trustee Hugh Harrison that his personal estimation of John Nason was quite high, adding "I do believe, Hugh, that no better choice could have been made." For the benefit of alumni and the public, Gould offered that he knew nobody better qualified for the position and that he thought it "especially fortunate" that the college would thus have a Carleton alumnus on the job when celebrating its 1966 centennial. Nason, said Gould, "has my complete confidence and my support in every way that I can be of use to the College through him."

With the announcement of a successor—and a precise date of retirement now definitely established—Gould's Carleton mailbox now filled with tributes and appreciations that helped to warm a notably cold Minnesota January.

A note from a Cal Tech geographer, while praising Gould's ability to select outstanding young faculty and then to keep most of them despite lucrative offers from other institutions, singled out for particular praise Gould's "key role" in helping to launch the American Universities Field Staff with a crucial ten-year Ford Foundation grant. This personal action, in the opinion of the letter writer, might well have been Gould's "greatest administrative contribution to the welfare of our country." Gould's response: "While I am sure you exaggerate the role I played in the early days of the American Universities Field Staff, I am none the less grateful for your friendly remarks."

A Carleton alumnus of 1931, who had in 1944 been among those enthusiastically endorsing the idea of Gould as president to the trustee search committee looking for the right man to succeed Cowling, now wrote Gould with thanks for the job he had done and to tell him that he was proud of his own foresight, for Larry's performance at Carleton had been "magnificent": "I truly have never met a man as brilliant as you and yet with an unbelievable common touch, a *wonderful* sense of humor and a warm and endearing personality. You are truly a complete person." Gould's answer: "If I had it to do over again I could do a better job. However, I am glad I have stayed."

An alumnus of 1945 wrote that every year of the Gould presidency he and his wife had become "a little prouder to be Carleton alumni." He thanked Gould for all he had done "for Carleton and for the cause of liberal education" and suggested that "few retiring college presidents can look back upon so much solid accomplishment, or can feel so secure in the affection of all those they have influenced for good."

Suggestions for further employment continued to come his way as well. President John Dickey of Dartmouth wondered whether Gould would be interested in exploring ways to make him "a part of the Hanover scene." The US State Department's science adviser wrote to inquire whether he might be interested in becoming a science attaché on government assignment abroad, perhaps in New Delhi or Tel Aviv.

By early February, however, Gould was ready to tell friends that it was "quite likely" that his next permanent residence would be Tucson, with a good chance that he would join the University of Arizona faculty on President Harvill's "do anything you want" basis. (The commitment to Arizona, starting with the second semester of the 1962-63 school year, would be finalized by mid-April.) To former dean Frank Kille, Gould outlined further plans:

> I know we shall spend our summers in Jackson Hole but for more
> extended periods than in the past.
> I shall continue as a trustee of the Ford Foundation and a member

of its Executive Committee, which together take a fair amount of time. I am not sure whether I shall continue as a member of the National Science Board or not.* However, I am still chairman of the Committee on Polar Research for the National Academy of Sciences, which suggests that I really ought to go back to Antarctica again. Indeed, I have made so many promises as to what I am going to do next year that the wisest course may be to do just that.

Gould's last few months in office at Carleton were dominated by activities driven by his end of June departure—by efforts (his own and that of others) to bring the Development Program to its $12 million goal by June 30; by making his own arrangements and preparations for retirement and what would come next; and, increasingly, as the calendar pages turned, by the round of tributes and farewells coincident to his stepping down.

Gould had first arranged, for his final Carleton commencement, for the centerpiece to be a speech by John J. McCloy, chairman of the board of the Ford Foundation and of the Council on Foreign Relations. When McCloy, however, found in mid-winter that he would after all be unable to attend, what Gould then described to Atherton Bean as "the whole confounded senior class" quickly—without giving the president time to secure another speaker—presented Gould with a petition entreating him to bow to the united wishes of the Class of '62 and deliver the commencement address himself. As Gould wrote McCloy: "So you see, I am 'stuck' and all on account of you!"

In mid-February he began the last of his periodic presidential western swings, speaking over the course of eighteen days at the alumni clubs of the Pacific coast and the Southwest. A few days after Gould's March 9 return to Minnesota, Bean announced that the Carleton Development Program had passed the $10 million mark—the campaign's original goal—in cash and pledges. At about the same time, Gould summarized for an interviewer his own plans for his first six months of retirement: a summer spent catching up on his trout fishing, followed by a fall and early winter trip to Antarctica in his capacity as chairman of the National Academy of Science's Polar Research Committee.

In Northfield, Mayor W. T. Nelson officially proclaimed April 12 as a civic "Larry Gould Day," and a committee of the Northfield Area Chamber of Commerce laid plans for a gala "red tie" banquet to be held that evening in Larry and Peg's honor. When the day arrived, many in town thought it perfectly appropriate, given Gould's polar pedigree, that the morning of Larry Gould Day brought with it a spring snowstorm. Despite the weather, over five hundred of the Goulds' Northfield friends and neighbors gathered at the St. Olaf College Center to demonstrate their affection. It was the largest testimonial dinner in town history. Five speakers vied with one another making highly complimentary remarks; former

---

* He would not. He allowed his term to expire in 1962 without seeking reappointment.

president Eisenhower wired praise and congratulations; gifts were bestowed;* and it was announced that St. Olaf College would at its June commencement join the ranks of institutions making Gould an honorary alumnus. The *Northfield News* that day praised Gould editorially for having "made the broad pursuit of excellence a practical reality" and for having "exemplified in himself and in what he has said and done the ideal of what an educated man, competent in today's world, should really be."

It is a fine thing to be the toast of the town, but Gould still had work to do besides resting on his laurels. "I have only about two and a half months," he had just written to a fellow college president, "to wind up enough work to last me two years." A number of prospective donors to the Carleton Development Program had been assigned to Gould as requiring the president's personal attention. Many he had been long cultivating; it was now time to harvest.

One friend apparently well-disposed toward Carleton was I. A. O'Shaughnessy, founder of the Lario Oil & Gas Company, who said of money that it was like manure: "It doesn't do any good unless you spread it around." O'Shaughnessy's substantial philanthropy was primarily directed toward Catholic higher education, but he and Gould had become warm friends, and Gould believed him ready to associate himself with the Carleton drive. Early in April Gould wrote O'Shaughnessy a reminder that his retirement was fast approaching, that he had "high hopes" of completing the Carleton Development Program by the time of his departure, and that "no matter how much money we shall have raised, however, the program will not be complete unless I. A. O'Shaughnessy is in it." By way of example, he mentioned that William McKnight (of 3M) was giving $100,000. ("I hoped he would give us $6,000,000," he told O'Shaughnessy. "I wish he could be infected by your public spirited generosity.") O'Shaughnessy's gift of $100,000 arrived a week later.

Gould wrote similarly to Henry Ford II, whose personal friendship he hoped might generate a substantial gift, perhaps under the canopy of the Gould Science Fund. Compared to O'Shaughnessy, Ford required a bit more shaking for the fruit to drop. A month later Gould wrote again:

> It was good to see you at the recent meetings of the Foundation in New York. I was very glad to have you tell me that you had read my special letter to you four times but that you had not yet decided how to answer it. May I suggest that you keep right on reading the letter until the right answer comes. That is a very good recipe.

Henry and Anne Ford's gift of $25,000 directed to the Gould Science Fund would arrive before the end of the calendar year.

---

* For Peg, a keepsake handbag; for Larry, a large framed sketch drawn at the request of Northfield's Larry Gould Day Committee by Carleton coach and artist Jim Nelson. Also presented was a handsome plaque inscribed "Larry Gould, Neighbor - Friend - Citizen - Educator."

On the last weekend in April, Gould played host to John and Elizabeth Nason, who were making their first visit to the college since Nason's selection as Gould's successor. On Saturday morning Nason addressed students and faculty at a special chapel convocation. In the evening both men were present for the annual senior-alumni banquet in the Tea Room, where the main address was given by a third college president, that of Iowa's Cornell College, Carleton alumnus Arland F. Christ-Janer (Class of 1943). At the college chapel service Sunday morning Gould delivered what Christ-Janer praised as "a very significant statement of your convictions with respect to a Christian way of life." In the evening, after hosting an afternoon reception in honor of the Nasons in Great Hall, Gould attended his second religious service of the day in the chapel, this a Jewish service that, Gould affirmed afterward to Rabbi Dudley Weinberg, would be ever memorable to him for the excellence of its sermon, the beauty of its music, and for "the spiritual uplift" it gave him.

In May, bit by bit, the four-year total of contributions toward the Development Program campaign continued to progress toward the $12 million goal. One memorable event that month was the organization, on the 14th, of a novel "conference call," whereby some eighty volunteers across the nation who were leading Carleton's Alumni Capital Gifts Program (ACGP) fundraising— a new initiative with a goal of raising $1,560,000 through alumni giving by Gould's last day in office—were connected by telephone to simultaneously hear messages spoken by Gould, Bean, and ACGP national chairman Bill Hulings. In some cities phone amplifiers were used to allow other area workers to listen as well, amounting to about three hundred alumni in all. Hulings was able during the call to announce that, although active solicitation for this program had begun only four weeks before, the ACGP pledge total had already exceeded the $1 million mark. A few days later, Vice President Bob Gale reported to Bean that the new grand total for the entire campaign stood at $11,018,701.82, and that his office would henceforth be preparing daily updates. The same day Gale, Bean, and Director of Development Bob McCarthy met with Gould to discuss plans regarding the president's remaining prospect "assignments"—the people he still needed to see in person—and the status of approaches already made.

By this point in the year, more and more events and activities on Gould's schedule began to signal the nearness of retirement—the approach of which he both welcomed and regretted. ("As the man said as he watched his mother-in-law drive his new Cadillac over a two hundred foot cliff," Gould wrote that month to trustee emeritus Louis Headley, "I have mixed emotions.") He was honored by Carleton's Chicago area alumni club on May 15. By the beginning of June he was, somewhat under protest, spending time sitting for his official presidential portrait, being executed by English artist A. Egerton Cooper. Gould had attempted to argue to Atherton Bean that a painted portrait of himself was quite unnecessary and that a photograph would do. Bean had overruled him: "You may have one vote against the fourth President having his portrait painted, but there are 35 other trustees of the College who vote the other way. There may be some times when one to 35 makes it about even, but this is not one of those times."*

Students celebrated the last campus Larry Gould Day on June 2, assembling en masse on the Bald Spot to cheer as Larry and Peg were driven slowly around the central campus in a bright red convertible. They were accompanied by a student dressed as a penguin, who, when the Goulds had been delivered, read a celebratory poem about Gould's accomplishments. Then, in remembrance of Gould's having voiced regret the year before that he and Peg had been unable to spend more time in Greece during his world trip for the Ford Foundation, the student body presented the Goulds with two round-trip tickets to Athens, to be used whenever they wished. In a subsequent note to Carleton Student Association president Dan Styron, who had presided over the June 2 festivities, Gould wrote that no words could possibly convey "how deeply touched my wife and I were with your magnificent and imaginative goodbye gift to us." He pledged, in accepting the tickets, that whenever the journey was made, he would return to Carleton afterward to tell students how it had gone.

Four days later it was the faculty's turn to say farewell. At an evening reception at the Northfield Golf Club on June 6, the faculty and administration presented the Goulds first with humorous remarks by Carleton professors Reed Whittemore and Alfred Hyslop and then with the surprise gift of a new red Jeep with white canvas top, perfect for use in the back country around the Goulds' Wyoming cabin. Peg was also given a pair of early Victorian earrings.

Meanwhile, another $100,000 came in for the Development Program, in the form of Laird Bell's creation of a professorship honoring his grandfather, William Laird. This was followed almost immediately by more great news: Dr. and Mrs. Harry Towsley of Ann Arbor, who now had sent two daughters to Carleton, were committing to provide the final $200,000 needed to finance the Women's Recreation Center. Gould reported this exciting development promptly to President Emeritus Cowling, knowing how pleased his predecessor would be that with regard to the gymnasium each had looked toward in successive inaugural addresses, "after 53 years we are able to redeem our joint promise." (The building, when finally dedicated in 1965, would be named in honor of Cowling's wife, Elizabeth.)

A week before Commencement, Carleton's "Commitment to Excellence" development campaign was coming tantalizingly close to completion.

***

The second week of June 1962 was effectively "honorary degree week" for Larry Gould. On June 9, he was hooded by the University of Minnesota. When

---

* Cooper's earlier portrait subjects had included King George VI and Winston Churchill. Writing in 1983 to Carleton's seventh president, however, Gould confessed that he had never liked "that G - D - portrait of me."

rain washed out the planned outdoor ceremony, Gould's degree was presented afterward in President O. Meredith Wilson's home. Gould wrote Wilson that the resulting warmth and informality in some ways made the occasion all the more memorable. The next day, it was the turn of St. Olaf College, where the degree came at the hand of President Clemens Granskou. That evening Gould flew to Cleveland and on the 11th was honored by the College of Wooster, where his citation read, in part:

> Sir, by your stature in your own field of learning, by your courage and vision in higher education, and by your sheer winsomeness and warmth as a man, you have worked a miracle. You have made every college and university in America feel that you somehow belong to it.

At Wooster, Gould's commencement speech emphasized that "beliefs are important." "Every one of you," he told the graduates, "will give your life for what you believe. Sometimes people believe in little or nothing at all. Then they give their lives for little or nothing at all. One life is all we have and we live it as we believe in living it." Three days after that, his fourth degree of the week was bestowed by Harvard University, where the fact that the honorary LLD was conferred by his good friend, President Nathan Pusey, made the honor for Gould "doubly wonderful."

Gould hurried home from Massachusetts, for the next morning was Carleton's own commencement, the college's eighty-eighth and the seventeenth under its fourth president. At 10 a.m. on what was a beautiful early summer Friday the colorful academic procession began. Double lines of gowned faculty and 262 graduates-to-be filed through the campus greenery and waiting audience to take places among the rows of folding chairs set up north of Skinner Memorial Chapel, which had housed or overlooked most important Carleton ceremonies since 1916. Among those present for the occasion was eighty-one-year-old Donald Cowling, the man whose vision had raised that chapel tower in the first place and who by the time Skinner was built had already presided over seven Carleton commencements. Once all were seated, College Chaplain David Maitland spoke an invocation, after which the choir, directed by Associate Professor of Music Enid Woodward, sang an anthem, "This is the Day," by Flor Peeters, based on the text of Psalm 118. By request of the senior class, Gould himself gave the morning's address, on the theme of "Noblesse Oblige."

Before the ceremonies were concluded the audience was witness to two surprises. One was board chairman Bean's electrifying announcement of the successful completion that very morning of the college's four-year $12-million development drive—which Bean noted had been "the largest short-term fundraising program ever attempted by a liberal arts college." (The result, said Bean subsequently, was "a tribute to, and the result of, the imagination and leadership which President

Gould, with Merrill Jarchow and Leith Shackel, receiving honorary Carleton degree

Gould has given.")* The other surprise, absent from Gould's script for the day's ceremony, began with Bean tapping the president on the shoulder and saying (as Bean remembered it), "Larry, I've got something I want to do." A startled Gould was momentarily unsure what was happening; Bean told him, "I'm taking charge of this meeting. You stand over there." Assisted by Dean of Men Casey Jarchow, who placed the hood, and Professor of English Reed Whittemore, who provided the citation, Bean then made Gould an official alumnus of Carleton College by conferring upon him the Degree of Doctor of Humane Letters, *honoris causa*. Whittemore's citation read, in part:

> Larry Gould has already his full measure of such tributes; his cup of honorary degrees runneth over. In marking, thus, his departure we are doing really nothing at all unless we can tell him that this community prizes less the academic distinction he has done so much to bring it than the spirit in which he has done so; to tell him that the money he has found to strengthen our enterprises has been little beside the strength of his leadership; to tell him that his magnificent performance in the role of president was only possible because of the humor, gentleness and humanity he brought to that role; and, perhaps most of all, to tell

---

*   In an interview years later, Bob Gale remembered waiting to see whether or not the morning's
    mail would bring in enough to put them over the top, with "several trustees standing there ready
    to write out a check" so that the news could be announced that day regardless. Bean himself,
    earlier that month, had told Gould that he would guarantee to make up any needed difference
    if necessary; Gould replied that he would "always cherish the wonderful assurance" thus given
    but that he would "hope we shall not need to capitalize on it." They did not. By that afternoon
    the official tally put the campaign $4,864.60 over goal.

him—as I now do tell him—that what we are doing now we are doing not out of a sense of duty but out of love.

In the afternoon, following the morning commencement, the Carleton board convened in the library for what would be the last trustees' meeting of the Gould era. Business included the formal election of Laurence McKinley Gould to the status of president emeritus of Carleton College, a step accompanied by Trustee Emeritus Laird Bell's moving statement of gratitude for the job Gould had done, followed by the board's standing ovation. (Regarding the "emeritus" honorific, Gould liked to explain to audiences from time to time that the title was derived from two Latin words: "e," meaning "without," and "meritus," meaning "merit." He also enjoyed telling the story of a woman who learned that her neighbor had just become professor emeritus and who went over and gushed to him, "Oh, what a wonderful honor, but you should have had this much sooner!")

The last report heard by the trustees that afternoon was the president's own, dealing with approvals for various faculty leaves, one promotion (that of Gould protégé Eiler Henrickson—his former student—from associate to full professor of geology), a gift covering the remaining cost of the college's IBM computer, and the establishment of the Ward Lucas Memorial Lectureship Fund in the humanities. At the completion of Gould's report, the board ended the meeting with a second standing ovation.

Eiler Henrickson

That evening Atherton and Winifred Bean hosted a dinner in Larry and Peg's honor at the Minikahda Club in Minneapolis, attended also by Dr. Cowling, Dean and Mrs. Gilman, and, with spouses, by nearly all living trustees who had served during the Gould presidency. There Larry was presented with one more gift: a very fine portable Questar telescope, bearing a plaque commemorating its presentation that day by members of the Board of Trustees of Carleton College "to Laurence McKinley Gould. Teacher, Administrator and Explorer of Far Places in the Minds and Ways of Men. Master Alike in Polar Colds and in the Warmth of Kindling Youth."

Two weeks now remained to the Gould presidency. On June 16, as part of the alumni reunion following Commencement, he addressed the early evening alumni banquet. In the week that followed he went to New York for two days of Ford Foundation meetings. During his last week in office Gould's outgoing letters included warm appreciations written to John Cowles and Laird Bell for the gift of their friendships—which of course, as he wrote Bell, "has no termination."

The correspondence of his final days as president also included one last letter in response to questions still being raised with regard to Professor Ken May and May's former involvement with the Communist Party. Baptist minister G. Archer Weniger had written an article once again "exposing" May in a spring issue of the fundamentalist publication *The Sword of the Lord*, and had recently followed that up with a letter demanding that Gould provide him with documentation regarding the sincerity "of the break that Professor May is alleged to have made with the Communist conspiracy." Gould replied to Weniger that he found his article to be "so completely misleading" that he thought it might be hopeless to respond, but he referred Weniger to May's sworn affidavit on file and added that "as a Christian college, Carleton is dedicated to the thesis that sinners—even those who sin by way of Communism—can repent." May, he assured the inquisitive Dr. Weniger, had long ago done that and become moreover "perhaps the greatest teacher and scholar on our campus."

On his last day before retirement, Gould sent a memorandum to the Carleton Business Office asking that in connection with having been promoted to full professor Eiler Henrickson receive a salary increase from $10,500 to $11,000.

And with that, he was done. His house, in which the Nasons were to live beginning July 9, was ready to be turned over its new occupants. "I am glad that both John Nason and his wife Elizabeth love gardens," Gould wrote to longtime Carleton groundskeeper D. Blake Stewart, "else I should have been reluctant to leave my wonderful peonies and other flowers for them."

Tributes continued to come his way both before and after the retirement date. *Newsweek*, in commenting on the transition in Northfield, noted that it was under Gould's tenure that Carleton had been transformed "from a little-known Congregational institution into one of the finest liberal-arts colleges in the nation." Music professor Henry Woodward, one of the dwindling number of professors still remaining in the classroom whose Carleton service predated Gould's becoming president, wrote a note telling Gould that "when Carleton people count their blessings," besides "what you have done for faculty salaries and in building up the faculty, in raising standards, in supplying fine buildings and excellent equipment, in encouraging the arts," and so forth, "what they think of more than anything else is the joy they have had in being associated with you in an exciting adventure."

Larry and Peg left town en route to the Tetons on July 5. Later that month, by way of a silent final farewell, some anonymous nocturnal artist one night painted high on the face of the Carleton water tower the image of a giant red tie.

***

"I dare say we shall miss this place more than it will miss us," Larry Gould had predicted to a member of his faculty that spring, "for it has been the center of the universe to me for thirty years." In an April message to the Carleton alumni, Gould recalled the circumstances of his coming to Carleton in 1932, admitting that:

> Quite frankly, Dr. Cowling offered me a larger salary than I would have gotten at the University of Michigan from which I was on leave. I don't believe I intended to remain at Carleton very long; I wanted to get back into

academic life and this seemed a good place to do it. I am sure I was planning at the time to go on eventually to a large university. It soon became evident to me, however, that if one loves to teach, there is no better atmosphere in which to work than a good, small, liberal arts college like Carleton.

"If I had my life to live over again," he concluded, "I could not invest it with greater satisfaction to myself than I have done at Carleton College."

The Goulds spent the balance of the summer at their Wyoming cabin—though Larry did return to Minnesota two or three times through September due to responsibilities he had agreed to take on as a local educational consultant and as a director of mutual funds managed by the Minneapolis-based Investors Diversified Services, Inc. Peg reported to Carleton's Editor of College Publications Bea Wardell that Larry was, for his fishing expeditions, loving "THE JEEP" to a degree that was "almost indecent." A little later Larry wrote, also to Wardell, that while his fishing had been wonderful, it was "terrible to have no secretary." He was, he said, "going on the assumption that if I keep stacking up my letters many will answer themselves." This complaint was confirmed by a *Carletonian* feature on the Goulds in their Wyoming retirement written for October publication by a student who had made a summer visit: "With no secretarial help, he has to answer all this correspondence himself, in longhand or 'pounding with his two fingers.'"

The *Carletonian* profile, by then-junior Peter Schwenger, also reported that during the summer Gould had read more than twenty scientific books as part of his service to a Phi Beta Kappa committee making selections for an annual best book award.* "He recuperates with detective stories," the article informed. The article also mentioned the "miniature irrigation system Mr. Gould dug on the grounds this summer" and the fact that "he cuts all the wood for the stove and he's building bookcases for the cottage." It was noted that the long narwhal tusk that had previously been a feature of Gould's Laird Hall office was now on display beneath the dinner bell hanging to the left of the Gould cabin's front door. Getting to that front door, the student observed, took some doing: "After making the turn at Hungry Jack's General Store" in "one-horse Wilson," "ahead of you are five miles of rough dirt road" before finally coming to a gate where the name "Gould" appears along with several others. "When you turn into it you can see the cottage half-hidden in a clump of aspens." Schwenger described the cabin's main room as full of character, though "easy and unassuming":

---

* The $1000 Phi Beta Kappa Award in Science, for books in the literature of science, had been established in 1959 at Gould's own suggestion. Its purpose (as stated by Hugh Odishaw in the journal *Science*) was pure Gould; "to honor scientists whose scholarly and literary interpretations of their work demonstrate that the sciences and the humanities are not 'two cultures' and that the search for wisdom is still a single enterprise." Natural science writer Loren Eiseley had been the award's fitting first recipient.

A couple of casual sofas scattered with pillows form an 'L' in one corner; and there is a Franklin stove in another with some unusual chunks of rock on the brick hearth before it. Handwoven Indian rugs lie on the floor. There are crowded bookcases, a paper-scattered desk, a personalized Carleton blanket. On one side of the ceiling a mobile by Carleton's Hyslop shies lightly away from the monster opposite: a grotesque combination of bird, fish, and cow usually hung above the cradles of Indonesian babies to scare away evil spirits.

And the walls are far from bare: a Daumier print showing a man at his desk distracted by visions of tiny fishermen; Mr. Gould's framed honorary membership in the class of 1962; a sampler embroidered on red cloth and decorated with penguins, reading "LIBER NON EST QUI NON ALIQUANDO NIHIL, AGIT," or "Workers of the World, Quit";* a number of bright Picasso posters; and finally a view of more than 50 miles, seen from the spacious windows.

In the latter half of August (coinciding with his sixty-sixth birthday), Gould, as the official delegate for the United States, took an active part in the five days of proceedings when the Sixth Meeting of SCAR, the international Scientific Committee on Antarctic Research, convened in Boulder, Colorado.

When fall came—the autumn that would include several days of tense international drama remembered as the Cuban Missile Crisis—the Goulds closed up their cabin for the season and moved temporarily to Albuquerque, where Peg would stay on near her brother while Larry for a month conducted other travels: to Tucson, Los Angeles, and the Antarctic.

On November 15, at the University of Arizona, Gould had agreed to deliver the honors convocation address. President Harvill provided the introduction, reminding the audience that Dr. Gould would be returning next semester as a member of the faculty.

Gould's address on that occasion, "Our Fractured Culture," was in part a reaction to C. P. Snow's "two cultures" dichotomy between science and the humanities, though it touched on much else besides. Gould asserted that, for our intellectual culture to be whole, we needed a positive faith, "some stronger unifying element in our intellectual life than any now widely accepted." Coming around, as he often did, to the "results and implications" of the International Geophysical Year experience, he told his listeners that, great as the IGY's scientific gains had been, "the social and human aspects may in the long run be more important." The IGY had taken place in "a time of unprecedented worldwide unrest and turmoil," but its effect had been to lower international barriers and heighten scientific cooperation. Nowhere else, Gould said, did collaboration "reach such a magnificent

---

* This Roman proverb is more commonly translated as something like "He is not free who doesn't sometimes do nothing."

level, perhaps, as it did in Antarctica," and so, he claimed with pride, it was on this icy continent that "the first notable thawing of the cold war" took place. He was very pleased to be headed there again in just a few days.

Gould's fourth trip to the Antarctic was made in company with the Rev. Theodore M. Hesburgh, the forty-four-year-old president of the University of Notre Dame and member of the National Science Board. (Father Hesburgh wrote later that "going to the Antarctic with Larry was like going to Africa with Dr. Livingstone.") The two departed from Los Angeles November 18, connecting in Fiji, after a long unscheduled delay, for a flight to New Zealand, and on to Antarctica from Christchurch. A major highlight of this trip for Gould was his first landing at the South Pole itself; in 1957 he had circled the pole by plane but had not landed. He and Hesburgh observed there the Thanksgiving Day change-of-command ceremony whereby Rear Admiral James R. Reedy relieved retiring Rear Admiral David M. Tyree as commander of US Naval support forces in the Antarctic. With the Amundsen-Scott South Pole Station temperature at 34 degrees below zero, the ceremony was kept to a brisk twenty-five minutes. While at the South Pole Station, Gould and Hesburgh decided that they should together take a walk "around the world," and so the two went out to the very point indicated as the global axis of rotation and ambulated in a complete circle around it, taking about thirty seconds to do so. Earlier that year astronaut John Glenn had become a national hero for his three orbits of the Earth in a space flight of under five hours, but that day in Antarctica, as Gould enjoyed pointing out, he and Hesburgh had gone around the world themselves "and beat Glenn's program" by doing so in far less time.

Gould caught a bad cold while in Antarctica, but otherwise, he reported, his trip was "magnificent" and the weather "generally very co-operative," which allowed him and "Father Ted" to be flown about all that they wished and so cover much territory. The trip filled Hesburgh with sufficient enthusiasm about the US Antarctic Program that he subsequently persuaded the National Science Board to set up an advisory committee on Antarctica, of which Gould (who had gone off the NSB itself) became chairman. Gould returned to the U.S. in the second week of December, in time to attend Ford Foundation meetings in New York. Just before year's end, during its annual meeting in Philadelphia, the American Association for the Advancement of Science chose Gould as its president-elect. He would assume the presidency of the world's largest scientific organization in a year's time, succeeding Alan Waterman.

Meanwhile, that month the Goulds completed the purchase of a house in Tucson, where Larry and Peg would take up residence shortly after Christmas. For Larry Gould, the "center of the universe" was shifting. Tucson, "the Old Pueblo," would now and for the rest of life—thirty-two years—be home.

CHAPTER 25

SUN AND ICE

Geology major Clark Arnold, of Jacksonville, Illinois, and sociology major Ardith Propst, from Omaha, Nebraska, were among those graduating from Carleton College with the Class of 1962. Carleton had been a fortunate choice of school for them both, in no small part because they had met each other there. By the time of their commencement they were engaged, planning to marry in Omaha the first week of September before moving to Tucson, where Clark would start graduate studies in geology at the University of Arizona.

At Carleton, neither Clark nor Ardi had had any significant personal association with their college president, though Gould certainly was, for students, prominent as a campus presence.* Students were often startled to find Gould unexpectedly greeting them by name as they walked across the campus—it was his habit to study the photos of new students in the freshman "zoo book" publication, and learn to associate faces with names. But at their graduation ceremony Clark and Ardith both were even more surprised, when walking across the stage to collect their diplomas, to have Gould say to each of them, as he shook their hands, "I'll see you in Arizona." (Ardith recalled: "At that point I had no idea that Larry knew that Clark and I were getting married or that we were going to Arizona. Absolutely astonished.")

That fall, as Gould went from Jackson Hole to Albuquerque to Antarctica, the newly wedded Clark and Ardi Arnold set up in Tucson, with Clark entering graduate school and Ardith getting a job in which she was entirely miserable: "I remember writing my father saying I was overqualified for the telephone company and that I hated what I was doing ... and my father wrote back and said, 'I didn't

---

* Interviewed years later, Ardith would mention that in her Carleton time the student name for Gould's beige-colored Lincoln Continental was "the Godmobile." Ardith considered that the short Tuesday morning chapel services that students were still required to attend at the beginning of her time at Carleton were special—had more character and more meaning—when conducted by Dr. Gould, whose voice and manner were so impressive. On the other hand, she remembered, it became a campus joke that, whenever the president was scheduled to speak at convocation, watch out! This was likely a sign that tuition would be raised the next year; his convocation appearances always seemed to include such an announcement.

send you to Carleton to get a job, I sent you to Carleton to get an education.'"
Then, at a university party midway through February, Ardith heard from an assistant professor that Larry Gould was now on campus and needed a secretary.
Ardi said, "You're kidding that Dr. Gould needs a secretary." The professor said
no. Ardith made Clark leave the party. They went home and composed a letter,
which Ardi had Clark take to the university at 2 a.m. on a Sunday morning and
put under Gould's door. At this point, in a joint retelling three decades afterward,
Clark took up the narrative:

> Everyone [in Arizona's Geology department] was pretty much in awe of
> this person they'd heard lots about, and that they really didn't know very
> well. And so when he moved into his little office—and it was a small
> office, it was not by any means an ostentatious or large, commodious
> office—somebody came down the hall with a certain amount of concern:
> 'Dr. Gould wants to see you!'—as if I were being called on the carpet,
> which I was pretty sure I wasn't, because I hadn't done anything yet. And
> I came in and the office was just a mess. There were boxes and books
> and papers and everything stacked around, and he had to unpile a chair
> so that I could sit down, and we exchanged pleasantries, and 'how was
> your summer?', and he had Ardith's letter in his hand, and he said, 'well,
> I understand that your wife is looking for a job, and I wish she had called
> me two weeks ago.' And my heart sank, because I thought 'well, he's hired
> someone.' And then he said 'I'm so damn far behind I don't know what
> to do. When can she start?'

Ardith Arnold would work as Gould's secretary for the next three and a half
years, until the birth of the Arnolds' first child. She admitted, when she first
went to talk to Gould about the job, that she didn't have shorthand, though she
could do some speedwriting and had a very good memory and was sure she could
manage taking dictation.* In Ardith's memory, the first letter Gould dictated to
her was addressed to Henry Ford II and, after saluting him as "Dear Henry,"
went on to thank him very much for his generous recent gift to Carleton College—the amount being sizable enough to cause Ardith to drop her pencil. As she
later recalled, Gould "obviously saw my surprise, and he laughed. And he said,
'You know, you have to ask for things. Lots of people will turn you down, but
every now and then they say yes. And if you don't ask, you won't get anything.'"
    Ardith strove to help Gould bring order out of the chaos of his Arizona of-
fice, but this was a battle that could never really be won, for good and all. By her
testimony, the typical state of Gould's office in those days approximated what it

---

* At Carleton, Gould had routinely dictated to tape, and a secretary—usually Dorothy Obaid—
  would type from the tape. For Dorothy, transcription was never dull, due to Gould's habit of
  interrupting the content of a serious letter by breaking out of the blue into song, perhaps a sea
  chantey, or by reciting a poem—or a poetic mash-up; in a 1995 interview Obaid recalled one
  example: "The boy stood on the burning deck ... his fleece was white as snow ... "

A new haircut, a new home, trips to Antarctica, his classes at the University of
Arizona, involvement in the founding of a liberal arts college in Prescott — Gould
and former secretary Sally Crandall (shown here in 1964) had much to catch up on
whenever he visited campus after "retiring."

would look like if you had simply thrown papers in the air and pushed books on the floor. He would go off on one of his frequent trips, to Washington or New York, perhaps, and while he was away she would clean up and organize. (They were both in the same small room, at first, with his desk in one corner and hers in another. Later, Gould was also given an adjoining office, and a door was put through between, so that they each had more space.) These episodic clean-ups, however, never lasted. He would return from his trip, arrive at the department as usual an hour or more before Ardith got in at 8 a.m., and by the time she would arrive all would look again as it had before. "He would grin at me, and say, 'I'm sorry, but I just can't work in a clean space.' But he generally knew where everything was."

The young secretary also struggled to interpret Gould's handwriting, which could be atrocious enough that he himself sometimes could not read notes he had written and would come to Ardith for assistance in interpreting. "I can remember one in particular," she would relate, "where he had studied it and studied it, and I studied it and studied it, and I finally figured out that it said 'Letters to Russians.' He had been in Russia, and he was trying to remind himself to write letters to them."

Nonetheless, filling the role of Gould's secretary was a pleasure for Ardith Arnold. "He did not believe in busywork," she remembered, "and if there was nothing to do I was perfectly free to read, or write letters... . In the morning he'd bring a paper in, and hand me part of it, and go in his office, read it, and then we'd trade." (At this point in their joint 1995 interview, Clark Arnold added that this used to annoy the Dean of the College of Mines—this was the college within which geology at Arizona was then placed—whose personality was such that "it just drove him to distraction to walk by the office and see Ardith reading the newspaper." But this dean, nicknamed "Froggy," "stood in great awe of Larry Gould" and "didn't dare say anything to Larry Gould's secretary. And besides, Larry was sitting on the other side of the room, reading the newspaper as well.") But, each of the Arnolds agreed, when there was work to be done Gould then "was all business, and generated lots of activity." "He was," summed up Ardith, "absolutely marvelous to work for."

Both Arnolds were to have a close personal relationship with Larry Gould— and with Peg Gould as well—lasting many times longer than Ardith's few years as secretary or Clark's as a graduate student in Larry's department. But even at the beginning, Ardith would say, it was quickly the case that the bond that was formed was a close one, "much more father-daughter than it was boss-secretary." Even then, in those first years in Tucson, said Ardith, "he referred to us as his children."

***

In moving to Tucson, the Goulds were shifting the backdrop of their future lives to the mesquite, saguaros, chollas, and prickly pears of the Sonoran desert.

The Tucson area, sixty miles north of the Mexican border,* is home to six species of rattlesnakes. The town had its origins in an eighteenth-century Spanish presidio, whose garrison on multiple occasions fought deadly encounters with the local Apaches. Tucson grew slowly through much of its history, but had experienced its most rapid population increase during the decade of the 1950s, expanding 368 percent from one decennial census to the next, from about 45,000 citizens in 1950 to 213,000 ten years later. (Tucson's population boom of the 1950s has been linked to the introduction of home air conditioners.)

In 1890—twenty-two years still before Arizona statehood—Tucson's recorded population was only 5,150, about 26 percent less than its numbers ten years earlier—making the 1880s the only post-Civil War decade during which Tucson actually shrank in size. Yet it was in the middle of that decade that Arizona's territorial legislature, meeting in Prescott, approved the chartering of the University of Arizona as a land-grant college and offered Tucson $25,000 to establish the school in or near its boundaries. This allocation came as something of a disappointment to Tucson, which had hoped to receive the $100,000 that went with the territory's insane asylum, but that superior political plum was given instead to Phoenix. (Tucson had hoped as well to convince, or bribe, the legislators of this session to move the territorial capital from Prescott back to Tucson—the capital from 1867 to 1877—and a group of businessmen had provided the Tucson delegation with $5,000 to "lobby" for this purpose. However, flooding on the Salt River prevented the Tucsonans from arriving in time for the start of the 1885 legislative assembly—they actually, in the end, had to detour through Los Angeles and Sacramento before reaching Prescott—and while they were still in transit a majority of the council had already met privately and reached agreement on a number of key decisions, including keeping the capital at Prescott.) This legislative session—officially the 13th Arizona Territorial Legislative Assembly but known to history as the "Bloody Thirteenth" or the "Thieving Thirteenth" due to its brawling and lax ethical standards in the awarding of its appropriations—concluded with Tucson being offered the consolation prize of the territorial university. The response of Tucson's citizens, when the news became known, was lukewarm. As a potential source of revenue for local business, the university was considered far inferior to recapture of the territorial capital. ("Who ever heard of a professor buying a drink?" was a much muttered dismissal.) In order to act on the university authorization (and keep from having to return the allocated money), Tucson needed to provide an appropriate plot of land on which the school could be sited. For a time nobody stepped up with an offer, and it appeared the authorization to charter the university would expire, but in the end two gamblers and a saloon keeper donated forty acres east of town, between what was then the

---

* Tucson was a part of Mexico until it was sold to the United States in 1854—it was at the geographical center of the swath of land acquired by the U.S. through the Gadsden Purchase, bought to make feasible a southern transcontinental railroad route.

edge of Tucson and Fort Lowell, which could be used for a campus, and Tucson indeed became home to the University of Arizona.

Leaping now across three quarters of a century of institutional history … in 1963, when Larry Gould joined its faculty, the university's course was being charted by Richard Anderson Harvill, an economist educated at Mississippi State, Duke, and Northwestern, who had taken office in 1951 as Arizona's fourteenth president.* Harvill's administration spanned a period of remarkable growth and expansion. In his first ten years as president, nineteen new buildings had been added to the campus. (Seven more would go up before his 1971 retirement.) During Harvill's entire twenty-year tenure, student enrollment would increase from 5,700 to more than 26,500, and faculty and staff numbers would expand from around 1,100 to nearly 8,600. By 1963 Harvill had guided the establishment within the university of two new colleges: those of nursing (1956) and of medicine (1961). Harvill's concern, however, was not simply to make the University of Arizona bigger but also to make it qualitatively better—enhancing the intellectual environment, in part by putting research and scholarship more significantly "on the agenda" than had previously been the case. His invitation to Gould to throw in his lot with the university in his "retirement"—further enhancing the intellectual environment simply by being present, and being able then through personal advice to assist Harvill in continuing "to develop a greater strategic vision" for the institution—was one of many manifestations of Harvill's strong desire to move Arizona forward.

Gould's official start date as a member of the Arizona faculty was February 1. In January, he and Peg spent some time living out of a Tucson motel, waiting for the (overdue) arrival of furniture to put into their new home; finally, it did arrive, and they settled in. The house that would be known as "Casa Gould," 9451 E. Rosewood Street, was a 1,524-square-foot ranch style house with stucco exterior, built in 1955 on a one and three-quarter acre lot ten miles east of the university down Speedway Boulevard, at the corner of Harrison and Rosewood. (In 1963 this was still quite far out from the main part of Tucson, and to drive there involved unpaved roads with big dips.) From Casa Gould the Santa Catalina Mountains rose to the north—a view the Goulds enjoyed from their patio—and the Rincon Mountains to the east. Most of the city of Tucson lay to the west. The neighborhood was just south of Tanque Verde Creek, not far from the eastern district of Saguaro National Monument. (The monument would be elevated to national park status in 1994.) Gould decorated his yard with new plantings of shrubs and trees and—on a bright sunny March day when the radio told him of a Midwestern blizzard that dumped seventeen inches of new snow in Minnesota—wrote of his intent to get started soon putting in a desert cactus garden. "Curiously enough," he wrote a Carleton correspondent, he no longer missed the snow.

---

*   In a contrast of very different rates of executive turnover, Larry Gould had been only the fourth
     president of Carleton, though Carleton was the older of the two institutions by nineteen years.

During his first semester at Arizona, Gould by choice taught, together with assistant professor Ed McCullough, the introductory course in geology, primarily to freshmen. This involved instruction for over a thousand students, handling the large numbers by giving lectures which would be taped and then broadcast three times per day. Although Gould would tell a local newspaper interviewer later that year that he preferred teaching freshmen, he would nonetheless, in subsequent semesters, shift his teaching to his specialty of glaciology, given to relatively small classes of graduate students.

Within a short while of taking up residence in Arizona, Gould began to involve himself significantly in an ongoing effort to bring the small, private, four-year liberal arts college model of education to the state in the form of a proposed new school, Prescott College. Charles Franklin Parker, a Congregational minister in the central Arizona "mile high" city of Prescott, had already for a number of years been the chief promoter of a dream to establish in Arizona a school following in the tradition of Congregationalist-founded "colleges of the New England type" that had begun with Harvard and eventually moved into the west in such places as Oberlin, Grinnell, Carleton, Colorado, Whitman, and Pomona. In 1960, Parker's "Leadership Council" had registered Prescott College with the state of Arizona as a nonprofit educational corporation, so that it could receive gifts and acquire property. Two years later, in March 1962, the Prescott College Founding Fund had been launched, with the slogan "It's up to you in '62! To Open the Door in '64!" By the end of July over a million dollars in pledges ($300,000 of it in immediate gifts) had been raised in the Prescott area in support of Parker's dream, and a larger campaign was begun to raise four and a half to five million dollars throughout Arizona and the Southwest. At the end of 1962 Parker resigned his pastorate to accept the office of founding president of Prescott College and to work fulltime toward opening the college on a sound financial basis. At the University of Arizona, Parker found Harvill very supportive of the Prescott College idea, as was Gould, who before the end of March had agreed to become a Prescott College trustee and chairman of its nascent Academic Advisory Council—envisioned as twenty-five to thirty educators and laymen who would define the academic purpose and design the academic program of the college-to-be. Among those accepting early membership on this council were Harvill and Gould's friend Hugh Odishaw of the National Academy of Sciences.

Not long after securing Gould's willing service on behalf of Prescott College, Parker spoke in Tucson to a group of potential Prescott supporters. There he expressed his pleasure in having the support and encouragement of both Dr. Harvill, representing the state institutions, and Dr. Gould, as one so closely identified "with the great private schools throughout the country." In words that would have been comfortably at home in Gould's own speeches, Parker described his vision for Prescott College as "a college that can and will be church-related in the sense of its traditions ... but free in terms of control ... and seeking to create an academic community where there will be a sharing and a seeking for the truth and the light that make men free." "We are seeking," he continued, "to build the kind of board of trustees that will move forward in the spirit of adventure and understanding, seeking to establish an institution of greatness. For, he stressed, "we who are interested in Prescott College are not interested in establishing a college of mediocrity. Very frankly, and very honestly, there are enough such schools." What the friends of Prescott College desired to do, Parker emphasized, was "to bring into being ... an institution that shall be worthy, that shall stand for excellence, that shall take its place in the great tradition of private schools, complementing and supplementing the work of the great state institutions." The prospect was an exciting one, Parker told his Tucson audience, and to underscore the point he drew upon the authority of his new Academic Advisory Council chairman: "Dr. Gould has said to me, and said to the Board, 'Did you ever stop to think ... what a privilege it is to share in the creation of a new college?'"

***

During an April trip to Minnesota to attend a meeting of the board he served on for a group of mutual funds administered by Investors Diversified Services, as well as a meeting of the Boy Scouts Region X council, Gould made a brief stop at Carleton, where he was interviewed by a reporter for the student newspaper. Asked about a new, extremely short haircut, the president emeritus confided, "the Arizona air dries out my hair, and it sticks out all over. So last week I asked the barber to give me a crew cut. He cut my hair and then had to even it up and I was left with this." He said that returning to Carleton was a little painful, simply because "I was here thirty years, and I left behind more of myself than I realized." Regarding retirement, he said that he had been afraid he would be home so much that he would drive Peg crazy, but instead he was so far traveling about as much as he did before retiring. He spoke of plans to teach one semester a year at Arizona and of his expectation that his recent trip to Antarctica would not be his last, as he was finding himself "now more than ever deeply involved in Antarctic affairs."

During the summer of 1963, which began with Gould collecting his twenty-first honorary degree, from Michigan's Kalamazoo College, Larry and Peg established themselves as usual in the familiar surroundings of their Wyoming cabin. Arrangements were made for Clark and Ardith Arnold to house sit in Tucson at Casa Gould while the Goulds were in Jackson Hole. (The Arnolds actually were invited to start living at the house in May, while the Goulds were still there for a couple of weeks, so that they could be introduced to how things were done with the place.) The Goulds paid the Tucson utilities and had their maid continue to come in once a week to clean, so the Arnolds' main duty, beyond simply being in residence and looking after things generally, was to do a lot of watering to keep the plants alive—which in the heat of a Tucson summer was no insignificant task. Ardith and Clark would live in the Goulds' house during four successive summers. The two were well aware that Peg's house—quite the opposite of Larry's university office—was always kept immaculately clean and tidy. Despite the maid service, they made it their pattern at summer's end actually to move out a week before the Goulds were expected back, so that evenings after work they could go back and clean and scrub and not undo their work by living there. Ardith remembered: "You kind of vacuumed as you backed out the door so that all the nap would be straight." (For the Arnolds the biggest house-sitting drama occurred the summer the roof went bad. During a monsoon electrical storm with heavy rain the young couple were sitting in the living room when suddenly water began to sheet down the wall—over the Goulds' record collection. The Arnolds leapt up and moved the records, but the water was calamitous. To inform the Goulds, who were without a telephone in Wyoming, Clark either sent a telegram or left a phone message at Hungry Jack's Country Store in Wilson—to be conveyed when the Goulds collected their mail—asking Larry to call home. When he did and the situation was explained, Gould asked the Arnolds to go ahead and arrange for a new roof and to send him the bill. Clark researched roofs thoroughly before committing the Goulds to such an expensive item, and the Decro-Coat roof selected would last the house for the next three decades.)

In September 1963, Gould flew to Cape Town, South Africa, to attend the seventh series of meetings of SCAR, the Scientific Committee on Antarctic Research. (Carleton's Dunc Stewart also attended.) There Gould was elected the international organization's second president, succeeding G. R. Laclavére of France, who had presided since 1958.

Then it was on to an October tour of Greece, where Larry and Peg enjoyed the trip that had been the gift of the Carleton student body in 1962. If they felt they had not had sufficient time in Greece during their world tour for the Ford Foundation in 1961, they now made up for it by making their 1963 visit more thorough. On the mainland: Athens, Delphi, and the Peloponnesus, including Corinth, Mycenae, Epidaurus, with its famous ancient theater, Nauplia, and the sanctuary of Olympia. Among the islands: Mykonos, Delos, Crete, and Rhodes. In Turkish Asia Minor: Ephesus. (Larry identified Delphi, on the slopes of Mt. Parnassus, as his favorite; he least enjoyed Mycenae, where it rained the whole time and the bloody history of the place depressed him—as did the symbolism of the royal road leading directly from the palace to the graveyard.)

Shortly after returning home, Gould took part in a rather exciting three-day symposium. Held November 7-9 at the Camelback Inn in Phoenix, it brought together nearly a hundred state and national leaders in the fields of higher education, finance, government, philosophy and religion to design the academic framework for Prescott College based upon a thorough discussion of philosophical underpinnings: assuming freedom to create, in the 1960s, an ideal college of the future to be located in the American Southwest, what should it look like; what ought to be its fundamental principles? Gould had been instrumental in bringing this symposium into being; he had been responsible for securing a $15,000 grant from the Ford Foundation's Fund for the Advancement of Education in partial support of the conclave, which, it was hoped, might serve not only to produce an academic blueprint specifically for Prescott, but also help to catalyze educational reform more broadly.

One goal of the symposium, suggested Franklin Parker, was determining how best "to transplant an educational tradition some three hundred years old, growing out of New England, to the locale of the Southwest, with its own peculiar overlays of culture, long heritage and emerging opportunities." Participants were asked to create a vision of a college that could produce leaders equipped through their developed skills, their moral foundation, and their visionary capacities to meet the changing challenges of the future: complex problems such as environmental degradation, poverty, and overpopulation, for instance, as well as the promotion of "peace and well-being among the world's peoples."

The conference proceedings and report, published eventually as *Emergence of a Concept: A Dynamic New Educational Program for the Southwest*, served as the fundamental reference for those continuing to bring Prescott into being over the next few years. Among the concepts endorsed by the symposium participants was what was called the "principle of unity," conceptualizing knowledge as a "seamless coat," only artificially divided into the distinct divisions and departments that defined the traditional college curriculum. Instead, the visionaries of Prescott College chose to emphasize the interrelationship of knowledge by declaring that in this new college there would be a single faculty, without individual departments or divisions between the humanities, social sciences, and natural sciences.

In addition to his clear influence on the "principle of unity," Gould led a discussion during the symposium on what it meant to be a "Christian" college. (His own answer is implied in what he would say two and a half months later to the Prescott Chamber of Commerce: "Implicit in the very structure of Prescott College must be the realization that education must be both moral and intellectual. From the beginning we must insist that the educated person cannot live detached from the moral issues being decided in the world.") More than two and a half years would still intervene between the end of the Phoenix symposium and the 1966 opening of Prescott College to its charter class of students, during which a full board of directors was appointed (with Laurence M. Gould as chairman), intense fundraising continued, and, early in 1965, Prescott's first dean (D. Mackenzie Brown) and first operational president (Ronald C. Nairn) were selected. Gould would remain on the Prescott board, deeply involved in this Arizona educational experiment, until 1970.

A few days after the end of the Prescott College planning symposium, Gould flew to Michigan to deliver at his alma mater's Rackham Amphitheatre the annual Sigma Xi Ermine Cowles Case Memorial Lecture, on the topic of "Antarctica as the Frontier of International Science." His principal themes on this occasion had been prominent in his speeches for years; they remained close to his heart: that the International Geophysical Year had constituted "the greatest revival in understanding, knowledge and human progress in history, not excluding the Renaissance"; that the international cooperation characterizing the IGY in Antarctica had led to the first real thaw in the Cold War; and that the Antarctic Treaty which had followed was "a document unique in history that may take its place in human events along side the Magna Carta."

The following week he had business in Minnesota, at Minneapolis and Rochester. He returned to Tucson by plane early in the day on Friday, November 22. At 11:30 that morning (Arizona time), an assassin in Dallas murdered President Kennedy. As Ardith Arnold would remember, Gould arrived at his university office but simply told his secretary, "Go home, and stay home the rest of the day. ... We need to go home."

***

In the waning days of 1963, between Christmas and New Year's, Gould went to Cleveland for the 130th annual meeting of the American Association for the Advancement of Science, of which he had become president-elect a year earlier. (In accordance with AAAS procedure, his presidential term would be one year—1964—followed by another single year as chair of the AAAS Board of Directors. It would be at the end of 1965 that he would close his three-year cycle of status within the organization by opening the AAAS annual meeting with what would be considered—a year after technically completing his presidency—his presidential address.)

In January 1964, Gould returned to Carleton to deliver a convocation address in fulfillment of his 1962 promise to report back to the student body after going to Greece. (By this time, of course, only the freshmen and sophomores of '62—now grown into the juniors and seniors of '64—remained present on campus as students with personal memory of his having been president.) Gould described his recent Greek travels and also told a personal tale of discovering stories, when in the fourth or fifth grade, about a fascinating guy named Socrates [SO-craytes], with whom he became obsessed and about whom he read all he could—and that it was not until he was well on in high school that he learned that his hero Socrates [SO-craytes] was indeed Socrates [SOCK-rah-teez]. He also commented on how difficult he was finding it to separate himself from Carleton, "for thirty years ... the center of the universe to me." "The faculty gave me a red jeep to get me on my way," he said at the convocation, "and the students gave me a ticket to Athens to get me even farther away. And—you won't believe this—the trustees gave me a Questar telescope to get me even farther away! I've never thought of the symbolism of that before ... ."

Despite his putative "retirement," Gould continued to be in great demand as a speaker, and for service on committees and boards of various organizations.

At the university, he settled into the pattern of teaching one glaciology course, to a limited number of graduate students,* one semester a year. He involved himself in his department in many ways beyond his own teaching. His former Arizona colleague George Davis (discussing a later period, but the words apply equally to earlier days) has said,

> Larry functioned in the Department of Geology as a close colleague, an ever-present individual in departmental meetings; a door always open as you walked down the hall on the first floor of the old Geology Building. Very welcoming, very engaging in conversation—not just in relationship to teaching or scholarship, but other things as well. He was subtle in his leadership.

Summers continued always to be spent mostly at the G2V cabin in Wyoming. (In an interview for a profile published early in 1964, Gould claimed to have discovered a good method for keeping himself young: "Winter in Tucson, summer at Jackson Hole, with an occasional visit to Antarctica. That's my recipe for retirement.")

The summer of 1964 was bracketed by two trips back to Minnesota. Late in May, mutual fund board meetings and three speeches he had agreed to make were combined with a visit to Carleton to be on hand for the dedication of the new Minoru Yamasaki-designed men's gymnasium, one of the major building projects funded by the Carleton Development Program campaign concluded in Gould's final days as college president. ("I am pleased indeed, at your comments about the architectural developments at the college," President Emeritus Gould wrote President Emeritus Cowling a few days after the dedication. "I am only sorry now that we didn't have the wisdom to find Yamasaki sooner. I believe along with you that he has added much beauty to the campus.") In mid-September, Gould presided over a symposium in Rochester, marking the centennial of the Mayo Clinic—the symposium had come into being as a result of Gould's own concept and suggestion to the Mayo Centennial Committee. Other participants included such notables of science, technology, education, and other fields as Loren Eiseley, Peter Brian Medawar, Lauris Norstad, Edward Teller, Arthur Larson, Constantinos A. Doxiadis, and O. Meredith Wilson. Following a panel discussion

---

* Limiting the number was not always easy. Clark Arnold has remembered: "He taught one course, in glacial geology ... and he wanted it limited to thirty students. And thirty students signed up within the first ten or fifteen minutes of the time courses opened. Then he said, 'We can't have any more than thirty, because that's all that will fit into the room.' And so they gave him a bigger room, and he said, 'Maybe we can accommodate fifty students in this room,' and within the next fifteen or twenty minutes fifty students had enrolled, and there was literally standing room ... and after the fifty students signed up, why another fifteen or twenty asked whether they could just come and audit the course, not take it for credit, but just come and participate. And he wouldn't say no, so the room ... every day was absolutely standing. He had the class at eight o'clock, three mornings a week. He thought that by having it at eight o'clock it would discourage participation. And it was always filled to capacity, and he was just adored by the students."

that had wrestled with such matters as the growing concern over environmental degradation through air and water pollution, Gould summed up on a positive note: "We are equal to all that we can understand, and to the extent that we can understand the products of science and technology and apply them for the benefit of all mankind, we have ... radiant hope."

That autumn also contained the national presidential election contest between Kennedy's Democratic successor, Lyndon Johnson, and his Republican challenger, Arizona Senator Barry Goldwater. The nomination of the archconservative Goldwater, whose core grassroots support came from "new right" groups and factions not previously dominant within the party at the national level, was a sharp turn to the right from all previous Republican standard-bearers since before the New Deal. Goldwater proposed radical reductions in the size and aims of government, favored repeal of the graduated income tax, and transformation of Social Security into a voluntary program. He opposed civil rights legislation, questioned the value of the United Nations, and took an extreme "hawkish" view on issues of war and peace, speaking with alarming casualness of the utility of giving NATO field commanders authority to use tactical nuclear weapons at their own discretion. He denounced the Johnson administration's so-far restrained policy with regard to the Communist insurgency in South Vietnam, pledging if he were elected to take a much harder line. At the Republican convention that summer, with Goldwater partisans firmly in control, the liberal Republican Nelson Rockefeller, who Gould had once said would be his top choice for president, was booed unmercifully when he attempted to address the convention in support of a civil rights plank proposed—and soundly rejected—for the platform.

Gould found the rightward lurch of the Republicans appalling. In particular, with regard to the senator from his adopted home state, he could not abide Goldwater's opposition to the Civil Rights Act of 1964, to the partial nuclear test ban treaty, and to his beloved Antarctic treaty. President Johnson, meanwhile, was heading a 1964 ticket that included Gould's friend, Hubert Humphrey, whom he had increasingly come to admire politically. Despite his heretofore lifelong allegiance to the GOP—for him, to the party of Lincoln, and of the progressive Teddy Roosevelt—by 1964 this had become a party moving out from underneath him in directions he could no longer stomach and to which he found he could no longer give his vote. Gould joined the group Scientists and Engineers for Johnson and Humphrey. He and Peg both registered in the Arizona voting rolls as Democrats, and, as the two parties continued to realign more distinctly along ideological lines in the years ahead, the more liberal party would remain his political home for the rest of his life.

***

Following that fall's electoral Democratic landslide, Lyndon Johnson told America in his January inaugural address that ours was a time of rapid and fantastic change, "baring the secrets of nature," but "placing in uncertain hands new weapons for mastery and destruction"; a world in which change and growth could "seem to tower beyond the control and even the judgment of men." For his part, speaking in the Twin Cities two days after the inauguration, Larry Gould highlighted the twin global threats of overpopulation and nuclear war. At a dinner marking the move of the Science Museum of Minnesota to a new St. Paul building, he noted that the supreme irony of the time as he saw it was that at the same moment that scientific and technological advances were opening the benefits of civilization to all mankind, mankind was also in increasing danger of becoming extinct. Two months later, he addressed in Philadelphia a conference of the National Association for Foreign Student Affairs, a professional association dedicated to advancing international education and exchange. In a speech titled "When the Barriers Are Down," Gould spoke hopefully regarding his "one world" ideal:

> In some places when I talk about one world … people do not like the idea. They don't want one world; they think it means a kind of uniformity. This is nonsense, of course. They are the kind of people who like to mouth such clichés as "the American way of life." There is no more nonsensical statement in the world. There is no such thing as "the American way of life." One of the reasons that you and I have great joy in life in these United States is the fact that there isn't one way—there are a thousand ways. It is the pluralistic character of our society that makes it stimulating. So will it be with the world as a whole. We can have unity and diversity. We shall find that strength derives from union, and vitality from diversity.

Summertime 1965 was spent as usual in the Jackson Hole country—the Goulds left Tucson on June 1 and, as recorded in the journal Peg kept for that year, returned September 9. (They were home at Casa Gould, however, for only six days before departing for another two weeks, including time seeing a variety of friends in Minneapolis, a three-day "annual reunion" with the Obaids of Carleton and St. Olaf friends Fred and Lenore Schmidt at the historic Seven Pines fishing lodge in Clam Lake, Wisconsin, and several days in New York—there were meetings to attend—accompanied by John and Betty Cowles.)

Though now in his seventieth year and retired (apart from his part-time teaching arrangement with the University of Arizona), Gould in "retirement" remained remarkably active. His titles during 1965 and 1966 included president, Scientific Committee on Antarctic Research; chairman, Board of Directors of the American Association for the Advancement of Science; chairman, National Academy of Science's Committee on Polar Research; chairman, National Science Foundation's Advisory Committee on Antarctic Programs; chairman, Board of Trustees of Prescott College; trustee (and member of the Executive Committee), Ford Foundation; senator at large, United Chapters of Phi Beta Kappa; member, Board of Governors of the Arctic Institute of North America; member, Geophysical Research Board of the National Academy of Science; and board member at large, University Center for Atmospheric Research.

He was continually accepting invitations to make speeches as well. During October and November of 1965, for instance, he spoke at the dedication of a new science building at Austin College in Sherman, Texas, and at the inauguration of former Carleton Dean Richard Gilman as the tenth president of Occidental College.* He also, in those months, addressed the question "Where is Science Taking Us?" at a regional meeting of the American Association of University Women in Minneapolis and talked on "Goals in Education" at the University of Arizona, on "The Technological Society" at a management seminar, and on "The Last Continent of Adventure" at the Waldorf-Astoria in New York. In those same weeks he also attended in New York the special Ford Foundation meeting at which McGeorge Bundy was chosen to succeed Henry Heald as foundation president and participated in Washington in a White House Conference on International Cooperation.†

In Berkeley, California at the end of December, Gould delivered his AAAS presidential address, later published in the journal *Science* as "Antarctica—Continent of International Science." Ten additional addresses are listed in his Arizona annual report for 1965-66, concluding with the commencement ceremony at Simpson College in Iowa, at which he was awarded yet another honorary degree.

* * *

Entries in the personal journal then being kept by Peg Gould ceased for a period of three months early in 1966. When she took up pen again on April 4, she explained: "This lapse represents 3 bad months. The bad accident to Larry; hospitalization, concussion and the 8 weeks of recovery. All the time trying to get back on my feet after the December shock, and going on with my secret project for Larry's birthday." The "bad accident to Larry" was a January 9 fall on his head resulting in five days in the hospital and several weeks of recuperation. (Ten days after his accident Gould was reporting that the event had slowed him down, but not very much. "Apparently," he wrote John Nason at Carleton, "as long as I land on my head everything is all right and all I need do now is have patience and not travel for awhile.") The "December shock" was the medical diagnosis Peg received

---

*   In order to keep his commitment to speak at the Gilman inauguration Gould unfortunately had to miss being present at the funeral of Laird Bell, who died October 21. Bell's widow Nathalie asked Gould to conduct the service, but he had to decline, telling Nathalie that even if he had not felt bound by the other commitment he would have doubted his ability to get through the service "because he loved Laird so."

†   The day before the start of this three-day conference, former Carleton president Donald J. Cowling, aged eighty-five, died in a University of Minnesota hospital. A memorial service was held in Minneapolis three days later, but Gould, still in Washington for the three-day White House conference, was—as with Bell five weeks before—prevented by his commitments from attending.

in the middle of that month that she was now diabetic. The "secret project for Larry's birthday" was Peg's effort to collect and present to her husband on his seventieth birthday letters of congratulations and recounted stories from a large swath of his extensive circle of friends.

When that great day, August 22, 1966, finally came, there was a party at the Goulds' Wyoming cabin, with some fourteen guests. After punch on the porch, followed by dinner on TV trays, Larry seated himself in his favorite rocking chair to open packages and begin to read through the impressive collection of birthday letters solicited by Peg. These greetings, stored thereafter in a special leather case Peg had made for the occasion and now preserved in the Gould Papers of the Carleton College Archives, amount to more than 250 letters and eight telegrams. Written on diverse dates in the days and weeks before and containing a surprising amount of bad original poetry, the birthday letters present a sort of epistolary *This Is Your Life* testimonial to the place Gould occupied in the hearts of so many. It would be conventional to say that the list of letter writers reads like a roster out of *Who's Who*—but in fact quite a large number of the contributors did have impressive entries in that publication.

Vice President Humphrey sent warm greetings, as did Secretary of Health, Education, and Welfare John W. Gardner. Writer and naturalist Joseph Wood Krutch, with whom the Goulds had become quite friendly in Tucson, conveyed congratulations on behalf of himself and his wife, Marcelle, saying, with reference to Marcelle, that his words were to be taken as coming not only from himself but also from "what a guide in Hong Kong told me one should refer to in public as 'My beautiful internal assistant.'" Messages came from numerous present and past Carleton College trustees, faculty, staff, and alumni, as well as other residents of Northfield, Tucson, and Wilson; from persons prominent in the work of the great foundations, Ford and others; from "fellow unfortunates" among the ranks of college and university presidents; and from numerous distinguished scientists and fellow Antarcticans, including several former co-inhabitants of the original Little America. Letters had arrived as well from scores of others, cumulatively recalling decades of shared memories.

Jacques and Marge Crommelin, among the original G2V shareholders who went in together in 1953 to buy land plots near Wilson, called to mind a 1954 picnic that had included Lily and Walt Disney, with Walt cooking the hamburgers—and later, in December 1956, as Gould was staying at the Crommelins' California home just prior to leaving for Antarctica during the IGY, being taken on a two-day tour of Disneyland with Walt himself as their guide: "He was so pleased and proud to show us everything from his own little apartment over the firehouse to the immaculate barns, the locomotive repair shop, and the machines that count the money." (Gould replied that this spell at the Crommelin home and Disneyland before taking off for Antarctica in 1956 had done him much good: "In all my 70 years I had never been at as low ebb as I was then. It may well be that you literally saved my life.")

The Goulds' G2V getaway in the Tetons, site of many restorative summer vacations—and of the celebration of Gould's seventieth birthday

A former Carleton student who had been among the first of his geology majors (Vic Church, Class of 1936) thanked Gould for having sparked in him the scientist's questioning attitude by being the first teacher to convey the lesson that just because something was in print did not necessarily mean it was true, and also for instilling in so many of his students "the joy of learning to live the full and meaningful life." Church recalled a number of incidents from the geology classroom but added how deeply impressed he had been at a college vespers service by Gould's likening of religious faith to how one felt when hearing "a Brahms symphony, beautifully played."

Colleagues from his teaching days at Carleton remembered the 1930s: Helen and Fred Hyslop sent fond memories of "simple delights shared with friends"—of "fishing trips, picnics, and delightful ribald evenings," holidays and birthdays celebrated together, of "luscious tomatoes, beans and peas from the Gould garden ... brought to our door by our favorite vegetable man," and of a costume party where Gould had dressed as a Buddha. Bertha Linnell, a Carleton teacher until retiring in 1953, wrote of the great pleasure she had in "thinking of those far-off times when you were the center of that magic circle composed of those I love dearly: Alfred, Helen [Alfred and Helen Hyslop], your own Peg, Gertrude, Harvey [Gertrude and Harvey Stork] and Lucile [Deen]. I can almost smell that burned steak now... ."

From a younger generation of Carleton faculty, those hired by Gould himself, one outstanding letter was that from Richard Ramette, in chemistry, who couched his memories in the form of "A Few Special Awards to 'LMG' on the Completion of His First 70 Years." Ramette's "awards" included choice Gould quotations for "Best Vision" ("I try to think of Carleton in terms of 500 years") and for "Best Summary of a Year's Speaking Engagements" ("... forty speeches. Of course, that's really one speech with forty different titles"). Ramette's award for "Best Evidence of Support" was Vice President Bruce Pollock's declaration, in a memorandum admonishing the faculty for bad parking habits, that "only the oil from the President's car doesn't hurt the grass."

Johnny Byrnes, an apartment neighbor from the Goulds' time in New York during World War II, shared memories of the Byrneses renting rooms, in 1944, in a Murray Hill brownstone beside that "immigrant couple" from Minnesota: "She was a lissome, fawn-eyed doll, as merry as a grig. He was some kind of professor, working hush-hush for the Air Force. 'Arctic survival,' he used to mutter, but it sounded more like a boondoggle scheme to nail down the Eskimo vote for Harold E. Stassen." Above them, in a skylight attic, resided "a mad artist, lewd and dissolute by repute," but who "ran his orgies (if indeed he ever orgied) as quiet as Mennonite funerals." Byrnes recalled summer nights sitting with his wife and the neighboring couple out on the terrace with "pans of ice water" by their feet and "flagons of bourbon" by their side, talking and singing and drinking and laughing. Byrnes remembered the professor wrestling with the question of whether to return to the "freshwater college" from which he was then on leave or to take the attractive job offer from Mr. Cowles, the "publishing tycoon," at double the salary to start and "the sky the limit." To ponder the choice seemed puzzling, Byrnes pretended, because "the backwardest sophomore in Dogpatch High could instantly have told him which side of the cake the caviar was buttered on." Byrnes wrote that he had the other day gone by the old brownstone where once they had all lived and that the changes had given him "pause, egad": "Where are the mad artists and orgies of yesteryear, I wondered, and how did things work out for that poor impractical blackavised professor?"

John Cowles, for his part, wrote that he still had regrets that Gould, who had "squeezed half a dozen different distinguished careers into a few years," had not, "in addition to everything else, become both a metropolitan newspaper editor and a United States Senator." Cowles evoked the personal memory of Larry, when the Goulds would visit the Cowles' summer home, "walking calmly, with folded arms, into the icy waters of Annie Battle lake" wearing a "red Egyptian fez and appearing unaffected by the almost freezing temperature." Cowles added a fine birthday compliment: "Although I never had the privilege of being one of your students in a formal educational course, I regard you as the best teacher I have ever known."

The letters, and the compliments, go on and on. Irwin Miller, another Ford Foundation trustee, wrote that "it is the greatest of privileges to be associated with a man who continues to demonstrate wholeness, integrity, and serenity in a fragmented and frightened world." Caltech geographer Edwin S. Munger wrote: "No man I have ever met in my sojournings on this planet better combines my ideal of a scientist with my ideal of a humanist." Writer and editor Hiram Haydn offered that he remembered vividly his first long conversation with Gould and that afterward he had asked Carl Billman, the national secretary of Phi Beta Kappa, "Is it possible that man can be a college president and be as good a man as that?" Haydn continued: "I admire many things about you, Larry, but most of all your wonderfully uninsistent cheerfulness and kindness, your honesty and your quiet strength. I don't think I have known anyone else who so consistently seemed to me to justify the words 'this is a man.'"

Also presented to the new septuagenarian that day was a resolution from The Antarctican Society electing him to honorary membership and conveying the news that arrangements had been made, with the assistance of the National Science Foundation, for a mountain in the Queen Maud range to be named in Gould's honor. Included in the Antarctican Society package was a photograph of, and a piece of rock from, the newly named Mount Gould. The rock, sent from the end of the Earth, took up new residence atop Gould's desk.

Gould claimed, in at least one post-birthday letter, that he did not think of his seventieth "as any different than any other birthday." In the four years since his Carleton retirement, he explained, he had decided that "retiring" was exactly the thing he did not want to do. He felt little if any abatement in his vigor. Nonetheless, though there may have been nothing inherently special about the numerical achievement—significant only because ten-fingered human beings had adopted base ten by which to count—Peg Gould's "secret project" had in fact made Larry Gould's seventieth birthday stand out among the string in a way that, in another letter, he admitted was "absolutely overwhelming."

CHAPTER 26

SEPTUAGENARIAN

SCAR, the Scientific Committee on Antarctic Research, met in September 1966 in Santiago, Chile. It was the international organization's ninth general meeting. (Convenings were annual from the founding two in 1958 through 1964 and biennial thereafter.) Among the SCAR business transacted in Santiago was the reelection of Gould, the American representative, to another term as president, extending to 1970.

Disembarking in Cuzco, Peru, 1966

The Goulds, Larry and Peg, expanded the five days of the SCAR meeting into a two-week South American trip, preceding their arrival in Chile with a week in Peru. There they visited friends and made a "long postponed" journey to Machu Picchu, which they had neglected to include in their Peruvian visit eleven years earlier.

From Santiago, they flew directly to New York, where Larry, whose twelve-year tenure as a Ford Foundation trustee was coming to an end, attended meetings of that board. The Ford Foundation, in the years just prior to 1966, had reached unprecedented peaks with regard to assets and expenditures. In the early 1960s it had become the largest private funding source for the arts, and in 1966 it made its largest contribution in that arena, $80 million "to retire the debt and enhance the financial stability of sixty-one symphony orchestras across the country." The foundation's continuing support for higher education had been substantial, and it had crucially assisted the worldwide beginnings of what later became known as the "Green Revolution" in agriculture. Beginning in 1966, however, the foundation's new president, McGeorge Bundy, persuaded the trustees to maintain Ford as a large foundation indefinitely, rather than continuing to expend capital (as its charter did allow) in a manner that would eventually have been self-liquidating. Annual expenditures, which reached $367 million in fiscal 1966, were curtailed sharply, to the neighborhood of $200 million, with the largest cuts coming in the area of support for American colleges and universities. Bundy, says one commentator, "saw that the bounding growth of American higher education was diminishing the impact foundations could have on it." So was ended, among other things, Ford's liberal arts college program that Gould, years before, had been instrumental in introducing. As Gould wrote to Carleton's John Nason the following April, though the budget trimming had "made necessary a number of sharp choices" and he was naturally reluctant to see the closing out of the program for liberal arts colleges (at his last board meeting, Gould wrote, "I made my last plea for the liberal arts college"), he found himself nonetheless "in general agreement with Bundy's policies."

Meanwhile in Arizona, as Gould attended the September Ford Foundation meetings in New York, the experiment in the liberal arts that was Prescott College was finally ready to launch. Prescott's pristine new 200-acre campus opened to a charter class of eighty eager students on September 26, and President Ronald C. Nairn was formally inaugurated in October. Prescott's board chairman Gould declared in connection with the opening that never had a college come into being at a more auspicious time:

> In the last two decades, specialization and fragmentation of knowledge has had a profoundly separative effect on our civilization. The need has become intense and urgent for a bringing-together. Understanding of all the historical and political forces at work throughout the world, and of the implications that science, technology and humane studies have for each other—these are needed for leadership in the complex future. It is on these needs that Prescott college focuses its attention.*

Two days before speaking at President Nairn's Prescott College inauguration, Gould was forced to face up to the fact that he needed to hire a new secretary. Ardith Arnold, who had provided him with office assistance since early 1963, was expecting her first child in mid-October. As her pregnancy progressed, Ardith would repeatedly remind Gould that he needed to think about finding a replace-

---

* Auspicious time or not, Prescott College opened on a financial foundation still far from firm. "The College had a brilliant opening year," Gould would write to another of the Prescott College founders, Victor H. Lytle, in June of 1967, "but must raise $600,000 by August 1." In 1967, Charles F. Kettering II, whose Kettering Family Foundation had substantial assets derived from the family's co-ownership of General Motors, joined the Prescott board, and for some years was an important source of support, with more expected to follow. By 1970, Prescott College had gained admiring national attention for its Wilderness Orientation program; it was the first college to incorporate the principles of Outward Bound into its curriculum. 1970 was Gould's last year on the Prescott board.

The Arnolds in 1969: Ardith, Joanna, Amy, and Clark

ment for her, pointing out that if he could hire this person while she, Ardi, was still working, she would be able to help train her successor. "Yes, yes," he would do that, Gould would agree—an assurance upon which he consistently failed to act. "Larry, you know I really should quit the first of September," Ardith would say. And Gould would counter: "Well, how about the middle of September?" Then when mid-September was reached, Gould took a new tack: "How about the middle of October?" "Ultimately," Ardith would later relate, "I was still working on the 20th of October, and Larry was out of town." That evening, with the doctor suggesting that the baby likely would not be born for three or four more days, Peg took Ardith and Clark to dinner, after which they all went to meet Larry's incoming plane, due in at about 10: 30. Larry said when he got off the airplane, "Oh, I'm so glad I still have a secretary!" The Arnolds drove the Goulds home. As it happened, Amy Christina Arnold was born only a few hours later, between 1 and 2 a.m. Clark Arnold called Gould early that morning, telling him, "You know that secretary you had last night? Well, you don't have her today."

***

The 1960s had developed into a notoriously difficult time for administrators at American colleges and universities; it was difficult to navigate smoothly through waters made turbulent by the rocks and shoals of an increasingly assertive youth culture, changing societal norms, and an energetic waxing of student activism. Student-administration conflict became a seemingly inescapable part of the academic *zeitgeist*. On campus after campus, students pressed for change on a variety of fronts. More and more often, they did so not through respectful request and petition but in the form of demands, stridently expressed. Equally strident in reaction could be the disapproving voices of alumni and other older observers who expected college administrators to hold the line and stand firm against the presumption and incivility that seemed to have taken hold of the young.

All of this was certainly the case at Carleton College, with the turbulence of "the Sixties" by and large emerging only after 1962, when Larry Gould departed as president and John Nason arrived to replace him. Nason, whose previous experience running a college had ended in 1953, quickly found at Carleton that with students much had changed, or was rapidly changing. Though adjusting was neither immediate nor effortless nor entire, Nason would come to realize that the administrative attitudes and styles that had worked for Gould, and for Nason, a decade and more earlier, now needed to change as well. In attempting to steer responsibly between the Scylla of student demands and the Charybdis of indignation among the college's older constituencies, it was often difficult for Nason to please anyone. In the space of a few years Carleton did change dramatically in significant ways, greatly reducing the formerly strict and rarely questioned *in loco parentis* regulation of student behavior with regard to parietal rules and other matters and reforming college governance so as to make it more open and more participatory. To some, such changes seemed to come with frustrating slowness; to others, they seemed to happen with dismaying rapidity. In the mid-1960s, to impatient students (and some younger faculty) Nason might seem a conservative old stick-in-the-mud, a vestige of the past stubbornly resistant to progressive and now overdue change needed for the school to align itself with the temper of the times. To others, including significant portions of the college's alumni body, he might seem a spineless appeaser, seen continually to be giving way to unruly students on traditional Carleton rules and practices. "This never would have happened under Larry" was—true or not—a sentiment muttered darkly by many in the latter camp as Carleton's student-administration discord grew acute in the years immediately after Gould's departure.

Indications exist that Larry Gould himself became unhappy over the conduct of campus affairs under his successor. In 1966, in a note to F. Champion Ward of the Ford Foundation (and formerly dean at the University of Chicago), Gould commented that Ward's name had been among his own suggestions conveyed to the Carleton Board of Trustees as they began in 1961 to search for the next Carleton president. (Ward had at the time promptly declined to be considered.) "Off the record," Gould on this occasion added, "I wish the hell you were there now." In a 1970 exchange of letters between Gould and his sister-in-law, Jean Rice Hoppin, written when Howard Swearer had been named to succeed Nason as Carleton president in a few months, Jean added the postscript that, although she and Dick faithfully continued to make annual contributions to their alma mater she "wouldn't send an eligible to Carleton these days on any account," adding a line about "the arrogance & sickening rudeness of the latter-day young," who "don't even consider how lucky they are to get IN to a good school." Gould responded: "I too have been unhappy with what has happened at our college since I retired and it need not have been so—a long story which I shall tell you some day but I am enthusiastic about Howard Swearer."

Ardith Arnold would later recall a memory from her time as Gould's secretary of Larry coming into her adjoining office "obviously very upset." "He'd been to Carleton for something," Ardith remembered, "and he came in, and he said, 'I will never go back to Carleton again as long as that man is president. ...I will not watch my seventeen years be destroyed.'" This, on the one occasion,* was the only time that Ardith remembered ever hearing Gould himself speak so bluntly in this vein. But, she added, "Peg, because Larry was upset [with Nason's handling of Carleton affairs], was just vehement about it." Peg Gould apparently shared her vehemence in a 1964 letter to Atherton Bean. While no copy of Peg's letter has been found, Bean's reply is extant and revealing. He said, in part:

> I knew, of course, how you felt about the Carleton situation, for [Trustee] Goley [Newhart] and Helen [Newhart, his spouse] had told me of their conversations with you last February—and I know further that there are a number of other people who have felt much the same way. The very difficult thing in situations like this is to appraise accurately just how wide-spread and just how deep these feelings are and whether they are really currently endangering the health of the institution that we all have so much affection for. With all due allowance for the fact that I cannot dive into the faculty and try to take soundings—for that would be completely destructive to the Administration, ... I have had lots and lots of contacts with faculty, students, (past and present) etc., etc., and my guess is that the very real rumblings which were there a year ago have quieted down. There were some true trouble makers on the campus. Most of them are gone. ... I appreciated your letter—and I am not going to show it to Larry. It was to me and that is all.

Whatever the state of Larry Gould's concern in 1966 regarding developments at Carleton since he had been president, he did return to the campus that fall to participate in one of the major public events forming part of the college's year-long centennial celebration. Over the course of the academic year Carleton was to host three centennial symposia, one each in the areas of science, the humanities, and international relations. The first of the three, the symposium on "Scientific

---

*   Ardith Arnold's anecdote comes attached to no definite date. Gould returned to Carleton during the Nason presidency, lasting until June 1970, on four public occasions: in April 1963, January and May 1964, and October 1966, during the college's centennial celebration. This memory as told could not well have followed Gould's 1966 return, coinciding as that did with Arnold's giving birth and ceasing to work as Gould's secretary. For a variety of reasons it seems most likely to fit 1964.

Discovery and Its Consequences," took place October 13-14, and Gould was on hand to deliver—in the new men's gymnasium for which he had helped to raise funds—the symposium's opening address, a talk he titled "Science and the Culture of Our Times."

Published in 1968, Gould's address that day distilled a number of his favorite themes into a forceful statement of his scientific-humanistic credo. "I do not subscribe," he said, "to the idea of two cultures. The gap exists, but the feud between science and the humanities is without substance. ... We must have humanists who comprehend and include scientific and technological knowledge in their dreams of the world, else we shall have no world at all." "The pursuit of wisdom," he declared (as he often had before), "must at long last

At Carleton's Centennial science symposium, 1966

be a single enterprise, or liberal education has no meaning." Gould identified pure science as having been historically, "along with religion and art, one of man's great avenues in his quest for truth." "Both the scientist and the poet," he said, "seek to explore and to understand. It is only the form of exploration which is different." Our fundamental intellectual plight, he posited, was that in a world of "shaken beliefs" where scholarship no longer developed, as it once had in the West, under an "all-covering canopy" of religious faith and "force from the classics," we are "adrift without an anchor." We need in our intellectual life, said Gould, a strong unifying element to anchor us now, to "help fill the void caused by the decay of the classical humanism." And science, he thought, which, "viewed historically, is the great untapped reservoir of humanism," was well suited to be the new unifier. Unlike such contending forces for allegiance as nationalism and racialism, science as an avenue to be followed in the quest for an orderly world has as its proudest claim its universal status. This also was its greatest opportunity: "In an age characterized by perfection of means and confusion of ideals," said Gould, "the disciplines of science, which admit no frontiers of race or creed, provide a basis for effective international cooperation. Science has long since made the world one community."

At the same time, at the University of Arizona, President Harvill was making use of Gould's presence in ways extending far beyond his course-a-year teaching contribution. Harvill asked Gould to lead a search committee to find a new head for the Department of Geology. This proved to be a tougher-than-expected assignment. In December 1967, nearly two years after being asked to do this, Gould told the Arizona Joint Economic Development Committee that professorial salaries in Arizona higher education were scandalously low and that this was proving highly problematic for the recruitment and retention of key personnel. Not only had he and his committee been unable to fill the department head position—"we have interviewed many able men," he reported, "but none has agreed to come to the University of Arizona, delightful as our climate is, for a salary two to three thousand dollars less than they receive in their present position"—but the College of Mines had also recently lost two senior professors who had accepted jobs elsewhere at considerably higher salaries. Although his examples were drawn from his personal experience within a particular college of the University of Arizona, Gould stressed that the situation was similar at that time in other areas in all three Arizona public universities.

During the same period, Gould was helping to promote the idea of creating a School of Earth Sciences within Arizona's College of Mines. The School of Earth Sciences—to include the Departments of Geology and Geochronology, Arizona's Tree-Ring Laboratory, and the Office of Arid Land Studies—was approved by the Arizona Board of Regents in the spring of 1967. Harvill then asked Gould not only to chair the committee to seek a permanent director for the new school but also to serve as acting director until a permanent replacement was found. This he agreed to do, thus finding himself living again for a time in the world of "budgets, personnel and things of that sort" from which he had thought to retire.

Harvill tapped Gould to deliver the principal address at the University of Arizona's end of May 1967 commencement. The speech he made, "Education and Change," was in essentials a reprise of the "Noblesse Oblige" address he had given several times before on similar occasions and which itself adapted remarks he had first offered in a 1937 talk to the Carleton student body. He added now, however, some reflections prompted by the character of more recent 1960s campus unrest:

> We have forgotten that freedom of speech is a two-way street—that the right to be heard is just as sacred as the right to speak. The intellectual does not shout down persons who disagree with him. He listens, for he knows that democracy's greatest self-correcting technique is dissent and debate. Do not misunderstand me. The courage of dissent is part of the responsibility of the intellectual but it carries with it the reciprocal responsibility of listening.

"Colleges and universities," he went on to assert, "have ever been the arenas for dialogue and debate, but the boorishness and the boisterous hoodlumism which have erupted on the campuses of some of our greatest universities are a disgraceful repudiation of the university's historic role." In changing times such as these, he suggested, the most important persons were not the ready followers of change "but the person of unchangeable values."

In September 1967, Harvill asked Gould, in consultation with other faculty, to put together a report describing the sort of facility needed by the new School of Earth Sciences. "Since we are starting from scratch," Gould urged his colleagues by memorandum, "no holds should be barred. Let us ask for what we consider the best kind of facility for our needs for a long time to come." Meanwhile, the Gould committee's search for a permanent director was leading to the 1968 appointment of James H. Zumberge, then the president of Michigan's Grand Valley State College.* Gould's duties as acting director of the School of Earth Sciences would terminate on June 30 of that year. Harvill wrote Gould a note of appreciation for the job he had done, telling him that his "outstanding achievements as administrative officer" and the skill with which he had brought together the various departments and personnel constituting the Earth sciences group "are examples of the kind of administration that makes the President of a university look good!" Adding that Gould's selection of Jim Zumberge and his influence in getting Zumberge to come to Arizona was "in and of itself ... a major achievement," Harvill wrote that all this "adds up to the inevitable conclusion that it was a great day for the University of Arizona when you and Peg decided to come and cast your lot with us."

*　*　*

Larry Gould's notable activities for the last third of the 1960s were little different in kind from what had kept him occupied during the middle third of the decade. He continued the teaching of a single course, "Glacial and Pleistocene Geology," which was conducted through informal lectures and discussions and which he was now striving to restrict in size to no more than twenty-five students. He continued his involvements in organizations such as the American Association for the Advancement of Science, Phi Beta Kappa (late in 1966 he delivered a pair of lectures at the University of Southern California as a Phi Beta Kappa Visiting Scholar, a program he had proposed while president of the United Chapters), SCAR, the Committee on Polar Research, and so forth. To ongoing involvements such as these Gould occasionally added new commitments, such as when, in 1968, he acted as chairman of a commission examining the feasibility of establishing a new Mayo-associated medical school in Rochester, to be affiliated with the University of Minnesota.

---

*　Zumberge, a Minnesota native, had, prior to becoming president of a small liberal arts college, taught geology at the University of Michigan and become a notable Antarctican. (During the International Geophysical Year he had been chief American glaciologist in Antarctica, studying the ice breakup patterns on the Ross Ice Shelf. Cape Zumberge on the Ronne Ice Shelf had been named in his honor in 1960.) Just what it was in the pattern of this résumé that might have appealed to Gould in bringing Zumberge to Arizona remains murky.

The Goulds continued to return to Jackson Hole for large parts of each summer, though sometimes Larry's ongoing commitments cut into that time. In June of 1967, for instance, Gould spent a week on SCAR business at the Scott Polar Research Institute in Cambridge, England, and at the end of August he spent four days attending the Alaskan Science Conference, in Fairbanks. The following summer he went to Tokyo in June, presiding over the Tenth Meeting of SCAR, and for a little over two weeks in July and August, he and Peg were again in England, where Larry, representing at once the Ford Foundation, the National Academy of Sciences, and SCAR, helped dedicate a new building for the Scott Polar Research Institute. In mid-July of 1969, Gould was in England during a third straight summer, attending meetings of SCAR's Executive Committee.

Outside of summers, although he was no longer giving addresses with the frequency that had prevailed before his putative retirement, speaking engagements on a variety of subjects still regularly dotted his schedule. Lectures on Antarctica and talks on one or another aspect of education continued to form a large part of his podium repertoire, but to these he was increasingly adding addresses on the environmental threats posed by overpopulation and pollution. In May 1967, for instance, he told the National Planned Parenthood Conference in Denver that mankind may be in the process of destroying itself by destroying its habitat, and in December of that year he said that he thought the single "greatest problem facing society today" was "man's relation to his environment."

Gould's chief statement in print on this issue of growing importance to him was an article, "While There Is Still Time," published early in 1969. In it he wrote that however "painfully aware" the world was of "the growing antagonism between man and the social environment he has created"—problems evident in "our racial woes, our Vietnams* and our urban messes which illuminate our failure to adapt human settlements to dynamic change"—yet "the most serious long-term problem facing mankind" was a situation "even more sinister" though of which people were, he regretted, less aware: "that is man's relationship to his deteriorating physical and biological environment." Man, he warned, "is fouling his own nest." "For the first time in human history," he wrote, "the chief danger to our survival comes from ourselves instead of the forces of nature. We have not yet learned that we cannot bully nature but that we must cooperate and negotiate with it." Even while science has enabled us to bring under control or eliminate diseases that once were major scourges, "now it is pollution and not disease that

---

* On the issue which dominated American political discourse in the late 1960s, the war in Vietnam, Gould said at the time very little. Interviewed early in 1973 for the Ford Foundation Oral History Project—speaking three days after President Nixon announced that peace talks in Paris had resulted in an agreement that would "end the war and bring peace with honor" and two days before the official ceasefire went into effect in Vietnam—Gould was asked what his 1960s viewpoint on the war had been during the time he was still on the Ford Foundation Board. He answered only: "I may have been a hawk ten years ago, I don't remember. At any rate I didn't disturb myself one way or another."

may do us in. If we continue to multiply without finding means of using our wastes, we will poison ourselves by them or bury ourselves in them." Related in peril was overpopulation. "There is no problem," he wrote, "which is not complicated by too many people. The size of the human population is the primary key to the significant problems that face mankind today." "We must establish," he urged, "some equilibrium between population and the limited resources of earth. Man's only hope is not to try to conquer nature, as he has been doing, but to try to live in harmony with it."

Gould was disappointed when his friend Hubert Humphrey lost the 1968 presidential election to Richard Nixon, but in January 1969 he did have the satisfaction of having one of his former students take office as a member of the Nixon Cabinet. This was Wisconsin Congressman Melvin Laird (Carleton Class of 1944), the new Secretary of Defense, who at Carleton in 1941-42 had taken Geology 101 and 102, Gould's general survey course at the time.

On the opposite end of 1969, in November and December, the decade ended memorably for Gould when, at age 73, he made his fifth journey to Antarctica.

His objectives in going were both scientific and sentimental. He traveled in an official capacity, given his status as chairman of the National Academy of Science's Committee on Polar Research, chairman of the National Science Foundation's advisory panel on Antarctic programs, and president of SCAR. "Since I had not been in Antarctica for six years," Gould was quoted at the time, "it seemed wise, because of these scientific responsibilities, to make a tour of inspection." However, he had added, "beyond my scientific objectives in Antarctica, I have a real sentimental desire to return." Gould had, earlier that year, been notified of his election as the tenth honorary member of The American Polar Society. Three other members of the first Byrd Antarctic Expedition had previously been so honored: Byrd himself, in 1938, Paul Siple in 1957, and Bernt Balchen in 1966. His trip would coincide with the fortieth anniversary of his dog sledge journey into the Queen Maud Mountains, as well as, on November 29, the fortieth anniversary of Byrd's historic flight over the South Pole, and he wished to be present at commemorative ceremonies to be held at the pole on that date. The trip coincided as well with the tenth anniversary of the signing of the Antarctic Treaty. His presence in Antarctica at this time, then, seemed fitting on many counts.

Gould afterward termed his three-week Antarctica trip "magnificent." For it, he again kept a diary.

In Los Angeles, before flying on to New Zealand, Gould was joined by geologist Grover Murray, the president of Texas Tech University, who was making the trip as a member of the National Science Board. Gould found Murray "a comfortable and delightful companion." In Christchurch, the duo became a trio with the addition of Gordon de Quetteville Robin, the Australian glaciologist who in 1958 had become director of the Scott Polar Research Institute at Cambridge University. Robin was then carrying out a survey of the thickness of the Antarctic ice cap by radar soundings from airplanes, and Gould hoped to include a flight with Robin to observe this work among his field activities on the trip.

After getting outfitted in Christchurch with the approved US Antarctic Research Program clothing, Gould arrived at the McMurdo base by plane early on
the morning of November 24. That day and the next four Gould spent touring
different stations in this sector of Antarctica where a variety of interesting scientific investigations were underway. One of the highlights, on the 26th, was the
mountain field station near the Beardmore Glacier, where vertebrate paleontologist
Edwin H. Colbert was working with an Ohio State University field party headed
by David Elliot. They were hunting for fossils to follow up upon the discovery two
years before of the first vertebrate fossil to be found in Antarctica, the jawbone of
a freshwater amphibian, a labyrinthodont. That discovery, Gould had indicated in
his pre-trip comments for press distribution, had constituted "one of the strongest
of many lines of evidence" for the theory that "many of us geologists have long
believed that Antarctica was once the heartland of a great southern continental
land mass, parts of which have separated and drifted away to form Australia, India,
Africa and South America." The forty-five persons populating this camp had just
settled in earlier in the week, and within hours (as noted in Gould's diary with
three exclamation points) "had found Triassic reptile bones!!!"* Another memorable visit, the day after, was made to the University of Minnesota seal behavior
project, of which Gould recorded: "Fascinating technological innovation. TV
camera immersed below ice. We could watch seals cavorting about unaware that
they were being watched—first time this ever done. Heretofore observers (divers)
intruded seals environment."

On the 29th, Gould and Murray were flown from McMurdo to the South
Pole—following, after first flying eastward to Little America, what had been
Byrd's flight route south forty years before. (They were also following, of course,
Gould's 1929 sledge route, up to a point.) At the pole—not, Gould recorded,
"the barber pole near the base which is what the usual visitor sees," but at the
exact geographic South Pole—a short service was held. Gould contributed brief
remarks about the significance of the historic flight forty years before and laid a
commemorative wreath. He had pictures taken of himself at the pole with flags
of the University of Arizona, the State of Arizona, and the Arizona-Sonora Desert
Museum. (The latter flag and accompanying photographs were to be returned to
the Desert Museum to aid in an upcoming fund drive.) Following the ceremony,
Gould was thrilled when the base's ham radio operator arranged a phone patch

---

* This November find was a thecodont. As Gould would explain in his 1971 article "Antarctica:
The World's Greatest Laboratory," skepticism about the theory of continental drift and of a
previously existing great southern continent—Gondwanaland—that had broken up into the
present day southern continents and India, had been fading for years as evidence accumulated of
plant and mineral connections among these lands. That now both an amphibian labyrinthodont
and reptilian thecodont had been found in Antarctica provided strong new evidence for the
correctness of the Gondwanaland hypothesis. As we shall see, a discovery at the Beardmore
site that provided even better evidence yet, and more precise dating, was only days away.

A fifth trip to Antarctica, this time in 1969 to commemorate the fortieth anniversary of the polar flight; (inset) Gould with the bust of Richard Byrd at McMurdo Station

by which he was able to converse with Peg from the bottom of the earth. After a meal, Gould and his party were flown back by way of the Beardmore Glacier, passing only some 500 feet above the ice—Gould called it in his diary the "most spectacular flight I have ever had"—and then, he wrote, "to add frosting to my cake the pilot flew us twice around Mt. Erebus [the active volcano near McMurdo base] and right over the crater which was spewing out a little steam." It was, he concluded in that day's entry, "a day in which everything worked out even better than I had dared hope."

Commemorations continued the next two days. At McMurdo on November 30, representatives from five countries spoke briefly at a mid-day memorialization of the ten-year anniversary of the signing of the Antarctic Treaty, held near the base chapel around the statue of Admiral Byrd. Later in the day Gould was at the center of a cake-cutting ceremony in the Mess Hall featuring two beautifully decorated cakes, one for the anniversary of the first South Polar flight and the other for the treaty anniversary. Then on December 1, back at Scott Base, there was a larger morning ceremony in honor of the treaty-signing anniversary, held outdoors beneath the flags of all sixteen signatory nations. Gould gave a brief speech, as did several other dignitaries, including the First Secretary of the Russian legation. Gould was flattered when the chancellor of Victoria University of Wellington afterward requested a copy of his remarks so that he might quote from them in an upcoming commencement address.

On the 2nd and 3rd, Gould toured Antarctica's snow- and ice-free "dry valleys" and made visits to the still extant huts left behind on the continent more than half a century before by Shackleton and Scott.

On December 4, at the Beardmore Glacier field camp where the Ohio State team was continuing its investigation of a great outcrop of early Triassic rocks, paleontologist Colbert identified a new vertebrate fossil find as Lystrosaurus, a freshwater reptile of the Lower Triassic living some two hundred million years ago, whose fossils had previously been found in abundance in Africa and the other major southern landmasses. Gould and Murray arrived at the Beardmore camp that same evening, and it was Gould who reported the find to the National Science Foundation, saying that he and Murray considered Dr. Colbert's Lystrosaurus "not only the most important fossil ever found in Antarctica but one of the truly great fossil finds of all time."

Gould's quick judgment as to the fossil's importance was quoted December 6 on the front page of the *New York Times* and sent out with an Associated Press story the same day. The AP further reported Gould as saying that the presence of this fossil within a few hundred miles of the South Pole "establishes beyond further question the former existence of the great southern continent of Gondwanaland." Later, in a 1971 article, Gould would explain what made the Lystrosaurus find more special than the earlier amphibian and reptile fossil finds from the same locale. "Labyrinthodonts and thecodonts are general terms," he wrote, whereas Colbert's Lystrosaurus "was the first fossil vertebrate from Antarctica identified as to specific genus. More than that, it is a fossil that literally dates a continent. If one had gone to Antarctica to find a specific fossil, this would have been it."

Gould's Antarctic tour concluded with a December 5 visit by helicopter to Cape Crozier on Ross Island, home to notable Adelie and Emperor penguin rookeries. The next day saw Gould and Murray flown back to Christchurch, where he found it a "great relief to shed the Antarctic clothing" and put on a light suit. The next three days in New Zealand combined sightseeing, shopping, collecting his letters ("2 from Peg!!" rated double exclamation points in the diary), and simply "being lazy." His final diary entry, on the 9th, was only, "Saw Grover off for Sydney, Australia at 5: 15. I shall leave just 24 hrs. later."

***

Two weeks prior to his departure for Antarctica on November 19, Gould's former Michigan student, former Carleton colleague, and fellow Antarctican Duncan Stewart had died unexpectedly in Northfield at age sixty-four. The November before, in 1968, Paul Siple—the Eagle Scout selected to accompany the 1928 Byrd expedition and later scientific leader at the Amundsen-Scott South Pole Station during the International Geophysical Year—had died in Washington at age fifty-nine. These untimely passings were on Gould's mind as he prepared for his trip. So also, perhaps, was the failing health of another good friend, his Tucson neighbor Joseph Wood Krutch, with whom he had formed a close bond both social and, through admiration for Krutch's writings, intellectual. Krutch had been diagnosed a year before with a malignant colon cancer, which chemotherapy and surgery had failed to arrest. In September 1969 he had been hospitalized for further surgery that left him now a semi-invalid. (The seventy-six-year-old Krutch would succumb to the cancer the following May.)

These evidences of mortality may have been part of the context for Gould's decision, two days before leaving for Antarctica, to write as follows to his sister-in-law, Jean Rice Hoppin, whom Peg had declared cut out of their lives ever since her disastrous Christmas visit of 1961:

> My darling Jean,
>
> For some reason or other you are very much on my mind. That is not unusual for I think of you 42 times a day. There never was another black piss ant in my life. And I don't see why I should be penalized because the three remaining Rice children are so uncivilized. I have loved you more than anyone else in the world except Peg and I don't understand why I should live out the remaining years of my life without seeing you.
>
> Your father's favorite word was "absolutely" and the three of you inherited it. But it isn't true, none of you is absolutely right about anything including your relations to each other!! Enough for now.
>
> Don't answer this now even if you are inclined to do so. As you will see [clipping enclosed] I am off to Antarctica again for about a month,

depending on the weather.

Of course Peg does not know I am writing this letter but when I return you may write me here at the University marking the envelope personal. You can also call me at my University number.

I have had a wonderful new career here in the midst of the friendliest people I have ever known. The president Dick Harvill is a particularly warm friend. I am having luncheon with him today (which will include 2 martinis!)

As B4

Larry

As it happened, the address to which Gould attempted to send this missive was not current, and eventually the now somewhat battered envelope was re-turned to him without having found the Hoppins. In the final week of February 1970, Gould enclosed it with a new note, addressed to Dick Hoppin at his Ohio State University office, saying that he hoped Dick would see that Jean got the November letter, even though "It is a bit of ancient history now in some ways." Jean quickly wrote back:

Larry, love ... sea-lion, the kind of that you are:

Great to hear from you again. Before Antarctic in November. You thought you might not get back ... and you weren't about to depart this world without a reaffirmation of steady fondness of us. At least, that was Dick's immediate thought when he opened your communication at school ... and mine, when I read your dear letters, on Dick's bringing them home. Your letter to me—before the Antarctic—did indeed get kicked around. But that's the postal situation for you these days. The more we progress, the more inefficient everything becomes.

Included within the several paragraphs of news and affectionate commentary that followed, Jean wrote this:

Don't be a hopeful idiot and take this home to Peg. The separation she created is tragically silly. But she has to stick to her hate of us or charge herself in a way she cannot nervously bear. She really CANnot. Let her, if the Arizona life is happy for her, continue in happiness. God knows that, after she was made so miserable as a girl to be growing at so unusual a rate—for then—that our mother took her out of school and had her tutored by Mrs. Pearson, she has never been solidly well.

Jean finished by affirming, "You were a nut when first I knew you (at, me, 10-years-old). You are still a nut. Blessedly. Don't lapse, Larry. Ever." She closed, "As B4, yourself ..."

Larry's reply to this letter was typed—wretchedly; when, on rare occasions,

Larry Gould produced his own letters, typographical errors were sure to be legion—on March 14. He told Jean, "I loved your letter but I wish you had not said 'The separation she created is tragically silly.'" "Whoever they are," he insisted,

> it still takes two at least to make a quarrel. I shall always be sorry that I di[d] not phone and warn you that Peg was vry vry tired and tense. You will never know the pressures under which a college president's wife works. She needed you and Dick. She often told me how much she enjoyed talking with you and Dick—in a way she could not talk with me. When you called to tell me she was coming home you intimated that she was quite mad. You should long since have learned that you cannot reason with a sick mind. I'm sure Peg has said much more terrible things to me than she did to you ... and then forgets entirely that she has said them.
>
> Have no illusions—she loves you as ever. When we moved to Tucson I was pleased and surprised to have her insist on keeping all you[r] "paintings." One wall of her room is covered with photographs and pictures; you and Dick are there—Peg and Gert etc. Some weeks ago when I told her about the 3 day symposium on Polar Research to be held by the OSU Institute of Polar Research in May for which I am invited to give one of the 3 key addresses, she instantly said: "I think you should accept; you could then see Jean." I was pleased and replied that I did want to see Jean and Dick—that in all the world I had loved you more than anyone else except her. "I love her just as much as you do."
>
> It is time the folly be ended Jean and only you can do it.

Gould then revealed the medical trouble which had come to Peg (and therefore to him) in the weeks since his previous letter: Peg was at Tucson's St. Joseph's Hospital, recovering from major surgery to remove her cancerous right breast. "It all happened quite suddenly," he wrote. Lumps had been detected by her regular doctor, and arrangements then made for "the earliest appointment possible" with a local surgeon, Dr. Robert Hastings, in whom he expressed great confidence. The mastectomy had apparently gone well, but Peg would be taking cobalt treatments after leaving the hospital. "Of course Peg was terrified at first, but she has adjusted quickly and is in good spirits." "It would be good," he typed on to Jean, "for the Rice sisters to really know the bliss of mutual forgiveness ... (my sermon for the day)."

Jean replied with speed, with sorrow over Peg's medical trial, but also with a review of how thoroughly crushing and "final" Peg's previous pronouncement of judgment against her and Dick had been and with the observation that the very fact that Larry had not told Peg that he was writing to them "seemed to us both a confirmation of her continued animus. ... Don't be over sure now she wants us back." Jean confessed that, given what had occurred, she thought she could not be happily in Peg's presence again, but that she could certainly write. "I'm going to write her a note now. Open. And you are to approve of it, seal it, and give it to her … or suppress it." Jean's note was enclosed.

As it transpired, Gould would wait nearly eight months to answer, eventually telling Jean that he had not given her note to Peg: "After much thought and worry I decided my idea would not work—not yet, anyhow." To that, Jean's response would term Peg's act of separation "a waste of years and essential affection," but she would accept Larry's decision as to what it was best (not) to do. Jean's December letter would close with "much and special Christmas and New Year's love to you both," even "though you can't carry ours home to Peggy."

Peg Gould had a very difficult time of it following her mastectomy. Although the original operation was deemed a full success, Dr. Hastings then had to be away for some days and Peg was (in Larry's later recapitulation to Jean) left "in the hands of another who promptly removed the stitches—much too soon." Almost immediately, Peg took a turn for the worse, oozing from her incision. "I was nursing and mopping up," Larry would eventually write Jean, "and when I called said surgeon in the morning he was quite casual and said it had to come out; take a bath etc. Then he became afraid of infection and started filling her with antibiotics; on her last visit, the day before Dr. Hastings returned he said quite casually 'I guess you will have to have some stitches put back in.'" When Dr. Hastings saw the situation he was "deeply disturbed." The end result saw Peg rehospitalized and undergoing a second surgery. "Then came eighteen cobalt treatments." Peg had an uncomfortable summer in Wyoming and in August had to forego accompanying her husband to Oslo for his last meeting as president of SCAR. Upon the Goulds' return to Tucson in September, Dr. Hastings prescribed elastic bandages or an elastic sleeve on her right arm during the day. Although sleeping was complicated by Peg's need to lie on her back with her arm raised up on pillows, her pain was finally decreasing. "Peg is not a patient sufferer and these months have been trying," Larry wrote Jean in November, "but I think [now] getting better."

***

During the spring and summer of 1970, as the Goulds privately struggled through the aftermath of Peg's operations, Larry cancelled most "outside" engagements but did continue—selectively and mostly locally—with some public speaking. Increasingly now, his subject was environmental stewardship and the dangers presented by pollution and overpopulation. April 22, 1970, the first Earth Day—often pointed to subsequently as the birth of the modern environmental movement—was observed as something like a national "teach-in" on environmental responsibility. During the month preceding it, Gould participated several times in related events. He delivered his address "While There is Still Time" both at a Tucson conference on environmental concern in the mining industry and at a symposium on pollution put together jointly by several Rocky Mountain institutions. He was active in a "Population Pollution" symposium sponsored by Planned

Parenthood and ten other local organizations. He spoke on "Our Deteriorating Environment" to the Tucson Rotary Club. On April 21, he moderated a campus panel on the environment as part of the University of Arizona's "Teach-in Week."

Months earlier, he had accepted an invitation to be keynote speaker at a May conference on the Antarctic at Ohio State University (a trip that also offered him the opportunity to see Jean and Dick Hoppin). That conference was ultimately cancelled, however, due to campus turmoil at Ohio State (as at scores of other colleges and universities across the country that month), beginning with mass protests following the U.S. invasion of Cambodia and intensifying after Ohio National Guardsmen killed four students at Kent State University. In June, the only speaking engagement on Gould's calendar was delivery of the main address at the Prescott College commencement.

A piece of pleasant news that arrived in May was official notification that the Carleton Board of Trustees had created the Laurence McKinley Gould Professorship in the Natural Sciences and that Richard Ramette of the Chemistry Department had been named its first holder—a choice in which President Nason, just before his own retirement, had allowed Gould to participate.

That August, on the closing day of the SCAR conference he presided over in Oslo, Gould turned seventy-four. He suggested to Arizona's President Harvill that perhaps it was time for him again to retire. Harvill's response, as reported later by Gould to Jean Hoppin, was to say, "Hell, I am going to extend your contract for twenty-five years!" "Curiously," Gould told Jean, "members of the staff seem to wish me to remain and I may for another year until the emerging College of Earth Sciences which I set in motion and of which I was acting director its first year, gets under way."

Harvill, notwithstanding his claim that he wanted to keep Gould active at Arizona for another twenty-five years, was himself preparing to retire in 1971. The selection of Harvill's successor, a task belonging to the Arizona Board of Regents (a body with authority over the entire public university system for the state, including all three major institutions), wound up being something of a messy affair, with too much open publicity about who the top candidates being considered were and camps forming in vocal support of, or in opposition to, one or another of these. In December, prior to a regents meeting at which it was expected that the Presidential Selection Committee would make its recommendation, it was widely (and apparently accurately) rumored that the choice had narrowed to two candidates already at the university: James Zumberge, the School of Earth Sciences director, and Marvin D. "Swede" Johnson, an Arizona alumnus who was then vice president for university relations. At this point Tucson's *Arizona Daily Star* newspaper ran a Sunday front-page editorial urging the regents to select Johnson rather than Zumberge, who the paper termed Harvill's "crown prince." Other newspapers and some politicians also felt free to weigh in on the matter. An Arizona alumnus writing a column on the front page of the *Yuma Daily Sun*, for instance, noting that the search was "raising blood pressures in Tucson," also expressed the hope that Swede Johnson, who had been "devoted to the school and its betterment" for the past twenty years would be "given an opportunity" to lead it. (That Zumberge was a distinguished scholar while Johnson had no PhD ought not to count against Swede, thought the alumnus, for though the PhD was certainly a mark of scholarship, it "does not certify to administrative ability," and in any case "a good administrator can employ an academic vice president if he wishes.") Lacking unanimity, the regents' committee failed to make a December recommendation, though it was reported that four-fifths of its membership had voted in favor of Zumberge. With the head of the selection committee stepping down after that meeting because he had been elected to the state legislature, another regent was appointed to chair a reorganized committee, and the search went on.

Gould's role in all this was small, though he was rightly seen as Zumberge's man. His only public comment on the matter came in January, while passions were still running high. Shortly before heading off for a couple of weeks in Mexico with Peg, in advance of another semester of teaching, Gould sent a statement to the *Tucson Daily Citizen* which that paper (one which had not taken sides in the selection controversy) printed under the title "How Not to Select a University President." "The academic community of the University of Arizona," Gould scolded,

> has been amazed, depressed, and greatly embarrassed by the irresponsible segments of the press which have presumed to arrogate to themselves the responsibility of selecting the next president of the University of Arizona.
>
> The whole campaign has been a great disservice not only to the university but to everyone who has been considered as a likely candidate to succeed President Harvill. It has reduced the present quest for a new president of the University of Arizona to the lowest level of irresponsible political campaigning. For the regents to yield to any kind of outside pressure in the selection of the presidents of our three state universities would be to abdicate their highest and greatest responsibility.

Finally, late in April, with Harvill's retirement barely more than two months distant, the Board of Regents named as Harvill's presidential successor a compromise candidate, thirty-six-year-old research chemist John P. Schaefer, then the dean of Arizona's College of Liberal Arts.

The year before, Carleton College had handled a presidential transition far more smoothly, with another young man, thirty-eight-year-old political scientist Howard R. Swearer, taking over in the summer of 1970 as John Nason retired. Gould and Swearer met at least twice before the new president's formal inauguration in January 1971 and liked one another immediately. Swearer told Gould that hearing his "refreshing views on Carleton, higher education and the state of the nation" was "as always … a tonic." Gould, for his part, thought that "through Howard" he could "again be of help to the college."

And so he was. For the next several years Carleton records show Gould becoming far more actively engaged—and strategically deployed—in assistance with alumni fundraising. Letters would go out under his name, both to Carleton alumni in general and to particular subsets, such as special letters to the classes in which he had honorary memberships. Additionally, he began at this time to make numerous appearances at alumni gatherings coordinated by the Carleton alumni office. In March 1971 Gould and Swearer were both present for a Carleton alumni event hosted by Brownie Cote, Class of 1921, at his Tanque Verde ranch near Tucson. In subsequent years, and during the administrations of several successive Carleton presidents, Gould's attendance at these annual "chuck wagon picnics" for Carleton alumni at Tanque Verde would be quite regular. Additional "solicitation forays" and other assistance involving Gould, and utilizing his extraordinary popularity with the alumni body, continue from 1971 on to be evident in the records of Carleton fundraising, year after year, for some time.

Gould's first visit back to Carleton while Swearer was president came in November of 1970, when he needed to be in Minnesota for other business and added on a night at the college. The Swearers gave a Thursday evening cocktail party for him, inviting all staff still present at Carleton who had served under him. The following June, Gould attended Swearer's first Carleton commencement. In November of 1971, Larry and Peg spent a full week at the college: a week of dinners with friends as well as a more formal reception and dinner at the president's house, a lecture and discussion with geology students, a Phi Beta Kappa talk and reception, a Twin Cities Alumni Club event billed as "An Evening with Larry Gould and Howard Swearer,"* and the main event, Gould's opening address (in the familiar surroundings of Skinner Memorial Chapel) for a two-day symposium on "Technology and Man's Future." At the end of this week at Carleton, a student writer for the *Carletonian*, impressed with his performance and presence, with exciting stories of the Antarctic told in his "rolling, wonderful voice" and with his podium trick of shuffling through his stack of note cards, discarding many ("It's too bad I know so much"), asked in wonder, "Who else could establish such an immediate and complete rapport?"

***

Larry Gould would live to be ninety-eight; two months shy of ninety-nine. The reader of this biography may find it startling to reflect at this point that on his seventy-fourth birthday more than a full quarter of his long life still lay ahead. The last fourth of his days, however, contain nothing like an equal measure of

---

* Passed on to Gould after the Twin Cities alumni event was this comment from a Carl of the 1950s who had not heard Gould speak in close to fifteen years: "I closed my eyes while he was speaking, and I could have sworn I was sitting in the chapel listening to him raise the comprehensive fee once again. He always did it in such a magical way that only a couple of hours after Convocation had ended did we realize he was picking our parents pockets for an additional $100."

biographical interest. Activity and accomplishment, in these years, are slowing; biographical pace, therefore, may quicken.

Even if the fourth quarter of Gould's life contains only a small portion of the significant accomplishment of that life, these years were rich in many personal satisfactions. Although he was by no means, in his seventies, yet ready simply to "rest on his laurels," laurels were, in these years, present in abundance.

Gould's twenty-third honorary degree came in May 1971 from the University of Alaska—he accepted the degree in Fairbanks one week after delivering the commencement address at the Alaska-Anchorage campus. Just prior to that, the Soviet Academy of Sciences had awarded him its Bellingshausen-Lazarev Medal, making him only the second American so honored.

On March 6, 1972, the University of Arizona renamed a space in the geology building from the pedestrian "Room 232 E" to the far more exciting "Laurence M. Gould Seminar Room." On the east wall of the room was placed a handsome plaque, bearing the inscription, "This room is dedicated to Laurence McKinley Gould, ScD, LLD, in recognition of his life-long contributions to the earth sciences as a teacher-scholar, explorer-scientist, academic statesman and international science diplomat..." The dedication and accompanying ceremony took Gould by surprise. (An article in the *University of Arizona Faculty & Staff Newsletter* was accompanied by a picture showing the honoree looking astonished, snapped as Gould was being shown into the room full of faculty, deans, and university vice presidents. Gould said that the picture had been taken just as he was exclaiming "well I'll be god-damned," which, he reported, "effectively broke the ice.") Among those on hand that day to "present" the room were Arizona's vice president for student affairs, the dean of the College of Mines, the acting dean of the college (who presented Gould that day with the University of Arizona Alumni Association's Distinguished Citizen's Award), Geosciences Department head Ed McCullough, President Emeritus Harvill, and Jim Zumberge, who, after not having been selected as Harvill's presidential successor had moved on from being dean of the College of Earth Sciences* to become chancellor of the University of Nebraska. Zumberge had recently given Gould appreciation of a different sort, telling him in a letter the month before that the few years they had spent together at Arizona had been "truly a wonderful experience in which the student learned from the master." "Next to my parents and wife," Zumberge told his mentor, "you have been the most influential person in my life."

Summers continued to be devoted to trout fishing at the G2V property in Wyoming—though the summer of 1974 climaxed with SCAR holding its five-day biennial meeting at Jackson Hole, with Gould, now president emeritus and an

---

* The School of Earth Sciences had been elevated to the College of Earth Sciences in 1971 prior to Zumberge's departure. Gould's old friend from IGY days, Hugh Odishaw, was chosen as the college's new dean after Zumberge resigned. The College of Earth Sciences would in the end be short-lived, however, and in the reorganization following its phase out the Department of Geosciences was moved into the College of Sciences.

The first four presidents of SCAR at Jackson Hole, 1974: T. Gjelsvik (Norway), G. de Q. Robin (U.K), L. M. Gould (U.S.A.), and G. R. Laclavére (France)

honorary life member of the organization, as host. Larry and Peg had also taken to making annual winter trips to Mexico. In 1972, in the course of recommending the Oaxaca valley to Jean and Dick Hoppin, Gould mentioned having been there with Peg in January and then having returned in early May to help promote a project archaeologist John Paddock wanted to develop, a study of distinctively non-violent communities living in the area. He reported having been successful in getting the Ford Foundation interested in Paddock's plans.

Gould continued, in these years, to be in regular correspondence with the Hoppins, most particularly with Jean, though he had felt compelled to ask that their responses always be sent to his office rather than home so as not to disturb Peg. This series of Gould's letters (eventually added to the Gould Papers at Carleton College by Dick Hoppin's brother Charles) provides helpful information about some of Gould's thoughts and activities during the remainder of his seventies. Some snippets:

> (January 29, 1973)
> I had my throat cut two weeks ago—first time in 76 years a surgeon ever had his knife in me. The node was benign anyhow and I am teaching again (just now going to see said surgeon).
> We have a cat of all things. She moved in on us a year and a half ago. She helps me about my yard and sleeps on my bed. I don't like cats so I call her "the dog."

(February 13, 1973)

We did have two quiet weeks in Guadalajara. [...] But in spite of its smog I love Mexico City. I assume you have seen their absolutely fantastic folklorico ballet.

(March 13, 1973)

Do you remember how you teased me because I transplanted some flowers because they were not comfortable together. Please read the enclosed "Love Among the Cabbages" and then return it. It is my only copy and it is important. I do most of my flower gardening in pots now and I have the heavy ones on dolleys so I can move them about easily—change the patterns from time to time and make sure they are all among friends! Soon I'll send you some pictures.

We have the most rain in the 105 years of weather records here. We shall soon have the greatest display of desert bloom ever! How I wish I could show them to you!

(April 20, 1973)

I am delighted with your pictures and I am green with envy at the picture of that handsome sephardic jewish husband of yours. I have long thought of growing a beard again. Dick's prowess may be just the push I need to do it this summer in Wyoming where we shall be for nearly 4 months.

I do remember your good luck on the pool as to the blooming date of my amaryllis in Northfield. I still grow a few every winter but plant them in the water wells about my citrus trees since we are gone so long. They do quite well.

Your sister is still a handsome woman and not quite as grim as she looks alongside the amaryllis. [photo enclosed]

(May 23, 1973)
My dear dears,

We plan to leave for Jackson Hole on the 29th, arriving on the 31st. ... Happily we have no phone. Better suspend your end of our correspondence, which I shall miss—Peg often picks up the mail at the post office.

However I'll send you a post card or note from time to time.

(July 8, 1973)
My dears,

I was so intrigued by the picture of Dick's beard that I decided to grow one up here this summer—so far unlike Dick I don't look like a sephardic Jew but a kind of dirty old man—and I am rather. In due time I'll send you a picture. Weather fine and the fishing good!

(August 22, 1973)

My dears,

This is my 77th birthday and it is a very depressing one. Not because I am 77 but because our beloved cat disappeared more than two weeks ago and now there is no reason to hope she will ever come back. Perhaps a coyote or other wild animal will have gotten her. It is incredible how empty the house is without her.

Our other pets left us, but they were all old and it [was] time for them to go, but Maydie [Medianoche] was not two years old. I don't believe someone could have stolen her; she had a bit of wild Persian streak in her. She did not like to have most people pick her up. She never jumped up on people's laps, except mine and then only rarely.

The enclosed photo is self-explanatory. Even Peg who was responsible for growing it decided that she didn't like it and so off it came. I decided I could never look very Jewish any way. Dick won!

The summer is grand here and I can still find good fishing. I have great fun with my Jeep which the Carleton faculty gave me when I retired from Carleton and I have made many beautiful wood piles with my power saw.

We shall be here as late into September as weather permits. Then a very busy year (teaching the second semester again) getting my papers in order to give to the Polar Center in the National Archives—that will be a helluva job.

(October 14, 1974)

I think of you more and more often and also miss you more and more.

We had 4 wonderful months in Wyoming with a new and winsome French poodle who looks quite like Jill did but who has quite a different but quite as intriguing a personality as Jill had.—name—Lonnie.

I thought at our age we should have no more animals but Peg persisted. I wanted another cat for I have never known as interesting an animal as was our black Medianoche but Peg was sure we could never find another like her so we compromised and got a dog.

I am to teach again next semester. I must be getting better (or perhaps it's senility) with age for I think I have never had a class which gave my course as high a rating as it got last year.

(February 4, 1975)

I have been urged by 2 or 3 publishers to write an autobiography but I can't think of a good subject.

(April 30, 1975)

My final exam is one week from tomorrow but I am committed to stay for Commencement but we should get up to Jackson Hole by the 23rd—in time for the wild flowers!

Peg will be 70 on the 11th as you know. Jack and Martha will come over for a dinner on the 10th which I am arranging at the Old Pueblo Club.

It breaks my heart that this can't be a family reunion.

I guess I told you that the President insists that I return next year. With inflation continuing I guess that is a good idea. Anyhow I still get a big bang out of my classes.

I have so much confidence in my longevity that I bought a new suit yesterday.

***

Another informative series of Gould letters begins early in 1974, when Henry T. Harrison started a periodic newsletter for members of the First Byrd Antarctic Expedition, keeping the shrinking number of men from that great adventure who still survived—Gould's special friend Bernt Balchen, for instance, passed on shortly before Harrison produced his first issue—in touch with one another and sharing personal news and thoughts. Gould, through letters addressed to Harrison, became a regular contributor.

For the newsletter's first issue Gould summarized his polar-related activities from World War II to his 1972 retirement from chairing the National Academy of Sciences' Committee on Polar Research, including his fifth trip to Antarctica in 1969 and its anniversary commemoration of the historic flight of Byrd and his three companions. The newsletter's second number, published at the end of November, featured extractions from multiple Gould letters to Harrison written at various times that year. In mid-June and then again in November, for instance, he wrote of his growing concern over the proliferation of nuclear power and its "hazards to all of us." "I am disturbed," he wrote, "that with the new energy bureaucracy the budget for nuclear energy is second only to that for military weapons etc. Only 10% goes for research in coal. … The ultimate source of energy must be the sun, and yet only 1% of budget goes for solar and geothermal research." In October, he sent Harrison a copy of personal reactions he had dictated in August immediately after hearing disgraced President Nixon's speech of resignation and (the following morning) remarks bidding farewell to his staff, which had combined, he said to give him "a spiritual hangover":

> My first reaction is that it is the same old Nixon; the same old malarkey on which he has built his career. These are just two more Checkers speeches.
>
> Indeed, Nixon was worse in his emotional remarks than I had expected. Nowhere was there the slightest indication of humility; nowhere the slightest admission of wrongdoing, just a very brief admission that he had made some mistakes. On the contrary his resignation remarks were an arrogant defense of his actions including the expected self pitying statement about the great personal sacrifice he was making for the good

of the country. His remarks were sheer blasphemy. I do not remember a more totally insecure and dishonest statement.

If ever a man was hoist by his own petard it is Richard Milhous Nixon.

His farewell remarks to his staff was even more sickening than the resignation speech. Indeed, it was the sort of talk that should not have been broadcast if he meant it sincerely. Here were the same self justifying remarks. Here more of the insincere pious platitudes which we have come to expect from him.

Nixon's administration was the most preachy and sanctimonious in our history and at the same time the most hypocritical and most corrupt. ...

I shall put these remarks aside to see what my reactions are as the weeks pass. It does not seem to me that there is anything under the sun that can possibly happen that will redeem Richard Milhous Nixon and his dishonest career from the time he entered politics.

One year later, in the next distribution of the BAE I newsletter (Harrison was bringing issues out every November 29, on the anniversary of the famed polar flight), Gould continued to be quoted in general opposition to nuclear energy—he described his membership in a local group opposing the building of a proposed reactor near Phoenix, which he described as "monstrous"—and in specific outrage over suggestions that nuclear wastes might be safely stored for the next 250,000 years in the ice sheets of Antarctica. This newsletter also reported that Eddie Goodale had that year visited Larry Gould in Tucson and found him to be "in high spirits and good health."

In October of 1975, with fall colors at their best in Minnesota, Gould returned again to Carleton, this time to assist in the dedication of the college's new Seeley G. Mudd Science Building, into which the Geology and Chemistry Departments had moved. To Carleton's director of development he wrote following this visit that the college was "still the center of the universe for me." To Jean Hoppin he reported that his opinion of Carleton's President Swearer continued to rise* and also that he had had a chance to visit with a new Carleton assistant professor of music, Steve Kelly, who had been mentored by Dick Hoppin in his graduate education at Ohio State, and he was happy to report to Jean that he had liked Kelly very much.

---

* Swearer, however, would in a little less than another year announce his departure from Carleton to become president of Brown University. When the search for Carleton's seventh president began late in 1976, Gould recommended to the search committee the name of Thomas L. Hughes, a Carleton alumnus (Class of 1947) then heading the Carnegie Endowment for International Peace. (Hughes appeared earlier in this biography delivering congratulatory remarks on behalf of Carleton students at the luncheon following Gould's presidential inauguration.) Hughes was given a top ("1A") rating by the committee, but when contacted by a committee representative he declined to be considered.

Early in 1976 Gould described himself as "fine but too busy." In addition to teaching again that semester, he reported being "up to my neck trying to stop the building of an unneeded boiling water reactor near Phoenix" and working to promote a university symposium on "the nuclear problem." "I am swamped," he wrote Jean Hoppin, "trying to put together a [written] piece raising hell with the nuclear industry. I want to get the issue on the ballot for the November elections. I think no more reactors should be authorized until we have learned how to neutralize radioactive wastes—storage won't do anywhere!" He had also gotten enthused by the campaign of his own congressman, Morris K. Udall, a liberal lion, for that year's Democratic presidential nomination. "I am all for Mo Udall," he wrote Harrison. "He is a man of complete integrity—the kind of man who could restore faith in our institutions in our bicentennial year." (Udall would finish second in primary after primary, however, and though he stayed in the race until the July convention, it was of course Georgia's Jimmy Carter who was nominated.)

In mid-April, Gould accepted another honorary degree, this from Michigan's Alma College. Making his concern over the safety of nuclear energy a part of his address at Alma, he said that if we as a nation had invested in solar energy only a small part of the billions that had been spent on nuclear research it was probable that we would now be "much nearer to the one energy source which is ever renewing and which man must eventually tap if he is to survive on his planet earth." "Some of my pessimistic friends tell me I am just whistling in the dark when I talk like this," Gould went on, "but surely it is better to whistle in the dark than to curse it. For I have found over a long life that while life has rarely been quite as good as I would have liked it to be, neither has it ever been as bad as I feared it would be. My faith in the resilience of man has not decreased over the years."

That August Gould turned eighty, his faith in the resilience of man still strong and his mind and spirit still very much engaged in the world and ready to grapple with some of its most troublesome issues—far more inclined, that is, to whistle (or better yet, to light a candle) than to curse the darkness.

CHAPTER 27

MR. ANTARCTICA

L arry Gould at eighty carried his years remarkably well—so well, in fact, that he would in 1977 carry them again all the way to Antarctica. This despite what he described as "a set to with angina pectoris [chest pain associated with coronary artery disease] in August" that slowed him for a bit. But only for a bit. By November 1976 he had passed all the necessary physical examinations to be cleared to make the January trip—a two-week tour of inspection, at the request of the director of the National Science Foundation, in the company of three members of the National Science Board and the board's executive secretary, Vernice Anderson. Grover Murray, with whom Gould had traveled in 1969, was a companion again, one of the National Science Board members making the 1977 trip. Gould left Tucson on New Year's Day and returned on the 17th. As usual, his route to the White Continent ran through New Zealand—where the party spent two unplanned days in Christchurch waiting out a blizzard on the other end of their flight further south. In Antarctica, the group visited many of the NSF-funded scientific projects underway at the bottom of the world. They stayed in barracks on Ross Island that Gould described as having "all the comforts of home, including running water for bathing." ("My God I slept between sheets!" he exclaimed in a letter to one of his old companions from Byrd Expedition days.) A newspaper interview after his return had Gould opining that, with the growing technology on the continent, some of the "romance" there had disappeared. Nonetheless, he said, the Antarctic remains the "one part of the world man has not spoiled," and his sixth journey there left him, he said, "feeling better than I have in years, both physically and emotionally." Already he was talking about plans to return for a seventh visit: "I'm only eighty. Why shouldn't I go back?"

At Arizona, Gould was still teaching his one course a year, now titled "Glacial and Quaternary Geology." His yearly travel mileage, though greatly reduced from earlier days, remained robust: during the year following his eightieth birthday, in addition to his Antarctic trip, Gould in December spent two days in Williamsburg participating in the Phi Beta Kappa bicentennial; in February he delivered an address ("The Emergence of Antarctica") in Denver as

part of a symposium on Polar Research at the annual meeting of the American
Association for the Advancement of Science; in March he was one of a committee of four that spent three days at the University at Buffalo helping to evaluate
the geology program there; and in June he absented himself from Jackson Hole
for a few days in order to make an appearance at the Carleton College alumni
reunion, there to accept an Alumni Association exceptional service award and
to meet the incoming Carleton president, Robert H. Edwards.* (He also spent
a night in Minneapolis, visiting with old friends Atherton and Winifred Bean
and with John Cowles.)

In August 1977, Larry and Peg were visited in Jackson Hole for a couple
of weeks by Peg's brother, Jack Rice, whose spirits needed bolstering following
the death of his wife earlier that year. The Gould cabin would be good for that
purpose, Larry wrote Jean Hoppin, for it is "a glorious place." He and Peg were,
however, Larry went on regretfully to state, trying to make a decision about putting their Wyoming property up for sale—something they knew that advancing
age would require them to do sooner or later. At the beginning of the summer of
1977 the cabin still had no telephone, a point of pride for the Goulds for many
years, but sometime that year or the next they finally had one installed, agreeing
that doing so had become a prudent step.

Though prudence on behalf of personal safety could eventually dictate a
concession to modernity in the case of a telephone for the cabin, on another
matter Peg was forever adamant that there would be no concession: She never
would entertain even the possibility of their acquiring a television. Apparently
well before Newton Minow's famous 1961 pronouncement on the low quality of
so much of what passed for TV entertainment, Peg Gould had concluded that
television fare was a vast wasteland or at least an uninteresting waste of time and
an annoyance that she would not allow into her home. At the time of a 1973
interview he gave for the Ford Foundation Oral History Project, Gould said he
believed that he had likely seen fewer than half a dozen television programs in
his life and that "my wife has such a thing about it, which I share, that if I were
to come home with a TV set I think she'd go out the other door."

In November, at age eighty-one, Gould's report to Jean read that he and Peg
each continued in essentially good health, but that "I tire of the heavy medication
I take for an angina pectoris more than a year ago." The angina "doesn't bother
me," he wrote "but I think it wise to follow my doctor's instructions (except he
thinks I drink too much—but he is a very conservative Lutheran). Anyhow I
restrict myself to two bourbon and soda before dinner, with rare exceptions.
And I do continue to raise a multitude of flowers." The following month Gould

* Gould had "a good visit" with Edwards and reported that he "liked him immensely. Beautiful
  clear mind, unusually articulate and fully aware of the problems of being a college president in
  the years immediately ahead." That Edwards' background included no academic experience,
  Gould thought, might actually be a great asset.

made a trip to New York that included attendance at a dinner for Henry Ford II. That same December he and his Arizona department officially requested, with Dean Odishaw's approval, continuation for 1978-79 of Gould's half-time teaching appointment. Previous requests had been submitted, and approved year by year by Presidents Harvill and Schaefer and the Board of Regents, despite the state of Arizona's mandatory retirement age of sixty-five. (The age of retirement had been reduced from seventy in 1974. Working beyond that age on public payrolls remained possible but only with special permission.) This year, however, would be different. The state legislature was getting tougher about exceptions, and in February Schaefer wrote Gould that he was under considerable pressure to reduce the number of faculty members over retirement age for whom he was requesting retention. Noting that the problem was greatest for individuals now well past the sixty-five year benchmark, he indicated, with sincere personal regrets, that he would be unable to offer Gould a continuing appointment beyond the end of the current academic year. He noted that the university, owing Gould "a significant debt" for his extraordinary contributions and counsel, would be honored to designate Gould as professor emeritus, that he could continue to occupy his office and use university facilities, and that he, Schaefer, hoped that Gould would continue to attend colloquia and to advise the president "as long as your interest in Geology and this university continues, and I hope that will be a long, long time."

Far from being upset at the discontinuance of his paid services, Gould professed simply to be grateful that the university had kept him on for so long to that point. "I've had a whole new career thanks to Richard Harvill and John Schaefer," he told the *Arizona Sunday Star*, and to Jean Hoppin he wrote, "I owe this university which has been so good to me." Schaefer had offered Gould the option of continuing to teach his course in glaciology beyond 1978, if he wished to do so without pay, and Gould eventually decided that he would indeed do that, at least for one more year.

In mid-April the university honored Gould and three other eminent UA scientists similarly situated by presenting them all with Creative Service Awards. The other three—Carl Shipp "Speed" Marvel, George Gaylord Simpson, and Ralph W. G. Wyckoff, all aged seventy-six to eighty-four—had, like Gould, each been brought to Tucson as they closed out stellar careers at other institutions or laboratories as part of President Harvill's successful strategy to attract older "superstar" scientists whose expertise could continue to be utilized for additional years to the benefit of the University of Arizona. Gould indicated to Jean a month after receiving his Creative Service Award that he likely would teach another year or two for no income, but he did confess that it had been "a tiresome year for a variety of reasons." He was looking ahead to summer in Jackson Hole, but he knew that "there we must think seriously about selling our beloved Wyoming home." "Though I think I do everything I used to do except climb mountains," he went on, "I do get tired dammit! My heart doctors insist

I must not climb. Our Wyoming cabin is 4,000 feet higher than [Tucson] so I am ordered to do nothing for at least 3 weeks after we arrive in Jackson Hole." His letter concluded: "P.S. There ain't nothing good about getting older."

***

George H. Davis joined the University of Arizona Department of Geosciences in 1970 as an assistant professor, later becoming full professor, department head, and a regents professor as well as serving the university in a number of administrative roles, including senior vice president for academic affairs and provost. Acknowledging Larry Gould to have been one of his principal mentors, Davis would write some years after Gould's death that Gould's "positive impact on students and faculty, and on everyone in the Tucson community who got to know him, was life changing." Looking back afterward at how Gould's influence on the development of Arizona's outstanding program in the geosciences had been made manifest, Davis stressed that it had happened "in extraordinarily personal ways." "That is," he said, "it's the impact on individuals, and it's the attention that he provided individuals in personal letters or personal conversations." Gould was always a very visible figure in the department, functioning, at least in the 1970s, Davis recalled, as an ever-present and ever-welcoming "close colleague" whose door was "always open as you walked down the hall on the first floor of the old geology building." He was, Davis noted, "subtle in his leadership" and very effective at picking his moments, recognizing when and where key decisions were to be made and "reaching the right people with the right recommendations at the right time." Davis identified three elements in the rise to excellence of the Arizona Geosciences Department in which he thought he could discern Gould's definite influence: the forward-looking change of name from "Geology" to "Geosciences," which reflected how traditional geology was increasingly being informed by interactions with chemistry, physics, and biology, and through mathematics; a resolve to identify those things that the Arizona department could "do really, really well" and to make those things "focus themes"; and becoming more demanding in terms of the prerequisites for degrees in geosciences—as Davis put it, the "setting of a benchmark that began to transform the quality of the students that came into the program."

Ed McCullough, head of the department for many of Gould's active years at Arizona, made a number of the same points when interviewed in 2002. He called Gould "great as an aider and abettor of 'the right thing to do,'" a provider of "always very sage advice," who "knew how to pick the right moment for pressing a point." McCullough also pointed to Gould's palpable charisma and his ability to get along with everyone. (Gould "knew everyone's name who worked in the building," McCullough observed, "and all about them and their families, etcetera." He was also "great with Regents. ... He could have been a fantastic politician or diplomat.")

Davis and McCullough were far from alone in their appreciation of Gould's many contributions at Arizona to departmental and institutional advancement. In 1980, President Schaefer gave public credit to the presence of Gould and George Gaylord Simpson for having, in the years they had been at the university, "made it easy to attract scholars of national renown to the faculty."

The arrangement that had brought Gould to Tucson had clearly been very beneficial to the University of Arizona. It had been highly satisfactory to Larry and Peg Gould as well. Both Goulds loved the desert and found Tucson a most congenial place in which to live—though Gould did regret some aspects of how the Tucson he first knew changed as it grew dramatically. In 1976, writing Frank Wright at Carleton of the city's having doubled in size since he and Peg had come there, he lamented that "we were well out in the desert when we bought our place and now we are getting closed in by quite unattractive housing."*

Gould's life in Tucson, as everywhere he had ever lived, was enriched by his friendships and much-enjoyed social interactions. He was often visited in Tucson by persons he had known elsewhere. It was memorable to Gould's Arizona colleague, Professor Paul Damon, that when New Zealander Hilton Willcox, a deckhand on the *City of New York* during the first Byrd Antarctic Expedition, visited Arizona, he said he wanted to see two things in the state: the Grand Canyon and Laurence McKinley Gould. Though Peg was an outstanding gourmet cook, the Goulds' houseguests were often treated to steaks grilled outdoors by Larry. (He "liked his steaks on the rare side of medium rare," Ed McCullough remembered, "and had trouble understanding anyone liking theirs any more well done.") Gould also enjoyed taking people to his favorite Tucson restaurants, notably the Pueblo Club, the Palomino (where he was particularly fond of the sweetbreads), or—best of all, in his estimation—the Iron Mask, run by Doug and Rita Marvin, where he was a favored customer. At the Iron Mask, Rita would reliably come up and greet him with a big hug and kiss, and Doug had a much-valued way of preparing a fish—cabrilla, a sea bass—that Larry would order—and usually get—whether it was on the menu that day or not.†

At some point—they are not certain when—Clark and Ardith Arnold began to make regular visits to the Goulds on most Sundays, following church. (They lived on opposite sides of Tucson, but the Arnolds' church lay halfway between.)

---

* Gould's 1970s aversion to the uncontrolled manner of Tucson's rapid growth echoed that of his friend and neighbor Joseph Wood Krutch, who in the 1960s, watching "as hamburger stands, filling stations, shopping centers, and housing 'developments' spread out toward his formerly isolated desert home," had "like a disillusioned lover," lamented how "everything looks improvised, random, unrelated to everything else, as though it had no memory of yesterday and no expectation of tomorrow."

† Clark Arnold recalled: "You had to call up and make sure Doug had some cabrilla. We'd call up and say, 'well, Larry Gould's coming …' 'Oh yes, I'll get some cabrilla.' He would fix it."

Also at some indeterminate time the Goulds' young friend Pete Kresan began to come "semi-regularly" to Sunday dinners at Casa Gould. Kresan had been a graduate student in Larry's course in 1971 and then later taught in the department. After Kresan and some others invited the Goulds to dinner on one occasion that year, an ever-deepening friendship had resulted.

Peg Gould used to say that, though she and Larry never had any children of their own, through special relationships with many younger people they in fact had children all over the world. Ardith and Clark, certainly, they informally "adopted," and they took great delight in being like an extra set of grandparents to the Arnolds' daughters, Amy and Joanna. Years later, at the memorial service held at Carleton in celebration of Gould's life, Joanna Arnold shared a story of herself as a four-year-old, playing "school" on the Goulds' patio with Larry her attentive pupil, instructing him in the letters of the alphabet. She recounted how her parents, scandalized at hearing her familiarly calling Gould "Larry," instructed her that he was more properly addressed as "Dr. Gould." This admonition produced an alteration in their formerly easy camaraderie for which, Joanna stated, Gould never fully forgave her parents, "contending that a certain charm had departed [the] relationship, never to be entirely regained." Gould's niece Jean Pensinger was once quoted as saying that "Uncle Larry only had one regret, and that was that he and Aunt Peg never had any children." Ed McCullough, however, when interviewed about Gould in 2002, marveled at the "amazing number of people who viewed Gould as like a father to them."

***

In the summer of 1978, the Goulds returned to their G2V cabin near Wilson, Wyoming, for what they expected would be one of their last seasons there before selling.

One day that August, several days in advance of Larry Gould's eighty-second birthday, Atherton Bean in Minneapolis—still a member of the Carleton Board of Trustees, as he had been since 1944—needed to communicate with the Carleton president emeritus regarding his college retirement resources. Knowing that telephone service had now been added to the Goulds' summer home, he sought to reach Gould there. Bean's call, and what he did after, may have been lifesaving.

Gould had that spring begun feeling a general malaise, which he assumed to be just "getting old." He thought that when he got back to his beloved Jackson Hole at the end of May he would improve. He did not; by late in the summer he had significantly worsened. Bean, when he called in August, grew seriously concerned by how ill Gould seemed to be. And Bean, chairman of the executive committee of the International Multifoods Corporation, was a person with the resources to act decisively on his concern: He sent his private plane to Jackson Hole, with a male nurse on board, to pick Gould up and fly him directly to Minnesota's Mayo Clinic. Bean had, for a number of years, been chairman of the board of the Mayo Foundation.

Gould, meanwhile, had grown sick enough that as they put him on the plane he may not even have realized what was going on. On arrival in Rochester, he was carried into the hospital on a stretcher. After much examination, the Mayo doctors concluded that the real problem likely stemmed from the effects of the medication he was taking. Since his trouble two years before, diagnosed as angina pectoris, Gould had been placed on a regimen of daily drugs. At Mayo the physicians determined that the diagnosis of two years before may have been wrong and "elected to terminate both Inderal and quinidine on the theory that [Gould] may not need these drugs and that they might be contributing" to his present illness.

Soon Gould was back in Wyoming and feeling much better. Before the month was out he wrote Clark Arnold: "It takes a bit of time to recover from an original wrong diagnosis and 2 years of wrong medicine (10 pills per day)," but, "Since Mayo took away all my medication I am getting better every day. I have been fishing the past 2 days and may go again this afternoon!" Some months later he wrote Jean: "They stopped all medications and I began to get well. I have taken no medication of any sort since August and I feel fine. I was literally being poisoned to death by over medication for an ailment I didn't have." Gould himself subsequently credited Bean and the Mayo Clinic with having saved his life. His health, vigor, and good spirits all rebounded remarkably quickly.

Even so, it remained clear that it would soon be necessary for the Goulds to give up spending their summers substantially alone at #28—G2V in Wyoming. Before their property could become available for public sale they were required by G2V by-laws to offer it first to their little corporation, whose members would have a thirty-day option to buy it. Given that by the end of August several of the G2V property owners had already shut their cabins down for the season and departed Wyoming, Gould thought it best to plan for one last summer in residence, when they could go through the selling process in unhurried fashion.

1979 was therefore to be a year of multiple "lasts." In the winter and spring, without pay, Gould taught his "Glacial and Quaternary Geology" course one last time. In mid-year the Goulds spent their last summer in Wyoming before selling.* And then in November, in order to participate in the observation of the fiftieth anniversary of the Byrd Expedition flight over the South Pole, Gould, now eighty-three, visited Antarctica for a seventh and final time.

The first half of 1979 was hard on Peg Gould due to months of failure to heal well from painful gum surgery at the end of 1978 and to the removal of a tooth due to bone deterioration. Her spirits were very low, which was hard on Larry as well. He did get away in March for two days at the Asilomar conference grounds

---

* Selling to, as it transpired, Minnesotan Jean Congdon Adams, a relative of Dorothy H. Congdon, an important Carleton College donor and Gould-era trustee of the college. The closing date for the transaction was September 15, 1979.

on California's Monterey peninsula, where he spoke to some 150 Carleton alumni and families, and in June he would again attend Carleton's alumni reunion.

Before that, though, in April, by joint invitation of the Antarctican Society, the National Academy of Sciences' Polar Research Board, and the National Science Board, Gould gave the Antarctican Society Memorial Lecture at the National Academy of Sciences Auditorium in Washington. The speech was entirely about the speaker: personal reminiscences of Gould's half century-long involvement with the continent, shared with an audience of Antarctic enthusiasts. It was titled "My 50 Years of Antarctic Exploration and Research." Pete Demas, another of the "forty-two men" who had wintered-over together at Little America on the first Byrd Antarctic Expedition, flew clear across the country from Los Angeles in order to be present for the event.

Glowing tributes were offered Gould that evening, both in the printed program, which called him "an Antarctic superstar," and in the warmhearted introduction given by his friend and protégé Jim Zumberge. "He is," said the program, "Mr. Antarctica in the United States, a true All-Antarctican." Interviewed afterward in connection with a Gould profile in *The Washington Star*, Zumberge recalled the thrill of "sitting in his family living room as a child of six and listening to the crackling radio messages sent by the Byrd party" from the unimaginably distant American outpost in Antarctica. Hearing the words "This is Little America calling" was "as exciting then," Zumberge said, "as getting the first messages back from space, especially for young boys at the beginning of the depression years."

Peg seems to have healed at last during the summer in Jackson Hole, but at season's end having to pack up and leave the place for the last time was difficult. Arizona Geosciences Department lecturer Pete Kresan came up from Tucson to help with the moving out. (As one token of Gould's gratitude for Kresan's friendship and his many services to the Goulds, Kresan would eventually "inherit" the red Jeep given Gould by the Carleton faculty in 1962 for his use in Wyoming.)

That autumn Peg's brother Jack Rice died of cancer. Larry went to see Jack a few days before his death. To the third sibling, Jean, Larry wrote, "I am glad that neither you [n]or Peg saw him in his last days." "Would to God," he went on, "that [Jack's] death would bring you and Peg together—the two people whom I love best in this whole world." "But," he admitted sadly, "there is no apparent basis for that hope."

In November, Gould took part in two commemorations of the fiftieth anniversary of the Byrd south polar flight. The first, in mid-month, took place in Byrd's birthplace of Winchester, Virginia. Principal speakers were Gould and Virginia Senator Harry F. Byrd, Jr., the admiral's nephew. Other participants included Ruth Siple, the widow of Paul Siple; Paul C. Dalrymple, the president of the Antarctican Society; and the US Navy Band, which performed for an hour before the speechmaking. "I thought it was going to be a great bore," Gould wrote Dalrymple later, "but the audience was so warm and friendly that I had a thoroughly good time. … The quality of my speeches always depends to a large extent on the audience." Gould's talk was titled "Mr. Antarctica."

The second commemoration, on the anniversary itself, took place in Antarctica. At that time only ten still lived of the forty-two men of the Byrd Expedition who had been on the continent at the time of the historic flight. Two of those ten—Gould and his former dog driving companion Norman Vaughan—were among the dozen notables who, beginning November 24, were to be flown as part of a "VIP junket" from Washington to Christchurch to the US base at McMurdo Sound and then on to the South Pole for a commemorative ceremony, with the last 800-mile leg retracing the route taken in 1929. Also in the VIP group were Senator Byrd and his nephew (the admiral's grandson), Robert Breyer, Jr., plus—accompanying Gould to Antarctica for a third time—Grover Murray of the National Science Foundation. The party reached McMurdo as planned, having been outfitted with cold weather gear in Christchurch. But then—a disaster intervened.

The day before Gould and the others were to be flown from McMurdo to the South Pole in a National Science Foundation C-130 Hercules, an Air New Zealand chartered DC-10 out of Auckland carrying 237 sightseeing passengers and a crew of twenty crashed on the side of Mount Erebus, the active volcano on Ross Island within sight of the McMurdo base. There were no survivors—this was the costliest disaster in lives lost in the history of the Antarctic and one of the deadliest crashes in aviation history. The tragedy ended commercially operated sightseeing by air in Antarctica for many years. It also, as a decidedly minor consequence, caused the planned fiftieth anniversary flight to the pole to be cancelled. (At a McMurdo meeting of their group called after the crash became known, someone—Gould thought perhaps Grover Murray—made the suggestion that they could be most helpful simply by getting out of the way and not diverting any McMurdo effort toward an unnecessary flight. Agreement was universal, and announcement of the cancellation was made late on the 28th.) At noon on the 29th Gould and the others in his group attended a memorial service for the 257 people who were killed. The chairman of the National Science Board then announced that the ceremony that had been planned for the pole would instead be carried out at 2 p.m. at McMurdo. There, a number of people spoke, and Gould to his "great surprise" found himself the final focus of attention when at the end of the ceremony the Science Board chairman honored Gould by presentation of the NSF's Distinguished Public Service Award, with accompanying gold medal.

"And thus I end my Antarctic ventures," Gould wrote his sister-in-law the following month. He did, "in spite of the misery" of the Air New Zealand tragedy, return with good memories from his seventh and last trip to the ice. It was great, he wrote Paul Dalrymple, to see Norman Vaughan again and also to spend time with Byrd's grandson Bob Breyer, "a great addition to the Byrd family." That the announcement of his Distinguished Public Service award was largely "lost in the shuffle" of news beside the reporting on the crash and its aftermath, Gould professed to be "a tragedy for my ego," which the publicity given the award would (he claimed to have told Peg) otherwise have bolstered. "Your ego was already healthy enough," he said his wife replied.

***

Old age came late to Larry Gould, but come it did in time, however gradual its arrival. At age eighty-three he found his last trip to Antarctica very strenuous and confessed to Jean that "I could not keep up with people 40 years younger than me." Writing in March to Carleton president Bob Edwards, he mentioned that though he still enjoyed splitting wood doing so now cramped his hands, which were a bit arthritic. Later that month he told Jean that he was about to go see a special cardiologist—"I hope he does not prescribe any pills"—and that doctors at the Mayo Clinic, who had in 1978 diagnosed him with calcific aortic valve disease, were suggesting possible aortic valve replacement for him. "But I think I'll carry on with the old one," he wrote. "At my age it would be folly to do otherwise. I saw wood, I work hard in my yard, I go to Antarctica. I do everything I want to do."

In 1980 Gould did not, in fact, do quite everything he wanted to do. He wanted, in June, to travel to Columbus to accept an honorary degree to be conferred upon him at the Ohio State University commencement. Doing so would have allowed a visit with Jean and Dick Hoppin, with whom he had been in semi-regular correspondence for several years now but whom he had not seen in person since before Peg's blow-up with them in 1961. After an initial acceptance of the invitation, however, Gould wrote again to the Ohio State president on the 9th of May, regretting that Mrs. Gould's "fragile health" mandated that he "remain close to home for the predictable future" and so he would be unable to attend the commencement. Peg, he wrote to the Hoppins the same day, "is teetering on the edge." Gould's degree (his twenty-fifth honorary one) was awarded him in absentia, and Jean wrote back that it was "just as well" he had not been able to come for she feared she "could not stand the impact of a meeting." To this Gould was slow to reply, explaining when he finally did the following April that her statement "took the wind out of my sails." "Such emotional impacts," he scolded Jean, "are never fatal, and I too would probably have wept 'like a bathtub overflowing' but what a wondrous talk we three would have had. If I had been near you at the receipt of your letter I would have beaten you up just as I used to."

Peg's poor health was still a concern in the spring of 1981—"arthritic degeneration of the lower spine, which means a painful back, a spur on the head, a spot on lung which isn't cancer but doesn't go away etc." were enumerated in Larry's letter to Jean—but while these things kept Peg from traveling much herself, they did not bind Larry entirely to home. That May he again attended a Carleton alumni gathering at Asilomar in California. ("As ever," Carleton's President Edwards wrote him afterward, "your presence warmed Asilomar, awing the males and dissolving the females.") In June he returned to Carleton to show the colors at a reunion weekend—"that will be my last," he wrongly predicted. In between, two days after a celebration of Peg's birthday at the Arnolds' home, he flew to Washington to receive a major honor: the Cosmos Club Award. ("It is a plush dress affair," he wrote Jean, "and Peg should be with me but she doesn't feel up to the trip.") In accepting the award—he was the eighteenth annual recipient of this honor, given "to persons of national or international standing in a field of science, literature, the fine arts, the learned professions, or the public service"—Gould delivered an address, "The Last Terrestrial Frontier." In it he called for the continuance of Antarctica's status under the Antarctic Treaty as "a continent for science" and "the only place left on earth where there are no boundaries." A large photographic portrait of Gould was to be placed beside like portraits of each of the previous recipients of the Cosmos Club Award, an illustrious list that included such luminaries as Helen Hayes, Archibald MacLeish, and John W. Gardner. Gould observed that he "could not be hanged in more distinguished company."

A couple of weeks after the highly satisfying Cosmos Club affair, the Goulds left Tucson for the location where, since the 1979 sale of their Wyoming property, they were now spending their summers: Pinetop,* in Arizona's White Mountains, only a two hundred-mile journey from home, where at an elevation of 7,300 feet they were annually renting a cabin that allowed them to escape Tucson's summer heat and where Larry continued to find good trout fishing.

In mid-summer of 1981, with Peg feeling sufficiently better to abide the travel, the Goulds took time to go to California to attend the Carmel Bach Festival. There they heard a German pianist whose performance both Goulds found outstanding. Afterward, in words Larry passed along to the Hoppins, "Peg remarked that Dick Hoppin was the only pianist she had rather hear." Seizing on any hopeful signs that Peg might be softening to where a reconciliation might be possible, Gould also informed the Hoppins that "Peg asks me from time to time if I keep in touch with you." "What a loss this [estrangement] has been to all of us," he bemoaned.

As he aged, Gould was often called upon to revisit the history of the years he had lived. Twice in 1981 he sat for oral history interviews—once over two days in Tucson with polar historian Peter J. Anderson, who was contemplating writing a Byrd biography, and then in November, while he was in Washington for meetings of the National Academy of Sciences' Polar Research Board (virtually the only such board upon which he was now still active), for the National Science Board Oral History Project. One obvious thing for him to consider by way of making a contribution to the historical record was to write an autobiography but—even though he was often urged to do so (publisher Alfred Knopf asked him several

---

* The name "Pinetop" is said to derive not, as might be expected, from the high-altitude ponderosa pines to be found in the vicinity but from the nickname of a saloon keeper who formerly served the soldiers at nearby Fort Apache. The Goulds spent half a dozen summers at Pinetop, often being driven there at the beginning of the summer and picked up again at the end by the Arnolds or by Pete Kresan.

times to write a memoir, and he had been offered an advance of several thousand dollars to commit himself to a book)—this he refused to do. "Parts would have to be too revealing and 'controversial,'" he had written Jean as long ago as 1972—sending her in the same letter an old cartoon he had once clipped, showing an executive saying to a trio of underlings, "I called for you creative people because I feel it's time to write my autobiography." In 1978 he had told another interviewer, Charles Neider, that if he ever did write an autobiography, he would make it about the things that he *didn't* do that he should have done. (This, he said, put him in mind of a lad's definition of a "sin of omission"—that is, "a sin one should have committed but didn't.")

***

Though Gould had now ceased teaching, he remained, in the early 1980s, actively involved with and invested in both Carleton College and the University of Arizona. At Arizona he continued to maintain an office and, for a time, went there during the school year more days than not, working, for instance, on going through his accumulated files, throwing some out and selecting others for donation to the university. In 1982, President Schaefer stepped down after more than a decade in office and was replaced by University of Massachusetts chancellor Henry Koffler. Gould wrote Schaefer of his admiration for the job he had done in moving the school "rapidly toward greater excellence," despite having been, in Gould's view, "handicapped by a naive, unsophisticated Board of Regents" with a "completely mistaken notion of what its functions should be," coupled with having "had to endure the mindless vendetta of a local sensational newspaper." "We in the Department of Geosciences," Gould wanted Schaefer to know, "will always remember that it was during your administration that we grew from a good to a great department."

In May of 1982, the University of Arizona presented Gould with his twenty-sixth honorary degree. It would be his last.

With regard to Carleton, the college continued to want to involve him in alumni and occasional campus events, and he continued to allow himself to be involved. In 1982, after one of the annual Tanque Verde alumni picnics at which Gould's presence was again a featured attraction, Carleton dean Peter W. Stanley wrote Gould that he and President Edwards "could not be more keenly aware than we are that Carleton's greatness is your legacy. We shall try to be good stewards." For his part, Gould a few weeks later wrote to Vice President for Planning and Development Dan Sullivan that he was "so happy with Bob Edwards' Carleton and the splendid staff he has built to support him" that being back on campus was now always a sure way to give him "a great lift." That June he—and Peg too—went to Northfield for the Carleton reunion. Part of the weekend festivities on that occasion was alumni celebration of the fiftieth anniversary of Gould's joining the Carleton faculty, for which a "red tie tea" was held in his honor. Chuck Donnell, president of the Carleton Alumni Association, introduced Gould and presented him with a gift. Richard Ramette, the Laurence M. Gould Professor of Chemistry, recalled interviewing for his job at Carleton during a 1950s Larry Gould Day on campus, and that "one of the most exciting features" of a tea held *that* day was "the emerging from the wings of a beautiful girl dressed as a penguin," who rushed in and gave Gould a big kiss. Not many minutes later, as Gould was beginning to make a few remarks of his own—to be kept concise, he said, because a speech "need not be eternal to be immortal"—he was interrupted by the appearance of a girl dressed as a penguin, who rushed in and kissed him.

The next spring Gould was back at Carleton again—flown up and back in Atherton Bean's private jet—to be on hand for a multi-day mid-April symposium, "Revolution in the Geological Sciences," being held to mark the fiftieth anniversary of the Geology Department established with Gould at its head. All of the symposium papers were given by alumni of the department, many of whom, of course, had once been Gould's own students.

During the year that followed, the renewal of the Carleton love affair with Larry Gould continued when the college—prompted, in Gould's words, by President Edwards having "gone quite daft" about Gould's book *Cold*—decided to bring out a new edition of the 1931 book. In addition to asking Gould to write an epilogue summarizing his post-Byrd expedition ventures in Antarctica and his help getting US Senate approval of the Antarctic Treaty, the college added a forward by Jim Zumberge (by then president of the University of Southern California) and put on the cover Gould's favorite photograph of himself, taken in Antarctica in 1957. The new edition of *Cold* was published a few months into 1984. Gould autographed copies at Carleton's June reunion and at Homecoming in September—each time being flown to Minnesota and back in Bean's private plane.

In mid-1982 Gould wrote Jean that his doctor had attributed trouble he had been having with his legs to hardening of the arteries. He was then, he reported, following a regimen of a shot in the buttocks every two weeks and thiamine tablets twice per day, plus six glutamate and one dyazide daily. By early 1984, following a scare where his heart "quite suddenly went wild with frightful chest pains" and aortic valve replacement surgery had again been considered but decided against in favor of additional medications, his daily pill total had risen to twenty-six.

If Gould's body, in the first part of the 1980s, was now an imperfect machine, yet his mind, in these years, remained healthy. In the summer of 1981, for instance, he mentioned in a letter from Pinetop that—having, in his mountain retreat, "only to read and go fishing"—he had that summer been immersed in the following eclectic selection of books: *Sentimental Imperialists* (an appraisal of the history of the American experience in China, Japan, and the Philippines), much of V. S. Naipaul, a biography of Nikola Tesla, Trollope's *Barchester Towers* (again), some of *The Best of Roald Dahl*, and "most of all Carl Sandburg's *Abraham Lincoln*—the same six volumes I had in my Antarctic winter 1928-30."

His mind was also very engaged in those years with political matters.

The conservative ascendancy in the national elections of 1980 had disappointed him and he found Ronald Reagan's subsequent performance in the White House increasingly infuriating. By the end of 1981, the first year of the Reagan presidency, Gould was expressing himself as appalled by "what Reagan is doing to us." A year later he was writing to Jean that he wished he were younger so that he "could expose a bit better the lunacy and dishonesty of Reagan and company." Leading up to the mid-term elections of 1982, he involved himself deeply in the grassroots movement to place on the state ballot and then pass in Arizona a nuclear weapons freeze initiative. Freeze initiatives, calling upon the United States and the Soviet Union mutually to agree to a halt in the production, testing, and deployment of additional nuclear weapons were voted upon that November in ten states, where, to the distress and opposition of the Reagan administration, they had reached the ballot either through citizen petition or legislative action. In Arizona, Gould's name appeared on the letterhead of the group Arizonans for a Bilateral Nuclear Weapons Freeze, and he was one of four persons (former UA president John Schaefer was another) whose signatures appeared on a statewide fundraising letter for the cause. Before election day, Gould went on television in support of the initiative. Freeze initiatives won in nine of the ten states voting on them. It lost only in ultra-conservative Arizona, where the state's largest newspaper, the *Arizona Republic*, refused to give the movement any positive news and, Gould complained to Jean, "printed outstanding lies."

In 1983 and 1984 Gould's loathing for Reagan-as-president grew ever more virulent. In February 1983 he enclosed to Jean a copy of the January 15 edition of the *Washington Spectator*, which contained, he said (in the article "President Reagan: The Bloom Is off the Rose"), the best "debunking" of Reagan that he had yet encountered. In April he sent Jean a copy of a column by Manhattan Borough president Andrew Stein, "Reagan's Wreckage," that had appeared in the March 28 *New York Times* and which Gould thought was "one of the best over all appraisals" of the damage done to America's communal fabric by Reagan's social policies. ("Whether or not Ronald Reagan's economic manipulations bear fruit," Stein had written, "he will leave America with a fundamental and devastating legacy: the wreckage of five decades of public policy aimed at creating a more equitable society.") Early in 1984, Gould vented further in letters to the Hoppins, fuming about the ubiquity of Reagan's "lies"—he noted that the *New York Times* had recently listed three hundred of them—and concluded, "Surely he will go down in our history as the worst president ever.... [T]hat includes such oafs as Nixon."

Gould's disgust and poor estimation, however, were not shared in equal measure by the mass of his countrymen, and a few months later Reagan was reelected to a second term with the electoral votes of forty-nine of the fifty states.

***

The Goulds in Arizona in 1986

Gould continued, as he moved through the years of his upper eighties, to record the principal occurrences and concerns of personal life in his letters. Extractions from these provide a convenient means of setting down, in Gould's own words, what must be communicated about this period of life, even though at this time his news reports—of himself and, especially in these years, of Peg—when placed all together read like an almost unrelenting litany of medical misfortune:

(February 3, 1983, to Jean Rice Hoppin)
    Peg is having a painful time with her arthritic back and knees. Sadly she has the mistaken idea that alcohol is good medicine for it.

(May [25?], 1983, to Jean Rice Hoppin)
    Peg has suffered much depression but is improving with good medical help and a splendid psychiatrist. She has a tricky memory which may mean brain damage from too much alcohol but the psychiatrist thinks it may just be dysfunction. I am not sure that she is not an alcoholic. I would not write that to anyone else.
    Hardening of the arteries in my legs is annoying but they don't appear to be getting any worse. Our wonderful little dog* is great

---

* The Goulds' treasured companion at this time was "Gray," a pound-rescue dog the Arnolds believe to have been "probably part Schnauzer and part Cairn Terrier."

medicine. Every morning we are up at 6 or earlier and I have no peace or breakfast until she has taken me on a long walk.

On February 17th an irresponsible driver in a borrowed car from California slammed into the right side of my 2 year old Volvo with only 23,000 miles and smashed it all to hell. "Totaled," they say. Neither one of us was injured beyond a minor bruise or two. I am convinced that I have not yet perpetrated my portion of mischief in this world—but I shall be 87 come August 22.

(October 20, 1983, to the Hoppins)

Peg is in Intensive Care at St. Joseph's Hospital after an operation which yesterday safely removed a tumor (cancer) from her liver. The operation was completely successful and she will get well.

We went up to our White Mountains at Pinetop on July 1 and during the second week she fell and crushed a vertebrae. The local medical service was good but still she didn't seem to be recovering as she should. Auto travel was too rough and I brought her home by air ambulance and got her into St. Joseph's Hospital under the care of her own doctor. The assumption was that all her misery was due to the crushed vertebrae but no orthopedics or others could give her much relief. She lost 17 pounds in a few weeks.

The good doctor Hastings who operated on her breast cancer 13 years ago insisted on a liver scan which showed a spot no doctor could safely identify. The good Dr. Hastings insisted on an angiogram on Monday which showed the spot to be hard. He pointed out the great hazards of toying with the liver but both Peg and I insisted we had to know. He operated yesterday and was completely successful in removing the "bad" part—a malignancy—a cancer which was inherited from the breast cancer 13 years ago. Strange world that Peg's crushed vertebrae probably saved her life. The cancer would have spread through the liver had it been left.

It seems likely that the loss of weight and Peg's general misery were largely due to the cancer. She will get well. She is now in Intensive Care but I saw her today and she wants to live. Oftimes in past weeks she has expressed the wish that she might not ever awake.

But enough of that. I shall continue being annoyed by hardening of the arteries in my legs and a persistent annoying bursitis in my left shoulder—but not enough to stop my gardening. ...

(December 12, 1983, to Jean Rice Hoppin)

I am glad to have your card and sorry to have neglected you so long. Everything has been neglected but Peg but I think she is improving. ... The good surgeon who did her breast operation 14 years ago removed a quarter of her liver. She lost 20 pounds but I really think she is improving. I hope so for the past 6 months have been a nightmare and my d-- heart began acting up last night and I am awaiting a call from my cardiologist! Isn't that enough?

I have shopped—cooked etc. The last may be why I have lost 12 pounds. But I see light at the end of the tunnel. I am now able to take Peg out for dinner. ...

I have not been able to spend half a dozen days here in my office since June 30. It will be better from now on.

P.S. The removal of so much of Peg's liver makes alcohol a forbidden drink—a situation she has accepted completely and gracefully. She actually urges me to keep up my drunken ways.

(February 7, 1984, to the Hoppins)

In my last letter I think I reported that Peg's breast cancer of 12 years ago had migrated (not the right word) last summer to her liver. The cancer was operated with the loss of about 1/3 of her liver. All this time from her fall in early July she had been suffering excruciating back pains. The orthop. insisted on another bone scan about a month ago. This revealed a tumor in her lower spine. The damned liver cancer had apparently migrated again. She had 15 radiation treatments which reduced back pains from a rating of ten to three—but the radiation had bad side effects: nausea, vomiting, diarrhea and frightful abdominal pains. Her oncologist put Peg in the hospital yesterday and already her back pains are abating and she may come home tomorrow. In all this Peg has lost 25 pounds. She looks like a starving peasant from the Sudan.

(February 14, 1984, to Jean Rice Hoppin)

You will have received my letter [2/7] ere now and know how pathetic Peg's condition is. Just when I thought the radiation had helped, her back pain is giving her hell again this morning. I believe her fall last July precipitated a chain of events which no medical service seems to have helped and I am at my wits end.

(April 6, 1984, to the Hoppins)

Perhaps you know Hugh Odishaw died of cancer some 3 weeks ago. He was one of my dearest friends and so I had to respond to Marian's (his wife) request that I speak a bit at a gathering of a few friends in the home the day after Hugh died. There was no other service and Hugh was cremated as he wished. It was a sudden tragedy. Hugh was a thoughtful person about others but procrastinated about Hugh. He just did not go to see his doctor in time—the same wonderful one who cares for my heart. ...

I am assuming that Peg will get better and have rented the same condominium in Pinetop ... which is almost as nice as our Jackson Hole cabin was. If all goes well we go up there July 1. May 16 one of my former students will drive Peg & me up to the Grand Canyon for 2 days to see how she stands up to it.

(December 6, 1984, to Jean Rice Hoppin)

Little change at Casa Gould. Peg has regained the 25 pounds she lost after her liver cancer operation more than a year ago but she suffers much from back pains [and] is only comfortable when lying down with a heating pad.

(January 10, 1985, to Peter J. Anderson)

Peg's chemotherapy medicine has been very upsetting and to add insult to injury she had a mild heart attack last week which will keep her quiet for 2 months.

(April 6, 1985, to Daniel Sullivan)

Sadly our household consists only of Gray and me just now. A week ago Peg fell in our living room and broke a hip and is now in St. Joseph's Hospital doing well (but not happily) and may be home by the end of next week.

(June 24, 1985, to Jean Rice Hoppin)

Replying to your letter of course I have neglected you and Dick. For the past 3 years most of my time has centered around Peg and I am way behind in accounting to you. I think I have neglected to tell you that a month or two ago Peg's severe stomach aches were diagnosed as ulcers. As if that were not enough she stubbed her foot on the carpet and broke a hip—some time toward the end of March I think.... She now gets around with a cane well enough so her surgeon says there is no reason why we should not go up to our mountains July 5 for 3 months. Whether we can do that or not apparently now depends on me. I'll know Monday July 1 and I'll call you.

On May 11, 1985, Peg turned eighty. In July, they were able to go on to Pinetop for another summer in the White Mountains. Physical ailments had created a rough stretch of time for the Goulds on so many counts—and, medically, there would soon be fresh calamities ahead—but that summer would also contain two developments that would, in the one instance, give to Gould a deep satisfaction and in the other bring him great joy.

George Davis had assumed the chairmanship of the Department of Geosciences at the University of Arizona in 1982 and was soon involved in university planning for the construction of a major new building to house that department and other tenants. Sometime around the beginning of 1985, Davis, with the enthusiastic backing of the rest of the geosciences faculty, submitted a proposal to Arizona president Henry Koffler that the new building be named to honor Gould and his departmental colleague, paleontologist George Gaylord Simpson, who had passed away in October 1984 at age eighty-two. (Gould and Simpson had been close; each had called the other "brother." Gould called Simpson as brilliant a man as he had ever known.) Davis's vision, as communicated to Koffler, was that when students or faculty went into the Gould-Simpson building and then came out again, they ought to feel "the way that an individual like myself feels when you go into Larry Gould's office and you come out—you just feel restored, you feel better than when you went in; you feel like you're supported."

There were some difficulties to conquer: Arizona's Board of Regents, said Koffler, had "historically demonstrated some reluctance to naming buildings for University employees or for living persons, and has placed procedural obstacles in the way." But these obstacles were overcome, and in mid-July Gould and Simpson's widow were informed of the impending honor. "When you called to tell me about the name," wrote Gould to Davis a few days later, "I was stunned in a most pleasant way! I have never been so surprised." Davis, in his memorandum to geosciences faculty and staff about the naming, reported that "Mrs. Simpson indicated that George Gaylord would have been so pleased to know that his name would be linked with Larry's in such a way; and Larry expressed a certain sorrow that George Gaylord could not be here to feel the honor firsthand."

The second joyous summer development also involved a surprise. On August 2, in Columbus, Ohio, Jean Rice Hoppin unexpectedly found that her mail contained a note from her sister, with whom (to Larry Gould's abiding sorrow) she had not been in direct contact since Christmas Eve of 1961. "Dear Jeanie," Peg had written. "Being 80 makes one ponder deeply. I know full well, therefore, that I am tired of the heavy lump in my heart. If I say 'I'm sorry' will that do it?" The note was signed: "Love from two to two, Peggy."

Jean's reply, if it took written form, has been lost, but on August 13 Peg wrote again:

> Jeanie, Jeanie—
>
> After all those barren years (forgive me Aldous) the first voice encounter is going to be hard on both of us. I know what's going to happen to me and I strongly suspect the same for you—we'll both bawl our heads off thus rendering us incoherent for a few moments. But, querida hermana, they'll be cleansing tears and will go far toward making us whole again.
>
> I wish my arms were long enough to reach to Columbus. Love from two to two,
>
> Peggy
> (the 2nd was our 55th anniversary—a helluva long time but a bit of a triumph these days)

Again, it is unclear precisely what response Jean made or sent. A letter from Jean to Peg dated August 18 is extant, but marked, apparently by Jean, "Letter <u>not</u> sent." In that letter, perhaps unsent because Jean thought better of pointing out that when the break had come in 1961 Peg had been "emotionally, psychically, desperately unwell," Jean termed "these barren years" an "idiocy," made more particularly so "because you and Dick and I had more fun together—important fun—than any other three people ensemble I know." She had closed her unsent letter: "Now, at the tag end of our lives, let us have done with backward looking (there ain't time) and go on with Love, two to two... Jean."

On August 22—Larry's eighty-ninth birthday—Jean telephoned Peg, completing the sisters' tearful, but full, reconciliation. Larry could not have been happier about the removal, at last, at last, of what had been for him an anguish of twenty-three years' duration. He wrote Jean after the call, calling the reconciliation the most precious and meaningful birthday gift he ever remembered receiving. "A load," he wrote, "seems to have been lifted from my spirit—and my body too. I swear I actually feel better physically than I have in a long time." Interviewed many years later about the Goulds, Ardith Arnold said that she "remembered vividly how excited Peg was" about the reconciliation and at the prospect that Jean and Dick were going to come visit.

That pleasure, however, was denied them. The reconciliation by phone and post produced real joy, but for purposes of a visit it came too late. Within a very short time Jean took ill, was found to have a terminal cancer, and suddenly was gone. (Her death in November came just ninety-nine days after the happiness of her call to Peg on Larry's birthday.) Dick Hoppin, however, came to the Goulds in Arizona in January and thereafter, until his own death late in 1991, continued to make periodic visits to Tucson.

***

Friday, March 21, 1986, was a very special day for Larry Gould. "His" building on the University of Arizona campus, the Gould-Simpson Building, had been completed and was that day dedicated. Ten stories tall, Gould-Simpson was now the university's largest building. At the morning dedication ceremony, featuring a keynote speech by Frank Press, the president of the National Academy of Sciences, Gould, and Simpson's widow, Anne, were the natural center of attention. The two—both beaming broadly in every photograph—were presented with keys to the building so that they would each always have access. The day continued with a noon luncheon, an afternoon open house in the building with mariachi band, and a reception and cocktails followed by a banquet and the showing of a newly made videotape which combined old silent film footage of the 1929 dog sledge journey to the Queen Maud Mountains with a modern narration recently recorded by Gould. Several persons had come from afar to be present at the dedication, including, from Carleton College, President and Mrs. Edwards, trustees emeriti Atherton Bean and John Musser, Dean Roy Elveton, and, from the Geology Department, Professors Shelby Boardman and Eiler Henrickson. The mood of celebration continued throughout the weekend as the Arnolds hosted a Saturday night dinner for the Goulds, and Sunday was the annual Tanque Verde Carleton

The University of Arizona's Gould-Simpson building

Larry Gould on his 91st birthday

alumni picnic, with Gould again prominently present.

In correspondence a few weeks later, Gould wrote that he had moved into a new office in the new building—"on the 5th floor north side so I have a magnificent view of the Catalina Mountains." He mentioned in the same letter that he was looking forward to attending in June the fifty-year reunion of the Class of 1936, one of the Carleton classes in which he had "membership," due to its members having entered Carleton as freshmen the same year he had first arrived as a young professor.

This hopeful plan for June did not come to pass. What happened instead that month is that Gould underwent a heart operation—bypass surgery at two months shy of ninety years of age. As Clark Arnold described the situation nine years later, Peg's health had again taken a turn for the worse, with a return of her cancer, now located in her lower spine. Her physician was warning that there would be difficult times ahead for her. Meanwhile, Larry was now having serious cardiac problems. He went, Arnold related, to a University of Arizona cardiologist, Dr. Gordon Ewy, and was told that, without surgery, his life expectancy was about six months. His alternative was to have a triple bypass. "And he was told," Arnold remembered, that if he survived he would "A. Be the second oldest person ever to survive a triple bypass, and B. That his life expectancy would be increased and he could expect to live for several years." Gould's choice to go ahead with the surgery, Arnold said, was tied to his determination "to remain alive to help care for Peg." He underwent the operation, and it did presumably extend his life. But, those who knew him best at that time agree, the heart surgery marked a clear point of division. According to Pete Kresan, "he was never the same after." In Clark Arnold's recounting, "he took a big step down. … He recovered physically from the surgery, but he never recovered his complete cognitive powers."

At the end of July, Gould wrote a note to Frank Wright, at Carleton, saying that "the wound of my surgery has temporarily left me confused. It has been very painful but I am assured I will recover. Somehow the impression seems to have gotten around otherwise." By November, however, he was back in the hospital for more surgery, this time for a prostate condition. This too, Clark Arnold recalled, was painful and involved a "very difficult convalescence," but he did then regain "some of his former vigor." A letter Arnold wrote to a number of Gould's physicians at the time of this second 1986 hospitalization noted that Larry "suffers occasional brief periods of confusion and disorientation. Momentary dizziness has recently contributed to three minor falls." At that time, noted Arnold's letter, Peg was also "subject to periods of confusion and disorientation." Arnold also felt it important to state in this letter that Peg had "a history of drug and alcohol dependence and has at least twice barely survived encounters with these substances."

Fortunately, the Goulds could rely in their growing need on the assistance of a number of caring persons. In place at home, five days a week, was a capable full-time housekeeper, Maria Rodriguez, who was, Ardith Arnold has said, "a saint." The Arnolds themselves took on increasing responsibility for managing the Goulds' situation and assisting with their affairs. "It was much like you'd care for a parent," Clark Arnold has stated. (The relationship between the Goulds and the Arnold family had long been in many ways like that of parents to children and grandchildren. At Christmas 1984, Larry had given the Arnolds a copy of the new Carleton-published edition of *Cold*, inscribing the volume "For my children Clark and Ardith with great affection." When at the end of the summer of 1985 the Arnolds' oldest daughter, Amy, was about to depart for her freshman year at Wooster College, Larry had written her a note congratulating her on the start of "a real adventure" and reminding her that he and Peg would be "following your years as though you were our own.")

In December Gould would admit to one correspondent that recent months "have been the worst of my 90+ years." In January he told Carleton's David H. Porter (a professor of classics and music who had then, for a single year on an "interim" basis, succeeded Bob Edwards as Carleton president) that "the months since I had the open heart surgery have not been kind to me. I guess I should say that I have run my course." "In spite of the above," he continued, "I have high hopes that I shall be able to come to the 25th reunion of my class." This last was a reference to the 1987 reunion of the Class of 1962, the class with which Gould himself had "graduated" from Carleton. (And also the class to which both Clark and Ardith Arnold belonged.)

In 1987, unlike in 1986, this hopeful plan for June *did* come to pass. Atherton Bean again sent his private plane, and Gould, accompanied by Ardith Arnold, was flown to Minnesota for the reunion. In Northfield, the two stayed comfortably at Eiler Henrickson's house. College and class both "went all out," in Ardith's words, to make Gould available and ensure his comfort. Afterward, President Porter wrote Gould that having him there for the occasion had been "absolutely wonderful … the high point for us all." This would be Gould's last visit to Northfield.

In March of 1988, Carleton's new president, Stephen R. Lewis, Jr., together with his wife Gayle, came to Tucson to attend the annual Carleton alumni gathering at Tanque Verde. After the picnic, the Lewises spent "a splendid three hours" with the Goulds at their home, prompting a gracious note sent back to them a few days later from Peg. Meeting the Lewises, she wrote, had been "a visit we'll never forget. We knew immediately how simpáticos we are and that Carleton will come to mean to you what it has never ceased to mean to us."

Though she was increasingly sick that year, Peg's death came peacefully and unexpectedly in her sleep on July 9. Her instructions, written long before, mandated no ceremonial observance of her passing and directed only that her cremated remains were to be "disposed of." In the fall, they would be scattered on Carleton College's "Lilac Hill." Carleton held a memorial "remembrance" for her in October which Larry did not—in a last minute decision—fly out for, but the Arnolds did. Peg's ashes had been carried to Northfield in September by Clark and Ardith's daughter Joanna, then entering Carleton as a freshman, and were scattered after the Carleton memorial event with a little secular ceremony by a small group that included the Arnolds, Tony and Dorothy Obaid, and Eiler Henrickson, who had come from Colorado to participate.

For Larry, the loss of his life's companion was felt to be, as he wrote one correspondent at the end of 1988, "the worst disaster of my life." For several weeks after Peg's death—"probably a period of two and a half months," Ardith Arnold would remember later—Gould was "so upset, distraught and confused. … He really wasn't dealing with the situation all that well." "But," Ardith related, "friends came in. … We were able to get people in to stay with Larry literally all the time, who were just friends." Ardith, Clark, Pete Kresan, university Geosciences Department secretary Betty Hupp, and others: "there was this whole group of friends who kind of rallied about." From afar, Atherton Bean—who Ardith Arnold described as "our angel with Larry"—wrote to the Arnolds to make clear that with regard to Gould's future care, they were not to worry about finances: "His 'appropriate way of life' should be our only concern. If his assets drop to zero, the College and/or Winnie and I will surely take care of him. This eliminates the necessity of calculating his 'life-expectancy.' Short or long, it makes no difference."

***

Of the seven years that remained to Larry Gould after Peg's death there is no need to present more than a bare sketch. To do more would read only as an essentially dismal chronicle of ineluctable decline and diminishment while adding nothing further to the story of his life of achievement. The man grew old, very old, and the final stage of his journey becomes non-singular, the common story: powers wane and frailties wax.

Gould's condition in his last years was a moving target: He would have good days and bad days, usually perking up for visitors or special occasions. But the overall slope, of course, was downwards. His command of language slipped. (Clark Arnold recalled that "he had many of the problems that you often associate with a person who's had a stroke," and Ardith added, "He was almost aphasic. He knew what he wanted to say, and he'd start to say it, and it was gone. Could not get it out. And he knew; and he would become so frustrated.") A Carleton College observer at the spring 1989 Tanque Verde picnic described him afterward as "remarkably alert and hearty for a 92-year-old" and "still charismatic," but "walking haltingly and with the aid of a cane," and showing "some loss of short-term memory." This was probably a good day. In March of 1991, Dick Hoppin, planning for a three-week visit the following month, reported that "he now seems to stay more cheerful when I'm there, so

I go more often."* Gould's hearing declined badly, and he had difficulty keeping his hearing aids in working order. "It's hard to know," Clark Arnold would communicate in 1993, "how much of his apparent confusion results from his inability to hear and how much is simply mental deterioration."

Gould continued to live in his own home for all but the last two months of his life. This was possible only because arrangements were made—following a fall in his driveway when he was alone—to provide him with round-the-clock caretaking. Maria Rodriguez stayed on as housekeeper, five days a week, eight hours a day. "She was our savior, toward the end," Ardith Arnold reported. "She could get Larry to do things that nobody else could get him to do." As Larry declined Maria became increasingly a care provider, staying at the house until the night person arrived. Continuous custodial care at home was expensive, but, as Clark Arnold explained, "our policy [was to] keep Larry in his home and maintain him as well as possible, as comfortably as possible and safely as possible, absolutely as long as we could." When this level of care began, Gould "had a trust fund that amounted to several hundred thousand dollars. And he had of course no heirs, so we thought, well, if you have a man who's 95 years old and several hundred thousand dollars, how far wrong can you go?"

Through the Carleton College network, at the University of Arizona, and elsewhere, Gould's well-wishers remained legion and did not forget him. Within the polar community, he remained "Mr. Antarctica." In the July 1991 issue of *The Antarctican Society Newsletter*, Gould was lauded as "certainly Antarctica's most legendary living American." "No one," this publication reminded, "who has ever heard Larry lecture or talk on Antarctica will ever forget the thrill of hearing this golden-tongued orator." In 1993, when Gould turned ninety-seven, his birthday celebration was attended by thirteen or so of his friends. Gould was presented with a collection of written birthday greetings that had been collected at that year's Carleton reunion. And he was informed of another tribute and birthday present: plans at the University of Arizona's Department of Geosciences to construct for the foyer of the Gould-Simpson Building a large, attractive, wood-and-glass case to house a permanent display of the colorful academic hoods from each of Gould's (and Simpson's) honorary doctorates. The finished case, with hoods in place, was dedicated that November, before an audience of several dozen people, including Gould and three University of Arizona presidents. Among those friends who had contributed financially to the project was Gould's old dog-sledging companion, Norman Vaughan, who regretted that he could not be personally present for the dedication. (In mar velous vigor at age eighty-seven, Vaughan was planning an upcoming return to Antarctica where he would ascend the mountain named for him there.) With his donation, Vaughan enclosed a note saying that Gould, to him, was "the

---

* Dick Hoppin also, however, would predecease Gould. He died November 1, 1991.

one man in the world in whom one could find no faults. ... Larry always did the right thing. I have tried to emulate his example all my life." The dedication of the doctoral hoods display case at the Gould-Simpson Building would be Gould's last major non-posthumous honor.

In January of 1995, Clark Arnold was informed by Gould's Bank One, Arizona trust officer that the expenses of his care had been so great that Gould's trust assets, except for his home, had nearly been exhausted. As Arnold would recount events some months later:

> We immediately contacted Atherton Bean. Atherton had told us on several occasions, "Now if there's anything that Larry ever needs, here's my phone number." And Carleton College had done the same thing; [President] Steve Lewis told me on a couple of occasions, at the Tanque Verde picnic, "Now if we can do anything, if Larry needs financial support, the college wants to do this." And both of them responded magnificently. Atherton sent funds immediately, which allowed us to cover expenses and to arrange for Larry to move into a care home. ... He was at this point sinking pretty rapidly.

On April 15, 1995, Gould was moved into the Something More Adult Care Home, located on Tucson's northwest side not far from the Arnolds. As Ardith Arnold would describe in May correspondence:

> We arranged for Larry to have a double room but as a single. We were able to move his own bed, dresser, chair and desk to his room. In addition, we took pictures and art work, including his beloved print of Abraham Lincoln. And we even took Oscar the Penguin.
>
> There are six others, all women, in the home. Meals are served at the dining room table. The manager of the home, who lives in one end of the house, has four very well-behaved children who will read to the residents and play their instruments for them if invited but are very unobtrusive. There is also a little black and white dog named Bandit Larry seems to like very much.
>
> The move went far more smoothly than we had anticipated. We arranged to have Maria at the new home when he arrived so that there would be someone he was very familiar with and for the first few nights we had one of the agency caregivers stay with him so that if he woke up and was disoriented there was someone with whom he was familiar to reassure him that everything was all right. The home has now assumed that responsibility. Needless to say Larry is somewhat disoriented but Clark and I truly do not feel he is aware that things are all that different. The first day he was there he introduced himself to the other residents as "Dr. Gould, Dr. Larry Gould" and told them he'd enjoyed having them to dinner and please to come again. His appetite is excellent and he often asks for second helpings.

Gould had "two pretty good months" in the care home, "perking up" when he got there, Clark Arnold would relate. "We assumed it was because there were people around, more stimulus. ... Generally the last couple of months were a bit of an uptick." "He never lost his sense of humor," Arnold remembered, and "could understand and laugh at a joke, even almost within hours of the time he died." This was so "even though he had trouble speaking and very little short-term or long-term memory at the end."

On June 14, after a fall necessitated a trip to urgent care, Gould was given extra oxygen, following which he had a window of time—five or six hours, Ardith remembered, where he became remarkably lucid and could talk about the university, about teaching at Carleton, and having been president of Carleton. Ardith related: "The Home called me at work, they were so excited, because he'd talked about the mountains, how beautiful the mountains were. ... He was very, very lucid when I was out there, and we talked and visited." For a few precious hours, something of the fog which had enveloped Gould's mind lifted, and he "knew who he was."

Gould died, as a consequence of his coronary artery disease, exactly one week later, at 8 a.m. on June 21, 1995, two months and a day before he would have turned ninety-nine. In Antarctica, it would be noted in connection with his passing, the 21st of June is the first day of winter and the darkest day of the year.

VISION AND CHARM

Now, like the personal hero whose portrait had accompanied him from office to office and home to Home, Larry Gould belonged to the ages.

Obituaries lauded his accomplishments, particularly in the Antarctic realm. The *New York Times* ran a fine memorial written by the "dean" of science reporters, Walter Sullivan. *Time* magazine took notice of Gould's passing, though it erred in identifying Antarctica's Gould Glacier as having been named for him. In London, the *Times'* tribute to Gould ran with a photograph of the young explorer headed for Baffin Land in 1927, aboard ship with pipe in hand. Publications in Arizona and Minnesota were more likely than others to give equal prominence to Gould's transformative impact on two institutions of higher education. The *Minneapolis Star Tribune* obituary quoted Carleton College's treasurer emeritus Frank Wright: "He walked on water." … He "made Carleton much more visible," and "the reputation of the college was carried on his shoulders." In Tucson, an editorial calling Gould "truly a wise and generous man who had seen much" included this from Arizona geosciences lecturer Peter Kresan: "He had done all these great things, had several careers, yet just the same he didn't live in the past but in the present, and the future." This editorial noted that for over thirty years Gould's presence at the University of Arizona had been a "grace" to the many younger geologists he had helped to train and to the whole UA community. The piece termed the totality of Gould's ninety-eight years "a life of vision and charm."

A eulogy written in advance of Gould's death by longtime Carleton professor Antonio Obaid, husband to Gould's Carleton secretary Dorothy, stated that, in Gould, "the dreamer and the doer have seldom been joined in a finer and more fruitful union." Obaid's tribute read further: "He could rub shoulders with kings and emperors as well as he could sit on a curb of a Northfield street to chat with a humble worker, and he was as comfortable with any of them as he made you feel with him. His true greatness left no room for pretense."

A memorial service for Gould took place at St. Mark's Presbyterian Church in Tucson on June 24, at which remembrances were shared by Pete Kresan, George Davis, and Clark Arnold. Davis asked, "How do you explain a Larry Gould?"

At least seven features of the Antarctic bear the name "Gould," but only three—
Mount Gould (top), Gould Bay, and the Gould Coast—honor Laurence McKinley
Gould. Also named in his honor are the NSF research ship, *R/V Laurence M.
Gould* (middle), and the Laurence McKinley Gould Library at Carleton (bottom).

and suggested that the answer "goes far beyond his extraordinary intellect." It resides, he thought, "in his enormous generosity." "He gave to us continually," Davis said. "He constantly recharged us through reminding us, through example, how to live and how to treat others." "Larry's office door was always open," Davis continued. "A 'force field' surrounding the opening would draw you in. Abraham Lincoln was on the wall close by. You were made to feel special. You were made to feel as if what you did really mattered. You always left feeling better about the world than when you entered."

At Carleton College, a public memorial was delayed until October, when school was back in session. "A Convocation in Celebration of the Life of Laurence McKinley Gould" was held in Skinner Memorial Chapel on the morning of October 13. It was fifty years to the week from the date of Gould's inauguration as Carleton president in the same space. Oscar, Gould's stuffed penguin (which the Arnolds had had crated up and sent to Carleton along with a rich store of Gould papers, memorabilia, and personal effects), shared the convocation stage, wearing a bright red tie in Gould's honor. Four personal remembrances were prepared for the "celebration" by persons who had known Gould well. The first, from Atherton Bean, was read in Bean's absence by Carleton President Steve Lewis. It mentioned, among much else, "that wonderful smile, that deep and rumbling laugh, that wonderfully expressive expletive, 'Holy Toledo!'" Geologist Eiler Henrickson, whose enthusiasm for geology had begun in Larry Gould's Carleton classroom, emphasized Gould's "wonderful sense of humor and ability to laugh at himself." Carleton's former college chaplain, David Maitland, stressed that Gould had been "a person whose inner life was at least as precious as his public person was impressive" and that the man's brilliance alone did not fully account for his effectiveness; that another important part of the mix had been his "combination of color and character." The remembrance shared by Joanna Arnold, who had graduated from Carleton three years before, related what it had been like to be, in effect, "Larry Gould's grand-daughter," even though he and Peg had raised no children of their own.

President Lewis closed the convocation with a dramatic announcement: The Carleton Library, built during the Gould years and identified by Gould himself as the intellectual heart of the whole college, was henceforth officially to be named the Laurence McKinley Gould Library. The news was greeted by an ovation of hearty approval. Inside the library at that moment was a major exhibit on the life of Gould. Now, appropriately, it would be the first exhibit hosted in the library bearing his name.

That afternoon, following a post-convocation luncheon, a small group progressed to Lilac Hill, on the other side of one of the small campus lakes, to spread Gould's ashes in the same location that had received Peg's seven years before. The group included eleven Carleton alumni: Tony ('41) and Dorothy ('42) Obaid, Ralph ('43) and "Jappy" ('42) Smith, Eiler ('43) and Kris ('88) Henrickson, Chuck ('54) and Zoe ('55) Donnell, and Clark ('62), Ardith ('62), and Joanna ('92)

Arnold. Also present were two non-alumni: Diana Anderson, the editor of the college magazine, *The Carleton Voice*, and David Maitland, the former chaplain. Maitland voiced a prayer, and Tony Obaid read a short statement. (In part: "Peg, we know how much you have missed Larry and how patiently you have been waiting for his return. ... Next spring, and every spring afterwards, you [both] will return to life with the leaves and flowers of this sacred lilac hill, and the birds will greet you ... with their songs of love and life everlasting.")

One further major honor for Gould was initiated the year he died. The National Science Foundation was planning to sponsor construction of a new Antarctic Research and Supply Vessel, a sister ship to the recently completed *R/V Nathaniel B. Palmer* that would shuttle regularly between Punta Arenas, Chile, and Antarctica's Palmer Station. It was determined in 1995 that this great ice-strengthened vessel, to be built in a Louisiana shipyard, would be christened the *R/V Laurence M. Gould*. Gould thus became only the second American after whom a polar research vessel was named, following Palmer, the Connecticut-born mariner and seal-hunter who had reached the Antarctic Peninsula in 1820. The *R/V Laurence M. Gould*, designed for year-round Antarctic operations, functions as a multi-disciplinary research platform, built to carry a complement of twenty-six scientists. It was eventually put into the water in 1997.

***

There is a great deal to admire in the person and character of Laurence McKinley Gould; he lived a life both extraordinary and exemplary. With near unanimity, those who knew him esteemed him—indeed, discerned in him alongside his eloquence and his charisma a quality of "greatness," however that might be defined. The prime of his years, and a long prime that was, abounded in achievement, and the number of persons who acknowledged his having been a positive influence in their own lives is remarkable. The man tended to inspire, at every stage from youth to old age, both respect and a great deal of affection. His praises were sung by the great—former U.S. National Security Advisor McGeorge Bundy wrote, "Larry Gould is one of the wisest and most constructive counselors that one can have on any problem requiring judgment and excellence and choice among possibilities"—and also by the small—in 1955, when her father was a visiting professor for a term at Carleton, ten-year-old Martha Grout informed him, "what a good baby sitter you would be, if you did not have to be president!"

What were the ingredients of Gould's greatness? If it is so that his was "a life of vision and charm," what were the crucial elements of character or capability that went into the making of it? Or, to ask again the question posed by George Davis at Gould's Tucson memorial service: "How do you explain a Larry Gould?"

He certainly was blessed, foundationally, with a profusion of natural gifts— the agility of his mind, the soundness of his constitution, the warmth of his humor, the apparently instinctive reliability of his judgments about people—that would have tended to favor success in any of a great number of possible careers. Gould did not waste the potential inherent in such foundations but worked hard to develop in himself a rich variety of competencies. When asked in 1984 what he thought made for success in life, he responded, "Discipline—it's indispensable to any successful thing, isn't it? The other essential is integrity. And you can't be lazy. If you have those, and you have any gifts at all, well, there you go."

During the long "wintering over" in Antarctica in 1929, one of the Byrd Expedition's young aviation mechanics, Epaminondas J. "Pete" Demas, nine years Gould's junior, solicited advice from the older scientist regarding his life ambitions and how best to prepare himself educationally. Demas copied Gould's written response into his diary in full:

Little America, Antarctica. / July 2, 1929

My dear Pete,
    You are already abundantly supplied with the most precious qualifications for becoming a good student. You are SINCERE and you have great capacity for WORK. In the course of my teaching at the University of Michigan more than two thousand students have passed through my classes and I can about literally count on the fingers of one hand those who have possessed these two qualifications and have yet failed. You are probably familiar with Edison's definition of genius. He says that genius consists of about two percent natural gift and ninety eight percent hard work. A great French musician, Sarasate, was once complimented by a friend who referred to him as a genius, "What," he replied, "for thirty years I have practiced fourteen hours a day—and now you call me a genius."
    Try always, Pete, to get a larger more general view of things, don't let the details obscure the bigger picture. Don't learn anything that you do not understand. This is the most real criticism I can make. Pete, after watching you I have sometimes had the opinion that you were reciting things to me without exactly understanding what they meant. Make sure you understand. Don't be afraid to ask questions.
    I have great respect for your old Greek proverb, Pete, but I cannot say anything that will make you weep. Indeed I do not want to. I think more than criticism, what you need is a little inspiration and appreciation. I gave you Pupin's book because I knew you would get much inspiration from it. I advised you to read Franklin's *Autobiography* because it contains the soundest advice I know. Anyone who can behold himself with the same degree of self criticism as you do needs no advice from me. I have never had the courage and will power to do it so completely with myself. I like to remember these lines from a poem by Wordsworth:
        "True dignity abides with him alone
        Who in the quiet hour of patient thought
        Can still suspect and still revere himself"

and again these lines from Shakespeare:

"This above all to thine own self be true and it must follow as the night the day—thou canst [not] to any man be false."

The most priceless thing any man possesses is his self respect. You can never afford to lose that. You may insult somebody else and stand a chance of getting into trouble. But [if] you offend yourself there is no escape—you insure [sic] trouble.

And lastly, Pete, find out the thing you like best to do and let nothing stop you from doing it. I believe any man who possesses a soul makes his greatest mistake in life when he turns aside from the thing he likes best to do. I am surer you will never need worry about your bread nor a roof over your head if you do this. There is no satisfaction so great as that which comes when you realize that you have achieved something. No man can be genuinely happy without a major capacity for the happiness that comes from within one. You have been taught that the Kingdom of God is within you. So it is with all things that bring lasting peace and satisfaction. The kingdom of beauty, of life, of success, of all things that are real is within you.

I am and shall always be glad to be your friend, Pete. I shall always watch you with more than friendly interest and I hope and in fact I know that you will some day have the joy of achievement.

> Faithfully yours,
> Larry Gould.

"Find out the thing you like best to do and let nothing stop you from doing it." This was Gould's prescription for himself as well. "Life means adventure," he would often assert. Without adventure, he said in a 1962 letter, life "can be a drab and dull thing." Gould's grandniece, Neita Trollinger, who described "Uncle Laurence" as her hero, said that he was a man who "took life by the throat and shook it until nothing was left." Adventure, for Gould, did not necessarily mean such excitements as exploring near the South Pole. It meant rather, as he explained in a 1973 address at Alma College, "investing one's life in something that will outlast it. There is no greater adventure than that."

Gould followed the call of adventure as scientist, explorer, and educator. High among the things outlasting himself in which Gould meaningfully invested his life was Antarctic science and Antarctica itself, whose "magnificent desolation" and "simple beauty" penetrated his soul and made the continent what he several times called his "spiritual home." Ultimately, however, it was neither in science nor exploration but rather in education where Gould felt he had made his greatest contribution. There he invested himself especially, of course, in the betterment of two beloved institutions, Carleton College and the University of Arizona. Gould affirmed several times that "of all the things I have done in my life, teaching has been the most rewarding." "I know of no designation equal to that of professor," he once wrote. It is "the most distinguished status our culture affords." At Alma College he said, "I have had a varied and exciting life. I have been on every continent and have explored at the ends of the earth." But "of my several careers that by which I most want to be remembered is my identification with the liberal arts."

Gould's passion for liberal education and belief in the importance and value of the small liberal arts college permeated his statements for decades. He thought such institutions could be particularly effective in developing the kinds of leadership and "excellence" that society needed. (When speaking of the ends of liberal arts education at its best, he liked to quote Rousseau: "It matters little to me whether my pupil is intended for the army, the church, or the law. Before his parents chose a calling for him, nature called him to be a man. When he leaves me, I grant you he will be neither a magistrate, a soldier, nor a priest; he will be a man.") Gould knew that colleges of his ideal type must always be changing, adapting, and incorporating new ideas—when a college "ceases to change," he wrote, "it will cease to be worthy of its heritage"—but he advocated change that stayed within the framework of certain assumptions, with "roots in the very origins of Western civilization." They are, he wrote:

> that such ideas as justice, goodness, truth, beauty, and virtue have content transcending place and time—that they are not merely names which men and women of all societies are free to interpret without regard to universal principles. It means that man does not live in a universe which has only such values as he himself gives to it, but that he lives in a universe which has a voice to which he can listen, a beauty to which he can respond, a perfection to which he can aspire.

Gould suggested that the best image to represent the sort of institution to whose advancement he devoted the greatest part of his life was not that of an ivory tower but rather of a lighthouse—"apt to be on an island apart from the mainland, and yet it sheds its light onto all roundabout it. It is both a kind of ivory tower and a beacon for all to see."

George Davis said that Larry Gould showed us by example how to live. In that sense, the image Gould offered to symbolize the benefit to society of a good college may also aptly be applied to himself. His own life shines still as a beacon for all to see.

Larry Gould, 1981

Office of the president, 1958

BOOKS AND SELECTED ARTICLES

Bain, Richard C., and Judith H. Parris. *Convention Decisions and Voting Records. (Studies in Presidential Selection* series.) Washington: The Brookings Institution, 1973 (2nd ed.).

Balchen, Bernt. *Come North With Me: An Autobiography.* New York: E. P. Dutton & Co., 1958.

Bartlett, Robert A. *The Log of Bob Bartlett: The True Story of Forty Years of Seafaring and Exploration.* New York: G. P. Putnam's Sons, 1928.

Behrendt, John C. *Innocents on the Ice: A Memoir of Antarctic Exploration, 1957.* Niwot, CO: University Press of Colorado, 1998.

Berg, A. Scott. *Lindbergh.* New York: G. P. Putnam's Sons, 1998.

Bursey, Jack. *Antarctic Night: One Man's Story of 28,224 Hours at the Bottom of the World.* New York: Rand McNally & Company, 1957.

Butler, Susan. *East to the Dawn: The Life of Amelia Earhart.* New York: Da Capo Press, 1999.

Byrd, Richard Evelyn. *Little America: Aerial Exploration in the Antarctic; The Flight to the South Pole.* New York: G. P. Putnam's Sons, 1930.

Carleton College Department of Geology. *Carleton's Century of Geology: A Look at the Past, Present, and Future of Geology at Carleton College.* Northfield, MN: Carleton College, 1975.

Carter, Paul A. *Little America: Town at the End of the World.* New York: Columbia University Press, 1979.

Chaturvedi, Sanjay. *The Polar Regions: A Political Geography.* Chichester: John Wiley & Sons, 1996.

Dowie, Mark. *American Foundations: An Investigative History.* Cambridge, MA: MIT Press, 2001.

Fogg, G. E. *A History of Antarctic Science.* Cambridge: Cambridge University Press, 1992.

Giblin, James Cross. *The Rise and Fall of Senator Joe McCarthy.* New York: Clarion Books, 2009

Glines, Carroll V. *Bernt Balchen: Polar Aviator.* Washington: Smithsonian Institution Press, 1999.

Gould, Laurence M. *Cold: The Record of an Antarctic Sledge Journey.* New York: Brewer, Warren & Putnam, 1931.

Gould, Laurence M. Foreword, in Edwin H. Colbert, *Wandering Lands and Animals.* Boston: E.P. Dutton, 1973), xv-xvii

Gould, Laurence M. "The Geological Sledge Trip," Chapter 15 in Byrd, *Little America.* New York: G.P. Putnam's Sons, 1930.

Gould, Laurence M. "Memorial to William Herbert Hobbs (1864-1953)," *Geological Society of America Proceedings 1953,* May 1954, 131-139.

Gould, Laurence M. "Some Geographical Results of the Byrd Antarctic Expedition," *Geographical Review,* Vol. 21, No. 2 (April, 1931), 177-200.

Gould, Laurence M. "World Trip Reveals Revolution of Rising Expectations," *The Voice of the Carleton Alumni* 26, No. 6 (May 1961), 2-6.

Grant, Philip A., Jr. "The 1952 Minnesota Republican Primary and the Eisenhower Candidacy," *Presidential Studies Quarterly,* Vol. 9, No. 3 (Summer 1979), 311-315.

Griffith, Robert. *The Politics of Fear: Joseph R. McCarthy and the Senate.* Second edition. Amherst, MA: University of Massachusetts Press, 1987.

Headley, Leal A., and Merrill E. Jarchow. *Carleton: The First Century.* Northfield, MN: Carleton College, 1966.

Henrie, Samuel Nyal. *Uncommon Education: The History and Philosophy of Prescott College, 1950s Through 2006*. Tucson, AZ: Wheatmark, 2008.

Hobbs, William Herbert. *An Explorer-Scientist's Pilgrimage: The Autobiography of William Herbert Hobbs*. Ann Arbor, MI: J.W. Edwards, Inc., 1952

Hobbs, William Herbert. *Exploring About the North Pole of the Winds*. New York: G. P. Putnam's Sons, 1930.

Hobbs, William Herbert. *The First Greenland Expedition of the University of Michigan*. New York: American Geographical Society. Reprinted from *The Geographical Review* Vol. XVII, No. 1, January, 1927, 1-35.

Hobbs, William Herbert. "Laurence Gould—Antarctic Explorer," *The Michigan Alumnus*, 36 (1929-1930), 315-316.

Hoyt, Edwin P. *The Last Explorer: the Adventures of Admiral Byrd*. New York: The John Day Company, 1968.

James, George Wharton. *Arizona, The Wonderland*. Boston: The Page Company, 1917.

Jarchow, Merrill E. *Casey: An Autobiography*. Northfield, MN: Carleton College, 1993.

Jarchow, Merrill E. *Donald J. Cowling: Educator, Idealist, Humanitarian*. Northfield, MN: Carleton College, 1974.

Knapp, Robert H. and Joseph J. Greenbaum. *The Younger American Scholar: His Collegiate Origins*. Chicago: Chicago University Press, 1953

Knopf, Alfred A. *Portrait of a Publisher 1915-1963 Vol. I: Reminiscences and Reflections*. New York: The Typophiles, 1965.

Lane, Kit. *The History of Western Allegan County*. Dallas: Curtis Media Corp., 1988.

Larsen, Erling. *The Educations of Laird Bell: Notes Toward a Brief Biography*. Northfield, MN: Carleton College, 1967.

Livingstone, Richard. *Education for a World Adrift*. Cambridge: The University Press, 1943.

Lynfield, Geoffrey. "Laurence Gould. Explorer-Educator: From Boca to Antarctica," in *The Spanish River Papers* (Vol. XI, No. 3. Spring 1983) published by the Boca Raton Historical Society, Inc.

Macdonald, Dwight. *The Ford Foundation: The Men and the Millions*. New York: Reynal, 1956.

Macdonald, Dwight. *The Ford Foundation: The Men and the Millions*. New Brunswick: Transaction Publishers, 1989.

Margolis, John D. *Joseph Wood Krutch: A Writer's Life*. Knoxville, TN: University of Tennessee Press, 1980.

Milanovsky E. E. "Three Sessions of the International Geological Congress held in Russia and the USSR (1897, 1937, 1984)," *Episodes* 27, No. 2.

Munger, Frank J., and Richard F. Fenno, Jr. *National Politics and Federal Aid to Education*. Syracuse, NY: Syracuse University Press, 1962.

Neider, Charles. *Beyond Cape Horn: Travels in the Antarctic*. San Francisco: Sierra Club Books, 1980.

Nielsen, Waldemar A. *The Big Foundations*. New York: Columbia University Press, 1972.

Porter, David H., and Merrill E. Jarchow, eds. *Carleton Remembered 1909-1986*. Northfield, MN: Carleton College, 1987.

Priestley, R. E., and C. E. Tilley. "Geological Problems of Antarctica," in *Problems of Polar Research* [American Geographical Society Special Publication No. 7]. New York: American Geographical Society, 1928, 315-328.

Putnam, George Palmer. *Mariner of the North: The Life of Captain Bob Bartlett*. New York: Duell, Sloan and Pearce, 1947.

Putnam, George Palmer. "The Putnam Baffin Island Expedition," in *The Geographical Review* Vol. XVIII, No. 1, January, 1928, 1-27.

Putnam, George Palmer. *Wide Margins: A Publisher's Autobiography*. New York: Harcourt, Brace and Company, 1942.

Rich, Doris L. *Amelia Earhart: A Biography*. Washington and London: Smithsonian Institution Press, 1989.

Rodgers, Eugene. *Beyond the Barrier: The Story of Byrd's First Expedition to Antarctica*. Annapolis: Naval Institute Press, 1990.

Romig, Walter. *Michigan Place Names: The History of the Founding and the Naming of More Than Five Thousand Past and Present Michigan Communities*. Detroit: Wayne State University Press, 1986.

Rose, Lisle A. *Explorer: The Life of Richard E. Byrd*. Columbia, MO: University of Missouri Press, 2008.

Ross, Walter S. *The Last Hero: Charles A. Lindbergh*. New York: Harper & Row, 1964.

Rowland, Captain O. W. *A History of Van Buren County Michigan: A Narrative Account of its Historical Progress, its People, and its Principal Interests* . Chicago and New York: The Lewis Publishing Co., 1912.

Shaw, Wilfred. *The University of Michigan*. New York: Harcourt, Brace and Howe, 1920.

Siple, Paul. *90° South: The Story of the American South Pole Conquest*. New York: G. P. Putnam's Sons, 1959.

Siple, Paul. *A Boy Scout With Byrd*. New York: G. P. Putnam's Sons, 1931.

Streeter, Daniel W. *An Arctic Rodéo*. Garden City, NY: Garden City Publishing Company, Inc., 1929.

Swithinbank, Charles. *An Alien in Antarctica: Reflections upon Forty Years of Exploration and Research on the Frozen Continent*. Blacksburg, Virginia: The McDonald & Woodward Publishing Company, 1997.

Tebbel, John. *A History of Book Publishing in the United States, Vol III: The Golden Age between Two Wars 1920-1940*. New York: R. R. Bowker Company, 1978.

Vaughan, Norman D., with Cecil B. Murphey. *With Byrd at the Bottom of the World: The South Pole Expedition of 1928-1930*. Harrisburg, PA: Stackpole Books, 1990.

Wagoner, Jay J. *Arizona Territory 1863-1912: A Political History*. Tucson, AZ: University of Arizona Press, 1970.

Walton, D. W. H., ed. *Antarctic Science*. Cambridge: Cambridge University Press, 1987.

West, Wallace. *Paramount Newsreel Men With Admiral Byrd in Little America: The Story of Little America with Pictures by Paramount Newsreel Cameramen and the Story of their Adventures*. Racine, WI: Whitman Publishing Co., 1934.

Willcox, Hilton L. *Beneath a Wandering Star*. Edinburgh: The Pentland Press Ltd., 1986.

DIARIES, JOURNALS, AND LOGS

Gould, Laurence M. "The Journal of Record of the events connected with the life of Private & Sgt. Laurence M. Gould for the year 1918 with a brief introduction covering the events of the past six months." National Archives Gift Collection of Materials Relating to the Polar Regions, Papers of Laurence M. Gould, RG 401.59. (Cited as: LMG 1918 Diary)

Gould, Laurence M. Diary of the 1926 University of Michigan Greenland Expedition: "An Arctic Summer." National Archives Gift Collection of Materials Relating to the Polar Regions, Papers of Laurence M. Gould, RG 401.59. (Cited as: LMG 1926 Diary)

Gould, Laurence M. "Personal Record or Diary of L. M. Gould Geologist and Geographer Byrd Antarctic Expedition." (1928-1930) National Archives Gift Collection of Materials Relating to the Polar Regions, Papers of Laurence M. Gould, RG 401.59. (Cited as: LMG BAE I Diaries)

Gould, Laurence M. "Diary of XVIIIth International Geological Congress (Russia) July 1-September 4, 1937." National Archives Gift Collection of Materials Relating to the Polar Regions, Papers of Laurence M. Gould, RG 401.59. (Cited as: LMG 1937 Diary)

Gould, Laurence M. Pocket diary kept for part of 1941. Carleton College Archives, Laurence M. Gould Collection (61). (Cited as: LMG 1941 Diary)

Gould, Laurence M. Diary of his 1969 trip to Antarctica, with entries from November 19 to December 9. National Archives Gift Collection of Materials Relating to the Polar Regions, Papers of Laurence M. Gould, RG 401.59. (Cited as: LMG 1969 Diary)

Gould, Margaret R. Travel diary covering the Goulds' trip to South America, February to March, 1955. Carleton College Archives, Laurence M. Gould Collection (61). (Cited as: MRG 1955 Travel Diary.)

Gould, Margaret R. Travel diary covering the Goulds' trip around the world for the Ford Foundation, January to March, 1961. Carleton College Archives, Laurence M. Gould Collection (61). (Cited as: MRG 1961 Travel Diary)

Gould, Margaret R. Journal for 1965-1966. Carleton College Archives. Laurence M. Gould Collection (61). (Cited as: MRG 1965-1966 Journal.)

Harrison, Henry T. Diary of the first Byrd Antarctic Expedition, 1928-1930. National Archives Gift Collection of Materials Relating to the Polar Regions, Papers of Henry T. Harrison, RG 401.86. (Cited as: Harrison BAE I Diaries)

McCarthy, John R. "Rumor, Grub, Bowels, and I: A War Diary: An Unvarnished, Unromantic Record of an Unconvinced Soldier." (1918-1919) Undated typescript. Photocopy provided to the author in 1998 by Tucky McCarthy Walker. (Cited as: McCarthy, "Rumor, Grub, Bowels, and I.")

Section 590, Unit B, United States Army Ambulance Service. Company Log, 1917-1919, recorded by Gus Reynolds and Howard D. Tubbs, with introduction by Ross McLean. Photocopy provided to the author by Zoe Donnell, to whom it had been given by Tucky McCarthy Walker in 1996; original at the University of Michigan. (Cited as: Company Log of Section 590.)

RECORDED INTERVIEWS

Arnold, L. Clark and Ardith P. Interview by Zoe Donnell for the Carleton Oral History Program, October 13, 1995, in Northfield, Minnesota. Carleton College Archives. (Cited as: 1995 Arnolds/Donnell interview, CCA.)

Arnold, L. Clark and Ardith P. Interview by Eric Hillemann for the Carleton Oral History Program, December 6, 2002, in Tucson, Arizona. Carleton College Archives. (Cited as: 2002 Arnolds/ Hillemann interview, CCA.)

Bean, Atherton. Interview by Robert L. Gale for the Carleton Oral History Program, July 10, 1994, in Minneapolis, Minnesota. Carleton College Archives. (Cited as: 1994 Bean/Gale interview, CCA.)

Carver, Wayne M. Interview by Zoe Donnell for the Carleton Oral History Program, December 4, 1992, in Northfield, Minnesota. Carleton College Archives. (Cited as: 1992 Carver/Donnell interview, CCA.)

Caton, John R. Interview by Eric Hillemann for the Carleton Oral History Program, May 28-31, 1991, in Northfield, Minnesota. Carleton College Archives. (Cited as: 1991 Caton/Hillemann interview, CCA.)

Davis, George H. Interview by Eric Hillemann for the Carleton Oral History Program, December 5, 2000, in Tucson, Arizona. Carleton College Archives. (Cited as: 2002 Davis/Hillemann interview, CCA.)

Gale, Robert L. Interview by Barbara Clark for the Carleton Oral History Program, June 18, 1993 and May 14, 1994. Carleton College Archives. (Cited as: 1993-1994 Gale/Clark interview, CCA.)

Gilman, Richard C. Interview by Richard Crouter for the Carleton Oral History Program, June 24, 1993, in Pasadena, California. Carleton College Archives. (Cited as: 1993 Gilman/Crouter interview, CCA.)

Gilman, Richard C. Interview by Eric Hillemann for the Carleton Oral History Program, June 16, 2006, in Northfield, Minnesota. Carleton College Archives. (Cited as: 2006 Gilman/ Hillemann interview, CCA.)

Gould, Laurence M. Interview by Charles T. Morrissey for the Ford Foundation Oral History Project, January 25-26, 1973, in Tucson, Arizona. Transcript University of Arizona Geosciences Department, Antevs Library. (Cited as: 1973 Gould/Morrissey interview, UAAL.)

Gould, Laurence M. Interview by Charles Neider, early February 1978. Published in Neider, Beyond Cape Horn. (Cited as: 1978 Gould/Neider interview, transcript in Neider, Beyond Cape Horn.)

Gould, Laurence M. Interview by Peter J. Anderson, March 16-17, 1981, in Tucson, Arizona. Transcript The Ohio State University Archives, Papers of Peter J. Anderson, RG 56.11. (Cited as: 1981 Gould/Peter J. Anderson interview, OSUA-AP.)

Gould, Laurence M. Interview by E. Vernice Anderson for the National Science Board Oral History Project, November 13, 1981, in Washington DC. Transcript copy Carleton College Archives, Laurence M. Gould Collection (61). (Cited as: 1981 Gould/E. Vernice Anderson interview, CCA-GP.)

Hansen, Eleanor H. Interview by Joan Reitz for the Carleton Oral History Program, August 23, 1994, in Northfield, Minnesota. Carleton College Archives. (Cited as: 1994 Hansen/Reitz interview, CCA.)

Jarchow, Merrill E. Interview by Tom Jeglosky for the Carleton Oral History Program, October 8, 1992, in Northfield, Minnesota. Carleton College Archives. (Cited as: 1992 Jarchow/Jeglosky interview, CCA.)

Maitland, David J. Interview by Joan Reitz for the Carleton Oral History Program, May 22, 1993, in Northfield, Minnesota. Carleton College Archives. (Cited as: 1993 Maitland/Reitz interview, CCA.)

Nason, John W. Interview by Chuck Donnell for the Carleton Oral History Program, August 12, 1992, in Keene, New York. Carleton College Archives. (Cited as: 1992 Nason/Donnell interview, CCA.)

Obaid, Dorothy P. Interview by Zoe Donnell for the Carleton Oral History Program, March 10, 1995, in Northfield, Minnesota. Carleton College Archives. (Cited as: 1995 Obaid/Donnell interview, CCA.)

Thurnblad, Jack M. Interview with Joan Reitz for the Carleton Oral History Program, October 15, 1992, in Northfield, Minnesota. Carleton College Archives. (Cited as: 1992 Thurnblad/Reitz interview, CCA.)

Tinnin, Alvis L. Interview by Robert L. Gale for the Carleton Oral History Program, March 20, 1994, in Green Valley, Arizona. Carleton College Archives. (Cited as: 1994 Tinnin/Gale interview, CCA.)

Vaughan, Norman D. Interview by Karen Nichols Brewster for the Byrd Polar Research Institute's Polar Explorers and Scientists Oral History Project, April 30, 2001, in Anchorage, Alaska. The Ohio State University Archives, Byrd Polar Research Archival Program, Polar Oral History Program; transcript available at https://kb.osu.edu/dspace/handle/1811/6062. (Cited as: 2001 Vaughan/Brewster interview, OSUA.) Wright, Frank I. Interview by Charlotte Smith for the Carleton Oral History Program, December 30, 1992, in Northfield, Minnesota. Carleton College Archives. (Cited as: 1992 Wright/Smith interview, CCA.)

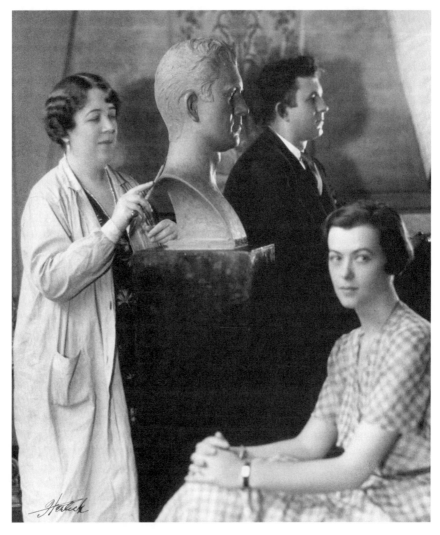

The Antarctic celebrity is immortalized, 1931.

ABBREVIATIONS

BAE I	First Byrd Antarctic Expedition (1928-1930)
BHL	Bentley Historical Library, University of Michigan
CCA	Carleton College Archives
CCA-GC	Carleton College Archives—Laurence M. Gould Collection
DJC	Donald J. Cowling
JRH	Jean Rice Hoppin
LMG	Laurence McKinley Gould
MRG	Margaret Rice Gould
NA	National Archives
NA-GP	National Archives—Laurence M. Gould Papers
NA-HP	National Archives—Henry T. Harrison Papers
OSUA	The Ohio State University Archives
OSUA-AP	The Ohio State University Archives—Peter J. Anderson Papers
OSUA-BP	The Ohio State University Archives—Richard E. Byrd Papers
REB	Richard Evelyn Byrd
UAAL	University of Arizona Department of Geosciences, Antevs Library

PROLOGUE — "WHAT WE WANT IS A PARAGON"

1 **1961 feature**—Chesly Manly, "Carleton Called 'Little Harvard,'" *Chicago Daily Tribune*, February 25, 1961.

2 **first joint meeting**—Referenced in Ralph Henry to Louis Headley, 26 July 1944, CCA.

3 **able man with ambitions**—See Laird Bell to LMG, 16 May 1945, CCA.

3 **"I simply cannot"**—Erling Larsen, *The Educations of Laird Bell, 151.*

3 **Bell's sense of responsibility**—See for instance Bell's August 23, 1944, letter to President James B. Conant of Harvard, where he writes: "I had fought off the chairmanship since my father's death but when Dr. Cowling's retirement became imminent I felt that our family had so large a stake in the College that I had to take the responsibility of the chairmanship, and of securing a successor." Laird Bell to James Conant, 23 August 1944, CCA.

3 **Cowling wrote Bell … "approximately three million."**—DJC to Laird Bell, 22 September 1943, CCA.

4 **Bell promised to give**—Bell's promise to consider the matter in the new year was referenced in Laird Bell to Horace Irvine, 3 January 1944, CCA.

4 **"might prove … "even radical."**—Ibid.

4 **"not merely a man" … "uncertain years ahead."**—Ibid.

5 **At the same meeting**—Minutes of the Carleton College Board of Trustees for 28 January 1944, CCA.

5 **references in a later letter**—Ralph Henry to Louis Headley, 26 July 1944, CCA.

5 **expecting that he would be free**—See for instance, LMG to DJC, 29 February 1944, CCA.

5 **Correspondence from April and May**—DJC to Chancellor Frederick M. Hunter, 27 April 1944, and DJC to LMG, 25 May 1944—both CCA.

5   **being pressed … "ever hope to achieve."**—LMG to DJC, 8 June 1944, CCA.

5   **During that first week … "looking the situation over."**—LMG to DJC, 8 June 1944 and 21 June 1944, CCA.

6   **"without first discussing"**—LMG to DJC, 21 June 1944, CCA.

6   **On July 7**—DJC to Hans Weigert, 8 July 1944, CCA.

6   **Cowling may have been quietly**—As early as the previous summer, Headley wrote Bell that "I know that Dr. Cowling has a suggestion as to his successor." (Louis Headley to Laird Bell, 14 July 1943, CCA.) That this suggestion may have been Gould is inferable from the several expressions of satisfaction voiced by Cowling upon Gould's eventual selection and by evidence such as Charles A. Culver's reference in a letter to Gould of "the fact that the retiring president strongly favored your selection." (Charles A. Culver to LMG, 29 May 1945, CCA.) Alternatively, Cowling's first suggestion as to his successor may have been his former assistant at Carleton, who had gone on to the presidency of Knox College, H. Carter Davidson. (See Bell to Headley, 10 September 1944, CCA.) It is clear, however, that Cowling was careful never to intrude his suggestions upon the trustee committee without express invitation to do so. (See Headley to Bell, 2 September 1944, CCA.)

6   **"very hot scuttlebutt" … be looked into.**—Dexter Lufkin to Malcolm B. McDonald, 11 July 1944, CCA.

6   **"I should think we ought"**—Laird Bell to Louis Headley, 14 July 1944, CCA.

6   **McDonald agreed … Minneapolis people**—Malcolm B. McDonald to Laird Bell, 17 July 1944, CCA.

6   **Accordingly, on the 19th**—Laird Bell to LMG, 19 July 1944, CCA.

6   **Recalling that … his immediate field**—Laird Bell to Louis Headley, 17 July 1944, CCA.

6   **Henry then provided … "though he is available."**—Ralph Henry to Louis Headley, 26 July 1944, CCA.

7   **Bell's reaction was**—Laird Bell to Louis Headley, 2 August 1944, CCA.

7   **Headley thought he sensed**—Louis Headley to Laird Bell, 28 July 1944, CCA.

7   **"We need as president"**—Louis Headley to A. Calvert Smith, 7 July 1944, CCA.

8   **in Chicago on the 18th**—Laird Bell to Horace Irvine, 19 September 1944, CCA.

8   **"general sense" of a conclave … "counsel of wisdom"**—"Memorandum" dated 12 October 1944, CCA.

9   **"We started with"**—Bell's letter quoted in Larsen, *The Educations of Laird Bell*, 152.

9   **Helpful evaluations**—John W. Nason to Malcolm B. McDonald, 4 October 1944; Nason to Laird Bell, 23 November 1944—both CCA.

9   **suggestion was made … Nason's attitude.**—Luther A. Weigle (Dean, Yale University Divinity School) to Louis Headley, 2 September 1944; Headley to Laird Bell, 18 October 1944—both CCA.

9   **almost regular succession of letters**—Elizabeth Oliver Hosick to Laird Bell, 24 October 1944; Nelson Vance Russell to Bell, 4 November 1944; Keith Clark to Bell, 14 November 1944; Peggy Porter Muirhead to Bell, 15 November 1944; Olin S. Pettingill to Bell, 20 November 1944; Azariah T. Lincoln to Bell, 21 November 1944—all CCA.

9n   **"If I were to leave"**—John W. Nason to Louis Headley, 8 March 1945, CCA.

10   **"it looks a little"**—Laird Bell to trustee committee members, 24 November 1944, CCA.

10   **"particularly in view"**—Laird Bell to Louis Headley, 25 November, 1944, CCA.

10   **"It would be unwise"**—Charles A. Culver to Laird Bell, 25 November 1944, CCA. It may be that Culver made a bit of a tactical error, however, in this letter to Democrat Laird Bell, when he noted parenthetically that he considered that month's reelection of FDR to have been "a long step in the direction of national socialism."

10   **"I am not sure what kind"**—Laird Bell to John W. Nason, 30 November 1944, CCA.

10   **"painfully aware"**—Laird Bell to Katharine E. McBride, 30 November 1944, CCA.

10 **"reduced to approximately"** ... **"in the east."**—Curvin H. Gingrich to Laird Bell, 4 December 1944, CCA.

10 **distressed to hear**—Laird Bell to Curvin H. Gingrich, 2 December 1944; Gingrich to Bell, 4 December 1944; and Horace Irvine to Bell, 7 December 1944—all CCA. False rumor was perhaps an inevitable accompaniment of such a search. In his letter of the 4th, Gingrich reports that it was being said on campus just then that a Stanford history professor was to be Carleton's next president.

10 **Letters urging**—W. R. Stafford to Laird Bell, 1 December 1944; John Sirjamaki to Bell, 2 December 1944; Carl Eklund to Bell, 7 December 1944; Victor Church to Bell, 14 December 1944; 19 December 1944, Hans Weigert to Bell—all CCA.

11 **On the 11th ... "to the Board of Trustees."**—LMG to Laird Bell, 11 December 1944, enclosing letter of Robert F. Leach to LMG, 27 November 1944, CCA. Bell's response was to acknowledge having received "quite a number of letters from alumni and others in your behalf" and to assure Gould that his answer to the one that embarrassed him by writing him directly was "quite correct." (Bell to LMG, 13 December 1944, CCA.)

11 **"president hunting"**—Laird Bell to Louis Headley, 2 January 1945, CCA.

11 **Attributing Gould's success ... "days if possible."**—George Miksch Sutton to Laird Bell, 9 January 1945, CCA.

11 **"The longer I turn"**—Charles A. Culver to Louis Headley, 9 January 1945, CCA.

11 **He was most impressed**—Laird Bell to Curvin H. Gingrich, 20 January 1945, CCA.

12 **interest in arranging**—Laird Bell to LMG, 22 January 1945 and 31 January 1945—both CCA.

12 **"very difficult to get ahead."**—Laird Bell to DJC, 31 January 1945, CCA.

12 **The faculty advisory ... "proper evaluation."**—Curvin H. Gingrich to Laird Bell, 1 February 1945, CCA.

12 **Louis Headley visited**—Louis Headley to Laird Bell, 13 February 1945, CCA.

12 **requested to compare**—Robert W. McEwan to Louis Headley, 30 March 1945. The responses which follow are taken from Curvin H. Gingrich to Laird Bell, 31 March 1945; David Bryn-Jones to Bell, 6 April 1945; Ralph Henry to Headley, 31 March 1945; Neil S. Dungay to Bell, 31 March 1945; and Robert W. McEwan to Bell, 30 March 1945—all CCA.

13 **"terrifying responsibility"**—quoted in Larsen, *The Educations of Laird Bell*, 153.

13 **"I am not happy"**—Ibid.

13 **Headley regretted ... "missed some material."**—Louis Headley to Laird Bell, 31 March 1945, CCA.

14 **A few days later, Bell ... "he will leave."**—Laird Bell to Louis Headley, 4 April 1945, CCA.

14 **"I'd like another year"**—quoted in Larsen, *The Educations of Laird Bell*, 154.

14 **Bewkes wrote**—Eugene G. Bewkes to Laird Bell, 3 April 1945, CCA.

14 **"a genuine contribution"**—Bell's compliment was relayed by Blayney to Peg Gould. (Lindsey Blayney to MRG, 6 June 1945, CCA.)

14 **[Blayney] began by observing ... all of the above heads.**—Lindsey Blayney to Laird Bell, 3 April 1945, CCA.

15 **"profoundly spiritually-minded" ... "unquestionably is."**—Ibid.

15 **"he enjoys far wider" ... "have in the hand."**—Ibid.

16 **[Fath] had changed his mind ... to Bell the next day.**—Malcolm McDonald to Laird Bell, 13 April 1945, enclosing copy of E. A. Fath to McDonald, 12 April 1945, CCA.

16 **Meanwhile, Louis Headley**—Louis Headley to the Rev. Wallace W. Robbins, 9 April 1945; Headley to Laird Bell, 11 April 1945; Headley to Bell, 17 April 1945—all CCA.

16 **"the recurring proposition" ... "just the right man."**—Louis Headley to Laird Bell, 17 April 1945, CCA.

16   **"we have no candidate"** ... **"have to say."**—Thomas C. McQueen to Louis Headley, 19 April 1945, CCA.

17   **"would be a serious handicap"**—Louis Headley to Thomas C. McQueen, 21 April 1945, CCA.

17   **again gone east**—Louis Headley to Laird Bell, 20 April 1945; Headley to Thomas C. McQueen, 21 April 1945—both CCA.

17   **feeling "sunk"**—Louis Headley to Laird Bell, 20 April 1945, CCA.

17   **"Carleton obligations cleaned up"**—Laird Bell to DJC, 24 April 1945, CCA.

17   **"this means either"**—Louis Headley to Laird Bell, 20 April 1945, CCA.

17   **"I don't believe we'll find"**—Laird Bell to Louis Headley, 24 April 1945, CCA.

18   **Russell April 26**—Louis Headley to Thomas C. McQueen, 21 April 1945, CCA.

18   **Millis on May 5 ... evening of the 9th**—Louis Headley to John S. Millis, 7 May 1945, CCA.

18   **accepted upon being assured**—LMG to Laird Bell, 21 May 1945, CCA.

18   **"This Board cannot permit"**—Minutes of the Carleton College Board of Trustees for 15 June 1962, CCA.

CHAPTER 1 — LAUNCHED: WHITHER BOUND?

21   **Forebears on both**—For the genealogical information of this and succeeding paragraphs I am indebted to the work of Gould family historians Marcia J. Tripp and Trudy Gould, in the form of genealogical sketches published in Lane, *The History of Western Allegan County* (1988), and as recorded on pedigree charts and family group records filed by Tripp with the Genealogical Library of the Church of Jesus Christ of Latter-day Saints in Salt Lake City, copies of which were graciously provided to me by family member Elizabeth A. Wagar, MD.

21   **Each of Gould's**—LMG's parents were Herbert Adelbert Gould, b. 5 September 1871, Cheshire Township, Allegan County, Michigan, and Anna Eliza Updike, b. 17 January 1873, Casco Township, Allegan County, Michigan. Paternal grandparents were William H. Gould, b. 16 February 1834, Sussex County, New Jersey, and Henrietta Fisher, b. 12 November 1848, Cooper, Kalamazoo County, Michigan. Maternal grandparents were Albert DeWitt Updike, b. 22 October 1846, Otsego, Allegan County, Michigan, and Sarah Ann Peck, b. 7 November 1852, Woodstock, Oxford, Ontario, Canada.

21   **Seven great-grandparents**—Great-grandfather Robert Gould is believed to have died between 1850 and 1860, probably in Pennsylvania. LMG's great-great grandparents who lived in Michigan were Gilbert and Laney Updike and Abram and Aseneth J. Loveless.

21   **would remarry twice**—Henrietta Fisher Gould m. (2) 14 September 1878, Henry Warfield; and (3) 8 June 1886, Henry Overhiser. Henrietta was William Gould's second wife; he m. (1) 21 July 1855, in Steuben County, Indiana, Martha F. Melendy.

21   **"unbearably bossy."**—This characterization, and all subsequent family information and anecdote through the end of this section of text (the next seven paragraphs) is all, except as noted below, to be found in the several genealogical sketches by Marcia J. Tripp and Trudy Gould in Lane, *The History of Western Allegan County.*

22   **some five miles north of South Haven.**—The Updike property, known after it passed out of the family as "The Hilltop," later became a commercial resort.

22   **Sarah's family had come**—LMG's grandmother, Sarah Ann Peck, was the daughter of Ephraim and Mary (Whitmore) Peck, who settled near Bangor, Van Buren County, Michigan, about 1859-60.

22   **They were married**—Sarah Updike continued to care for her in-laws during their lifetimes, with the farm, upon which Albert built his own cider mill and Sarah tended the garden, eventually becoming their own. Eliza Updike d. 15 August 1884; Garret Updike d. 10 May 1888.

22 **These Updike grandparents were important**—1995 Arnolds/Donnell interview, CCA; also e-mail communications to the author from Elizabeth A. Wagar, granddaughter of LMG's sister, Cecile, 1998.

23 **family of seven children**—The entire family was Ralph Albert, b. 27 October 1892; Cecile Fern, b. 29 October 1894; Laurence McKinley, b. 22 August 1896; Neita Hazel, b. 25 March 1898; Betty Alice, b. 16 August 1901; Helen Marie, b. 10 June 1908; and Bonnie Anne, b. 14 March 1911.

23 **"always cherished the illusion"**—LMG to REB, 31 December 1954, NA-GP.

23 **"I disliked it heartily"**—LMG to William L. McKnight, 10 November 1955, CCA.

23 **Herb Gould avoided … "let them rest."**—E-mail to the author from Elizabeth A. Wagar, September 8, 1998. The same story is told by Marcia J. Tripp in her sketch of LMG in Lane, *The History of Western Allegan County*.

23 **Another relative reports**—E-mail to the author from Neita Trollinger, granddaughter of LMG's sister, Neita, 10 January 2001.

23 **kind of boy of whom**—LMG, "Ten Years From Now," Carleton College commencement address, 6 June 1955, unpublished transcript, CCA.

24 **Irvington in commemoration … Varnum Dilley**—Romig, *Michigan Place Names*, 310.

24 **In 1912 Lacota**—Rowland, *A History of Van Buren County Michigan*, 500.

24 **Goulds apparently associated**—The obituary for Anna E. Gould (*South Haven Daily Tribune*, August 11, 1950) mentions her membership in Lacota's Methodist church.

24 **"Quite distinctly we remember"**—"Gould Rescued by Comdr. Byrd," *South Haven Daily Tribune*, March 20, 1929.

24 **On several occasions later**—For example, LMG to S. Spencer Scott, 30 December 1953; LMG to Arlie Russell, 15 September 1958—both CCA. Also, *St. Paul Pioneer Press* feature, June 24, 1962.

24 **Later he is known**—Handwritten reminiscence of Phyllis Simpson Vydareny, October 1, 1988, CCA.

25 **Larry later recounted**—Gould's telling of this story of his father's attempting to teach him to shoot was recalled in a 1995 interview with L. Clark Arnold. (1995 Arnolds/Donnell interview, CCA.)

25 **When he entered … new high school.**—Rowland, *A History of Van Buren County Michigan*, 169.

25 **Gould rather wished**—"When he was home the last time," his mother told a journalist in 1929 while Gould was temporarily "lost" in Antarctica, "he censured me because I wouldn't allow him to play football when he was in school. At that time, I was afraid he might be seriously hurt, but perhaps it would have been just as well for him to have broken his neck at football as to have been lost down there." ("Mother Tells Gould's Last Visit at Home," *South Haven Daily Tribune*, March 19, 1929.)

25 **In his Latin teacher**—In the mid-1940s, while visiting family in Michigan, Gould called on Eva Carnes in South Haven and was "immensely pleased and honored" to find over her mantelpiece pictures of himself and the prominent theologian Reinhold Niebuhr, who Carnes recalled "with fondness and affection … as her two particular boys." In subsequent correspondence with Niebuhr, Gould wrote that "we have one tie in common and that is we both owe a great deal to [this] great teacher of Latin." (LMG to Reinhold Niebuhr, 26 July 1948 and 9 February 1950, CCA.)

25 **"he might have carried away"**—"Gould Rescued by Comdr. Byrd," *South Haven Daily Tribune*, March 20, 1929.

25 **His message, as reported**—*South Haven Daily Tribune*, June 20, 1914.

26 **Gould's ambition now**—Gould's two-year stint teaching school in Boca Raton is the subject of a useful article by Geoffrey Lynfield, "Laurence Gould. Explorer-Educator: From Boca to Antarctica," published by the Boca Raton Historical Society, Inc., in *The Spanish*

River Papers XI, No. 3, (Spring 1983). Except where indicated below, this is the (unpaginated) source for all information presented here about Gould's time in Boca Raton.

26 Gould scored high—In a 1978 interview, Gould told Charles Neider: "I had never had any exposure to education as such. I bought two books on elementary education. I boned up on them and I took the teachers' examination and I passed with higher grades than anybody else in Florida except a man with a Masters of Arts from Columbia Teachers College. That just shows you the status of education in Florida in 1914." (1978 Gould/Neider interview, from transcript in Neider, *Beyond Cape Horn*, 326.)

26 story passed along by a grandniece—E-mail to the author from Elizabeth A. Wagar, September 8, 1998.

27 Many of Gould's ... "and sometimes Y."—1981 Gould/Peter J. Anderson interview, OSUA-AP.

27 Another anecdote ... matter in private.—E-mail to the author from L. Clark Arnold, December 16, 2002.

27 "These two years"—Quoted in Lynfield, "Laurence Gould" (unpaginated).

28 traditional business and pleasures—An historian of the University of Michigan wrote in 1920: "During the years just preceding the entrance of the United States there was probably no part of the world as little touched by the actualities overseas as the mid-western portion of the United States." (Shaw, *The University of Michigan*, 306.)

28 3,254 undergraduate students—*Catalogue of the University of Michigan, 1916-1917*, Ann Arbor, MI: University of Michigan, 1917, 704.

28 three credits of—A transcript of Gould's academic record at Michigan is available through the university's Office of the Registrar. A certified copy was issued to the author July 29, 2002.

28 intent of emulating—Gould often mentioned his original aim of studying law. See, for instance, LMG to Arlie Russell, 15 September 1958, CCA.

28 Thus it was—Gould, "Memorial to William Herbert Hobbs," 134.

28 required headwear ... "Sleepy Hollow."—Shaw, *The University of Michigan*, 184.

28 Phylon—Information about Phylon, including its original constitution, may be found in the Records of Pi Kappa Alpha (Beta Tau Chapter) at the University of Michigan's Bentley Historical Library (hereafter BHL). That Gould's association with the group dates from his first year at Michigan is clear from his letter of January 2, 1919, addressed to "Andy" (probably Phylon president Einer B. Anderson), located in Box 1 of these records.

29 "The outbreak of war"—Introduction by Ross McLean, former instructor in the History Department at the University of Michigan, to the Company Log of Section 590, Unit B, United States Army Ambulance Service (hereafter cited simply as "Company Log." A copy of this document, a crucial source of information for the following chapter, was provided to the author by Tucky McCarthy Walker; the original is at the University of Michigan.

29 Some three hundred ... "University to enlist."—Shaw, *The University of Michigan*, 308.

29 On May 8—McLean, Introduction to Company Log of Section 590.

30 article in the Michigan Daily—McLean, in his Introduction to the Company Log, wrote: "On Saturday, May 12th, there appeared in the *Michigan Daily* an article inserted by the Intelligence Bureau to the effect that the Government proposed to organize an Army Ambulance Service to be recruited very largely from the colleges and universities of the nation, which should 'carry on' the work begun with the French army by the American Field Service. The men were to enlist in the Enlisted Reserve Corps, Medical Department, U. S. A. for the duration of the war.

30 It was widely believed—The motivating factor of this belief in the early opportunity for service in France—which proved to be entirely mistaken (Gould did not sail for Europe until nearly a year after enlistment)—is mentioned both by McLean in his introduction to the Company Log of Section 590 and by LMG in the introductory paragraph to his diary of military service (LMG 1918 Diary, NA-GP).

30   **Within eight days ... formed at Ann Arbor.**—McLean, Introduction to Company Log.

30   **In late May ... "university town." [end of chapter]**—Ibid. McLean's introduction is the source for all information and quotes for the rest of the chapter, excepting the report of Gould's grades, from his university transcript.

CHAPTER 2 — DOUGHBOY

31   **Almost the first thing**—LMG 1918 Diary, introduction.

31   **By noon ... after 10 p.m.**—McLean, Introduction to Company Log.

31   **Early morning found ... making roads**—LMG 1918 Diary, introduction; Company Log, 23-25 June 1917.

32   **Six months after ... "poorly managed."**—LMG 1918 Diary, introduction.

32   **The company was increased**—New men joined the section and others were reassigned to other service nearly every month, and so the original all-Michigan character of the unit became increasingly diluted over time. The company's first non-com officers, all from the men enlisted at Ann Arbor, were Sgt. 1Cl. Glenn M. Coulter, Sgt. Earl E. Pardee, and Corporals Harry R. Louis and George W. Williams. See McLean, Introduction to Company Log,

32   **Days were filled**—LMG 1918 Diary, introduction; Company Log, 28 July 1917 and other entries.

32   **At the end of August ... orders to sail.**—LMG 1918 Diary, introduction; Company Log, 4 September 1917.

32   **On September 1, Gould**—Company Log, 1 September 1917.

32   **When it became evident**—LMG 1918 Diary, introduction.

32   **"Battle of Guths Station" ... materials at hand.**—Company Log, 31 October 1917, and "November" entry. (Though "eighteen-hundred-man" figure from LMG 1918 Diary, introduction.)

32   **Gould and three other ... on December 8.**—LMG 1918 Diary, introduction.

32   **The shift involved**—Company Log, 8 December 1917.

32   **Though many ... comes to a close.**—LMG 1918 Diary, introduction.

34   **Late on New Year's ... under quarantine.**—Company Log, 2-3 January 1918; LMG 1918 Dairy, 2 January 1918.

34   **formed a section forum**—Company Log, 10 January 1918.

34   **new daily schedule**—Company Log, 7 January 1918; LMG 1918 Diary, 7 January 1918.

34   **On Saturdays ... appreciate jazz.**—LMG 1918 Diary, 9-27 January 1918.

34   **Many weeks passed ... 4th of March.**—Ibid., 14 January to 4 March 1918.

34   **On February 10 ... should he be called.**—Ibid., entry for 1-11 February 1918.

34   **new hope that ... "uneasy and restless."**—Ibid., entries for 12-14 February and 15 February 1918.

34   **Some from the section**—Ibid., entry for 16-19 February 1918.

35   **"I do not know just"**—Ibid., 15 February 1918.

35   **"most joyous" ... their section, separately.**—Ibid., entry for 20-21 February 1918.

35   **only "tentative." ... heavy artillery.**—Ibid., entry for 22-25 February 1918.

35   **On the last day ... "granted to me soon."**—Ibid., entry for 26-28 February 1918.

35   **In mid-March 175 men**—Ibid., 18 March 1918.

35   **Gould had applied ... "drive an ambulance."**—Ibid., 4 March 1918.

35   **Instead, he and three**—Ibid., entry for 10-18 March 1918.

35   **promoted to sergeant**—Company Log, 21 March 1918.

35   **By the end of ... "very good men."**—Ibid., 28 March 1918.

35   **Three men added**—Ibid., entries for April 1918.

35   **On the 1st of April**—Ibid., 26 April 1918.

36   **Sergeant Gould drilled ... new men.**—LMG 1918 Diary, 4 May 1918.

36   **brought back up ... William H. Woolverton.**—Company Log, entry for 12-13 June 1918.

36   **"was able to make arrangements"**—Hobbs, "Laurence Gould—Antarctic Explorer," 315.

36   **telegram authorizing**—LMG 1918 Diary, 27 May 1918.

36   **At long last ... ship left harbor.**—Ibid., 13 June 1918.

36   **After a day ... to Gibraltar.**—Ibid., entries for 15 June to 23 June 1918.

36   **"glad to see us,"**—Ibid., 23 June 1918.

36   **A day later ... five fierce escorts.**—Ibid., 24 June and 26 June 1918.

36   **The next day**—Company Log, 27 June 1918.

36   **"It seemed as though"**—LMG 1918 Diary, 27 June 1918.

37   **They were given ... and pillows.**—Company Log, 27 June 1918.

37   **After a day ... squad tents.**—LMG 1918 Diary, entries for 28 June and 29 June 1918.

37   **interest in photography**—On August 20, 1918, Pvt. McCarthy wrote in his journal, "'Larry' (the Serg.) is a good fellow in spite of being an optimist. We call him Burton Holmes because he runs around all over taking pictures." (McCarthy, "Rumor, Grub, Bowels and I" (undated typescript), entry for 20 August.)

37   **carrying the Italian flag**—LMG 1918 Diary, 4 July 1918.

37   **All this while ... "last night in Genoa."**—Company Log, entries for 19 August to 22 August 1918; LMG 1918 Diary, entries for 19 August to 22 August 1918.

37   **Three nights later ... August 27**—Ibid., entries for 25 August to 27 August 1918.

37   **Section 590 had been ... north to Souilly**—Ibid., entries for 5 September to 15 September 1918.

38   **overflown by a German plane**—LMG 1918 Diary, 16 September 1918.

38   **"gaunt looking"**—Ibid., 18 September 1918.

38   **"Larry Gould rode"**—McCarthy, "Rumor, Grub, Bowels and I," entry for 22 September 1918.

38   **Finally, on the night ... heaviest barrage**—Company Log, entries for 25 September and 26 September 1918.

38   **"our busy time"**—Ibid., entry for 26 September-1 October 1918.

38   **climbed onto the right mudguard**—LMG 1918 Diary, 27 September 1918.

38   **Soon, Section 590 ... at Fromerville.**—Company Log, entry for 26 September-1 October 1918.

39   **"The place where we"**—LMG 1918 Diary, 2 October 1918.

39   **During the same ... "cases were dead."**—McCarthy, "Rumor, Grub, Bowels and I." entry for "October 1 or 2." 1918.

39   **"We oozed into town"**—Ibid.

40   **"always ailing" ... Yeckel's place.**—Ibid., 4 October 1918.

40   **"the night is unusual"**—LMG 1918 Diary, entry for 3 October to 8 October 1918.

40   **One night ... had been sleeping.**—Company Log, 4 October and 5 October 1918.

40   **Gould was not present**—LMG 1918 Diary, entry for 3 October to 8 October 1918.

40   **"The road was mighty rough"**—Ibid.

40   **On the 9th ... above their heads.**—Ibid., 9 October 1918.

40   **The Section stayed ... returned to Italy.**—Ibid., 12 October 1918.

40   **By the 14th ... first fatal losses.**—Ibid, 14 October 1918; Company Log, 14 October

1918. The company would suffer a third death after the armistice, when on Feb. 14, 1919 Pvt. Sisok H. Darbinian died of pneumonia in Germany. (Company Log, entries for February 1919 and Log "dedication.")

40 **Regarding being relieved**—McCarthy, "Rumor, Grub, Bowels and I," entry for 15 October 1918.

41 **From then until**—See entries of mid-October to mid-November 1918 in both the Company Log and LMG 1918 Diary.

41 **November 7 … no excitement!**—Company Log, 7 November 1918; LMG 1918 Diary, 7 November 1918.

41 **Section 590's work … city of Trier**—Various November and December entries in both the Company Log and Gould's diary, especially LMG 1918 Diary, 19 December 1918. The phrase "proper command" from LMG to "Andy" [probably Einer B. Anderson] 2 January 1919, Box 1, Records of Pi Kappa Alpha, Beta Tau Chapter, University of Michigan, BHL.

41 **"adjutant, stenographer"**—Company Log, 8 December 1918. Readers who were undergraduates at Carleton College in the years that Gould was its distinguished and irreproachable president will be shocked, *shocked*, by the December 28 entry in the journal of Private McCarthy: "The night after Christmas three of us tried to go to the opera but found the theatre sold out. On the way home we were picked up by M.P.'s for being down town without a pass. . . . The next day the Looie [Lt. Woolverton] swiped some pass blanks and Larry forged the surgeon general's name on them so all 590 became possessors of phoney passes that gave us a right to be 'anywhere in the third army area at any time.'" (McCarthy, "Rumor, Grub, Bowels and I." entry for 28 December 1918.)

41 **"doing nearly all"**—LMG 1918 Diary, 19 December 1918.

41 **December 20 they moved**—Ibid., 22 December 1918,

41 **Already in December … "real work to do."**—Company Log, 11 December 1918.

42 **In March … "will be over."**—Ibid., 13 March 1919.

42 **On March 15 … transportation home.**—Ibid., entries for 14 March to 1 April 1919.

42 **about forty-five of the old**—Ibid., 7 April 1919.

42 **At last … civilian life.**—Ibid., entries for 19 April to 8 May 1919; also McCarthy, "Rumor, Grub, Bowels and I." entry for 19 May 1919, for the soaking by rain and being "fixed out with new clothes" at Camp Morrison.

CHAPTER 3 — ENTERED UPON A SCIENTIFIC CAREER

43 **As the University … "Ann Arbor's skyline."**—Shaw, *The University of Michigan*, 189, 322, and Table IV.

43 **The university advanced him**—LMG academic transcript, University of Michigan. This is the source for all later information concerning courses taken, and grades received.

43 **Gould was influenced**—Gould acknowledged Hobbs' decisive influence upon the direction of his life at this time in many places. When Hobbs' retired, Gould sent him a letter stating "My whole career in geology and all that it has led to, derives from the infectious character of your personality and the intellectual stimulus I have absorbed from you." (Quoted in Hobbs, *An Explorer-Scientist's Pilgrimage*, 141.)

43 **By November, Hobbs**—Proceedings of the University of Michigan Board of Regents, November 1919, BHL; Gould, "Memorial to William Herbert Hobbs," 133.

43 **"I probably owe more"**—Gould, Memorial to William Herbert Hobbs, 134.

43 **"the Lord in Sepia" … "a lively" … "he could take"**—Ibid., 133.

44 **During that first year**—Important news at Michigan that year was the announcement, made December 29, 1919, that Marion LeRoy Burton, then president of the University of Minnesota, would take over the following summer as the fifth president of the University of Michigan. Burton had received his undergraduate degree in 1900 from then little-known

Carleton College in Northfield, Minnesota, and one might well suppose that the first mentions Gould may have heard about his future academic home for thirty years were in connection with the news of Burton's selection at Michigan. In 1919, thirty-nine-year-old Donald J. Cowling, who Gould would eventually succeed, had already been president of Carleton for ten years.

44   **the Phylon Club**—See Records of Pi Kappa Alpha, Beta Tau Chapter, University of Michigan, BHL.

44   **Throughout the years**—Pi Kappa Alpha pages in the *Michiganensian* yearbooks of 1922-26 and 1928-30, BHL. An article by Hobbs in a 1930 issue of *Michigan Alumnus* notes that Gould's connection with Pi Kappa Alpha "resulted in bringing many students from that fraternity into the geological department.... No less than four members of this fraternity went to Greenland in connection with the three expeditions of the University."

44   **confirmed in June 1920 ... set at $1,800.**—Proceedings of the University of Michigan Board of Regents, June 1920, November 1920, and June 1921, BHL

44   **summer of 1921**—Gould, "Memorial to William Herbert Hobbs," 133.

44   **In later years ... "semester to go."**—Carleton College Department of Geology, *Carleton's Century of Geology*, 33.

46   **Miss Margaret Rice**—Margaret Rice was born in Detroit May 11, 1905, the daughter of Alfred Rice, born in Woodstock, Ontario, and Bertha Marker, born in Wayne, Michigan.

46   **In 1922 she entered**—A transcript of Margaret Rice's academic record at Michigan is available through the university's Office of the Registrar. A certified copy was issued to the author July 29, 2002.

46   **"lingered to marry"**—Carleton College Department of Geology, *Carleton's Century of Geology*, 33.

46   **His dissertation subject ... maps of the range.**—Hobbs, "Laurence Gould—Antarctic Explorer," 315.

46   **It was Hobbs' hope ... shales hypothesis**—Gould, "Memorial to William Herbert Hobbs," 134; Gould, "The Role of Orogenic Stresses in Laccolithic Intrusions," 119-120.

46n **During 1922-23, Margaret Rice**—*Michiganensian* yearbook for 1923, BHL.

47   **"reconnaissance studies"**—Gould, "The Role of Orogenic Stresses," 120.

47   **It was at the end**—This anecdote, and the quotation beginning "While passing through" from Hobbs, "Laurence Gould—Antarctic Explorer," 315-316.

47   **"within a fortnight"**—Another account of this event appeared in a profile of Gould in the *South Haven Daily Tribune* of March 20, 1929. Accentuating the peril to life with what has the whiff of journalistic license, as compared with Hobbs' statement that Gould was teaching again in a fortnight, the newspaper profile had it that, after driving the car "over the precipitous side of a mountain," Gould "was in the hospital for many weeks" and that "for some time there was little hope that he would survive."

48   **his evidence regarding ... "consequences may be."**—Gould, "Memorial to William Herbert Hobbs," 134.

48   **Though Hobbs himself**—Ibid.

48   **Hobbs' "championing"**—"Laurence M. Gould, a Great Alumnus," in the University of Michigan's *Geoscience News*, December 1995, 3.

48   **A few months later**—Proceedings of the University of Michigan Board of Regents, February 1926, BHL.

48   **Gould's daily routine ... deepened into romance.**—Information and quotations from a profile (under headline "Gould Rescued by Comdr. Byrd") in the *South Haven Daily Tribune*, March 20, 1929.

48   **"accounted one of the two"**—Ibid.

48   **"no one of [my] acquaintance"**—Ibid.

48n   **In a poem written**—Jean's poem for Gould's sixtieth birthday (located in CCA-GC) reads:

> Solemn he looked in hornrimmed glasses;
> Elderly, in a thick moustache.
> This was his hope, at least—but futile:
> One-who-was-ten remarked the clash
> Patent between his eyes and make-up;
> Tried out her strongest sauce and found—
> Joyfully—that, in lieu of Grandpa,
> There was a gay young man around!
> Yet he persisted in the aspect
> Till he had gained some honest age;
> Then, by miraculous inversion,
> Younger he grew, as he grew sage.
> Out went the grave falseface and manner;
> Safe in his astral course, he dared
> Show in his look the leaping spirit
> Shrewdly the child at once had bared.
> Ten knew the inside Twenty-seven...
> Thirty-three years confirm her there!
> Larry, at SIXTY, is most truly
> LARRY HIMSELF, the DEBONAIR!!!

49   **The object ... later expeditions**—Hobbs, *An Explorer-Scientist's Pilgrimage*, 104; Hobbs, *Exploring About the North Pole of the Winds*, 6-7.

49   **Gould gladly accepted**—In his 1978 interview with Charles Neider, Gould recalled: "I thought I was going to become an oil geologist and make a lot of money. And I had a tentative offer of a job with an oil company in Mexico when Professor Hobbs ... organized a small expedition to go to Greenland, on which he took me along in the summer of 1926." (1978 Gould/Neider interview, from transcript in Neider, *Beyond Cape Horn*, 326.).

49   **It was necessary ... retrieved in September.**—Hobbs, *An Explorer-Scientist's Pilgrimage*, 103-104; Hobbs, *Exploring About the North Pole of the Winds*, 5-7.

49   **He made a promise**—"Prologue" to LMG 1926 Diary, NA-GP.

49   **On June 23**—LMG 1926 Diary, 24 June 1926.

CHAPTER 4 — AN ARCTIC TENDERFOOT

50   **When Gould and Belknap ... Bartlett**—LMG 1926 Diary, 26 June 1926.

52   **"weather-beaten face**—Ibid.

52   **"You never saw" ... "warmth of heart"**—Edward M. Weyer, Jr., "Obituary for Captain Bob Bartlett," *The Explorers Journal*, Spring-Summer 1946.

52   **"He is I think"**—LMG 1926 Diary, 26 June 1926.

52   **swear for ten**—Comments by Joanna Arnold, Carleton College videotape recording of "A Convocation in Celebration of the Life of Laurence McKinley Gould, Skinner Memorial Chapel, October 13, 1995, CCA.

52   **The following morning ... "boots in Greenland."**—All information and quotations in this paragraph from LMG 1926 Diary, entries dated June 28th" [sic—actually 27 June 1929] and June 29th.

52n   **"magic carpet"**—Putnam, Mariner of the North, 158.

53   **Bartlett's mother had ... "meant to do."**—Putnam, *Mariner of the North*, 26-27.

53   **pair of explorer's lectures**—The question of who first kindled Gould's interest in polar exploration inspires this biography's longest endnote. Many years later, enough for imperfect memory to blur strict accuracy, Gould mentioned these lectures in the course of correspondence with his friend the Canadian ethnologist Vilhjalmur Stefansson and with the distinguished Australian Sir Douglas Mawson. To Stefansson, he wrote: "I really believe my interest in polar exploration started one day at a convocation at the University of Michigan many, many years ago, when as a young undergraduate I heard you speak on 'The Northward Course of Empire.'" (LMG to Stefansson, 1 November 1954, NA-GP.) Four years later in another letter, Gould told Stefansson that "a lecture you gave at the University of Michigan many years ago on 'The Northward Course of Empire' was the beginning of my own interest in the ends of the earth. Whether you like it or not, therefore, Stef, I am sort of a protégée of yours." (LMG to Stefansson, 11 October 1958, NA-GP.) In his reply, Stefansson recalled the occasion well, giving reasons for his having been that day in "an exalted, intellectually intoxicated mood." Contemporary issues of the University of Michigan's student newspaper, *The Michigan Daily*, confirm that Stefansson's convocation address titled "The Northward Course of Empire" was delivered in Michigan's Hill Auditorium one morning in March 1923. Gould's memory was correct except for the minor matter of his having asserted that he had been a "young undergraduate" at the time of the lecture—for he had received his undergraduate degree in 1921.

More problematic, possibly, is Gould's memory of another lecture, shortly preceding Stefansson's. In the late 1950s, responding to a letter from the Antarctican Sir Douglas Mawson, Gould wrote as follows: "You may have long since forgotten a visit to the University of Michigan so many years ago that I cannot remember the number. You were a guest of Professor Hobbs, who became my own chief. I went to the University of Michigan to study law and was deflected into geology by the infectious enthusiasm of his personality. I still remember your magnificent pictures, and I think my own polar interests stem from hearing that lecture by you and one shortly afterward by Stefansson. In my polar genealogy, therefore, the name of Sir Douglas Mawson occupies a very important place." (LMG to Mawson, 19 March 1957, NA-GP.) Mawson's reply to this, if any, has not been found. The problem is that staff at Michigan's Bentley Historical Library have been unable to locate evidence of any early 1920s Ann Arbor address by Mawson. Requested to search for such a lecture shortly before the March 1923 convocation given by Stefansson, as indicated by Gould's letter to Mawson, the Bentley's reference assistant instead found reporting of a February 28, 1923, visit and lecture by the American Arctic explorer Donald B. MacMillan. (*The Michigan Daily*, March 4, 1923.) While Gould, once he had formed serious interest in the polar regions a few years later, certainly would not have confused the Australian Antarctican with the American explorer of the Arctic, it does seem plausible that Gould may in fact have attended *MacMillan's* lecture in 1923—his first real exposure to the subject of polar exploration, perhaps—and then later, when mentally reconstructing incidents that led to the forming of his own polar interests, thought wrongly that the lecturer he had heard many years previously had been *Mawson.*

54 **Will Bartlett ... "Virgin Mary!"**—LMG 1926 Diary, 30 June 1926.

54 **once proposed marriage**—Bartlett, *The Log of Bob Bartlett*, 119-120.

54 **"It seemed inappropriate"**—Putnam, *Wide Margins*, 252.

54 **invited Gould to switch**—LMG 1926 Diary, 30 June 1926.

54 **"continuous nightmare" ... Twain's third.**—LMG 1926 Diary, 4 July 1926.

54 **Describing how ... lift on July 4**—LMG 1926 Diary, 5 July 1926.

54 **cowboy saluted patriotically**—Streeter, *An Arctic Rodéo*, 58.

54 **morning of the 6th ... in to Holsteinsborg.**—LMG 1926 Diary, 6 July 1926.

55 **Before us lay**—Streeter, *An Arctic Rodéo*, 67.

55 **The expeditions' credentials ... steep rocky hill.**—LMG 1926 Diary, 8 July 1926; Streeter, *An Arctic Rodéo*, 70-71.

55 **absence of trees made it**—LMG 1926 Diary, 8 July 1926.

55 **eager to barter**—Ibid., and Streeter. *An Arctic Rodéo*, 73.

55 **Gould wrote that the Eskimos**—LMG 1926 Diary, 8 July 1926.

55 **banquet of sorts ... "an indefinite stay."**—Streeter, An *Arctic Rodéo*, 71-73

55 **After a time ... their summer base.**—Ibid., 73; LMG 1926 Diary, 8 July 1926.

55   **An early morning stop ... beached sharks**—LMG 1926 Diary, 8 July 1926; Streeter, An Arctic Rodéo, 84.

56   **The native dwellings ... "some days previously."**—Streeter, An Arctic Rodéo, 87-88.

56   **The party introduced ... by a stream.**—Ibid., 91-93; LMG 1926 Diary, 8 July 1926.

56   **Farewells were said**—The historian of the Putnam expedition wrote: "Saying goodbye to the pedagogues was rather depressing. We'd been shipmates for some time now and after a look at the scenery the suspicion grew strong in us that we'd never see them again." (Streeter, An Arctic Rodéo, 92.)

56   **departed until September**—Hobbs and Putnam had agreed that, unless other plans were arranged by radio, the Morrissey would aim to return to Holsteinsborg by September 18, where Hobbs and his men would be ready to embark. If no ship and no news had arrived by October 10, the Michigan party was to assume that the ship had met with difficulty or disaster, notify the Danish authorities, and then shift for themselves. (Hobbs, Exploring About the North Pole of the Winds, 6.)

56   **After she was gone ... "tin cans."**—LMG 1926 Diary, 8 July 1926.

56   **"It seems like 85 degrees"**—Ibid.

56   **disputed the notion ... "more ferocious."**—Streeter, An Arctic Rodéo, 91.

56   **On the 8th ... "all the trouble."**—LMG 1926 Diary, 8 July 1926.

56   **performance of one kayaker**—Ibid.

57   **On July 10**—The story of the capsized canoe is told in LMG 1926 Diary, 11 July 1926; Hobbs, Exploring About the North Pole of the Winds, 34-37; and Hobbs, An Explorer-Scientist's Pilgrimage, 106.

57   **"Before I half realized"**—LMG 1926 Diary, 11 July 1926.

57   **"seemed continually"**—Ibid.

57   **with "wonderful speed"**—Hobbs, Exploring About the North Pole of the Winds, 34,

57   **"In a few hours"**—Ibid.

58   **Gould supposed ... "more than ever now."**—LMG 1926 Diary, 11 July 1926.

58   **next two weeks ... ptarmigan pie**—LMG 1926 Diary, entries from 11 July to 23 July 1926.

58   **month's journey inland**—Except where otherwise indicated below, the source of all statements in subsequent paragraphs about the journey to the inland ice is Gould's 1926 diary. Specific entry dates are noted for direct quotations only.

58   **Their intent was**—Hobbs, The First Greenland Expedition of the University of Michigan, 5; and Hobbs, Exploring About the North Pole of the Winds, 69.

58   **"our strong man Gould"**—Hobbs, Exploring About the North Pole of the Winds, 70.

58   **"I have been learning"**—LMG 1926 Diary, 27 July 1926.

58n **"blood curdling gurgles" ... modicum of peace.**—LMG 1926 Diary, 16 July and 17 July 1926.

59   **"our pemmican is"**—Ibid, 30 July 1926,

59   **"three of Professor Hobbs' miles"**—Ibid., 31 July 1926.

59   **"beautiful sunset effects"**—Ibid.

59   **"With my face raw"**—Ibid.

59n **Hobbs estimated that**—Hobbs, Exploring About the North Pole of the Winds, 75.

60   **"starvation rations."**—Ibid., 2 August 1926.

60   **Eskimos had nearly used up**—Hobbs, Exploring About the North Pole of the Winds, 80; LMG 1926 Diary, 5 August 1926. Gould states that the Eskimos had expected to make the trip to the ice shelf in four or five days, whereas with the party's heavy load of scientific equipment it had actually taken ten.

60   **Some of the party ... Nordenskjöld Glacier**—Hobbs, Exploring About the North Pole of the Winds, 79-80.

60   **The following morning ... "ice-cap air circulation."**—Ibid., 82.

60   **"rather a plain talk"**—LMG 1926 Diary, 5 August 1926.

60   **"Our condition is not"**—Hobbs, *Exploring the North Pole of the Winds*, 81-82.

60   **Retracing their steps**—Hobbs, *Exploring the North Pole of the Winds*, 86-87.

60   **At the base ... earlier in September**—Hobbs, *An Explorer-Scientist's Pilgrimage*, 107; Streeter, *An Arctic Rodéo*, 184-189, 192-195. ("[L]eaking like a funnel" from Streeter, 194.)

61   **Lake Laurence M. Gould**—Hobbs, *The First Greenland Expedition of the University of Michigan*, 10.

61   **September 7 set sail**—Hobbs, *An Explorer-Scientist's Pilgrimage*, 107.

61   **its passengers now ... cubs were female.)**—Streeter, *An Arctic Rodéo*, 287, 291; Putnam, *Mariner of the North*, 164-165.

61   **A post-supper poker game ... simply a passenger.**—Streeter, *An Arctic Rodéo*, 294; Hobbs, *An Explorer-Scientist's Pilgrimage*, 107.

62   **"in the twinkling"**—Streeter, *An Arctic Rodéo*, 294

62   **"like liquid mountains" ... "instead of a sailor"**—Streeter, *An Arctic Rodéo*, 296.

62   **"no recourse but" ... "better get busy."**—Hobbs, *An Explorer-Scientist's Pilgrimage*, 107.

62   **"a roaring gale came"**—Streeter, *An Arctic Rodéo*, 304.

62   **Hobbs describes ... "in his element."**—Hobbs, *An Explorer-Scientist's Pilgrimage*, 108.

62   **major Miami hurricane ... thirty years.**—Ibid., 109.

CHAPTER 5 — BAFFIN TO BYRD

63   **Their purpose was**—Putnam, *Mariner of the North*, 156; Gould, "Contributions to the Geology of Foxe Land, Baffin Island; Part I," 19; Putnam, "The Putnam Baffin Island Expedition," 3. Collateral work was also conducted on behalf of the Heye Foundation's Museum of the American Indian, the National Research Council in Medicine, the American Museum of Natural History, and the Buffalo Society of Natural Sciences. Personnel responsible for these collateral efforts were anthropologist Donald A. Cadzow, doing ethnological and archaeological work; Dr. Peter Heinbecker, whose medical investigations among the Eskimo included blood-typing and studies of starvation symptoms; and taxidermist Fred Limekiller. Other members of the expedition, in addition to Putnam, Gould, and the crew of the *Morrissey*, included Gould's surveying assistants George Weymouth of Philadelphia, Monroe G. Barnard of New York, and John A. Pope of Detroit, as well as engineer and assistant Robert E. Peary and Wallace R. Hawkins, radio director Edward Manley, motion picture photographer Maurice Kellerman, botanist Junius B. Bird, and youngsters David Binney Putnam and Deric Nusbaum. (See Putnam, "The Putnam Baffin Island Expedition," 3-4.)

63   **In that interval**—For a fuller account of Putnam's role in signing Lindbergh to a contract and bringing out *We*—including an interesting foofaraw over an initial ghostwriting assignment for the book, which Lindbergh first approved and then rejected, see Putnam, *Wide Margins*, 231-235. In this account, Putnam refers to pressures and discussions in "late June," without any indication in the text that at this time he was aboard the *Morrissey* en route to Baffin Island. Presumably he remained in contact with the G. P. Putnam's Sons office by radio. Under pressure to provide at least forty thousand words in a hurry, if he was to insist on writing the promised book himself, Lindbergh produced a manuscript in about three weeks time, and *We* was published July 27, 1927. It sold close to 200,000 copies within a month—all while Putnam was on his Baffin expedition—and continued near the top of bestseller lists well into the following year, with total sales surpassing $650,000. See also Ross, *The Last Hero*, 139-141, and Berg, *Lindbergh*, 165-167.

64   **By June 20**—Putnam, "The Putnam Baffin Island Expedition," 4. For pictures of the expedition's welcome to Brigus and of Bob and Will Bartlett's parents, presumably taken by Gould, see Gould's photo album of the 1927 expedition, CCA-GC. Photographs from this album, largely arranged in chronological order, are the basis for some statements that follow concerning details of the expedition. Otherwise, except as indicated below, the steady source for the account of the Putnam expedition that follows is Putnam's article "The Putnam Baffin Island Expedition." Specific pages are noted for direct quotations only.

64   **"vast drifting fields" ... "through 'tickles.'"**—Putnam, "The Putnam Baffin Island Expedition," 5.

64   **"thorough-going archaeological study"**—Ibid., 6.

64   **"well beset"**—Ibid.

65   **"an unrecorded tidewater"**—Ibid., 7.

65   **"freakish gorge"**—Ibid., 8.

66   **"In a matter of ten"**—Ibid., 9.

66   **"remarkable" for the perfection**—Gould, "Geological Results of Putnam Baffin Island Expedition," 149.

66   **"long finger of rocks"**—Putnam, "The Putnam Baffin Island Expedition," 13.

66   **"Out of sixty days"**—Ibid., 4."

67   **"the conditions were not"**—Ibid., 13.

67   **"wilderness of ... dead monotony."**—Ibid., 3.

67   **"ribbon of granite"**—Ibid., 16.

67   **"The shore itself"**—Ibid.

67   **"dodging along close" ... "between us and bottom."**—Ibid., 17.

68   **"even more out of harmony"**—Ibid., 16.

68   **"cartographically ... sunk"**—Ibid., 1.

68   **"Blue Goose Prairie."**—Putnam, *Mariner of the North*, 156.

68   **"one distinctive landmark"**—Putnam, "The Putnam Baffin Island Expedition," 3.

68   **Gould was delighted ... back to the boat.**—Gould, "Contributions to the Geology of Foxe Land, Baffin Island; Part I," 22. Gould's Putnam Highland fossils were assessed and written up in reports published in tandem with Gould's geological report by two other scholars, Aug. F. Foerste and Russell C. Hussey.

69   **three-month flying tour**—Ross, *The Last Hero*, 142; Berg, *Lindbergh*, 164, 167.

69   **Sponsored by ... surf of Ver-sur-Mer.**—Rodgers, *Beyond the Barrier*, 9-11; Hoyt, *The Last Explorer*, 131-154; and Glines, *Bernt Balchen*, 37-53.

70   **first person ever**—Rodgers, *Beyond the Barrier*, 12.

71   **"I do not think we could"**—Isaiah Bowman to Putnam, 11 October 1927, with handwritten notation "To Dick B from G.P.P.", OSUA-BP, folder #512.

71   **Gould wrote directly ... and Professor Hobbs followed**—LMG to REB, 12 November 1927, OSUA-BP, folder #1766; telegram William H. Hobbs to REB, 15 November 1927, OSUA-BP, folder #512.

71   **The Tuesday evening**—1981 Gould/Peter J. Anderson interview, OSUA-AP; REB to Hobbs, 16 November 1927, OSUA-BP, folder #512.

71   **"hit it off extremely well."**—1981 Gould/Peter J. Anderson interview, OSUA-AP.

71   **"the probable selection"**—*Detroit News*, November 23, 1927.

71   **Even so, Byrd hesitated ... interesting to attempt.**—1981 Gould/Peter J. Anderson interview, OSUA-AP; REB to LMG, 29 February 1928, OSUA-BP, folder #1766.

71   **Gould declared himself ready**—LMG to REB, 5 March 1928, OSUA-BP, folder #1766.

71   **Byrd wrote that, at least**—REB to LMG, 14 March 1928, OSUA-BP, folder #1766.

72	**In mid-March … geographer and geologist.**—LMG to REB, 21 March 1928, OSUA-BP, folder #1766. Byrd's book, *Skyward*, was ghost-written by Fitzhugh Green, a naval commander and Arctic explorer who had joined the editorial staff at G. P. Putnam's & Sons in 1927 and completed the work on Lindbergh's *We.*

72	**Byrd, however, subsequently … American Geographical Society**—REB to LMG, 26 March 1928; LMG to REB, 2 April 1928 and 14 April 1928—all OSUA-BP, folder #1766.

72	**Finally, in April**—REB to LMG, 20 April 1928, OSUA-BP, folder #1766.

72	**"we are very glad"**—Clarence Cook Little to REB, 10 May 1928, OSUA-BP, folder #5336.

72	**For months on end (and information following)**—See Rodgers, *Beyond the Barrier*, 24-25 and following.

73	**Meanwhile Gould … American Geographical Society**—LMG to REB, 26 April 1928; REB to LMG, 24 May 1928—both OSUA-BP, folder #1766.

73	**established an understanding**—1978 Gould/Neider interview, from transcript in Neider, *Beyond Cape Horn, 307*: "Just before I left for Antarctica I became engaged to Margaret Rice."

73	**Gould came to New York**—LMG BAE I Diaries, 28 September 1928, NA-GP.

73	**expedition's library**—REB to Putnam, 23 April 1928, OSUA-BP, folder #2739; Gould, *Cold*, 64.

73	**In the end … party in Antarctica.**—Byrd, *Little America*, 3; Rodgers, *Beyond the Barrier*, 37.

73	**(Gould later recalled**—1981 Gould/Peter J. Anderson interview, OSUA-AP.

74	**portraits of each member**—Ibid.

74	**prewritten obituaries**—Rodgers, *Beyond the Barrier*, 36.

74	**The newspapers and other … ships to depart.**—Rodgers, *Beyond the Barrier*, 35, 37.

74	**That ship, the *City* … on to Antarctica.**—Byrd, *Little America*, 26-28, 34, 37-38; Carter, *Little America*, 35-36; Rodgers, *Beyond the Barrier*, 34.

75	**Larry Gould shipped**—LMG BAE I Diaries, 28 September 1928; Byrd, *Little America*, 37; Carter, *Little America*, 36 (including the "worn iron pot" quotation); Rodgers, *Beyond the Barrier*, 40.

75n	**"good-bye son"**—LMG BAE I Diaries, 23 October 1928.

CHAPTER 6 — HIGH VENTURINGS

76	**His first entry**—LMG BAE I Diaries, 28 September 1928. Gould's diary entries are the source for all information concerning the voyage to New Zealand except as noted. Specific entry dates are given below for all direct quotations.

76	**roll in dry dock**—Willcox, *Beneath a Wandering Star*, 87.

76	**Even so, he … perverse satisfaction.**—LMG BAE I Diaries, 28 September 1928.

76	**praise for the work**—Ibid., 13 October 1928.

76	**"waste in making" … "always be one."**—Ibid., 28 September 1928.

78	**West Indies climate**—Ibid., 3 Oct. 1928.

78	**While their ship … before it was over.**—Ibid., 8 October 1928 and 12 October 1928.

78	**"brazenly open" … "poured aboard."**—Ibid., 8 October 1928.

78	**personal reading**—Information about Gould's reading during the voyage is from the undated insert found with the BAE I Diaries that is titled "Books Read—in order from time of leaving Norfolk."

78	**King Neptune … "break in the monotony,"**—LMG BAE I Diaries, 18 October 1928.

78 **"an inexplicably delicious"** … **"dislocated jaw."**—LMG BAE I Diaries, 3 November 1928.

79 **comparatively unhappy ship**—See, in addition to Gould's diary, Carter, *Little America*, 52; and Rodgers, *Beyond the Barrier*, 46-48. At least one of the privileged expedition members, physicist Frank "Taffy" Davies, voluntarily switched his mess from the officers' to the common men's, desiring to retain, according to historian Eugene Rodgers (47), the goodwill of men with whom he would soon be confined on close terms "for over a year in Antarctic huts."

79 **Gould's journal records** … **"same mess."**—LMG BAE I Diaries, 3 November 1928,

79 **Gould described as awe-inspiring** … **in high school.**—Ibid., 16 November, 1928.

79 **"the end of privation"** … **"seem petty."**—Ibid., 11 November 1928.

79 **The Ross and Larsen** … **green hillsides.**—LMG BAE I Diaries, 6 December 1928 (including the "quintessence" quote about Harold Tapley); Rodgers, *Beyond the Barrier*, 52; Byrd, *Little America*, 49.

80 **The day after** … **on the continent.**—Rodgers, *Beyond the Barrier*, 52-53; Balchen, *Come North With Me*, 151; Byrd, *Little America*, 53-54.

81 **Thus, when** … **additional cargo**—LMG BAE I Diaries, 6 December 1928.

81 **low in the water** … **to the foremast.**—Byrd, *Little America*, 54-55.

81 **Fine weather prevailed** … **"ship itself."**—LMG BAE I Diaries, 6 December, 8 December, 9 December, and 10 December 1928; Byrd, *Little America*, 60-63;

81 **On the second** … **bobbing behind.**—LMG BAE I Diaries, 10 December ("again"); Byrd, *Little America*, 65-69; Rodgers, *Beyond the Barrier*, 57-58.

81 **Movement through** … **through the ice.**—Byrd, *Little America*, 70-76.

81n **Byrd noted that**—Byrd, *Little America*, 54-55.

82 **Larry Gould, meanwhile** … **soon followed.**—LMG BAE I Diaries 16 December 1928; Rodgers, *Beyond the Barrier*, 59.

82 **"calm sober judgment"**—from LMG BAE I Diaries, 13 December 1928.

82 **Official confirmation**—An "Expedition Order" of December 28, 1928 specified Gould's appointment as second-in-command at the base of operations, but third-in-command of the expedition. Remaining for a time as the nominal second-in-command was Dick Brophy, whose "disintegrating performance" due to nervous exhaustion—he was well on the way to an imminent mental breakdown—had led to Byrd's subtracting Brophy from his Antarctic roster, though leaving him in charge of operations in New Zealand. Brophy became increasingly erratic, and the seriousness of his mental collapse resulted in his eventual resignation about two months later. Thereafter Gould was second-in-command of the expedition in both name and fact. See Byrd, *Little America*, 82, 161; Rodgers, *Beyond the Barrier*, 54, 79, 111.

82n **"My mind as to"**—Byrd, *Little America*, 81.

83 **When the C. A. Larsen**—Byrd, *Little America*, 76; Rodgers, *Beyond the Barrier*, 60-61.

83 **Many years later** … **spiritual home**—1978 Gould/Neider interview, from transcript in Neider, *Beyond Cape Horn, 310.*

83 **turkey and cranberry**—LMG BAE I Diaries, 25 December 1928.

83 **enlivened by** … **"starboard bow!"**—Rodgers, *Beyond the Barrier*, 61; Bursey, *Antarctic Night*, 51.

83 **"There was a clatter"** … **back pounding.**—Byrd, *Little America*, 77.

83 **muter reception** … **"carved in ice."**—Balchen, *Come North With Me*, 163.

83 **Hours later** … **turned east**—Rodgers, *Beyond the Barrier*, 61-62.

83 **"feeling like pigmies"**—Bursey, *Antarctic Night*, 51.

83 **"white silence"**—Balchen, *Come North With Me*, 163.

83 **"It was so still"**—Bursey, *Antarctic Night*, 52.

83   **The next day ... easterly course**—LMG BAE I Diaries, 26 December 1928; Carter, *Little America,* 63-64; Byrd, *Little America,* 79-80; Rodgers, *Beyond the Barrier,* 63-64.

84   **Sailing all the next ... "indescribable blue."**—LMG BAE I Diaries, 27 December 1928.

84   **It was early morning**—Ibid., 28 December 1928; Byrd, *Little America,* 84-86.

84   **Unfortunately, the expedition ... Little America.**—Byrd, *Little America,* 88; LMG BAE I Diaries, 28 December 1928; Rodgers, *Beyond the Barrier,* 66-67. On the naming of Little America, see Rodgers, *Beyond the Barrier,* 70.

84n   **"All of Little America"**—Rodgers, *Beyond the Barrier,* 301.

85   **"Desire to Live"**—LMG BAE I Diaries, 30 December 1928.

86   **Gould went in ... the entire distance.**—Ibid., 29 December 1928, 3 January 1929, and entry dated "January 6th," which appears to be an error, actually 5 January 1929.

86   **Taking charge of ... "Construction Company."**—Balchen, *Come North With Me,* 167; LMG BAE I Diaries for early January, 1929; Siple, *A Boy Scout with Byrd,* 53.

86   **"overpowering quiet"**—LMG BAE I Diaries, entry dated "January 8th" [sic—7 January 1929].

86   **"a silence which fairly"**—Ibid., 28 December 1928.

86   **In a blizzard ... "he was standing."**—Ibid., entry dated "Wednesday Jan 10th" [sic—9 January 1929].

86   **When work resumed ... put on a roof.**—Ibid., 11 January 1929, and entry dated "Sunday Jan 14th" [sic—13 January 1929]."

86   **Gould then went back**—This paragraph and the next based on LMG BAE I Diaries, 20 January to 26 January 1929; also Byrd, *Little America,* 100-101.

89   **written instructions for assuming**—LMG BAE I Diaries, 26 January 1929.

89   **The meteorologist's go-ahead**—Description, in this paragraph and the next, of the January 27 flight from LMG BAE I Diaries, 27 January 1929; Byrd, *Little America,* 117-125.

89   **The arrival of the *Eleanor Bolling***—This paragraph and the next based on Byrd, *Little America,* 126-127 and 132; Rodgers, *Beyond the Barrier,* 76.

89n   **"steady as a rock"**—Byrd, *Little America,* 125.

89n   **"after the signature"**—Carter, *Little America,* 76.

90   **Gould stayed a day**—This paragraph and the next based on LMG BAE I Diaries, 28 January to 1 February 1929; also Byrd, *Little America,* 128-129.

90   **After supper, Gould**—This paragraph and the next based on LMG BAE I Diaries, 1 February 1929; Byrd, *Little America,* 130-132; Rodgers, *Beyond the Barrier,* 77-78; Balchen, *Come North With Me,* 171 (including the remark attributed to Taffy Davies).

91   **In the weeks that followed**—This paragraph and the next based on LMG BAE I Diaries, 3 February 1929 to 17 February 1929.

92   **A further cause ... year and more.**—Ibid., 3 February 1929.

      Marie Byrd Land—Credit for first spotting a peak of the new range was claimed personally by Byrd in connection with his flight on the *Virginia,* though the actual discovery was apparently made by the crew of the *Fairchild,* piloted by Dean Smith, flying after the *Virginia* had returned to base. For discussion, see Rodgers, *Beyond the Barrier,* 96-101.

92   **Byrd noted ... was lacking.**—Byrd, *Little America,* 146, 152, 155.

92   **fell to Gould to inform**—LMG BAE I Diaries, 2 March 1929.

92   **"Larry had promised"**—Siple, *90° South,* 41.

93   **Gould recorded that**—LMG BAE I Diaries, 2 March 1929.

93   **On February 22**—Rodgers, *Beyond the Barrier,* 83; Byrd, *Little America,* 148.

CHAPTER 7 — FEARED LOST

94 **Early in March 1929**—News items are from *New York Times*, page one stories of March 1-3. 1929.

94 **Inauguration Day blizzard**—See for instance LMG BAE I Diaries, 4 March 1929; Byrd, *Little America*, 159-61; Rodgers, *Beyond the Barrier*, 85.

94 **A few days later ... delay their return.**—Owen, "Byrd Fliers Survey Rockefeller Range," *New York Times*, March 10, 1929.

95 **The expedition had forwarded**—*New York Times*, March 4 and March 5, 1929.

95 **On the first**—Ibid., March 10, 1929.

95 **A week later**—"Wilkins Hails Byrd in Radio Greetings," *New York Times*, March 17, 1929.

95 **On March 17**—Owen, "Byrd to Fly to Aid of Mountain Party," *New York Times*, March 18, 1929.

96 **"Commander Byrd was all" ... "may be the explanation."**—Owen, "Byrd's Dog Teams Hitch Up For Dash to Isolated Men," *New York Times*, March 19, 1929.

96 **Other newspapers ... "not giving up hope."**—*Detroit Times, Ann Arbor Times News, South Haven Daily Tribune*, all March 19, 1929.

96 **Professor Hobbs declared**—Unidentified newspaper clipping headed "Byrd to Hunt U.M. Aide," in scrapbook titled "Larry's Book," CCA-GC.

96 **At Little America**—Byrd, *Little America*, 175.

97 **Excited by ... rest until morning.**—Byrd, *Little America*, 162, 180; Gould, *Cold*, 8-11; Hoyt, *The Last Explorer*, 221; Rodgers, *Beyond the Barrier*, 102.

97 **The next day ... [end of chapter]**—Except where otherwise indicated, the parallel sources for the rest of this chapter are LMG BAE I Diaries, entries dated "Mar 9th" [sic—8 March 1929] to 28 March 1929, and Gould, *Cold*, Chapter 1, 12-34. Direct quotations from the diary and from Cold are given specific citation.

98 **"a sharp retort"**—Balchen, *Come North With Me*, 173.

98 **"The plane has moved!"**—LMG BAE I Diaries, entry dated "Saturday Mar 10th" [sic—9 March 1929.]

98 **When the wind slackened**—Balchen, *Come North With Me*, 174, is a source for this and following paragraphs, along with the LMG diary and book.

98 **"like a madman"**—LMG BAE I Diaries, entry dated "Saturday Mar 10th" [sic—9 March 1929.]

98 **"Another feather,"**—Ibid.

99 **"seemingly endless" ... "numb with cold"**—Balchen, Come *North With Me*, 174.

99 **"worse than needles"**—LMG BAE I Diaries, entry dated "Saturday Mar 10th" [sic—9 March 1929.]

99 **"a veritable sand blast."**—Gould, *Cold*, 15.

99 **"Turkish-bath" sleeping bags**—Ibid., 16.

99 **"quivered and shook"**—LMG BAE I Diaries, entry dated "Saturday Mar 10th" [sic—9 March 1929.]

100 **"Little America will look"**—Ibid., 11 Mar. 1929.

100 **"it was no use." ... "and breathe."**—Gould, *Cold*, 21-22.

101 **"With infinite trouble"**—Ibid., 22.

101 **"One time Bernt and I"**—Ibid., 23.

101 **"quivering ... and lifting"**—LMG BAE I Diaries, 15 March 1929.

101 **"a snow-bound lake"**—Gould, *Cold*, 24.

101 **it "was evident"**—Ibid.

102 **"Along about midnight"**—Balchen, *Come North With Me*, 175.

102 **"I think we had all"**—Gould, *Cold*, 26.

102 **"There are no words"**—LMG BAE I Diaries, 15 March 1929.

102 **120 to 150 miles per hour**—They did not really know. Gould's diary (15 March 1929) recorded June's estimate that the wind must have blown fully 120 miles an hour to have carried the plane away. Two years later Gould wrote in *Cold* (29) that "we judged that the wind which caused all this must have blown at least 150 miles an hour." In his 1958 book, Balchen wrote that he calculated the speed of the gusts that night to have been in excess of 200 miles per hour. Clearly, it was blustery.

102 **"sit still and contemplate"**—Gould, *Cold*, 27.

102 **"just sitting tight"**—LMG BAE I Diaries, 15 March 1929.

103 **"We had brought"**—Gould, *Cold*, 28.

103 **"disheartening" and "pitiful"**—LMG BAE I Diaries, 16 March 1929.

104 **"preserved its equilibrium"**—Gould, *Cold*, 29.

104 **"refreshed in body"**—LMG BAE I Diaries, 16 March 1929.

104 **"a reasonable length" … "good weather lasts."**—Ibid., 17 March 1929.

104 **"Now the sky"**—Ibid.

105 **"It is so hard"**—Ibid., 18 March 1929.

105 **"And so we shall sit"**—Ibid.

105 **("'Tanks God,'"**—Ibid.

105 **In Byrd's account … "had to smile."**—Byrd, *Little America*, 178-179.

106 **No two accounts**—Crossing a boundary between a natural emphasis on the most dramatic elements of the situation and outright fancy is a 1934 publication for a juvenile audience, *Paramount Newsreel Men With Admiral Byrd in Little America*, with text by Wallace West. Freely employing fiction to heighten drama, as does the Paramount film about the Byrd Expedition (*With Byrd at the South Pole*, 1930), here the reader is led to believe that "everything useful was wrecked" in the crash of the Fokker, that Gould, Balchen, and June were thus "thrown back into the primitive," and that while they had "managed to save a little food," particles of which were "doled out … like jewels," the men if not rescued might have starved to death in three more days. (West, *Paramount Newsreel Men With Admiral Byrd in Little America*, 54-56.)

106 **Balchen's has the sound**—Balchen, *Come North With Me*, 177.

106 **Russell Owen's dramatic dispatch (and accompanying long quotation beginning "All we knew")**—Owen, "Byrd Flies to Mountains, Finds Missing Men Safe," *New York Times*, March 20, 1929.

107 **prepared to walk west**—Byrd, *Little America*, 183.

107 **passed over the sledge … thirteen hours.**—Ibid., 186.

107 **stormiest month**—Ibid., 187.

107 **some glaciological studies**—Gould, "Summary Report on the Geology of the Rockefeller Mountains," in *New York Times*, June 16, 1929.

107n **Apparently, however, Gould**—LMG, "My 50 Years of Antarctic Exploration and Research," Antarctican Society Memorial Lecture, National Academy of Sciences Auditorium, 19 April 1979, unpublished transcript, CCA-GC. Also 1981 Gould/Peter J. Anderson interview, OSUA-AP.

108 **"a silly, silly thing"**—LMG, "My 50 Years of Antarctic Exploration and Research," op. cit., CCA-GC.

108 **"That was all my fault"**—1981 Gould/Peter J. Anderson interview, OSUA-AP.

108 **"Now that the aviation unit"**—Rodgers, *Beyond the Barrier*, 109.

108   **concern to preserve Gould's morale**—Hoyt, *The Last Explorer,* 221; Rodgers, *Beyond the Barrier,* 101-102.

108   **"He [Byrd} has been so kind**"—LMG BAE I Diaries, 16 March 1929.

108   **regret would in time be tempered**—See Gould, *Cold,* 126, and 1981 Gould/Peter J. Anderson interview, OSUA-AP.

CHAPTER 8 — FORTY-TWO MEN

109   **"A man is not lost"** ... **"Lost in Mountains Gould."**—Gould, *Cold,* 34.

109   **In any case ... pale green.**—Gould, *Cold,* 37-42; LMG BAE I Diaries, 31 March to 7 April 1929. (Direct quotations in this paragraph are from Cold, 41.)

109   **On the 19th ... the physical.**—Gould, *Cold,* 42; LMG BAE I Diaries, 19 April 1929; Byrd, *Little America,* 197-198; Rodgers, *Beyond the Barrier,* 118.

111   **"each man's true self"**—Balchen, *Come North With Me,* 180.

111   **to his taste**—Gould, *Cold,* 65, for instance.

111   **practical weapons**—Byrd, *Little America,* 198.

111   **Camp chores**—Balchen, *Come North With Me,* 180; Gould, *Cold,* 45; LMG BAE I Diaries, 23 April and 18 June 1929.

111   **"with an unswerving"**—Byrd, *Little America,* 199.

111   **"if any man"**—Ibid., 209.

111n **Sleeping and living quarters**—See descriptions in Byrd, *Little America,* 211-216, as well as the map of Little America between 232 and 233; also Rodgers, *Beyond the Barrier,* 114-116.

112   **"Simon"**—Gould, *Cold,* 55; LMG BAE I Diaries, 29 June 1929.

112   **On a typical**—"typical day" information from Gould, *Cold,* 53-59, and Byrd, *Little America,* 199-200, 205-206, with direct quotations cited below.

112   **"special accomplishment"**—Byrd, *Little America,* 206.

112   **"the one time of quiet"**—Gould, *Cold,* 58.

112   **"luxury of an hour"**—Ibid.

112   **"As the cold air"**—Ibid., 58-59.

112   **Saturday nights ... deprivation.**—LMG BAE I Diaries, 23 April 1929; Gould, *Cold,* 49.

112n **By midwinter ... "Simon Doodle Bug."**—LMG BAE I Diaries, 29 June 1929.

113   **Card games filled**—LMG BAE I Diaries, several entries, for instance 8 April 1929; Gould, *Cold,* 48.

113   **camp library**—Gould, *Cold,* 64-65; Carter, *Little America,* 98; LMG BAE I Diaries, numerous entries, plus undated insert "Books Read—in order from time of leaving Norfolk." Gould's journal entries sometimes include reactions to his reading. Some sample reviews: 16 May 1929: "Last night I read Hudson's "Green Mansions"—what a book what a book—I wonder how many more times I shall read it. If there was ever a more exquisite love story written—a more perfect picture of etherealized passion then I have not heard of it—so poignant that it hurts—the sort of book that leaves one with the feeling that he never wants to read anything else. He wants to preserve always the precious, the delicate, the fragrant memory of this story. I am actually reluctant to pick up another book." 14 September 1929: "I have just finished reading Romain Rolland's "Jean Christophe." ... I believe I can without hesitation call it the greatest work of fiction I have ever had my hands on. ... It is filled with writing that thrills one with its sheer beauty—it is the rarest combination of all the elements or sides of life. It is the first book I have ever read that has seemed to me to be genuine realism. Here is a deep perception of the spiritual forces behind life—but never with eyes that are blinded to the ugly facts that often constitute the major part of a life."

In an introduction Gould wrote in 1965 for a new printing of George Gaylord Simpson's book *Attending Marvels*, Gould noted: "During the long winter night on the First Byrd Antarctic Expedition I had time to read all of Shakespeare's plays. To pass the time of day I recorded his allusions to geology and was astounded both by their number and accuracy."

113 **"As for myself."**—Gould, *Cold*, 65.

113 **religious observation ... unlikely people.**—LMG, "My 50 Years of Antarctic Exploration and Research," op. cit., CCA-GC; Carter, *Little America*, 97.

114 **"University of Antarctica"**—Gould, *Cold*, 48; LMG BAE I Diaries, entry dated "Monday. May 5th," [sic—6 May 1929], 8 May, 15 May, entry dated "Monday June 11" [sic—10 June 1929]; Byrd, *Little America*, 221.

114 **"teaching people who are"**—LMG BAE I Diaries, entry dated "Monday June 11" [sic—10 June 1929].

114 **Gould himself spent**—Ibid., 5 May, 15 May, and 29 May 1929 (including "quite wooden headed").

114 **altered plans ... "making preparations."**—Ibid., 2 May 1929.

114 **learning to ski ... too dark.**—Ibid., entries for 3 May to 12 May 1929.

114 **"just an average" ... "thought it would be."**—Ibid., 9 April 1929.

115 **"He tried for three"**—Ibid., entry dated "Tuesday May 6" [sic—7 May 1929].

115 **"an aurora of auroras" ... "up there anyhow."**—Ibid., 13 May 1929.

116 **On the 9th of May**—Description from ibid, 12 May 1929; Rodgers, *Beyond the Barrier*, 131.

116 **"pretty gay" ... "fell off his seat."**—LMG BAE I Diaries, 12 May 1929,

116 **"It was a grand party"**—Ibid.

116 **"a spectacular and riotous"**—Harrison quoted in Rodgers, *Beyond the Barrier*, 131.

116 **two men began siphoning ... ski boot.**—Carter, *Little America,* 104; Rodgers, *Beyond the Barrier*, 132; LMG, "My 50 Years of Antarctic Exploration and Research," op. cit., CCA-GC; 1981 Gould/Peter J. Anderson interview, OSUA-AP.

116n **nearly experienced a fatality**—See the account in Rodgers, *Beyond the Barrier*, 131-132.

117 **"When I remember"**—LMG BAE I Diaries, 12 May 1929.

117 **"Liquor is a bad thing"**—Ibid., 27 May 1929.

117 **"The recent drunk"**—Ibid., 29 May 1929.

117 **"did not want to give"**—Rodgers, *Beyond the Barrier,* 132-133.

117 **As Gould recalled ... "people to drink."**—LMG, "My 50 Years of Antarctic Exploration and Research," op. cit., CCA-GC; also 1978 Gould/Neider interview, transcript in Neider, *Beyond Cape Horn*, 323; 1981 Gould/Peter J. Anderson interview, OSUA-AP.

118 **"dopey" feeling**—LMG BAE I Diaries, 24 May 1929.

118 **"There has been so much"**—Ibid., 31 May 1929.

118 **"Yesterday found me"**—Ibid., entry dated "Monday June 11" [sic—10 June 1929].

118 **"There are so many"**—Ibid., 31 May 1929.

118 **"Incredible how the time"**—Ibid., entry dated "Monday June 11" [sic—10 June 1929].

118 **On June 12 ... "establish you everlastingly."**—Radiogram, Putnam to REB via *Times*, 12 June 1929, OSUA-BP, folder #1761.

118 **"quite the most" ... "off the map."**—LMG BAE I Diaries, 12 June 1929.

118 **early in 1930**—While Gould on the sledge trip trail back to Little America early in 1930. Byrd sent him the message: "Putnam is back from Europe sends his regards and he tells us the submarine trip is probably off." (From folder "Messages Sledge Journey Part 2," in Box 2 of NA-GP.)

118 **Gould was surprised**—Gould, *Cold*, 67.

118   **65 degrees over twenty hours**—Byrd, *Little America*, 231.

118   **"balmy" ... "cloth parka."**—LMG BAE I Diaries, 6 June 1929.

118   **"unparalleled quiet" ... "expanding sort of silence,"**—Ibid., 23 June 1929.

118   **"It is the natural"**—Gould, *Cold*, 65.

118   **"the whining and screeching ... "when it is so dark."**—Ibid., 67.

118   **"a soft pastel" ... "graceful curves."**—LMG BAE I Diaries, 23 June 1929.

118   **"The whole snowscape,"**—Ibid.

119   **"should be sorry for"**—Gould, *Cold*, 66-67.

119   **"butters his bread"**—1981 Gould/Peter J. Anderson interview, OSUA-AP.

119   **Experienced explorers had warned**—Rodgers, *Beyond the Barrier,* 135, quoting radiogram of 8 August 1929, REB to Hilton H. Railey. [Railey was Byrd's business manager.]

119   **Personalities did clash ... depression**—See Rodgers, *Beyond the Barrier,* Chapter 8, throughout.

119   **A falling out between**—2001 Vaughan/Brewster interview, OSUA.

119   **as has been suggested**—Rodgers, *Beyond the Barrier,* 134.

119   **frequent butts**—Rodgers (*Beyond the Barrier,* 143-144) identifies Tom Mulroy as meeting "the psychic needs of the men to have a target for their hostility" and Russell Owen as meeting "the need to have a target for their contempt."

119   **character of Richard Byrd**—The literature on Byrd is voluminous, and the characterizations made here are based on no single source, though I have found Rodgers' book on the 1928-30 expedition especially useful. Gould was reluctant throughout his life to offer any public criticism of Byrd. The frankness of his 1981 interview with Peter J. Anderson, who was then hoping to write a new Byrd biography, is helpful. In addition to the interview recording and transcript, see also Anderson's handwritten notes in Box 5, Folder 7 of the Peter J. Anderson Papers, OSUA. In his Anderson interview Gould supposed that Byrd came to resent him and the attention that came to him and perhaps that Byrd was jealous of his facility in getting along with people, saying "he wanted people to like him—but he didn't know how." (1981 Gould/Peter J. Anderson interview, OSUA-AP)

119   **managed without difficulty**—Or maybe not entirely without difficulty. Gould always got on easily with people, but at times that winter he regretted his "unruly" tongue. See for instance this diary entry from early June: "Of my infinitude of faults none seems to come more often and more conspicuously to the front than my tongue—like no other aspect of my being is it unruly. I must write again that I may the more often recall it the admonition of Epictetus 'Nature hath given man one tongue but two ears, that we may hear from others twice as much as we speak.' I talk every day but tonight it seems as though my tongue has been more two edged to-day than usual." (LMG BAE I Diaries, 8 June 1929.)

119   **Gould significant credit ... "kept morale high"**—Rodgers, *Beyond the Barrier,* 153. Another historian of Little America wrote similarly that Gould was "in many respects the real backbone of the wintering-over party." (Carter, *Little America*, 100.)

119   **Fourth of July**—Information from LMG BAE I Diaries, entry dated "Sunday, July 6th" [sic—actual date either Saturday July 6 or Sunday July 7, 1929]; Gould, *Cold*, 50-51; Rodgers, *Beyond the Barrier,* 137-138, with direct quotations cited below.

120   **"a curious combination" ... "vocal ability."**—Gould, *Cold*, 50.

        "Don't tell Simon"—LMG BAE I Diaries, entry dated "Sunday, July 6th" [sic—actual date either Saturday July 6 or Sunday July 7, 1929].

120   **break up two fights.**—Ibid.

120   **Ashley McKinley ... "son of a bitch!'"**—1981 Gould/Peter J. Anderson interview, OSUA-AP.

120   **unsanctioned after-hours drinking parties**—Rodgers, *Beyond the Barrier,* 139.

120n   **"a pest of hell" ... make him sick.**—1981 Gould/Peter J. Anderson interview, OSUA-AP.

121 **"arrested" Taffy Davies ... "sphinx to smile."**—LMG BAE I Diaries, 19 July 1929.

121 **sleeping during the day ... on the 30th.**—LMG BAE I Diaries, 1 August 1929; Byrd, *Little America*, 230-231 (for temperature and wind velocity recordings).

121 **"There is an increasingly" ... "actual polar flight."**—LMG BAE I Diaries, 9 August 1929.

121 **On August 19**—Byrd, *Little America*, 271.

121 **"again the very atmosphere" ... returning presence.**—LMG BAE I Diaries, 21 August 1929.

121 **August 22** Information from LMG BAE I Diaries, 21 August and entry dated "August 23rd" [sic—24 August 1929]; Byrd, *Little America*, 272; Carter, *Little America*, 108; and Rodgers, *Beyond the Barrier*, 153-154; with direct quotations cited below.

122 **"plenty wet."**—LMG BAE I Diaries, entry dated "August 23rd" [sic—24 August 1929].

122 **"rigged up as"**—Harrison quoted in Rodgers, *Beyond the Barrier*, 153.

122 **"A mild tornado"**—Quoted in Byrd, *Little America*, 272.

122 **Gould "was the first"**—Rodgers, *Beyond the Barrier*, 154.

122 **"stuck for the next"**—Carter, *Little America*, 108.

122 **"those few who drink"**—Demas quoted in Rodgers, *Beyond the Barrier*, 154.

122 **"Larry gave the boys" ... this time, kept.**—Ibid.

122 **only month of their entire stay**—Gould, *Cold*, 104; Byrd, *Little America*, 273.

122 **Most of Gould's ... "taken care of."**—See Gould, *Cold*, 103; LMG BAE I Diaries through September 1929. "Of paramount importance" is from 21 August 1929; the quotation beginning "There are accumulating" is from the entry misdated "Wednesday September 5th." [sic—September 5 was a Thursday].

123 **"the wings of expectancy"**—Byrd, *Little America*, 273.

123 **"another busy day" ... "months on end."**—LMG BAE I Diaries, 26 September 1929.

CHAPTER 9 — THE TRAIL SOUTH

124 **"On the 11th"**—Amundsen, Roald, "The First Account," in Vol. I. of *The South Pole: An Account of the Norwegian Antarctic Expedition in the "Fram," 1910-1912*, trans. by A. G. Chater. London: John Murray, 1913, xii; viii-xix.

124 **In 1908 ... (and paragraphs following)**—All of this is standard information on the much-documented Antarctic expeditions of Shackleton, Amundsen, and Scott, derivable from summarizations to be found in any number of online websites.

126 **Therein, noting that ... "evidence of this."**—Quotations from Priestley and Tilley, "Geological Problems of Antarctica," 315, 321, and 324.

126 **85° 27' S**—Gould, "The Geological Sledge Trip," in Byrd, *Little America*, 406.

126n **"Find out some place"**—LMG, "My 50 Years of Antarctic Exploration and Research," op. cit., CCA-GC.

128 **The composition of the geological**—Rodgers, *Beyond the Barrier*, 48, 86, 134, 160; Gould, "The Geological Sledge Trip," in Byrd, *Little America*, 397.

128 **multiple aims**—Gould, *Cold*, 69-70; Byrd, *Little America*, 249; Gould, "The Geological Sledge Trip," in Byrd, *Little America*, 396; Gould, "Some Geographical Results of the Byrd Antarctic Expedition," 180-181.

128 **"curious and unnatural-seeming"**—Gould, "Some Geographical Results ...", 181.

128 **Ninety days**—Gould, Cold, 70.

128 **logistical planning**—The third chapter of Gould's book *Cold*, "How We Planned To Do

It," contains the best summary of problems faced in planning the Geological Party's sledge journey and of the solutions employed.

129 **Gould's six-man … making ready.**—Rodgers, *Beyond the Barrier,* 160; Byrd, *Little America,* 254; Gould, *Cold,* 106; LMG BAE I Diaries, 4 October and 6 October 1929.

129 **first clean shave … thick snow.**—LMG BAE I Diaries, 30 September 1929.

129 **On the 4th … "made of lead."**—LMG BAE I Diaries, 4 October 1929.

129 **Another problem emerged**—LMG BAE I Diaries, 7 October 1929; Gould, *Cold,* 107; Rodgers, *Beyond the Barrier,* 161.

129 **Departure was retargeted … postponed departure.**—LMG BAE I Diaries, 9 October 1929, 12 October 1929 ("off my feed"), 13 October 1929 ("a bit queer amidships"); Byrd, *Little America,* 281.

130 **conference in the camp library**—Harrison BAE I Diary, 13 October 1929, NA-HP; Rodgers, *Beyond the Barrier,* 161-162.

130 **"an unsatisfactory session"**—Harrison BAE I Diary, 13 October 1929, NA-HP.

130 **"clearly acrimonious"**—Rodgers, *Beyond the Barrier,* 161.

130 **"hectic confused takeoff"**—Harrison BAE I Diary, 13 October 1929, NA-HP.

130 **After four exhausting … to move again.**—Byrd, *Little America,* 284-285; LMG BAE I Diaries, 13 October 1929; Harrison BAE I Diary, 13 October 1929, NA-HP. The day's experience added to some of the men's growing disenchantment with Byrd. Harrison's diary entry for October 13 observed that "The Commander caused considerable confusion unnecessarily, much misunderstanding and even a little hard feeling through his seemingly thoughtless tactics today," also observing that "under stress or at close range the idol usually topples from the pedestal." That same evening, expedition general hand Arnold Clarke was telling his diary that "the farce reached a chaotic condition today. If there is one here who still respects [Byrd], it is because there is something wrong with him." (Quoted in Rodgers, *Beyond the Barrier,* 162

130 **The next day … "in the morning."**—Byrd, *Little America,* 285; LMG BAE I Diaries, 14 October 1929.

130 **The combined parties**—Information for this and the succeeding paragraph from Gould, *Cold,* 114-118; Byrd, *Little America,* 287-289; and LMG BAE I Diaries, 17 October 1929, with direct quotations cited below.

131 **"evident beyond any"**—LMG BAE I Diaries, 17 October 1929.

131 **"Frightfully tired"**—Ibid.

131 **air support**—Hoyt, *The Last Explorer,* 239; Rodgers, *Beyond the Barrier,* 164; Gould, *Cold,* 73, 118.

131n **clear explanation … "second method."**—Gould, *Cold,* 71-73.

132 **at the conference convened**—Information for this and the succeeding paragraph from Byrd, *Little America,* 290-291; Rodgers, *Beyond the Barrier,* 164.

132 **Ford snowmobile**—Gould expressed himself as "doubtful as to its possible usefulness," noting that the snowmobile's performance the previous fall had left much to be desired and that "in order to help our sledging parties now it would have to go so far out as to make it expensive in getting to the starting point where our heavy loads are." (LMG BAE I Diaries, 22 October 1929; also in Gould, *Cold,* 120.)

132 **Two days later (October 20)**—LMG BAE I Diaries, 20 October 1929; Gould, *Cold,* 119. The date printed in *Cold,* October 25th, is an error.

132 **Vaughan's depot-laying … to No. 3**—Gould, *Cold,* 119-122; Byrd, *Little America,* 292-296. Vaughan's message to Gould regarding "important deficiencies" and "much overhauling necessary" is quoted in Byrd, *Little America,* 293.

133 **While the rest … fairy palace.**—LMG BAE I Diaries, 25 October 1929 (including "celestial room"); Gould, *Cold,* 109-111.

133 **A few days later**—LMG BAE I Diaries, 29 October 1929.

133 **recovered and photographed ... "far as they could see."**—Byrd, *Little America,* 297.

133 **radio carried even to**—Carter, *Little America,* 110; Rodgers, *Beyond the Barrier,* 170.

133 **A communiqué on the 30th ... beyond imagination.**—Byrd, *Little America,* 298.

134 **"Great upheavals" ... now marked trail.**—Ibid., 300-301.

134 **In Little America ... "toward the mountains."**—LMG BAE I Diaries, 1 November 1929.

134 **in the early afternoon**—Ibid., 4 November 1929; Gould, "The Geological Sledge Trip," in Byrd, *Little America,* 397.

134 **They drove ... malted milk.**—Gould, "The Geological Sledge Trip," in Byrd, *Little America,* 394-395.

134 **For entertainment**—Ibid., 405; LMG BAE I Diaries, 16 December 1929; Gould, *Cold,* 240.

134n **"Tea, not coffee"**—LMG to Hyme Loss, 28 July 1948, CCA.

135 **snowmobile party carried no radio.**—Byrd, *Little America,* 296.

135 **Gould's group met ... twenty-mile depot.**—Ibid., 302, 304; LMG BAE I Diaries, 4 November 1929; Gould, *Cold,* 125. The first two of these sources put the snowmobile breakdown at seventy-five miles out, while the third says eighty-five miles.

135 **For some days ... "the next month."**—LMG BAE I Diaries, 6-8 November 1929. ("For some of us" quotation from entry of November 8.)

135 **"How many times" ... snow blindness**—Ibid., 10 November 1929.

135 **"The blister, the size" ... the whole party.**—Vaughan, *With Byrd at the Bottom of the World,* 97-98. Vaughan wrote of Gould's blister as being on his left heel. In *Cold*, Gould says that it was his right. Vaughan wrote of Gould as uncomplaining, but Gould remembered this time as excruciating: "Never before or since have I ended a day in such complete and hopeless misery as I did this second day of independent travel on skis. Every stride of my right ski sent pains shooting up from my heel. I never would have believed that my legs could get so lame and sore without actually falling off." (Gould, *Cold,* 132.)

136 **A heavy hoar frost ... two lashed units**—LMG BAE I Diaries, 13-14 November 1929; Gould, *Cold,* 134-135.

136 **On the 15th**—LMG BAE I Diaries, 15 November 1929.

136 **often held their breath ... "seemed quite black."**—Gould, *Cold,* 136.

136 **all in all, milder**—LMG BAE I Diaries, 15 November 1929.

136 **Depot No. 4**—Ibid., 17 November 1929; Rodgers, *Beyond the Barrier,* 201.

136 **The effect of added**—LMG BAE I Diaries, 18 November 1929.

136 **"Disheartening and dreary"**—Gould, *Cold,* 138.

136 **"I tried to beguile"**—Ibid., 139.

136n **Though blistered ... rest of the trip.**—See Gould's 1986 narration to silent film footage of the Geological Party Sledge Trip to the Queen Maud Mountains, videotape copy, CCA.

137 **altered order of march.**—Ibid., 138, and Rodgers, *Beyond the Barrier,* 203.

137 **About noon that day**—Gould, *Cold,* 139; Byrd, *Little America,* 311.

137 **"frightful mess" ... continued on its way.**—Byrd, *Little America,* 311-312.

137 **"covering in about four"**—Gould, *Cold,* 139

137 **One thought that ... "kill so many."**—Gould, *Cold,* 139-140.

137 **Meanwhile, Byrd ... "but little comfort."**— Ibid., 140 (including all quotations). Also Rodgers, *Beyond the Barrier,* 180; LMG BAE I Diaries, 19 November 1929.

138 **On the morning ... day in repose.**—Gould, *Cold,* 142-43.

138 **"things began to go better."**—Gould, "The Geological Sledge Trip," in Byrd, *Little America,* 398.

138   **Depot No. 5**—Gould, *Cold*, 145; LMG BAE I Diaries, 22-23 November 1929.

138   **shoot four dogs … for the purpose.**—Rodgers, *Beyond the Barrier*, 203-204; LMG BAE I Diaries, 22 November 1929. Gould in his 1981 interview with Peter J. Anderson (1981 Gould/Peter J. Anderson interview, OSUA-AP), was still appreciative of Vaughan's "grand gesture" in taking over that responsibility for everyone, and Vaughan, in his 2001 interview with Karen Brewster (2001 Vaughan/Brewster interview, OSUA), said that shooting those dogs was "a terribly hard thing to do."

138   **"The crack of the revolver"**—LMG BAE I Diaries, 25 November 1929.

138   **From the crevassed … of supper.**—Gould, "The Geological Sledge Trip," in Byrd, *Little America*, 398; Carter, *Little America*, 114-116; LMG BAE I Diaries, 23-24 November 1929.

139   **one change of underwear … "for the whole trip."**—Vaughan, *With Byrd at the Bottom of the World*, 121-122.

139   **Through twenty-one days … before them.**—LMG BAE I Diaries, 25-26 November 1929; Gould, *Cold*, 149.

140   **nerves … and irascibility**—Dana Coman to LMG, letter begun 25 November and completed 28 November 1929, NA-GP. This letter was part of the packet of mail dropped for the Geological Party as the polar flight passed by on the 28th.

140   **Worried by the news … forecast in camp.**—Rodgers, *Beyond the Barrier*, 182.

140   **perfect local weather … later that afternoon.**—Gould, *Cold*, 151; Rodgers, *Beyond the Barrier*, 182.

140   **Enjoined from … traveling time.**—Gould, *Cold*, 151, 154.

140   **At 3:29 p.m. … headlines everywhere.**—Gould, *Cold*, 154-155; Rodgers, *Beyond the Barrier*, 184-191.

140   **While their expedition … "or bust."**—Gould, *Cold*, 161.

140   **Bitter winds**—Ibid., 162.

140   **"countless crevasses" … "being the latter."**—LMG BAE I Diaries, 30 November 1929.

140   **"maze of chasms"**—Gould, *Cold*, 167.

141   **"an almost grim necessity."**—Ibid., 165.

141   **With great partially … four feet wide.**—Ibid., 168.

141   **"We were able to"**—Ibid., 169.

141   **"frozen inferno,"**—Ibid.

141   **About a mile from**—Rodgers, *Beyond the Barrier*, 206.

141   **"practically before they hit" … hot supper before bed.**—Gould, *Cold*, 169.

141   **"One of the boys" … "long sought mountains."**—Ibid., 170.

CHAPTER 10 — "NO SYMPHONY I HAVE EVER HEARD …"

142   **some hypotheses … flat-topped tabular mountains**—Gould, *Cold*, 171.

142   **"immediately suggested horsts"**—Gould, "Some Geographical Results …", 187.

142   **"were covered with" … "story of it all."**—Gould, *Cold*, 171.

142   **Their next challenge**—Ibid., 172.

142   **Their first attempt … "of any consequence."**—Ibid., 172-173.

142   **A mile or two … returned to camp.**—Ibid., 173-174.

143   **All the while … and adding ten.**—Ibid., 174.

144   **Discouraged by … reaching Mt. Nansen.**—Ibid., 175-176.

144   **The team spent … flexible sledges.**—Ibid., 176-178. Also LMG BAE I Diaries, 3 December and 4 December 1929, and Rodgers, *Beyond the Barrier*, 207.

144 **"most depressing day" ... human feces.**—LMG BAE I Diaries, 5 December 1929.

145 **"reasonable conjecture"**—Priestley and Tilley, "Geological Problems of Antarctica," 321.

145 **on the 6th ... the next day.**—LMG BAE I Diaries, 6 December 1929; Gould, *Cold*, 180 (including "hard grind"). Gould put the day's mileage at thirteen in his diary and fifteen in his book. Hence, "some fourteen" seems fair to record.

145 **"It was the same old story."**—Gould, *Cold*, 181.

145 **The rocks were found ... "Queen Maud Mountains."**—Ibid., 181-182.

145 **Finally, three or four ... desired outcrop.**—LMG BAE I Diaries, 7 December 1929 (including "spine sort of tingle"); Gould, *Cold*, 181-183.

145 **"I had had the unhappy"**—Gould, *Cold*, 183.

146 **significance of the sandstone**—See Gould, "Some Geographical Results ...", 189; Gould, *Cold*, 184; Carter, *Little America*, 140-142.

146 **"the most stupendous"**— Gould, *Cold*, 184.

146 **The climbers were further... yet been found.**—Gould, Some Geographical Results ...", 189; Gould, *Cold*, 185.

146 **Gould immediately anticipated ... low-grade coal.**—Gould, *Cold*, 186-187.

146 **it implied that ... "sub-tropical climate."**—Gould, "An Antarctic Sledge Journey," 6 (including quotations); also Gould, "Some Geographical Results ...", 194.

146 **Determining after another ... to Strom Camp.**—LMG BAE I Diaries, 9 December 1929; Gould, *Cold*, 188.

147 **En route, they made ... eighteen years before.**—Ibid., 9-10 December 1929; Gould, Cold, 189-190.

147 **Alas, when they ... soon be pointed.**—LMG BAE I Diaries, 10 December 1929; Gould, Cold, 191.

147 **Gould decided ... would yield success.**—Gould, *Cold*, 192.

147 **On December 11 ... too much for them.**—LMG BAE I Diaries, 11 December 1929; Gould, *Cold*, 191-192 ("untidy ways" on 192).

147n **"They ... approached very gingerly"**—Gould, *Cold*, 190.

148 **The next day**—Gould, *Cold*, 192 (including "with but little difficulty"); LMG BAE I Diaries, 12 December 1929 (including "very safe margin"). "Approximately thirty miles" and "two hundred-some pounds": Gould's diary says 29.5 miles and 250 pounds; Gould's book says 34 miles and 200 pounds. You pick.

148 **brilliant sunshine ... "complete fairyland."**—Gould, *Cold*, 193-195.

148 **awoke on the 14th ... delighted to move on.**—Gould, *Cold*, 195-199 ("godsend," 196); LMG BAE I Diaries, 13-17 December 1929.

149 **familiar trouble ... Thorne Glacier.**—Information from LMG BAE I Diaries, 17-19 December 1929; Gould, *Cold*, 198-207; Vaughan, *With Byrd at the Bottom of the World*, 117; with direct quotations cited below.

149 **"quite the grandest"**—Gould, *Cold*, 201.

149 **"There seemed,"**—Ibid., 206.

149 **supposed "Carmen Land"**—Gould, *Cold*, 201-204.

149 **no intention ... before turning about.**—Gould, *Cold*, 205.

150 **Accordingly, on the 20th**—Information for this and two following paragraphs (to "the journey home") from Gould, *Cold*, 207-212; LMG BAE I Diaries, 20-21 December 1929; Vaughan, *With Byrd at the Bottom of the World*, 117; with direct quotations cited below.

150 **"Put your hats on!"**—Gould, *Cold*, 208.

150 **"a dependency" ... "soil in the Antarctic."**—Gould copied a replica of the note left behind into his trip log. (LMG BAE I Diaries, 21 December 1929.)

150n **It was the official ... take them up.**—Chaturvedi, *Polar Regions*, 74.

151 **similar difficulties**—LMG BAE I Diaries, 22-25 December 1929; Gould, *Cold*, 213-214.

151 **On Christmas Day**—Information for this and two following paragraphs from Gould, *Cold*, 216-221, and Carter, *Little America*, 146, with direct quotations cited below.

151 **"as a last hope"**—Gould radio message to Byrd quoted in Carter, *Little America*, 146.

151 **"did not seem conceivable"**—Gould, *Cold*, 218.

151 **"seemed to be just"**—Ibid., 219.

151 **"The nearer we came"**—Ibid.

151 **"a tin can with"**—Ibid., 220.

151 **"We did not need"**—Ibid.

152 **"His simple gesture"**—Vaughan, *With Byrd at the Bottom of the World,* 126.

152 **That night the group … they were off.**—LMG BAE I Diaries, 27-30 December 1929; Gould, *Cold*, 222-223 and 227-228.

152n **"Here is the hammer"**—Swithinbank, *An Alien in Antarctica*, 94-95.

153 **"As though for a good"**—LMG BAE I Diaries, 30 December 1929.

153 **Unanimous in wanting … on the 31st.**—Gould, *Cold*, 237.

153 **Nineteen more days … reverse direction.**—See LMG BAE I Diaries, entries for 1 January-19 January 1931, and Gould, Cold, 238-256.

153 **limited themselves … six or seven hours.**—Gould, *Cold*, 239.

154 **skiing naked**—LMG BAE I Diaries, 7 January 1930.

154 **Camping on the edge … on either side.**—LMG BAE I Diaries, 10 January 1930.

154 **It was in this area … Gould's way for days;**—Information from Gould, *Cold*, 248-250; LMG BAE I Diaries, 11 January 1930; with direct quotations cited below.

154 **"quite the most foolish"**—Gould, *Cold*, 248.

154 **"turned and looked down"**—Ibid.

154 **"very meekly"**—Ibid., 249.

154 **As Vaughan would later note**—Vaughan, *With Byrd at the Bottom of the World,* 134.

154 **Beset a day later … northward march.**—Gould, *Cold*, 250-251; LMG BAE I Diaries, 12-14 January 1930 ("a spider web" quotation from entry of January 12).

155 **an uneasy month … through that season.**—See Rodgers, *Beyond the Barrier*, 223-224 and throughout Chapter 14; Carter, *Little America*, 144, 148-150.

155 **It was feared … evident in morale.**—Byrd, *Little America*, 365-366.

155 **no other situation**—Ibid., 365.

155 **Gould was kept informed … "arduous journey."**—Ibid., 367.

155 **In the middle … dogs to death.**—Rodgers, *Beyond the Barrier*, 225-227; Byrd, *Little America*, 370-373; Gould, *Cold*, 253-254 (including "much discussion" quote, 254).

156 **That day, the 17th … "see it end."**—LMG BAE I Diaries, 17-18 January 1930.

156 **Setting out that night … back at camp.**—Gould, *Cold*, 256.

156 **boisterous greeting … of the 19th.**—LMG BAE I Diaries, 19 January 1930; Byrd, *Little America*, 374; Henry Harrison, BAE I Diary, 19 January 1930.

156 **"As they topped … Abdul"**—Byrd, "The Conquest of Antarctica By Air," *The National Geographic Magazine* (August 1930): 220. Apparently the full form of Gould's new nickname was "Abdul the Camel Driver." (Henry Harrison, BAE I Diary, 19 January 1930.)

156 **"A bath—and Paradise!"**—Goodale quoted in Byrd, *Little America*, 374.

156 **As the layers … men now looked.**—Ibid.

156n **"On the trail bound"**—Frederick E. Crockett to LMG, 18 January 1930 ("On the trail bound for Little America"), NA-GP.

157 **"a new place" ... "peace and security"**—Henry Harrison, BAE I Diary, 19 January 1930.

157 **became clear to Gould ... "on their way out."**—1981 Gould/Peter J. Anderson interview, OSUA-AP.

157 **As for himself ... "curious feeling."**—LMG BAE I Diaries, 24 January 1930.

158 **At one point ... "interesting, if true"**—Byrd, *Little America*, 378.

158 **on January 20 ... her way through.**—Rodgers, *Beyond the Barrier*, 228, 236-237.

158 **diarist Harrison wrote**—Henry Harrison, BAE I Diary, 28 January 1930.

158 **Gould reportedly broached**—Rodgers, *Beyond the Barrier*, 233.

158 **"feared that the ships"**—Siple, *A Boy Scout With Byrd, 141*.

158 **such activities as**—LMG BAE I Diaries, 7 February 1930.

158 **Finally, on February 7 ... "might prove serious."**—Byrd, *Little America*, 381-382.

158 **As it happened ... ferocious winds.**—Ibid., 383-386.

158 **On the 15th ... "here in camp."**—LMG BAE I Diaries, 15 February 1930.

158 **It was early evening ... for the last time.**—Ibid., 19 February 1930 (including "Detention Camp"); Byrd, *Little America*, 387-388.

159 **Loading was directed ... they were away.**—Byrd, *Little America*, 389; Rodgers, *Beyond the Barrier*, 242.

159 **"colored by romance."**—Gould's words at age 81, as told to writer Paul Carter, quoted in Carter, *Little America*, 155.

159 **"I must confess"**—LMG BAE I Diaries, 19 February 1930.

159 **Aboard ship ... return to Dunedin.**—Willcox, *Beneath a Wandering Star, 69-71* (including "more than most" quote); Byrd, *Little America*, 390-391; LMG BAE I Diaries, 1 March 1930.

159 **It was March 10 ... "The Conquering Hero."**—*Ann Arbor Daily News*, undated clipping pasted into scrapbook of the Byrd Expedition titled "Larry's Book," CCA-GC.

159 **how very green ... fresh fruit.**—Carter, *Little America*, 155.

CHAPTER 11 — ENDINGS AND BEGINNINGS

160 **Departing New Zealand**—Rodgers, *Beyond the Barrier*, 248.

160 **shipboard mate**—Willcox, *Beneath a Wandering Star*, 87.

160 **"a sorry pair" ... "aptly named."**—Ibid., 88.

160 **Following a week's**—Ibid., 96.

160 **on May 22**—Rodgers, *Beyond the Barrier*, 250.

160 **seventeen-day tow**—Willcox, *Beneath a Wandering Star*, 102.

160 **Associated Press interviewer**—The AP report ran in numerous papers; see for instance the *Detroit Free Press*, May 24, 1930.

160 **returned to sea ... June 19.**—Rodgers, *Beyond the Barrier*, 250.

160n **After the seasickness**—Willcox, *Beneath a Wandering Star*, 133-134.

161 **Both the *City* ... slowly up Broadway.**—Willcox, *Beneath a Wandering Star*, 136-137; Rodgers, *Beyond the Barrier*, 251-252.

161 **In the lead car ... and Goodale.**—Vaughan, *With Byrd at the Bottom of the World*, 152.

161 **The caravan unloaded ... overnight to Washington.**—Willcox, *Beneath a Wandering Star*, 137-139; Rodgers, *Beyond the Barrier*, 252-253.

161 **On the 20th ... With Byrd at the South Pole.**—Willcox, *Beneath a Wandering Star,*

139-141; Rodgers, *Beyond the Barrier*, 253 (including "almost everybody who was anybody"); *New York Times*, June 11, 1930.

162   **A train carried … state capitol.**—Rodgers, *Beyond the Barrier*, 254; Rose, *Explorer*, 285.

162   **morning of the 26th**—*Detroit News*, June 26, 1930; *Ann Arbor Daily News*, June 26, 1930.

162   **to Boston … "of distinguished citizens."**—Willcox, *Beneath a Wandering Star*, 141-143.

162   **In July, Gould**—Willcox, *Beneath a Wandering Star*, 157.

162   **university had just**—Proceedings of the University of Michigan Board of Regents, June 1930, BHL. Securing a boost in salary at a time of deepening economic depression was doubtless most welcome, but it would never in fact be collected, as Gould would ultimately be granted leaves of absence without pay for both the 1930-31 and 1931-32 academic years, "to permit him to complete, if possible, certain duties which have devolved upon him in connection with the Byrd Antarctic Expedition." (Proceedings of the University of Michigan Board of Regents, September 1930 and January 1931, BHL.) Gould's principal income during these years came from his lecturing, supplemented, at least at the beginning, with some continuing salary paid by Byrd. Between July 7 and October 10, 1930, for instance, Byrd paid Gould $1,235 for expenses and salary. (Referenced in REB to LMG, 28 November 1931, OSUA-BP, folder #6613.) Gould noted that most of his time during that period was given over to expedition affairs, including negotiating the sale of the *Eleanor Bolling*. (LMG to REB, 2 December 1931, OSUA-BP, folder #6613.)

162   **for Christmas sales.**—Rodgers, *Beyond the Barrier*, 259.

162   **"consummated in a few days"**—LMG to REB, 29 July 1930, OSUA-BP.

162   **The couple then … life as newlyweds.**—REB to LMG, 8 August 1930; LMG to REB, 16 August 1930; LMG to REB, 21 August 1930—all OSUA-BP, folder #6613.

162n   **"The entire theme"**—Willcox, *Beneath a Wandering Star*, 141.

164   **settling within a short time**—Correspondence to and from Gould show the currency of the 435 East 57th St. address at least from late October 1930 until the Goulds' departure from New York in 1932.

164   **It was envisioned**—Rodgers, *Beyond the Barrier*, 268.

164   **On September 2 … labor of love."**—LMG to REB, 2 September 1930, OSUA-BP, folder #6613.

164   **Byrd responded reassuringly … "see you through it."**—REB to LMG, 5 September 1930, OSUA-BP, folder #6613.

165   **Gould had already … in his appearances.**—LMG to REB, 2 September 1930, OSUA-BP, folder #6613; Rodgers, *Beyond the Barrier*, 266; Rose, *Explorer*, 290.

165   **Accordingly, in September … District of Columbia.**—LMG to REB, 22 September 1930, and "Pond Bureau List of Lecturers for 1930-31," brochure—both OSUA-BP, folder #6613; "With Byrd to the Bottom of the World" publicity flyer, with schedule of bookings, CCA-GC.

165   **Gould received a number**—REB to LMG, 10 September 1930; REB to LMG, 17 September 1930; REB to LMG, 18 September 1930—all OSUA-BP, folder #6613. (All quotations in this paragraph from the 17 September letter.)

165n   **Pond's list**—"Pond Bureau List of Lecturers for 1930-31," brochure, OSUA-BP, folder #6613.

165n   **Byrd was counting … "to the expedition."**—Rose, *Explorer*, 223.

166   **Byrd also offered**—REB to LMG, 10 September 1930, OSUA-BP, folder #6613.

166   **After first suggesting**—LMG to REB, undated but supposed to be 21 or 22 September 1930, OSUA-BP, folder #6613.

166   **declined as not adequate**—REB to LMG, 23 September 1930; REB to LMG, 27 September 1930—both OSUA-BP, folder #6613.

166   **Gould eventually agreed**—LMG to REB, 22 September 1930; REB to LMG, 23 September 1930; REB to LMG, 27 September 1930—all OSUA-BP, folder #6613.

166   **"a frightfully poor" ... departed for Chicago**—LMG to REB, 26 October 1930—all OSUA-BP, folder #6613.

166   **series of Midwestern lectures.** "With Byrd to the Bottom of the World" publicity flyer, with schedule of bookings, CCA-GC.

166   **rather grudging permission**—LMG to REB, 21 August 1930; REB to LMG, 10 September 1930; REB to LMG, 27 September 1930—all OSUA-BP, folder #6613.

166   **"discouraged [O'Brien] in his desire"**—LMG to REB, 9 September 1930, OSUA-BP, folder #6613.

166   **Byrd was being petitioned ... "about the expedition."**—REB to LMG, 27 September 1930, OSUA-BP, folder #6613.

166   **At Denison ... Livingstone medal.**—"With Byrd to the Bottom of the World" publicity flyer, with schedule of bookings and quoted testimonials, CCA-GC.

166n **"dirty deal" ... "do his job."**—Rodgers, *Beyond the Barrier*, 232-233.

167   **One of the earliest ... famed Byrd Expedition.**—*Carletonian*, October 11, 1930, 1.

167   **Following his well-received ... "agreed very warmly."**—"President Gould Says" column, *The Voice of the Carleton Alumni*, July 1957, 19. Gould was also known to suggest in later years that the true reason he wanted to return to the state after his 1930 lecture at Carleton was because on this occasion he had his first taste of Minnesota wild rice, which he liked immediately and later termed as "one of Minnesota's chief claims to enduring greatness." (See LMG to Laurence A. Rossman, 27 December 1945, and 18 January 1950, CCA.)

167   **Byrd sought Gould's critical ... "sorry not to have had them."**—REB to LMG, 2 November 1930, and LMG to REB, 22 November 1930—both OSUA-BP, folder #6613; see also Rodgers, *Beyond the Barrier*, 259-260.

168   **Early that month ... "less than 1500 miles.")**—LMG to Edward E. Goodale, 8 December 1930, National Archives Gift Collection of Materials Relating to Polar Regions—Edward E. Goodale Papers (hereafter NA-Goodale Papers).

168   **"without question one"**—"With Byrd to the Bottom of the World" publicity flyer, with schedule of bookings and quoted testimonials, CCA-GC.

168   **Blayney had followed through ... "one of the 'family.'"**—Lindsey Blayney to LMG, 15 January 1931, CCA.

169   **Toward the end of 1930 ... "eventually forthcoming."**—LMG to REB, 8 December 1930, OSUA-BP, folder #6613.

169   **work as practically stopped**—Ashley McKinley to REB, 11 December 1930, OSUA-BP, folder #6613.

169   **"please outline for me"**—REB to LMG, 20 December 1930, OSUA-BP, folder #6613.

169   **dated January 10 ... "that you speak of."**—REB to LMG, 10 January 1931, OSUA-BP, folder #6613.

169n **"Always sharp and quick"**—Carleton College Department of Geology, *Carleton's Century of Geology*, 36.

169n **Byrd biographer ... "considered disloyalty."**—Rose, *Explorer*, 5, 289.

170   **"I am genuinely disturbed"**—LMG to REB, 12 January 1931, OSUA-BP, folder #6613.

170   **"First—About medals." ... "O'Brien write such a book."**—LMG to REB, 17 January 1931, OSUA-BP, folder #1762.

171   **Gould repeated ... "O'Brien publish book."**—LMG telegram to REB, 19 January 1931; REB telegram to LMG, 20 January 1931; LMG telegram to REB, 26 January 1931—all OSUA-BP, folder #1762.

172   **"I cannot and will not" ... and aerial photography.**—REB to LMG, 3 February 1931 (three separate letters); REB to LMG, 6 February 1931—all OSUA-BP, folder #1762.

172   **"a pity for us" ... "purely for this reason."**—LMG to REB, 12 February 1931, OSUA-BP, folder #1762.

172n Byrd's post-expedition ... "scientific project."—Rodgers, *Beyond the Barrier*, 272-273.

173 The two did apparently ... "'full speed ahead.'"—Byrd's letter to Haines, of 2 March 1931, is quoted in Rodgers, *Beyond the Barrier*, 274.

173 When Byrd wrote Gould again—REB to LMG, 31 March 1931, OSUA-BP, folder #6613.

173 Putnam, who had sold—Tebbel, *A History of Book Publishing in the United States, Vol. III*, 525, 544-545.

173n The petrographical study—Carleton College Department of Geology, *Carleton's Century of Geology*, 51-52.

174 presented Larry with a gift copy—The book, now residing in the Carleton College Archives along with other personal effects of the Goulds, bears the inscription "A valentine for my husband."

174 wrote of his pleasure—Willcox, *Beneath a Wandering Star*, 335.

174 "This hero, now happily"—Ibid., 338-339.

174 Lincoln Ellsworth apparently approached—LMG to REB, 5 June 1931, OSUA-BP, folder #6613.

174 Gould wrote Paul Siple ... "by waiting for us."—LMG to Paul Siple, 24 April 1931, as quoted in Rose, *Explorer*, 291-292.

174n acquired in November 1932—Tebbel, *A History of Book Publishing in the United States, Vol. III*, 545.

175 Towards the end of May ... "privately and publicly."—LMG to REB, 27 May 1931; LMG to REB, 5 June 1931—both OSUA-BP, folder #6613.

175 Gould informed Byrd ... "the parties concerned."—LMG to REB, 5 June 1931, OSUA-BP, folder #6613

175 dated the preface ... American Geographical Society—Gould, *Cold*, 2-3.

175 verses of his kid sister-in-law—Ibid., 35.

175 desire to go back—Ibid., 268.

175 On the 17th ... "wish you all success."—REB to LMG, 20 May 1931; LMG to REB, 2 July 1931; REB to LMG, 30 June 1931—all OSUA-BP, folder #6613; also Rodgers, *Beyond the Barrier*, 275.

176 mother fell critically ill—LMG to REB, 8 July 1931, OSUA-BP, folder #6613.

176 "a crushing blow."—MRG to Marie Byrd, 9 September 1931, OSUA-BP, folder #6613.

176 telegram of sympathy—Telegram, REB to Mrs. L. M. Gould, 4 August 1931, OSUA-BP, folder #6613.

176 Byrd took exception ... "as a rule not possible."—REB to LMG, 28 July 1931, OSUA-BP, folder #6613.

176 Byrd had heard ... "know anything about them."—These two paragraphs are following Rodgers, *Beyond the Barrier*, 275-277, including Rodgers' quotations from REB to Ashley McKinley, 26 July 1931; also REB to Edward E. Goodale, 28 July 1931, NA-Goodale Papers.

177 In September ... conspicuously uninvolved.—Rodgers, *Beyond the Barrier*, 277-278.

177 "Dear Dick, / I am sorry not"—LMG to REB, "Friday afternoon" [presumably 11 September 1931], OSUA-BP, folder #6613,

177 "I am sorry if"—REB to LMG, 13 September 1931, OSUA-BP, folder #6613.

178 Early in October, Gould—LMG to REB, 7 October 1931, OSUA-BP, folder #6613.

178 Another signal pleasure ... played in it.—LMG to REB, 7 November 1931, OSUA-BP, folder #6613.

178 introducing his friend ... flying solo.—Glines, *Bernt Balchen*, 103-104.

178 The affair concerned ... "dupe an unsuspecting public."—Typescript transcript from the *Martinsville Democrat*, September 4, 1931 ("Ocean Vagabond Talks to Lions"); clipping from the *Mooresville Times*, October 22, 1931 ("Investigation Proves 'Explorer' A Fraud"), including Gould's letter beginning "I hasten to answer." Both in OSUA-BP, folder #6613.

178n   **"only baggage"**—Glines, *Bernt Balchen*, 103.

179   **Mercola's audacity ... "to us post haste."**—R. B. Pickard to LMG, 30 October 1931, OSUA-BP, folder #6613. Gould's letter to Byrd soliciting a statement followed promptly. (LMG to REB, 3 November 1931, OSUA-BP, folder #6613.)

180   **Despite Pickard's prediction ... "at the Naval Academy"**—The story can be followed from LMG telegram to REB, 4 November 1931; REB to R. B. Pickard, 4 November 1931; LMG to REB, 20 November 1931 ("insane or making"); LMG to REB, 27 November 1931 ("all so damned stupid" ... "drop the case"); LMG to REB, 6 February 1932; REB to LMG, 22 February 1932; REB to LMG, 12 March 1932 (not mailed, though the relevant paragraph here was sent separately on 23 April); LMG to REB, 4 May 1932; REB to LMG, 6 May 1932 ("it helped that")—all OSUA-BP, folder #6613.

180   **Pressed in November**—REB to LMG, 12 November 1931, OSUA-BP, folder #6613.

180   **Gould responded ... "informed about it."**—LMG to REB, 20 November 1931, OSUA-BP, folder #6613.

180   **"I think practically"**—REB to LMG, 24 November 1931, OSUA-BP, folder #6613.

180   **"vital to all" ... "one beyond that."**—LMG to REB, 9 January 1932, OSUA-BP, folder #6613.

180   **definite offer**—The terms were spelled out in DJC to LMG, 31 December 1931, CCA.

180   **After "much correspondence" ... offered at Carleton.**—LMG to DJC, 24 December 1931, CCA.

181   **highest-paid professor**—"Carleton College Salaries, 1932-1933," CCA.

181   **made possible by ... "ought to have."**—F.S. Bell to DJC, 2 January 1932, CCA.

181   **"regretfully accepted"**—Proceedings of the University of Michigan Board of Regents, January 1932, BHL.

181   **definite commitment**—LMG to DJC, 9 January 1932, CCA.

CHAPTER 12 — CARLETON PROFESSOR

183   **excited reporting**—*Carletonian*, January 16, 1932, 1.

183   **the school which Gould**—Much of the information about Carleton College that follows in this and succeeding paragraphs and in particular the numerical information, is conveniently available in the college's annual catalog, published in March 1932, for instance, as the *Carleton College Bulletin: 65th Annual Catalog Number*. Direct quotations are given specific citations below. More general historical statements about Carleton, here and elsewhere, may derive less from specific or enumerable sources than simply from the knowledge and understandings that come with having served for more than twenty years as Carleton's college archivist.

184   **"The College is especially"**—*Carleton College Bulletin: 65th Annual Catalog Number*. (March 1932), 41.

184   **"In all matters"**—Ibid, 100.

184   **"of national reputation"**—Ibid., 93.

184   **"A student may not"**—Ibid., 101.

184   **"supplied with electricity"**—Ibid., 43.

185   **one out of every ninety-four**—Headley and Jarchow, *Carleton: The First Century*, 22-23. The year referenced was 1936.

185   **Cowling to New York**—DJC to LMG, 16 January 1932; MRG to DJC, 21 January 1932—both CCA.

185   **statement outlining his thoughts**—LMG to DJC, 29 January 1932, CCA.

185 **Early in February, Gould alerted**—LMG to REB, 1 February 1932, OSUA-BP, folder #6613.

185 **The playwright ... "sense of proportion."**—"The World Waits," by George F. Hummel, script in Frances Cosgrove, ed., *Scenes for Student Actors, Volume 1,* online at books.google. com/books; see also Rodgers, *Beyond the Barrier,* 266-267.

185 **As Gould would inform ... matter really was.**—LMG to REB, 9 February 1932, OSUA-BP, folder #6613.

185n **The department had already**—Carleton College Department of Geology, *Carleton's Century of Geology,* 6-7.

186 **In April ... his personal approval.**—LMG to REB, 28 April 1932, OSUA-BP, folder #6613.

186 **unclear that Byrd ever**—Rodgers, *Beyond the Barrier,* 267.

186 **given the title *The World Waits***—"The Theatre: New Plays in Manhattan," *Time,* November 6, 1933, located online at www.time.com; Internet Broadway Database, online at www.ibdb.com. *The World Waits* eventually opened on Broadway in October 1933 with a warning in the program that it was based on fact "in no sense other than purely creative." It closed the next month after running for only thirty performances.

186 **Byrd, during this time ... various scientific reports.**—Rodgers, *Beyond the Barrier,* 279-280.

186 **In March, Saunders ... "expense of the expedition."**—Saunders' March 4, 1932, letter to Gould, and Gould's March 14 reply are quoted in Ibid., 281.

186 **"almost threatened with bankruptcy"**—REB to Ashley McKinley, 11 July 1932, quoted in Ibid., 282.

186 **"Won't you try to"**—REB to Ashley McKinley, 17 March 1932, quoted in Ibid., 281.

186 **The following January**—LMG to REB, 10 January 1933 and 19 January 1933—both OSUA-BP, folder #6613.

186 **"pretty much at a standstill"**—Saunders to LMG, 17 March 1933, quoted in Rodgers, *Beyond the Barrier,* 282.

186 **could not personally spend**—REB to Dana Coman, 15 April 1933, as quoted in Ibid.

186 **"during the summer."**—LMG to REB, 14 April 1933, OSUA-BP, folder #6613.

186 **By late September**—LMG to REB, 25 September 1933, OSUA-BP, folder #6613.

187 **forced to acknowledge ... never be resumed.**—Rodgers, *Beyond the Barrier,* 282, 284.

187 **"most of the scientific"**—Ibid., 287.

187 **Rodgers, in his 1990 ... all "guesswork."**—Ibid., 283-284.

188 **A Day in the Life**—Butler, *East to the Dawn,* 266-267; Glines, *Bernt Balchen,* 105; and Rich, *Amelia Earhart,* 132.

188 **In the summer of 1932**—http://timelines.ws/20thcent/1932_1933.HTML, retrieved 4 September 2012.

189 **In June, Byrd ... "Mount Gould."**—REB to LMG, 10 June 1932, OSUA-BP, folder #6613.

189 **nature camp at Holderness ... on to Northfield**—LMG to DJC, 7 July 1932, CCA.

189 **"economic conditions within"**—Ibid.

189 **upper floor of a college-owned**—The house in which the Goulds lived was Sperry House on Nevada Street, named for an early Carleton professor of the physical sciences whose courses in the 1880s had included some of Carleton's first offerings in the field of geology. By chance, in 1990 the author of this biography, with wife and year-old daughter, happened to be assigned during his own first few months as Carleton archivist to live in the same rooms once occupied by the Goulds, though he was not aware of this history until several years later.

189 **For the academic year 1932-33 ... fossil collections.**—*Carleton College Bulletin: 66th Annual Catalog Number.* (March 1933); "Annual Report of the Chairman for 1932-33, Department of Geology and Geography," CCA (including the "tedious and meticulous"

quotation). Regarding Miss Macgowan's work organizing specimen collections, Gould went on at some length in his first annual report for the department about the disarray to which what had once been fine collections of rocks, minerals, fossils, and casts had fallen: "That these collections should have been so misused and scattered about as to be now largely junk is nothing short of criminal. Collections whose value must have run into the thousands of dollars are now worth but a few hundred dollars because of the irretrievable loss of labels and other identification data." Gould pointed out that "the task of trying to bring order out of chaos ... is much more difficult and tedious than would be the task of organizing new materials" and noted that "the major part of Miss Macgowan's time and no small part of my own, during the past year have been devoted to this task." In his first annual report Gould made a strong plea for providing the department with adequate storage space and proper drawers and cabinets for organizing the "heterogeneous 'mess' of material which constitutes the major portion of our collections."

190   **Gould and the other ... president's house.**—Minutes of the Carleton College Faculty for 19 September 1932, CCA;

190   **featured speaker ... "excellent impression"**—DJC to F. S. Bell, 5 October 1932, CCA.

190   **"as different from" ... "essentially a farmer."**—LMG to REB, 5 October 1932, OSUA-BP, folder #6613.

190   **Emerson Bureau**—1981 Gould/Peter J. Anderson interview, OSUA-AP.

190   **public addresses remained ... Missouri.**—*Carletonian*, October 19, 1932, 3; LMG annual reports for 1932-33 and 1933-34, CCA.

190   **"one of the first impressions"**—LMG to William L. Ayres, 19 July 1949, CCA.

191   **In October he accepted ... awful puns.**—*Carletonian*, October 12, 1932, 3; November 2, 1932, 1; November 5, 1932, 1; November 9, 1932, 1; November 23, 1932, 3; November 30, 1932, 1; December 3, 1932, 1; December 10, 1932, 1.

191   **straw poll**—*Carletonian*, November 2, 1932, 1. Carleton's student straw vote result was Republican Hoover 458, Democrat Roosevelt 122, Socialist Norman Thomas—who had recently spoken on campus—40, and Communist William Z. Foster 1. Straw balloting results in subsequent elections show Carleton remaining, as regards quadrennial presidential elections, an overwhelmingly Republican campus through the 1960 election and then overwhelmingly Democratic ever since. Gould and the Carleton student body in this respect remained ever in sync, as Gould's own political affiliation underwent precisely the same change, also starting, at the presidential level, in 1964.

191   **Though Carleton had been ... "in this connection."**—DJC, statement of 12 December 1933, submitted to the Carleton College Board of Trustees for their March 1, 1934 meeting, CCA; also Jarchow, *Donald J. Cowling*, 294.

191   **The spring before Gould's arrival**—Minutes of the Carleton College Faculty for 25 April 1932 and 6 June 1932, CCA.

191   **Nonetheless at the end ... end of the college year.**—Minutes of the Carleton College Board of Trustees for 12 November 1932 and 25 January 1933, CCA.

191n   **told of the waggish**—*Carletonian*, November 12, 1932, 4.

192   **In the spring ... payrolls of 1933-34.**—Minutes of the Carleton College Board of Trustees for 21 April 1933; DJC, "Statement Regarding The Financial Condition of the College Made at a Meeting of the Board of Trustees Held on March 1, 1934"—both CCA.

192   **In February, Gould ... at St. Olaf.**—*Carletonian*, February 8, 1933, 1, 3; March 11, 1933, 1; March 18, 1933, 3.

193   **"last week I thought I was"**—LMG to REB, 19 January 1933, OSUA-BP, folder #6613.

193   **Minnesota Academy of Science**—*Carletonian*, April 22, 1933, 1. Gould himself would be this organization's vice-president for 1934-35.

194   **Also in April ... rock specimens**—LMG to REB, 14 April 1933, OSUA-BP, folder #6613.

194   **He then suggested ... "half my time instructing."**—Duncan Stewart to LMG, 5 May 1933, Duncan Stewart file, Ser. 58A, CCA.

194   **Definite announcement … six thousand spectators**—*Carletonian*, May 17, 1933, 1, 3; May 20, 1933, 1.

194   **"to wish you bon voyage"**—LMG to REB, 10 July 1933, OSUA-BP, folder #6613.

194   **though private correspondence would**—See, for instance, correspondence quoted in Rodgers, *Beyond the Barrier*, 282-283; also, for example, LMG to Howell W. Murray, 27 February 1954, CCA.

195   **Decades later Gould … "too seriously."**—1981 Gould/Peter J. Anderson interview, OSUA-AP.

195   **"downright homesick" … "enrolled in them."**—LMG to REB, 25 September 1933, OSUA-BP, folder #6613.

195   **acknowledged a keen desire … "just an avocation."**—*Carletonian*, October 4, 1933, 1.

CHAPTER 13 — ANY BRIGHT COLOR, SO LONG AS IT IS RED

196   **Testimony abounds**—The particular instances that follow here are all taken from Carleton College Department of Geology, *Carleton's Century of Geology*, 91-102, with direct quotations from, in order, Carleton alumni Jane Darby Scholl '39, James F. Anderson '41, Chandler W. Swanson '37, Robert M. Chapman '39, John R. Lewis '40, Sheldon B. Vance '39, and Shirley Shale '39.

196   **A magazine profile**—John Sirjamaki, "Among Those We Know," in *Golfer and Sportsman*, March 1934.

196   **A student from one of Gould's first years**—1991 Caton/Hillemann interview, CCA. The author can attest that the appropriateness of Caton's Carleton nickname of "Laughing Jack" remained joyously evident decades after his student days.

198   **"One hour each week"**—Russell W. Harper to Dean Lindsey Blayney, 26 February 1937, located in Dean of the College Records (Ser. 18A), alumni correspondence on the subject of student cheating, CCA.

198   **Student demand … nine years.**—Carleton College Department of Geology, *Carleton's Century of Geology*, 35, 89-102.

198   **As chairman, Gould pushed**—See Annual Reports of the Chairman, Department of Geology and Geography, for 1933-34, 1934-35, and 1935-36, CCA.

198   **He praised … "teaching and research."**—Quotes are from the Annual Reports of the Chairman, Department of Geology and Geography, 1934-35, 1935-36, CCA; sentiments are echoed in each report from 1932-33 through 1936-37.

198n   **memory of Gould interrupting**—Reminiscence of Jane Andrews '41, Porter and Jarchow, eds., *Carleton Remembered*, 54.)

198n   **account of a sleepy student**—*Carletonian*, November 11, 1936, 2.

199   **but she miscarried**—The information that Peg Gould had had a miscarriage "after which she never tried again to have a child" came to me first from two telephone conversations, 12 September and 10 October 2002, with Robert L. Gale, the Carleton alumnus hired by President Gould in 1957 to be Carleton's vice president for public relations and development. Gale told me that Peg spoke about her miscarriage with his wife Barbara, who had become close to Peg Gould for awhile and who had the experience of a miscarriage herself. That Peg had at some point suffered at least one miscarriage was confirmed for me in a conversation of 6 December 2002 with Clark and Ardith Arnold at their home in Tucson, Arizona. The Arnolds, who became very close to the Goulds after the early 1960s, remembered Peg having termed the event a "terrible miscarriage." Clark Arnold further told me that it was his understanding that, prior to miscarrying, Peg had not welcomed the pregnancy—that Larry had told him that she had been "very upset when she discovered that she was pregnant."

199   **The Carletonian's mythologization … "'Spring.'"**—*Carletonian*, April 1, 1933, 2.

199   The following fall the paper ... "vest begins."—*Carletonian*, November 15, 1933, 2, 3.

199n   Carletonian declared him—*Carletonian*, December 6, 1933, 3.

201   chapel talk to Carleton's senior class—LMG, undated senior chapel talk [Spring 1934], unpublished transcript, CCA. This is the source for all quotations in this section's four paragraphs, ending with "seem so precious."

203   In both 1934 and 1935 ... via Glacier Park.—March 1935 Utah State Agricultural College bulletin on summer session ("scenic and scientific"); LMG to DJC, 26 June 1934; LMG to DJC, 18 July 1935 ("took a holiday"); LMG to DJC, 1 August 1935; LMG to DJC, 22 August 1935 ("I surprised myself")—all CCA; *Carletonian*, May 15, 1935, 1; *Carletonian*, September 25 1935, 1.

203   Gould was touched—1981 Gould/Peter J. Anderson interview, OSUA-AP; also 2001 Vaughan/Brewster interview, OSUA.

203n   reprinted in the 1936—*The Algol 1936*, 18.

204   Cowling wrote to inform ... vacant for a year—DJC to LMG, 18 July 1935; Minutes of the Carleton College Board of Trustees for 7 August 1935—both CCA.

204   During 1934-35 ... Cap and Gown Day service.—Annual Report of the Chairman, Department of Geology and Geography, 1934-35, CCA; *Carletonian*, November 7, 1934, 1; *Carletonian*, January 16, 1935, 1; *Carletonian*, March 13, 1935, 1; *Carletonian*, May 22, 1935, 1.

204   "interesting" Dr. Gould's love—*Carletonian*, May 8, 1935, 2.

204   in October Gould sent him—LMG to REB, 21 October 1935, OSUA-BP, folder #6613.

204   In 1936 the financial ... as toastmaster.—Jarchow, *Donald J. Cowling*, 324-325.

205   Citing increasing interest ... war work.—Annual Report of the Chairman, Department of Geology and Geography, 1935-36; faculty file for Leonard S. Wilson—both CCA.

205   In 1935-36 ... fabled monster.—Annual Report of the Chairman, Department of Geology and Geography, 1935-36, CCA; *Carletonian*, May 14, 1936, 3; *Carletonian*, October 14, 1936, 3.

205   "a veritable festival" ... "quite in love"—LMG to DJC, 4 August 1936, CCA.

206   Early in December the chancellor ... "good business"—George R. Throop to DJC, 10 December 1936; DJC to F. S. Bell, 11 January 1937; F. S. Bell to DJC, 13 January 1937—all CCA.

206   decided by May—DJC to F. S. Bell, 11 May 1937, CCA.

206   "the chief needs ... "with the President."—Annual Report of the Chairman, Department of Geology and Geography, 1936-37, CCA.

206   During the winter of 1937 ... "your generation?"—*Carletonian*, February 10, 1937, 4.

207   One of the first ... English and Russian.—Milanovsky, "Three Sessions ..." 103.

207   Following an ocean ... on July 19.—LMG to Lindsey Blayney, 21 May 1948 (re passage on the *Europa*); LMG to DJC, 29 July 1937—both CCA.

207   "internal upset" ... "dusty roads."—LMG 1937 Diary, 10 July 1937, NA-GP.

207   Traveling the next ... "not in Russia, I fear."—Ibid., 11 July 1937.

208   Skeats, whose company—Ibid., 26 July 1937.

208   Seeing a newspaper ... "jail of nations."—Ibid., 13 July 1937.

208   "obvious and childish" ... "the U.S.S.R. plans."—Ibid., 16 July, 1937.

208   "A number of Soviet Congress participants"—Milanovsky, "Three Sessions ...", 104.

208   the more interesting city—LMG 1937 Diary, 24 July 1937.

208   Visiting the Hermitage—Ibid., 25 July 1937.

208   Far duller ... "at every opportunity."—Ibid., 27 July 1937.

208   In Leningrad ... "except Stalin."—LMG to DJC, 29 July 1937, CCA.

209   On July 29 ... "left behind."—LMG 1937 Diary, 29 July 1937.

209 **The Arctic journey**—LMG to DJC, 26 August 1937, CCA; LMG 1937 Diary, entries for 4 August ("tang and real chill"), 11 August, and 16 August, 1937.

209 **"Finland and Free"**—LMG 1937 Diary, 22 August 1937.

209 **"all in all" ... people in control.**—LMG to DJC, 26 August 1937, CCA.

210 **"spinster instructor" ... "ends this journal."**—LMG 1937 Diary, 4 September, 1937.

210 **Gould's speaking engagements**—Annual Report of the Chairman, Department of Geology and Geography, 1937-38, CCA. Gould spoke on Russia to a Carleton audience in November, with his subject described by the campus newspaper as "a frank discussion of conditions as he found them, and their relation to both scientific work going on in the country and world affairs." (*Carletonian*, November 17, 1937, 1.)

210 **introduced a new course ... taken in college**—Annual Report of the Chairman, Department of Geology and Geography, 1937-38, CCA.

210 **painted portrait of Al Smith**—*Carletonian*, January 26, 1938, 1. According to the *Carletonian*, Gould told the story of Al Smith while lecturing at the University of South Dakota and then had subsequently received a communication from a member of the audience, Blanche Harrington, "well-known for her paintings of reproductions of pre-historic animals, and animal pictures in general," that she would like to paint a picture of Al Smith, if Gould would be good enough to provide a picture. The paper quoted Gould as saying that whether or not the result was "good art," "it is my dog, and I like it."

212 **That same winter Gould**—*Carletonian*, January 19, 1938, 1.

212 **Bartlett stayed overnight**—*Carletonian*, February 23, 1938, 1.

212 **"liable to cover"**—*Carletonian*, March 2, 1938, 1.

212 **The Carletonian reported ... "with his vocabulary."**—*Carletonian*, March 9, 1938, 1, 4. Bartlett was reportedly delighted with the Carleton campus, which he wandered all over during his short stay, greatly preferring it to Chicago, from which he had just come, which Bartlett characterized as "as close to the Nether regions as a man could get." The paper also reported that Bartlett was an especially big hit with geology instructor George Gibson's three-year-old son Randall, who had a picture book at home of famous explorers and had startled Bartlett upon meeting him with the eager question, "Do you know Rasmussen?" The boy was thrilled when Bartlett presented him with a signed photograph of himself to add to his explorers book.

212 **interview with student reporter Alan Cason ... "neighborhood awake."**—*Carletonian*, April 6, 1938, 4.

213 **A deeply moved Exner**—Franz F. Exner to LMG, 5 July 1938, CCA-GC. The copy of *Cold* given by Gould to Exner on Commencement Day 1938 now resides in the Carleton College Archives. Gould's inscription reads: "Dear Dr. Exner, Emerson once said that some persons were content just to be influences. He might have said it of you and I hope you know that 'influence' has been an inspiration to your colleague across the hall—who now begs you will accept this modest token of his personal esteem, admiration and indebtedness to you, Laurence M. Gould."

213 **proposed that Carleton undertake ... summer and fall of 1939.**—LMG to DJC, 4 April 1938; LMG to DJC, 22 June 1939; MRG to DJC, 3 January 1940—all CCA; also see Topical File "Gould House," CCA.

214 **wedding of Peg's sister**—*Northfield News*, December 28, 1938, 12.

214 **uncooked tomato**—Gould's dislike of raw tomatoes (but little else) was mentioned in a 1995 Carleton oral history interview with Clark and Ardith Arnold. (1995 Arnolds/Donnell interview, CCA.)

214 **"You have no idea"**—LMG to DJC, 29 May 1941, CCA.

214 **In June 1939 ... high school in South Haven.**—Information in these paragraphs is all from Annual Reports of the Chairman, Department of Geology and Geography, 1938-39 and 1939-40, CCA.

CHAPTER 14 — WARTIME AND NEW TASKS

216   In November ... economic self-interest.—While Gould's November 1939 chapel talk went unreported in the *Carletonian* at the time, some outline of what he must have said is evident from the commentary printed a year later, following his "change of heart" Vespers talk. See *Carletonians* of November 15 and 29, 1940.

217   Shortly before the general ... Willkie Clubs.—*Carletonian*, November 1, 1940, 1. The *Carletonian* straw poll of 532 Carleton students and 87 faculty members showed these results, including Socialist candidate Norman Thomas:

	Roosevelt	Willkie	Thomas	Undecided
Faculty	21.8%	71.3%	4.6%	2.3%
Seniors	9.2	80.7	4.6	5.5
Juniors	21.2	65.1	6.4	7.3
Sophomores	13.3	81.6	2.9	2.2
Freshmen	18.7	74.6	2.8	3.9
Totals	16.6	75.2	4.0	4.2

217   Less than a week after ... "almost infallible."—*Carletonian*, November 15, 1940, 4 (Bud Jacobson's "Ye Gods, Another Week" column, and 8 (letters by Jack Bunday, by Clarke A. Chambers, John Deason, and John Unumb, and letter by "Antarctic News Service"); *Carletonian,* November 29, 1940, 8 (editorial "Good Sign ..." and letter by Jean Knapp).

218   During the second ... Oklahoma, and Texas.—*Carletonian*, January 17, 1941, 2; LMG 1941 Diary, entries of 17 January-13 February, CCA-GC; Annual Report of the Chairman, Department of Geology and Geography, 1941-42.

218   4th of March ... such as the Sierra Nevada.—LMG 1941 Diary, entries of March-May; LMG to DJC, 10 April 1941 and 10 May 1941, CCA; *Carletonian*, February 20, 1942, 3; Annual Report of the Chairman, Department of Geology and Geography, 1941-42, CCA.

218   decision by Duncan Stewart ... no increase in pay.—LMG to DJC, 10 April 1941 ("whatever arrangements"); Duncan Stewart to DJC, 14 April 1941; DJC to LMG, 26 April 1941—all CCA.

218n   "I had hoped"—LMG to DJC, 10 May 1941, CCA.

219   When Gould heard ... "been let down."—LMG to DJC, 30 April 1941, CCA.

219   Somewhat affronted ... "compare with ours."—DJC to LMG, 5 May 1941, CCA.

219   A chastened Gould ... "lose faith in you."—LMG to DJC, 10 May 1941, CCA.

219   Cowling concluded ... "near to affection."—DJC to LMG, 19 May 1941, CCA.

219   in late May he finalized—LMG to DJC, 20 May 1941; LMG to William Fiedler, 20 May 1941—both CCA.

220   The Goulds left ... Dakota County.—LMG 1941 Diary, entries of June-July; LMG to DJC, 10 April 1941, CCA.

220   309 new freshmen—*Carletonian*, September 26, 1941, 1.

220   108 students enrolled—Annual Report of the Chairman, Department of Geology and Geography, 1941-42, CCA.

220   homecoming festivities ... Stassen.—Ibid., September 19, 1941, 1, and September 26, 1941, 1.

220   note to Dick Byrd—LMG to REB, 10 October 1941, OSUA-BP, folder #1763. Exactly at this time a *Carletonian* poll of the student body found that 59 percent of Carleton students—83 percent of the men—disagreed with Colonel Charles Lindbergh's isolationist views on American foreign policy (*Carletonian*, October 10, 1941, 3). A month later, another poll found 54 percent of Carleton students agreeing that defeating Hitler was more important than keeping America out of the war (*Carletonian*, November 14, 1941, 5).

220   **"Wild Tie Day"**—*Carletonian*, December 5, 1941, 2.

220   **student play**—LMG 1941 Diary, 3 December 1941.

220   **Sunday in Northfield ... International Relations Club**—See remembrances of "December 7" in the 1942 Carleton College yearbook, *The 1942 Algol, 8*.

220n **Co-winners were chosen**—*Carletonian*, December 5, 1941, 2.

221   **At Carleton an evening ... with Fiedler.**—Minutes of the Carleton College Faculty for 8 December and 17 December 1941, CCA.

221   **In the end ... interest in the Arctic.**—Annual Report of the Chairman, Department of Geology and Geography, 1941-42, CCA; J. Brian Bird, "Trevor Lloyd (1906-1995)," in *Arctic* 48, No. 3 (September 1995), 308-309.

222   **some while to be felt**—As late as the second semester of 1942-43 Carleton's male student enrollment remained robustly above three hundred, but for the fall of 1943 it plunged to eighty-seven and thereafter continued slowly to sink through the end of the war. By the spring of 1945 there were only fifty-four men enrolled as Carleton students, as compared with 573 women. (*Carleton College Catalogs for 1942-43, 1943-44, and 1944-45*.)

222   **army of 3.6 million**—*Carletonian*, February 13, 1942, 8.

222   **91 former Carleton students**—*Carletonian*, February 20, 1942, 3.

223   **would top fifty.**—After the war Carleton published a booklet memorializing its war dead. (They Shall Grow Not Old: A Memorial to the Carleton Men who gave their lives in World War II. Northfield, MN: Carleton College, 1946.)

223   **On March 31 ... COTC commandant.**—*Carletonian*, April 1, 1942, 1-3, and April 24, 1942, 1; Minutes of the Carleton College Board of Trustees for 7 April 1942, CCA. The site ultimately selected for the Carleton airfield, the William J. Dack farm near Stanton, about eight miles east of campus, was acquired within the next month. The field was readied over the summer and, despite unavoidable delays in completing hangar construction, received planes and became operational in October. (*Carletonian*, October 2, 1942, 1).

223   **During the next month ... recruiting program.**—*Carletonian*, May 15, 1942, 1, 9; "Information Submitted [by Carleton College] in Connection With 'A Study of the Accelerated Program In a Sampling Selection of Privately Controlled Colleges of Liberal Arts," dated 29 August 1942, in President's Office subject file: "Military Training & Issues, 1942-44," CCA.

224   **"as the news from"**—LMG to DJC, 16 July 1942, CCA.

224   **Late in October, even as ... duties at Carleton.**—*Carletonian*, October 2, 1942, 1; LMG to DJC, 23 October 1942 ("immediately on the merry-go-round") and 24 October 1942 ("the sense of frustration")—both CCA.

224   **Gould's father died**—*South Haven Daily Tribune*, November 2, 1942.

225   **Public announcement ... "or someplace else."**—*Carletonian*, December 4, 1942, 1; 1973 Gould/Morrissey interview, UAAL.

225   **One of Gould's early acts**—Jean Rice Hoppin's biographical statement for the Carleton Class of 1935 50th anniversary publication (1985), CCA.

225   **For the first several**—LMG to DJC, 26 January 1943, CCA.

225   **By mid-July ... in those matters.)**—LMG to DJC, 21 July 1943, CCA.

225   **In the fall of 1943 ... work at the college.**—LMG to DJC, 2 September 1943 and 10 December 1943—both CCA.

226   **national change of course ... technical in nature.**—*Carletonian*, January 15, 1943, 1.

226   **At Carleton, a group ... mid-February of 1944.**—*Ibid.*, December 11, 1942, 1, January 15, 1943, 1, February 5, 1943, 1, and February 12, 1944, 1, 5; *The Algol of 1943*, 33.

226   **second large influx ... by fall 1943.)**—Minutes of the Carleton College Board of Trustees for 25 June 1942, CCA; *The Algol 1944*, 12; "Carleton College Enrollment, 1943-44," sheet located in President's Office subject file "Army Specialized Training Program, 1943-44," CCA.

227   **disbanding of the ASTP**—*The Algol 1944*, 12; *Carletonian*, March 25, 1944, 3.

227   **ratio of ten to one**—*Carleton College Catalog for 1944-45.* School opened in September
      with 591 women and 59 men.
227   **institutional search for his replacement.**—This narrative has already been told, and
      sources cited, in the "Prologue" chapter of this biography.
227   **Gould's department during that year**—*Carleton College Catalog for 1944-45.*
228   **talk on "Arctic Survival" ... upperclass teams.**—*Carletonian,* October 21, 1944, 1,
      November 4, 1944, 1; November 18, 1944, 1.
228   **Also in November ... the chapel.**—LMG to DJC, undated but noted as received 15
      November 1944, CCA; *Carletonian,* March 10, 1945, 1; LMG to J. Margaret Carter, 24
      March 1945, CCA; *The Algol 1945,* 49.
228   **Arctic Institute of North America ... military release.)**—Robert MacDonald,
      "Challenges and Accomplishments: A Celebration of the Arctic Institute of North America,"
      in *Arctic* 58, No. 4 (Dec. 2005), 440; "Albert Lincoln Washburn (1911-2007)," in *Arctic* 60,
      No. 2 (June 2007), 212.
228   **Cowling received a letter**—Virgil M. Hancher to DJC, 27 March 1945, CCA.
229   **"It would be entirely"**—DJC to Virgil M. Hancher, 28 March 1945, CCA.
229   **seventy-five names**—Faculty Advisory Committee's Concluding Report to the Carleton
      Faculty on the Presidential Search, 16 May 1945, CCA.
229   **On the 12th of May**—LMG to Louis S. Headley, 21 May 1945, CCA.
229   **Two days later ... allowance for expenses**—Minutes of the Carleton College Board of
      Trustees for 14 May 1945, CCA.
230   **dinner in the Carleton Tea Room**—*Carletonian,* May 19, 1945, 1.
230   **Cowling—who had also been informed**—DJC to Mrs. George C. Christian, 12 May
      1945, CCA
230   **Public announcement ... "is dependent."**—*Carletonian,* May 19, 1945, 1.
230   **letters to Trustees Bell and Headley**—LMG to Laird Bell, 21 May 1945 ("unbelievable
      enthusiasm") and LMG to Louis S. Headley, 21 May 1945, CCA.
230   **"find ourselves standing"**—*The Algol 1945,* 116.

CHAPTER 15 — BUILDING A CATHEDRAL

231   **Just four days ... Stewart quickly agreed.**—See correspondence of 18 May to 19 June
      1945 in Duncan Stewart file, POF Faculty Files (Ser. 58A), CCA. Stewart's appointment
      was approved by the Carleton Board of Trustees on June 4, and Stewart's formal assent soon
      followed. Stewart was thus Gould's first presidential hire in his own right. (Already in May
      President Cowling had involved Gould in the final stage of selecting Louis L. Curcio as an
      assistant professor of Romance languages, and it was Gould whose name was on the May 19
      telegram to Curcio with a firm job offer, but this is most accurately cast as one of Cowling's
      last appointments rather than as Gould's first.)
231   **Gould thought it best ... "professional scientists."**—LMG to Laird Bell, 21 May 1945;
      LMG to John W. Nason, 31 May 1945, and Nason to LMG, 4 July 1945—all CCA.
231   **Gould met with Kille ... academic dean.**—LMG to Frank Kille, 25 July 1945; Minutes
      of the Carleton College Board of Trustees for 26 July 1945; LMG to Merrill E. Jarchow, 18
      August 1945—all CCA. A less accurate projection Gould made that summer was the hope
      he expressed, in a 10 July letter to Kille, that by the fall of 1946 he might find it possible
      himself to resume the teaching of "one class at least." (It may be helpful to note, by the way,
      that the pronunciation of Kille rhymes with "Billy.")
232   **English, Gould thought**—LMG to William Thomson, 27 June 1945; LMG to Frank L.
      Huntley, 10 July 1945—both CCA.

232   **It was Louis Bredvold**—Louis I. Bredvold to LMG, 11 July 1945, in Arthur Mizener file, POF Faculty Files (Ser. 58A), CCA. Bredvold advised Gould that Mizener reportedly "was suffering at Yale from concern over the poor, and he was supposed to be communist-inclined; but reports at Yale and Princeton are that he is now devoting his attention to literature, and is probably only moderately leftish."

232   **Gould followed up ... on the 22nd.**—LMG to Louis Bredvold, 13 July 1945; LMG to Arthur Mizener, 9 August, 20 August, and 22 August 1945; Mizener to LMG, 17 August, and (telegram) 22 August 1945—all CCA.

232   **Though President William Weld ... outstanding program.**—LMG to William E. Weld, 23 August 1945, CCA. Weld was not really mollified by Gould's note, replying: "Thank you for your letter of August 23. There seems to be some misunderstanding. Dr. Mizener was not released but left us with four or five days notice. It seems to me that there is a morale [sic] principle involved which is not avoided because of the beneficence of your offer." (Weld to LMG, 27 August 1945, CCA.)

232   **How to build ... "too many majors."**—Laird Bell to LMG, 16 May 1945; LMG to Bell, 21 May 1945; LMG to William Thomson, 27 June 1945—all CCA.

232   **Gould elaborated ... "the chaotic future."**—LMG to Laird Bell, 17 August 1945, CCA.

234   **In pushing forward ... "their whole life.")**—Ibid.; LMG to Robert Leach, 18 May 1945—both CCA.

234   **Another aim Gould expressed**—See for instance LMG to Arthur Mizener, 20 August 1945, CCA.

234   **trustees authorized that summer**—Minutes of the Carleton College Board of Trustees for 26 July 1945, CCA. On the same date Allied leaders meeting in Potsdam issued an ultimatum stating that Japan now faced the alternative of either the unconditional surrender of their armed forces or "prompt and utter destruction."

234   **week-long holiday ... the following month.)**—LMG to Merrill Hutchinson, 28 June 1945; LMG to John Cowles, 12 July 1945; LMG to John and Betty Cowles, 12 July 1945; John Cowles to LMG, 21 July 1945; LMG to John Cowles, 25 August 1945—all CCA.

235   **off to Chicago ... at the Palmer House**—LMG to Renzo Bianchi, 2 August 1945 and 10 August 1945—both CCA.

235   **trout fishing trip**—LMG to Hans Weigert, 11 August 1945 ("positively be my last"); LMG to Malcolm B. McDonald, 18 August 1945—both CCA.

235   **"These are times for rejoicing"**—LMG to Reine Myers, 16 August 1945, CCA.

235   **At home, Peg's ... invasion of Okinawa.**—*Northfield News*, October 4, 1945, 3; "Richard H. Hoppin," in *Carleton College Class of 1936 50th Reunion Book*, CCA.

235   **ratio of about six to one**—*Carleton College Annual Catalog for 1945-1946*.

235   **Gould delivered ... "super-imposed from above."**—LMG to John Cowles, 19 September 1945, CCA. The relevant Carleton faculty meeting minutes simply report that President Gould "gave an outline of vital policies." (Minutes of the Carleton College Board of Trustees for 17 September 1945, CCA.)

236   **Since mid-summer a working group**—See the Carleton Archives' topical file on the 1945 presidential inauguration. Overseeing the planning as chairman of Carleton's Committee on Public Occasions was Professor Curvin Gingrich.

236   **excursion to Montreal**—LMG to John Cowles, 8 October 1945, CCA.

236   **tragic occurrence ... six somber pallbearers.**—*Northfield News*, October 11 and October 18, 1945; *Carletonian*, October 13, 1945, 6; LMG to Leonard S. Wilson, 13 October 1945, CCA. See also Weigert file, POF Faculty Files (Ser. 58A), for additional details.

236   **Inauguration Day 1945**—Sources for everything written in this and succeeding paragraphs concerning the details of Gould's presidential inauguration (through "memorable day" on page 243) are as follows: *Carletonian*, October 13, 1946; *St. Paul Pioneer Press*, October 17, 1945; programs for the inauguration ceremony and inaugural luncheon, found in the Carleton College Archives' topical file (TF) "Inaugurations—1945:

President Gould"; and the publication "The Inauguration of Laurence McKinley Gould as the Fourth President," *Carleton College Bulletin* 42, No. 2 (November 1945), which contains the full text not only of Gould's inaugural address but also of remarks delivered by all speakers at both the induction ceremony and at the inaugural luncheon.

243   *Time* **magazine ... father of one of his Carleton students.**—*Time*, October 29, 1945, 77; LMG to Lt. Merrill E. Jarchow, 7 November 1945, CCA.

244   **"I had known, of course"**—LMG to William A. Fiedler, 14 November 1945, CCA.

244   **The situation "is hopeless"**—LMG to Mrs. I. M. Cochran, 5 April 1946, CCA.

244   **764 important addresses**—Headley and Jarchow, *Carleton: The First Century*, 122.

244   **seventy-some speaking invitations**—LMG to Rev. Homer J. Armstrong, 10 June 1946, CCA.

244   **eight outside commencement**—LMG to Olin S. Pettingill, 20 June 1946, CCA.

244   **Titles of his talks**—Titles of specific talks are to be found in various clippings and correspondence files, CCA.

244   **("no one can talk"**—LMG to Rev. Homer J. Armstrong, 10 June 1946, CCA.

244   **"assume ... that speaking" ... any surplus.**—LMG to Bruce Pollock, 8 July 1946—all CCA.

244n   **"I once suggested"**—LMG to Atherton Bean, 30 January 1950, CCA.

245   **Two weeks after ... a few months later.**—LMG to John Cowles, 3 November 1945; LMG to Trevor Lloyd, 8 November 1945; LMG to Hugh Keenleyside, 9 November 1945; Verbrugge file, POF Faculty Files (Ser. 58A)—all CCA.

245   **"Peg is not being swamped"**—LMG to Thomas Job, 12 November 1945, CCA.

245   **"I don't believe Peg"**—LMG to Ray M. Conger, 14 November 1945, CCA.

245   **five and a half weeks ... brother Jack.**—LMG to Jenny Cullen, 29 April 1946, CCA.

246   **less of a hardship ... "president's wife."**—LMG to Dr. C. E. Lyght, 2 April 1946;

246   **Late that first fall ... "EXPLODED it!"**—LMG to Atherton Bean, 6 March 1946; Bean to LMG, 23 July 1946; LMG to Bean, 19 November 1946; LMG to Laird Bell, 3 December 1946—all CCA; remarks prepared by Atherton Bean (but delivered in Bean's absence by Stephen R. Lewis, Jr.) for Carleton's memorial convocation in Gould's honor, 13 October 1995 ("Did I hit it?").

246   **curriculum committee ... alternate weeks**—"The President's Report for 1945-46" (*Carleton College Bulletin* 43, No. 2, November 1946); Minutes of the Carleton College Faculty for 10 December 1945; LMG to Frank Kille, 20 February 1946—both CCA.

246   **Fourteen tentative proposals ... "in due time."**—"The President's Report for 1945-46," op. cit.

247   **international relations with political science**—LMG to David Bryn-Jones, 28 March 1946; LMG to Frank Kille, 26 April 1946—both CCA.

247   **moving to combine**—LMG to Kille and Profs. Waggener and Dungay, and also to Olin S. Pettingill, 20 June 1946, CCA.

247   **"to inaugurate another unfortunate"**—Bruce Pollock to [unknown], 15 December 1945, CCA.

247   **luncheon address on "The Independent College"**—Clipping [page number unrecorded] from *The Coe Cosmos*, December 1945.

247   **During the month following ... Carleton's dean of men.**—Merrill E. Jarchow, *Casey: An Autobiography* (1993), 92; 95-97; letters of 1945 and early 1946 in Jarchow file, POF Faculty Files (Ser. 58A), CCA; LMG to James V. McDonough, 19 March 1946, CCA ("what might be called"). Upon learning of Jarchow's acceptance Dean Kille wrote to his new assistant congratulating him on his decision to come to Carleton and telling him how fortunate they both were in their chief: "From my point of view, a happy and effective administration depends a great deal upon the President. President Gould is rapidly building a community interest on the part of the faculty, the Board, the students, the graduates and the staff, which I feel sure

will not only maintain Carleton College as a good college but will some day make it a truly great one. I have heard college presidents speak of this point of view as if it were theirs, but I have not known many who actually operated on this basis." (Kille to Jarchow, 26 January 1946, CCA.)

247 **Also in January ... institution like this."**—LMG to Marian F. Adams, 7 January 1946, CCA.

248 **At this juncture Gould wanted**—LMG to Charles A. Culver, 18 January 1946, CCA.

248 **"While the most critical"**—"President's Report for 1945-46," op. cit.

248 **ten-day eastern trip ... not previously met.**—LMG to Atherton Bean, 28 January 1946; LMG to Ralph Sargent, 31 January 1946—both CCA.

248 **"This is a resource"**—LMG to N. K. Chaney, 11 February 1946, CCA.

248 **"a renewed interest"**—LMG to C. Whit Pfeiffer, 16 September 1946, CCA.

248 **envisioned improvements**—LMG to Ralph Henry, 13 February 1946 ("to carry news"); LMG to Bob Matteson, 19 June 1946 ("more definitely tied")—both CCA.

248 **Gould proposed ... "toward their achievement."**— LMG to Ralph Henry, 13 February 1946, CCA.

248 **debut in September 1946**—*The Voice of the Carleton Alumni* 12, No. 1 (September 1946).

248 **Partially in the interest of better**—Minutes of the Carleton College Board of Trustees for 17 January 1946, CCA.

248n **At the Philadelphia meeting**—Related in John W. Nason to Alfred J. Hyslop, 9 June 1964, CCA.

249 **One week before ... later that month.**—LMG to Mrs. A. J. McGuire, 5 June 1946, and Minnesota United Nations Committee to LMG, 13 June 1946—both CCA.

249 **Over the course of ... forty-six married couples.**—*Carleton College Annual Catalogs* for 1945-1946 and 1946-1947; "President's Report for 1945-46," op. cit.; LMG to Dr. C. E. Lyght, 2 April 1946 ("by the very nature"); Minutes of the Carleton College Board of Trustees for 10 June 1946—both CCA. The admissions committee at this time, chaired by Director of Admissions Donald Klinefelter, also included Dean of Men Frank Kille, Dean of Women Hazel Lewis, and Professors Bertha Linnell and Arthur Mizener.

249 **a long weekend ... Annie Battle Lake)**—LMG to Frank Kille, 6 July 1946 and 16 July 1946; LMG to John Cowles, 23 July 1946—all CCA.

249 **two weeks ... "sit in the sun."**—LMG to Frank Kille, 6 July 1946; LMG to Olin S. Pettingill, 21 July 1946 ("fish and sit"); LMG to Constance Hampl, 31 July 1946; LMG to Atherton Bean, 26 August 1946—all CCA.

250 **"I was interested to know"**—LMG to Arthur Mizener, 30 July 1946, CCA.

250 **Between February and mid-September ... future employment**—Various POF Faculty Files (Ser. 58A), CCA; *Carleton College Annual Catalog* for 1946-1947.

251 **The housing shortage was responsible**—See for instance LMG to Ida Walz Kubitz, 21 February 1946; LMG to Stanley W. Oexemann, 26 April 1946; LMG to Mrs. A. J. Ecklund, 29 April 1946; LMG to R. H. Wollin, 22 May 1946—all CCA.

251 **"The housing situation becomes"**—LMG to Cyrus C. DeCoster, 30 May 1946;

251 **In the letter of appointment ... "at all for you."**—LMG to Eiler L. Henrickson, 30 May 1946, CCA.

251 **"You have no idea"**—LMG to Olin S. Pettingill, 20 June 1946, CCA.

251 **"there are plenty of mediocre"**— LMG to Bertha Linnell, 3 July 1946, CCA.

251 **He pressed the trustees ... graded accordingly.**—LMG to Leonard S. Wilson, 9 February 1946, CCA.

251 **In June the board**—Minutes of the Carleton College Board of Trustees for 10 June 1946; LMG to Floyd A. Bond, 11 June 1946—both CCA.

251 **"It may sound reckless"**—Laird Bell to LMG, 29 July 1946, CCA.

251 **"Much of my summer"**—LMG to Laird Bell, 3 September 1946, CCA.

251 **fully 46 percent …forty-one academic appointments.**—LMG to Laird Bell, 18 September 1946, CCA.

252 **"I wonder if"**—Arthur Mizener to LMG, 18 September 1946, CCA.

252 **"complexion has changed" … "risen considerably."**—LMG to Laird Bell, 27 September 1946, CCA.

CHAPTER 16 — THE WAY AHEAD

253 **fall term student enrollment**—Figures for the years before 1946 come from the Carleton College Annual Catalogs. The figures for the fall of 1946, slightly higher than those reported in the annual catalog, are those given in *The Voice of the Carleton Alumni*, December 1946, 8, or in *"The Report of the President to the Board of Trustees of Carleton College, 1946-1947,"* 3-4.

253 **Class of 1950 the school's largest**—Shifting classifications among the 407 students considered freshmen in the fall of 1946, many of whom started with a variety of previously earned credits, means that a substantial number are not now counted as alumni of the Class of 1950 but rather of 1949 or another year. Nonetheless, by any count, those who entered in 1946 would remain Carleton's largest cohort until the arrival of a new era of expansion some years into the 1960s.

253 **Although a few ex-soldiers … feared to miss.**—1992 Jarchow/Jeglosky interview, CCA.

253 **message he would voice**—Testimony abounds among Carleton alumni that such a message was consistently conveyed by President Gould year after year, but—though the Carleton Archives is frequently asked to provide the quotation—there is no canonically correct wording or precise phrasing for his annual welcome to new students. Gould rarely spoke from a prepared text, and these occasions were not recorded. We do, however, fortunately find in writing the following excerpt from Gould's 1951 talk to new students, prepared for the *Chicago Tribune*: "In words honored by long tradition you have now completed your matriculation, and I declare you members of Carleton College forever. We hope all of you will graduate; but whether you do or not, you are forever a part of this College and it is forever a part of you. I have high hopes as I welcome you that none of you will be disappointed in it, but that you will learn to cherish it as you live in it and that it will become for you as it has for many before you a beloved community of memory and hope for all the years of your lives. You are to remember that wherever you go, whatever you do, however long you live, whatever happens to you will be a concern of Carleton College, and whenever we can be of help to you in your work or in your play you are to call upon us."

254 **election as one of the twenty-seven**—Carleton College news release of 25 September 1946, CCA.

254 **number of other matters**—In addition to the matters mentioned in the text, at this time (September 27) came family news from Lacota that Gould's beloved "Grandmother Dike" (Sarah Ann Updike), who had been so important a part of his Michigan upbringing, had just died at age ninety-four.

254 **A group of prefabricated**—LMG to Lindsey Blayney, 24 September 1946, CCA.

254 **"somewhat low spirits"**—LMG to Reine Myers, 26 September 1946, CCA.

254 **"Thorough examinations" … "cares at all."**—LMG to Dr. C. E. Lyght, 26 September 1946, CCA.

254 **"the fraternity of the itching palm"**—LMG to Charles Dolllard, Carnegie Corporation, 16 May 1947, CCA.

254 **"Dr. Gould had confined"**—Headley and Jarchow, *Carleton: The First Century*, 107.

254 **decided against launching**—LMG to Laird Bell, 29 October 1945 {"to build up"); Minutes of the Carleton College Board of Trustees for 17 January 1946 ("long time low")—both CCA.

254 **"somewhat disappointing."**—LMG to Laird Bell, 6 July 1946, CCA

254 **Cowles had impressed … "coming year."**—LMG to John Cowles, 5 September 1946, CCA.

255 **"we made a major" … was insufficient.**—LMG to Atherton Bean, 24 September 1946, CCA.

255 **"we have missed" … "start from today."**—Bean to LMG, 28 September 1946, CCA.

255 **new tradition for the fall**—Minutes of the Carleton College Board of Trustees for 10 June 1946, CCA; 1973 Gould/Morrissey interview, UAAL.

255 **At this meeting … of sixty-five.**—Minutes of the Carleton College Board of Trustees for 26 October 1946, CCA.

255 **Gould presented a rough summary**—Minutes of the Carleton College Board of Trustees for 23 January 1947; LMG to Howell W. Murray, 10 March 1947—both CCA.

256 **$100,000 from Mrs. Edward C. Congdon**—LMG to Mrs. Edward C. Congdon, 27 November 1946; LMG to Mrs. Congdon, 7 March 1947 (gumdrops); Mrs. Congdon to LMG, 12 March 1947; LMG to David Bryn-Jones and Lucile Deen, 13 March 1947; LMG to Bruce Pollock, 13 March 1947 ("I am afraid")—all CCA. Later additions to the Congdon gift brought to total to $200,000 by October 1956.

256 **The Congdon gift would be announced**—*The Voice of the Carleton Alumni*, June 1947, 1.

256 **Also in mid-March … "indication of impatience."**—LMG to Frank Kille, 17 March 1947, CCA. See also Minutes of the Carleton College Faculty for 16 December 1946, CCA, for the faculty action on comprehensive examinations.

257 **"I want to be a good president"**—Arthur Mizener to LMG, 8 February 1947, CCA.

257 **first Midwestern college to require**—Minutes of the Carleton College Board of Trustees for 9 June 1947, CCA; *Carletonian*, January 15, 1949, 2. Gould explained the new admissions policy at commencement time in 1947, after which trustee Malcolm McDonald wrote as follows: "To me this is a matter of growing pains. We are shifting our method of judging students, with emphasis upon the college boards. Carleton has developed from a Minnesota to a Middle Western and now to a National institution. When people understand this, they will realize the desirability of college boards and will appreciate the fact that the College cannot admit all applicants, even though their parents are alumni." (Malcolm B. McDonald to LMG, 17 June 1947.)

257 **Some now were essentially … to Ann Arbor.**—Elledge, Whittemore, Boyd, Rayment correspondence in POF Faculty Files (Ser. 58A), CCA.

258 **attention by Walter Rogers**—LMG to Malcolm B. McDonald, 3 May 1947, CCA.

258 **May had previously … entirely behind him.**—Ibid. Also Kenneth O. May to LMG, 25 September 1950, CCA.

258 **"above all things else"**—LMG to Kenneth O. May, 18 June 1946, CCA.

258 **unsigned and undated memorandum … fact and error.**—"Memorandum re: Unsigned, undated memorandum 'Re: Kenneth Ownsworth May,'" dated April 15, 1947, signed by Kenneth May; LMG to Malcolm B. McDonald, 3 May 1947—both CCA. The original anonymous memorandum was returned to McDonald with Gould's letter of May 3, and no copy was retained for May's faculty file; its precise content, therefore, is not known, though much is clear from the above-referenced responses. Among the statements flagged by May as in error were assertions that May had been a member of the California Central Committee for the Communist Party in 1940, that he had been State Educational Director of the CP, that he had been a member of the California State Committee for the CP, and that he had been a candidate for the Oakland city council on the CP ticket, which was doubly inaccurate. May called "completely false … fabricated out of whole cloth or based on rumors" statements concerning his actions while in service or after his discharge, stating that "the fact is that I have not attended a Communist meeting or otherwise participated in CP activities since

1942, when I resigned from the CP before entering the army. Immediately upon discharge I returned to the University of California, [devoting] myself exclusively to studies and research."

259 **Gould stated that ... "proud of his son."**—LMG to Malcolm B. McDonald, 3 May 1947, CCA.

259 **Gould looked upon ... "crucified in this way."**—Ibid.

259 **The whole matter ... "Communism on the outside."**—Ibid.

259 **At the same April ... "any other position"**—LMG to Louis S. Headley, 19 April 1947, CCA.

260 **the following week ... socially in Northfield**—Peter Olesen to LMG, 3 May 1947, CCA.

260 **"we cannot very much longer"**—LMG to Atherton Bean, 2 May 1947, CCA.

260 **That summer ... "situations like Carleton College."**—LMG to Laird Bell, 23 July 1947, CCA.

260 **two African-American students**—These were Franklin B. McDaniel, enrolled 1874-1876, and Angelina Weld Grimké, 1895-1897. (See student transcripts for the Carleton Preparatory Department and Academy, CCA.) Grimké later became a noted poet, playwright, essayist, and lecturer.

260 **"one request for the admission"**—Minutes of the Carleton College Board of Trustees for 24 October 1947, CCA.

260 **"universal interest" ... "in the Carleton community."**—LMG to Donald H. Klinefelter, 26 October 1947, CCA.

260n **"We really have progressed"**—LMG to Laird Bell, 23 July 1947, CCA.

261 **Alvis Lee Tinnin**—1994 Tinnin/Gale interview; Tinnin's alumni file—both CCA.

261 **During his first ... show him the door.**—1994 Tinnin/Gale interview, CCA.

261 **activities external ... Community Research Council.**—Assorted correspondence, including LMG to Atherton Bean, 1 December 1947; LMG to Alex Wetmore, 3 February 1947; LMG to Laird Bell, 12 April 1947; LMG to Luther W. Youngdahl, 28 July 1947; LMG to Malcolm B. McDonald, 7 September 1947; LMG to Laird Bell, 23 September 1947; LMG to Atherton Bean, 20 November 1947; LMG to Sumner T. McKnight, 7 September 1947—all CCA; *Northfield Independent*, February 9, 1950.

262 **Also in vain ... "to go fishing."**—LMG to Duncan Stewart, CCA.

262 **Alfred Knopf ... "breathing it.")**—Knopf, *Portrait of a Publisher 1915-1963 Vol. I.*

262 **When in September 1947 ... honorary degree.**—LMG to George L. Weaver, 23 September 1947 and 21 February 1947; LMG to Edwin D. Dickinson, 13 September 1947 ("fear at this moment"); Minutes of the Carleton College Faculty for 13 October 1947—all CCA.

263 **In October he spoke ... on the subject**—Reginald D. Lang to LMG, 10 October 1947, CCA.

263 **"I want you to know" ... "fearlessly examined.")**—Philip H. Phenix to LMG, 16 October 1947, CCA.

263 **"how to defend"**—LMG to Robert F. Creegan, 20 October 1947—CCA.

263 **"We need to remind ourselves"**—*The Voice of the Carleton Alumni*, September 1947, 5.

263 **"very real ... interdependence"**—LMG to Frank W. Abrams, 18 January 1948, CCA

264 **Recommending to Laird Bell**—LMG to Laird Bell, 23 December 1947, CCA. Frank Abrams, the author of this article, would in later years become Gould's close friend through their joint service with the Ford Foundation.

264 **"It is a slow" ... "before we run."**—LMG to John M. Musser, 11 June 1947 and 17 November 1947—both CCA.

264 **"It beats the dickens"**—LMG to Donald Klinefelter, 1 December 1947, CCA.

264 **It was about a week later … end of April.**—LMG to Charles J. Miel, 27 October 1947 and 23 January 1948 ("for lengthening"), as well as other items in the Miel file, POF Faculty Files (Ser. 58A), CCA; also Minutes of the Carleton College Board of Trustees for 22 January 1948, CCA.

265 **insisted on the use of Mankato stone**—LMG to Reine Myers, 24 November 1948, CCA.

265 **at $250,000.**—Minutes of the Carleton College Board of Trustees for 23 January 1947, CCA.

265 **By December the estimate … other "free" funds.**—Ibid. for 7 June 1948, CCA.

265 **"on behalf of" … "this is wrong."**—Laird Bell to LMG, 16 July 1948, CCA.

265 **assurance that all fundraising**—Gould wrote Bell that "as I have thought about the proposition concerning the Art Building my feeling becomes more and more clarified that we should abandon every other project until that $75,000 is raised. I think the Student Union should be relegated to a place of quiescence and all of our fund raising activities directed toward the Art Building." (LMG to Laird Bell, 24 July 1948, CCA.)

265 **Hutchinson to open bids**—LMG to Laird Bell, 28 July 1948, CCA.

265 **Ground was broken … fall of 1949.**—*The Voice of the Carleton Alumni*, September 1948, 5; *Carletonian*, September 24, 1949, 1.

265n **The Boliou Fund**—See Boliou file, Biographical Files (Ser. 2A), CCA.

266 **In January 1947 … next two years.**—Minutes of the Carleton College Board of Trustees for 23 January 1947, CCA.

266 **Preliminary drawings**—*The Voice of the Carleton Alumni*, June 1947, 9 and back cover.

266 **A year later … Gridley Hall**—Ibid., September 1948, 20 (reporting on the June 5, 1948, annual meeting of the Carleton Alumni Association).

266 **At the trustee meeting … "with prospective donors."**—Minutes of the Carleton College Board of Trustees for 7 June 1948, 16 October 1948, 5 February 1949, 6 June 1949, and 22 October 1949—all CCA.

266 **Early in 1948 Gould pushed**—LMG to Edward A. Fath, 24 February 1948, CCA.

266n **"Probably one of the reasons"**—LMG to Hyme Loss, 29 August 1946, CCA.

267 **"one of the most exciting"**—LMG to Dave M. Okada, 12 April 1948, CCA.

267 **"This course represents"**—"*The Report of the President to the Board of Trustees of Carleton College, 1947-1948*," 7. The same page of this report, by the way, contains a short paragraph, inserted by Gould between various curricular matters, which reads: "I wonder if members of the Board of Trustees read these presidential reports. I shall think of some special way to reward anyone who informs me that he has read this far." I have no knowledge as to whether the offered reward was ever claimed. For my part, I wonder whether anyone reads these footnotes. If you do, dear reader, I hope that the inherent pleasures of close reading provide their own reward.

267 **Prompted by the receipt … "matter in the least."**—LMG to John Phelan, 1 March 1949, CCA.

268 **"the success of a course"**—John Phelan to LMG, 9 March 1949, CCA.

268 **"the idea has not" … "next time."**—LMG to Neil Gillam, 23 March 1949, CCA.

268 **Interviewed and hired … Capek in philosophy.**—Harrison, Fjelstad, and Capek correspondence in POF Faculty Files (Ser. 58A), CCA.

268 **George F. Baker Trust**—*Carletonian*, September 18, 1948, 1; LMG to Arthur Mizener, 14 May 1948, CCA ("one of the greatest").

268 **In June, he was asked … "Trustees continues.")**—Dean B. Webster to LMG, 8 June 1948; LMG to Webster, 16 June 1948—both CCA.

268 **Larry Gould Bay**—Radiogram dispatch from Finn Ronne to LMG, 14 January 1948, NA-GP.

269 **"I ofttimes long"**—LMG to Milic Capek, 24 June 1948, CCA.

269 **"Strategy and Politics ... "future of mankind."**—LMG, "Strategy and Politics in the Polar Areas," in *Annals of the American Academy of Political and Social Science* 255 (January 1948): 105-114.

269 **Dick Byrd wrote twice ... "be in the plane."**—REB to LMG, 12 June 1948 and 14 June 1948, NA-GP.

269 **Gould responded ... assistance to Henson.**—LMG to REB, 16 June 1948, NA-GP.

269 **"ranting and raving" ... "selfishness of some people."**—Finn Ronne to LMG, 2 November 1948 and 1 March 1949; LMG to Finn Ronne, 3 March 1949—all NA-GP .

270 **Gould had first thought ... delegation in Washington.**—LMG to Erling Christophersen, 18 November 1948, CCA; *Northfield Independent,* 20 January 1949.

270 **"rightful role"**—"President Gould Says:" column, in *The Voice of the Carleton Alumni,* March 1949, 10.

270 **On January 26 ... precious Amundsen note.**—Ibid., 9-10; LMG to Erling Christophersen, 31 January 1949, CCA (including "detailed knowledge").

270 **("You can be sure"**—LMG to Bernt and Bess Balchen, 31 March 1949, NA-GP.

270 **Senate bill 246 ... come in 1949.**—Munger and Fenno, *National Politics and Federal Aid to Education,* 10, 124, 138.

271 **academic freedom as the mother**—Phrase appearing in LMG to Earl Bunting, 13 April 1947, CCA.

271 **In April, he first ... "of the schools."**—LMG to Gideon Seymour, 6 April 1949; LMG to Paul H. Good, 20 April 1949; LMG telegram to Senators Thye and Humphrey, 25 April 1949; Hubert H. Humphrey to LMG, 26 April 1949—all CCA.

272 **Gould's address to the US Chamber ... "dare not take."**—LMG, "On Federal Aid to Education" (address at the 37th Annual Meeting of the Chamber of Commerce of the United State, Washington, D.C., May 3, 1949.)

272 **On May 5 ... "I do believe."**—Munger and Fenno, *National Politics and Federal Aid to Education,* 10, 140; LMG to Arch N. Booth, 11 May 1949, CCA.

272 **Hearings were held ... vote of 13-12.**—Munger and Fenno, *National Politics and Federal Aid to Education,* 10-11 and 125-126; *New York Times,* March 15, 1950, 1.

273 **"the coming of the welfare state"**—See, for instance, LMG to Frank G. Jewett, 26 July 1949, or LMG to Laurence A. Rossman, 29 December 1949—both CCA. In the latter letter, Gould writes: "I have been encouraged by the number of people I have met in the last weeks whose opinions have changed within the course of the last year. They are awakening to the fact that education is central to all other things and that unless we do want a socialized state we had better stop in the realm of education among all things else."

273 **He worked with ... "people in the country."**—LMG to Paul H. Good, 31 January 1950; also LMG to Laurence A. Rossman, 1 February 1950 (regarding editorial advice from Cowling)—both CCA.

273 **"Education and the Welfare State" ... "system of education."**—LMG, "Education and the Welfare State," *The Minnesota School Board Journal* 2, No. 7 (March 1950).

273 **America's Town Meeting of the Air**—"What Should We Do About Federal Aid to Education?" – Town Meeting of the Air, March 21, 1950. The published transcript of this program is the source of all information for three paragraphs of text, ending with "hurt you for the world.'"

274 **board chairman was urging ... "off for the present?"**—Laird Bell to LMG, 4 May 1950, CCA.

274 **convocation on the subject of academic freedom**—LMG, "On Academic Freedom," Carleton College convocation address, 22 April 1949, unpublished transcript, NA-GP. Gould sent a copy of the address to Atherton Bean, noting that he had spoken only from notes but that the convocation had been recorded and then transcribed by a secretary. (LMG to Atherton Bean, 29 May 1949, CCA.)

275 **"The Way Ahead"**—LMG, "The Way Ahead," commencement address, undated (presumably from circa 1949 or 1950), unpublished transcript, NA-GP.

275 **"sunshine-favored"**—*The Voice of the Carleton Alumni*, June 1949, 1. (Description of the commencement exercises and honorary degree recipients follows, 1-2.)

276 **"the most perfect" ... "have been President."**—LMG to Carter Davidson, 20 December 1948, CCA.

277 **Cowling had previously ... own honorary degree.**—LMG to Carter Davidson, 7 February 1949, CCA.

277 **Davidson directed Gould**—Carter Davidson to LMG, 13 February 1949, CCA.

277 **spontaneous standing ovation**—*The Voice of the Carleton Alumni*, June 1949, 1.

CHAPTER 17 — THE THINGS THAT HAVE MADE US GREAT

278 **pressure for entry had diminished**—Minutes of the Executive Committee of the Carleton College Board of Trustees for 10 March 1949, CCA.

278 **Commenting in a Carleton ... on remaining small.**—"President Gould Says: Notes on the Progress of the College from the Desk of the President," *Carleton College Bulletin* 46, No. 1; LMG to Laird Bell, 21 June 1949, CCA. In the "Five-Year Report" on his presidency issued a year later in the summer of 1950, Gould wrote: "I should hesitate to state a positive, definite figure as the 'ideal' size for Carleton College; but we who have experimented with and thought about the problem during the post-war years are convinced that for us it is certainly less than one thousand students." (LMG, "The Report of the President," in "Five-Year Report; Carleton College: 1945-1950," published as *Carleton College Bulletin* 47, No. 1 (August 1950), 3-4.)

278 **Assisted by some ... while he was away.**—LMG to Laird Bell, 13 July 1949; Atherton Bean to LMG, 1 July 1949 ("A good enough job"); LMG to Lucile Deen, 16 July 1949; LMG to Bruce Pollock, 21 July 1949—all CCA.

278 **alumni magazine declared that "progress"**—"College Opens Year of Progress," in *The Voice of the Carleton Alumni* 15, No. 1 (September 1949), 1.

279 **address at the centennial banquet ... "material civilization."**—October 20, 1949 address, "Minnesota Today and Tomorrow." Excerpts printed in the *Minneapolis Star*, November 14, 1949; LMG to Rex Lang, 17 November 1949 (in which Gould writes that he thought he got the major idea for his address from Professor Hayek's article in the spring issue of the *University of Chicago Law Review*—that would be Hayek, "Intellectuals and Socialism," 417-433). In transmitting a copy of the speech to Bell, Gould wrote that he was "increasingly convinced that unless the point of view I express is accepted we shall one day find ourselves a completely socialized state without realizing that we have gotten there. As a Democrat, that probably concerns you less than it does me." (LMG to Laird Bell, 16 November 1949, CCA.) Bell replied, even while congratulating Gould on the "excellence" of the address: "I do not despair of the Republic as much as you seem to. It has seemed to me inevitable that in the kind of mass production industry we have developed there is need for increasing control and a good deal of security legislation." (Laird Bell to LMG, 29 November 1949, CCA.)

279 **"As is so often" ... "quite so severe."**—LMG to Laird Bell, 5 December 1949—both CCA.

280 **major report on public relations ... dissipating Gould's efforts.**—Charles Miel, "Comments on Public Relations"; LMG to William Benton, 10 November 1949; Charles Miel to William Benton, 24 January 1950—all CCA.

280 **Bell soon strongly seconded**—Bell wrote Gould in February that he thought Gould had "reached the point where you can ration your speechmaking and take only those jobs where widespread results may be anticipated. I think you are completely right in making the building and maintenance of a good faculty your main concern. Unhappily there is no escape from trying to raise money at the same time. And I think you need to conserve your nervous energy, as well as your time, for those two major tasks." (Bell to LMG, 9 February 1950, CCA.)

280 **the president should become … "talks by the President."**—Charles Miel, "Comments on Public Relations, " CCA.

280 **The goal was … "was encouraging."**—Ibid.

281 **"a worthy physical shrine"**—LMG, "Five-Year Report," (1950), CCA.

281 **by January 1950 … winter meeting.**—Minutes of the Carleton College Board of Trustees for 19 January 1950; John Lindstrom memorandum to LMG and others of 6 January 1950—both CCA.

281 **"As you probably guessed "**—Laird Bell to LMG, 20 January 1950, CCA.

281 **"I do hope that"**—LMG to Laird Bell, 20 January 1950, CCA.

281 **"gingerbread"**—Ibid.

281 **"I don't think the plan"**—Laird Bell to LMG, 9 February 1950, CCA

281 **"from Missouri" … "side of economy."**—Ibid.

282 **Gould replied that … "gadgets" and so forth**—LMG to Laird Bell, 13 February 1950, CCA.

282 **"so ambitious" … "come to that issue."**—Laird Bell to LMG, 16 February 1950, CCA.

282 **by telephone … "I am objecting to."**—LMG to Laird Bell, 28 February; Bell to LMG, 4 March 1950—both CCA.

282 **"of such shape and appearance"**—Bruce Pollock to LMG, 5 July 1950, CCA.

282 **He also acceded … gift from Adams.**—LMG to Marian Adams, 14 March 1950, and 5 July 1950 ("auspicious beginning"); Marian Adams to LMG 1 June 1950—all CCA. See also LMG to Willard Thorp, 21 September 1954, CCA. Adams had, that March, indicated to Gould that she was considering leaving Carleton at the end of the academic year, but a distressed Gould had convinced her to stay, telling her that the prospect of her departing at year's end depressed his spirit too much to allow it just then; that for her to stay another year at least would give him "a real breathing space" for finding a suitable replacement for what he recognized as "one of the most critical positions in the whole life of the College." (LMG to Marian Adams, 10 March 1950, CCA.)

283 **On the 18th of January … "come of this."**—Memorandum from Kenneth O. May to LMG, 18 January 1950, CCA.

284 **"a fraud and a hoax"**—These widely-quoted words from the Tydings Committee majority report are to be found, for instance, in Griffith, The Politics of Fear, 325.

284 **Dorothy Kenyon**—Two years after Kenyon's confrontation with McCarthy, Gould's invitation to her to come give an address to students and faculty at Carleton drew criticism in the pages of an anti-Communist Catholic magazine, The Wanderer, which Gould dismissed as an "organ of prejudice." See Atherton Bean to LMG, 27 May 1952, and LMG to Bean, 29 May 1952—both CCA.

284 **"He's a lowdown worm"**—Kenyon's statement to reporters was widely reported in American newspapers of March 10, 1950 and shortly after.

284 **"a coward to take shelter"**—From Kenyon's testimony before McCarthy's investigative committee, a quotation found online at, for instance, http://en.wikipedia.org/wiki/Dorothy_Kenyon, retrieved 10 October 2012, citing the New York Times, "Judge Dorothy Kenyon Is Dead; Champion of Social Reform, 83," February 14, 1972.

284 **She was promptly … another political appointment.**—Ibid.

284 **State Department official Haldore Hanson**—Information in this and subsequent paragraphs (through "an end in 1953") from Haldore Hanson student transcript and

biographical file; Haldore Hanson to LMG, 31 March 1950, with transcript of Hanson's statement of March 28, 1950 to the Senate Subcommittee on the Investigation of Loyalty of State Department Employees (Tydings Committee); LMG to Hanson, 10 April 1950—all CCA; Griffith, *The Politics of Fear*, 84-85; *Wisconsin State Journal*, 30 December 1952, Section 1, 8.

287 **"irresponsible sensationalism" ... "fear, ignorance, bigotry, and smear."**—Quotations from Margaret Chase Smith's "Declaration of Conscience," June 1, 1950, *Congressional Record*, 81st Congress, 2nd Session, 7894-95.

287 **changeover to be managed in the college chaplaincy**—See LMG to James C. Flint, 16 February 1950; Flint to LMG, 14 March 1950; LMG to Philip Phenix, 3 January 1950 and 27 February 1950; LMG to Howard Conn, 6 March 1950 and 29 April 1950; LMG to Atherton Bean, 14 April 1950—all CCA.

287 **Curt Friese**—See LMG's correspondence with Edward J. Thye, or with Thye's administrative aide Carl Weicht, in POF4 correspondence, CCA; or with Friese himself, in POF Faculty Files (Ser. 58A), CCA; from 1 March 1950 until midway through 1953.

287 **$60,000 by the end of June**—LMG to Alexander G. Ruthven, 21 April 1950.

287 **decision to reduce enrollment ... salary for 1950-51.**—LMG to John M. Musser, 18 March 1950; LMG to Charles L. Horn, 29 March 1950; Minutes of the Carleton College Faculty for 22 May 1950; LMG to Professors Mizener, Thomas, and Verbrugge, 20 May 1950, LMG to Wally Hass, 5 June 1950, and LMG to Jane Andrews, 20 June 1950—all CCA.

288 **"It seems to us" ... "our admissions standards."**—Arthur Mizener, Thurlo Thomas, and Frank Verbrugge to LMG, 29 May 1950, CCA.

288 **Gould responded ... "fiercely proud."**—LMG to Mizener, Thomas, and Verbrugge, 30 May 1950, CCA.

289 **"Our Competition,"**—Dean DeVane's article was referenced in a 1956 Carleton brochure on the Cowling Foundation in Philosophy, CCA.

289 **In Chicago in May ... "values for us."**—LMG address delivered May 17, 1950. Originally titled "The Welfare State As I See It," all quotations come from the version printed later as "Are We Ashamed of the Things that Have Made Us Great?" The same address was also printed separately with the title "America's Passing Greatness." For the approach taken in this address and similar restatements, Gould acknowledged an intellectual debt to Felix Morley and Morley's 1949 book, *The Power in the People*. (See LMG to Felix Morley, 2 July 1951, CCA.)

289 **He then focused ... "he can respond."**—All from LMG, "Are We Ashamed of the Things that Have Made Us Great?" (Address before annual convention of Millers' National Federation, Chicago, May 17, 1950).

290 **What is needed ... "institutions are founded."**—Ibid.

290 **embodied in but two traditions**—Here and elsewhere in his writings and addresses, including elements of his inaugural address as president, Gould was influenced and inspired by his reading of the president of Corpus Christi College, Oxford, Sir Richard Livingstone. In *The Future in Education* (1941) and *Education for a World Adrift* (1942) Livingstone provided Gould with several ideas and quotations that he would return to again and again in his own communications and which he often (though not always) specifically acknowledged. In addition to the observation that the spiritual life of European civilization comes "from two sources, and only two, Greece, and Palestine," Gould was fond of quoting Livingstone's precept that "the good schoolmaster is known by the number of valuable subjects that he declines to teach." It likely was Livingstone as well who introduced Gould to the quotation from Alfred North Whitehead's *The Aims of Education* which he often repeated: "Moral education is impossible apart from the habitual vision of greatness." Livingstone referenced Whitehead's statement in *Education for a World Adrift*, saying that "outside Plato, there is no profounder saying about education."

290 **"We don't need a lot"**—LMG, "Are We Ashamed of the Things that Have Made Us Great?", op. cit.

290   **surprise awarding**—LMG to Catherine Fath Sherry, 24 July 1950, CCA.

290   **"never forget the expression"**—Ibid.

290n   **"previously (and lovingly)"**—*The Voice of the Carleton Alumni*, June 1950, 1.

291   **somewhat bewildered and uncertain ... "period of years."**—LMG to Leonard S. Wilson, 21 July 1950, CCA.

291   **"listen to no radio"**—LMG to Thurlo B. Thomas, 25 July, 1950, CCA.

291   **May's confidential grand jury testimony ... "the most careless."**—Kenneth O. May to Charles J, Miel, 28 July 1950, with enclosed typed statement of same date, CCA; *Minneapolis Tribune*, August 4, 1950; *St. Paul Dispatch*, August 4, 1950.

292   **"would rather be" ... long confidential report.**—Kenneth O. May to Charles J. Miel and Carolyn Pettet, 8 August 1950, CCA. The "long confidential report" to the president which May referenced in this letter is not present in May's faculty file where one might have expected to find it.

292   **Sally Crandall sent along ... not been possible.)**—LMG to Charles J. Miel, 14 August 1950, Kenneth O. May File, POF Faculty Files (Ser. 58A), CCA. For the Minneapolis Tribune response to Gould's criticism, see Gideon Seymour to LMG, 15 August 1950, Kenneth O. May File, POF Faculty Files (Ser. 58A), CCA.

292   **In March, Miel had written ... "to the Ford Plant."**—Charles J. Miel to Laird Anderson, 21 March 1950; Anderson to Miel, 4 August 1950—both CCA.

292   **A few days later ... "cannot be overstated."**—Rollo F. Hunt to LMG, 7 August 1950, CCA.

293   **Responses to these ... "explain the situation."**—Memorandum Charles J. Miel to LMG, 15 August 1950, in Kenneth O. May File, POF Faculty Files (Ser. 58A), CCA.

293   **It was decided ... "defending him."**—Charles J. Miel to Kenneth O. May, 28 August 1950 (containing excerpts from LMG to Miel, 21 August 1950 ("stronger position if we had a signed statement") and LMG to Miel, 24 August 1950 ("understand the urgency" and "He owes it to us")—all in Kenneth O. May File, POF Faculty Files (Ser. 58A), CCA.

293   **May readily agreed ... "anti-communist denouncer."**—Kenneth O. May to LMG, 1 September 1950, CCA.

293   **By late September ... friends, or country.**—Kenneth O. May to LMG, 25 September 1950, CCA.

294   **provided, in condensed ... Weinberg case.**—Charles J. Miel to Kenneth O. May, 21 December 1950; May to Miel, 25 December 1950—both in Kenneth O. May File, POF Faculty Files (Ser. 58A), CCA.

294   **named him chairman**—Memorandum LMG to Frank Kille, 27 November 1950, in Kenneth O. May File, POF Faculty Files (Ser. 58A), CCA.

294   **That fall, when pressed ... "good old times."**—LMG to Charles L. Horn, 20 October 1950, in Kenneth O. May file, POF Faculty Files (Ser. 58A), CCA.

294   **Carleton, Gould reminded ... "soul if I did so."**—Ibid.

295   **Gould advised the Carleton professoriate**—Minutes of the Carleton Faculty, 18 September 1950, CCA.

295   **Trustees officially directed**—Minutes of the Carleton College Board of Trustees for 13 October 1950, CCA.

295   **"Even now, young men"**—LMG to John E. Baer, 25 September 1950, CCA.

295   **"a little troubled" ... "give up this view.")**—LMG to Nathan Pusey, 25 October 1950; Pusey to LMG, 28 October 1950—both CCA.

295   **"a kick in the teeth"**—LMG to John M. Musser, 23 April 1951, CCA.

296   **"Am not reflecting"**—LMG to Hubert H. Humphrey, 20 April 1951, CCA.

296   **explanation arrived from**—Thomas K. Finletter to LMG, 17 May 1951, CCA.

296   **stopping the application process**—LMG to Colonel Millard Thompson, 30 July 1953, CCA.

296	**Estimates that ... could not remain.**—LMG to Leonard S. Wilson, 22 November 1950; Minutes of the Executive Committee of the Carleton College Board of Trustees for 14 December 1950—both CCA.

296	**"This is a dreadful"**—LMG to the Rev. Peter J. Jansen, 13 January 1951, CCA.

296	**trustees agreed to postponement**—Minutes of the Carleton College Board of Trustees for 22 January 1951, CCA.

296	**Budgeting that winter ... in the same place.**—LMG, "The State of the College," talk to Chicago area alumni meeting, 5 February 1951, unpublished transcript, CCA. A few days later Gould fretted in his correspondence that he supposed that "at no time since its origin has this college faced a more uncertain future." (LMG to Laurence A. Rossman, 11 February 1951, CCA.)

297	**"never in our history" ... "loss of its own soul."**—LMG, "The College in a Time of Peril," address delivered at the opening of Ripon College's Centennial Year, 31 January 1951, unpublished transcript, NA-GP.

297	**Minnesota Editorial Association ... "Communism itself."**—LMG, "Freedom of the Press in a Time of Peril," address of 16 February 1951, published in *Proceedings, the Eighty-fifth Annual Convention, Minnesota Editorial Association*. Gould began this address with an amusing story on himself that ought to be fitted in somewhere, even if only as a footnote. He said that it was "the story of a college president in a small college in the Upper Middle West who, when he became president of the college, was quite sure that he knew most of the answers and spoke very freely and authoritatively about education. He was invited to speak one time before an educational association in a town not very far from the one in which he lived. He went down and told the school teachers all about education and how desperately the world needed it, and he noticed that someone in the front row was taking copious notes; but he was not prepared for the headline in the local paper a few days later, as follows: 'College President Shows Need of Education.'"

298	**William Benton**—Biographical information and Benton quotations from "clippings" folder in Benton biographical file (Ser. 1A), CCA; also, regarding Gould's first meeting with Benton when in New York for the Eisenhower inauguration. see LMG to Atherton Bean, 18 October 1948, CCA. That UNESCO was very much Benton's idea was stated in the Benton memorial tribute of Hubert Humphrey, *The University of Chicago Record*, September 11, 1973, 230.

298	**"May I tell you that"**—LMG to William Benton, 2 February 1951, CCA.

299	**politically quixotic resolution ... "in and out of Government."**—Griffith, *The Politics of Fear*, 158-163; LMG to William Benton, 9 October 1951, CCA ("so pleased and proud"); Giblin, *The Rise and Fall of Senator Joe McCarthy*, 131.

299	**hospitalized in December ... at least June.**—LMG to Atherton Bean, 6 December 1950 and 9 March 1951; LMG to Winifred Bean, 5 January 1951; Atherton Bean to LMG, 1 February 1951 ("almost all general")—all CCA.

299	**private plane crash**—See LMG to Mrs. Alfred Lindley, 1 March 1951, CCA, for Gould's expression of sympathy.

299	**announced regretfully ... reading material**—Arthur Mizener to LMG, 15 February 1951; LMG to Mizener, 28 February 1951—both CCA.

299	**"fishing" trip**—LMG to Leonard S. Wilson, 16 February 1951, CCA.

299	**terrific cold**—LMG to Laird Bell, 28 February 1951, CCA.

299	**exceptionally snowy ... "negotiate the snow."**—LMG to Betty Carman, 17 January 1951; LMG to Mrs. A. N. Farmer, 19 March 1951 (since leaving Antarctica); LMG to Edwin D. Dickinson, 19 March 1951 ("a dog team")—all CCA.

299	**(Peg Gould, ... "sort of way."**—LMG to Mardy Murie, 12 February 1951; LMG to Atherton Bean, 9 March 1951 ("a personal affront"); LMG to Mrs. A. N. Farmer, 19 March 1951 ("but in a revolting"); LMG to Edwin D. Dickinson, 19 March 1951—all CCA.

300	**By the fifth of April ... "playing snowball."**—LMG to Edward A. Fath, 5 April 1951, CCA.

300   **fun between Gould and … Nancy's dormitory.**—E-mail to the author from Nancy Neller Springsteen of 8 January 2001, reporting upon her review of her 1951 letters home from Carleton.

300   **"as a lesser president"**—Anthony Downs to LMG, 14 May 1951, CCA. (In the same note, Downs also thanked Gould for having recently delivered a requested semi-serious address to the student body "concerning spring, emotions, and other germane topics." Echoes of a memorable talk Gould would sometimes give to students on controlling one's youthful passions in springtime have come to my ears from more than one Gould-era alumnus. It is a great pity that no recording nor transcript is available.)

300   **he and Laird Bell had scotched**—LMG to Laird Bell, 22 December 1950; Bell to LMG, 6 March 1951—both CCA.

300   **"I suppose at no time" … "must be maintained."**—LMG to Laurence A. Rossman, 11 February 1951, CCA.

300   **"Whether Carleton College needs"**—LMG to Edward A. Fath, 5 April 1951, CCA.

300   **"devote the rest"**—LMG to Leonard S. Wilson, 21 March 1951 (not sent), CCA.

300   **Henrickson, who was eyeing … "worth it."**—LMG to Eiler Henrickson, 13 July 1951, CCA.

301   **Larry Gould Day … the Gould home.**—*Carletonian*, May 12, 1951, 1.

301   **"probably 750 or less."**—LMG to Leal Headley, 7 June 1951, CCA.

301   **"we face the prospect"**—"President Gould Says" column in *The Voice of the Carleton Alumni*, June 1951, 11.

301   **Within a few days … brighter than heretofore.**—LMG to Nelson Vance Russell, 15 June 1951, CCA.

301   **"So much brighter"**—LMG to John M. Musser, 22 June 1951, CCA.

301   **projections were for 863 students**—Minutes of the Executive Committee of the Carleton College Board of Trustees for 12 July 1951, CCA.

301   **higher yet … "year starts splendidly."**—LMG to A. N. Farmer, 17 September 1951, CCA.

301n **Jill "grows rapidly"**—LMG to Ellwood and Helen Newhart, 16 May 1951, CCA.

CHAPTER 18 — I LIKE IKE

302   **reported to Laird Bell**—LMG to Laird Bell, 6 September 1951, CCA.

302   **earlier he had critiqued**—LMG to Laird Bell, 17 June 1948, CCA.

302   **gratified that week**—See LMG to Laird Bell, 12 September 1951, CCA.

302   **"a very opinionated" … president himself.**—Paul Christopherson to LMG, 3 October 1949, CCA.

302   **Gould had laid out … in faculty salaries.**—LMG to Charles L. Horn, 29 March 1950 , and 16 July 1951; LMG to Laird Bell, 12 September 1951 ("some long overdue")—all CCA.

303   **(Soon after , however… future gifts.)**—Malcolm B. McDonald to Atherton Bean, 4 October 1951 (conveying Horn's "could not expect"); LMG to Charles L. Horn, 2 June 1952 and 12 June 1952; Horn to LMG, 9 June 1952; Ellwood H. Newhart to Charles Miel, 26 June 1952—all CCA.

303   **out of which Gould hoped**—LMG to Seymour A. Smith, 14 September 1951, CCA.

303   **Gould had spoken … "have been the case."**—LMG to Nancy Wegner, 19 November 1951; LMG to Mrs. George C. Christian, 20 November 1951; LMG to Seymour A. Smith, 4 December 1951 ("the actual experience"); LMG to Laird Bell, 7 December 1951—all CCA.

303   **"still cause me" … neglecting other things.**—LMG to Howard Mundt, 23 February 1952; LMG to Lindsey Blayney, 24 December 1951; LMG to Laird Bell, 3 January 1952 ("demoralizing result")—all CCA.

   Professor Philip Sheridan, who began teaching in Carleton's English department in 1952, recalled, in typed reminiscences written decades later and present in the Carleton College Archives, that Larry Gould "was a well-read man in literature and knew a lot about it." Sheridan reported hearing Gould talk with admiration about special favorites Jane Austen and Robert Browning, "though he read very widely." The saying that his mind "was a library and not a debating hall," first applied to a former president of Cornell, "could well apply to Larry," wrote Sheridan, who also recorded that Gould "had an especial fondness for Milton" and had once told Sheridan that he wished he could give a course in his works. "When it comes to be written," Sheridan's reminiscences mistakenly assert, "none of these things are going to appear in Larry Gould's biography." (So there.)

   Non-fiction also always figured largely in the breadth of Gould's reading, and comments on books or articles with which he had recently been impressed are rife in his correspondence. In December of 1951 (correspondence of 14 December, CCA) he told history professor Carlton Qualey that "good biography or autobiography" was of particular interest, mentioning plans to soon pick up Catherine Drinker Bowen's *John Adams in the American Revolution* and Louise Hall Tharp's *The Peabody Sisters of Salem*. A couple of years before he had been particularly effusive about the autobiography of Albert Schweitzer, Laird Bell's Christmas gift to him that year. Gould called Schweitzer's memoir "a liberal education in itself." (LMG to Laird Bell, 2 February 1950, CCA.)

304   **confided to a friend … "good opportunities."**—LMG to Leonard S. Wilson, 25 February 1952, CCA.

304   **candidate for governor**—After Gould had mentioned the first of these suggestions, humorously, he thought, over a dinner with trustees Atherton Bean and Malcolm McDonald and their wives, Bean was concerned enough that Gould seemed to be "half seriously considering" the idea that he wrote a note of caution:

   "As you well know, I have the very highest regard for Larry Gould's abilities in almost every line. I have no question that from the standpoint of giving the State an honest, straightforward, well-managed administration, within the limits that are politically possible, he would do it. I question, however, whether this same Larry Gould would enjoy at all the necessary pulling and hauling, compromising and conceding that are necessary …

   "You now have a job which I feel you enjoy and where you certainly can look back on six years of real accomplishment. You can look forward to more years of real accomplishment as the problems of a college in the current 'Sturm und Drangzeit' are presented and solved. … I do not think that a political job would bring the same personal satisfactions or even possibly the same results.

   "May I say that my interest in this matter is not at all in what is good for Carleton, although I am sure that your staying there is good for it. I think it is also and in many ways more important, good for Larry Gould. As the preacher says, 'Here endeth the lesson.'" (Bean to LMG, 20 July 1951, CCA.)

   Gould responded with thanks for the friendly comments, but said he could reassure Bean, as he had all of his other friends, that in reality not "all the king's horses" nor "all the king's men" could possibly persuade him to get involved in the upcoming Minnesota gubernatorial race. (LMG to Bean, 23 July 1951, CCA.)

   A second suggestion that Gould run for governor came in September from Carleton alumnus Bob Matteson, an assistant to former Minnesota Governor (and then president of the University of Pennsylvania) Harold Stassen. Matteson wrote that he had heard a number of people express the thought that Gould would make an excellent candidate for governor and that he himself felt "very strongly the same way" and hoped he would consider it. (Robert E. Matteson to LMG, 13 September 1951, CCA.)

304   **an extraordinary letter … balance of power.**—Andrew J. Galambos to LMG, 12 February 1952, CCA.

304n   **"I have read and re-read"**—LMG to JRH, 27 March 1948, CCA.

305   **few weeks earlier … "science fiction."**—LMG to Robert W. Feyerharm, 5 February 1952, CCA.

305   **"deeply touched"** ... **"in that direction."**—LMG to Andrew J. Galambos, 27 February 1952, CCA.

305   **aligned himself with**—See, for instance, among many possible relevant sources, LMG to Rex Lang, 21 July 1949, CCA, or Gould's published address to the Minnesota Editorial Association of 16 February 1951, "Freedom of the Press in a Time of Peril."

305   **"if Stassen is not elected"**—LMG to Alfred D. Lindley, 9 July 1947, CCA.

305   **rejoiced to his friend John Cowles**—LMG to John Cowles, 29 September 1950, CCA.

306   **"Harold [Stassen] is still"**—LMG to Robert E. Matteson, 6 September 1951, CCA.

306   **he attended ... "or General Eisenhower."**—LMG to Mrs. George C. Christian, 22 September 1951, CCA. Gould's unfavorable view of President Truman at this time can be seen, for instance, through the prism of his reaction in correspondence to the 1951 *contretemps* over Truman's firing of General MacArthur as commander in Korea over public comments by MacArthur bordering on insubordination. While acknowledging that "the supremacy of our civilian elected president had to be established over that of any military commander, no matter whom he might be," Gould thought it "unfortunate," however, "that this particular civilian is not a man of greater stature." "Heaven knows," he added, "we need leadership of competence and inspiration as we have perhaps never needed it before." (LMG to Leonard S. Wilson, 18 May 1951, CCA.)

306   **Eisenhower's stature ... "Eisenhower boom"**—Quotations are from *Time*, January 14, 1952.

306   **"doing a great job"**—Taft quoted in *Time*, March 31, 1952. This in contrast to Gould's writing that winter to Senator Benton, then McCarthy's leading Senatorial nemesis: "I hope very much that your objection to Senator McCarthy still continues and may bear fruit. Some day people who have supported that man will be so ashamed of themselves that they will wonder how they could ever have been so grossly misled. Your forthright and honest exposure of him is but one of the many reasons why we are so proud of you and glad to have you on our Board." (LMG to William Benton, 12 February 1952, CSA.) Benton replied that he was not letting up, but that he was losing: "I'm being pushed to the wall. Your Republican friends are winning out. ... I'm doing the best I can but the odds against me are rising weekly." (William Benton to LMG, 17 February 1952, CCA.)

306   **likely winner in November, if he could only be nominated**—A Gallup poll in February 1952 as to which of the possible GOP candidates had the most appeal to independents showed 42 percent choosing Eisenhower, as opposed to 16 percent for Taft, and lesser numbers for Earl Warren, Douglas MacArthur, Harold Stassen, or Thomas Dewey. At the same time, Gallup showed *Republican* voters as evenly split between Eisenhower and Taft at 33 percent each, with MacArthur (aligned with Taft on the conservative side of the party) next at 14 percent, and Warren, Stassen, and Dewey, all considered moderates like Eisenhower, combining for 18 percent. With Taft supporters largely in control of party machinery in the various state organizations, it was by no means clear that Eisenhower's popularity would mean that the nomination was his for the taking. (see *Time*, February 18, 1952.)

306   **asked Gould to become ... elected as a delegate**—LMG to Andrew J. Galambos, 27 February 1952, CCA.

307   **"I have lost my chance"**—LMG to Ellis H. Dana, 10 March 1952, CCA.

307   **Minnesota primary ... securing the nomination.**—See Philip A. Grant, Jr. "The 1952 Minnesota Republican Primary and the Eisenhower Candidacy," in *Presidential Studies Quarterly* 9, No. 3 (Summer 1979), 311 (including quotations from the New York Times); *Time*, March 31, 1952, 19-20.

308   **not actually present ... reached Albuquerque.**—Various correspondence, such as LMG to Robert Adamson, 10 March 1952; LMG to Reginald D. Lang, 10 March 1952; and LMG to Edward A. Fath, 14 March 1952; plus list of LMG addresses for 1952—all CCA.

308   **friendly ten-dollar bet ... "smoke filled rooms."**—LMG to Howell W. Murray, 25 April 1952 and 13 May 1952—both CCA.

308   **"setting the pattern and policy"**—LMG to DJC, 8 March 1952, CCA.

308   **dinner most Thursday evenings**—LMG to Hazel Lewis, 15 April 1952, CCA.

308   **initiation of a five-year**—LMG to J. R. Dunning, 13 May 1952; Minutes of the Carleton College Faculty for 12 May 1952—both CCA.

308n **"Somehow," Gould wrote**—LMG to Edward A. Fath, 14 March 1952, CCA.

309   **faculty hiring**—See POF Faculty Files (Ser. 58A) for James H. Richards, Robert Adamson, Albert E. Elsen, Elvan E. Kintner, Jean M. Calloway, William A. Butler, and Eleanor H. Hansen—all CCA.

309   **As Hansen would later recall**—1994 Hansen/Reitz interview, CCA.

309   **"I don't think you should be depressed."**—Laird Bell to LMG, 12 February 1952, CCA.

309   **"I have never dabbled" … "blow off steam."**—LMG to Charles M. Horn, 18 May and 17 July, 1952; Thomas L. Daniels to Charles Miel, 3 September 1952 (reporting "blast over the telephone"); LMG to Daniels, 8 September 1952—all CCA.

310   **"right hand," … "rest of the year."**—LMG to Howard Mundt, 23 February 1952, CCA.

310   **shocked in March … Coman's funeral.**—LMG to Carl and Harriet Eklund, 10 March 1952 ("in rare spirits"); Carl Eklund to LMG, 28 April 1952—both CCA.

310   **Colonel Bernt Balchen … great pleasure.**—LMG to Bess Balchen, 5 June 1952, NA-GP.

310   **"The situation looks"**—LMG to Ellis H. Dana, 19 June 1952, CCA. (Also "expressed some optimism" below.)

310   **"greatly depressed at"**—LMG to Laird Bell, 26 June 1952, CCA.

311   **"desperately in need" … become a Democrat.**—Ibid.

311   **"If you Democrats" … at the convention.**—LMG to William Benton, 1 July 1952, CCA.

311   **Gould left for Chicago … University Club**—LMG to Laird Bell, 26 June 1952, CCA;

311   **historic convention … "liked Ike."**—For the information and quotations of these two paragraphs, see account of the convention proceedings in Bain and Parris, *Convention Decisions and Voting Records.*

311n **"positively disgraceful"**—LMG to Carl Eklund, 30 April 1952, CCA.

312   **"Illuminating" … for another.**— LMG to Scott Elledge, 13 July 1952, CCA. See also LMG to DJC, 12 July 1952, CCA.

312   **"in spite of" … "no little enthusiasm."**—LMG to Mrs. Edward C. Congdon, 16 July 1952, CCA.

312   **Miel had worried … "will come true."**—Charles J. Miel to LMG, 24 April 1951; LMG to Carlton Qualey, 26 April 1951—both CCA.

313   **Qualey agreed … "on this campus."**—Qualey to LMG, 27 April 1951, CCA.

313   **"I want," Bell began … $1.5 million.**—Laird Bell to LMG, 1 July 1952, CCA.

313   **Gould shared early news … "at least $1,500,000."**—Howell W. Murray to LMG, 14 July 1952; LMG to Atherton Bean, 15 July 1952; LMG to James H. Richards, Jr., 15 July 1952; Minutes of the Executive Committee of the Carleton College Board of Trustees for 16 July 1949; LMG to Laird Bell, 16 July 1952; Bell to LMG, 19 September 1952—all CCA.

314   **at least as early as 1940.)**—See Alfred Hyslop to DJC, 8 May 1940, CCA.

314   **put away his portable radio**—LMG to Ralph Henry, 3 August 1952, CCA.

314   **climbed mountains somewhat less**—LMG to Bruce Pollock, 10 August 1952, CCA.

314   **fished somewhat more … "as well as I do.")**—LMG to Mrs. George C. Christian, 29 August 1952, CCA.

314   **welcome repeat of the pattern**—Minutes of the Executive Committee of the Carleton College Board of Trustees for 9 September 1952, CCA: "President Gould submitted Mr. Klinefelter's figures on enrollment as of September 9, 1952. Whereas last spring's budget figures were based on an enrollment of 790, it now appeared likely that the registration would

be approximately 865 students ..." Later in September, actual enrollment stood at 875. (See LMG to Haven A. Requa, 24 September 1952, CCA.)

314 **Eisenhower's speech ... "security and prosperity."**—Information for two paragraphs from LMG to Laird Bell, 16 September 1952, CCA; *The Voice of the Carleton* Alumni, September 1952, 7; *Carletonian*, September 20, 1952, 1, 2.

314n **"very bad tennis" ... "wish to cherish."**—Quotations are from LMG to Atherton Bean, 10 February 1950 and LMG to E. S. Hjortland, 5 June 1952—both CCA.

316 **ask Dulles to "soft-pedal" ... Eisenhower's ear.**—John Cowles to LMG, 12 September 1952; LMG to Cowles, 16 September 1952—both CCA.

316 **"pull the carpet out from under"**—LMG to Arthur Mizener, 27 July 1953, CCA.

316 **At Carleton during ... less than two years.**—Minutes of the Carleton College Board of Trustees for 17 October 1952, CCA.

317 **On Saturday afternoon ... had ever received.**—LMG to Atherton Bean, 21 October 1952, CCA (including "off the ground"); *The Voice of the Carleton Alumni*, December 1952, 7-8.

317 **At Carleton a poll**—77 percent figure cited by Gould in LMG to Nat S. Finney, 5 November 1952, CCA.
   Carleton campus straw poll results for most U.S. presidential elections since 1884 have been reported in the campus paper, the *Carletonian*. These show campus sentiment as overwhelmingly favoring Republican candidates throughout the Roosevelt and Truman years and indeed through 1960, since when the campus has to date equally overwhelmingly favored Democrats. As Gould himself also voted Republican through 1960, but, it is fairly clear, never again thereafter at the presidential level, in this respect Gould and Carleton always remained in synch.

317 **"heartened by the fact" ... "political neck."**—LMG to Laird Bell, 5 November 1952;

317 **"Though I am" ... McCarthy's political power.**—LMG to William Benton, 6 November 1952, CCA.

318 **Shortly after ... at year's end.**—LMG to Trevor Lloyd, 23 November 1952; LMG to Charles L. Horn, 21 December 1952; LMG to Laird Bell, 30 December 1952—all CCA.

318 **for $10,000**—LMG to Charles L. Horn, 18 November 1952, CCA.

318 **"I am convinced,"**— LMG to Charles Miel, 20 November 1952, CCA.

318 **"dwelt unduly" ... marks of quality.**—LMG to Charles L. Horn, 1 December 1952, CCA.

318 **"The Olin Foundation is being"**—Charles L. Horn to LMG, 8 December 1952, CCA.

319 **Gould replied to Horn ... "one I am following."**—LMG to Charles L. Horn, 21 December 1952, CCA.

319 **off to Los Angeles for**—LMG to Carlton Qualey, 1 January 1953, CCA.

319n **though in December Gould wrote**—LMG to Laird Bell, 2 December 1952, CCA.

319n **ties hung "very lightly"**—LMG to the Rev. Kyle Hasenden, 7 June 1950, CCA.

319n **"I think religion is like"**—LMG to Wilder Crane, 23 October 1947, CCA.

319n **"What Christianity means"**—LMG to F. A. Bean, 26 January 1953, CCA.

320 **study by two Wesleyan to Charles Horn.**—The book was titled *The Younger American Scholar: His Collegiate Origins*, by Robert H. Knapp and Joseph J. Greenbaum. LMG to Leonard S. Wilson, 6 February 1953; LMG to Charles L. Horn, 6 February 1953—both CCA.

320 **"I have just learned" ..."melt them."**—LMG to S. Spencer Scott, 6 February 1953; Scott to LMG, 17 February 1953—both CCA.

320 **Notwithstanding Gould's stout ... "from your office."**—LMG to Charles L. Horn, 21 December 1952; LMG to Director, FBI, Minneapolis, 13 February 1953—both CCA.

320 **seem to have involved ... Rosenberg**—LMG to Kirk W. McVoy, Jr., 24 February 1953; McVoy to LMG, (29?) February 1953 [this letter is dated 9 February, but is apparently in

response to Gould's letter of 24 Feb., so I take the letter to have been misdated]; LMG to McVoy, 15 March 1953 ("jocose manner" etc.)—all CCA.

321 **FBI promptly designated**—W. G. Banister to LMG, 16 February 1953, CCA.

321 **Gould spoke with ... next morning.**—LMG to Alden D. Sheffield, 23 February 1953, CCA.

321 **"completely confident"**—LMG to Kirk W. McVoy, Jr., 24 February 1953, CCA.

321 **With May he ... "circumstances suggest."**—LMG to Alden D. Sheffield, 23 February 1953, CCA.

321 **"token of his sincerity"**—Ibid.

321 **letter of resignation**—Kenneth O. May letter of resignation dated 21 February 1953, CCA.
    May's letter read, in part: "In these troubled times I know that the presence of an ex-communist on the faculty causes the college some embarrassment. While I am not in a position to judge all the factors involved, I realize that a situation might develop in which it would be in the best interests of the college for me to leave. ...
    "I do not know of or anticipate anything that would justify my dismissal 'for cause' under normal tenure procedures. Also I do not wish to waive any of the tenure rights that are justly prized by my colleagues. On the other hand I wish to give you a free hand to do whatever you consider necessary.
    "Accordingly, I am now submitting my resignation from the faculty, to take effect at the end of the current academic year."
    Two days after meeting with Gould May wrote to President Eisenhower stating that he now wished to withdraw his previous letter to President Truman in which he had urged the president to commute the death sentences against the Rosenbergs. He wrote that while he had previously judged from what he had read in the newspapers that "current popular emotions" had likely influenced the Rosenbergs' trial and sentence, he had recently read the entire transcript of the trial and appeals, and it had now become clear to him that he had earlier not fully realized "either the extent of their guilt or the lack of extenuating circumstances." "While clemency may be justified on humanitarian grounds," he concluded, he wished to "set the record straight" by withdrawing his previous statement. May gave Gould a copy of this letter, as well as his never-accepted resignation. (Kenneth O. May to "The President," 23 February 1953, CCA.)

321 **Gould wrote to three professors**—Memorandum, LMG to Renzo Bianchi, 26 February 1953, with penciled note that the same memorandum had gone to Professor [Samuel] Strong and Mr. [Milic] Capek, CCA.

321 **received but one letter ... then seemed necessary.**—statements dated 3 March and 17 March 1953 from Kenneth May POF Faculty File; Malcolm B. McDonald to LMG, 10 March 1953; LMG to Ellwood "Goley" Newhart, 11 March 1953 (including "the less publicity")—all CCA.

321 **awarded a prestigious**—see LMG to Clarence H. Faust, The Fund for the Advancement of Education, 24 March 1953, CCA.

322 **$100,000 pledge**—LMG to Atherton Bean 18 February 1953 and 3 March 1953—both CCA.

322 **half a million dollars by the end of March**—LMG to Charles A. Culver, 23 March 1953, CCA.

322 **Gould maintained some hope ... "one's hide off."**—LMG to Howell W. Murray, 16 March 1953 (including "hard nut to crack" and "one's hide off"); LMG to Olivia Coan, 10 March 1953 ("all friendliness")—both CCA.

322 **"I have never been treated"**—LMG to Howell W. Murray, 16 March 1953, CCA.

322 **"whom I have got to"**—LMG to Olivia Coan, 10 March 1953, CCA.

322 **attention focused on William McKnight**—LMG to A. N. Farmer, 24 February 1953; LMG to Laird Bell, 5 April 1953 ("opening wedge"); LMG to Howell W. Murray, 7 April 1953 ("could build us")—all CCA.

322 **"extensive" search ... offer accepted**—LMG to Howard Conn, 11 April 1953; LMG to David M. Stowe, 6 May 1953—both CCA.

322 **"tempted to invite"**—LMG to Floyd A. Bond, 8 May 1953, CCA.

322 **another automobile accident ... running into others.**—LMG to Atherton Bean, 29 April 1953, CCA.

323 **attempt to interest Gould**—LMG to Howell W. Murray, 26 May, 1953; LMG to Ellis H. Dana, 17 June 1953 ("I am sensible enough")—both CCA.

323 **when he informed ... in that way.**—LMG to Howell W. Murray, 26 May, 1953, CCA.

323 **Nathan Pusey had just ... "very great opportunity."**—LMG to Nathan Pusey, 9 March 1953; John Cowles to LMG, 1 June 1953; Nathan Pusey to LMG, 23 June 1953—all CCA.

CHAPTER 19 — "CARISSIMA MIA"

324 **Carleton commencement weekend of 1953**—*The Voice of the Carleton Alumni,* June, 1953, 7-10.

324 **already become an entrenched**—See for instance, Gould's letter that summer from a Carleton graduate of 1950: "Say, what happened to your fabled powers of weather prognostication and control this year? My informants report that doting mothers had to forego parading specially purchased picture hats, and proud fathers lacked the bright sunshine necessary for brilliant color snapshots. Can this be true?" (Robert E. Will to LMG, 29 July 1953, CCA.)

324 **Nothing observable**—Phil Phenix to LMG, 16 June 1953, CCA.

324 **On Thursday night ... troubles with arthritis.**—LMG to R. D. Musser, 9 June 1953 ("collapsed"); LMG to Malcolm B. McDonald, 10 June 1953; LMG to Laird Bell, 11 June 1953; LMG to Dr. E. H. Hammes, 25 June 1953; LMG to Leonard S. Wilson, 30 June 1953—all CCA.

325 **"Mrs. Gould hasn't been"**—LMG to Laurence A. Rossman, 2 July 1953, CCA.

325 **"for the past four or five years."**—LMG to Peg Gould, note dated "Sunday morning," identified as 28 February 1954, CCA-GC.

326 **Gould cancelled ... stand in.**—Nels Minne, Winona State Teachers College, to LMG, 6 June 1953, CCA.

326 **budget balanced**—LMG to Leonard S. Wilson, 30 June 1953, CCA.

326 **events as planned**—List of LMG addresses for 1953, CCA.

326 **wrote to James O. Wynn**—LMG to James O. Wynn, 16 June 1953, CCA.

326 **carried on ... at the Gould house.)**—*Northfield News,* July 2, 1953, 8.

326 **Dr. Hammes reported ... "better for her."**—LMG to Dick Hoppin, 25 June 1953; LMG to E. H. Hammes, 25 June 1953—both CCA.

326 **eager and impatient**—LMG to Leonard S. Wilson, 30 June 1953; LMG to Samuel M. Strong, 30 June 1953; LMG to Renzo Bianchi, 1 July 1953—all CCA.

326 **finally allowed ...** LMG to Mr. and Mrs. Laird Bell, 1 July 1953

326 **by mid-month ... at the Square G.**—LMG to Martha L. Rice, 15 July 1953 and 28 July 1953, LMG to Laird Bell, 19 July 1953, LMG to Atherton Bean, 28 July 1953—all CCA.

327 **Gould was concerned ... forty acres in 1955**—LMG to Olaus J. Murie, 14 April 1953, 3 June 1953, and 26 September 1953 ("so as to be sure"); LMG to Laird Bell, 29 April 1953; Murie to LMG, 1 May 1953; LMG to Charles E. Lyght, 3 November 1955—all CCA.

327 **reported to multiple correspondents**—See, for instance, LMG to Olin S. Pettingill, 14 September 1953, and LMG to Jesse Robinson, 16 September 1953; LMG to Mrs. George C. Christian, 25 September 1953 ("better than she has been")—all CCA.

327n **The Goulds' friendship**—See LMG to Olaus J. Murie, 22 September 1950; Murie to LMG 19 April 1951; LMG to Murie, 23 April 1951—all CCA.

328 **Gould thought it a part**—LMG to Dorothy Obaid, 27 February 1954, CCA.

328 **anonymous gift of stock**—LMG to John M. Musser, 15 September 1953; Minutes of the Carleton College Board of Trustees for 31 October 1953—both CCA.

328 **formally solicited ... "this year and next."**—LMG to Charles L. Horn, 5 October 1953; Horn to LMG, 4 January 1954—both CCA.

328 **"moving along as it should" ... "uproarious laughter.")**—LMG to Atherton Bean, 30 November 1953, CCA.

328 **owed his position on the short list**—1981 Gould/E. Vernice Anderson interview, transcript copy in CCA-GC.

329 **in November, Gould was**—Robert M. Lester to LMG, 19 November 1953, CCA.

329 **Bernt Balchen came to visit ... room at home)**—*Carletonian*, November 21, 1953, 1; LMG to Erwin S. Barrie, 23 December 1953; LMG to Bernt Balchen 31 January 1954—all NA-GP.

329 **"There's no doubt"**—Bernt Balchen to LMG, 22 October 1953, NA-GP.

329 **Gould sympathized ... "as I do."**—LMG to Bernt Balchen 23 December 1953, NA-GP.

329 **Gould did encourage**—LMG to Howell W. Murray, 31 January 1954, CCA.

329 **"it seems that"**—LMG to Howell W. Murray, 27 February 1954, CCA.

329 **"the mean extremes" ... "do so now."**—Ibid.

329 **weather cooperated ... "a lot of good."**—LMG to Charles C. Mierow, 12 November 1953 "phenomenal"); LMG to Richard H. Hoppin, 21 January 1954—both CCA.

330 **"Carissima mia, I wonder if"**—LMG to Peg Gould, 14 January 1954, CCA-GC.

330 **"Carissima mia, I am so"**—LMG to Peg Gould, 28 February 1954, CCA-GC. [This note, dated only "Sunday morning," has been assigned the above date in accordance with its internal clues.]

330 **largely undertaken to continue**—See LMG to Dorothy Obaid, 27 February 1954, or LMG to Charles Miel, 4 March 1954, for example—both CCA.

331 **1954 had begun with ... quite another scale.)**—LMG to Carter Davidson, 5 January 1954 (including "if the people"); Richard Drew Musser to LMG, 6 January 1954 (for $12,500); Bruce Pollock to LMG, 11 January 1954; LMG to Howell W. Murray, 16 July 1954—all CCA.

331 **signed the papers establishing**—John H. Myers to LMG, 14 February 1954, CCA.

331 **"M.P.M. Account," ... "Gould in particular."**—John H. Myers to LMG, 14 May 1954, CCA.

331 **less than $300,000 away**—Carleton College news release dated 15 March 1954, CCA.

331 **In January and February**—See POF Faculty Files (Ser. 58A) for Robert A. Reitz, and Richard W. Ramette, CCA.

332 **called out of a dinner**—LMG, "My 50 Years of Antarctic Exploration and Research," op. cit., CCA-GC.

332 **Gould had known since**—LMG to Edward C. Rosenow, 29 October 1949, CCA.

332 **follow-up call to Gould ... "not yet quite clear"**—LMG to Lloyd V. Berkner, 19 March 1954, CCA.

332 **evening of March 21 ... by his friend John Cowles**—LMG to Donald K. David, 22 March 1954; LMG to John Cowles, 17 April 1954—both CCA.

332n **Years later Gould told**—See LMG, "My 50 Years of Antarctic Exploration and Research," op. cit., CCA-GC.

333 **"a large body of money" ... by far the largest foundation**—Macdonald, *The Ford Foundation*, 1956, 3. In 1954 the Ford Foundation would spend nearly $68 million, about four times the usual annual spending of the Rockefeller Foundation and ten times the annual spending of the Carnegie Corporation, the second and third largest foundations, respectively.

333 **Immediately confirming his interest**—LMG to Donald K. David, 22 March 1954, CCA.

333 **"bad impression"**—LMG to Winnie and Atherton Bean, 29 March 1954, CCA.

333 **"the unanimity with which" … forever doing for Carleton.**—Charles E. Wyzanski, Jr. to LMG, 5 April 1954; LMG to John Cowles, 17 April 1954; LMG to Claude Robinson, 18 April 1954—all CCA.

333 **day or two of trustee orientation**—LMG to Donald K. David, 16 April 1954; LMG to John Cowles, 17 April 1954—both CCA.

333 **Gould told Laird … thought was fertile.**—LMG to Laird Bell, 24 May 1954, CCA.

334 **interestingly fraught juncture**—The principal source of information for the paragraphs that follow on the internal and external "politics" surrounding the Ford Foundation in the early 1950s is Nielsen, *The Big Foundations,* 82-85, supplemented to some extent by Macdonald, *The Ford Foundation,* 1989 reprint, viii; 27-31. Specific pages are noted for direct quotations only. Dwight Macdonald suggested that the Reece Committee's investigation of the foundations may be best understood as an episode in Republican factional politics, stemming from the bad blood between the Eisenhower and Taft factions at the 1952 Republican National Convention. Noting that the Fords and Rockefellers had been conspicuous as "among those who won the nomination for the Eisenhower internationalists against the Taft isolationists, while Paul Hoffman, then head of the Ford Foundation, was not only the former head of 'the Marshall Plan squanderbund' but also one of Eisenhower's chief political advisers," (Macdonald, 28) and further observing that Rep. Reece, on the other hand, had been one of Taft's campaign managers, Macdonald described Reece's call for a new investigation as motivated by disappointment over the Cox Committee's "failure to 'get' the Fords' and the Rockefellers' foundations." (Macdonald, 29)

334 **"one of the favorite"**—Nielsen, *The Big Foundations,* 82.

334 **"determine whether they"**—Statement of purpose of the Cox Committee from the Wikipedia entry: http://en.wikipedia.org/wiki/United_States_House_Select_Committee_to_Investigate_Tax-Exempt_Foundations_and_Comparable_Organizations, retrieved 21 October 2011.

334 **"there is little basis"**—Ibid.

334 **"clean house"**—Nielsen, *The Big Foundations,* 83.

334 **"mild and reflective"**—Ibid., 84.

334 **"this fateful stroke"**—Ibid.

334n **"the Fund's first" … "subsidiary of the Ford Foundation."**—Macdonald, *The Ford Foundation,* 1989 reprint, 69-70.

335 **"the last of the great" … "Socialism in the United States."**—Reece quoted in Macdonald, The Ford Foundation, 1989 reprint, 29.

335 **Larry Gould Day**—*Northfield News,* May 20, 1954, 2; additional detail from a newspaper clipping unidentified as to paper and date.

335 **Miel's report … "better eastern colleges."**—Minutes of the Carleton College Board of Trustees for 7 June 1954, CCA.

336 **The trustees approved … was insisting.**—Ibid.; also see LMG to Harvey Stork, 7 July 1954—both CCA.

336 **afternoon flight to Ann Arbor … "hell to pay."**—LMG to Atherton Bean, 11 June 1954; LMG to Harlan Hatcher, 17 June 1954; LMG to Henry Margenau, 22 June 1954; LMG to Harry A. Towsley, 22 July 1954—all CCA.
     The ceremony-canceling storm in Ann Arbor was the last episode in a year-long string of bad weather incidents starting with the rain-soaked Carleton Commencement following Peg Gould's nervous collapse. In early March, while Gould spent eight days pursuing potential donors in Florida, the weather was worse than he had ever seen it in that state, with Gould reporting that he had "shivered much of the time and slept under a down puff at night." (LMG To Wadsworth A. Williams, 18 March 1954, CCA) As he returned from that trip via a National Science Board meeting in Washington, Gould's night flight return to Minnesota ran into a

nasty blizzard, keeping him two hours in the air over Minneapolis before being allowed to land. Early in May, a flight he was to take from Washington to New York was cancelled due to heavy rain, forcing him to take the train instead. When asked about the Michigan storm, however, and why his vaunted ability to control the weather had not kept undesirable elements at bay that day, Gould protested that he wished to "disinfect" himself from all responsibility for the weather at commencement time in Ann Arbor, stating forthrightly that "no college president in his right mind would pretend omniscience and omnipotence beyond his own campus." (LMG to Harry A. Towsley, 7 September 1954, CCA.)

336 **Gould claimed that**—LMG to Jesse S. Robinson, 7 July 1954, CCA.

336 **his address "Noblesse Oblige**—"Noblesse Oblige," *Michigan Alumnus Quarterly Review*, 1954 Autumn Number, 1-7.

336 **check for $250 ... "giving the address."**—LMG to Harry A. Towsley, 22 July 1954, CCA.

337 **In May he had asked ... "with pleasure."**—LMG to Paul A. Siple, 6 May 1954 and 4 June 1954; LMG to Bernt Balchen, 5 May 1954; Siple to LMG, 9 June 1954 ("highly problematical" etc.); LMG to REB, 25 May 1954 and 12 December 1954; Byrd to LMG, 23 December 1954 ("with pleasure")—all NA-GP.

337 **Writing Lloyd Berkner ... "person to do it."**—LMG to Lloyd V. Berkner, 24 May, 1954, CCA.

337 **pair of IGY-related ... "until fall."**—LMG to Atherton Bean, 11 June 1954; LMG to Hubert Humphrey, 17 June 1954 ("most important cooperative"); LMG to Carleton Qualey, 6 July 1954 ("I think")—all CCA.

338 **maintained for one final season**—LMG to Tom Morgan, 17 June 1954, CCA.

338 **"go fishing with a clear"**—LMG to Carlton Qualey, 6 July 1954, CCA.

338 **$140,000**—LMG to Howell W. Murray, 16 July 1954, CCA.

338 **therapeutically "imperative"**—LMG to Laird Bell, 22 July 1954, CCA.

338 **"calm and peace"**—LMG to Laird Bell, 9 August 1954, CCA.

338 **"with the hope that"**—LMG to Howell W. Murray, 16 July 1954, CCA.

338 **conscience cleared ... "from fainting."**—LMG to Howell W. Murray, 27 July 1954; LMG to Laird Bell, 17 November 1954—both CCA.

338 **While in the West ... Wayne Carver.**—1992 Carver/Donnell interview; also LMG to Wayne Carver, 16 August 1954—both CCA.

338 **anticipated making arrangements**—LMG to Laird Bell, 9 August 1954, CCA.

338 **intended on this vacation ... with it himself.**—LMG to Lucile Deen Pinkham, 10 September 1954, CCA.

339 **Another familiar guest ... forwarded his way.)**—John M. Musser to LMG, 18 August 1954; Charles J. Miel to John M. Musser, 19 August 1954; LMG to John M. Musser, 9 September 1954—all CCA.

339 **night of August 29 ... or other persons**—Charles J. Miel to LMG, 30 August 1954; Charles J. Miel to Laird Bell, 1 September 1954; LMG to James R. Thorpe, 9 September 1954; Charles J. Miel to James R. Thorpe, 14 September 1954—all CCA.

339 **Additional amounts would indeed**—LMG to Richard D. Musser, 11 September 1954; LMG to Wadsworth A. Williams, 11 September 1954—both CCA. In the end, Carleton would take advantage of Thorpe's generous offer to fill any remaining gap to the amount of only an additional $4,000. (See LMG to James R. Thorpe, 23 September 1954, CCA.)

339 **Laird Bell went ahead ... "and your confidence."**—LMG to Laird Bell, 9 September 1954; LMG to Willard Thorp, 21 September 1954—both CCA.

339 **Later that month ... long-sought library.**—LMG to Thurlo B. Thomas, 23 September 1954, CCA.

340 **At the trustees ... "for the time being."**—Minutes of the Carleton College Board of Trustees for 22 October 1954, CCA.

340   **Bianchi's suggestion**—Renzo Bianchi to LMG, 22 November 1954, CCA.

340   **Gould himself hoped**—LMG to Merrill Hutchinson, 28 October 1952, CCA.

340   **"that there will be"**—Carlton Qualey to LMG, 10 March 1954, CCA.

340   **"kind of let down" ... "take a holiday."**—Ibid.

340   **One month later ... such a purpose.**—Ellwood H. Newhart to Laird Bell, 27 October 1954, with draft of proposed letter to be sent to Trustees, in Bell Papers, CCA.

340   **Bell informed ... South America.**—LMG to Thurlo B. Thomas, 27 October 1954, CCA.

341   **"the trustees insisted"**—LMG to Frank Sparks, 1 February 1955, CCA.

341   **informal dinner for twelve**—LMG to Laird Bell, 17 September 1954, CCA.

CHAPTER 20 — SOUTH AGAIN

342   **law of averages ... "championship football team!"**—LMG to Laird Bell, 8 November 1954, CCA.

342   **Gould added one touch ... "no longer man."**—LMG to James H. Richards, Jr., 27 October 1954, CCA.

342   **"about as fine"**—LMG to Th. Siqveland, Royal Norwegian Consul General, 7 June 1956, CCA.

342   **(Bell's instructions**—Laird Bell to LMG, 30 September 1954, CCA.

343   **eight formal meetings**—Gould's USNC-IGY Antarctic Committee meetings were held on these dates: October 13, 1954, January 20, 1955, April 7, 1955, May 19, 1955, August 24, 1955, October 14, 1955, March 12, 1956, and July 13, 1956. The committee's responsibilities were summarized as being fivefold: (1) formulation and implementation of final plans for the US-IGY Antarctic program, (2) preparation of budget estimates and justifications in support of the scientific program, (3) selection, screening, outfitting and indoctrination of all scientific personnel who were ultimately assigned to the Antarctic stations, (4) liaison with private institutions, government, and military agencies concerning scientific programs and equipment, transportation, communications, housing, and command relationships, and (5) liaison with other countries who participated in the IGY Antarctic program, including U.S. representation of the committee at appropriate international conferences. (From the *Report on the U.S. Program for the International Geophysical Year July 1, 1957 - December 31, 1958.* IGY General Report No. 21 (November 1965). National Academy of Sciences—National Research Council.)

343   **at which it was decided**—Ibid.

343   **"keep intruding" ... "than I want to do."**—LMG to REB, 12 December 1954; LMG to Scott Elledge, 10 December 1954—both CCA.

343   **"that confounded virus" ... "forget the difficulty.")**—LMG to Laird Bell, 24 December 1954, CCA.

344   **promptly sent a copy ... no harm.**—LMG to Waldemar A. Nielsen, 4 January 1955, CCA.

344   **roundly attacked ... of the Ford Foundation.**—Macdonald, *The Ford Foundation*, 1989 reprint, 34.

344   **Accordingly, shortly before ... "proposals in education."**—LMG to H. Rowan Gaither, Jr., 3 February 1955; Waldemar A. Nielsen to LMG, 8 March 1955—both CCA.

344n **Dwight Macdonald ... "concepts and principles."**—Macdonald, *The Ford Foundation*, 1989 reprint, 31-33.

345   **Spanish "at odd moments,"**—LMG to Mona Lloyd, 18 January 1955, CCA.

345   **The plan evolved**—LMG to William B. Dunham, 17 January 1955, CCA.

345   **seven-week holiday [South America]**—Sources for description of this trip in this and

succeeding paragraphs are Peg Gould's South American trip diary and Peg's long travel letter to her siblings, the Hoppins and the Rices, written near the end of the trip—both located in the CCA-GC; also the "President Gould Says:" column in the June issue of *The Voice of the Carleton Alumni*, 19. Specific citations are given for direct quotations only.

345   **"bright sun"**—MRG 1955 Travel Diary, 6 February 1955.

345   **"we were lulled"**—MRG sibling travel letter, undated [early April 1955], CCA-GP.

345   **"what a reunion"**—Ibid.

345n   **The trip's timing ... as college treasurer.**—Bruce Pollock to Frank Wright, 17 February 1955, CCA.

345n   **"seldom have we had"**—LMG to Earl Bunting, National Association of Manufacturers, 7 October 1949, CCA.

345n   **A second momentous ... first been trained.**—See Ian G. Barbour to LMG, 19 March 1955; LMG to Barbour, 18 April 1955—both CCA.

346   **"all too short"**—Ibid.

346   **"first-class earthquake"**—Ibid.

346   **"I had all I could" ... "enchanting"**—Ibid.

346   **"warm and royal"**—LMG, "President Gould Says:" column, *The Voice of the Carleton Alumni*, June 1955, 19.

346   **termed "wonderful" ... "lovely."**—Ibid.

346   **"ghastly" ... "ever made."**—MRG 1955 Travel Diary, 1 March 1955.

346   **"God deliver us" ... "all get out."**—MRG sibling travel letter, undated [early April 1955], CCA-GP.

347   **The thorny business ... "as I would like."**—*Report on the U.S. Program for the International Geophysical Year, op. cit ("to explore the need")*; Bernt Balchen to LMG, 19 November 1954, NA-GP; LMG to William Benton, 10 April 1955, CCA; LMG to Paul A. Siple, 12 April 1955, NA-GP.

347   **"We are now in"**—LMG to Thomas B. Morgan, 24 April 1955, CCA.

348   **late April visit ... "ill health."**—LMG to Paul A. Siple, 30 April 1955, NA-GP.

348   **In May ... "weight and endurance."**—LMG to REB, 4 May 1955; REB to LMG, 12 May 1955—both NA-GP.

348   **"Command structure" ... "before too long."**—LMG to Laird Bell, 8 November 1954, 24 December 1954, and 12 May 1955 ("good arrangement"); Bell to LMG, 22 December 1954; Atherton Bean to LMG, 5 May 1955 —all CCA. Regarding Bean's "splendid" qualifications for board leadership, consider Gould's opinion as expressed to Bean's wife Winnie: "In my association with the members of the Board, there has been no mind which I have enjoyed more than that of Atherton. His capacity for listening to varying points of view and then tying it all together neatly is a source of delight to watch in operation." (LMG to Winifred Bean, 5 May 1955, CCA.)

348   **At the start ... so it happened.**—Howell W. Murray to LMG, 18 April 1955; LMG to Murray, 2 May 1955 ("under no circumstances"); Laird Bell to LMG, 18 May 1955; LMG to Margaret F. Bell, 23 May 1955—all CCA.

349   **"Immediately after vespers"**—*Northfield News*, May 19, 1955, 1.

349   **"drafted into doing" ... "number of givers."**—LMG, "Ten Years From Now," Carleton College commencement address, 6 June 1955, unpublished transcript, CCA.

350   **he foresaw that ... "idea of quality."**—Ibid.

350   **"I said then," ... "maternal ground."**—Ibid.

350   **"the accomplishments" ... "Everybody else has."**—Laird Bell to LMG, 8 June 1955, CCA.

350   **visited with Peg's brother**—LMG to Martha and Jack Rice, 14 June 1955, CCA. This letter also contains a little story that does not quite fit anywhere in the biographical narrative yet is

too amusing not to slip into the book somewhere. Gould spoke the letter into his dictation recorder for later typing by his secretary, Dorothy Obaid, married to Spanish professor Tony Obaid and mother to four-and-a-half-year-old Stephen. Gould says: "Another reason for dictating this letter is that Dorothy will be typing it, and perhaps she will tell you Stevie's latest term of endearment for his father. I should hesitate even to dictate the word, but she may somehow if she wishes imply it in a footnote." Dorothy duly added her own note to the letter: "Such decorum as the Pres. displays—Tony called Steve in for lunch the other day, and the reply was, 'O.K. you s__ of a b_____!!!!!!!'"

351   **Boulder at the home of**—LMG to Raymond Jacobson, 20 June 1955, CCA.

351   **"completely succumbed,"**—LMG to Harry W. Osborne, 12 July 1955, CCA.

351   **"neither had time"**—LMG to Charles Shain, 12 July 1955, CCA.

351   **"a significant place" ... "Antarctic Treaty."**—D. W. H. Walton, ed., *Antarctic Science*, 33.

351   **The potential for discord ... "international scientific cooperation."**—Information for these paragraphs from LMG, "My 50 Years of Antarctic Exploration and Research," op. cit., CCA-GC; LMG, "Emergence of Antarctica: The Mythical Land." *Science and Public Affairs, Bulletin of the Atomic Scientists* 26, No. 10 (December 1970) ("this was a significant"); Walton, ed., *Antarctic Science*, 33 ("an enthusiasm for"); LMG, "Antarctica, Continent of International Science," *Science* 150 (December 1965) ("willingness to adjust"); Fogg, A *History of Antarctic Science*, 172-173; and Siple, *90° South*, 99.

351n **While in Colorado ... position for him.**—See Raymond Jacobson file, POF Faculty Files (Ser. 58A), CCA.

352   **first day in the new cabin ... "cane and crutches."**—LMG to Reine Myers, 22 August 1955; LMG to Atherton Bean, 1 September 1955—both CCA.

353   **"been concerned with"**—LMG to Robert L. Gale, 19 September 1955.

353   **"one of the outstanding"**—LMG to James H. Richards, Jr., 1 July 1955, CCA.

353   **inviting him to come**—LMG to Archibald MacLeish, 15 September 1955, CCA.

353   **To foundation staff ... "South Again."**—List of LMG addresses for 1955, CCA; Carl T. Rowan exclusive, *Minneapolis Tribune*, October 20, 1955, 1.

353   **In remarks delivered ... "ever undertaken."**—National Academy of Sciences - U.S. National Committee - IGY press release of 14 November 1955.

354   **finalization of a stunning ... at least $550,000.)**—"President Gould Says" column, *Voice of the Carleton Alumni*, January 1956, 1-2.

354   **The opportunity for ... "continuing need is."**—LMG to Sister Mary William, Pres. College of St. Catherine, 14 December 1955, (referencing "The Great Grant"); Minutes of the Carleton College Board of Trustees for 24 January 1956—both CCA; Nielsen, *The Big Foundations*, 86-88; 285 ("appease some of", 86); Macdonald, *The Ford Foundation*, 1989 reprint, 4; "President Gould Says:" column, *Voice of the Carleton Alumni*, January 1956, 2 ("exciting, thrilling").

354   **turned down offers**—LMG to Reuben A. Holden (Yale), 16 January 1956; LMG to Robert W. McEwen (Hamilton), 19 January 1956; LMG to John Dickey (Dartmouth), 21 January 1956—all CCA.

355   **wrote Charles Horn**—LMG to Charles L. Horn, 30 January 1956, CCA. Gould, whose personal distaste for Horn still ran strong but who wanted very much to stay on his good side for the largesse which might from that source flow, told Horn that "it would be a great compliment to you and the role you play in the Upper Midwest to symbolize your influence in such a structure here in this college, which already owes so much to you and to men like you." When Horn replied that the Olin Foundation now felt that it should put its money into scientific projects, Gould, in passing the reply on to Vice President Miel, wrote across the top, "At least I didn't offend him." (Horn to LMG, 8 February 1956, CCA.) Later in the spring, following a social evening arranged at the Cowles' home to include the Horns and the Goulds, Horn began addressing Gould by his first name for the first time, which Gould

took as "a good sign, and if I use proper techniques, mayhap the Olin Foundation will build a much-needed laboratory of physics and biology here at Carleton College." He regretted, however, having during the course of the evening, pointed out an inaccuracy in something Horn was holding forth upon, for "he doesn't like that sort of thing, and … I want to please him." (LMG to John Cowles, 12 May 1956, CCA.)

355 **he himself handled**—See 1993 Maitland/Reitz interview; LMG to Miller Upton, 27 August 1956 ("more people than")—both CCA. During the weeks when Carleton's director of athletics position was open, English professor Phil Sheridan sent Gould a tongue-in-cheek proposal that the Departments of English and Athletics be combined into one. Gould responded in like spirit, saying that Sheridan's "exciting" idea "fits in well with my general thesis that there is too much specialization in this college and that we could do a better educational program if we had about a third as many departments as we do now."

355 **"yielding to demands" … "namely, teach.")**—LMG to Charles Shain, 9 April, 1956, CCA.

355 **"secured $200.00 from" … "from Mr. Henrickson."**—LMG to Eiler L. Henrickson, 10 April 1956; LMG to Bruce Pollock, 10 April 1956—both CCA. Henrickson successfully passed his doctoral examination later that spring. (See LMG to Mrs. Eiler L. Henrickson, 7 June 1956, CCA.)

355n **"man will not be"**—Unidentified newspaper clipping, CCA-GC.

356 **He also, that month**—Reginald D. Lang to LMG, 18 April 1956; LMG to Lang, 24 April 1956—both CCA.

356 **"Am undergoing wholly" … "and me also.")**—Telegram, Archibald MacLeish to LMG, 1 May 1956; telegram, LMG to MacLeish, 2 May 1956; LMG to Mrs. Archibald MacLeish, 7 May 1956; MacLeish to LMG, 2 June 1956—all CCA. MacLeish's dedicatory address had indeed already been sent on to Gould prior to MacLeish's confirmation that he could reschedule for September, and Gould indicated that he found the address "exciting reading" but shared it in advance with no one but John Cowles. (LMG to MacLeish, 5 June 1956, CCA.) In his June 2 letter, MacLeish wrote that he supposed he ought out of courtesy to send the current Librarian of Congress a copy "somewhat in advance—but not too much." "That is," he explained, "I should like to give him an opportunity to set me straight on the facts if I am wrong (which I am not) but not anticipate me with an answer. I think, therefore," he advised Gould, "the less prior circulation the better. At least, there should be none among librarians. They can't resist forwarding."

356 **"Project 'L' Day"**—George Nicholson, in the *Carletonian*, May 19, 1956, 1; Sherry Cornell, in the *Carletonian*, May 26, 1956, 2 (including "Women manned" and "in fine form" quotations).

357 **"in line with" … "health sanitation."**—LMG to John Cowles, 7 July 1956, CCA.

357 **eighth and final meeting**—*Report on the U.S. Program for the International Geophysical Year, op. cit.*

358 **broke a rib … Geographical Review.**—LMG to Marcie and Dick Ajello, 11 September 1956 ("sort of a mixed"); LMG to Scott Elledge, 17 July 1956—both CCA.

358 **"I continue to define"**—LMG to Bertha Linnell, 5 October 1956, CCA.

358 **running a profile … "not a spectator."**—Victor Cohn, "A Man of Books and Blizzards," *Minneapolis Sunday Tribune*, August 19, 1956, Feature Section, 1.

358 **MacLeish painted … "will not yield."**—Archibald MacLeish, "Dedication of the Carleton Library: An Address Delivered September 22, 1956," *Carleton College Bulletin* 53, No. 2 (November 1956).

358 **greatest he had heard**—LMG to James H. Richards, Jr., 24 September 1956, CCA.

359 **too ill to continue.**—Nielsen, *The Big Foundations*, 89.

359 **"Remember, if you fall"**—Behrendt, *Innocents on the Ice*, 40.

359 **Blackburn (Class of 1958), later remembered**—Thomas R. Blackburn e-mail to Carleton alumni listserve, 2 December 2000.

359 **called for greater encouragement**—LMG, "Use It or Lose It." *New York American Weekly Magazine.* Reprint of address to Grocery Manufacturers of America, New York, November 14, 1956.

359 **found slumped ... "compete with him."**—*The Voice of the Carleton Alumni,* January 1957, 11, 17.

359n **This appointment came through**—Detlev W. Bronk to LMG, 2 November 1956, CCA.

360 **Consideration of ... promptly accepted.**—LMG to John Cowles, 18 November 1956; LMG to Robert L. Gale, 13 December 1956 and 25 March 1957; LMG to Ellwood H. Newhart, 20 December 1956; Atherton Bean to Newhart, 22 January 1957; Gale to LMG, 24 April 1957—all CCA.

360 **finalized during November ... "even greater place."**—See various letters in Robert E. Will Faculty File (Ser. 58A), CCA. Quotations are from LMG to Will, 12 December 1956.

360 **gained much satisfaction ... "much lighter heart."**—LMG to Dr. Harry A. Towsley, 14 December 1956; LMG to DJC, 17 December 1956—both CCA.

360 **"healing."**—LMG to MRG, 1 January 1957 and 8 January 1957, CCA-GC. The characterization which follows of Gould's state before leaving on his trip is derived from both a variety of written evidences—the above letters and others such as LMG to Sally Crandall, 6 January 1957, CCA—and inferences extrapolating just a little from the same.

361 **"struck low physically"**—LMG to Miller Upton, 4 December 1957, CCA.

361 **"have the good judgment" ... "finish the race."**—LMG to Robert H. Edwards, 3 July 1984, CCA.

361 **first expected to fly ... "loss to me,"**—LMG to REB, 14 December 1956; telegram, REB to LMG, 25 December 1956—both NA-GP.

361 **"I was very, very" ... "do that again."**— LMG to Sarah Crandall, 6 January 1957, including news for Carleton College, CCA; LMG to MRG, 1 January 1957 (postmarked January 5 on the USS *Curtiss*), CCA-GC. Later in the trip Gould wrote Cowling that he was the sort of college president "who needs to get away from his job from time to time—both to regain a proper perspective and to re-charge his batteries." For that, Gould told Cowling, "this place is ideal—no possible presidential worries, no parents, no alumni, no faculty, no trustees, no budget and no possibility of fund raising." (LMG to DJC, handwritten note of 6 February 1957, CCA.)

361 **almost immediately to improve ... "all right too."**—LMG to MRG, 1 January 1957 (postmarked January 5 on the USS *Curtiss*) and 8 January 1957 (postmarked aboard the *Curtiss*)—both CCA-GC.

362 **tenth day ... particularly lovely.**—LMG to MRG, 5 January 1957 (a continuation of the letter begun January 1), CCA-GC.

362 **The *Curtiss* arrived ... "we depart here."**—LMG to MRG, 13 January 1957, 14 January 1957, and 15 January 1957 ("the Antarctic will begin")—all in CCA-GC; also LMG to Carleton College from the USS *Curtiss*, 20 January 1957, CCA.

362 **At the edge of ... for the *Glacier* were lost.**—LMG to Carleton College, 20 January 1957, CCA. Gould's letter also relates his surprise and pleasure to discover aboard the *Glacier* Carleton alumnus Carl Eklund, Class of 1932, who had been designated as station chief for the Wilkes Station on the Knox Coast.

363 **Later, as the *Curtiss* ... wherever he wished.**—LMG to Carleton College, dictated at McMurdo Sound, 23 January 1957, CCA.

364 **suggestion advanced by Byrd**—See LMG to REB 28 November 1956, NA-GP.

364 **Gould served as dedication ... "darkness toward light."**—LMG to Carleton College, dictated at McMurdo Sound, 23 January 1957; LMG dictation sent to *Chicago Daily News,* New York bureau, 23 January 1957 (including "to the high purposes")—both CCA.

364 **Following the dedication ... "Yes, they do."**—LMG to Carleton College, dictated at McMurdo Sound, 23 January 1957; LMG, press conference at Minneapolis-St. Paul International Airport/Wold-Chamberlain Field, 16 March 1957, unpublished transcript

("Yes, they do.")—both CCA.

364 **The next two days … "anywhere in the world"**—LMG to Carleton College, dictated at McMurdo Sound, 26 January 1957.

365 **When the plane … anything like it.**—Ibid.

365 **Gould stayed aboard … "more fun."**—LMG to Carleton College, 1 February 1957, CCA.

366 **During one of the days … accumulated snow cover.)**—Carleton College News Release dated 13 February 1957; LMG to Carleton College, 1 February 1957—both CCA.

366 **The *Curtiss* redelivered … return north.**—LMG to Carleton College, 14 February 1957, CCA; LMG to MRG, undated but in envelope postmarked on the *Curtiss* 14 February 1957, CCA-GC; "President Gould Says:" column, *The Voice of the Carleton Alumni* May 1957, 20. Regarding the visit to Scott's 1910-12 headquarters, Gould reported February 12 for the *Chicago Daily News* that he "was astounded to see the manner in which things had been preserved. Near one side of the house, where once had been a kind of back porch, were the carcasses of lambs. They still looked quite solid and little changed after more than 50 years in this natural cooler."

366 **"heart-warming" reunion**—LMG to MRG, 19 February 1957, CCA-GC.

366 **From Tucson, he wrote … "in the past."**—LMG to MRG, 7 March 1957, CCA-GC. The resolve never again to "overdo" was expressed to others as well as to Peg; for instance, LMG to Carl Weicht, 20 March 1957, CCA.

367 **a love note … "And that's that."**—LMG to MRG, 10 March 1957, CCA-GC.

367 **that afternoon he indicated**—LMG, press conference at Minneapolis-St. Paul International Airport/Wold-Chamberlain Field, 16 March 1957, unpublished transcript, CCA.

367 **"very humble to be included"**—LMG to Hubert H. Humphrey, 29 March 1957, CCA.

CHAPTER 21 — THE PURSUIT OF EXCELLENCE

368 **When he stepped off … back to Northfield.**—*Carletonian*, March 16, 1957, 1; *Northfield News*, March 21, 1957, 1.

368 **"One of the most"**—LMG to Rabbi Dudley Weinberg, 22 March 1957, CCA.

368 **most dramatic change … fall term of 1958.**—LMG to Charles L. Horn, 1 April 1957; Minutes of the Carleton College Board of Trustees for 2 November 1956 and 24 January 1957—all CCA.

369 **Gould wrote Horn … "many other requests."**—LMG to Charles L. Horn, 1 April 1957 and 5 May 1957; Horn to LMG, 9 May 1957—all CCA.

369 **Gould now expected … attain its objectives.**—Charles A. Anger, of John Price Jones Company, to LMG, 25 April 1957; LMG to Anger, 27 April 1957; Minutes of the Executive Committee of the Carleton College Board of Trustees for 7 May 1957; Minutes of the Carleton College Board of Trustees for 10 June 1957 and 11 October 1957—all CCA.

370 **At the June 1957 meeting**—Minutes of the Carleton College Board of Trustees for 10 June 1957, CCA.

370 **Earlier the same day … "World Peace I."**—*The Voice of the Carleton Alumni*, July 1957, 1.

370 **drove Peg and Jill**—LMG to Harvey Stork, 11 July 1957, CCA.

370 **consultant study … center on Larry Gould**—All information and quotations in these paragraphs from "Development and Public Relations Potentials at Carleton College: A Survey, Analysis and Plan prepared by the John Price Jones Company, Inc." (September 1957), CCA.

371 **"certain reservations" … "future action."**—Minutes of the Executive Committee of the Carleton College Board of Trustees for 7 October 1957, CCA.

372   **discussion by the full board ... "volunteer workers."**—Minutes of the Carleton College Board of Trustees for 11 and 12 October 1957, CCA.

372   **Bean subsequently agreed**—LMG to Robert L. Conway, John Price Jones Company, 17 October 1957, CCA.

372   **nine hundred parents ... "so let it be."**—Information and quotes are from clippings in the CCA, one from the "Dispatch News Service" dated October 22, 1957, and another from the *Minneapolis Tribune* of October 25, 1957.

373   **tried to steer Humphrey**—LMG to Hubert Humphrey, 21 October 1957, CCA.

373   **written a number of times**—For instance, see LMG to Humphrey, 14 June 1955 and 28 November 1956; LMG to Thomas L. Hughes in Sen. Humphrey's office, 15 June 1956—all CCA.

373n   **"source of immense pride"**—LMG to Hubert H. Humphrey, 28 November 1956, CCA.

374   **sent off a promised article**—LMG to Howard E. Kasch, 28 October 1957, CCA.

374   **go with them on a car trip**—LMG to Dr. and Mrs. Charles E. Lyght, 31 October 1957, CCA.

374   **Gould had been asked ... "aviation in Antarctica."**—Andrew Stevenson to LMG, 30 August 1957; LMG to Stevenson, 16 October 1957—both CCA; LMG to George Dufek, 16 October 1957, NA-GP.

374   **dictated a note ... "expressing it."**—LMG to Sally Crandall and Dorothy Obaid, 9 November 1957, CCA. Eight years earlier, at a Carleton Founder's Day convocation, Gould had remarked, "I long ago discovered that if the janitor is sick for ten days, we have to get a substitute. The president of the college can be away for a month, and things seem to go right on happily." (LMG, Carleton College Founder's Day convocation, 11 November 1949, unpublished transcript, CCA.) Gould's regularly fixing afternoon tea for Sally and Dorothy was remembered by Dorothy Obaid in the 1995 Obaid/Donnell interview, CCA.

374   **Gould left campus ... Amundsen-Scott station.**—*The Voice of the Carleton Alumni*, January 1958, 12, and March 1958, 3-4 ("President Gould Says..." column); program for Thanksgiving Service, Chapel in the Snow, U.S. Naval Air Facility, McMurdo Sound, in CCA-GC.

375   **misgivings in advance**—See, for instance, LMG to Harvey Stork, 3 January 1958, CCA, where Gould wrote: "I had looked toward my Antarctic journey with some reservations, since I was to go with six Congressmen."

375   **"The Congressmen were interesting,"**—LMG to Laird Bell, 16 December 1957, CCA.
       A few weeks after their return, Gould sent committee chairman Harris and committee advisor Andrew Stevenson red curling tams such as he himself had worn prominently on this Antarctic trip. (LMG to Andrew Stevenson 2 January 1958; LMG to Oren W. Harris, 2 January 1958; both CCA.)
       A color photo of Gould from this trip, wearing the curling tam, became Gould's own favorite of himself; "the most flattering photograph of me from my standpoint," he wrote to a friend. (LMG to Mr. and Mrs. Anatole Mazour, 19 April 1958, CCA.) This photograph was later used for the book jacket front of Carleton College's 1984 reprint of Gould's *Cold*.

375   **To Dufek he reported ... "program in Antarctica."**—LMG to George Dufek, 19 December 1957, NA-GP.

375   **Harris would forward**—Oren Harris to President Dwight D. Eisenhower, 17 January 1958 (copy), CCA.

375   **memorial service for Bianchi**—*Carletonian*, December 14, 1957, 2; *The Voice of the Carleton Alumni*, January 1958, 10-11.

375   **case of a full professor who had developed**—Particulars, with LMG memoranda to file, are present in the relevant POF Faculty File, CCA. The "few sadder experiences" quote is from LMG to John H. Myers, 4 January 1958, CCA.

376   **at their January meeting**—Minutes of the Carleton College Board of Trustees for 24 January 1958, CCA. The "Carleton should continue to be" quote is also given in Carleton's

summer 1958 publication of the Gould address "Education and Survival": LMG, "Education and Survival," *Carleton College Bulletin* 55, No. 1 (August 1958).

376　**"Carleton will never go above 1,000"**—"Carleton College's Trademark is Quality" article in the December 20, 1953, *St. Paul Sunday Pioneer Press.*

376　**In letters of December**—LMG to Laird Bell, 16 December 1957 ("in steps" and "sacrifice"); LMG to William Benton, 23 December 1957—both CCA.

377　**Bean reported that trustee … eighteen feet.**—Minutes of the Carleton College Board of Trustees for 24 January 1958, CCA.

377　**Bean also spoke …social environment.**—Ibid.

377　**Following discussion … to 35 percent.**—Ibid.

377　**That same week … to succeed Lewis.**—Hazel Lewis to LMG, 26 January 1958. See also Leith Shackel to LMG, 1 June 1957; both CCA. Lewis's enjoyment of her retirement would be sadly short. She died in Northfield Hospital of a heart ailment on December 21, 1958.

377　**Isaiah Bowman Memorial Lecture**—LMG, "The Polar Regions in Their Relation to Human Affairs," *Bowman Memorial Lectures, American Geographical Society, New York,* 1958.

377　**conference as US representative**—LMG, "My 50 Years of Antarctic Exploration and Research," op. cit., CCA-GC.

377n　**"With such a ratio"**—"*In Pursuit of Excellence*: A Statement from the Trustees About the Plans of Carleton College," Autumn, 1958, 12.

378　**testified in closed-door session**—Gould's statement of 21 January 1958 was made public on 13 March 1958.

378　**"Education for Citizenship" … "and quality."**—*Minneapolis Sunday Tribune,* February 9, 1958, Upper Midwest Section, 1, 6. Included in the same issue of the paper, by the way, inside a nationally syndicated Sunday magazine supplement, was another opinion piece on education, this by a Syracuse University professor, proposing—as a solution to projected overcrowding in colleges of the future—that the number of women allowed to go to coeducational schools be drastically cut back. This professor, though claiming that he admired women students "for their industry, enthusiasm, and abilities" and that in his own teaching it was "a real pleasure to see those pretty faces bent over their notebooks," declared that "just the same, ladies, … it looks very doubtful that in 10 years (or less) there will be room for both you and all the men who want to go to college. And it's more vital that men should have that college education." Two-year junior colleges, the professor asserted, "can equip most women sufficiently to be good wives, mothers, citizens, or temporary job-holders." (Philip Ward Burton, "Keep Women Out of College!," *This Week Magazine,* February 9, 1958, 10.) This nationally circulated opinion piece ran just sixteen days after the Carleton Board of Trustees found itself unanimously in favor of significantly increasing the percentage of men to women in Carleton's own future enrollments.

378　**"a gap" … Desert Willow guest ranch**—Minutes of the Carleton College Board of Trustees for 24 January 1958; LMG to Robert T. Mathews, 6 March 1958—both CCA.

378　**"sit as quietly"**—LMG to Andrew Stevenson, 11 February 1958, CCA.

378　**out-of-state stops**—List of LMG addresses for 1958, CCA.

379　**Balchen sought Gould's advice … "very apprehensive"**—Bernt Balchen to LMG, 17 February 1958 and 2 April 1958; LMG to Balchen, 12 April 1958—all NA-GP.

379　**eight-page letter … "truth of course."**—LMG to Balchen, 12 April 1958, NA-GP.

380　**tended to agree … "directly with it."**—Ibid.

380　**twenty outstanding Minnesotans**—*Northfield News,* April 24, 1958, 2A.

380　**pleased also by Senator Humphrey's … "safeguarded these things."**—Hubert H. Humphrey to LMG, 17 February 1958 and 7 May 1958; LMG to Humphrey, 13 May 1958 (including quotes)—all CCA. Though Gould reversed, or at least tempered, his opposition to federal aid to education after Sputnik, Carleton Treasurer Bruce Pollock remained true to the old faith. In a June 10, 1958, memorandum to Gould (CCA), Pollock wrote: "In my opinion, objections to federal aid are as cogent now as they were when you so valiantly campaigned against it but urgency on the part of its proponents has arisen from a state of emergency. Under the long Democratic administration of our federal government beginning in 1933, we were in a repeated, if not constant, state of emergency and under that urgency we adopted many of the principles and practices of socialism so that our government and our life now can hardly be said to be purely democratic. I believe it was a Harvard professor that remarked that we had adopted all of the bad features of European governments and none of the good ones, which is not far off line. I have a remnant of faith in the American people and a sustaining faith in the provisions of the Constitution which is our inheritance, which, however, has been distorted by legislation and misconstrued by courts. I believe, if given a chance, the ingenuity and integrity of our people will meet the emergency in education as they have formerly met emergencies without the aid of a paternal government." In August, Pollock wrote Humphrey himself to record his opposition to the National Defense Act of 1958's federal aid to education provisions, making clear that his opinion was his own and "not necessarily that of President Gould, formerly an ardent campaigner against federal aid." (Bruce Pollock to Hubert H. Humphrey, 4 August 1958, CCA.)

380   **decision by Phil Phenix**—Telegram, Philip H. Phenix to LMG, 9 May 1958. Gould began to sound Phenix out about the possibility of his returning to the college as dean in mid-January of 1958 and had initially received a regretful "no," but Phenix subsequently reconsidered, after which the appointment came speedily. (See LMG to Phenix, 15 January 1958, and Phenix to LMG, telegram of 19 March 1958 and letter of 6 April 1958—all CCA.)

380   **illness with which Gould was hit ... to the Tetons.**—LMG to Oren Harris, 27 May, 1958; LMG to Carlton Qualey, 2 June 1958; Minutes of the Carleton College Board of Trustees for 9 June 1958—all CCA; Sally Crandall to Bernt Balchen, 13 June 1958, NA-GP; LMG to Lillian M. Wilson, 23 June 1958; LMG to Louis S. Headley, 23 June 1958; LMG to Philip H. Phenix, 25 June 1958—all CCA.

381   **"case statement"**—John Price Jones Company, "Up-dated Outline Plan of Action," dated 3 July 1958, CCA.

381   **report, transmitted to Gould**—Henry Woodward to LMG, 22 July 1958, transmitting "Report of the Faculty Committee on Curricular Revision," CCA.

381   **"Education and Survival." ... "from its beginning."**—LMG, "Education and Survival," *Carleton College Bulletin* 55, No. 1 (August 1958). The lines identified here as the most widely quoted statement from this address received particularly wide notice when they were featured on the inside cover page of the January 4, 1959, edition of *This Week*, a national Sunday magazine supplement with circulation of over 13,000,000, under the title "Why Men Survive." The item was then later reprinted in *Reader's Digest*. (See Minutes of the Carleton College Board of Trustees for 19 January 1959, and LMG to Lindsey Blayney, 13 May 1959—both CCA.)

382   **one July day ... "posts in Washington."**—Sources for the account of the White House phone call to Gould at the Wilson general store are the author's 12 September 2002 telephone conversation with Robert L. Gale and the 21 November 1958 Founder's Day remarks of Robert K. Gray at Carleton College, CCA. Gray's helicopter landing at Carleton is reported in *The Voice of the Carleton Alumni*, July 1958, 34.

383   **"It was very nice to talk"**—LMG to Robert K. Gray, 18 August 1958, CCA.

383   **"Every time I greet"**—LMG to Andrew Stevenson, 14 September 1958, CCA.

383   **"If you had to choose" ... "human spirit can be."**—Arlie Russell to LMG, 4 July 1958; LMG to Russell, 15 September 1958; both CCA. Gould's tribute to his hero continued: "Coming from about as unpromising a background as anyone possibly could come, this man became one of the transcendent figures in history. Beyond the qualities of his character, his unbelievably great leadership during the Civil War, his military knowledge which in many ways exceeded that of any of his generals, he was without a peer; but he was more than all that. I continue to be fascinated with his writing and his speeches. I have but recently read the Lincoln and Douglas debates again with great profit."

384 **Friday, October 24**—Information for this and following paragraphs from LMG to Howell W. Murray, 20 October 1958; Minutes of the Carleton College Board of Trustees for 24 October 1958; "*In Pursuit of Excellence*: A Statement from the Trustees About the Plans of Carleton College," Autumn, 1958—all CCA; special "Development Issue" supplement to *Carletonian*, October 24, 1958; *St. Paul Dispatch*, October 24, 1958, 1, 21; *The Voice of the Carleton Alumni*, October 1958, 2-11, and December 1958, 2-3; with direct quotations cited below.

384 **"the year when retirement"**—"*In Pursuit of Excellence*: A Statement from the Trustees About the Plans of Carleton College," Autumn, 1958.

384 **"heart and nerve" ... "our free society."**—"Development Issue" supplement to *Carletonian*, October 24, 1958, 1.

384 **"to be used in turning"**—Quoting Carleton Student Association president Robert Stout, in The Voice of the Carleton Alumni, December 1958, 3.

385 **"ringing close"**—*The Voice of the Carleton Alumni*, December 1958, 3.

385 **"most ambitious effort" ... "So let it be."**—Phrases from Gould's statement to alumni concerning the new development program, excerpted in "Development Issue" supplement to *Carletonian*, October 24, 1958, 2.

CHAPTER 22 — A NEW RENAISSANCE

386 **reconvened for further business ... new science building.**—Minutes of the Carleton College Board of Trustees for 24 October 1958, CCA.

386 **"all possible fanfare"**—LMG to Charles L. Horn, 7 October 1958, CCA.

388 **"the very best possible architect" ... on November 20.**—John H. Myers to LMG and the members of the trustees' Buildings and Grounds Committee, 14 October 1958; Minutes of the Carleton College Board of Trustees for 25 October 1958; LMG to Charles L. Horn, 8 November 1958—all CCA.

388 **Gould told Yamasaki ... for Carleton's needs,**—LMG to John H. Myers, 15 November 1958, LMG to Charles L. Horn, 8 November 1958—both CCA.

388 **pressed by Horn ... "fancy" design.**—LMG to John H. Myers, 16 November 1958, CCA.

388 **worried by an article ... "to lose $1,500,000."**—LMG to John H. Myers, 17 November 1958, CCA.

388 **"We are in a terrific"**—LMG to John M. Musser, 20 November 1958, CCA.

388 **"thoroughly competent"**—LMG to James O. Wynn, 22 November 1958, CCA.

388 **"combination of imagination"**—LMG to John M. Musser, 21 November 1958, CCA.

388 **He assured Gould that**— LMG to James O. Wynn, 22 November 1958, CCA.

388 **Early in December ... "proceed with his plans ..."**—LMG to Charles L. Horn, 3 December 1958 and 16 December 1958—both CCA.

389 **Late in November ... "its immediate products."**—Charles E. Wyzanski, Jr. to LMG, 23 November 1958, CCA.

389 **warmed the cockles ... campaign publications.**—LMG to Wyzanski, 2 December 1958; LMG to Robert L. Gale, 14 December 1958—both CCA.

389 **This conference resulted**—National Academy of Sciences, National Research Council, *Annual Report for Fiscal Year 1958-1959* (Washington: Government Printing Office, 1960), 79.

390 **For Christmas 1958 ... be his godfather.)**—LMG to Bette Bianchi, 22 November 1958 and 27 December 1958; also LMG to Olin S. Pettingill, 22 February 1959—all CCA. Also Glines, *Bernt Balchen*, 270.

390   **"Penguins & Scholars"**—"Penguins & Scholars," *Time*, December 29, 1958, 30

390   **Gould was quite pleased … "stomp" when he walked.**—LMG to Jonathan Rinehart, 4 January 1959, CCA.

390   **pair of New Year's resolutions**—LMG to Stephanie Brown, 22 December 1958, CCA.

390   **"new intellectual lease on life."**—LMG to Charles A. Culver, 2 January 1959, CCA.

390   **In January the Twin Cities' … "over his environment."**—"Antarctica Move Series for TV Produced in St. Paul," *Minneapolis Star*, January 20, 1959.

391   **Gould reported to the trustees … "make it worthwhile."**—Minutes of the Carleton College Board of Trustees for 19 January 1959; LMG to John M. Musser, 21 January 1959; LMG to William P. Van Evers, 5 April 1960—all CCA.

391   **At 11 a.m. … any Minnesota institution.**—This account of the all-college convocation at which the Olin Foundation gift was publicly announced blends the reporting of Richard Kleeman in the *Minneapolis Tribune*, February 7, 1959, 1, 6; the *Carletonian*, February 14, 1959, 1 ("a buzzing semi-silence"); and *The Voice of the Carleton Alumni*, March 1959, 2-4.

392   **The next day … "particular source."**—Frank Kille to LMG, 7 February 1959, CCA.

393   **After Representative … "all the way along."**—LMG to Oren Harris, 15 February 1959, CCA. The White House replied to Harris on March 2, saying that "Your understanding is correct that we will withdraw U.S. personnel from Little America, but the station will not be abandoned and supplies for future use in that area will be stored there." This response also indicated that "the Administration will not abandon our recognized interests in the presently unclaimed sector nor any other part of Antarctica" and, in a preview of the Antarctic Treaty that would eventually be signed that December, indicated that President Eisenhower was "also having an evaluation made of current prospects for achieving an international arrangement among the interested nations to keep the area open for peaceful scientific activity, regardless of claims to sovereign control." (White House to Oren Harris, 2 March 1959 (copy), CCA.)

393   **telegram to the chairman**—LMG telegram to Representative Albert W. Thomas, 17 February 1959, CCA.

393   **contracting from five to two**—In a follow-up letter to his telegram, Gould wrote: "I think it a great misfortune that our own U.S.A. program in the first post-IGY year has in reality been reduced from its original five stations to two scientific stations; namely, the Pole and Byrd Station. To be sure, we have the co-operative one with New Zealand known as Hallett Station, but ourselves relinquished three—Ellsworth, Wilkes and Little America. Scientific work at Ellsworth and Wilkes will, we hope, be carried out by the Argentines and the Australians, respectively. Little America is closed and so a scientific gap begins which, to say the least, is unfortunate." (LMG to Albert W. Thomas, 22 February 1958, CCA.)

393   **To Lloyd Berkner, Gould confessed**—LMG to Lloyd V. Berkner, 22 February 1959, with a copy of Berkner's memorandum to J. R. Killian, Jr., special assistant to the president for science and technology, 14 February 1959, CCA.

393   **"Not since Copernicus"**—Unidentified newspaper clipping, 20 February 1959, CCA-GC.

393n   **"bumped into some"**—LMG to Andrew Stevenson, 16 March 1959, CCA

394   **remarks later published …"renaissance can be ours."**—LMG, "Education's Greatest Task," address at Carleton College Reception and Dinner, the Harvard Club, New York City, April 16, 1959.

394   **two Gould speeches**—List of LMG addresses for 1959, CCA.

394   **symposium on basic research …"single enterprise."**—Gould, "Basic Research and the Liberal Arts College," address of May 14, 1959, Symposium on Basic Research, AAAS, Washington, DC, 73-85.

394   **"a superb statement"**—LMG to Alfred P. Sloan, Jr., 18 May 1959, CCA.

394   **Ideal weather graced … $3 million pledged**—*The Voice of the Carleton Alumni*, July 1959, 2-3.

395   **at Dartmouth …tropical explorers!**—Story related in LMG to L. Emerson Tuttle, 22 May 1985, CCA-GC.

395   **Larry and Peg left ... not to talk for two months.**—LMG to Ben Wickersham, 5 July
       1959; LMG to Laura Bergquist, 23 July 1959; Atherton Bean to LMG, 5 August 1959; LMG
       to Clarence H. Faust, 20 August 1959; LMG to Bruce Pollock, 20 August 1959; LMG to
       Donald C. Balfour, 16 September 1959—all CCA.

395n   **Gould had been able**—*The Voice of the Carleton Alumni*, April 1959, 2.

396   **pair of ad hoc committees**—LMG to Miss Hansen, Miss Berwald, Dean Shackel, Mr.
       Jacobson, and Dean Phenix, 11 September 1959; LMG to Messrs. Kintner, Bailey, Jacobson,
       and Woodruff, 15 September 1959—both CCA.

396   **In October, Gould received**—LMG to Frank H. Boles, 19 October 1959, CCA.

396   **Pollock resigned the latter ... become treasurer.**—Minutes of the Carleton College
       Board of Trustees for 23 October 1959, CCA.

396   **Then in November Dean**—Phil Phenix to LMG, 23 November 1959, CCA. Resigning a
       position to Gould for the third time, Phenix wrote: "I can understand and accept any anger
       you may feel toward me for raising your hopes of some greater degree of permanence in my
       association with Carleton, and now disappointing them."

396   **honored October 12 ... "or anyone else."**—LMG to George Dufek, 27 September 1959,
       NA-GP. Gould's working relationship with Dufek had been very effective and satisfactory
       throughout the IGY period, and there had developed between the two a high level of mutual
       respect and admiration. The previous November, when Dufek had requested information
       from Gould that would assist him in preparing an article on IGY Antarctic operations for
       National Geographic, Gould had added to his response the following: " I hope there is some
       place in the article for me as Director of the U.S.-IGY Program to put in print the debt the
       scientific program owes to your leadership. The honorary degree you received from Carleton
       College was a token in this direction, but I do want the readership of such a public as the
       National Geographic magazine to know it. There may still linger in the minds of some people
       that some other admiral may have had something to do with it. I want the right admiral to
       receive the right credit." (LMG to George Dufek, 21 November 1958, NA-GP.) Readers will
       of course recognize the obliquely referenced "other admiral" as the late Admiral Byrd.

397   **faithfully attended ... to the Executive Committee.**—LMG to Henry T. Heald,
       16 September 1959 ("perhaps the Ford") and 12 December 1959; LMG to Laird Bell, 27
       September 1959 ("boring from within"); LMG to Charles E. Wyzanski, Jr., 29 September
       1959; LMG "Ford Foundation" memorandum for the record, 20 December 1957—all CCA.
       Gould's election to the Executive Committee filled a vacancy left by the departure of Frank
       W. Abrams, the former chairman of the board of Standard Oil of New Jersey.

397   **head a committee of six**—Minutes of the Carleton College Board of Trustees for 23
       October 1959, CCA.

397   **not called upon for much service.**—LMG to Scott Elledge, 21 December 1959, CCA.

397   **Also in October ... for political office.**—*St. Paul Pioneer Press*, October 16, 1959
       (clipping in CCA)

398   **in November the First**—*Northfield News*, November 26, 1959.

398   **in January he was compelled ... his present post.**—John C. McDonald, "Gould Won't
       Enter Senate Race in '60," *Minneapolis Sunday Tribune*, January 10, 1960, Upper Midwest
       Section, 1.

398   **Even so, in March ... "stand a chance"**—editorial by Herman Roe in the *Northfield
       Independent*, March 28, 1960.

398   **own ballot for the Democrat Humphrey.**—LMG to William Benton, 7 November 1959,
       CCA. Gould wrote Benton: "You know that I am nominally a Republican but it may please
       you to know that both my wife and I will vote for Hubert Humphrey for Senator tomorrow.
       He has long been a good friend of mine and I have real admiration for his statesmanlike
       record on both domestic and foreign policy issues. I think Hubert knows I am going to vote
       for him but just for fun I am going to send him a note today to tell him so.
           A few days after the election (which Humphrey easily won), Humphrey wrote Gould
       that "of all the letters I received these past weeks one was most pleasing to me—yours of

November 7. I am sure you know of my admiration and respect for you. Therefore your personal note telling me of your support for my re-election was like miracle medicine for a tired and weary body." (Hubert H. Humphrey to LMG, 17 November 1960, CCA.)

398 **On November 2, 1959 ... "shall always cherish."**—*The Voice of the Carleton Alumni*, January 1960, 21; LMG to Peg Gould, 4 November 1959, CCA.

399 **Gould told his audience ... "for radiant hope"**—Paraphrasings and quotes for three paragraphs are from LMG, "Education and Society," address delivered November 2, 1958, printed in Proceedings of the One Hundredth Anniversary Convocation Cooper Union (New York, 1959), 15-26.

399 **The next day, Gould ... Alfred P. Sloan Foundation.**—LMG to Atherton Bean, 8 November 1959, CCA.

400 **feature on "Gould the man"**—Richard P. Kleeman, "Laurence Gould of Carleton College," *Minneapolis Sunday Tribune*, November 8, 1959, 26-29.

400 **black tie reception ... "these barriers."**—Information on the dinner and quotes from James R. Killian are from the publication of Killian's address, "Education in a World of Conflict and Change," from a dinner at the Minneapolis Club, November 16, 1959, in honor of Gould's fifteenth year as president of Carleton College,

400 **"a wonderful thing" ... "the day's work."**—Gould's closing remarks are as reported in LMG to Elizabeth Wallace, 23 November 1959, CCA.

400 **"a dean to whom I can"**—LMG to John M. Musser, 12 December 1959, CCA.

400 **first been suggested ... until mid-April.**—1993 Gilman/Crouter interview; Phil Phenix to LMG, 23 November 1959; LMG to Frank Kille, 12 February 1960; LMG to John Musser, Atherton Bean, and Ellwood Newhart, 25 February 1960; LMG to Richard C. Gilman, 29 February 1960; Minutes of the Carleton College Faculty for 11 April 1960—all CCA.

401 **passed the $4 million mark**—*The Voice of the Carleton Alumni*, January 1960, 11.

401 **While there, Wayne State's dean ... "over the years."**—LMG to Frank Kille, 12 February 1960, CCA. An annual salary of $18,000 to teach as little or as much as wanted was indeed a handsome offer in 1960. This was a little less than Gould's salary as president in 1959-60, but not a lot less. That year the salary of Carleton College's highest paid member of the teaching faculty, Thurlo B. Thomas, was $12,000.

402 **(As early as 1949 ... "when we retire.")**—LMG to Arthur L. Rautman, 23 October 1949; LMG to R. F. Brownlee Cote, 3 January 1950—both CCA.

402 **Goulds spent the first two ... Reuben G. Gustavson,**—LMG to Laird Bell, 28 March 1960; LMG to Reuben G. Gustavson, 29 March 1960—both CCA.

402 **"I shall be 64"**—LMG to Reuben G. Gustavson, 29 March 1960, CCA.

402 **"I can readily"**—Gustavson to LMG, 25 April 1960, CCA.

403 **"a first rate human being"**—LMG to Melvin H. Taube, 24 February 1960, CCA.

403 **"I received a phone call"**—1992 Thurnblad/Reitz interview, CCA.

403 **truly collaborative decision**—See POF Faculty File of Bardwell L. Smith (Ser. 58A), CCA.

403 **90 percent of Carleton's "yeasty young faculty"**—Laura Bergquist, "What is a College President?", *Look*, June 7, 1960, 80.

404 **"3-3" plan ... in September of 1961.**—Minutes of the Carleton College Faculty for 24 November 1958, 21 March 1960, and 11 April 1960; LMG to Philip H. Phenix, 26 January 1960; LMG to Everett N. Case, 25 February 1960; 1993 Gilman/Crouter interview—all CCA.

404 **By January Yamasaki ... "mouth holds $1,500,000."**—Minutes of the Carleton College Board of Trustees for 15 January 1960; LMG to D. Blake Stewart, 15 February 1960, CCA.

405 **ground-breaking ceremony for Olin**—*Carletonian*, May 13, 1960, 8; *The Voice of the Carleton Alumni*, July 1960, 10.

405 **On May 21 ... toward its $10 million goal.**—Richard P. Kleeman, "Carleton Gets $1,000,000 for Faculty Pay Raises," *Minneapolis Sunday Tribune*, May 22, 1960, Upper Midwest Section, 1, 6.

406 **The same day ... for higher education.**—LMG to John S. Dickey, 2 June 1960, CCA.

406 **On June 3 ... "outside the Carleton family."**—*The Voice of the Carleton Alumni*, July 1960, 10; Minutes of the Carleton College Board of Trustees for 3 June 1960, CCA.

406 **urgent call for Gould ... "other political boundaries."**—LMG to Atherton Bean, 4 June 1960; LMG to Louis B. Wright, 17 June 1960 ("against various"); LMG to Hubert H. Humphrey, 8 July 1960—all CCA; LMG, "My 50 Years of Antarctic Exploration and Research," op. cit., CCA-GC ("just didn't think"); LMG, testimony of June 14, 1960 before the Senate Committee on Foreign Relations on ratification of the Treaty on Antarctica signed December 1, 1959, transcript, CCA.

407 **The following week ... "man was dead."**—LMG to Frank Stinchfield, 10 June 1960; LMG to Ellwood H. Newhart, 12 June 1960; LMG to Neele E. Stearns, 25 June 1960 ("Mr. Johansson almost")—all CCA.

407 **"a great increase in"**—LMG to William H. MacLeish, 28 June 1960, CCA.

407 **separate luncheons ... still desirable**—LMG to Robert Gale, 26 June 1960, CCA.

407 **subsequently suggested ... "comprehensive picture."**—LMG to Atherton Bean, 8 July 1960, CCA.

407 **Sadly, the night ... sudden heart attack.**—*The Voice of the Carleton Alumni*, September 1960, 42. The praise quoted is from LMG to Albert Teacher's Agency, Chicago, re: Lucile Deen, 18 December 1946, CCA.

408 **Gould asked Carlton Qualey**—LMG telegram to Carlton Qualey, 25 June 1960, CCA.

408 **Services would ... pallbearers.**—*The Voice of the Carleton Alumni*, September 1960, 42.

408 **"it is going to take"**—LMG to Bill Steven, 5 July 1960, CCA.

408 **He had learned ... "mere hypocrisy."**—LMG to Hubert H. Humphrey, 26 July 1960, CCA.

408 **Gould alerted ... "its voice heard."**—LMG to Bill Steven, 5 July 1960, CCA.

408 **"deeply concerned that"**—LMG to Hubert H. Humphrey, 8 July 1960 , CCA.

408 **invitation of Senator Thruston Morton**—LMG to Atherton Bean, 8 July 1960, CCA. Bruce Pollock to LMG, 21 July 1960, CCA, confirms that Gould's appearance was televised.

408 **preferred a ticket headed**—LMG to Ellis H. Dana, 30 November 1959, CCA. See also Dana to LMG, 11 October 1960, CCA, where Dana writes: "So far as our mutual interest in politics go, I presume whatever you find lacking in Nixon may be made up in Lodge. Although this is certainly not the same as having Rockefeller at the head of the ticket. My own candid opinion is that Kennedy now leads and will probably win unless some unforeseen international developments begin to favor Nixon. You see, I am already pulling for Rockefeller in 1964, which probably isn't the loyal party way of expressing myself at this time." To this, Gould responded: "I find myself in hearty agreement with you about the Republican candidates. ... Had there been a presidential primary rather than a convention, I am perfectly sure the Republican citizens of this country would have nominated Rockefeller. I too hope to vote for him in 1964." (LMG to Dana, 16 October 1960, CCA.)

408 **invited to take twenty minutes**—LMG to Atherton Bean, 8 July 1960, CCA.

408 **"intellectual renaissance" ... "our national purpose."**—LMG, statement to the Republican National Convention's Committee on Resolutions, 19 July 1960, transcript, CCA.

409 **"I shall be interested to see,"**—LMG to Paul C. Reinert, 24 July 1960, CCA.

409 **"deep appreciation" ... "our scientific enterprise."**—LMG to Hubert H. Humphrey, 26 August 1960, CCA.

409n **"became one of the major"**—Munger and Fenno, *National Politics and Federal Aid to Education*, 98.

CHAPTER 23 — SHAKING THE FOUNDATIONS

410   **Gould's team for this meeting**—See LMG to Alfred P. Sloan, Jr., 26 August 1960 and 14 September 1960, both CCA.

410   **Sloan was accompanied**—LMG to Arnold J. Zurcher, 28 September 1960, CCA.

410   **friendly personal terms**—A year and a half earlier, Stewart McDonald had written Bob Gale of a conversation he had just had with Warren Weaver, a Sloan Foundation vice president. McDonald reported: "Warren told me that late in January he received a telephone call from Alfred Sloan saying that he had just had lunch with Larry. In his telephone call, Mr. Sloan asked Warren, 'Can it be true that Dr. Gould is as good a man as he appears to be?'" W. Stewart McDonald to Robert L. Gale, 12 March 1958, CCA.

410   **In light of ... "might be asked for."**—Robert L. Conway to LMG, 5 January 1960, CCA.

411   **Sloan's parting words**—LMG to Robert L. Gale, 26 June 1960, CCA.

411   **Sloan and Gould had expected**—Alfred P. Sloan, Jr. to LMG 8 July 1960; LMG telegram to The Homestead at Hot Springs, 14 July 1960; LMG to Sloan, 26 August 1960—all CCA.

411   **"we had a thoroughly good"**—LMG to Arnold J. Zurcher, 28 September 1960, CCA.

411   **Gale's recollection**—1993-1994 Gale/Clark interview, CCA.

411   **difficulties that stood in the way**—See LMG to Alfred P. Sloan, Jr., 2 November 1961, CCA, for an after-the-fact recounting of these considerations, plus the additional one, very unlikely to have been voiced at the time, that "some very substantial changes in the Board of Trustees needed to be made in which I had to be involved."

411   **In town then for ... Sloan Foundation support.**—LMG to Everett Case, 5 October 1960; Robert L. Gale memorandum to Eileen Larson of 25 November 1960 (concerning Gale's notes jotted as Gould related facts about his recent trip to New York at a steering committee meeting)—both CCA. (Quotations from the Gale memorandum.)

412   **"my right arm" ... "things that Bruce did."**—LMG to G. Slade Schuster, 3 October 1960, CCA.

412   **conference on science and the news**—Victor Cohn, "Parley in the Pines," *Minneapolis Sunday Tribune*, October 16, 1960, Picture Magazine section, 4-5, 7-8; Minutes of the Carleton College Board of Trustees for 29 October 1960, CCA. See also Bill Steven to LMG, 17 December 1959, CCA.

412   **a venomous rupture**—See LMG to Frederick B. Leighton, 26 August 1960 and 3 October 1960; Leighton to LMG, 6 September 1960; Gould note to Leighton personnel file dated 12 September 1960—all CCA.

412   **"the best man we"**—LMG to Laird Bell, 16 October 1960, CCA.

412   **Gilman would be introduced ... fall of 1962.**—Minutes of the Carleton College Board of Trustees for 28-29 October 1960, CCA.

413   **mixture of trepidation and joy**—See LMG to Duncan Stewart, 25 September 1960; LMG to Ward Lucas, 16 October 1960—both CCA.

413   **Then on September 21 ... "going to the Antarctic."**—Duncan Stewart, "My First Visit to Antarctica," *The Voice of the Carleton Alumni*, January 1961, 8-9.

413   **"When you know"**—LMG to Duncan Stewart, 25 September 1960, CCA.

413   **8 a.m. on Monday the 17th**—LMG to Ward Lucas, 16 October 1960, CCA.

413   **reporting that class ... "trade places with him."**—LMG to Russell Langworthy, 26 October 1960—all CCA.

414   **In the third week ... "Building at Carleton College."**—LMG to Atherton Bean, 11 October 1960, CCA.

414   **"doubly sorry not" ... "Wesleyans and the Carletons."**—LMG to John Cowles, 1 October 1960, CCA.

414 **wrote Gould of his ... same at the Rockefeller Foundation.**—John Dickey to LMG, 30 September 1960; LMG to Dickey, 5 October 1960—both CCA.

414n **"The independent college"**—John Dickey to LMG, 30 September 1960, CCA.

415 **"Here again," ... "liberal arts colleges."**—LMG to Donald K. David, 5 October 1960, CCA.

415 **To Ford Foundation vice president ... "a particular institution."**—LMG to Clarence Faust, 5 October 1960, CCA.

415 **"the new program" ... "matter of semantics."**—LMG to Clarence Faust, 18 December 1960, CCA.

415 **hoped at one point ... had "compromised"**—LMG to Andrew Stevenson, 10 October 1960, CCA.

415 **granted the president leave**—Minutes of the Executive Committee of the Carleton College Board of Trustees for 25 August 1960, CCA.

416 **"Had I known that" ... "by the outcome."**—LMG to Torbert H. Macdonald, 27 November 1960, CCA.

416 **"immensely impressed ... "being a Democrat!"**—LMG to William Benton, 3 January 1961, CCA. In March 1961, after Kennedy's first two months in office, Gould would write Hubert Humphrey that he was growing "increasingly enthusiastic about the present administration and the way the President and you other leaders are moving us forward." (LMG to Hubert H. Humphrey, 21 March 1961, CCA. The new administration had, at this time, not yet suffered through the blunder of the failed Bay of Pigs invasion in Cuba, then still four weeks ahead.)

416 **"You sounded like an ancient" ... "being, named Laird Bell.")**—Laird Bell to LMG, 23 November 1960; LMG to Bell, 13 December 1961—both CCA.

416 **elected chairman of the board of the Carnegie Foundation**—Carleton College News Release SP60-136, 16 December 1960, CCA.

416 **"informal conversation by thoughtful"**—Christian A. Herter to LMG, 1 November 1960, CCA.

416 **Gould's talk ... "as a single enterprise."**—LMG, "Science, Engineering, and the Humanities in the University," address at the Conference on Science in International Educational and Cultural Affairs, at MIT, December 16-17, 1960. (Printed in Public and Private Association in the International Educational and Cultural Relations of the United States, Office of the Special Assistant to the Secretary for the Coordination of International Educational and Cultural Relations, February 15, 1961, 76-82); LMG, "One Culture Only," *Carleton College Bulletin* 58, No. 1 (1961).

416 **short note to his wife**—LMG to MRG, 1 January 1961. Larry signed his note, "As always, Tiglath Pilezer." With a significance to the couple unknown to this sadly non-omniscient biographer, styling Larry "Tiglath Pilezer" was something he and Peg affectionately did, across many years. Tiglath-Pileser was the name of three kings of ancient Assyria.

416 **Larry and Peg were leaving ... selected in the spring.**—LMG to Andrew Stevenson, 6 January 1961; Minutes of the Carleton College Board of Trustees for 7 January 1961—both CCA.

417 **Gould's travel mission**—Sources for all details concerning the Goulds' 1961 trip around the world are either the 1961 travel diary kept by Margaret Rice Gould (CCA-GC), the post-trip report by L. M. Gould to the Carleton alumni, "World Trip Reveals Revolution of Rising Expectations," in *The Voice of the Carleton Alumni*, May 1961, 2-6, or Gould's (undated) 15-page report to the Ford Foundation, titled "Comments on Around the World Trip January 8 through March 9, 1961," CCA. Specific citations are given for direct quotations only.

417 **entering through a basement ... "taken with them."**—*Minneapolis Morning Tribune*, January 10, 1961, 11; *Northfield News*, January 12, 1961, 2.

417 **"were moderately dull"**—MRG 1961 Travel Diary, 13 January 1961.

417 **"we learned more"**—Ibid., 16 January 1961.

418 **"a most interesting cross section"**—Gould, "World Trip Reveals Revolution of Rising Expectations," 2.

418 **"so very beautiful"**— MRG 1961 Travel Diary, 21 January 1961,

418 **"absolutely thrilling"**—Ibid., 22 January 1961.

418 **"wonky ear"**—Ibid., 1 February 1961.

418 **"Pain minimal"**—Ibid., 8 February 1961.

418 **"pleasant and easy"**—Ibid., 5 February 1961.

418 **"Whereas I did not"**— Gould, "World Trip Reveals Revolution of Rising Expectations," 2.

418 **"clear that the Indonesian"**—LMG, "Comments on Around the World Trip January 8 through March 9, 1961," CCA.

418 **"very poor & dull"** ... **"traditional style"**—MRG 1961 Travel Diary, 11 February 1961.

419 **"people not concerned to"**—Gould, "World Trip Reveals Revolution of Rising Expectations," 5.

419 **"crowded land"** ... **"would be India"**—Ibid., 5-6.

419n **"diplomatic Col. Blimp"** ... **"sorry representative."**—MRG 1961 Travel Diary, 11 February 1961.

419n **"two dull daughters"** ... **"incredibly stupid."**—Ibid., 26 January 1961.

419n **"intelligent, interesting"**—Ibid., 14 February 1961.

420 **"no retreat from"** ... **"toward the West."**—LMG, "Comments on Around the World Trip January 8 through March 9, 1961," CCA.

420 **"somewhat smaller and"**—MRG 1961 Travel Diary, 25 February 1961.

420 **"thrilling beyond belief."**—Ibid., 27 February 1961.

420 **"in the Parthenon"**—Gould, "World Trip Reveals Revolution of Rising Expectations," 6.

420 **"utterly enchanted"**—MRG 1961 Travel Diary, 1 March 1961.

420 **"one of the most exciting"**—LMG, "Comments on Around the World Trip January 8 through March 9, 1961," CCA.

420 **"Nothing left & I fall apart"**—MRG 1961 Travel Diary, 2 March 1961.

421 **"despite Larry's malaise"**—Ibid., 6 March 1961.

421 **"still feeling miserable"**—Ibid., 7 March 1961.

421 **"picked up Ste. Chapelle"**—Ibid., 8 March 1961.

421 **Early in January** ... **"stack up pretty well,"**—LMG to Richard C. Gilman, 5 January 1961; 1993 Gilman/Crouter interview—both CCA.

421 **Gilman flew to Denver ... on February 13**—1992 Wright/Smith interview; 1993 Gilman/Crouter interview (including all quotations this paragraph); "Profile of Carleton College 1951 to 1971"; Minutes of the Executive Committee of the Carleton College Board of Trustees for 5 February 1961—all CCA.

422 **What had once been ... "problem that has arisen."**—Warren Weaver to LMG, 12 January 1961; John W. Nason to LMG, 14 February 1961; Robert L. Gale to Nason, 17 February 1961—all CCA.

423 **When Gould returned ... "release from the College."**—Robert L. Gale to W. Stewart McDonald, 16 March 1961; LMG to Alfred P. Sloan, Jr., 14 March 1961; LMG to Weaver, 14 March 1961—all CCA.

423 **In an address the following June**—LMG, "The New Dimension in Philanthropy," published address given 24 June 1961 at The Johnson Foundation, Racine, Wisconsin, on the occasion of the dedication of "Wingspread." (The Wingspread house was originally designed by Frank Lloyd Wright as the Herbert F. Johnson residence, but was adapted after 1959 for use by The Johnson Foundation as an educational conference facility.)

For a different take on the appeal of foundation work, however, consider Dwight Macdonald's warning that "giving away money through a foundation is a wearisome and complicated business, vexing to the soul and wearing on the liver." Robert Hutchins, when he was associate director of a foundation, used to quip, "it's a nice job; you meet so many interested people." (Macdonald, *The Ford Foundation, 1989 reprint*, 109, 111.)

424   **Horn's ire was ignited … "start of the school year."**—Charles L. Horn to LMG, 20 February 1961; A. W. Pickford to Horn, 22 February 1961—both CCA.

424n   **"this wise selection"**—LMG to Alfred P. Sloan, Jr., 15 June 1961, CCA.

424n   **"I agree with you"**—Alfred P. Sloan, Jr. to LMG, 21 June 1961, CCA.

424n   **"very friendly letter"**—LMG to Alfred P. Sloan, Jr., 2 November 1961, CCA.

425   **Gilman also wrote … "great deal of publicity."**—Richard C. Gilman to Horn, 22 February 1961; Horn to Gilman, 24 February 1961—both CCA.

425   **Following his return … "you to dedicate [in October]."**—LMG to Charles L. Horn, 29 March 1961, CCA.

426   **It required further lobbying**—See LMG to A. W. Pickford, 21 April 1961; Pickford to Horn, 24 April 1961; James O Wynn to LMG, 3 May, 1961—all CCA. On April 10 Gould observed to Atherton Bean that so far Horn was "still adamant" about not allowing any move of equipment into Olin prior to dedication, which "makes our situation chaotic," but that he had promised to come down and talk with Gould about the matter. (LMG to Atherton Bean, 10 April 1961, CCA.) A few days later (the letter of 21 April), Gould protested to Pickford that it was necessary to make the move of equipment in physics and biology out of Laird Hall in summer, so that Laird Hall could in turn receive other equipment, etc., from Williams Hall, which was to be demolished and that "such a transfer of property and personnel could hardly be carried out after the college is in operation." Wynn wrote Gould (the letter of 3 May) that he saw no need for "this idea that we had to dedicate a building before any use whatever could be made of it" and promised to "talk to Charlie further about it."

426   **complimentary feature article … "intelligence and character."**—Chesly Manly, "Carleton Called 'Little Harvard,'" *Chicago Daily Tribune*, February 25, 1961.

426   **"trying to help make this college"**—LMG to Ellwood H. Newhart, 29 November 1960, CCA.

426   **The article placed … "extraordinary distinction."**—Manly, "Carleton Called 'Little Harvard,'" op. cit.

427   **"I think we have reached" … "prospects in Florida."**—Atherton Bean to LMG, 13 March 1961, CCA.

427   **prospect visits in Florida … ultimately closed.**—Ibid. (for Bean's prospect potential judgments); LMG to Atherton Bean, 10 April 1961; Robert L. Gale to Robert L. Conway, 12 April 1961—all CCA. By the end of August, Gale would be concerned enough by Gould's lack of success on recent big-ticket solicitations that he would suggest to Bean that in future "it might be a very good idea if the President were accompanied by some Trustee on each one of his visits so that we had a two-hand team, using the President's prestige and then having the second man on the team be sure that an actual pitch is made." (Gale to Bean, 31 August 1961, CCA.)

428   **in Washington … "about the Antarctic treaty."**—LMG to Robert Matteson, 23 May 1961, CCA.

428   **Perfect weather … new chairman.**—*The Voice of the Carleton Alumni*, July 1961, 2; Minutes of the Carleton College Board of Trustees for 2 June 1961, CCA.

428   **Earlier in that … construction contracts.**— of the Carleton College Board of Trustees for 2 June 1961, CCA.

429   **reunion weekend**—*The Voice of the Carleton Alumni*, July 1961, 8-12.

429   **In mid-June … "didn't dare say so."**—LMG to Margaret and George Cameron, 28 June 1961, CCA. That the Towsleys were seen as possible principal contributors to the women's gymnasium is clear from Atherton Bean to LMG, 13 March 1961, CCA.

429   **"depressing" … "its primary mission."**—LMG to Robert E. Matteson, 3 June 1961, CCA.

429 **"a mile wide"**—1993 Gilman/Crouter interview, CCA.

429 **Late in 1960 ... Which he did.**—*Carletonian*, December 7, 1960, 1; author's telephone interview (unrecorded) with Robert L. Gale, 12 September 2002.

429 **Horn had begun to allude**—LMG to Atherton Bean, 11 October 1960, CCA.

430 **As Gilman related ... no honorary degree.**—1993 Gilman/Crouter interview; LMG to John M. Musser, 15 May 1961—both CCA.

430 **Triennial Council meeting**—*The Voice of the Carleton Alumni*, November 1961, 22.

430 **two days of Ford ... "precipitate Heald's ouster."**—Nielsen, *The Big Foundations*, 90-91.

431 **"very productive" ... "overseas operations."**—LMG to F. F. Hill, 23 September 1961, CCA.

431 **"good for the trustees" ... "fact very much."**—LMG to Henry Heald, 23 September 1961, CCA.

432 **write Cowles of his interest ... "exciting and fruitful."**—LMG to John Cowles, 22 November 1961, CCA.

432 **approved the "ferment" ... "ought to be."**—LMG to Henry Ford II, 13 December 1961, CCA.

432 **foundation publicly announced ... by June 20, 1964.**—Joseph M. McDaniel, Jr., to LMG, 2 October 1961, CCA; *The Voice of the Carleton Alumni*, November 1961, 9.

432 **"recognition of the fact" ... "history of the College."**—LMG to Robert L. Gale, 19 September 1961, CCA.

CHAPTER 24 — "YOU CAN DO ANYTHING YOU WANT"

433 **"I must tell you" ... "recommended you in vain."**—LMG to Floyd A. Bond, 10 September 1954, CCA.

433 **"Larry Gould has come as close as anyone."**—Editorial: "Who Said 'Retirement'?," *Minneapolis Morning Tribune*, March 15, 1962, 4.

433 **Joseph Kaplan ... "in the same league."**—William Carmen to LMG, 30 October 1957, CCA. Kaplan's words had been reported to Carmen by Ruth Chance, the widow of one of Carman's partners, who had been present to hear them.

433 **he could complain ... "the elusive dollar."**—LMG to Floyd A. Bond, 10 September 1954; LMG to John M. Musser, 17 June 1956—both CCA.

434 **Robert M. Hutchins ... "prepared to be."**—Macdonald, *The Ford Foundation*, 1989 reprint, 78. Macdonald likened Hutchins' career to that of "a bright young sophomore who becomes a college president without ever ceasing to be a sophomore," showing "vivid potentialities"—"great verve and courage in pushing unorthodox and in general sensible ideas—but 'muted actualities'"—his potential for achievement to some degree thwarted by "superficiality, arrogance, poor judgment about people, and a congenital lack of maturity both in understanding specific situations and in effectively dealing with them."

434 **"finding time for leisurely reading" ... "before I go to sleep."**—"President Gould Says…" column in *The Voice of the Carleton Alumni*, April 1958, 2; LMG to Ralph Henry, 7 May 1956, CCA ("my customary hour's").

434n **"beautiful beyond belief"**—LMG to Bess and Bernt Balchen, 25 October 1956, NA-GP.

434n **"I've become sufficiently"**—LMG to Jack Lucas, 16 January 1958, CCA.

434n **"indifferent" to jazz**—Interview in the *Carletonian*, 6 April 1938, 4.

434n **"not received sufficient"**—LMG to Margaret F. Bell, 2 March 1949, CCA.

435 **thought it most likely**—See, for instance, LMG to Admiral David M. Tyree, 14 September 1961, NA-GP: "I expect this to be my last year as president of Carleton College, for I am due

to retire in June, 1962, though I have not yet persuaded the trustees to agree to this as yet."

435 **Bean was chary of diminishing**—Atherton Bean to Frank Hammond, 26 September 1961, CCA.

435 **dedication of the Olin Hall of Science**—*The Voice of the Carleton Alumni*, November 1961, 2-5; LMG to Atherton Bean, 3 August 1961, CCA ("quite frankly").

436 **enjoyed a week at the University ... "to him some day."**—LMG to Reuben G. Gustavson, 23 October 1961, CCA (including "splendid" visit); Interview with Gould by Lori Stiles, excerpted in University of Arizona publication *Lo Qué Pasa*, March 21, 1986.

436 **suggestion made in September ... "enjoyed teaching most.")**—LMG to Laird Bell, 26 September 1961; LMG to Frank W. Abrams, 4 October 1961, 20 November 1961 (including "beyond the normal"), and 24 November 1961 ("it may well be")—all CCA.

436 **business that included ... matching basis.**—Minutes of the Carleton College Board of Trustees for 27-28 October 1961, CCA.

437 **letter to alumni from Bean**—Atherton Bean to "Dear Fellow Alumnus," 27 October 1961, CCA.

437 **"a tactical error"**—LMG to Atherton Bean, 31 October 1961, Robert L. Gale to Bean, 1 November 1961—both CCA.

437 **and then on radio.**—After hearing the news on the radio, Carleton's former Dean Lindsey Blayney telegraphed his mingled dismay and congratulations, alluding as well to the memory that he and his wife had been the first to suggest, following Gould's 1930 lecture at Carleton on the Byrd Expedition, that Gould might wish to join the Carleton faculty. (Lindsey and Ida Blayney to LMG (telegram), 2 November 1961, CCA.

437 **$100,000 to get the building ... within three years.**—LMG to Eleanor H. Hansen, 31 October 1961; Laird Bell to LMG, 1 December 1961; LMG to Margaret Bell Cameron, 11 December 1961; LMG to John M. Musser, 13 December 1961—all CCA.

437n **No one at the college had realized ... "of the administration."**—LMG to Atherton Bean, 31 October 1961, CCA.

438 **"great incentive to our"**—Carleton College press release of January 1962 regarding the "challenge gift" for a women's gymnasium, CCA.

438 **"At current prices," ... "critical than now."**—LMG to Frank J. Miller, 14 December 1961, CCA.

438 **Peg left on December 18 ... "a magpie.")**—LMG to Mr. and Mrs. Walter Rudlin, 19 December 1961; LMG to Margaret Bell Cameron, 20 December 1961 ("I am the principal'")— both CCA.

438 **later confessed ... "her nerves were."**— LMG to JRH, 8 November 1970, CCA-GC.

438n **"probably further behind"**—Carleton College press release of January 1962 regarding the "challenge gift" for a women's gymnasium, CCA.

438n **"I understand that Dr. Cowling"**—John W. Nason to Margaret Bell Cameron, 26 July 1962, CCA.

439 **Christmas eve ... "Dick did go with her."**— JRH to LMG, 17 March 1970, CCA-GC.

Jean related, in her letter of 17 March 1970, that the argument started with *Time* magazine, with Arthur Schlesinger, Jr., on the cover. In letter dated 18 August 1985, but not sent, she recalled this again, lamenting Peg's "having declared us dead on Christmas Eve of 1961— because Arthur Schlesinger Jr. was on the cover of TIME Magazine." Only ... this is wrong. Arthur Schlesinger, Jr. appeared on the cover of *Time* once: in December 1965. On the cover of the Dec. 22, 1961, issue, the most likely one to be in the Hoppins' living room on Christmas Eve of 1961, was Moise Tshombe, of the Congo, who it would be extremely difficult to confuse with Arthur Schlesinger, Jr. (If the issue pre-dated December 29 was already present on the Sunday of Christmas Eve, that cover featured comedian Jackie Gleason.) Specific memory, after several intervening years, is notoriously unreliable; the detail is unimportant. The point of Jean's relation of "what happened" is that the entire quarrel, leading to a breach of decades, began over something that was itself unimportant.

439 **Jean called Larry ... "was quite mad."**—LMG to JRH, 14 March 1970, CCA-GC.;

439 **Apparently before leaving ... "to exist for you."**—LMG to JRH, 8 November 1970 ("turn to ashes"); JRH to LMG, 7 December 1970 ("we've just joined")—both CCA-GC.

439 **Larry remembered Peg ... "didn't last long."**)—LMG to JRH, 8 November 1970, CCA-GC.

439 **When, a few months ... "had ceased to exist."**—JRH to LMG, 17 March 1970, CCA-GC.

440 **"Of course, Larry, we"**—Ibid.

440 **In November he ... "if you ask it."**—LMG to Bea Wardell, 3 November 1961, CCA.

440 **"I am almost swamped"**—LMG to DJC, 20 December 1961, CCA.

440 **At 9:30 a.m. on January 13**—Minutes of the Carleton College Board of Trustees for 13 January 1962, CCA.

440 **evidence that his own preferred candidate**—See, for instance, 1994 Bean/Gale interview; 1993-1994 Gale/Clark interview; 1993 Gilman/Clark interview, and 2006 Gilman/Hillemann interview—all CCA.

440 **"on the record" responses**—LMG to Robert Conway, 14 January 1962 ("superb choice"); LMG to Hugh H. Harrison, 15 January 1962—both CCA; *The Voice of the Carleton Alumni*, March 1962, 2 ("especially fortunate").

441 **from a Cal Tech geographer ... "friendly remarks."**—Edwin S. Munger to LMG, 16 January 1962; LMG to Munger, 24 January 1962—both CCA.

441 **thanks for the job ... "glad I have stayed."**—Robert F. Leach to LMG, 16 January 1962; LMG to Leach, 24 January 1962—both CCA.

441 **"a little prouder" ... "influenced for good."**—Neil Gillam to LMG, 25 January 1962—all CCA.

441 **President John Dickey ... or Tel Aviv.**—John S. Dickey to LMG, 20 January 1962; Walter G. Whitman to LMG, 16 February 1962—both CCA.

441 **"quite likely" ... "to do just that."**—LMG to John S. Dickey, 3 February 1962; LMG to Reuben G. Gustavson, 17 April 1962; LMG to Frank Kille, 3 February 1962—all CCA.

442 **Gould had first arranged ... "account of you!"**—LMG to Atherton Bean, 7 February 1962; LMG to John J. McCloy, 28 March 1962—both CCA.

442 **$10 million mark**—*Minneapolis Morning Tribune*, March 15, 1962, 20.

442 **summarized for an interviewer his own plans**—*Minneapolis Morning Tribune*, March 14, 1962, 16.

442 **"Larry Gould Day," ... "should really be."**—*The Voice of the Carleton Alumni*, May 1962, 27; *Northfield News*, April 12, 1962, 2A.

443 **"I have only about"**—LMG to Miller Upton (president of Beloit College), 12 April 1962, CCA.

443 **who said of money that**—Many online sources reference O'Shaughnessy's use of this statement, for instance http://www.philanthropyroundtable.org/topic/excellence_in_philanthropy/i_a_oshaughnessy_foundation, retrieved 23 April 2012.

443 **Early in April Gould ... a week later.**—LMG to I. A. O'Shaughnessy, 4 April 1962; Robert L. Gale to John H. Myers, 11 April 1962; CCA. Gould responded to O'Shaughnessy's gift with this note: "Bless you, my good friend. I shall say some Protestant prayers for you. They won't do you any harm and, on the other hand, one never knows—they might help!" (LMG to I. A. O'Shaughnessy, 11 April 1962, CCA.)

443 **Gould wrote similarly ... "a very good recipe."**—LMG to Atherton Bean, 30 March 1962; LMG to Henry Ford II, 6 April 1962 and 8 May 1962—all CCA.

444 **On the last weekend ... "uplift" it gave him.**—*The Voice of the Carleton Alumni*, May 1962, 28; Arland F. Christ-Janer to LMG, 3 May 1962; LMG to Rabbi Dudley Weinberg, 20 April 1962—both CCA.

444 novel "conference call" ... exceeded the $1 million mark.—*The Voice of the Carleton Alumni*, May 1962, 2.

444 Gale reported to Bean ... approaches already made.—Robert L. Gale to Atherton Bean, 19 May 1962, CCA.

444 ("As the man said as he watched"—LMG to Louis S. Headley, 18 May 1962, CCA.

444 By the beginning of June ... "not one of those times.")—LMG to Hal Bly, 1 June 1962; LMG to Atherton Bean, 12 April 1962; Bean to LMG, 20 April 1962—all CCA.

445 campus Larry Gould Day—*The Voice of the Carleton Alumni*, July 1962, 3-4; *Northfield News*, June 14, 1962, 3A; *Carletonian*, January 8, 1964, 1; LMG to Dan Styron, 4 June 1962, CCA.

445 reception at the Northfield Golf Club—*The Voice of the Carleton Alumni*, July 1962, 4; *Northfield News*, June 14, 1962, 3A.

445 Meanwhile, another $100,000 ... "our joint promise."—LMG to Laird Bell, 5 June 1962 and 7 June 1962; LMG to DJC, 7 June 1962—all CCA.

445 rain washed out ... more memorable.—LMG to O. Meredith Wilson, 18 June 1962, CCA.

445n "that G - D- portrait"—LMG to Robert H. Edwards, 7 October 1983, CCA.

446 hand of President Clemens Granskou.—*Northfield News*, June 14, 1962, 1A.

446 "Sir, by your stature"—College of Wooster honorary degree (D.Let) to LMG, 11 June 1962; CCA-GC.

446 At Wooster, Gould's commencement speech—LMG commencement address at Wooster College, 11 June 1962, unpublished transcript, CCA.

446 "doubly wonderful."—LMG to Nathan Pusey, 24 January 1962, CCA.

446 Carleton's own commencement—Information for two paragraphs, except as noted below, is from *The Voice of the Carleton Alumni*, July 1962, 20-21; *Northfield News*, June 21, 1962, 1A.

447 began with Bean tapping ... "stand over there."—Bean/Gale interview, CCA.

447 "Larry Gould has already"—Carleton College honorary degree (L.H.D.) citation to LMG, 15 June 1962, CCA.

447n Bob Gale remembered waiting—1993-1994 Gale/Clark interview, CCA.

447n "always cherish the wonderful"—LMG to Atherton Bean, 7 June 1962, CCA.

447n $4,864.60 over goal—Minutes of the Carleton College Board of Trustees for 15 June 1962, CCA.

448 Carleton board convened in the library ... standing ovation.—Minutes of the Carleton College Board of Trustees for 15 June 1962, CCA.

448 (Regarding the "emeritus" ... "much sooner."—1981 Gould/Peter J. Anderson interview, OSUA-AP.

448 The last report heard—Minutes of the Carleton College Board of Trustees for 15 June 1962, CCA. In a note the next day informing Eiler Henrickson of his promotion to full professor, Gould wrote: "I need not dwell upon the fact that it meant much to me to do this and especially as my last official act as president of Carleton College. You know how proud I am of you and how much I have appreciated your personal friendship and affection." (LMG to Eiler Henrickson, 16 June 1962, CCA.)

448 That evening Atherton and Winifred ... "Kindling Youth."—*The Voice of the Carleton Alumni*, July 1962, 20-21; plaque present in the CCA-GC. Years later, Gould gave the Questar telescope to his friend Clark Arnold, who had far more interest in using it than Gould himself ever actually did. In an oral history interview, Arnold related: "So one day, Larry decided that he would give me the telescope, because he didn't want it, and he knew I liked it. So he gave to me, and then looked at it and said, 'Well, I suppose I ought to keep the plaque.' So he took a screwdriver and pried the plaque off the front of the telescope, and he looked at the plaque, and he looked at the telescope, and he said, 'I don't know why in the hell they couldn't have given me a real good fly rod.'" (1995 Arnolds/Donnell interview, CCA.)

448 **two days of Ford Foundation meetings**—At these meetings Gould moved to endorse an expansion of the foundation's grants program for liberal arts colleges. (See LMG to James Shannon, 26 June 1962, CCA.) The trustees also at this time received the report of the committee established the year before to review foundation programs and procedures as part of the board's redefinition of relations with president Henry Heald. The report directed Heald to work far more closely with the trustees on all policy and program questions and instructed him very specifically to expand the foundation's efforts in the field of civil rights, including support for projects promoting the full exercise of voting rights and equal opportunities to persons of all races in areas such as education, employment, and housing. Heald, according to observer Waldemar Nielsen's later evaluation, accepted realistically the outcome of "the power struggle that had taken place" with the foundation board, and "positive results followed." Nielsen judged that Heald's acceptance of the new operating procedures dictated by the board lessened tensions enough for him to continue as president for another three years, before new strains emerging by 1965 would finally lead to Heald's ouster. (Nielsen, *The Big Foundations*, 91-92.) In his January 25-26, 1973, interview for the Ford Foundation Oral History Project, Gould stated that Heald had wanted the trustees' role to be almost a pro forma ratifying of decisions made without them and that "we didn't like it." (1973 Gould/Morrissey interview, UAAL.) Gould entirely supported the board's reassertion of control during 1961 and 1962.

448 **warm appreciations written**—LMG to John Cowles, 2 July 1962; LMG to Laird Bell, 25 June 1962—both CCA.

449 **letter demanding that Gould ... "on our campus."**—G. Archer Weniger to LMG, 20 June 1962; LMG to Weniger, 28 June 1962—both CCA.

In another letter written the same week, Gould mentioned to Carleton professor John Dyer-Bennet that in 1958 when the AAUP had established the Meiklejohn Award for college administrators who had made outstanding contributions to academic freedom, he had been asked, in part due to the statements he had made defending Ken May, to be its first recipient but had declined out of reluctance to bring the "long since resolved" May matter again to the surface and perhaps cause May new embarrassment. (LMG to John Dyer-Bennet, 28 June 1962, CCA.)

449 **asking that in connection**—LMG to Business Office, 30 June 1962, CCA.

449 **His house, in which ... "flowers for them."**—LMG to John B. Faegre, Jr., 23 June 1962; LMG to D. Blake Stewart, 28 June 1962—both CCA

449 **transformed "from a little-known"**—*Newsweek*, June 25, 1962, 84

449 **"when Carleton people count"**—Henry L. Woodward to LMG, 25 June 1962, CCA

449 **Later that month ... giant red tie.**—*Northfield News*, July 16, 1962, 6B. When the Goulds left for the Tetons on July 5, the red jeep given by the Carleton faculty as a parting gift was already waiting for him at the G2V cabin, having been driven there by Gould's arrangement with Tom Tollman, Carleton Class of 1960, who had been working at Carleton for the past two years as an admissions counselor.

449 **"I dare say we shall miss"**—LMG to Lyle O. Estenson, 25 March 1962, CCA.

449 **"Quite frankly" ... "done at Carleton College."**—LMG, *Prologue to Rebirth: A Message to the Alumni of Carleton College from the President of the College.* Northfield: Carleton College, April 16, 1962.

450 **director of mutual funds managed by**—LMG to John B. Faegre, Jr., 23 June 1962; LMG to John Cowles, 2 July 1962—both CCA.

450 **Peg reported ... "will answer themselves."**—MRG to Beatrice Wardell, 12 July 1962; LMG to Wardell, 15 August 1962—both CCA.

450 *Carletonian* **feature ... "spacious windows."**—Peter Schwenger, "Goulds Move Life, Memories to Tetons," *Carletonian*, October 3, 1962, 2.

451 **active part in the five days**—"Sixth meeting of SCAR, Boulder, 20 to 24 August 1962." *Polar Record*, 11, (1963), 479-499.

451 **On November 15 ..."cold war" took place.**—LMG, "Our Fractured Culture," address at the University of Arizona, 15 November 1962, unpublished transcript, NA-GP.

452 **Gould's fourth trip to the Antarctic**—*Minneapolis Morning Tribune*, November 6, 1962, 9; LMG to Peg Gould, 20 November 1962; LMG, "My 50 Years of Antarctic Exploration and Research," op. cit. (including "beat Glenn's program")—both CCA-GC; Theodore M. Hesburgh to Mark E. Kronholm, 25 October 1995 ("going to the Antarctic with Larry"); LMG to Bea Wardell, 11 December 1962 ("magnificent" and "generally very co-operative")—both CCA; 1981 Gould/E. Vernice Anderson interview, transcript in CCA-GC.

452 **purchase of a house in Tucson**—LMG to Bea Wardell, 11 December 1962, CCA.

CHAPTER 25 — SUN AND ICE

453 **Geology major Clark Arnold ... "as his children."**—1995 Arnolds/Donnell interview, CCA. (The entire first section of this chapter, eight paragraphs of text, is based on a single source, the oral history interview recorded with Clark and Ardith Arnold by interviewer Zoe Donnell on October 13, 1995.)

454n **For Dorothy, transcription**—1995 Obaid/Donnell interview, CCA.

457 **Arizona's territorial legislature ... home to the University of Arizona.**—"A Proud Beginning," http://www.arizona.edu/about/ua-history-traditions, retrieved May 29, 2012,; Wagoner, *Arizona Territory 1863-1912*, 206-213; James, *Arizona, The Wonderland*, 225.

458 **Richard Anderson Harvill**—"Richard Anderson Harvill," http://president.arizona.edu/president/richard-anderson-harvill, retrieved May 29, 2012,.

458 **qualitatively better ... move Arizona forward.**—2002 Davis/Hillemann interview, CCA.

458 **out of a Tucson motel**—LMG to Bea Wardell, 14 January 1963, CCA.

458 **1524 square foot ... missed the snow.**—"Zillow.com" listing for 9451 E. Rosewood St., Tucson, retrieved May 29, 2012; 2002 Arnolds/Hillemann interview; LMG to Bea Wardell, 21 March 1963 ("Curiously enough")—both CCA.

459 **During his first ... preferred teaching freshmen**—Author's notes of personal interview (unrecorded) with Edgar J. McCullough, Jr., Tucson, Arizona, 5 December 2002; article by Carle Hodge, in undated (but 1963) newspaper clipping from the *Arizona Star*, found in Gould Biographical File, UA Geosciences Department: "He prefers teaching freshmen, as he did last spring. But next semester he will preside, instead, over a course in glaciology."

459 **Prescott College ... Hugh Odishaw**—Henrie, *Uncommon Education*, 8-15; LMG to Bea Wardell, 21 March 1963, CCA; article "Dr. Gould to Head Council," in clipping of May 12, 1963 from unidentified newspaper, found in Gould Biographical File, UA Geosciences Department.

459 **Parker spoke in Tucson**—All quotations this paragraphs are from "Discussion of the Development of Prescott College," Charles Franklin Parker (Tucson, Arizona, 1963). Sharlot Hall Museum Archives Audio History Collection. (Recording available for listening at http://azmemory.azlibrary.gov/cdm/singleitem/collection/shmoralhist/id/55/rec/1.)

460 **During an April trip ... "Antarctic affairs."**—Article by Frank Gniffke, *Carletonian*, April 24, 1963, 1.

460 **Arrangements were made ... next three decades.)**—1995 Arnolds/Donnell interview (including ""You kind of vacuumed"), and 2002 Arnolds/Hillemann interview—both CCA.

461 **flew to Cape Town**—*The Voice of the Carleton Alumni*, September 1963, 39.

461 **tour of Greece**—LMG, Carleton College convocation address, 14 January 1964, unpublished transcript, CCA-GC.

461 **three-day symposium … a "Christian" college.**—Information for three paragraphs and a sentence regarding this symposium is from Henrie, *Uncommon Education*, 15-30.

462 **"Implicit in the very"**—LMG, "What Should Education Mean," address to the Prescott, Arizona, Chamber of Commerce annual dinner, 24 January 1964, unpublished transcript, NA-GP.

462 **Sigma Xi Ermine … "Magna Carta."**—Clipping from the *Ann Arbor News*, November 14, 1963 [page number not indicated], located in CCA-GP.

463 **business in Minnesota**—LMG to Bea Wardell, 12 November 1963, CCA.

463 **He returned … "need to go home."**—2002 Arnolds/Hillemann interview—both CCA.

463 **convocation address … "symbolism of that before… ."**—LMG, Carleton College convocation address, 14 January 1964, unpublished transcript, CCA-GC.

464n **"He taught one course"**—1995 Arnolds/Donnell interview, CCA.

464 **"Larry functioned in the Department"**—2002 Davis/Hillemann interview, CCA. Another small example of departmental involvement: In the spring of 1964, Clark Arnold was preparing to defend his master's thesis, dealing with the supergene mineralogy of a small mine not far from Tucson. As Arnold wrote to this undergraduate geology mentor at Carleton, Duncan Stewart, his work was to come before a committee of four Arizona professors, the last being L. M. Gould. "I'm a bit worried about that last chap," Arnold wrote. "He keeps wanting to know about ice and I keep telling him that the principal use is to cool highballs, but he doesn't seem satisfied somehow, so I anticipate trouble." (Clark Arnold to Duncan Stewart, 27 April 1964, CCA.)

464 **"Winter in Tucson, summer at Jackson Hole"**—Jim Cook, "Especially, An Adventurer," *Arizona Days and Ways Magazine*, February 16, 1964.

464 **("I am pleased indeed")**—LMG to DJC, 25 May 1964, CCA-GC.

464 **Gould's own concept**—Constantinos A. Doxiadis to LMG, 22 August 1966, 70th Birthday Letters (and replies), CCA-GC.

464 **following a panel … "radiant hope"**—*Mayo Clinic Proceedings* 40, No. 1 (January 1965): 111.

465 **Rockefeller, who Gould had once**—See, for instance, LMG to Ellis H. Dana, 16 October 1960, CCA.

465 **Gould found the rightward … rest of his life.**—Interview with LMG by Victor Cohn, printed in the *Minneapolis Tribune*, December 28, 1964 and January 3, 1965; 2002 Arnolds/Hillemann interview, CCA.

466 **speaking in the Twin Cities … "vitality from diversity."**—LMG, "Our Fractured Culture," address delivered 22 January 1965, unpublished transcript, CCA-GC; LMG, "When the Barriers Are Down," address delivered 30 April 1965, unpublished transcript, NA-GP.

466 **left Tucson on June 1**—Alfred J. Hyslop to John W. Nason, 7 June 1965, CCA. (The Hyslops, Fred and Helen, who had long been the Goulds' fellow G2V cabin owners in Wyoming, had also retired to Tucson upon Fred's 1963 retirement from Carleton.)

466 **returned September 9 … John and Betty Cowles.)**—MRG 1965-1966 Journal, entries for September 1965; John W. Nason to Alfred J. Hyslop, 20 September 1965, CCA.

466 **titles during 1965 and 1966 … yet another honorary degree.**—Information for three paragraphs on late 1965 activities from LMG, "1965-66 Annual Report," found in Gould Biographical File, UA Geosciences Department; MRG 1965-1966 Journal, entries for October and November 1965; news release of 28 November 1965, found in Gould Biographical File, UA Geosciences Department; Gould, "Antarctica—Continent of International Science," *Science* 150 (December 1965): 1775-1781.

467 **"This lapse represents" … now diabetic.**—MRG 1965-1966 Journal, entry for 4 April 1966; LMG to John W. Nason, 19 January 1966, CCA.

467n **Bell's widow Nathalie asked**—MRG 1965-1966 Journal, entry for 22 October 1965.

468 **party at the Goulds' Wyoming cabin**—Nine-page "album" of photographs of the celebration of LMG's seventieth birthday, accompanied by captions describing the day's

activities, given the title "Wilson Gazette * Special Issue: Jackson Hole Celebrates Birthday of Favorite Son," CCA-GC.

468 birthday letters —70th Birthday Letters (and replies), CCA-GC. All letters referenced in the eight paragraphs that follow (to "'this is a man.'") are located in this collection, arranged alphabetically by correspondent.

471 resolution from The Antarctican Society ... atop Gould's desk.—LMG to Henry M. Dater, 3 September 1966. 70th Birthday Letters (and replies), CCA-GC; clipping from the *Minneapolis Star*, September 12, 1966 [page number not indicated], located in CCA-GC.

471 Gould claimed ... "absolutely overwhelming."—LMG to John B. Howard, 6 September 1966; LMG to William M. Fiedler, 9 September 1966; both in 70th Birthday Letters (and replies), CCA-GC.

CHAPTER 26 — SEPTUAGENARIAN

472 "long postponed" journey—LMG to Frederick Schmidt, 9 September 1966, CCA-GC.

472 directly to New York—Ibid.

472 unprecedented peaks ... "with Bundy's policies."—Dowie, *American Foundations*, 170 (including "to retire the debt"), 173; Francis X. Sutton, introduction to Macdonald, *The Ford Foundation*, 1989 reprint, xi-xvii (including "saw that the bounding," xvii); LMG to John W. Nason, 11 April 1967, CCA.

473 charter class of eighty—Henrie, *Uncommon Education*, 48.

473 chairman Gould declared ... "focuses its attention."—*Northfield News*, December 1, 1966, 3.

473 Ardith would repeatedly ... "don't have her today."—1995 Arnolds/Donnell interview, CCA.

473n "The College had a brilliant"—Quoted in Henrie, *Uncommon Education*, 278.
    Events at Prescott subsequent to Gould's involvement are outside the scope of this biography, but do make for a fascinating story. In December 1971, Charles F. Kettering II was hit and killed by a car while chasing a runaway dog onto a highway, and his family, which "did not share his enthusiasm for Prescott College, ... withdrew any pledges." Shortly after that, another important trustee and financial supporter, George Farnham, also died. (Henrie, *Uncommon Education*, 83.) Poor financial management led, at the end of 1974, to a very sudden closing down of the school, two days before the normal end of a semester, after the trustees were told that the college's liability insurance was lapsing. A declaration of bankruptcy followed, but a group of faculty and students determined not to let their college altogether die arranged for spring semester classes to continue in homes and a hotel basement, and, in what becomes rather an inspiring tale, against all odds the school survived—for many years reconstituted as the Prescott Center for Alternative Education. Balancing an intense commitment to environmentalism with the liberal arts, it won reaccreditation in 1984, and would eventually regain the rights to its old name, becoming Prescott College once again in 1999 (Henrie, *Uncommon Education*, 1, 87-93, 305).

475 Nason would come to realize—In an oral history interview recorded in 1992, Nason would reflect: "When I went out in 1962, I was not as aware, as I quickly became, of the need for some sort of change at the College. ... There was a certain restlessness there and dissatisfaction with the tight control, albeit with great admiration and affection, of course, for Larry Gould. And so I found very soon after I got there that one of my jobs was to try to ease the College from this authoritarian atmosphere of administration to one in which faculty and students took a more active part, and in which the College would find itself closer to the temper of the modern era."
    Later in the same interview Nason said: "My relation with the students began, if not badly, at least not very well. I had been out of the academic world for a decade. ... I had not been aware of some of the cultural, psychological changes that had been taking place

on college and university campuses. … Part of my job was to move Carleton from the early 20th-century parietal rules and restrictions to the kind of free-wheeling society where we could have coed dormitories, no more in loco parentis control by the College. We gave up the chapel attendance, we gave up a single convocation attendance, we gave up a restriction on alcohol on campus, we gave up the attempt to control the behavior of the students in their personal and sexual relations, as they demanded that they be treated as adults. This took a lot of explaining to parents. It took a lot of explaining to alumni. And I suppose that one of the few real advantages that I had in this situation lay in the fact that I was an older alumnus, and I could say to the alumni who would call me up or write letters, 'I know exactly how you feel. I lived at Carleton in the same era that you did, and I was amazed at the sort of things I'd find, but we are living in a different world. We can't reconstruct or keep going that older world; we've got to face the fact that this is a different world. We may regret it, I regret it in many ways, but there it is.' And I think by the time I left Carleton the whole College community had pretty well accepted the changes in the social and cultural structure of the College." (1992 Nason/Donnell interview, CCA.)

475   **In 1966, in a note … "were there now."**—LMG to F. C. Ward, 6 September 1966, 70th Birthday Letters (and replies), CCA-GC. In 1971 Gould told Nason's successor as Carleton president: "As a bit of history you probably do not know that when I was retiring from Carleton and the Trustees asked me for suggestions as a successor I immediately named Champ Ward. It took him only a few seconds, however, to disinfect himself from being considered." (LMG to Howard R. Swearer, 17 February 1971, CCA.)

475   **In a 1970 exchange … "enthusiastic about Howard Swearer."**—Jean Rice Hoppin to LMG, 28 February 1970; LMG to Hoppin, 14 March 1970; both in CCA-GC.

476   **Ardith Arnold would later … "vehement about it."**—2002 Arnolds/Hillemann interview, CCA.

476   **"I knew, of course"**—Atherton Bean to MRG, 19 October 1964, CCA-GC.

477   **Published in 1968 … "world one community."**—LMG, "Science and the Culture of Our Times," address delivered 13 October 1966 at Carleton College; recording, CCA; published in the *UNESCO Courier* 21 (February 1968): 4-11.

478   **Harvill asked Gould … public universities.**—LMG, Remarks at final meeting of the Arizona Joint Economic Development Committee, 1 December 1967, unpublished transcript, NA-GP.

478   **During the same … thought to retire.**—LMG to Bea Wardell, 29 September 1967 and 10 January 1968 ("budgets, personnel"), CCA-GC.

478   **Harvill tapped … "historic role."**—LMG, "Education and Change," University of Arizona commencement address, 31 May 1967, unpublished transcript, CCA-GC.

479   **"but the person of unchangeable values."**—Clipping from the *Arizona Citizen*, June 1, 1967 [page number not indicated], located in CCA-GP.

479   **In September 1967 … "lot with us."**—LMG memorandum to Drs. Anthony, Bannister, and McGinnies, and Prof. Smiley, 22 Sept. 1967, Richard A. Harvill to LMG, 29 May 1968; both in Gould Biographical File, UA Department of Geosciences.

479   **Larry Gould's notable activities**—Information for three paragraphs from LMG to Frederick Schmidt, 9 September 1966; LMG to Frank I. Wright, 21 July 1968 and 26 November 1968; LMG to Jane Andrews, 26 August 1968; all in CCA-GC; and LMG, 1969-70 Annual Report, found in Gould Biographical File, UA Department of Geosciences.

480   **"greatest problem facing"**—LMG, Remarks at final meeting of the Arizona Joint Economic Development Committee, 1 December 1967, unpublished transcript, NA-GP.

480   **"painfully aware" … "harmony with it."**—LMG, "While There Is Still Time," *Bell Telephone Magazine* 48, No. 1 (January/February 1969): 2-9.

480n   **"I may have been a hawk"**—1973 Gould/Morrissey interview, UAAL.

481   **in 1941-42 had taken**—Carleton College academic transcript of Melvin R. Laird, CCA.

481   **His objectives in going … fitting on many counts.**—Quotations located in *Northfield News*, December 4 1969, p. 3, though derived from a University of Arizona News Bureau

release supplied to many papers, based upon information supplied by Gould in LMG to Hal Marshall (UA News Bureau), 31 October 1969, copy in CCA-GC.

481   **Gould afterward ... "magnificent."**—LMG to Dick Hoppin, 22 February 1970, CCA-GC.

481   **kept a diary**—Gould's travel diary for his 1969 trip to Antarctica, with entries from November 19 to December 9, is to be found in Box 2 of the Laurence M. Gould Papers in the National Archives. It is the source of all the description of this trip that follows, except where otherwise noted. Specific entry dates are noted for direct quotations only.

481   **"a comfortable and delightful"**—LMG 1969 Diary, [21?] November 1969.

481   **Robin was then carrying**—*Northfield News*, December 4, 1969, 3.

482   **That discovery, Gould had indicated**—Ibid.

482   **"had found Triassic"**—LMG 1969 Diary, 26 November 1969.

482   **"Fascinating technological"**—Ibid., 27 November 1969.

482   **"the barber pole"**—Ibid., 29 November 1969.

482   **returned to the Desert Museum to aid**—*Tucson Daily Citizen*, November 6, 1969.

484   **"the most spectacular" ... "dared hope."**—LMG 1969 Diary, 29 November 1969.

484   **On December 4 ... "would have been it."**—In addition to the December 4 entry in Gould's 1969 travel diary, sources for these two paragraphs are the *New York Times*, December 6, 1969, 1 ("not only the most"); Associated Press reporting of December 6, 1969, located in Gould Biographical File, UA Department of Geosciences ("establishes beyond"); LMG, "Antarctica: The World's Greatest Laboratory," *American Scholar* 40 (Summer 1971): 412. See also; and Gould, Foreword, in Edwin H. Colbert, *Wandering Lands and Animals* (1973), xv-xvii.

485   **"a great relief"**—LMG 1969 Diary, 6 December 1969.

485   **"2 from Peg!!"**—Ibid., 8 December 1969.

485   **"being lazy" ... "24 hrs. later."**—Ibid., 9 December 1969.

485   **Krutch had been diagnosed ... semi-invalid.**—Margolis, *Joseph Wood Krutch*, 228.

485   **"My darling Jean,"**—LMG to JRH, 17 November 1969, CCA-GC.

486   **As it happened ... "in some ways."**—LMG to Dick Hoppin, 22 February 1970, CCA-GC.

486   **"Larry, love ... sea-lion" ... "As B4, yourself ..."**—JRH to LMG, 28 February 1970, CCA-GC.

486   **Larry's reply ... "can do it."**—LMG to JRH, 14 March 1970, CCA-GC. Regarding the "wretched" typing, Gould's March 14 letter to Jean included this explanation, original typos included: "I think my typiny is improving but I can8t seem to get the hang of my Mexiczn American Eloise's electric typewriter." Eloise Grijalva, then Gould's university secretary, was a woman both, as Gould informed Jean, good natured and hefty. Her desk at the time bore a sign that read: "I am not too fat. I am just a foot too short." (from same letter of 14 March 1970.)

487   **Gould then revealed ... "sermon for the day)."**— Ibid .

487   **Jean replied with speed ... was enclosed.**—JRH to LMG, 17 March 1970, CCA-GC.

488   **"After much thought" ... "home to Peggy."**—LMG to JRH, 8 November 1970; JRH to LMG, 7 December 1970—both CCA-GC.

Jean and Dick Hoppin were not unique in their status as persons once close to Peg Gould with whom she had a falling out. At some point in the mid-60s she quarreled with—and similarly "cut off"—Alfred and Helen Hyslop, longtime friends from Carleton and G2V partners in Wyoming. At another point she fell out with Martha Rice, wife to her brother Jack. At Carleton, according to information provided the author by former Vice President for Development Bob Gale, Peg first befriended, but later "turned against" Bob's wife, Barbara. Ardith Arnold, Larry Gould's first secretary in Tucson, has reported being "one of the few people to get crosswise with Peg and eventually to get back in her good graces." In Ardith's case, a coolness set in some while after the birth of her first child. It began over a meal the two were having while Clark Arnold and Larry attended an Arizona football game. Peg was critical of choices Ardith and Clark were making that had slowed Clark's progress toward his PhD, which Peg thought ought to be the couple's first priority, baby or no baby. With Ardith no longer working for pay, it had become necessary for Clark to do so, and—Ardith has related—"Peg was afraid he would never finish his Ph.D." With Peg implying that Ardith ought not to allow anything like a baby to stand in the way of Clark's getting that PhD and Ardith naturally becoming "very defensive," the meal ended with anger on both sides, and for a few years after "things were pretty cool." Relations subsequently improved again, permanently. Clark has said: "It was only cool one way ... I think Peg was just upset, and then, slowly, she kind of got over it. And I think that the reason was that we didn't make a big deal out of it; we didn't ever respond to her ... we were just very calm about it... . I got my Ph.D. [in 1971], and everything was fine, and we held no grudge, and finally things just kind of smoothed over." Ardith has said that "our relationship with Peg ... had certainly warmed again by the time Joanna was born." [February 25, 1970, just prior to Peg's mastectomy in the same hospital.] (2002 Arnolds/Hillemann interview; e-mail from Ardith Arnold to Eric Hillemann, 6 July 2012.)

488   **Peg Gould had a very ... "getting better."**—LMG to JRH, 8 November 1970, CCA-GC.

488   **cancelled most "outside" engagements ... Prescott University commencement.**—Information for two paragraphs on Gould's 1970 activities from LMG, 1969-70 Annual Report; Ronald C. Nairn to LMG, 15 June 1970; both found in Gould Biographical File, UA Department of Geosciences; and LMG to JRH, 8 November 1970, CCA-GC.

489   **piece of pleasant news**—LMG to John W. Nason, 27 May 1970, CCA.

489   **He suggested ... "gets under way."**—LMG to JRH, 8 November 1970, CCA-GC.

489   **a messy affair ... search went on.**—University of Arizona *Desert Yearbook*, Class of 1971, 94-95; author's notes of personal interview (unrecorded) with Edgar J. McCullough, Jr., Tucson, Arizona, 5 December 2002; *Yuma Daily Sun*, December 17, 1970, 1.

490   **seen as Zumberge's man.**—Author's notes of personal interview (unrecorded) with Edgar J. McCullough, Jr., Tucson, Arizona, 5 December 2002.

490   **"The academic community" ... "greatest responsibility."**—Clipping of LMG, "How Not to Select a University President," Tucson Daily Citizen, January 14, 1971[page number not indicated], located in CCA-GP.

490   **compromise candidate**—Author's notes of personal interview (unrecorded) with Pete Kresan, Tucson, Arizona, 3 December 2002.

490   **Gould and Swearer met ... "help to the college."**—LMG to JRH, 8 November 1970, CCA-GC (including "through Howard"); Howard R. Swearer to LMG, 15 January 1971, CCA.

491   **Gould's first visit back ... "complete rapport?"**—LMG to JRH, 8 November 1970; Kate Ligare, "Larry Gould: The Humanist, The Explorer, the Eccentric," *Carletonian*, November 18, 1971, 7.

491n   **"I closed my eyes"**—Reported in Jon M. Nicholson to LMG, 24 November 1971, CCA.

492   **On March 6, 1972 ... "in my life."**—Dick Haney, "'Gould Room' Honors Noted Geoscientist," *University of Arizona Faculty & Staff Newsletter* 5, No. 8 (April 1972); LMG to Jean and Dick Hoppin, 3 May 1972 ("well I'll be god-damned"), CCA-GC; James H. Zumberge to LMG, 5 February 1972 (photocopy provided by George Davis during an interview with the author in Tucson, 5 December 2002).

493   **recommending the Oaxaca ... Paddock's plans.**—LMG to JRH, 31 October 1972, CCA-GC.

493   **felt compelled to ask**—See LMG to JRH, 17 November 1969, CCA-GC ("You may write me here at the University marking the envelope personal"), as well as later references in their subsequent correspondence.

493   **Some snippets (to "new suit yesterday.")**—LMG to JRH (or to both Hoppins), 29 January 1973, 13 February 1973, 13 March 1973, 20 April 1973, 23 May 1973, 8 July 1973,

22 August 1973, 14 October 1974, 4 February 1975, and 30 April 1975—all in CCA-GC.

496 **For the newsletter's first ... "he entered politics."**—LMG to Henry T. Harrison, 7 February 1974—excerpt printed in *Byrd Antarctic Expedition I News* 1, No. 1 (1974); LMG to Harrison, 13 June 1974, 3 October 1974, and 19 November 1974—excerpt printed in *BAE I News* 1, No. 2 (November 29, 1974).

497 **One year later ... "and good health."**—LMG to Henry T. Harrison, 13 February 1975, 10 July 1975, and 10 November 1975—excerpts printed in *Byrd Antarctic Expedition I News* 2, No. 1 (November 29, 1975).

497 **returned again to Carleton ... Kelly very much.**—LMG to Walter Reeves, 17 November 1975, CCA; LMG to JRH, 9 October 1975, CCA-GC.

497n **Gould recommended to the search**—Files of the Presidential Search Committee, 1976-77, CCA.

498 **"fine but too busy" ... "nuclear problem."**—LMG to Henry T. Harrison, 12 February 1976—excerpt printed in *Byrd Antarctic Expedition I News* 3, No. 1 (November 29, 1976).

498 **"I am swamped"**—LMG to JRH, 10 March 1976, CCA-GC.

498 **"I am all for Mo Udall"**—LMG to Henry T. Harrison, 7 April 1976—excerpt printed in *Byrd Antarctic Expedition I News* 3, No. 1 (November 29, 1976).

498 **In mid-April ... "over the years."**—LMG, "Some Divided Point in Time," Alma College commencement address, 17 April 1976, unpublished transcript, CCA-GC.

CHAPTER 27 — MR. ANTARCTICA

499 **"a set to with angina" ... board's executive secretary**—LMG to JRH, 22 November 1976, CCA-GC.

499 **Grover Murray ... Byrd Expedition days.)**—"Scientist, 80, is back from Antarctica trek," *Tucson Daily Citizen*, January 28, 1977 ("all the comforts"); *Carleton Voice*, Winter 1977, 6; LMG to Henry T. Harrison, 30 November 1976, and LMG to Jim Feury, 6 October 1977 ("My God I slept")—excerpts printed in *Byrd Antarctic Expedition I News* 4, No. 1 (November 29, 1977).

499 **A newspaper interview ... "Why shouldn't I go back?"**—"Scientist, 80, is back from Antarctica trek," *Tucson Daily Citizen*, January 28, 1977.

499 **At Arizona, Gould was ... with John Cowles.)**—LMG to JRH, 17 March 1977, 2 May 1977, and 9 May 1977, CCA-GC; LMG to Nena Thames Whittemore, 1 June 1977, CCA.

500 **The Gould cabin ... do sooner or later.**—LMG to the Hoppins, 11 July 1977, CCA-GC.

500 **still had no telephone**—LMG to Nena Thames Whittemore, 1 June 1977, CCA-GC. Gould was concerned, when attending the Carleton reunion, that it meant leaving Peg alone for three nights, at a time early enough in the season that they were still the only ones then in residence in the nearby cabins. A telephone had apparently been installed by the following summer, when Atherton Bean's call to Gould in Jackson Hole would result in his sending a plane to take Gould to the Mayo Clinic for emergency care. (See 2002 Arnolds/Hillemann interview, CCA.)

500 **Peg was forever adamant ... "out the other door.")**—2002 Arnolds/Hillemann interview, CCA; 1973 Gould/Morrissey interview, UAAL.

500 **At age eighty-one ... "multitude of flowers."**—LMG to JRH, 4 November 1977, CCA-GC.

501 **dinner for Henry Ford II. ... half-time teaching appointment.**—LMG to Jim Feury, 6 October 1977—excerpt printed in *Byrd Antarctic Expedition I News* 4, No. 1 (November 29, 1977); LMG to Henry T. Harrison, December 1977—excerpt printed in *Byrd Antarctic Expedition I News* 5, No. 1 (November 29, 1978); Gould Biographical File, UA Department of Geosciences.

501   **legislature was getting tougher ... "long, long time."**—John Schaefer to LMG, 20 February 1978, CCA-GC. See also "This Gang is Not Over the Hill," University of Arizona News Bureau Press Release 784.12, 12 April 1978, copy in CCA-GC.

501   **"I've had a whole new" ... "good to me."**—"Professor May Relive Byrd Trip," *Arizona Sunday Star*, April 16, 1978; LMG to JRH, 22 May 1978, CCA-GC.

501   **without pay ... one more year.**—LMG to JRH, 28 December 1978, CCA-GC.

501   **In mid-April ... "superstar" scientists**—"This Gang is Not Over the Hill," University of Arizona News Bureau Press Release 784.12, 12 April 1978, copy in CCA-GC.

501   **Gould indicated to Jean ..."about getting older."**—LMG to JRH, 22 May 1978, CCA-GC.

502   **Acknowledging Larry Gould ... "was life changing."**—George H. Davis, "It's Simple: Achieving Excellence Costs Money," "Perspective," published by the *Tucson Citizen*, August 14, 2000.

502   **Looking back afterward ... "into the program."**—2002 Davis/Hillemann interview, CCA.

502   **"great as an aider" ... "politician or diplomat.")**—Author's notes of personal interview (unrecorded) with Edgar J. McCullough, Jr., Tucson, Arizona, 5 December 2002.
          Regarding "how to pick the right moment": With President Harvill, McCullough reported, Gould would say that "he'd let down after the third martini." With Dean Odishaw, at least on one occasion in McCullough's retelling, the right moment was when the dean was out of town. In 1979, according to McCullough, the department was very interested in luring Bill Dickinson away from a full professorship at Stanford. They "wowed him" at an interview, part of which included dinner at one of Tucson's best restaurants, with Larry Gould as host. But Odishaw balked at trying to go after Dickinson, having the idea that "if someone would be willing to leave Stanford for Arizona, he couldn't be any good." Gould counseled McCullough to wait until Odishaw was on vacation, at which time they did all the paperwork, got signatures approving the hire from the president and provost, and presented Odishaw upon his return with a successful *fait accompli*. Dickinson would spend the rest of his career as an outstanding luminary of the Arizona geosciences faculty.

503   **Schaefer gave public credit**—University of Arizona President's Report 1979-80, 48.

503   **"we were well out"**—LMG to Frank Wright, 23 June 1976, CCA.

503   **It was memorable ... Laurence McKinley Gould**—Author's notes of personal interview (unrecorded) with Paul Damon, Tucson, Arizona, 3 December 2002.

503   **outstanding gourmet cook**—1995 Arnolds/Donnell interview, CCA. Peg developed an all-purpose Italianate spice of which she was justifiably proud, that became known as PGHC, standing for "Peg Gould's Herb Compound." The recipe for PGHC was a closely guarded secret for many years—kept in the Gould's bank safe-deposit box, according to Clark Arnold—though eventually Peg passed it along to Ardith Arnold and some other friends, who continue to give it good use. (L. Clark Arnold to Jewelnel Davis, 3 October 1988, "Gould File" maintained by Clark and Ardith Arnold at their Tucson home.)

503   **houseguests were often ... "well done."**—Author's notes of personal interview (unrecorded) with Edgar J. McCullough, Jr., Tucson, Arizona, 5 December 2002.

503   **favorite Tucson restaurants**—1995 Arnolds/Donnell interview, and 2002 Arnolds/Hillemann interview—both CCA. Gould's particular affinity for the Iron Mask was also mentioned in LMG to Robert H. Edwards, 5 February 1979, CCA, and Denis McCarthy to LMG, 18 November 1988, CCA-GC.

503   **At some point ... friendship had resulted.**—1995 Arnolds/Donnell interview, CCA; author's notes of personal interview (unrecorded) with Peter L. Kresan, Tucson, Arizona, 3 December 2002.

504   **children all over**—1995 Arnolds/Donnell interview, CCA.

504   **Joanna Arnold shared a story**—Remarks of Joanna E. Arnold, on Carleton College videotape recording of "A Convocation in Celebration of the Life of Laurence McKinley Gould, Skinner Memorial Chapel, October 13, 1995.

504 **"Uncle Larry only had one regret"**—Quoted in an undated 1992 clipping from unidentified *Tribune*, apparently a Michigan paper near Lacota—clipping in CCA-GC.

504 **"amazing number of people"**—Author's notes of personal interview (unrecorded) with Edgar J. McCullough, Jr., Tucson, Arizona, 5 December 2002.

504 **One day that August ... Mayo Clinic.**—LMG to JRH, 9 January 1979, CCA-GC.

505 **may not even have realized**—1995 Arnolds/Donnell interview, CCA.

505 **on a stretcher ... his present illness.**—LMG to JRH, 9 January 1979, CCA-GC; 1995 Arnolds/Donnell interview, CCA; Dr. James C. Broadbent, Mayo Clinic, to Dr. James L. Parsons, Tucson, 22 August 1978 ("elected to terminate"), copy in CCA-GC).

505 **"It takes a bit ... "again this afternoon!"**—LMG to L. Clark Arnold, 27 August 1978, CCA-GC.

505 **"They stopped all"**— LMG to JRH, 9 January 1979, CCA-GC.

505 **subsequently credited ... remarkably quickly.**—1995 Arnolds/Donnell interview; 2002 Arnolds/Hillemann interview—both CCA.

505 **Before their property could ... unhurried fashion.**—LMG to L. Clark Arnold, 27 August 1978, from the "Gould File" maintained by Clark and Ardith Arnold in their Tucson home.

505 **winter and spring, without pay**—LMG to JRH, 28 December 1978 and 7 February 1979—both CCA-GC.

505 **months of failure to heal ... Carleton alumni reunion.**—LMG to JRH, 28 December 1978, 29 March 1979, and 8 May 1979—all in CCA-GC; Nena Thames Whittemore to LMG, 21 June 1979, CCA.

506 **in April, by joint ... present for the event.**—*Byrd Antarctic Expedition I News* 6, No. 1 (November 29, 1979).

506 **Glowing tributes ... "the depression years."**—Christine Russell, "Dr. Laurence Gould: Superstar of the Antarctic," *The Washington Star*, April 25, 1979.

506 **Pete Kresan came up**—Author's notes of personal interview (unrecorded) with Peter L. Kresan, Tucson, Arizona, 3 December 2002.

506 **Kresan would eventually "inherit"**—1995 Arnolds/Donnell interview, CCA.

506 **Larry went to see Jack**—LMG to JRH, 10 March 1980, CCA-GC,

506 **"I am glad" ... "basis for that hope."**—LMG to JRH, 31 October 1979, CCA-GC.

506 **The first, in mid-month ... "Mr. Antarctica."**—LMG to JRH 31 October 1979, CCA-GC; Chronology for November 1979," in *Byrd Antarctic Expedition I News* 6, No. 2 (December 31, 1979); LMG to Paul C. Dalrymple, 16 January 1980—excerpt printed in *Byrd Antarctic Expedition I News* 7, No. 1 (December 17, 1980).

507 **only ten still lived**—Jason Eberhart-Phillips reported in the October 11, 1979 *Arizona Daily Star* that "Just 11 from the original crew are still living." The following month, Gould was packing for his departure when he was called by Henry Harrison with the news that Pete Demas had died on November 17. See "Chronology for November 1979," in *Byrd Antarctic Expedition I News* 6, No. 2 (December 31, 1979).

507 **Two of those ten ... gear in Christchurch.**—"Chronology for November 1979," in *Byrd Antarctic Expedition I News* 6, No. 2 (December 31, 1979).

507 **The day before ... to be cancelled.**—"Chronology for November 1979," in *Byrd Antarctic Expedition I News* 6, No. 2 (December 31, 1979); "Jetliner Crashes in Antarctic; All 257 Aboard Believed Dead," clipping from the *Richmond* (VA) *News Leader*, November 28, 1979 [page number not indicated], located in CCA-GP.

507 **(At a McMurdo ... accompanying gold medal.**—LMG to Paul C. Dalrymple, 16 January 1980—excerpt printed in *Byrd Antarctic Expedition I News* 7, No. 1 (December 17, 1980); LMG to JRH, 28 December 1979, CCA-GC (including "great surprise").

507 **"And thus I end"**—LMG to JRH, 28 December 1979, CCA-GC.

507   **"in spite of the misery"** ... **"lost in the shuffle"**— LMG to Paul C. Dalrymple, 16 January 1980, op. cit.

507   **"a tragedy for my ego"** ... **his wife replied.**—LMG to Robert H. Edwards, 15 February 1980, CCA.

508   **"I could not keep up"**—LMG to JRH, 28 December 1979, CCA-GC.

508   **Writing in March** ... **"I want to do."**—LMG to Robert H. Edwards, 6 March 1980, CCA; LMG to JRH, 10 March 1980, CCA-GC.

508   **He wanted, in June** ... **"as I used to."**—LMG to the Hoppins, 9 May 1980; LMG to JRH, 17 April 1981—both in CCA-GC.

508   **Peg's poor health** ... **"dissolving the females."**—LMG to JRH, 17 April 1981, CCA-GC; Robert H. Edwards to LMG, 12 May 1981, CCA.

509   **"that will be my last"**—LMG to JRH, 17 April 1981, CCA-GC.

509   **birthday at the Arnolds'**—Ardith Arnold to Robert H. and Ellen Edwards, 12 May 1981, CCA.

509   **"It is a plush"**—LMG to JRH, 17 April 1981, CCA-GC.

509   **In it he called for**—LMG, "The Last Terrestrial Frontier," address at the Cosmos Club, Washington, D.C., 14 May 1981, unpublished transcript, CCA-GC.

509   **A large photographic** ... **"distinguished company."**—LMG to JRH, 17 April 1981, CCA-GC.

509   **Carmel Bach Festival** ... **"to all of us,"**—LMG to the Hoppins, 22 September 1981, CCA-GC.

509   **often urged to do so** ... **"committed but didn't.")**—Gould profile by Alan Thurber, *Arizona Republic*, 16 May 1982; LMG to JRH, 29 May 1972, CCA-GC; 1978 Gould/Neider interview, transcript in Neider, *Beyond Cape Horn*, 309.

510   **At Arizona he continued** ... **"to a great department."**—Gould profile by Alan Thurber, *Arizona Republic*, May 16, 1982; LMG to John Schaefer, 19 February 1982, UAAL.

510   **"could not be more"** ... **"great lift."**—Peter W. Stanley to LMG, 26 March 1982; LMG to Daniel Sullivan, 18 May 1982—both CCA.

510   **That June he** ... **and kissed him.**—"Gould honored on Milestone 50," *Northfield News*, June 24, 1982, 11.

511   **The next spring** ... **Gould's own students.**—LMG to JRH, 6 April 1983, CCA-GC.

511   **During the year that followed** ... **Bean's private plane.**—LMG to the Hoppins, 7 February 1984, CCA-GC (including "gone quite daft"); LMG to Henry Harrison, 15 June 1984—excerpt printed in *Byrd Antarctic Expedition I News* 11, No. 1 (November 29, 1984).

511   **In mid-1982** ... **risen to twenty-six.**—LMG to JRH, 2 June 1982 and 7 February 1984, CCA-GC.

511   **In the summer of 1981** ... **"Antarctic winter 1928-30."**—LMG to Peter W. Stanley, 26 August 1981, CCA.

512   **appalled by "what Reagan"**—LMG to JRH, 20 November 1981, CCA-GC.

512   **wished he were younger** ... **"outstanding lies."**—LMG to JRH, 8 November 1982; undated fundraising letter on Arizonans for a Bilateral Nuclear Weapons Freeze stationary—both in CCA-GC.

512   **In February 1983** ... **"oafs as Nixon."**—LMG to JRH, 14 February 1983, 6 April 1983 (with photocopy of Stein's article), 8 April 1983 ("one of the best"), and 14 February 1984 ("Surely he will go down"); LMG to the Hoppins, 7 February 1984 (300 of Reagan's lies)—all in CCA-GC.

513   **litany of medical misfortune:**—LMG to JRH (or to both Hoppins), 3 February 1983, [25?] May 1983, 20 October 1983, 12 December 1983, 7 February 1984, 14 February 1984, 6 April 1984, 6 December 1984, and 24 June 1985—all in CCA-GC; LMG to Peter J. Anderson, 10 January 1985, OSUA-AP. LMG to Daniel Sullivan, 6 April 1985, CCA.

516 **George Davis had assumed ... "like you're supported."**—2002 Davis/Hillemann interview, CCA; author's notes of personal interview (unrecorded) with Peter L. Kresan, Tucson, Arizona, 3 December 2002 (called the other "brother").

517 **"historically demonstrated some"**—Henry Koffler to Robert H. Edwards, 23 April 1985, CCA.

517 **in mid-July Gould ... "honor firsthand."**—George H. Davis to Geosciences Department faculty and staff, 15 July 1985; LMG to George H. Davis, 20 July 1985—both in Gould Biographical File, UA Geosciences Department.

517 **On August 2 ... "two to two, Peggy."**—MRG to JRH, undated note, marked "Received 8/2/85," CCA-GC.

517 **"Jeanie, Jeanie—"**—MRG to JRH, 13 August 1985, CCA-GC.

517 **"Letter not sent" ... "two to two... Jean."**—JRH to MRG, 18 August 1985, marked "Letter not sent," CCA-GC.

518 **On August 22 ... to come visit.**—LMG to JRH, 22 August 1985, CCA-GC; 2002 Arnolds/Hillemann interview, CCA.

518 **in Arizona in January**—Referenced in Dorothy Obaid to Richard H. Hoppin, 15 January 1986, CCA-GC.

518 **periodic visits**—2002 Arnolds/Hillemann interview, CCA, where Ardith Arnold remembered that Dick Hoppin, after Jean's death, would make visits to Tucson "with great regularity ... and for considerable periods of time."

518 **morning dedication ... again prominently present.**—*The Antarctican Society Newsletter* 85-86, No. 5 (April 1986), 4; photographs of 21 March 1986 dedication ceremony, CCA-GC; author's notes of personal interview (unrecorded) with Peter L. Kresan, Tucson, Arizona, 3 December 2002; Laurence M. Gould file, Central Records microfiche, CCA.

520 **"on the 5th floor north"**—LMG to Carole Warner, 18 April 1986, CCA.

520 **bypass surgery ... "complete cognitive powers."**—1995 Arnolds/Donnell interview, CCA; author's notes of personal interview (unrecorded) with Peter L. Kresan, Tucson, Arizona, 3 December 2002.

520 **"the wound of my surgery"**—LMG to Frank I. Wright, 29 July 1986, CCA.

520 **By November, however ... "with these substances."**—1995 Arnolds/Donnell interview, CCA; L. Clark Arnold to Dr. James L. Parsons with copies to Drs. Copeland, Drach, Ewy, Hastings, Mullon, Sibley, and the East Side Pharmacy Service, 3 November 1986, CCA-GC

520 **In place at home ... "care for a parent."**—1995 Arnolds/Donnell interview, CCA.

521 **"For my children"**—LMG Inscription in copy of 1984 edition of *Cold*, viewed in 2002 in the Arnold home in Tucson.

521 **start of "a real adventure"**—LMG to Amy Arnold, 12 August 1985, copy in CCA-GC.

521 **"have been the worst" ... "reunion of my class."**—LMG to Frank I. Wright, 29 December 1986; LMG to David H. Porter, 15 January 1987—both CCA.

521 **Atherton Bean again ... last visit to Northfield.**—Class of 1962 25-year Reunion booklet; David H. Porter to LMG, 30 June 1987; 2002 Arnolds/Hillemann interview—all CCA; e-mail to the author from Ardith Arnold, 17 August 2012 (including "went all out.") Only Ardith Arnold accompanied Gould to the Carleton reunion because Clark was away at the time on a job in Ecuador.

521 **"a splendid three hours" ... "to mean to us."**—Stephen R. Lewis, Jr. to John M. Musser, 15 August 1988; Margaret R. Gould to Gayle and Stephen R. Lewis, Jr., 17 March 1988—both CCA.

521 **Peg's death**—L. Clark Arnold to Jewelnel Davis, 3 October 1988, "Gould File" maintained by Clark and Ardith Arnold at their Tucson home; 2002 Arnolds/Hillemann interview, CCA.

522 **"the worst disaster of my life."**—LMG to Denis McCarthy, 22 December 1988, CCA-GC.

522 **For several weeks ... "rallied about."**—1995 Arnolds/Donnell interview, CCA.

522   **"our angel with Larry"**—2002 Arnolds/Hillemann interview, CCA.

522   **"His 'appropriate way of life'"**—Atherton Bean to L. Clark Arnold, 24 November 1988, copy CCA-GC.

522   **Gould's condition ... "mental deterioration."**—1995 Arnolds/Donnell interview (including "he had many of"), and 2002 Arnolds/Hillemann interview; Perry Mason, "Contact Report," 5 March 1989 ("remarkably alert"); Richard H. Hoppin to Stephen R. Lewis, Jr., 14 March 1991; L. Clark Arnold to Dr. and Mrs. Stephen R. Lewis, Jr., 28 September 1993—all CCA.

523   **fall in his driveway**—1995 Arnolds/Donnell interview, CCA.

523   **round-the-clock caretaking ... night person arrived.**—Charles Donnell, Carleton College "Call Report" filed 14 February 1992; 1995 Arnolds/Donnell interview, and 2002 Arnolds/Hillemann interview (including "She was our savior")—all CCA.

523   **"our policy [was to]" ... "wrong can you go?"**—1995 Arnolds/Donnell interview, CCA.

523   **"certainly Antarctica's most legendary"**—*The Antarctican Society Newsletter* 91-92, no. 1 (July 1991).

523   **attended by thirteen or so ... "example all my life."**—George H. Davis to Stephen R. Lewis, Jr., 30 July 1993, CCA; University of Arizona news release dated 17 November 1993, copy CCA-GC (including quotation from Norman Vaughan"); Jim Erickson, "UA Geology Legend Honored Again at 97," *Arizona Daily Star*, November 27, 1993.

524   **In January of 1995 ... "sinking pretty rapidly."**—Diantha Ellingsworth to L. Clark Arnold, 27 January 1995, copy CCA-GC; 1995 Arnolds/Donnell interview, CCA.

524   **On April 15 ... "for second helpings."**—Ardith Arnold to Ralph Christenson, 4 May 1995, copy CCA-GC.

525   **"two pretty good" ... "at the end."**—1995 Arnolds/Donnell interview, CCA.

525   **On June 14 ... "knew who he was."**—Ibid.

525   **consequence of his coronary artery disease**—The certificate of death (copy CCA-GC), signed by John T. Boyer, M.D., read "Immediate cause: arrhythmia. Due to or as a consequence of: coronary artery disease. Other significant conditions: Alzheimer's Disease."

525   **it would be noted in connection**—Jeff Harrison, quoting Orlo Childs, a friend and former student of Gould's, in the University of Arizona publication *Lo Que Pasa*, July 3, 1995.

500n   **Gould had "a good visit"**—LMG to JRH, 11 July 1977, CCA-GC.

503n   **Gould's 1970s aversion ... "no expectation of tomorrow."**—Author's notes of personal interview (unrecorded) with Edgar J. McCullough, Jr., Tucson, Arizona, 5 December 2002; Margolis, *Joseph Wood Krutch: A Writer's Life*, 217.

503n   **"You had to call up"**—2002 Arnolds/Hillemann interview, CCA.

505n   **Selling to, as it transpired**—Salisbury Adams to LMG, 8 May 1978; LMG to Jean C. Adams, 14 April 1980; and other material relating to the sale of Gould's G2V property, from the "G2V – Sale" folder, CCA-GC.

EPILOGUE — VISION AND CHARM

526   **Obituaries lauded**—Walter Sullivan, "Laurence McKinley Gould, a Polar Explorer And Innovative College President, Dies at 98," *New York Times*, June 22, 1995, B6; *Time*, July 3, 1995, 15; *The Times* (London), July 10, 1995, 21.

Sullivan's informed text was slightly marred by the accompaniment of a file photograph of "Gould" from Byrd Antarctic Expedition days that, unfortunately, depicted not the expedition's chief scientist, but rather Charles F. "Chips" Gould, the expedition's young carpenter.

526   **pipe in hand.**—In later days, any reference Gould might make to his former pipe habit was likely to be followed by his story about going to the doctor for a physical exam and being advised to give up smoking and start drinking. "Best damned advice I ever had!" Gould would declare. (Personal e-mail from L. Clark Arnold, 1 September 1995.)

526   **"He walked on water"** ... **"vision and charm."**—*Minneapolis Star Tribune*, June 22, 1995, 18A; "Laurence McKinley Gould," editorial, *Arizona Daily Star*, June 23, 1995, 14A.

526   **eulogy written in advance**—"It is with profound sorrow ..." statement written by Antonio H. Obaid in July 1991 as a draft for inclusion in Carleton faculty minutes following Gould's death, CCA.

526   **A memorial service ... "when you entered."**—"Memorial Service Celebrating the Life of Laurence McKinley Gould," St. Mark's Presbyterian Church, June 24, 1995.

527   **At least seven features of the Antarctic**—As this caption notes, at least seven features of the Antarctic bear the name "Gould," but only three are in honor of Laurence McKinley Gould: Mount Gould (named by Admiral Byrd), Gould Bay (named by Commander Finn Ronne), and the Gould Coast (named by the New Zealand Antarctic Place-Names Committee). Gould Peak, in the Rockefeller Mountains, is named for "Chips" Gould. Gould Glacier and the Gould Nunataks are named for Rupert T. Gould, the British naval officer, polar historian, and polymath. (Also known as the restorer of John Harrison's historic eighteenth-century timepieces, Rupert T. Gould was the character portrayed by Jeremy Irons in the film *Longitude*.) Gould Island is named for Lt. Stuart S. Gould, a dental officer at McMurdo Station.

528   **At Carleton College ... children of their own.**—Carleton College videotape recording of "A Convocation in Celebration of the Life of Laurence McKinley Gould," Skinner Memorial Chapel, October 13, 1995.

528   **President Lewis closed ... bearing his name.**—Ibid. That the Carleton Library ought to be named for Gould had first been suggested even while Gould was still Carleton's president. In making the case for doing so, for instance, as Gould retired in 1962, Vice President Gale had written Board Chairman Bean that he thought the college could do no more exciting thing for Gould than to name "the most important building on campus" for him, and added that "if Larry has said to me once, he has said forty times in the last five years, that the most important single thing he feels he has done is the Library. He is proudest of it of anything. I suspect if you really pinned him down, he would say the Faculty, but for one individual so-call[ed] small thing, the Library is it." (Robert L. Gale to Atherton Bean, 25 May 1962, CCA.)

528   **That afternoon ... "and life everlasting.")**—Memorandum of Charles A. Donnell to Eric Hillemann, 23 October 1995, with attached statement and prayer, CCA.

529   **One further major ... water in 1997.**—E-mail from John Goodge (Carleton Class of 1980) to Tim Vick, posted to Carleton's alumni listserve 21 Sept. 1995; National Science Foundation Office of Polar Programs website (http://www.nsf.gov/od/opp/support/gould.jsp) retrieved 21 August 2012.

      The vessel was responsible, early in its life, for a startling moment for at least one Carleton College alumnus, who reported being aboard another ship in southern waters in a very thick fog with zero visibility. At one point, from not far away in the impenetrable fog was heard a stern voice amplified over a powerful bullhorn: "This is the *Laurence M. Gould* ..." "My God!" thought the Carleton alumnus, feeling a chill run through his bones. "He's OUT there!"

529   **"Larry Gould is one of the wisest"**—McGeorge Bundy to Henry Koffler, 1 April 1985, copy CCA-GC.

529   **"what a good baby sitter"**—Referenced as a comment "I shall always cherish," in LMG to Donald J. Grout, 5 February 1962, CCA.

530   **"Discipline—it's indispensable"**—Ed Severson, "Antarctic Bred Tale of Heroes," *Arizona Daily Star*, November 18, 1984.

530   **Demas copied Gould's**—Demas' transcribed diaries, 1928-1930, are in the National Archives. A copy of the diary entry containing Gould's letter of July 2, 1929, was sent by Andy Shrader to Clark and Ardith Arnold and viewed by me in the "Gould File" maintained by the Arnolds at their Tucson home.

530   **A great French musician, Sarasate**—Pamplona-born Pablo de Sarasate is more usually described as a Spanish musician, though he also lived much in France.

530   **I gave you Pupin's book**—Presumably scientist and inventor Michael I. Pupin's 1923 autobiography, *From Immigrant to Inventor.*

530   **a poem by Wordsworth ... and again these lines from Shakespeare**—Neither of Gould's remembered quotations, from Wordsworth and Shakespeare, were rendered in his letter quite with word-for-word accuracy. But they were close.

531   **Without adventure, he said**—LMG to Betty Girling, 6 June 1962, CCA.

531   **"Uncle Laurence" ... "until nothing was left."**—E-mail from Neita Trollinger to the author, 10 January 2001.

531   **"investing one's life in"**—LMG, "Is the Ivory Tower Obsolete?" address at Alma College, 26 October 1973, unpublished transcript, CCA-GC.

531   **"magnificent desolation" and "simple beauty"**—Phrases, along with a reassertion that Antarctica was his "spiritual home," taken from the 1978 Gould/Neider interview, transcript in Neider, *Beyond Cape Horn, 310.*

531   **"of all the things I have done"**—Gould expressed this sentiment many times. This quotation of it is from LMG to George H. Davis, 27 July 1985, Gould Biographical File, UA Geosciences Department.

531   **"I know of no designation"**—LMG to John Gilbert, 12 April 1973; photocopy provided me by George Davis at the time of our 2002 interview.

532   **"I have had a varied"**—LMG, "Is the Ivory Tower Obsolete?" address at Alma College, 26 October 1973, unpublished transcript, CCA-GC.

532   **"It matters little to me"**—Quoted, for instance, in LMG to Howard Conn, 17 November 1949, CCA.

532   **when a college "ceases to change" ... "he can aspire."**—LMG, *Carleton College Annual Report for 1959-1960.*

532   **Gould suggested ... "beacon for all to see."**—LMG, "Is the Ivory Tower Obsolete?" address at Alma College, 26 October 1973, unpublished transcript, CCA-GC.

B

C

K

Kaplan, Joseph–332, 370, 433
Keeler, Stephen E.–3, 238
Kellogg, Frank B.–183, 204
Kellogg, Hamilton–430
Kelly, Stephen K.–497
Kendrie, Frank–238
Kenyon, Dorothy–284
Kille, Frank R.–231, 233, 246-247, 256, 267, 293, 310, 361, 374, 376, 392, 401, 441
Killian, James R., Jr.–400, 410
King Edward VII Land–124, 126, 152
King, Harry–75
Kintner, Elvan–309
Klinefelter, Donald–260, 335, 396
Knopf, Alfred–262, 509
Koffler, Henry–510, 516-517
Kolb, William–386
Kresan, Peter–504, 506, 509, 520, 522, 526
Krutch, Joseph Wood and/or Marcelle–468, 485, 503

L

Laclavère, George R.–351, 378, 493
Laird, Melvin–481
Laird, William H.–3
Lang, Reginald–356
Larry Gould Day–2, 301, 335, 442, 445, 511
 first time and tenth–230, 349
Larsen, the–81
Laurence McKinley Gould Library. *See* **Gould Library**
 See also **Carleton Library, the**
lecture circuit–164-166, 190, 571
 appearance at Carleton–167
Leverett, Frank–150
Leverett Glacier–150, 364
Lewis, Hazel–377
Lewis, Stephen R., Jr.–521, 524, 528
liberal arts colleges–207, 241, 247, 394, 406, 414-415
Library Campaign–266, 328, 335, 338
Library, the Carleton–302, 312.
 See also **Gould Library**
 architecture of–282

Lincoln, Azariah T.–10
Lindbergh, Charles A.–63, 69-70, 73, 188, 220, 554
Lindley, Al–299
Linnell, Bertha–469
literature and reading
 books read–55, 72, 78, 174, 285, 299, 305, 379, 450, 511
 favorite authors–241, 304, 356, 511, 531, 562, 642
 reading habits–48, 303, 314, 434
 reading in Antarctica–73, 79, 111, 113, 134, 556
Little America, Antarctica–176, 506
 Byrd discourages re-use of site–175
 fifth incarnation–365
Little America by Richard Byrd–89, 165, 167
Little, Clarence Cook–72
Liv Glacier–141-142, 364-365
Livingstone, Richard–593
Lloyd, Trevor–68, 222, 228
Lofgren, Charles–176
Look magazine–403
Loss, Hyme–266, 328
Lucas, Scott–273-274, 297
Lufkin, C. Dexter–6
Lyman, Elaine–328

M

Macdonald, Torbert H.–415-416
Macgowan, Helen–190
MacLeish, Archibald–297, 346, 353, 356, 358, 509
 library dedication–353, 358
MacMillan, Donald B.–552
Maitland, David–355, 414, 446, 528-529
Mason, Howard–106
Mathis, Paul C., Jr.–250
Matteson, Robert–429
Mawson, Douglas–552
May Fete–194
May, Kenneth O.–250, 258-259, 283, 291-294, 318-321, 448-449, 628
 and Joseph W. Weinberg–291, 321
 Communist ties before war–258
 Gould's support of–258-259, 318